INTELLECTUAL PROPERTY LAW AND TAXATION

INTELLECTUAL
PROPERTY
LAW AND
TAXATION

Richard J Gallafent, BSc, CPA, EPA, RTMA, ETMA, MITMA, CPhys, MInstP
Gallafent & Co, Chartered Patent Attorneys and European Patent Attorneys

Nigel A Eastaway, FCA, FCCA, FTII, FHKSA, FTIHK, FCMA, FCIS, FOI, TEP, AIIT, MBAE, MEWI, SBV
TaxServe

Victor A F Dauppe, BSc, FCA, ATII, AIIT, TEP
Hughes Allen, Chartered Accountants

FIFTH EDITION

Sweet & Maxwell

Published by
Sweet & Maxwell Limited of
100 Avenue Road
London NW3 3PF
Set by Kerrypress Ltd, Luton
Printed in Great Britain by Biddles Ltd, Guildford

A CIP catalogue record for this book
is available from the British Library

ISBN 0752 004670

No natural forests were destroyed to make this product,
only naturally farmed timber was used and re-planted

Contents

PART 3   INTELLECTUAL PROPERTY TAXATION

PART 5   SPECIFIC TAXATION APPLICATIONS

Preface

Intellectual property law and taxation have been the subject of very considerable development over the past few years and the authors expect this development to continue. Against this background it is convenient to consider intellectual property primarily in the individual areas of patents, designs, trade marks, service marks, copyright, design right and the various rights which are given common law protection (ie, passing-off, unfair competition, know-how, show-how and endorsement). However, these various areas interact and overlap and many real life situations contain components from more than one of them. It is in these messy situations that the possibilities for proper or incompetent planning are to be found and it is hoped that this book will assist in inclining practitioners and beneficiaries to the former rather than allowing a gradual slide to the latter.

This book is addressed primarily to those who wish to use intellectual property law and taxation for legitimate ends. The intricate nature of these subjects provides a fascinating set of ground rules which may be used by the skilled operator to his advantage. Those who wish to take advantage of those rules must first know them, in general if not in detail, and Part One of this work therefore deals with the main areas of intellectual property law. Each area is discussed within a single chapter but, for ease of comparison with the other areas, all the chapters in Part One follow the same format: an introduction explains the basic concepts behind the particular branch of intellectual property law concerned, followed by more detailed sections on the method of obtaining protection, the form of protection, exploitation, international systems and comparisons with other countries' laws on the subject.

This edition has, at the request of readers, been expanded and reorganised and Part Two now covers the principles of taxation in the UK.

In Part Three each type of intellectual property is discussed within a single chapter, but from the tax point of view. Part Four is concerned with tax planning generally and applies to all types of intellectual property. Part Five covers specific taxation applications where intellectual property normally plays a key role in the taxation situation.

In Part Six of the book we give practical examples, cautionary tales and what we hope is a clear illustration of how intellectual property law and taxation interact in the form of case studies which follow the progress of intellectual property based structures from the inception of the idea to the resolution of the tax planning problems.

Abbreviations

ACT	advance corporation tax
CA 1956	Copyright Act 1956
CA 1985	Companies Act 1985
CAA 1990	Capital Allowances Act 1990
CCR	County Court Rules
CDPA 1988	Copyright, Designs and Patents Act 1988
CFC	controlled foreign company
CTMO	Community Trade Marks Office
DSS	Department of Social Security
FA	Finance Act
IHTA 1984	Inheritance Tax Act 1984
IM	Inland Revenue Manual
IRS	Internal Revenue Service (US)
NIC	National Insurance contributions
p	page (*pl* pp)
PA 1977	Patents Act 1977
RAPs	retirement annuity policies
RDA 1949	Registered Designs Act 1949
SA 1891	Stamp Act 1891
SERPS	State Earnings Related Pension Scheme
SI	Statutory Instrument
SP	Statement of Practice
TA 1970	Income and Corporation Taxes Act 1970
TA 1988	Income and Corporation Taxes Act 1988
TCGA 1992	Taxation of Chargeable Gains Act 1992
TMA 1938	Trade Marks Act 1938
TMA 1994	Trade Marks Act 1994
TMA 1970	Taxes Management Act 1970
VAT	value added tax
VATA 1994	Value Added Tax Act 1994

Table of Cases

United Kingdom

Australia

Canada

Hong Kong

Irish Republic

Jersey

New Zealand

United States of America

Table of Statutes

Australia

Belgium

Canada

Table of Statutory Instruments

Table of European Provisions

Table of Treaties and Conventions

PART 1

LAW

1 Introduction

Broadly speaking, intellectual property is about copying, and the temptation to do so is an ever present human condition. The emergence of legal protection and legal remedies reflects this, and sets limits, trying to define boundaries between what may legitimately be done and what is illegitimate, between the areas of new development which are, for longer or shorter periods, fenced off and what then passes into (or always is in) that pool of common knowledge from which all may freely take.

Being able to stop copying is a desire of many businesses, for the straightforward reason that it impels customers to come to the originator for the product of service in question; accordingly, intellectual property law has a major impact on the actual conduct of business across a very wide range of human endeavour.

This impact has increased in recent years, in the face of a general move against monopolies or trade restrictions of any type. The impact, however, continues to be dissipated: there is no overall 'unfair copying' statute, only the well-established patent, trade mark and copyright laws and the more recent additions such as the protection of registered designs and the new UK 'design right'. All of these areas of law have been subject to revision, which reflects a desire to match and adapt intellectual property law to meet the desire for the protection in all the multifarious areas of modern technology and newly developed marketing methods. Matching the law to the new developments is important. The high speed development in communications and the 'information business', for example, initially left the practical application of copyright law and protection in disarray, while franchising and endorsement have led to a general questioning of the functions of the very rights which they exploit. The new technology of genetic engineering has raised a whole new issue of ethical dimensions: should new plants and animals be patented? The pace of change in the area of intellectual property law is increasing, and the boundaries between it and other areas of commercial, property and consumer law become ever less definite. Accordingly the term 'intellectual property law' becomes less and less exact as time goes on.

The general caveat notwithstanding, however, one can still discern not only various branches of the subject but also some common themes which various branches share, and it is the purpose of this brief introduction to bring these elements together. Once this has been done certain aspects of the law discussed in the following chapters should appear, if not more logical, at least more comprehensible.

The principal characteristic of all forms of intellectual property is the so-called 'incorporeal' nature of that property. It is an abstraction, intangible, and as such more difficult to protect than other less nebulous forms of property. The distinction between the two types of property is best made by comparing the rights over a book of its owner and its author. The owner has absolute control over it as an object and is at perfect liberty to do what he will with it. He may also benefit from the ideas contained in it but — and here the author's rights take over — he cannot treat the author's presentation of them as his own: he cannot republish the book in any form himself and neither can he make an adaptation or translation of it for publication. The author still retains a legal interest in the book by virtue of his work in preparing its contents, no matter how great or how meagre the intellectual effort which that involved. Not only can the author prevent the unauthorised copying of his work but he can also control its transformation into some other form, whether by translation, dramatisation, animated cartoon or any other means. An inventor or designer may have similar rights: if, for example, he designs a new gearbox or a new way of making a button he can prevent others from copying the basic design or process involved.

The second characteristic of intellectual property law, however, is that it is not solely intellectual. To be eligible for legal protection the author's or inventor's work must have been rendered into some tangible form, be it a book, a gearbox or whatever. There is no copyright in mere ideas. Legal protection would have been available for the creators of *La Grande Jatte* of the *Communist Manifesto* but Seurat could not have claimed any rights over the idea of pointillism nor Marx and Engels over that of communism. Whatever example of intellectual property, properly so-called, is discussed it will be seen that something embodying it already exists in a tangible form and is therefore capable of being copied: were it not, there would be no need, according to the theories and public policy considerations which have been responsible for shaping this branch of the law, for legal protection.

In practice, therefore, the term 'intellectual property' denotes the rights relating to producing tangible objects which copy in some way an original made by a person whose mental efforts created that original. To a very large extent, this has dictated the form of the rights granted to that person: ideas are not protected but copying the outcome of the application of those ideas is prevented. Obviously, only something which is likely to be copied needs protection but, if it is genuinely useful, that protection should be granted in such a way that it does not prevent or discourage the dissemination of it. The law does not make a value judgment as to whether or not the property it is desired to protect really is useful, but instead provides enough sticks and carrots to ensure that anything which could be exploited by copying is protected and, at the same time, to encourage the owner of the property to exploit it himself. Thus the author or inventor is given the right to prevent unauthorised copying (a right which he can exploit commercially by making copies himself or by selling subsidiary rights), but this right is usually limited in time (which encourages the owner to make use of his monopoly while he still has it). In many instances this system is backed up by a state agency (eg, the Patent Office) whose function is to assist the inventor in protecting his intellectual property rights while also ensuring, through the public registration of the inventor's work, that the benefits of that work are not lost to the community at large. Most countries now have such agencies, but thay have all been established on an *ad hoc* basis and do not necessarily cover the whole field of intellectual property law. The UK, for example, does not have a copyright office, although the US does.

Ideas and copying know no national boundaries, so intellectual property law systems in different countries need to interact. Many countries are party to various international agreements which have been formulated as mutual protection societies to ensure that rights in one country are not rendered worthless by an absence of such rights in another country. There are international organisations to develop and monitor international progress, most notably the World Intellectual Property Organisation in Geneva, and a trilateral interest group in the patent area (Europe/US/Japan) has started to develop thinking for the future in the intellectual property field. In recent years, intellectual property systems have even attracted attention in multilateral trade talks; the Uruguay Round of GATT negotiations identified trade-related aspects of intellectual property systems as a specific subject for study and reflection and this resulted, at the end of that round of negotiations, in the Trade-Related Aspects of Intellectual Property Rights (TRIPs) treaty by which an increasing number of states are bound.

All international work in this area is slow, not only because of the intergovernmental negotiating process, but also because of the difficulty of producing a centrally accepted approach which will suit all parties despite the differing origins of the legal systems of the various countries concerned: Roman-Dutch law, the Napoleonic code and Anglo-Saxon common law. Progress towards an international patent has already been made, and certain regional patent, design and trade mark offices are already in operation. More will follow.

It can be seen from this brief analysis that although what the law of intellectual property is really concerned with is the protection of original intellectual effort, it is commerce, rather than intellect, which is the principal factor in the development of this area of law. Intellectual property rights are marketable commodities and it is therefore not surprising to find that on occasions they are subject to the general rules of commercial, particularly competition, law. As mentioned earlier, intellectual property rights allow their owners to limit the activities of others. If those others are competitors, the question arises at once as to whether or not that restraint it too anti-competitive: if it is, it may be illegal. Over the past three decades intellectual property law has received a great impact from competition law, particularly in the developing field of so-called 'EU anti-trust' law, which is based largely on Articles 85 and 86 of the Treaty of Rome (*see* Appendix 3). The concepts of the exhaustion of rights and their possession (as opposed to their exercise) have been the subject of detailed government and professional scrutiny and the law in this area is still developing. However, with the general governmental view that competition should be stimulated, other ways of preventing competitors doing what they wish are becoming less available and less effective, thus placing an ever greater burden on the intellectual property systems to hold a fair balance between preventing copying in order to provide a legitimate reward to originators and allowing copying so that all may freely use new developments. Much recent development in the legislative area may be seen as altering this balance, sometimes consciously.

Various recent developments are discussed at various stages in the remainder of Part I but the point to be emphasised again here is that intellectual property of all forms is subject to a diverse body of laws which offers great scope, when approached from the right angle, for commercial exploitation. The following chapters examine those laws predominately from this viewpoint.

2 Patents

Introduction

These used to be called *letters patent* and many years ago (in countries which were still monarchies) were issued under the seal of the sovereign. Letters patent for inventions were but one of the variety of letters patent which the sovereign granted and, indeed, letters patent for UK life peers, for example, are still granted by the sovereign. All the somewhat archaic phrase means is royal or state document which is open to inspection by anybody, which might well be headed by the time-honoured phrase 'To whom it may concern'. Letters patent for inventions were awarded to inventors as part of a bargaining system between the state or Crown on the one hand and the inventor on the other. Nowadays, in the operation of a modern patent system, those participants are conventionally replaced by the state on the one hand, acting through the Patent Office, and the company which employs the inventor on the other. Letters patent continue, of course, to be granted to individual inventors, some of whom still exist and even thrive.

In order to understand the basis of the patent system it is convenient still to take the metaphor of a bargaining system between the state and the inventor. The impetus to set up the bargaining system arises from a view held by certain states that the progress of technology can be advanced by encouraging people to publish their new discoveries, techniques and the like. They therefore bargain with the inventor on the following basis: if the inventor comes to the state with an invention and reveals that invention to the state, then in return the state will reveal the invention to everyone else but, for a limited period of time, will restrict the use of the invention only to the person who brought the invention to the state, or those whom he permits to use it. Early patent laws more explicitly reflect this bargaining approach as the underlying basis of patent law than more recent attempts at statutory codification.

This simple approach to the state/inventor bargain requires more detailed consideration of two aspects before it can be fully appreciated. The first of these is the nature of 'invention' itself, and the second is the way in which the state restricts the use of the invention to the 'patentee', as the person to whom the letters patent are granted is conventionally called.

Turning first to the question of the nature of an 'invention', it should first of all be appreciated that not everything that is new is within the scope of patent law. Fundamentally, inventions in respect of which patent protection is available have to do with manufacture, either because they consist of manufactured articles, or because they relate to manufacturing processes. These are clearly capable of being contrasted with certain things which are undoubtedly inventive but which do not have the same directness of application to manufacture. Mathematical theories, medical treatment methods, ways of playing games and, now of particular relevance, ways of programming computers, are not in themselves capable of being protected by patents, although certain aspects of them may be the subject of copyright protection (*see* Chapter 5).

Secondly, the restriction of the use of the invention to the patentee is effected by forbidding others to use the invention rather than giving the patentee positive clearance to use it. Thus a patentee's manufacturing or processing activities may be circumscribed by the patents of others but are generally in no way affected by his ownership of his own patents. It is, of course, to be hoped that the possession of a patent, by keeping competitors off, will enable the inventor or his company to exploit an invention without the normal attack from the competition, at least for the number of years that the patent monopoly can run.

The fundamental bargaining approach between the state and inventor is nowadays very difficult to discern, since it is overlaid by the practical considerations of running the bargaining system. As soon as the industrial revolution started there was an immediate and enormous increase in the number of people inventing things and wanting state protection to enable them to develop their inventions, ie, wanting patents. The system accordingly developed from a system of contacting various court officials and securing a royal grant to a highly systematised operation run by a special government office set up for the purpose and acting under the authority of a statute (currently the Patents Act 1977) and rules made under the statute (the Patents Rules 1995). Some aspects of this growth in the mechanics of the system deserve detailed consideration.

First of all, it soon became necessary for the inventor not merely to allege that an invention had been made connected with, for example, ploughs or leather, undertaking to make the information concerning the invention available to third parties, but to explain in detail in writing of just what the invention consisted. This grew into a statutory requirement for filing a description of the invention with the government office concerned, and for obvious reasons, principally that others need to be able to carry out the invention after the statutory period of protection has come to an end, the description has to be adequate, ie written in adequate detail to enable others in the field (conveniently thought of as competitors) to carry the invention into effect.

In addition to the requirement to provide a full description of the invention, the practice arose of asking the inventor to supply a definition of his invention as well. This definition had to be designed to do two things: first, it had to act to distinguish the invention in question from what had been done before, ie from the so-called 'state of the art'. Secondly, it was used to delimit the monopoly claimed, ie to define that area out of which, by virtue of the grant of a patent, other people were meant to keep. These definitions, which have come to be known in jargon as 'claims', are little more than an attempt in wording accurately to identify an invention in terms which will enable someone assessing the patent to judge whether a given process, article or the like does or does not embody the invention, or does or does not fall within the scope of the claims, to put it in more formal language.

Much time is taken up in patent matters with the consideration of whether an invention is obvious or not, or whether it involves an inventive step or not, compared with what people were doing before. It is a matter for skilled value judgment and much time and effort has been expended over the years in the courts in arguing obviousness or lack of it in respect of inventions on which patents have been granted. While several lines of approach and, indeed, certain principles have emerged from all that litigation, every case on obviousness or lack of inventive step is peculiar to its own facts, and what is obvious to one judge at one stage in time does not affect what another judge or judges consider as obvious in some other field of technology at some other time. Much can be written about obviousness and, indeed, much has been written about it, both in the court reports and elsewhere, but it is beyond the compass of this volume to do more than indicate the problem area. It is sufficient for present purposes to say that obviousness usually represents the chief attack on a patent made by someone who wishes to destroy that patent.

Following the developments indicated above, most industrialised countries now have specialised Patent Offices which operate to grant several tens of thousands of patents per year in each of the major industrialised countries. These patents range over the entire field of subject matter and vary from very simple to very complex inventions. Of course, the system as operated by the government Patent Offices does little more than provide a preliminary sieving and evaluation process. Detailed consideration of whether an invention is new and unobvious, against a background of expert evidence in the particular field and very thorough searching of the prior literature, is simply impractical for the vast majority of patents. However, the system is self-adjusting to this extent: if an invention is of little commercial value, then it does not merit having that sort of money spent on it. The originator may put it into practice, but it is perhaps unlikely that it will be widely copied, certainly not on a sufficient scale to make it worthwhile bothering to take any proceedings for patent infringement. If, on the other hand, an invention is important, sufficiently important to make it worthwhile for parties other than the patentee to consider whether or not to put the invention into practice, then an attempt may be made to destroy the patent or to limit its effects by the interested third party. Such an attempt is not very often made as a mere academic exercise; rather the approach often adopted is that of commencing to use the invention and considering the position if the patentee decides to take action.

Obtaining protection

Patent protection is obtained by asking the government for it and paying the fees. Grant is not automatic in most countries.

In the UK the grant of patents for inventions is now subject to the provisions of the Patents Act 1977, and it is useful to consider what is necessary to secure a patent under that Act.

Patentable inventions

First of all, the Act defines the categories of patentable invention for which a patent may be obtained. Thus, PA 1977, s 1(2) states that the following (amongst other things) are not patentable inventions:

Anything which consists of:

    (a)   a discovery, scientific theory or mathematical method;

(b)   a literary, dramatic, musical or artistic work or any other aesthetic creation whatsoever;

(c)   a scheme, rule or method for performing a mental act, playing a game or doing business, or a program for a computer;

(d)   the presentation of information.

However, this exclusion is stated to apply 'only to the extent that a patent or application for a patent relates to that thing as such', a phrase which has so far received little judicial consideration.

A time-honoured category of invention which has often been stated to be unpatentable, though on no very clear statutory basis, is a process for treating the human body for the prevention or cure of disease. However, this approach is currently subject to erosion and was criticised heavily in a decision in the High Court of New Zealand ([1980] RPC 305). In some countries, notably the USA, it has been possible to obtain patents for the medical treatment of human beings for some time. More recently, the ban on patenting computer programs 'as such' has been shown to be of narrow application; there is an increasing tendency for patent offices to grant patents for 'computer-related' inventions where there may be a need to use 'software' to put the invention into practice, but where the invention is arguably not *just* in the programming.

Recently the boundary between the 'patentable' and the 'excluded from patentability' categories has received close scrutiny in the biotechnology field, where there has been (and continues to be) widespread debate as to whether an individual 'gene sequence' is patentable, or is just a discovery. Because one can always lose an existing patent, but never acquire one if one applies too late (*see* Novelty, *below*), there is much activity in this area at present, but no patent on a gene sequence has yet been tested in a court.

Still under the heading of what constitutes an invention, it is necessary to have something which is new and inventive or, in the wording of PA 1977, s 1(1)(*b*) 'involves an inventive step'. In addition, PA 1977 sets out the additional requirement that an invention must be 'capable of industrial application' (s 1(1)(*c*)) and this last requirement is the current basis on which the British Patent Office would undoubtedly reject a medical treatment claim (for the definition of industrial application *see* PA 1977, s 4).

Novelty

As noted above, an invention, to be patentable, must be 'new'. The necessity for this in a patent system reflecting the bargaining approach described above is that there is no virtue in the state granting a patent in return for a disclosure of something which was already known, in the legal phrase, something 'in the public domain'. There is now a statutory guideline to the meaning of the word 'new' in this connection in PA 1977, s 2 where it is stated that an invention is new if it does not form part of 'the state of the art' and that splendid phrase covers everything which has been made available to the public in any way at all, eg by printed publication, oral disclosure or use. From a consideration of this it follows that for an invention to be new at a given date, no one else but the inventor must know about it unless those people that the inventor has told are duty bound not to reveal it any further. In the classic words of Lord Parker in *Re Bristol Myers Co's Application* [1968]

RPC 146 'if the information has been communicated to a single member of the public without inhibiting fetter that is enough to amount to a making available to the public' and a valid patent cannot subsequently be obtained. Thus, in order to obtain a patent, ie in order to come to a bargain with the state, the inventor must tell the state about the invention first, before he reveals the invention to the public in any other way.

The stress on timing reflects the fact that the consideration of novelty must be related to a given point in time—what was new last week is not new now. In patent law, the all-important point in time is the date on which the invention was first communicated, by way of an application for a patent, to a government patent office. This date is usually known as the 'priority date', as the first filing creates a right of priority which can be invoked later in a second application for a patent filed within a year of the first one.

As noted above, in addition to the requirement of novelty at the priority date, in order to be patentable an invention must involve 'an inventive step'. This is another way of saying that the invention must not be obvious. There are all sorts of ways of making obvious modifications to articles and processes which will render the modified article or process new, but there may be nothing inventive about doing so. For example, the motor car having a door held on to the chassis by five separate hinges may be totally novel, but could hardly be described as embodying an inventive step. As with assessing novelty, the question of whether an invention was obvious is also related to the priority date; it is obviousness at the priority date which should be considered.

The application

Against this background, it is useful to see how these general ideas are reflected in practice in the working of the current Patents Act and the associated Patents Rules, 1995, made thereunder.

The general structure of the system is as follows: the inventor (or someone else entitled to apply for a patent) writes down the invention and takes the papers to the Patent Office and requests on an official form that he be granted a patent (the process is still paper-ridden, though moves to reduce dependency on paper are afoot). The Patent Office examines the technical papers to see if they are in good order and to see if the invention is patentable, and publishes the papers, essentially as filed, in order to disseminate the information. If, after examination, the Patent Office thinks a patent ought to be granted, then the patent is granted. The examination process is split into two main parts, in the first of which the papers are checked for formal requirements and a search among literature, mostly patent literature, is made in order to establish the technical background against which the invention is to be judged. In the second stage detailed scrutiny of the papers is effected to ensure that they are clear and internally consistent and the question of whether the invention as set out is really an invention having regard to the prior art known to the examiner is then carefully considered.

Broken down into fine detail, the normal procedure is as follows: first of all, it is necessary for the inventor to write down a description of his invention and take it along to the Patent Office, 'filing', before the invention has become public knowledge. This clearly needs to be done early, usually in order that the inventor, by his own efforts, does not make his own invention part of 'the state of the art' (*see* p 9 *above*), whereafter it cannot be validly patented. The filing date, ie the day on which the Patent Office receives the papers, becomes the priority date for the patent application in question. Normally the inventor applies or, if he is employed, his employer applies. The application is usually, though not always, made in the name of the person to whom it is intended that the patent should be granted (*see* PA 1977, s 7(2)). Questions of entitlement to the grant of a patent may be dealt with by the Patent Office in the case of disputes (*see* PA 1977, ss 8–12). In order to secure a filing date, the requirements are fairly minimal (PA 1977, s 15(1)), *viz*, that the fee is paid, a patent is requested, the applicant is named and there is a description of the invention. These four things constitute the minimum requirement for securing a date but they do not, of course, enable the Patent Office to deal fully with the application. All that the Patent Office does do if an application is filed with the minimum requirements is check that the subject matter is not 'information the publication of which might be prejudicial to the defence of the realm' (PA 1977, s 22(1)) (if it thinks so it lets the applicant know that and imposes an interim secrecy order—but this is rare) and then simply waits for the remaining requirements to be fulfilled. If they are not fulfilled, the application lapses. The remaining requirements for the first stage are to file claims (brief definitions of the invention) and an abstract (a brief description of what the invention is and, usually, what it is useful for—to aid those who look at the published application papers later) and, if the application is to proceed, a request for preliminary examination and search.

Search All these matters being taken care of, the Patent Office examiner looks at the case from two points of view, first, that of compliance with the miscellaneous formalities concerning typing, pagination, drawings and the like and, secondly, he makes a search to see what material should be cited in the search report as the appropriate technical background against which the invention is going to be judged. This search is carried out, usually expeditiously, under PA 1977, s 17. It has to be carried out fairly fast if the request for preliminary examination and search is not filed until the last possible day (one year after the priority date), since there is a requirement (PA 1977, s 16) that as soon as practicable after 18 months from the priority date the Patent Office must publish the application papers as filed and a practice that, unless the papers as filed are inadequate to enable a sensible search to be effected, the search report is published at the same time. Thus, the Patent Office is geared to make both formalities examination and the preliminary search within the space of a few months and to communicate the results of such examination and search to the applicant.

At this stage the applicant can consider whether or not he wishes to proceed further with the application. If the search has turned up material which quite clearly discloses the invention, or something so close as to make the invention really rather obvious, then the applicant can simply abandon the matter at that stage. Indeed, if the applicant acts sufficiently fast, as soon as he knows the results of the search report, he may be able to withdraw the application before preparations for its publication are complete and in those circumstances the papers are never published. This is not adverse to the public interest since the invention is effectively already known. The applicant does not have to react in any way to the search report, though he may do so if he wishes, eg by submitting amended claims. In contrast, if the preliminary examination has revealed deficiencies in the formalities—usually inadequately drawn drawings or the lack of a statement of how the applicant (if he is not the inventor) is entitled to apply for the patent, and giving the inventor's name(s)—then those deficiencies must be remedied. If this is not done, the Patent Office will simply deem the application withdrawn. Usually there is no possibility of reinstatement if that happens and if, by then, the invention has become known (eg by virtue of commercial use having started) the ability to secure a patent is wholly lost. It is thus very important to react to problems raised by the formalities examination at this stage.

If the applicant does not withdraw the case, and provided any requirements identified in the preliminary examination report are met, the Patent Office, a little while after the 18-month period has elapsed, publishes the application papers as a printed patent specification. These are numbered in a series starting at 2,000,000 and the number is followed by a suffix letter A to indicate that this is the publication of the specification as originally filed, and *not* of the specification of a granted patent. Publication does two things: first, it disseminates technical information thought to be for the common good. Secondly, it enables third parties, who may be aware of material much more relevant when considering patentability, to draw the existence of such material to the attention of the Patent Office (which in turn alerts the applicant with the details), so enabling more constructive examination to take place.

Examination Within six months of that publication, if the applicant wants to proceed with his application, a request for substantive examination must be filed. This once done, the examiner then, under the provisions of PA 1977, s 18, investigates, to the extent that he considers necessary in view of the results of the search previously carried out, whether the application complies with the requirements of the Act and the rules. The principal areas which the examiner considers are whether the invention, as described and particularly as claimed, is new and possesses an inventive step relative to 'the state of the art' and whether the documents are internally self-consistent. To do this the examiner looks at the claims which have been submitted and holds them up as a yardstick against what has been described or done before the application was filed. If he finds, for example, that the claims, looked at as definitions, contain within their scope matter which forms part of the state of the art, then he will point out this fact to the applicant, who then has a chance to amend the definitions in order to exclude them from the earlier known subject matter. Quite clearly, the definitions cannot be any good as definitions of an invention if they include within their scope something that is not new, or something which is effectively obvious. Another example is if the examiner decides that the claims cover more than one invention. This can happen it there is more than one ingenious idea underlying a new mechanism or process. In such a case, the application may be split up into two or more applications, each capable of becoming a separate patent.

The examiner may carry out this substantive examination process several times, each time giving the applicant a further chance to amend the papers in order to overcome the objections which he has raised, but finally the examiner has to make a decision either to pass the application to grant or to refuse it. In the former case, the Patent Office grants a patent to the applicant and appropriate entries are made in the Register of Patents kept at the Patent Office for that purpose. From the date of grant onward the applicant, now the patentee, can in theory stop other people using his invention. If the examiner, despite the pleas of the applicant, is not convinced of the patentability of the invention and issues a decision refusing the application the applicant may appeal to the Patents Court, a special court established by PA 1977, s 96 and forming part of the Chancery Division of the High Court. If the applicant still fails to convince the Patents Court that a potential invention is present, then, provided that the Patents Court itself gives leave, a further appeal may be made, under PA 1977, s 97(3), to the Court of Appeal.

It can be seen from the above observations that securing a patent usually takes considerable time, eg three or more years from when the inventor first applies. This can be very disadvantageous in certain industrial and commercial circumstances. However, if the Patent Office receives requests for search and examination (and the respective fees) simultaneously, it combines search and examination, thus shortening the procedure, and time to grant can be further shortened by asking the Patent Office to publish the application before the 18 months from the priority date have elapsed. The Patent Office will not usually move a case through to grant before three months after publication, so that anyone who wants to make observations on patentability has time to do so.

Patent agents

As can be seen, the system under the current Patents Act, as in previous systems before it, is fairly complex and since the last century a separate profession has evolved to act on behalf of people seeking patents. In the UK they are called patent agents or patent attorneys and the use of these titles is statutorily controlled. Under CDPA 1988, s 276 no one may describe themselves as a patent agent or patent attorney unless they are duly entered on the Register of Patent Agents kept for the purpose under the authority of the Patent Office by a registrar and in order to have his or her name entered on that register it is necessary to pass qualifying examinations which are administered by the relevant UK professional body, the Chartered Institute of Patent Agents.

The background to this legislation is the feeling that the public should be entitled to distinguish between qualified practitioners and unqualified practitioners whose competence it would be beyond the power of the applicant to determine. Quite clearly, an inventor who made a very good invention could be wholly denied his just rewards if his patent matters were not handled properly. Of course, the right of a person to file and prosecute his own patent application is still available to individuals and, indeed, is still made use of by some. It is not, however, a course that can be unreservedly recommended, particularly since the inventor himself is not always best able to take a detached or objective view of what he has invented, certainly not one sufficiently detached or objective to enable him, or her, properly to assess what has actually been invented. The skill of patent agents, however, is not merely the intellectual one of assessing wherein an invention may lie, but the practical ones of being able to reflect the invention in clear and adequately broad wording, and of knowing the extensive rules and formalities in the system of applying for patents at the UK Patent Office (and elsewhere *see below*). Since failure to observe the rules can lead to the application being deemed withdrawn—however meritorious or brilliant the invention—and since (because of the novelty requirement) it is often not possible to 'go round again', the benefits of using only qualified patent agents are clear. Mention should be made of the fact that in addition to the profession of patent agents qualified by examination, solicitors are able to act before the Patent Office in all matters as agent for an inventor or applicant. Most solicitors, however, prefer to see such work done by a patent agent, particularly if the matter in question is of a highly technical nature. Only a small proportion of solicitors is qualified technically, while almost all patent agents have university degrees in science or engineering.

It is, of course, necessary in making and pursuing an application for a patent to pay certain government fees and if an agent is used his professional fees will also need to be paid.

Form of protection

Turning now to consider that other aspect of the bargain noted above, *viz*, the way in which the state restricts the use of an invention to patentees or those whom they permit to use the invention, it is important to note carefully how the so-called patent monopoly works. The act of trying to secure a patent publishes the invention so that all may know about it, but the grant of the patent to the successful applicant restricts people other than the patentee from using the invention. It is important to remember that the restriction is placed on the people who are not the patentee, rather than a positive permission to operate the invention being granted to the patentee. A brief consideration of the results, were the latter course to be followed, will show why this is so.

Consider the first man to invent safety glass, ie two sheets of glass stuck either side of a sheet of transparent plastics. Assume that he invents it against a background 'state of the art' consisting only of single sheets of glass which tend to shatter and do damage. Safety glass is clearly an invention, judged against that background, and he secures a patent. Consider now the man who ten years later comes along and invents a much improved safety glass by the use of a particular material for the plastics interlayer. This, let us assume, is also inventive, so he obtains a patent too.

Now, if the grant of a patent is an entitlement to work the invention, the grant of the second patent for the improved safety glass clearly diminishes the 'monopoly' held up to that time by the first patentee, the man who actually invented safety glass in the first place. The grant of permission to the second man to operate would clearly detract from the previous 'monopoly' held by the first man.

In contrast, the system works the other way, and the grant of the patent simply gives the patentee a right to stop third parties. Thus the first patentee is in a position to stop anybody else making safety glass. This position continues to exist even when the second man comes along and secures his patent, which enables him in turn to stop anybody producing the improved safety glass, which includes stopping the original patentee of safety glass doing so. In this simple illustration neither party can produce the improved safety glass without the permission of the other. Of course, two reasonable men wishing to operate their inventions in the best possible fashion would each agree to let the other do so, but it might pay the second man to wait until the first man's patent runs out and then hope to take away his entire business by selling a better product which the first man could not produce.

The time period for which the state agrees to prohibit third parties from using an invention is currently 20 years in the UK and much the same sort of period outside it. The practice in the UK and most other countries is to pay for the operation of the patent system by means of fees collected from applicants and patentees. Since running a Patent Office is rather an expensive business, particularly in view of the necessity to employ technically competent examining staff, as well as the substantial cost of printing and publishing the patent documents, costs would be very high to the applicant if he had to pay for all those services as he used them. This would act as a deterrent to patenting, clearly not seen as good public policy, so for many years many countries have adopted an alternative approach by charging patentees annual 'renewal fees'. These must be paid annually if the patent is to be kept in force. They usually start very low but tend to finish up very high, on the theory that if after 15 or more years the patent is still doing useful work for a company or inventor in excluding others from a certain field, then it is worth his while to pay for it.

As noted, the patent gives the right to the patentee to stop other people using the invention, ie to stop other people infringing. Infringement is a very straightforward concept and while in detail, in practice, it is sometimes a little difficult to apply, the principles can be very simply stated: the claims at the end of the specification of the granted patent are definitions, usually of articles or processes, which, it is alleged, embody the invention which has been made. In order to determine whether infringement has occurred, it is only necessary to take the yardstick of the wording of the claim and hold it up, mentally, adjacent to the possibly infringing process or product and see if it fits. The sort of question which is simply posed is: does the product or process under consideration fall within the category of all products or processes embraced by the definition constituting (usually) claim 1 of the patent in question? If it does, then there is infringement and if not, not. This sort of question is sometimes difficult to answer, especially if it is difficult to see just what the allegedly infringing process or product does or is. It also depends on the construction of the wording of the claims (definitions), and that can be difficult sometimes. In addition even words with straightforward meanings should, at least on occasion, be given a 'purposive' construction (see Lord Diplock's remarks in *Catnic* [1982] RPC 183 at 244).

If a patentee decides that his patent is being infringed by a third party, his usual course of action is to ask the third party to stop, pointing out that he has a patent monopoly. This may or may not immediately have the desired effect and, indeed, in practice usually does not, though it may bring the parties together for discussions to settle the matter on an amicable basis. This is discussed more fully below in terms of licensing.

If, on the other hand, there is no question of settlement on an amicable basis, and the infringement continues, then the patentee has no alternative but to ask the government to stand by its side of the bargain and stop the infringer infringing. The patentee does this by commencing an action before the relevant court, usually, in England and Wales, the Chancery Division of the High Court up until 1990, but nowadays in the Patents County Court. Cases may be brought in Scotland or Northern Ireland if desired in the appropriate court (*see* PA 1977, ss 98 and 130).

The major object of the action is usually to seek an injunction stopping the infringer from continuing with his infringement or from infringing the patent in any other way.

The normal response given by an infringer to being sued falls into two parts. First of all, there is usually a denial that infringement is actually taking place. That denial may be more or less substantial in different cases. More fundamentally, however, in most cases there is an attack on the validity of the patent which has been granted to the patentee. In other words, what the infringer will say is that even if what he is doing falls within the scope of the claims, the patent cannot be used against him because it is a bad bargain made between the inventor and the state. The bargain can be bad for one of two types of reasons. It may be intrinsically bad, for example, because the invention is not one for which a patent may properly be granted or because the description of the invention provided by the applicant is insufficient. Alternatively, it may be bad because unbeknownst to the Patent Office and the inventor, what they thought was an invention, ie what they thought was new and unobvious, is not really so at all, but rather something that has been done before or something so close to what has been done before that there is no inventive step in doing what the applicant or patentee describes. Technically, the defendant in such a case raises a defence that the patent is invalid and, normally, counterclaims against the plaintiff patentee for the revocation of the patent. The matter proceeds as a normal civil action brought between two civil litigants and the usual rules and practice of the particular court apply. Trial is ultimately before a single judge, usually, though not invariably, one of the specialist judges with patents experience, and judgment is usually reserved. After judgment is delivered there is an automatic right to appeal to the Court of Appeal. The judge will normally issue an order, if he finds in favour of the patentee, restraining the defendants from continuing to infringe. The order may also compel delivery up of infringing material and may direct an inquiry as to damages which have been suffered by the patentee as a result of the unauthorised infringement.

If an appeal is filed and subsequently lost there is a further right of appeal to the House of Lords, but only, in accordance with the usual rules, on a point of law and with leave of the House of Lords.

Many cases which are brought in the UK do not even reach trial, the parties preferring to settle their differences in some amicable fashion rather than face the time and expense of a legal patent action. It is not unusual for patent actions to require the assistance of expensive expert witnesses, the performance of experiments, attendance on demonstrations and possibly weeks in court, though this is now rare.

Although the provisions are little used, it is also possible to bring infringement actions before the Patent Office, rather than before the court, but only if both parties agree (PA 1977, s 61(3)). Also, if there is a question of whether a particular process or product is or is not an infringement, the person who wants clearance can, if the patentee refuses to give it, apply to the Patent Office or Patents County Court for a ruling (PA 1977, s 71).

The Patents County Court, which started operations in 1990, is now the preferred forum for settling patent infringement disputes. It has its own special rules of procedure (CCR Ord 48A) and the ability to deal with any patent or design matter which previously would have had to be litigated in the High Court. A major difference in practice is that the High Court 'standard legal team' of barrister, solicitor and patent attorney can be dispensed with—all three may conduct the litigation and may appear before the court to plead the case, individually or in any combination. A further difference is that written pleadings are extensive and they, and case conferences, are intended to serve rapidly to clarify what is in issue between the parties and move the genuine issues to expeditious resolution. Most cases take less than a year from start to judgment. Since the Patents County Court commenced operations there have been major improvements in the practical aspects of High Court litigation, and rapid resolution of problems can be achieved in that forum as well.

Exploitation

Turning now to the commercial rather than the technical aspects of patents, it is as well to reiterate that the patent does not give the patentee any right to use the process or in any way enhance directly the patentee's ability to manufacture or sell the product in question. His rights are determined by the patents of others, but his own patent is like an agreement with the state, whereby the state grants him a right to stop others using the invention.

This right, once technically known merely as a 'chose in action' but now as a patent, is regarded, in the UK at least, simply as personal property, which can, however, be licensed and can be assigned (*see* PA 1977, s 30).

Assignment

Assignment is the easier concept. In exactly the same way as fishing rights along a river bank can be sold, patent rights can be sold by the patentee to anyone who is willing to buy them. It is customary (and necessary if the subsequent proprietor of the patent wants to take any legal action) to register the change in ownership at the Patent Office. In the UK this is governed by PA 1977, ss 30–36 and it is worth observing in passing that the effect of these sections is to render the registration of an assignment very desirable. If an assignment from A to B is not registered by B, B will certainly lose out on the possibility of collecting damages from an infringer C until B's name is entered on the register. Possibly more importantly, if A then purports to sell to C, and C registers his assignment before B has registered his, then, by virtue of PA 1977, s 33, the assignment to B is void. It accordingly behoves assignees to record at the UK Patent Office the fact that they are the new proprietors.

Licensing

Licensing is a very broad field in which a wide variety of arrangements is possible. The easiest way of thinking of licences is to think of a contractual arrangement between the patentee, who is the licensor, and someone who wishes to do something which, if done in the absence of a licence, would render him liable to a suit for infringement of the patent. Such a position should be at the heart of any licensing arrangement, but straightforward 'no strings' arrangements between a patentee and a user, although the simplest cases to analyse, are not particularly common. Quite often, parties come to arrangements which cover more than one patent or more than one product type or more than one market. Different patents may apply to different products and patent licences may contain agreement clauses between the parties which deal with collateral matters such as exchange of technical information, purchase of special materials, communication of improvements and the like. However, patent licence matters can often be broken down into a number of component parts each of which is relatively straightforward to understand.

The licence granted by a patent licence to a licensee is a permission to do that which, in the absence of the licence, would be restrainable. Accordingly, patent licences should make it quite clear just what patent or patents are being licensed and what, if any, restrictions are placed on the licensee in terms of the availability of the whole of the patented field. Thus, if the consideration for the licence is a royalty payment on products sold, it is quite clear that in most cases that royalty should be payable only on products the manufacture of which, if carried out by an unlicensed party, would be an infringement of the patent. This is, however, a purist approach which is not always observed, sometimes for sound practical reasons and sometimes for no apparent reason at all. Patent licences have been known where the patents have been recited but royalty has been payable on royalty bearing products which have been defined in a way not coextensive with the protection afforded by the broadest claims of the patent. Such arrangements need to be looked at very carefully in practice, though they rarely give rise to very much difficulty as between a willing licensor and a willing licensee. Care should, however, be taken not to attempt to hang too much on too slender a patent licence peg, since if that attempt is made difficulties may arise, for example, in terms of the fundamental propriety of the licence or its effect, particularly its effects in relation to competition and anti-trust law. In this connection, it is noteworthy that one area of very substantial activity in recent years by the EEC Commission has been an attempt to regulate patent licensing, particularly to prevent abuse of patents (and for that matter other industrial property rights) by their being used to cloak with apparent propriety an agreement between undertakings which was contrary to Article 85(1) of the Treaty of Rome (*see* Appendix 3).

Most licence arrangements take the form of a licence being granted from the licensor to the licensee with a payment by the licensee to the licensor as a result. However, the way in which licence payments are made varies very widely and, as will be seen subsequently, this can have a quite substantial effect on the ultimate return to the patentee.

The classical approach is to pay a licence royalty either as a percentage of net sales price or in terms of some fixed sum per article processed or manufactured. Percentage royalty arrangements have the advantage of being self-adjusting when the sales price rises. Fixed price royalties, however, need to be looked at rather more carefully and consideration should always be given in any licence agreement to including some form of escalation clause, either at a predetermined rate or, for example, tied to the general rate of inflation using some appropriate index. Additionally, or alternatively, royalty rates may vary in accordance with the amount of material produced or processed and in this respect, depending upon circumstances, it may be entirely appropriate and agreeable to the parties that the royalty rate rises or falls with increasing manufacture under licence.

In some cases, in contrast, the parties will agree for the purchase of a licence for a fixed sum, either by way of an immediate total payment or by way of appropriate deferred payment terms. Such arrangements are relatively unusual, however, not least because they saddle the patentee with a licensee from whom he may not be able to detach himself. This can be embarrassing if the licensee does not in fact operate the patent and some other party wants to take a licence. While the first licence is still in existence, the second party may be prevented from doing so.

To avoid this sort of problem, minimum payments are often specified in licence arrangements, partly to ensure return to the patentee and partly also to act as an incentive to the licensee to commence manufacture. Care invariably needs to be taken to ensure that the intentions of the parties concerning any minimum royalties are clearly expressed. In particular, attention needs to be given to the question of whether the licensee can keep a licence in force merely by paying the stipulated minimum royalties, even if no manufacture whatever has taken place.

In addition to the obligations normally placed on the licensee in a patent licence to work the invention and pay appropriate monies, obligations are sometimes placed on the licensor. For example, it is not unusual for a licence arrangement to require the patentee to keep patents in force and neither is it unusual to find provision made in the agreement for the situation where an unlicensed third party starts to infringe. In those circumstances, a wide variety of options is open to licensor and licensee, ranging from no obligations on the licensor at all through to a positive obligation to sue. This last could be an extremely expensive obligation and more than erode any profit from the licence. It is accordingly one which should be adopted only with adequate safeguards.

A particularly important area of licensing practice is the question of termination. While, quite obviously, the parties are always capable of agreeing mutually to terminate, many circumstances arise where it is in the patentee's interest to terminate, for example, if production by the licensee is inadequate or fails to meet standards of quality or if the licensee goes into liquidation or is taken over by some third party whom the licensor feels is undesirable as a licensee. Very varied clauses may be set out in licence agreements to meet the varying circumstances of varying parties and various types of licensed product or process.

No discussion of patent licensing is complete without reference to the terms 'sole' and 'exclusive'. The patentee who has (unless circumscribed by the patent rights of others) the ability to work his invention may wish to extend that ability to not more than one licensee. If so, then the patentee simply grants a sole licence and the effect of that is simply to leave the patentee and the sole licensee as the only two licensed parties. This may be advantageous from the commercial point of view but of course it excludes the possibility of granting a third licence to an infringer who appears and leaves open, should third party infringement commence, only the possibilities of ignoring it or commencing suit to stop it. The first may not be very satisfactory and certainly cannot be expected to improve the relationship between the licensor and the sole licensee; the second can be very expensive.

In contrast, in the case of an exclusive licence, the licensee becomes the only person entitled to work under the patent, ie the patentee himself is excluded. Exclusive licences have been entered into on many occasions in the past and they can be very attractive to the patentee from a financial point of view. They suffer, however, from problems with regulatory agencies, notably the EEC Commission, which has expressed the view that in appropriate circumstances the existence of an exclusive licence can itself give rise to a contravention of Article 85(1) of the Treaty of Rome. The argument is that an exclusive licence is an agreement between two parties which has as its object or effect the prevention or restriction or distortion of competition since the patentee himself is no longer able to compete with the licensee.

In substitution for one or more separate licences with individual payments, royalties and the like, it is possible to come to package deal arrangements either from a patent holder to a non-patent holder or as between patent holders who may 'cross-license' relevant patents or bundles of patents which they wish mutually to exploit. In some such arrangements, there may be no need for money to pass from one party to another, but consideration always needs to be given when such complex arrangements are being contemplated as to whether it is desirable for each party to have no net receipts and no net outgoings. Additionally, anything with a hint of a 'patent pool' or 'cartel' about it tends to interest regulatory authorities, either transnational ones like the EEC Commission, or national ones (eg UK Office of Fair Trading, German Bundeskartellamt).

Finally, consideration always needs to be given when considering patent licences to questions of the ability to sub-license or sub-contract manufacture or processing on the part of the licensee and questions of so-called 'exhaustion' in respect of the goods where patented goods are in question. It does need to be made quite clear to the licensee whether or not he is entitled to extend a sub-licence under his main licence and, if so, whether any restrictions are placed on such sub-licensing. Likewise, if the subject matter is a patented product, consideration should always be given as to whether a licence to manufacture and sell the product includes the possibility of the manufacturer sub-contracting the manufacture rather than doing it himself.

Exhaustion

'Exhaustion' is a term which has received much consideration in recent years in connection with alleged attempts by patentees to partition markets, most notably the European Common Market, by the use of patents and restrictive licences. The approach which has been adopted is to say that once a patented article has been placed on the market with the consent of the patentee, or indeed by his direct actions, then the rights in such patents as the patentee may hold are effectively exhausted, as far as that article is concerned, in such a fashion that neither the patent in the country where the article is first placed on sale nor any corresponding patents in other countries can subsequently be used as a barrier to the free movement of those goods. Generally speaking, what is important to remember is that a potential licensee needs to take great care to ensure that the licence he receives from the licensor gives him all the freedom necessary to do what he wants to and, in addition, that his customers are likewise free to use the goods or process in the way contemplated.

International systems

Until now only the basic structure of the patent system and the way it is put into effect in the UK have been considered. Patents, however, are considered by almost all countries to be a Good Thing and were even obtainable behind the former Iron

Curtain. In all cases the general approach is the same, save with the important exception of the USA in connection with the approach to novelty and filing. With the exception of the USA (and the Philippines where law closely follows American law in this area), all countries require application to be made *before* the invention is disclosed publicly (*see* pp 9–10 *above*), to a government Patent Office which subsequently grants patents which have much the same effect as UK patents in the UK. In the USA, the application can be made after public disclosure, though only within certain limits. It must be made, for example, before any other patent is granted on the invention, and within a year of the first printed publication describing the invention.

There are some exceptions in some countries to the usability of patents by their owners and, for example, the so-called third world countries increasingly have provisions written into their law which discriminate against those who secure patents in the countries concerned but do not attempt to work those patents by manufacture in the particular country. Such action is seen as possibly having the effect of stifling local industry (because there are areas of technology out of which they can be kept) and meeting local demand only by imports, with consequent loss of foreign exchange.

The South American countries, particularly, increasingly insist on patents being worked in the countries concerned by, or with the licence of, the patent owner and many countries now reserve the right to grant licences compulsorily if working does not take place.

The International Convention

Most countries' patent systems require the applicant to apply before the invention is disclosed. As noted above, the date on which the first application is made is called the 'priority date', and the 'state of the art' noted above is all that was known or used before the priority date. Since most countries require application to be made before the invention is known, inventors who want protection in a lot of countries would obviously be faced with a very major problem of expenditure if they had to apply in all of them before the invention was disclosed anywhere, and thus, generally, before the inventor has any idea whether the invention is 'commercial'. This problem was solved in the last century by means of an international treaty which is formally known as the *International Union for the Protection of Industrial Property*. Informally, it is known as the *Paris Union* (referring to the diplomatic conference in Paris in 1883 which settled the basic form of the treaty) or the *International Convention*.

While this convention deals with a wide variety of matters affecting industrial property law, it is of particular note as setting up a mutual arrangement between its member states which avoids the problem just noted. A provision in the treaty ensures that the signatory states enact in their national industrial property laws provision enabling a so-called claim of priority to be made by an applicant for an industrial property right (the treaty covers designs and trade marks as well as patents). Applied to patents, the system is quite straightforward: if an applicant makes a first application for a patent at a Patent Office in any member country (called a 'regular national filing') then, within one year of making that original application in the original country, he may make applications in other Patent Offices in the other member countries claiming the original priority date. In other words, he asks the Patent Offices in each of the other countries to consider the application as though it had been filed on the same day as the original application in the original country. That original application is normally, for reasons of convenience and sometimes necessarily for reasons of domestic law and internal security, in the home country of the applicant.

About 140 countries are members of the treaty now and these include all the principal European countries and the majority of the developed world. Certain states have bilateral arrangements with other countries which work on much the same basis: India and the UK have an arrangement of this sort. There is nowadays a major incentive to join the Paris Union as membership is a prerequisite to membership of the Patent Co-operation Treaty (*see below*), and compliance with its major provisions is required by the TRIPs agreement which emerged from the Uruguay Round of GATT negotiations.

Using the provisions of the Paris Union treaty, therefore, an inventor or company can make a single application in their home country relatively inexpensively and then proceed to try to exploit the invention. The subsequent publicity does not adversely affect their ability, within one year of the original filing, to file patents for the invention in the other countries. If the invention is a failure and there is no commercial need to continue, the expenditure has been relatively small and the initial application may be allowed to lapse or pursued just in the applicant's home country. If, on the other hand, the invention is by that time shown to have potential or, even better, has actually started to make a profit for the applicant, then at that stage he can make a reasoned decision as to how much to spend and where he wants to secure foreign patents. The system thus enables the inventor to protect himself widely but at a low initial cost.

Even the International Convention arrangements do not render the cost of filing foreign patents trivial, nor of protecting an invention in a number of countries something which is lightly undertaken. In recent years there have accordingly been attempts to set up supra-national patent systems with a view to making life easier for applicants and particularly with a view to granting strong patents in a number of countries without unnecessary duplication of search and examination effort.

The Patent Co-operation Treaty and the European Patent Office

So far, international co-operation in the patent field has led to the detailed formulation of three systems, two of which are already in force. These two might be described conveniently as central systems intended to avoid the duplication of effort but which nevertheless grant national patents as the end result. The third system, which has yet to come into force, proposes the grant of a single patent having effect in all countries of the European Union.

In 1973 a number of states signed the Patent Co-operation Treaty in Washington. That treaty has as one of its principal objects the avoidance of the duplication of search and examination in various different countries. It is administered by the World Intellectual Property Organisation in Geneva and works on the following basis: if an inventor wishes to secure patents in some of the member countries, he files an application at the Patent Co-operation Treaty Office (in fact, physically, with his own national Patent Office) which then remits the papers to a Patent Office with good search facilities. This is known as an international searching authority and the examiner there carries out a search and finds any literature which he thinks relevant to the consideration of patentability. Furthermore, under the system, if the applicant so wishes, a patentability report (called the 'international preliminary examination report') is made on the application which sets out whether or not the examiner thinks the invention is patentable in view of the material he has found in the search.

Search and preliminary examination are the so-called international phase of processing an application under the Patent Co-operation Treaty. In addition to these international stages, the papers are sent by the central organisation to each of the national Patent Offices in the various countries designated who thereafter can process the patent application in accordance with their national law. This may range from continuing the examination proceedings and making the applicant argue his case if he wants to get a patent, at one end of the scale, to simply granting a patent without any guarantee of its validity at the other.

The Patent Co-operation Treaty system is useful when it is desired to delay the cost of patenting, particularly if it is desired to put off the cost of making translations into foreign languages of the specification. This can be delayed until 20 months after the priority date (or 30 if preliminary examination is requested in the international processing phase). The usefulness of the system is somewhat restricted by the fact that some important industrialised countries (most notably Taiwan) are not members of the treaty, but efforts are being made to increase membership, which in mid-1997 totalled over 90 countries.

The other treaty currently operative is the European Patent Convention, which led to the setting up of the European Patent Office. This organisation, which has its headquarters in Munich but branches elsewhere, operates in a fashion very similar to a national Patent Office but with this difference: when the application is filed, in addition to asking for a patent, it is necessary to specify the countries of the system in which it is desired to have a patent. The search and examination by the European Patent Office examiner then proceed and, if the examiner is convinced that patentable subject matter is present, once the papers are brought into order and the claims directed to that subject matter, the European Patent Office grants not a single European patent but rather a bundle of patents in each of the national states designated. These patents then rank equally with patents in the particular designated state but obtained through the national Patent Office rather than the European Patent Office. Certain formalities must be observed if the patents are to be effective everywhere, most notably (and expensively) the filing of translations into the local languages. The way in which the European Patent Office operates has, of course, necessitated very substantial harmonisation of patent laws throughout the member countries and the substantive conditions set out in the national statutes of each individual country for patentability, the nature of patentable invention and the like, are now common to all member countries.

Within a few years, it is expected that the third system will come into operation using the European Patent Office organisation to grant a single patent effective throughout the countries of the European Union. Implementation of the Community Patent Convention (CPC) was for many years held back, as neither Eire nor Denmark had ratified the European Patent Convention. However, both did so some time ago, leading to a revival of efforts to bring the CPC into force. Concern continues to be expressed that patentees might be unwilling to put all their eggs in one (European) basket, but this pales into insignificance compared with the problems of the costs consequent on the need to produce a translation of the patent specification and claims into all community languages at the time of grant, costs which will predictably increase if the eastwards expansion of the EU leads to substantial enlargement.

It should be noted in passing that a national application can be used as a priority basis for filing an application under the Patent Co-operation Treaty or the European Patent Office systems, the priority date concept being preserved. In addition, it is possible using the Patent Co-operation Treaty to designate most European countries in one of two ways: either the Patent Co-operation Treaty organisation is asked to send the documents for national processing in the various European countries desired, or the Patent Co-operation Treaty authority is requested to send the documents to the European Patent Office with a notice designating the states in which ultimately patents will, the applicant hopes, be granted.

A further recent development is the concept of 'extension states'. If, when applying for a European patent (either direct or via the PCT system) the applicant designates an 'extension state', then when the European Patent Office finally grants the patent it can be made effective in each 'extension state' by taking care of certain simple formalities and providing a translation into a local language. So far Latvia, Lithuania, Slovenia, Albania and Romania have agreed to operate in this way, though national applications at their respective national Patent Offices may still be made. Most other states of the former Soviet Union are members of the Eurasian Patent Office system, which operates for those states in a fashion analogous to that of the European Patent Office for its member states.

The international systems not only keep down costs by reducing the duplication of efforts by national patent officers, but also by reducing duplication of work by patent lawyers throughout the world. Most UK patent agents are also European patent attorneys, the restricted class of people who are allowed to act for others before the European Patent Office. In PCT matters, for many countries, local patent lawyers do not need to become involved until around 30 months from the priority date, after due initial application has been made, the search carried out, the papers published and the preliminary examination report also settled.

Canada and the USA

In the USA (and until 1989 in Canada—but not subsequently: Canadian law is now in line with that of most other industrialised countries) the approach to patenting is somewhat different. Canadian law tended to follow American law for obvious geographical and economic reasons, though it also borrows heavily from English law. However, the USA is still distinguished from the rest of the world in the stress placed on the role of the inventor.

Indeed, the American constitution reserves to inventors the fruits of their labours and for this reason in the USA the inventor's employer, who may be entirely entitled to the invention, cannot apply for the patent initially. Instead, the inventor must apply and in Canada application could be made by the company only if it were accompanied by, or rapidly followed up with, proof of assignment from the inventor, who must in any case be named.

In the USA, the emphasis on the inventor is further reflected in the concept of granting the patent, not to the first man to come to the Patent Office with the invention, but to the first to invent. Thus if two inventors make the same invention at different times and the later inventor files an application at the USA Patent Office before the earlier inventor does, that does not stop the patent for the invention being awarded to the earlier inventor, even though he applies later. For the same reasons, the novelty requirements are different in the USA from those in other countries. The invention has to be new and inventive, but the relevant date at which the 'prior art' ends, for most categories, is not the date of filing but, in the USA, one year earlier (in Canada it used to be two years earlier). Note, however, that the detailed rules applicable are not as simple as this: see 35 USC, s 102 and the Canadian Patent Act, 1952, s 28. Thus in the USA it is possible to invent, reduce to practice and come out on the market and find that the invention is worthwhile commercially before applying for a patent.

Quite clearly, there had to be some limit on that activity and that is why the arbitrary one- and two-year periods are chosen. In addition, the application had to be made in the USA or Canada before any corresponding patent issued elsewhere.

In practice, these differences of approach in North America do not lead to very great difficulties or incompatibilities between the patent systems there and those elsewhere in the world. There is, however, one caveat which should be carefully noted: it has long been the practice in the USA and Canada to 'wait and see' before filing. As noted above, this does not jeopardise the validity of the American or 'old' Canadian patents which might subsequently issue on the invention but, of course, public use or disclosure in the USA or Canada before filing there and accordingly setting up a priority date may well make it quite impossible for the patentee to secure any valid patent protection outside the USA or Canada. Unless, therefore, interest is going to be limited only to the USA or Canada, it is wise for the North American inventor or his company to file an application at his local Patent Office, or at least a Patent Office in a country which is a member of the Convention, before the invention is released to the public.

Pressure has been brought on the USA in recent years to 'come into step' with the rest of the world. It may happen: there is a firm proposal for a trade-off: if the USA abandons its first-to-invent system, in favour of a first-to-file system, other countries would introduce a 'grace period' rule, discounting disclosures by the inventor before filing from counting as part of the 'state of the art'. In view of the need for primary legislation to effect such a proposal, even if agreement in principle can be reached, it will be several years before such a system could be introduced in practice. This problem has stalled progress with the 'Patent Law Treaty' which has been in negotiation for several years under the auspices of the World Intellectual Property Organisation in Geneva, but the negotiations continue and good progress is being made in agreeing further harmonisation between many participating countries. The advantage of a slow pace in these negotiations is that by the time the treaty comes into force, most countries will have had time to bring their local legislation into line with its provisions.

Petty patents

Not all inventions make the same technical contribution to progress in their particular field. They may nevertheless be useful, and many legislatures, particularly those requiring a high standard of inventiveness for patentability, have felt in the past that some sort of protection was needed for 'minor inventions'. A variety of systems have grown up in individual jurisdictions and there is no uniformity of indentifying name. The term 'petty patent' may be applied to the concept generally for English-speaking countries, though the normal English language term for the Japanese type is 'utility model'. The French and Italians have 'certificates of utility', while the German variety is almost invariably known by its German term 'Gebrauchsmuster'.

Protection by way of petty patent is generally characterised by being:

(1)   of shorter term than protection by patent, and

(2)   being obtained with no or relatively little formality.

Thus, for example, a German Gebrauchsmuster may be secured by filing an application to receive one, accompanied by a specification and claims drafted exactly as they would be drafted for a patent application. However, there is no examination or search, and grant occurs immediately and automatically.

In some countries, petty patent protection is restricted to mechanical subject matter, or at least to subject matter which can be illustrated in a drawing. However, in other countries the system can, for example, protect chemical inventions as well.

Because of the rapidity of obtaining them and the relative lack of formality, petty patents can be a useful form of protection, particularly where a product with relatively short market life is concerned, and where there might be doubts as to whether the item had sufficient inventiveness to support a normal patent. Manufacturing industry in countries which have petty patent systems tends to use such systems and in recent years several countries which did not previously provide such protection have chosen to enact petty patent laws to provide it. There is no immediate prospect of such being enacted in the UK, though there is potential pressure by way of a projected European Union directive. This was proposed on the basis that the current differences in availability of this sort of protection within the EU could distort inter-state trade and hamper the completion of an internal free market. The evidence for this proposition is thin. Generally, EU 'small industry' enthusiastically supports the introduction of petty patent protection throughout the EU as it is perceived as a cheaper route to protection than the patent system. Large industry is generally opposed, mindful of the extra burden on industry *as a whole* of the existence of a large number of unexamined rights which materially would increase the difficulty of being able to be sure that one could proceed with any particular product or process without fear of infringement.

In terms of exploitation, petty patents may be considered as equivalent to patents for most practical purposes, though in view of their shorter term, licence arrangements tend to be shorter term also. If exploitation needs to be offensive, by way of an infringement suit, a prerequisite to bringing such suit may be to have a novelty search carried out by the national Patent Office of the country concerned so that the court and defendant may both have a chance of assessing the likelihood of validity immediately an action is started. Such a requirement acts as a deterrent to the owner of the petty patent right bringing actions for infringement casually and possibly oppressively, eg against smaller companies or individuals, but large industry fears it might be 'held to ransom' if use of the petty patent systems (and the systems themselves) become more international.

Conclusion

Patents are useful, and can act at least for a short time to keep others away from encroaching on new technology, on the exploitation of a new invention. They can be built up into a portfolio to secure a technological lead in a field and ensure that any competitor is kept at bay.

However, there is a need to have ideas which are new, and not obvious, and to use the complex technical legal systems to secure protection. Once protected, the invention can be exploited by licence or by the patentee's own manufacture, or both.

Patents are useful pegs on which to hang know-how and licensing deals and can assist in transferring funds. The printed specifications also constitute an enormous body of literature on technology (rather than science) which is generally available and can be usefully studied because it is all classified by subject matter, and is increasingly becoming available in computer database form enabling relevant technical material to be located with ease and precision. In particular, all patents now in force in all the major industrialised countries which are members of the Paris Union can now be found by computer searching, making infringement clearance searches materially easier, though not easy.

3   Designs

Introduction

This chapter is concerned with the protection of designs by registration where a design is, broadly, something to do with the shape or configuration of, or the pattern or ornament applied to, an article. It is *not* concerned with pictures, or symbols, or logotypes which are used as trade marks and which are sometimes referred to as 'designs' (in contrast to 'words').

Design law borrows concepts both from patent law and from copyright law. From patent law it takes the notion of a restricted term of monopoly with registration giving the right to stop others producing articles to the same design, and the concept of novelty as a requirement for a design to be registrable. From copyright law, it borrows the concept of a design being the actual physical embodiment or manifestation of an idea, rather than the idea itself.

Design law is selective in its application: it is particularly useful in areas such as fabric designs and in other areas where the design is applied to the article in question for the purpose of imparting 'eye appeal' to it. However, it may be used to protect appearance where the motivation leading to the appearance has both functional and aesthetic components. Design law was fairly unchanging from 1950 to 1968, but following the amendments to the Copyright Act 1956 made by the Design Copyright Act 1968 (*see* Chapter 5, at p 48), its use underwent major changes, and in particular declined as industry found it preferable to rely on copying and copyright law than to seek protection via the Registered Designs Act. Despite that, it is still sufficiently used to merit its retention. The maximum term of protection was increased from 15 to 25 years in 1989.

In many industries registration of designs should not be overlooked by manufacturers since registering a design generally provides a quick, relatively inexpensive way of securing some immediate protection for the shape, configuration, pattern or ornament of an article. The pattern is, of course, of particular importance in respect of textiles, such as cloth and lace, and wallpaper. The lack of a requirement to prove copying in order to succeed in an infringement action can be very advantageous, particularly if copying takes place overseas.

Obtaining protection

In the UK, the registration of designs is governed by the Registered Designs Act (RDA) 1949, which defines design as 'features of shape, configuration, pattern or ornament applied to an article by any industrial process and applies to the design only so far as it applies to features which, in the finished article, appeal to and are judged solely by the eye' (s 1). It is specifically stated in RDA 1949, s 1(3) that a 'design' shall not be registered if it consists of a method or principle of construction or, and possibly more importantly, 'includes features of shape or configuration which are dictated solely by the function which the article has to perform'. This last exclusion is intended to direct use of the Act to protect designs where the aesthetic is predominant, and exclude those where function has wholly dictated form.

Leaving that aside, if a design is to be registered it must be 'new'. 'New' means that at the time of applying for registration the design has not been published before or, at least, not as applied to an article. Trivial differences or differences which, in respect of the type of article in question, are common trade variants, do not make a design 'new' as required. In addition, so-called 'artistic use' of a particular design will not be prejudicial to the novelty of the design. Thus, the publication of a strip cartoon including a distinctively presented koala bear called Kim Koala will not prejudice a subsequent application to register the Kim Koala design for a soft toy. However, it is, of course, very advisable to register if protection is to be sought by way of a registered design before the strip cartoon ever appears in print, since unauthorised manufacture of Kim Koala soft toys would still destroy novelty.

If a design is new or, rather, if the Registrar's office believes it to be new—and they do make a search—then registration is effected and a registration certificate issued which gives the normal formal data and to which are attached so-called representations of the design. These may take the form of line drawings or photographs, or some other suitable two-dimensional representation of the design.

These representations form part of the original papers which are filed at the Registry when applying to register. They must be filed in quadruplicate and accompanied by an application form (which gives the formal details of the applicant and makes the formal request for registration) and a statement of novelty (saying wherein the novelty of the design resides, eg, in its shape, ornament or whatever). The applicant must be the proprietor of the design, but he need not be the designer nor the owner of any copyright in the design; someone who has the exclusive right by virtue of contractual arrangements with a designer to exploit the design, eg on wallpaper, is the proprietor of the design as applied to wallpaper and may apply to register the design in respect of such goods.

As noted above, a design registration must be in respect of an article, but a series of design registrations may also be obtained in respect of a series of different articles to which essentially the same design is applied. In this case, the later registrations are not prejudiced by the earlier ones, provided that, in each case, at the date of applying for each later registration no use has been made of the design on the articles in respect of which the fresh registration is sought.

Thus, for example, a motor car manufacturer may register the design of a motor car initially and, if the motor car is then about to be launched, may register an associated design in respect of toy motor vehicles. As in the case of Kim Koala, it is wise to decide what range of goods seems appropriate before any of the range has reached the public domain.

The Registrar of Designs maintains a register of all designs in force and it is possible to secure information from that register as of right (though on payment of a fee). It is also possible to secure copies of the representations filed in respect of any design registration if its number is known. Searching of designs by the public in the UK designs registry is not possible. However, a manufacturer who wants to check whether a proposed item would infringe any registered design in force can ask the Registry to carry out a check (Design Form 21, Design Rule 71). Two specimens of the design proposed or two representations showing the design, eg photographs or drawings, have to be supplied and a fee paid. The Registrar's view expressed as a result of such a search is not conclusive, but it is a prudent step to take if it is proposed to launch a new item in a field where design protection is often taken out. Although it is not possible for the public to search the designs register by way of subject matter, a name index is maintained by the British Library.

Form of protection

When a registration certificate is issued (usually within a few months of applying) the proprietor of that registration then acquires the exclusive right in the UK and the Isle of Man to make or import for sale or hire or for use, or to sell, hire or offer for sale or hire, any article in respect of which the design is registered, either an article to which the exact registered design has been applied or an article to which a design 'not substantially different' from the registered design has been applied. As with patents, the right given is a right to stop other people, and it includes a right to prevent both manufacture and importation of articles bearing the registered design or a design substantially the same. The question of whether or not a design is substantially the same is one which is very straightforward: do the two articles look the same? If they do not, it is unlikely that there is any design infringement. If they do, then infringement will be established, provided of course that the article in question falls within the scope of the design registration. It is particularly noteworthy in this connection that the question of whether the infringement was derived from the original, eg by copying, is irrelevant.

In the UK, registration lasts initially for five years, counted from the original date of application. It may be extended four times, each time for a further five years, on payment of a fee. There is one exception to this if a design is registered which is based on a 'corresponding artistic work' where the copyright in the artistic work runs out before the expiry of the possible maximum 25-year term of the design registration. In such a case, when the copyright runs out (*see* Chapter 5 at p 48) the registered design runs out too (*see* RDA 1949, s 8(5)).

It is of very great importance to remember that infringement of a registered design can take place without any ill-intent or bad faith and without any copying taking place. If two parties independently conceive the same, or substantially the same, new teapot shape, one registers and the other produces, then since the shapes are substantially the same, the teapot as produced will infringe the registered design. In such a case, the so-called 'innocent infringer' does get let off damages (RDA 1949, s 9(1)) but can still be enjoined from further manufacture (RDA 1949, s 9(2)).

There is provision (RDA 1949, s 11) for cancelling registered designs by any person interested on the basis that the design was not at the date of registration new or original, or indeed on the basis of any other ground on which the Registrar should have refused to register. Such actions are rarely brought before the Registrar, registered designs usually being attacked only by defendants in infringement proceedings brought in the Patents County Court or the High Court.

Exploitation

As noted above, once the proprietor has his design registration, he can stop other people producing or offering for sale items which infringe it. The procedure parallels that for patent infringement (*see* pp 17–20 *above*). Equally, the proprietor can permit such activity to take place in return for a licence fee, either a lump sum or a royalty, or a combination of the two, or in certain cases some other form of consideration. Licences and other documents affecting the registered design may be registered on the register kept for that purpose. Registration is valuable if court proceedings are contemplated as, by RDA 1949, s 19(5), documents in respect of which no entry has been made in the Register of Designs shall not be admitted in any court as evidence of the title of any person to a registered design or share or interest in a registered design unless the court otherwise directs. Quite clearly, the court will always take registration of a licence, or an assignment, in the register as *prima facie* evidence of entitlement.

As just noted, an assignment can be registered and, indeed, should be, in order to claim entitlement if the registration is sold or otherwise transmitted.

International systems

Many countries protect so-called 'industrial designs' and this is usually effected by means of a registration system which varies quite widely from country to country. There is not that uniformity often encountered in patent and trade mark law, although design laws are covered by the provisions of the International Convention.

In a manner analogous to the one-year priority period for patents, there is a six-month priority period for designs, ie, if an application to register the design is made in, for example, the UK, then within six months an application can be made to register in other countries claiming the UK priority date and the applications in those other countries will be considered as though they had been filed on the same date as the UK application. The British Registry will provide a certificate for use abroad, if so requested.

Although in many overseas countries design registration is virtually automatic and little searching is carried out, there is one notable exception and that is the USA. In that country, the Patent Office carefully examines applications for 'design patents' and the procedure is very similar to the normal patent prosecution procedure there. The American examiner will quite often issue an official action on a design patent application, citing earlier designs which bear some resemblance to the design applied for and asserting that the differences are insubstantial. Prosecuting design applications in the USA is accordingly generally much more costly than prosecuting design applications elsewhere, and 'unobviousness' is a requirement for design patent validity. There is no direct parallel in the USA to the 'Industrial Design' registration systems of other countries.

There are two multinational systems for protecting designs, an 'International Design' deposit system run by the World Intellectual Property Organisation, which provides protection in up to 20 countries via a single deposit (the relevant treaty is called the Hague Agreement) and the Benelux Countries have a combined Designs Register and Designs Office. A proposed European Community Designs Regulation was widely discussed, but never achieved much support. More recently, however, a directive to harmonise design law in the EU has made much progress, and is likely to be adopted in 1998. However, the divisions between spare parts manufacturers and original equipment makers have proved intractable, and this important area of application of design law is likely to continue unharmonised as countries will be able to adopt different (and incompatible) solutions. The basic approach set out in the Directive will however, in time provide a more 'level playing field' at least within the EU, but its wider extension is fraught with difficulty.

Conclusion

In summary, the simple major rules about industrial designs are:

1. Consider whether registration is appropriate before the design becomes public in any way.

2. If design application is to be sought, make sure the articles to be covered are carefully thought out and that more than one application is made if more than one type of article is to be covered.

3. Remember that it may be much easier to prosecute a copyist under a clear design registration than under copyright or unfair competition law, even if either of the latter can be made to apply, which is not always the case.

4. Remember that design registration is probably the quickest and cheapest form of protection available for a manufactured product. It is restricted in its scope, but it may serve as a rapidly usable weapon to keep down competition from competitors who copy your products.

4 Trade marks

Introduction

For many centuries craftsmen and traders have sought to leave their marks on goods, as a means of identifying those goods. The motives for doing so may be mixed, but at least one central component has always been to attempt to identify the product in order to promote repeat business. In some technical areas, for example, the manufacture of precious metal wares and ceramics, very extensive marking systems have been in operation for centuries and these serve as an invaluable guide to the historian or even to the archaeologist. Their original purpose, however, was simply to identify the trade source, whether that was a manufacturer in post-industrial revolution times or a craftsman. Additionally, particularly after the industrial revolution, trade sources included an increasing number of people who were not manufacturers but merely traders who placed identifying marks on goods which passed through their hands with a view to spreading their own reputation and thus promoting repeat business.

With the use of marks to identify goods with their maker or trader arose the use of counterfeit marks, ie marks used improperly by those who wished to trade on the reputation of the original genuine manufacturer or trader. The object of doing so was to enhance the commercial prospects of the improper user at the expense of the legitimate user. It has long been held that attempts of this nature to secure a 'free ride' or improper commercial advantage are wrong. Originally such attempts generally involved an element of dishonesty on the part of the perpetrator but nowadays, with very substantial international trade in marked goods, dishonesty is not a necessary component. What is, however, almost invariably present is an ability, if not an intention, to cause deception or confusion among the purchasing public. This has for many years been regarded as unacceptable and strong trade mark laws are one of the weapons in the state armoury against public deception.

As usual, 'trade marks' developed only gradually over the centuries and various types of marking have come to be known generally under the term 'trade mark'. Markings may be indicative of attributes other than source, such as quality, type, fitness for purpose, compliance with standards or endorsement. Markings may also be more or less associated with the goods in question, and, with the rise in literacy and of service industries, marks (so-called 'service marks' in many jurisdictions) are widely used to identify a source of services and so promote repeat business. The law in the UK changed on 1 October 1986 to protect 'service marks' originally in parallel fashion to 'trade marks'. The current legislation (Trade Marks Act 1994) regards marks as trade marks applying equally to goods or services.

However, other than the mention in this paragraph, the chapter does not concern itself with three particular categories of trade mark. The first of these is defensive marks. These were trade marks registered by a trader in respect of goods on which he did not use the mark but in order to prevent others from using it on those goods since the mark was so well known that it would be deceptive if so used, despite the fact that the trader did not use it himself on the goods (*see* Trade Marks Act (TMA) 1938, s 27 in the UK). The second and third categories are certification marks and collective (or guarantee) marks, both of which types of mark are open to use by a number of traders and so do not serve as an unambiguous indicator of origin. Use of a collective mark may be restricted to members of a given trade association or some other grouping, while use of a certification mark may be restricted only to those whose goods meet some set of independent criteria. Typical examples of this last sort of mark are the British Standards Institution 'Kitemark' and the Woolmark. The use of certification marks is generally controlled independently of any particular trade or manufacturing source (for a statutory basis in the UK see TMA 1994, s 50 and Sched 2).

Thus, in what follows, the term 'trade mark' is used to denote exclusively marks used by an individual trader, or sometimes a consortium of traders or more than one trader by agreement, to denote origin or identify source, either on or in connection with goods or in connection with services.

The use of trade marks expanded enormously with the coming of the industrial revolution and the colossal expansion in trade in manufactured goods, and accordingly, in the legislative history of many countries there appears during the nineteenth century a realisation of the necessity to set down quite clearly the law relating to trade marks and to unify practices which may have differed as between different areas of trade. This unification generally adopted as its central element the creation of so-called trade mark registers, ie lists of trade marks together with their respective goods or services and proprietors which were maintained by the governments concerned. It had long been the practice in certain industries to control trade marks by the creation of a central register, often operated by the regulating body of the industry itself, and in some cases these systems were simply taken over by the states, which set up a central state-controlled register. In almost all the then industrialised countries by 1900 there was some sort of codified trade mark law and a register of trade marks.

The system of registering trade marks on an independently maintained statutory register still left the individual tradesman, craftsman or manufacturer free to adopt and use any trade mark which he pleased (provided, of course, that such use was not misleading or confusing) and there has never been any necessity, at least as far as most countries are concerned, to secure trade mark registration before a mark could be used and trade commenced. Instead, what the registration system provides is a register covering all classes of goods and services on which traders may enter notice of their rights, both as a warning to others of their existence and to form a statutory right on the basis of which action can be taken.

Trade mark registers are open to inspection by any member of the public in order that they may be searched with a view to ascertaining the freedom or otherwise to use a particular mark. Of course, such a search cannot be exhaustive in the sense of giving a positive clearance, since not all marks in use are necessarily on the register, but it does provide a valuable starting point and nowadays a check at the trade mark registries of several industrialised countries is a *sine qua non* prior to the application of a new trade mark to a new line of goods which is to be manufactured and sold in substantial quantities or to the adoption of a new mark for a service business. The risks of running into a problem if such a check is not carried out, and the consequent possible expense of renaming and remarking products, or reprinting stationery, are generally unacceptable.

Obtaining protection

In the UK, the registration of trade marks is governed by TMA 1994 under which is maintained the Register of Trade Marks (TMA 1994, s 63) on which details of all registrations are entered, and which continues the statutory office of the Registrar. This office is common with that of the Comptroller General of Patents, and the Trade Marks Registry forms a branch of the Patent Office and operates from the same premises.

Registrable marks

Any sign capable of being represented graphically and which is capable of distinguishing goods or services of one undertaking from those of other undertakings can be registered. Thus, both word marks and so-called device marks or symbols can be registered as trade marks, but they must be capable of being distinctive of goods or services rather than merely being descriptive. Thus a picture showing the type of goods in question or a word describing the nature or quality of the goods or services in question will not be registrable unless (usually due to very unusual circumstances) it has in fact become distinctive. A word with no direct reference to the quality or character of the goods or services, or a picture of some different good may well be registrable: for example, a picture of a swallow is registrable in respect of ballpoint pens, or of a penguin in respect of dry cleaning services. The most distinctive sort of mark which has the merit of memorability is, of course, the invented word. The most famous invented word mark is probably the word 'Kodak'. Care must always be taken when inventing words in one language to ensure that they do not have some specific meaning, particularly a pejorative or improper meaning, in another.

When applying to register a trade mark, it is necessary to specify the goods or services in respect of which registration is desired (Trade Marks Rules 1994, rule 8). An application to register can be made in respect of goods or services in one class only, or for both goods and services, and for any number of classes.

The goods or services for which registration is sought are generally expressed in general terms but for convenience of classifying them it is also necessary to state the class in which they fall. Most countries now use the so-called International Classification of Goods and Services. The 34 classes of goods and eight classes of services covered by this classification appear as Schedule IV to the Trade Marks Rules 1994.

The application

Under TMA 1994, in order to secure registration of a trade mark application must be made on the prescribed form and the prescribed fee paid. The application needs to state the name of the proprietor, and his address, include a representation of the mark, and state the goods or services in respect of which registration is desired. The Trade Marks Registry then conducts an examination of the application to see whether the mark qualifies for registration.

Under this examination, both intrinsic and extrinsic registrability are considered. Intrinsically, detailed consideration is given as to whether the mark is of a type which can be registered as a trade mark as falling within TMA 1994, s 3.

A mark cannot be registered if it cannot be 'represented graphically'. Subject to the condition that if one can prove by evidence that a mark is distinctive in fact, it can be registered, the following types of mark cannot, *prima facie*, be registered:

(a)   marks devoid of any distinctive character;

(b)   marks consisting exclusively of signs or indications which may serve in trade to designate characteristics of the goods or services in question, eg their type, quality, geographical origin, purpose or value;

(c)   marks consisting exclusively of signs or indications customary in current language or in *bona fide* and established practices in the trade in question.

In such cases, evidence of acquired distinctiveness must be supplied if the objection is to be overcome (TMA 1994, s 3(1)).

Under the heading of intrinsic registrability, the registry can also object to registering marks the use of which would not be entitled to protection in the courts for any reason, or the use of which would be contrary to public policy or morality, or is deceptive (TMA 1994, s 3(3) and (4)).

Turning now to extrinsic registrability (*see* TMA 1994, s 5), the registrar conducts, as part of the examination, a search of other marks on the register or the subject of earlier filed applications to see if there are any identical or similar marks already registered or applied for in respect of identical or similar goods or services. This includes, on a somewhat *ad hoc* basis, looking at marks applied for or registered in respect of services where those services are intimately connected with the goods applied for or *vice versa*. The search is also carried out in the European register and through Community trade mark applications, and in the international register where the UK is a designated state. If the registrar finds any other relevant mark or marks when the search is effected, depending upon the degree of identity or similarity of the marks or goods or services as the case may be, the registrar may flatly refuse to register, though such refusal may be overcome if consent to registration can be secured from the proprietor(s) of the other mark(s). Often some of the objections raised by the registrar on the basis of earlier marks can be overcome by written or oral argument, particularly if the goods or services are more narrowly specified to avoid overlap.

If the registrar is satisfied as to intrinsic and extrinsic registrability he then 'accepts' the application and causes the details of it to be published in the weekly *Trade Marks Journal*. Within three months from publication, an opposition may be filed by any interested third party on the basis of any grounds on which the application might be refused, both extrinsic and intrinsic. If no one opposes, or if an opposition is resolved in favour of the applicant, then the mark is registered with effect from the date on which application was made. This is subject to a small caveat: if someone, on seeing an application advertised, does not wish to oppose, but does feel that for some reason the mark should not be registered, he or she can file 'observations' at the Trade Marks Registry. These are communicated by the registry to the applicant. If the registrar thinks the observations reveal problems, then these must be resolved before the mark is registered.

In the UK, it usually takes (for an unopposed application) between nine months and two years to obtain registration. However, if evidence of distinctiveness needs to be collected, or if a third party opposes registration, the time from application to registration (if achieved) can be several years.

Once registration has been secured it can be retained forever, provided that the registration is kept in force by paying renewal fees every ten years and by use. This gives a very substantial term to arrangements involving trade marks but this term perforce reflects the long term over which genuine trading reputations can extend. Of course, if a mark ceases to be used, then that reputation starts to evaporate and after a given time (five years in the UK (TMA 1994, s 46)) the mark can be removed from the register ('revoked') for non-use.

Form of protection

Entry of a mark on the register gives the proprietor the ability to say effectively: 'My trade mark is on the register. It is therefore up to anyone who trades, and who can of course see that my mark is registered, to keep away from using, on goods like mine or in respect of services of the same kind as I provide, any mark which is the same or confusingly similar. If despite this someone does use such a mark, then the fact that I have registered my mark gives me a *prima facie* right to stop them using their confusingly similar mark and, if they will not stop when asked politely, I will take action in the courts to compel them to stop.' This conversion of what might be described as a common law right (*see* Chapter 6 for discussion of passing off) to a so-called prescriptive right is of very substantial importance. Not only does it create a position in which the original trade mark adopter and user can take legal action on the basis of a specific statutorily registered right, but it relieves him of the initial responsibility of demonstrating that the right in question is one which he ought to enjoy. In the contrasting case where a trader has had his mark appropriated by a third party improperly but the mark is not registered, the first trader always had to demonstrate, as a prerequisite for any success in court, that he had used his mark and thereby acquired a reputation or 'goodwill' arising out of its use. This prerequisite is still necessary in passing-off cases, but the burden of proof is difficult, and indeed can be very expensive, to discharge. Discharging that proof might also have adverse consequences such as the necessity of revealing the trading pattern of the original trader, including figures for trading, how the trade is carried on and the provision of examples and evidence from people in the trade. The provision of the statutory register and trade mark statute law avoids the trouble and expense of proving reputation and use, at least as a necessary step to stopping improper use. The ability to rely on such a prescriptive right, to say 'this is my territory and you infringe on it at your peril', vastly simplified trades disputes concerning marking.

Registration gives the proprietor of the mark the exclusive right to use it in respect of the goods or services save for two notable exceptions (*see* TMA 1994, ss 10 and 11). The first of these allows the use of a trade mark in connection with goods adapted for use in connection with particular trade marked goods, for example, as accessories or spare parts. The second exempts from infringement of a registration of mark 'A' the use of mark 'B', where the marks are identical or nearly resemble each other and have both been registered, if mark 'B' is used only on goods or services in respect of which it has been registered. These exceptions operate only if the use in question is in accordance with honest business practice.

Infringement

Basically, the right to proceed against others is limited to cases where the use is of the same or a confusingly similar mark on goods or services which are the same or similar to the goods or services in respect of which the mark is registered. Thus, if someone had registered a mark for 'silverware', use of the same or of a similar mark on 'goldware' by an unauthorised third party would be an infringement, Likewise, a registration in respect of 'insurance services' could well be infringed by the use of the same mark by a third party for banking services, but that would be the case only if consumers saw the services as similar or likely to be related. Much will depend on the particular circumstances of each case. Thus, in the celebrated *British Sugar* case ([1996] RPC 281) a 'toffee spread' for putting on, eg, toast was found to be not too similar to a dessert topping syrup.

Additionally, the 1994 Trade Marks Act introduced a new form of infringement where the mark registered has a reputation, and the use by a third party is on non-similar goods or services. If the use would cause detriment to the registered mark, it will infringe. Section 10(3) is thought to have analogous effects to the 'anti-dilution' sections in some foreign trade mark laws (notably those in the USA), but has not yet been tested in a reported case.

If someone infringes, and refuses to stop after the infringement has been drawn to their attention, action can be taken in the High Court to restrain infringement. The relief sought is usually an injunction and an inquiry as to damages, the former being by far the more important. The defences to infringement are usually simply that the respective marks are not confusingly similar, or that the goods or services in respect of which the alleged infringement is taking place are not covered by the registration.

Validity of the registration is rarely called into question; however, a counter-attack is sometimes mounted if the owner of the registration has allowed his mark to become generic, so that it ceased to function as a trade mark, so enabling the defendant, if successful, to have the mark removed from the register.

In the UK, registration also gives the proprietor a different form of protection, against encroachment by other would-be registrants or mark users. The search which the registrar carries out is done, in a sense, on behalf of the existing registrants, and a refusal to register a third party's mark on the ground of it being too close to one already on the register can often cause the third party to think again and adopt another mark, so protecting the existing registrant. Since the existing registrant does not, in general, know of the subsequent attempt at registration by a third party, many registrants are unaware of this aspect of protection which they enjoy in the UK and in other countries where the Trade Mark Office carries out a search and can reject an application on the basis of its search results.

Exploitation

Positive exploitation of registered trade mark rights (other than relying on them merely as a defensive measure) is a relatively modern phenomenon.

Originally, a very harsh approach was taken to the question of use of a registered trade mark by anyone other than its originator and original user, even if the trade mark proprietor was prepared to agree, it being felt that use by anyone other than the registered proprietor of the mark was effectively deceptive. With the liberalisation of trade and the growth of extensive trade practices inconsistent with this idealist approach, this is no longer the case and the practice has grown up of enabling marks to be properly used either by their original proprietor or by somebody who is licensed or permitted to use the mark.

Licensing and permitted use arrangements

Nowadays, the use of a particular trade mark on particular goods or services may be genuine in one of two different sets of circumstances: the first is, of course, the case where the goods are produced or the services rendered by the actual owner of the trade mark, who is usually the proprietor of the trade mark registration. The second is that the goods are produced or services rendered by some third party which may or may not have any other commercial connection with the proprietor, but which has an arrangement with the proprietor whereby the goods or services are in some way sanctioned or franked with the proprietor's approval. The usual approach is to say that the mark may be used by the third party under licence provided that the goods or services in question meet standards of quality laid down from time to time by the registered proprietor. Thus, to the member of the public who sees the goods or an advertisement for the services, the trade mark now indicates either that the goods or services emanate from the original proprietor of the trade mark, or that they are offered in the market with his approval. It is usually assumed that the proprietors of trade marks will jealously guard the reputation of their own manufacture, their own goods or their own services by ensuring that all products or services placed on the market under licence meet the high quality standards of their own product or service and, indeed, it is clearly commercially desirable in many cases to ensure that they do so. However, it should be remembered that there is nothing to stop a trade mark proprietor allowing a third party to manufacture under licence products of a markedly inferior nature with the proprietor's mark still stamped on them and with the manufacturers of the inferior goods securing an advantage for which they are prepared to pay the proprietor by virtue of the enhanced sales which the use of the mark is presumed to confer. Whether it does and whether it will continue to do so in the case of goods that are not of adequate quality is, of course, a very interesting question; generally speaking, proprietors effectively reserve to themselves the right to vary the quality of the goods they sell in response to market demand, availability of materials and so on, but they rarely allow such latitude to their licensees. Similar considerations apply in respect of services.

In the UK (and some other countries) it is possible (though not mandatory) to register permitted use arrangements, registration generally conferring the benefit that use by a licensee is deemed to be made by the proprietor and can be relied upon in any attack on the mark by virtue of alleged non-use. In the UK the provisions of TMA 1994, ss 28–31 govern the position of licensees.

Trade mark licence arrangements can be made as such or they may form part of overall arrangements between trade mark owners and users of the mark in a wide variety of circumstances. Trade marks can be particularly useful in identifying new products, particularly when the products are incapable of being protected by patents from exploitation by others.

Assignment

It should be observed that in addition to being licensed a trade mark registration is something which can be assigned. Generally speaking, trade marks are assigned with the business in respect of which the marks are used, but this need not always be the case. Sometimes assignments are effected of marks 'without goodwill', either because there is effectively no subsisting goodwill or because of certain other difficulties which can arise. For example, where a registration is used on goods both for home consumption and for export, the proprietor may wish to sell the overseas business, and if so he may wish to assign the marks in the exporting countries and additionally to assign the registration of the mark in the country of manufacture only in respect of exports. Part assignment of a registration in this way is permitted, as is assignment in respect of part only of the goods or services in respect of which the mark was registered. The registration then effectively splits into two (or more) registrations, each of which must be separately maintained if the registration is to continue.

Franchising

One particularly important area, particularly in recent years, of exploiting trade mark rights especially in the service industries is the use of so-called franchise arrangements in which the proprietor of a business pays a fixed fee or royalty for the right to use a licensor's name and trade mark. A classic example of this kind is the trade mark 'Wimpy' in respect of the provision of fast food services, both in terms of the sale of items such as hamburgers and in respect of the provision of restaurant services. The franchisor takes care of product and market development and national advertising, which of course enures to the benefit of all the franchise holders, or franchisees as they are called. Franchisees in turn secure the benefit of the reputation and, they believe, do better business than they otherwise would. Franchise agreements often include a number of other contractual terms; in particular, they often require the franchisee to obtain his supplies of raw materials from the franchisor or from an approved source. The subject of franchising agreements is, however, one of substantial complexity and capable of great development. Reference should be made to specialist works on the subject for detailed forms and precedents.

International systems

The basic framework

The International Convention (*see* p 21) covers trade marks as well as patents (though coverage of trade marks used on services is not as effective as that for goods marks). There is a priority claim system with a priority period of six months, *not* one year as for patents, but it is little used since there is no requirement (cf patents and registered designs) to apply to register before use has commenced. In some countries (for example, the USA and Canada), although application can be made prior to use, registration will not be effected prior to use commencing. It also provides that member countries will legislate to give special protection to 'famous marks'—in the UK this is reflected in TMA 1994, s 56—and enable the retrieval of a principal's mark for which the agent has, without authorisation, secured registration (TMA 1994, s 60).

The intricacies of trade mark law and registration are substantial and there is much variation in detail throughout the world. Accordingly, as with patents, a profession has grown up to deal with the matter. Most patent agents or patent agencies handle trade mark work, and in many countries, of which the UK is one, there is in addition a substantial professional body which deals solely with trade marks.

Most countries use the International Classification of Goods and Services, but some still do not (particularly the South American countries) and Canada does not use a classification system at all. There are two slightly different approaches which are adopted in various countries to the question of specificity in terms of goods and services. Some countries make the registrant specify very precisely the goods or services on which he is using the mark and will, in practice, allow registration only in respect of a relatively narrow specification. However, in those countries it is general that infringement will be committed by a trader who uses the same or a confusingly similar mark on those goods or services or on goods or services of a like kind.

The EU system of registration

The EC, as part of its work towards facilitating a true 'common market', provided two initiatives in the Trade Marks area. The first was a Directive on harmonisation of national trade mark laws. This Directive was collateral to the 1992 completion of the internal market and compelled all EU countries to adopt certain basic common elements in their trade mark law. It also laid the ground for the second, namely the Community Trade Mark Regulation. The latter sets up a system of trade mark registration which is operated by the Office for Harmonisation in the Internal Market (Trade Marks and Designs), more often simply referred to (since there is no EU design system as such as yet) as the Community Trade Marks Office ('CTMO'). It opened for business (in Alicante, Spain) on 1 April 1996, and grants trade mark registrations which are unitary throughout the EU.

The working languages of the CTMO are English, French, German, Spanish and Italian, though applications can be filed in any one of the other six official languages of the EU (though in such a case a second language, which must be one of the five specified, must also be chosen, in which communications with the CTMO are carried out).

The CTMO examines applications for intrinsic registrability, and advises those national trade mark offices which have indicated a desire to carry out searches of marks it has received. The national offices search their own registers for possibly conflicting marks, report any they find to the CTMO, and the CTMO forwards the report(s) to the applicant, but the CTMO does not, at that stage, make any assessment of the possible conflict, even in the case of its own search (limited to earlier Community applications and registrations).

If the CTMO is satisfied that a mark is intrinsically registrable, it advertises the details in the *Community Trade Mark Bulletin*. Advertisement starts a three-month term for oppositions by third parties, expected to be based on rights which those parties hold, eg in a national registration in an EU country. In opposition proceedings, the CTMO can adjudicate if a later mark is too similar to an earlier one to allow registration.

If no opposition is filed, or one is resolved in favour of the applicant, then (subject to the payment of a quite substantial registration fee) the mark is registered. The registration is renewable every ten years. A Community registration ranks equally in all countries of the EU with its national registrations, and, to the extent that a proprietor may have overlapping national registration of the same mark, the effects of the national registration(s) are suppressed while the Community registration remains in force.

If the opposition succeeds, it may be on the basis of a conflict which is only effective in one or a few member states of the EU. In such a case, there are arrangements for converting the Community trade mark application into one or more national applications, each of which is then processed by the respective national office in the usual way, each retaining the original filing date of the Community trade mark application.

The Madrid Arrangement and Protocol

A different approach to providing an international trade mark system has existed for several decades. It is called the 'Madrid Arrangement'. If did not (and still does not) apply in the UK since the UK is not a member. Basically, the Madrid Arrangement provides a system where, having secured registration in your original home country, you file a single international application with the central authority (the World Intellectual Property Organisation in Geneva) designating as many member states of the system as you want to have your registration effective in, and paying the appropriate fees. The international organisation then publishes details of the mark (and of the original home registration) and if, in countries where there is the possibility of objecting by way of opposition proceedings, someone opposes, the matter is then sorted out at a local level. The language of the Madrid Arrangement international registration system is French.

This system has worked well for several decades, but had certain technical drawbacks which prevented some countries joining. These were addressed at an inter-governmental level, and this resulted in the creation of a slightly moderated arrangement (known as the Madrid Protocol) which came into operation on 1 April

1996, with a relatively small number of adherent member countries, but with one of them being the UK.

Almost all EU countries are signatories to the Madrid Protocol, and now that Protocol is in force, more are expected to ratify than had done so by the date it entered into force. Additionally, a 'link' is proposed between the Madrid Protocol system and the Regulation which set up the EU system run by the CTMO, and this may be expected to operate by the year 2000. Even when the 'link' is in place, however, the possibility will remain of securing registration in a number of EU countries via the Madrid Arrangement or the Protocol, though the 'international registration' so obtained will still be a sort of 'bundle' of individual national registrations, not a single unified 'Community trade mark registration'.

The rest of the world

Most countries have trade mark registration systems, though in some third world countries no such laws yet exist and the only protection available is at common law and effected by publishing 'cautionary notices'. In many smaller countries, particularly British Colonies, registration is granted to proprietors only on the basis of a first registration in a 'major' country, for example, the UK.

Most countries are signatories to the 1883 International Convention, which sets out some very basic requirements for the trade mark laws of individual countries to comply with, and which sets up the 'priority term' scheme. However, that Convention allows very wide variations between national laws to co-exist. In an effort to make life easier for trade mark owners (and trade mark offices) a more recent treaty (the Trademark Law Treaty or 'TLT') was agreed, which harmonises the laws and practices of the member countries much more. So far, it has only a few ratifications, but the general picture of trade mark protection is becoming, globally, much more uniform, to the benefit of international brand owners and users.

Conclusion

Possession of a trade mark registration gives rise to an ability by its proprietor to do two things: first, by using his trade mark and by defending its integrity, for example by proceeding against anyone who uses the trade mark or one deceptively similar without authorisation, he can attempt to maintain a captive market. He can create a reputation by selling high quality goods in a particular brand and the hope is always that the use of a trade mark will ensure that his brand is purchased rather than that of a rival manufacturer. Nowadays, no one goes into a tobacconist's and asks for a packet of cigarettes; rather, they ask for a particular brand of cigarettes and the trade marks applied to such brands are of course invariably registered, if at all possible, and those registrations are jealously guarded. The registration offers a proprietary right, saving the proprietor very substantial sums of money in any litigation against a third party who unfairly uses the mark or a similar one on the right sort of goods or services and thereby injures the proprietor's trade or reputation.

Secondly, the reputation that has been built up may be traded on not only by the proprietor himself, but by licensing, with appropriate conditions to ensure that the reputation is not tarnished. Such licences can provide a very valuable source of income.

5 Copyright and design right

Introduction

Copyright law was originally designed to protect creators from exploitation of their works by others without permission. Certain categories of creation easily lent themselves to reproduction and it was not felt right that the creator should be denied the profits from that reproduction. Thus, originally literary works, and subsequently musical, dramatic and artistic works, came to be recognised as worthy of copyright protection and gradually the area was widened and the protection codified to give the various complex systems in operation today.

One thing common to all aspects of copyright law is the concept of a copyright 'work' and this stresses, rightly, the creative aspect just noted. The term 'work' in this sense includes a very wide variety of things such as books, pictures, music, sculpture and photographs, but one feature common to them all is that they have a tangible or otherwise perceptible specific form. A work is conveniently to be contrasted with an idea. Thus the idea of composing music based on bird song is not something over which copyright law has any control, but a piece of music by Oliver Messiaen based on that approach is a work in which copyright can and does subsist; pointillism is an idea, but the paintings of Seurat and his school each possess copyright; the idea of a reusable space shuttle contrasts with the actual design of one.

It follows from this approach that copyright is a right associated with and based on a particular perceptible expression usually, though not always, the conscious product of an original mind. Both skill and labour are normally employed in the production of a copyright work and the copyright comes into being when the work itself comes into being.

Copyright in three-dimensional works outside the fine arts and architectural areas should logically operate in parallel with its operation in them. However, this can give rise to practical problems, and a new right, so-called 'design right', was invented in the late 1980s to complement copyright and regulate the position in the three-dimensional design field.

Obtaining protection

Patent and trade mark law are fairly easy to grasp and both are voluntary in their application. The patent system is optional in the sense that inventors have a choice of whether or not to avail themselves of the bargaining system. Likewise, registration under a trade mark registration system is also voluntary, at least in most industrialised countries. The number of people inventing things and choosing to avail themselves of the patent system each year is relatively small, as is the number of persons who choose to use trade mark registration systems. In marked contrast, copyright law in many countries, and in particular in the UK, is not in the nature of a voluntary system but is a mandatory system which gives protection automatically on creation and reduction to a permanent form. Thus, every painting done by each member of a school class, every essay done for the English master, every technical drawing of each part that goes up to make a modern jet engine and every letter, report or memorandum may be the subject of copyright protection. Copyright law thus tends to embrace or touch upon very varied fields of activity and it has developed in somewhat haphazard fashion in many countries, with the inevitable result that, in detail, copyright law is often anomalous, piecemeal and almost invariably difficult to understand.

British copyright law was thoroughly revised in 1987 and provides a modern up-to-date framework which attempts to cover the whole field of literary, artistic and musical endeavour, the areas of computer programs, sound recordings, cinematograph films, television broadcasts and sound broadcasts and published editions of works. The Act (Copyright, Designs and Patents Act 1988) aims to give a homogeneous treatment to works which are the classical products of original creation by authors, artists and others such as books, plays, music, sculptures, drawings and engravings, and more recent types of work such as holograms, video recordings and computer programs. The Act also gave statutory birth to the design right, a sort of industrial copyright applicable where the work created is a tangible, physical, three-dimensional, useful article.

The nature of the protection available under copyright or design right depends centrally on the nature of the 'work' created. Copyright law tends to try to categorise works under several headings, but the terms used are not always very clear. Indeed, in some cases, such terms are defined very broadly, such as the definition of an artistic work in CDPA 1988, s 4, but this definition itself requires careful study to decide what it means and even then the boundaries are not clear. Consider a climbing frame built in the garden from old plumbing fittings and piping and set in the ground in some concrete. This is unquestionably a structure in the normal dictionary meaning of the term and 'building' is stated to include 'any fixed structure' in CDPA 1988, s 4(2). Artistic work in CDPA 1988, s 4(1)(*b*) is defined as including a work of architecture, being a building or a model for a building. Is the climbing frame a 'work of architecture' or will its creator have to rely on his design right to prevent copyists?

The term 'musical work' is defined in CDPA 1988, s 3(1) as meaning a 'work consisting of music'. If, working on some mathematical formula, a composer produces a spiked drum which, when inserted into a musical box movement and rotated, causes the box to produce 'music', is the spiked drum a musical work?

Protection, if obtainable, ie if the work is of a kind susceptible of protection, is usually obtained merely by making the work (when it is, of course, initially 'unpublished') provided that the maker was a 'qualified person' (CDPA 1988, ss 151, 152) or that first publication occurred in the UK (CDPA 1988, s 153). 'Qualified person' includes all British subjects and all persons (of any nationality) resident or domiciled in the UK. The application of these provisions is extended by the relevant Statutory Order to citizens of, or publication in, all of the member countries of the Berne and Universal Copyright Conventions.

Copyright ownership usually belongs in the first instance to the creator of the original work, called for convenience the author of the work, a reflection perhaps of the original roots of copyright law in literary copyright (CDPA 1988, ss 9, 11). Generally speaking, the author of the work is entitled to the copyright in it, but that copyright may be transmitted in the usual way by the author who can sell it to a third party for an appropriate consideration or it can be given away or passed by testamentary deposition. There are some cases, however, where copyright initially vests with someone other than the author by operation of law, and of course two parties can always agree that one will carry out original work and the copyright in that work shall belong to the other. Thus CDPA 1988, s 11 provides for automatic ownership of the copyright in the literary, dramatic, musical or artistic works of an employee by his employer unless there is agreement to the contrary. It should be remembered, however, that if any works such as drawings, photographs, paintings, engravings or portraits are commissioned, the commissioner does not automatically own the copyright in the work unless the parties have agreed so, explicitly.

Form of protection

Copyright and design right protect against unauthorised *copying*. The fundamental principle is that if someone has taken the time and trouble to produce a work in respect of which copyright or design right subsists, then others should not, at least not without appropriate permission, and/or payment, make a 'copy' of that work, ie reproduce it in some way involving an act of copying. The number of ways in which a work can be reproduced is large and, of course, dependent upon the nature of the work itself. Current UK legislation (CDPA 1988, s 16) tries to cover the various infringing acts, enumerating copying the work, issuing copies of the work to the public, performing, showing or playing the work in public, broadcasting the work, including it in a cable programme service, or making an adaptation of the work, or doing any of the proscribed acts in relation to such an adaptation. Definitions of these various categories of action are contained in CDPA 1988, ss 17–21. The copyright owner is given the exclusive right to carry out these various acts, and by virtue of CDPA 1988, s 16(2) it is an infringement of copyright to do, without the licence of the owner, any of these exclusive acts and it is also an infringement to authorise another person to do so.

All of these exclusive acts or acts which constitute infringement can broadly be described as 'copying'. In some way, the copyist/infringer reproduces the actual physical detailed perceptible form of the original work, possibly transmuted into an almost unrecognisable form compared with the original, but nevertheless a copy.

Certain minor corollaries follow from this approach to copyright law. The first is that a copy of a copy is a copy of the original. Thus if a novel is written by A and illegally copied by B, C who copies B's illegal copy can still have proceedings brought against him by A and can be restrained from copying without licence.

Secondly, the other side of the coin is that independent conception is always a complete answer to a charge of copying. Even if the final works are effectively identical, as if perforce the case with certain works such as mathematical tables, copyright can still subsist in the works but is not infringed by the later independent producer of the same work.

Returning to the point raised earlier concerning ideas, it should be stressed that copyright in a particular work is not infringed by somebody who takes the idea behind the work and then produces their own reworking of that idea. Thus a line is to be drawn between making an adaptation of a work and making an analogous work starting from the same first principles.

The term of copyright, during which 'copying' is restricted, is usually substantial, being in most cases (not, for example, typographical arrangements of a published edition) from the work's coming into existence until the expiry of 70 years from the end of the year in which the death of the author occurred. In the case of sound recordings, films and broadcasts, the term of protection dates from the year of their manufacture or release. Complex provisions apply to works where the author died more than 50 years before 1996 but less than 70 years before that date.

It should be pointed out, however, that the term of any protection under the CDPA 1988 in respect of ornamental surface designs registrable under the Registered Designs Act 1949 is limited by CDPA 1988, s 52 to a period of 25 years from the date of first marketing the item. The copyright protection in a drawing may continue to subsist and, for example, making a copy *drawing* will infringe after the 25-year period. Likewise, if a design right is exploited by making reproductions of an article created first as a drawing of that article, any protection under the copyright in the drawing cannot be used to stop the article being made or copied (CDPA 1988, s 51).

Design right

As explained above, copyright law evolved from the desirability of protecting the result of labour and skill in the fine arts, whether they were literary, artistic or musical. In contrast, registered design law was designed to provide protection for the applied arts, and specifically to ornamentation, shape and configuration as applied to industrially manufactured articles. In many countries these two sorts of protection exist, but separately and with little interaction. However, in the UK, there has been much interaction between the two.

The chief cause of the interaction was the ability to sue, for copyright infringement, the manufacturer of a three-dimensional article which was preceded by a drawing. The drawing attracted copyright (as drawings do, irrespective of artistic quality) and UK law has for many years (CDPA 1988, s 17(3)) deemed the making of a copy in three dimensions of a two-dimensional work an infringement of the copyright in that artistic work. Until 1968 there was, however, a specific exclusion separating protection by way of copyright and protection by way of registered design: if something was registered as a design, or could have been so registered, then no action was possible under the Copyright Act.

This had the effect that those who did not choose to register their designs but did exploit them commercially lost all protection. By an amendment to CA 1956, which became known as the Design Copyright Act 1968, the previous exclusion of suit under the Copyright Act was removed. This gave rise to substantial litigation by manufacturers of industrially produced articles, who sued the copiers of those articles for infringement of the copyright in the original design drawings.

This approach led to anomalies, particularly that if the drawings were of such a nature that the article in question was not susceptible of registration as a design under RDA 1949, the period of protection effectively given to such industrial designs under the Copyright Act was very substantial. If the design was not protectable under RDA 1949 for lack of sufficient originality, the anomaly arose that good innovative design was effectively protected for only 15 years, while trivial design was effectively protected for much longer.

After much debate, a new form of protection has been devised, known as 'design right' protection. This is a new attempt to protect design endeavour in respect of industrially produced articles and one which has not yet been adopted in any other country, though the scheme has aroused European interest. Whether the experiment will be successful and the innovation in intellectual property law followed is not known. The provisions have been in force since 1989 but eight years later only a handful of cases have reached the courts, so it is too early to say how useful the system is.

Design right applies narrowly, only to features of the shape and configuration of articles (or parts of them) and only when they are original—the 'commonplace' is excluded (CDPA 1988, s 213).

Design right arises once the relevant design is done, whether by drawing, sculpting, model making or otherwise, but only if the designer or commissioner of the design is an EU national (personal or corporate) or if that does not apply, if whoever markets the articles first is exclusively authorised to do so in the UK and first marketing takes place in the EU. The nationality and location requirements may be extended outside the EU countries in due course, but are not expected to be so extended unless reciprocal protection arises in those countries, possibly an unlikely early eventuality.

The extent of protection is the right to sue others who copy the design so as to produce articles exactly or substantially to that design (CDPA 1988, s 226(2), (3)).

Like copyright, design right arises automatically, but it lasts far less long, a maximum of 15 years from the end of the calendar year in which the design right arose, but as little as ten years from the end of the calendar year in which articles made to the design are first made available for sale or hire (CDPA 1988, s 216). For the last five years of the period of protection, a licence to copy the design is available as of right, the terms of such licence to be settled by the Comptroller General of Patents, Designs and Trade Marks in the absence of agreement between the parties.

In contrast to the position concerning copyright, the owner of design right, where the design is commissioned, is the commissioner, not the person who created the design (CDPA 1988, s 215(2)).

Design right may be assigned or licensed in the same way as other intellectual property rights and it may co-exist with registration under RDA 1949 for articles embodying the design. Ownership of any registered design protection and of the design right in respect of the same article will normally be the same, but need not be so.

Design right is a new attempt to hold the legislative balance between the creators of original designs who should enjoy, it is felt, a certain amount of protection, and the interests of industry in being able to use designs, and indeed copy industrially produced designs, after a reasonable period of time. There are a number of areas where such copying is deemed acceptably legitimate, most notably in the so-called spare parts industry. Whether design right will have much effect in that industry is unclear, having regard to the developments which took place in the UK in connection with an action brought under the Copyright Act in connection with the design of exhaust pipes. The House of Lords ruled in a case brought by British Leyland against Armstrong Manufacturing about replacement exhaust pipes, that the owner of the original vehicle was entitled to have it repaired, was entitled to have someone manufacture a copy exhaust pipe for that purpose, and by extension that manufacturers were legitimately entitled to manufacture copy exhaust pipes not to the specific order of someone who needed one but in the expectation that those who in due course would need to repair their vehicles would need to purchase one. The decision emerged against the background of the previous legislation, and it is far too early to say what effect the design right legislation will have in this area, or how the law concerning spare parts will develop further.

It should be stressed that all of the above observations concerning design right, and indeed the majority of those concerning the protection of industrially applied design by the use of copyright, are applicable centrally only in the UK, and have been followed in general terms in only a relatively few countries. In many countries, copyright law does not provide any remedy for the copying of industrially produced articles, and in the case of that occurring, the originator of that article may have to fall back on unfair competition law or slavish imitation law as developed in those jurisdictions in order to try to secure any relief. In some countries, copying of industrial design for which no protection has been sought under the registered design law of that country is effectively legitimate.

The interactions between copyright, design right and registered design protection should be remembered, recalling that for many articles, these types of protection are not mutually exclusive, and two or all three types may tend to be complementary. Despite the broad copyright and/or design right protection given by the CDPA 1988, it is still useful to register a design for an article which may be protected under both headings for a number of reasons. The major reason is that registration gives a clearly defined monopoly which is infringed by somebody who produces an article looking the same, whether or not copying has taken place. Thus in any action against a copyist, if action is brought under the RDA 1949, there is no need to *prove* copying. Sometimes copying is very difficult to prove, particularly if it takes place outside the jurisdiction. Secondly, the simple affixing of a copyright or design right notice to an article does not allow the competition to see in just what copyright or the design right subsists. If a design is registered then the articles may bear the registered design number and anyone can then discover precisely what the registered design covers and, if they are so minded, take care not to infringe. Naturally, if they move away from infringement of the registered design, they are most likely (though not inevitably) to move sufficiently far to avoid copyright or design right infringement also.

This discussion has shown how very strong copyright law can be in certain areas. It should not, however, be taken as too strong since, by appropriately conducting themselves, manufacturers can still compete legitimately without copying, as follows: if a manufacturer A brings out a new range of products and manufacturer B wants to copy them, clearly manufacturer B cannot simply proceed to do so without risk. However, if there is some underlying new design idea or the like which, stripped of its particular physical embodiments, can be appropriately expressed, then manufacturer B is entitled to go to a designer (or indeed use his own) and ask to have a range of designs produced embodying that concept. Since each of those designs would be original and not copied, no copyright or design right infringement can take place even if the ultimately produced designs bear an uncanny resemblance to the original designs of manufacturer A. Independent origination is a total defence to an allegation of copying. Care should, of course, be taken in embarking on any such course of action to make quite certain that the subsequently made designs are truly independently done. The temptation must also be avoided, if manufacturer B is not quite happy with the designs produced by his designer, for manufacturer B to review and alter the new designs to render them more marketable while at the same time making them resemble manufacturer A's designs more. Such changes may convert an original work into a copy.

Action for copyright infringement can be taken in the High Court, Chancery Division, the usual remedies of an injunction against further copying, delivery up of infringing copies and an inquiry as to damages or an account of profits being normally available. Conversion damages, which were available in appropriate cases under CA 1956, are no longer available as such, though in any particularly flagrant case of copyright infringement the court can award additional damages (CDPA 1988, s 97(2)), which could clearly be substantial. Design right cases can be taken in the Patents County Court.

Exploitation

Copyrights are generally exploited by manufacture of the copyright work normally by some form of printed publication or recording or by licensing others to do so. Licences need to specify carefully what acts are permitted. The payments may be by way of lump sum or royalty. Licences to perform are often administered by societies set up for the purpose; in the UK the Performing Right Society grants such licences.

However, exploitation by total reproduction, performance, or the like is not the only way in which a return for investment of skill and labour to produce the copyright work can be secured. One related area which relies on copyright law for regulating the conduct of parties operating in it is that of character merchandising.

In recent years it has become widespread practice to attempt to sell goods on the back of usually fictional characters. In most cases (though by no means all) the origin of the character is literary and in many cases of major impact the original literary work is made into a film. If the film is widely promoted, and has particular characters or images associated with it, then it is to be expected that a wide range of articles will have their sales potentially increased by being made in the form of, or ornamented with, the representations of the characters in question. In particular, clothing is of increased appeal to certain sections of the purchasing public if it bears a representation of a well-known character.

Underlying character merchandising programmes is copyright law. It is simply not open to would-be riders on the bandwagon of success of any particular film or comic strip to avail themselves of the copyright manifestations of the particular character. Their representation cannot be used with impunity and action can often be brought very quickly to stop misuse (*see*, for example, the Jaws T-shirt case, *Universal Studios v Mukhtar & Sons Ltd* [1976] FSR 252, and the Kojakpops case, *Tavener Rutledge v Trexapalm* [1977] RPC 275). In another case, the proprietor of a film was able to stop the sale of posters corresponding to frames in the film (*Spelling Goldberg Productions Inc v BPC Publishing* [1981] RPC 280 CA).

However, there are limits to the application of copyright: the refuse contractor who had the bright idea of riding on the popularity of certain furry creatures who allegedly live near and keep clean Wimbledon Common was, at least at the interlocutory level, not felt by the British courts to be reprehensible when the plaintiff, as assignee of the copyright in certain characters, sued the unlicensed user of the characters' name, for passing off (*Wombles v Wombles Skips* [1977] RPC 99). Exxon were unsuccessful in their plea that copyright would enable them to stop a third party setting up as 'Exxon Insurance Consultants International Ltd' though they did succeed on a passing-off basis ([1982] RPC 69).

The use of copyright in character merchandising should be carefully distinguished from the use of trade marks in that connection. The two may be complementary but are not the same and may require substantially different treatment (*see* Chapter 4, and the *Hollie Hobbie* case [1984] FSR 199).

International aspects

It cannot be stressed too much that copyright law, in contrast to patent, design and trade mark law, tends to vary very widely from country to country, both in respect of its detailed provisions and in respect of the degree of formality necessary to secure protection. Accordingly great care needs to be taken in any matter where there is a substantial copyright element in order to secure good local advice in all the relevant countries. This is particularly important where the exploitation of the copyright is otherwise than by classical means such as the publication of books or the printing of pictorial reproductions.

Just which works are protected and which works are not is an interesting area and there is wide variation from country to country and indeed from time to time. However, the often quoted maxim of copyright law that 'what is worth copying is worth protecting' implies that, at least in the Anglo-Saxon law countries, the law will be interpreted broadly in this respect where possible.

In some countries in order to secure adequate copyright protection certain registration formalities may be necessary. The UK is not one of those but it is worth noting that the USA is.

As in the case of other intellectual property law, it early became desirable for countries to come to multilateral agreements concerning copyright and there are two major copyright conventions known colloquially as the Berne Convention and the Universal Copyright Convention. The first of these is an attempt to preserve some uniformity of law between the various member countries and fundamentally it is a mutual agreement between its members that, as expressed in Article 4, 'authors, the nationals of any of the [member countries] shall enjoy in countries other than the country of origin of the work for their works, whether unpublished or first published in a [member country], the rights which the respective laws do now or may hereafter grant to natives'.

One of the fundamental planks of the Berne Convention is that such protection must be granted without any formalities. Formalities may be necessary in certain countries if copyright proceedings are to be taken against an infringer, but the protection is effectively automatic.

The Universal Copyright Convention is a younger convention but one which is, by virtue of its wider membership, perhaps the more important.

Under the provisions of that convention, each member agrees to give the nationals of all the other member countries the same protection for their unpublished works as it gives to the unpublished works of its own nationals. It also undertakes to give the nationals of other contracting states in respect of published works and to the nationals of any country if the work is first published in one of the member states, the same rights as it gives to works first published in its own territory. Also, if published works first published outside the territory of the contracting state in question are not the work of a national author, then the protection is to be enjoyed without formality of any sort, provided only that all published copies bear the so-called Universal Copyright Convention marking, which consists of the well-known © device, followed by the year of first publication and the name of the copyright owner (*see* UCC, Article III). The Universal Copyright Convention does not, however, stop the member countries from requiring formalities to be observed if copyright is to be enjoyed in its territory either in respect of works first published in its territory or in respect of work of its nationals wherever first published. In addition, the member countries may require compliance with formalities if action is to be brought in the courts of that country.

As noted above, copyright affects not only dealing in physical items embodying the copyright (books, prints, tapes, magnetic discs) but also broadcasting works or performances. In the international sphere, the Rome Convention on Satellite Broadcasting seeks to provide some international regulation and acts as a harmonising influence on domestic law in this area.

Conclusion

Copyright laws cover all dealings with copyright works, and specifically with reproducing those works, often in a form different from their original. Copyright adheres to the creator or part creator of the work and a work may accordingly have more than one copyright owner associated with it.

Copyrights can be exploited by making copies and selling them, by performing a 'performable' work, or by licensing others to do either of these. They last for a long time and, at least in the central fields of literary, dramatic and musical works, are of wide geographical application.

What is worth copying is worth protecting, morally if not caught by statute. Independent conception is a total defence to an allegation of copying.

6   Common law protection

Introduction

To a greater or lesser extent, each of the various forms of intellectual property discussed in the previous chapters stands on its own as a relatively clearly defined and easily distinguished subject, governed for the most part by statute law under which formal procedures have been established for the protection of the particular rights involved. There are some other forms of intellectual property, however, which are less easily defined and for which no formal protection is offered, other than that available from the courts. As a result, the legal rules governing such matters as breach of confidence, unfair competition and the protection of trade secrets are a good deal less clear than those regarding, for example, patents and copyright. Nonetheless, certain basic principles can be derived from the reported cases and their practical application is discussed in this chapter.

Passing off and unfair competition law

The concept of unfair competition between commercial undertakings is of relatively recent origin when compared to the patent and trade mark systems and it has grown up very much as a result of activities by companies being felt to be in some way unsatisfactory or unfair.

Unfair competition law varies very widely from country to country and interacts in many ways with intellectual property law. Cases of unfair competition often involve an intellectual property aspect and likewise intellectual property cases often involve an unfair competition aspect. Both should be remembered if action needs to be taken, both by a plaintiff wishing to assert his rights or by a defendant wishing to continue with an activity which has been complained of.

Often the law on this subject has developed on a very piecemeal basis, drawing from various other areas of law. In some countries there has been subsequent codification, but even codification in this field tends to be of a very general nature, leaving much to be decided by the courts.

In terms of unfair competition there is no question of taking any formal steps to obtain protection. Whoever trades in a particular country is protected automatically by the unfair competition law of that country, however undeveloped or highly developed that body of law may be. The form of protection is, however, usually relatively similar and consists in an ability to secure an injunction against a third party, forcing it to stop the act of unfair competition in which it is engaged. Sometimes, it is also possible to recover damages from such third parties, but damages are not usually nearly so important as stopping the abuse. Occasionally, however, damages can be of importance, particularly in the USA in connection with anti-trust law where so-called 'treble damages' can be awarded in appropriate cases.

The reason for including a brief discussion of unfair competition law in this book is simply that many unfair competition cases have as one or more of their ingredients a violation of patent, registered design, trade mark or copyright rights.

In terms of patents, the major area of interaction between patenting and unfair competition law is in the so-called anti-trust field. The anti-trust law was first developed in the USA under the Lanham and Sherman Acts and many volumes have been written on its detailed application. More recently a substantial body of European anti-trust law has emerged following cases brought under the provisions of Articles 85 and 86 of the Treaty of Rome. The situation most commonly met with in this area is an arrangement, concerning a patent, between two parties which is felt by a third to be improper and unfair. Much can hang in these cases on whether a patent monopoly is or is not valid and on the ability or inability (or unwillingness) of the patentee to grant licences on reasonable terms.

Although, theoretically, there is no barrier to similar problems arising in respect of registered designs, very little activity in this field has taken place compared with that in the patents field.

Turning now to the question of trade marks, as well as being an infringement of a trade mark registration, the adoption by a third party of a trade mark which is the same as, or confusingly similar to, a registered trade mark of another trader is considered in many countries to be of itself an act of unfair competition. In the UK, for example, the application of the same or a confusingly similar trade mark may well be a central plank in an allegation by a plaintiff in proceedings that the defendant is attempting thereby to pass off the defendant's goods as those of the plaintiff. 'Passing off' is a very well-established common law wrong in British jurisprudence and the courts have never been slow to act to restrain those who attempt to pass off their goods as those of others, ie, those who attempt to trade unfairly on a reputation previously established by others. Thus in litigation in the UK where trade marks have been copied or almost copied, it is common practice for suit to be brought not only in respect of the infringement of a trade mark registration but also in respect of an attempt to pass off. Of course, if the trade mark is used and has a reputation but is not registered no action can be brought under the Trade Marks Act 1994 (*see* s 2(2)) and in such a case the only remedy available to the owner of the unregistered trade mark is to sue for passing off.

Passing off has received a thorough judicial overhaul in the UK in recent years. In the *Advokaat* case ([1980] RPC 31) an attempt was made to set out clearly the ingredients necessary for the plaintiff to succeed. They must include (per Lord Diplock):

> (1) a misrepresentation (2) made by a trader in the course of his trade (3) to prospective customers of his or ultimate consumers of goods or services supplied by him (4) which is calculated to injure the business or goodwill of another trader (in the sense that it is a reasonably foreseeable consequence) and (5) which causes actual damage to a business or goodwill of the trader by whom the action is brought or (in a *quia timet* action) will probably do so.

The judgement in *Advokaat* carefully expressed the reservation (as passing-off cases traditionally do) that no set of rules for determining the presence or absence of passing off was likely to cover every possibility, but it remains a good guide.

However, the 'classic trinity' formulation—reputation, misrepresentation and damage—may provide a simpler yardstick in most cases.

In somewhat similar fashion copyrights often figure in unfair competition cases. The range of instances vary from the use of copyright material, such as customer lists or price lists, by a defecting employee setting up in his own business, to the use of similar designs for business forms or packaging. It is of particular value to remember in respect of items which in themselves may be, for lack of substantiality, on the borderline of copyright protection that, if they are copied, the act of copying may in appropriate circumstances be an act of unfair competition, even though the material may ultimately be shown not to enjoy copyright protection. In one particular area, that of so-called slavish imitation, copying is often actionable as an act of unfair competition even though, for technical reasons, the item being copied may not enjoy copyright protection.

Overall, it must be stressed that what does and what does not constitute unfair competition can vary from time to time and particularly from country to country. For example, the laws on comparative advertising, which often incidentally uses other people's trade marks, vary very widely from country to country. In some, certain types at least of comparative advertising are unquestionably legitimate. In the UK, fair comparative advertising is sanctioned and legitimate despite the fact that much of it appears at first glance to constitute a trade mark infringement. The formulation adopted to avoid infringement is to exempt use to identify goods or services of the legitimate proprietor or licensee, provided such use is in accordance with 'honest practices in industrial or commercial matters' and does not without due cause take unfair advantage of, or be detrimental to the distinctive character or repute of the trade mark.

Another area of particular variability from country to country is the ability of manufacturers to make free offers, give away free prizes, on either a lottery or some other basis, and generally use tough marketing techniques, which in many other countries are accepted as part of the normal commercial rough and tumble.

Manufacturers, traders and their advisers, therefore, need to remember that behind the specific intellectual property laws is the body of general and common law in the various countries concerned, particularly the unfair competition law, which interacts in many peculiar and sometimes changing ways with intellectual property situations. The general background should be borne in mind when making arrangements and contracts, particularly when making restrictive contracts, while if problems arise during the exploitation of the contract as a result of buccaneers, pirates or sharp operators, the unfair competition law should be checked to see whether it may not provide a simpler and often more rapid approach to commercial effectiveness than conventional litigation based on an alleged misuse of an alleged intellectual property right.

Of course, it is as well to remember that the whole situation can be looked at from the opposite point of view, in order to determine how far a trader may go in competing with other traders who have protected intellectual property rights.

Whenever action is contemplated under an intellectual property right it is as well to consider whether, in addition to mere technical infringement of that right, there is not also an unfair competition aspect of the case which may be prayed in aid. The practice of looking at things this way has developed rapidly in recent years in the USA because of the anti-trust laws. Many patent cases in the USA include a so-called anti-trust counterclaim where the defendants often allege, *inter alia*, that the patent in question was obtained by a fraud on the Patent Office and that an attempt to maintain it is accordingly an anti-trust violation entitling the defendant to treble damages. This approach, while understandable, is felt by many to be a regrettable situation, leading as it does to a very substantial increase in the costs, duration and complexity of American patent cases.

However, it has also led, paradoxically, to the increased use of legislation outside the strict field of patents where the allegedly infringing manufacturer or importer is outside the USA. In such a case it is now commonplace not to sue for infringement the importer or user of the pirated goods in the USA, but rather to commence an action before the USA International Trade Commission seeking to exclude the goods from the USA on the basis that patent infringement is occurring and American domestic industry is threatened by the therefore illegitimate importation. This alternative approach is highly effective and relatively rapid in many cases.

Know-how and show-how

The ability of manufacturers and traders to carry on their businesses legally depends not only on their being free of restrictions of the types discussed under the headings of patents, designs, copyright and trade marks, but also on their having the knowledge, skills and abilities to do what they want to do. To take a very simple example, a man may wish to set up in business manufacturing electronic calculators. This may look a good field to enter, but if the man has no knowledge and expertise he will have to acquire it. He may be able to do this by a diligent reading of the literature coupled with home experimenting but this is likely to be time-consuming and not very efficient. Clearly, he could employ people versed in those particular skills, but any employees who come to him would be expected to operate with the ordinary skills of the skilled persons in that field, and not to use particular trade secrets, confidential practices and the like, which their previous employers had regarded as part of that employer's 'confidential information'. If access to that information is required, it must be paid for, assuming that the possessors of the information are willing to sell it. Surprisingly often these days people are willing to sell confidential information, possibly due to the increasing industrial espionage which will render the sale impossible if not concluded fairly soon after the new techniques have been developed and put into practice. Indeed, the very existence of industrial espionage is but the other side of the know-how and show-how coin.

Conventionally speaking, the term 'know-how' is used to denote information that can be committed fairly straightforwardly to paper or some other tangible form while 'show-how' is used to cover information which really can be transmitted effectively only by in-house training. The person selling the show-how undertakes to train the purchaser's employees, for example, in how to polish and bloom lenses to obtain optical instruments of the highest quality. It goes without saying that paying know-how and show-how fees can generate much greater respect in an industry than trying to poach the competitors' skilled personnel.

Effectively, know-how and show-how can be transferred only once between the same two parties and any fee which passes is accordingly effectively the consideration for either information in tangible form, in the case of know-how, or a certain amount of demonstration or training in the case of show-how. Once the information has been passed or the demonstration given the contract is effectively concluded, save for any continuing obligations on the parts of the originator and purchaser. In this respect, the purchaser will usually want some guarantee from the originator that the same information will not be widely disseminated, or at least not without the purchaser's consent, for a certain period of time. Likewise, the vendor will probably want the purchaser to undertake to keep information secret or maintain skills, working practices and the like confidential. Usually, such obligations cease in any case when the information comes into the public domain, but care needs to be taken when considering any such arrangement as to just what continuing obligations are placed on both parties to the transaction.

Endorsement

In recent years the practice of endorsement, ie, of a well-known person recommending this or that product in an advertisement launched to promote sales at the expense of competing products, has become very widespread. Certain categories of public figure, most notably sportsmen and women and 'television personalities' can command very high fees by agreeing to support some particular manufacturer of goods which are sometimes only remotely connected with the person's particular claim to public fame. Thus boxers may be called upon to extol the virtues of a particular male cosmetic or newscasters may report glowingly on their predilections for a particular make of car. For such services they are paid a fee. They are not, of course, paid a fee if the same predilection is simply revealed as an item of news. The fact that a leader of a punk rock group eats a packet of Krunchy Krisps daily for breakfast may do wonders for the sale of that product, but its mere appearance in a newspaper report attracts no fees. Advertisers generally take the trouble to agree an endorsement fee with a personality if they wish to use an item of information such as this in their advertising but, of course, it is sometimes difficult to draw the line between what can and what cannot fairly be said about the person, either in advertising or non-advertising copy, having regard to the laws of libel and defamation.

In the UK the laws of libel and defamation and, to some extent, passing off govern the use by third parties of reference to particular living persons. In some countries, however, most notably the USA, legislators have directed their attention to the specific problems arising from the use of personalities' names, photographs and the like and widely varying local laws exist. As in other areas, therefore, care should always be taken when contemplating making money by endorsement to determine just what law is applicable and the extent to which the proposed activity could be restrained if it were unauthorised.

Endorsement fees, as with so many other fees which are paid in order to be able to do something legally which could otherwise not have been done legally, may be paid by way of a lump sum, or, for example, in dependence upon the amount of use made of the particular endorsement. The endorser may also wish to place limits on the amount to which that endorsement is used, particularly limits in terms of time. Many personalities are happy to receive a fee for endorsing some particular product at one stage of their career, but a repeat run of the advertisement five years later at a very different stage of that personality's career might be embarrassing.

7 Commercial exploitation of intellectual property

The preceding chapters of this book have attempted to break down intellectual property into its classic divisions and to provide general details with regard to each area relating to obtaining rights, and to the validity and enforceability of rights. This has been done without any specific attempt being made to relate those rights to actual businesses. Clearly, the applicability of individual rights will vary very substantially from one business to another. The relative importance of individual types of right will vary depending upon the nature of the commercial undertaking owning and exploiting such rights, and the relative importance of intellectual property to an undertaking will vary from cardinal, in the case of a business whose business is the exploitation of such rights, for example a copyright licensing agency, to peripheral, for example in the case of a firm of central heating maintenance engineers.

Wherever a business or organisation is situated on this scale, however, it is likely to have some intellectual property rights but even in those cases where there is a very conscious history and policy of obtaining those rights which do not arise automatically and without effort, there has been a tendency in many cases to see obtaining rights almost as an end in itself and certainly with a view to using the rights as little as possible.

Intellectual property rights can be thought of as a resource, and like many resources can be exploited more or less as the owner of that resource chooses. In many cases in practice, however, intellectual property rights are regarded as a somewhat arcane area, at best ancillary to the central business of the organisation, and not regarded as a resource to be exploited. This is regrettable, particularly in times when economic conditions may make it more and more difficult for an organisation to generate profits from its core business.

As will be apparent in Part 2 various aspects of taxation impinge on the acquisition or transmission of intellectual property rights, but larger sums of money (and accordingly larger benefits from getting it right and larger disbenefits from getting it wrong) are generally associated with the exploitation of rights. The most obvious example of this is the licensing of technology, be it patent or design protected, of reputation (such as in franchising, often based on trade mark protection), and in publishing or performance, based on copyright.

Policy

Many organisations have scant internal consciousness of the existence and usefulness of intellectual property rights, but even in those which do not suffer in this way, there is often a reluctance to analyse the actual or prospective business and to settle down and try to construct some sort of indentifiable policy for the exploitation of those rights. A prerequisite for a clear formulation of policy is the identification of what intellectual property rights the business or other organisation actually has, and for this an important starting point is to carry out some form of intellectual property audit.

Audit is perhaps a term covering both what you have and what you do with it, and the first part of an audit must accordingly be regarded as a 'stocktake'. It is a source of constant surprise to many practitioners in the intellectual property field to find that the ignorance and perhaps fear which surround intellectual property issues translate into an inability among business people even to appreciate what they have. This unconsciousness is, for obvious reasons, most pronounced in those areas which do not require positive and conscious intervention in order to secure intellectual property rights. Thus, companies owning patents and registered designs generally know that they own them. On the other hand, it is not at all uncommon to find that companies remember that they have copyright only when something adverse happens, such as a product being copied together with its packaging or some rather more obvious (and potentially commercially damaging) copying takes place. Perhaps the most widely ignored area is that of trade and service marks. A trade mark is too often equated with a brand name and overall marks of identity, for example the particular way a company represents its name as a logotype on letterhead, or particular unifying symbols, are not seen as being fully functional trade marks, despite the fact that their use is sometimes considerably more widespread than the use of a particular brand name would ever be. This often leads a company to rely on a (mistaken) belief that no one else can use its name, and to consternation when faced with the greater risk of failure, and much-increased cost, of litigating to stop a third party, rather than being able simply and quickly to secure the desired result by relying on a trade mark or service mark registration.

Accordingly, when contemplating the exploitation of intellectual property, stage one in many cases is simply to sit down and try to identify what intellectual property a particular business or organisation has. Clearly, the intellectual property can be categorised into the divisions represented by Chapters 2–6 and their relative impact on the company or organisation's business can be assessed.

Having identified what intellectual property is around, two immediate questions arise: the first is whether it is enough. Thus, for example, a company engaged in the manufacture of new domestic electrical appliances may well find, on carrying out an intellectual property stocktake, that it owns lots of design rights. However, it may own only a few registered designs, or indeed none at all. While, on account of the novelty rules explained in Chapter 3 (*see* p 29 *above*), protection by way of registered design may not be available for products already on the market, a decision may well be made that, as a matter of principle, it would be highly desirable to protect items by way of registered design, conferring a potential monopoly for a maximum of 25 years, rather than simply relying on a right against copying absolute for five years, qualified for the next five and then extinguished.

Analogously in respect of trade marks, but with the major difference here that there is no barrier on securing registration subsequent to adoption and use, and, indeed, at any time following adoption, the decision can be made to seek explicit and identifiable protection by way of registration rather than relying on being able to do something downstream if a problem arises on the basis of some common law passing-off or unfair competition aspects.

The second question which arises is how can one make more of the intellectual property rights one finds one has. Here commercial considerations obviously come into play, particularly in manufacturing industry. There is little merit in licensing your technology to competitors who, for whatever reason, can cheerfully pay you a licence royalty but then proceed to make the same or a similar product, sell it in direct competition with yours, and thereby reduce your sales (and the profit consequent on those sales) to an extent greater than the compensation received for allowing the activity to take place. On the other hand, technologies may well have applications outside the immediate market area of commercial interest to their owner, and so-called field-restricted licences can provide a valuable additional source of income.

Away from technology and purely into reputation, it may well be that a company which acquires expertise in a particular servicing field cannot exploit that reputation simply by expanding, and the problems of over-optimistic expansion are well documented in management textbooks. However, a company with a high reputation in a particular field but which works only in one area of a country may well find it highly profitable to share that expertise with someone who is willing to work a different area of the country. There is no essential reason why a London-based business with a strong reputation should not license others in the provinces to carry out the same business under the same banner for an appropriate fee. Such arrangements do not have to have the normal attributes of a franchising operation.

Looked at more internationally, the choice is clear in the case of an owner of copyright in a literary work, be it a novel or a book about mending your car. Copyright may be acknowledged on the back of the title page but wholly under-exploited. Both novels and car maintenance manuals are useful outside the country in which they are originally written, but too often little vigorous attempt is made to come to arrangements abroad involving translation and other possible localisation of the book in question with subsequent local publication and the return of royalty income.

Not so often appreciated is the fact that overseas consumer markets are not restricted to translations of books, but rather in general are not so dissimilar from one's home market that exploitation of rights there should be ignored. While clearly time and effort may be involved in securing someone abroad to exploit your ideas, be they market oriented as with the case of a good trade mark or a good design or technology oriented as in the case of a manufacturing process or product, nevertheless if you are able to make a success of the business in your own country, it is probably reasonable to suppose that someone else can make a like success of a like business in a similar country. An inducement when looking for someone to make money for themselves and give you a cut of it in an overseas country is of course, that you are offering protection. Particularly in the case of patents and designs but also in the case of trade marks, the up-front cost of securing the protection in the overseas territory may well be something which can easily be recovered by a downpayment from a willing licensee, even if the licensee insists that the payment has to be set off against initial royalties. Arranging with someone local to exploit markets overseas can often be much simpler and much less worrying than trying to do it yourself, whether by local manufacture and export on the one hand or by setting up a local operation in the country concerned on the other. Obviously if you are an existing multinational, that sort of thing presents no problems, but although multinational companies are large and there are many of them, they are vastly outnumbered by the small and medium-sized enterprises on which, it is now widely acknowledged, most economies' economic success actually depends in overall terms.

Once an organisation has identified its stock of intellectual property and taken a policy decision to try to exploit it, working through that policy decision will, if successful, generate new business and/or income. It may also give rise to certain extra outgoings. The taxation treatment of both income and outgoings is dealt with in the next part of this book and this is again broken down into individual subject headings since tax treatment is not uniform across the whole spectrum of intellectual property rights. Thus, the application of an overall intellectual property exploitation policy requires consideration of a myriad of details, with a view to securing a satisfactory return on the 'intellectual property capital' which a person or an organisation can build up. It suffers from the problem of all intellectual property: it is undervalued because you cannot see it. What you can see, however, is that by exploitation individuals and organisations may make money. The following chapters give guidance as to how the money you make splits between those authorities who feel entitled to a share and the organisation which is left with the residue.

8 Specific applications

Introduction

The aim of this chapter is to be illustrative, but not exhaustive, of the ways in which intellectual property rights interact with business activities. The various examples given have been selected as identifiable business areas, each with its own distinctive mix of intellectual property relevance. As will appear below, however, the nature of the mix and which ingredients of the recipe predominate vary widely.

Some of the illustrations also touch briefly on the interaction between intellectual property and much wider areas, such as the ethical impact of advances in biotechnology and the globalisation of trade and commerce, particularly in what might be described as information-based systems.

Biotechnology

Over the last two decades, this has suddenly assumed major industrial and commercial importance. Of course, biotechnology existed before and, indeed, some areas, most notably brewing and wine making, date back for centuries, as, indeed, do techniques of selective breeding. In recent years, however, the discoveries in biology in the 20th century have spawned the biotechnology industry we have today, and the pace of discovery and development in this area shows no signs of slowing, not least because of the enthusiasm with which the investment community has embraced the fledgling industry.

By is very nature, biotechnology is breaking new ground and is being seen as a possible source of effective weaponry in the fights against hunger and disease. The potential commercial rewards are substantial and accordingly the demand for protection is acute, particularly having regard to the intrinsic reproducibility of many biotechnological materials once they have been initially 'created'.

The major important form of intellectual property protection used by the biotechnology industry is the patent system. This can be seen to stem traditionally from the use of the system by the old biotechnology industry which relied on micro-organisms to operate novel and improved processes. Indeed, although clearly 'living material', due to their unprepossessing nature, most micro-organisms were regarded as just another material and, indeed, new strains could be patented. As the technical ability to manipulate life forms started to edge up towards the higher organisms, other considerations emerged, culminating, at the time of writing, in a vigorous debate which continues, and no doubt has many years to run, concerning the patenting of higher life forms and/or of methods or materials which can be used to generate new types of higher life form.

Much attention has been focused on the so-called 'Harvard oncomouse' which, by providing a real live creature genetically predisposed to develop cancer, gave researchers a further weapon in the armamentarium they are deploying to try to combat that disease. The case highlighted (though it is not the only case to do so) the previously rather dormant consideration common to patent law for a long time which allowed in this case the European Patent Office to refuse protection to an invention the use of which would be contrary to morality. Although in the past, in certain jurisdictions, such provisions had been used to prevent manufacturers of contraceptive devices securing patent protection for their products, the value of the prohibition had almost been forgotten until biotech cases started to emerge.

There has been much ill-informed debate on the subject, but what is important to remember is that those who invest in biotechnological development expect a return, and expect the entity in which they have invested to take prudent steps to protect its own technology with a view to maximising its profits and thereby the return on the original investment. It is thus hardly surprising that, in this fast-developing field, substantial amounts of effort have been directed to seeing how far the patent system can be used to protect the fruits of research from being overly harvested by others.

Those active in the field have also realised that, potentially, the scope of protection given by way of a patent is substantially broader and more effective than that which could possibly be achieved by use of the nearest previous attempt at providing protection in the biotech field, namely plant variety protection.

It is worth looking briefly at plant variety protection since, although relevant to only a very small proportion of industry at large, the system does exist, there is an international treaty, and, particularly in the field of crop seed, there can be substantial economic effects.

It is easy to see that the plant variety protection system was erected, in a fashion similar to that for the patent system, in order to stimulate selective plant breeders to intensify their efforts and produce new strains of useful plants or, of course, ornamental ones. The proposition, essentially, was to set up a registration system whereby someone who developed a new variety was entitled to a limited period of protection against copying. The requirement for protection is simply to produce a new variety, but in order to be protectable under the various national laws (most of which are consistent with the international treaty in the area, known as the UPOV Treaty) the variety must be stable, uniform and distinct. Provided that these criteria are satisfied (and, for example, the UK Plant Varieties Office does examine the point), protection can be secured for a period of time which can vary with the general type of plant, but is usually between 15 and 25 years.

The plant varieties legislation (and the underlying Convention) is, however, directed to the protection by an individual right of an individual plant variety. Thus, no protection is given, for instance, to a technique which may improve the pest resistance of a number of different varieties of, eg maize. Such a technique does not give rise to a new variety of maize, potatoes or whatever, but may be effective in improving the yield of many different varieties. If the technique is new and non-obvious (it is clearly 'industrially applicable') it ought to be protectable by way of a patent.

Although there is, as mentioned above, an international treaty relating to plant varieties and national laws exist in the countries which have ratified that treaty, there is no parallel in respect of animal varieties, something which was not of particular significance many years ago, but which is important to remember now, and the absence of which undoubtedly increased the pressure on using the patent system to protect investment in development of better animals.

The argument which has raged (and which continues to rage) in connection with the patenting of living material is whether, ethically, it is correct to give anyone, even for the limited monopoly term, control over something possessing a quality of 'life'. A point often missed by animal rights activists and others is that at least the patent system does provide the patentee with a certain amount of control, for a limited period of time, with respect to the exploitation of his invention. If, as has been argued, no patents should be granted in the area for ethical reasons, then the possibility of controlling development of any particular invention in the field or, indeed, the development of the field itself is diminished, and this hardly seems consistent with the views expressed by some that animals should simply not be used in certain ways for what are essentially industrial purposes. At least if there is a patent, use without the patentee's permission can be stopped, so reducing the amount of (in some people's views) deplorable activity.

When considering the biotechnology industry's use of patents, mention should also be made of the very considerable regulatory barriers which are placed in the way of commercialising many inventions in the field. These will undoubtedly give rise in the years to come to attempts to extend the life of patents in this area in a fashion similar to the supplementary protection certificate schemes which operate for pharmaceuticals and agrochemicals, where their commercial introduction may be delayed by regulatory processes, effectively eroding the term of patent protection which the patentee could expect.

There have been suggestions that copyright protection might be available (or even design type protection) for huge, complex bioactive molecules, some of which can, for example, be expressed in typographic form or by way of their shape and configuration, but little progress has been made in enlisting either of these types of right in the cause of protecting biotech developments. Know-how and secrecy, however, may well provide an adequate period of protection, enabling a commercial lead to be built up which it may be difficult for competitors to erode. However, the control of source material will not prolong a *de facto* monopoly. The grant of patents for any biotechnological invention which depends on a micro-organism requires it to have been deposited in a culture collection and for samples to be available to third parties.

As usual, major players in the field will have corporate identities and as the whole biotechnology industry develops, trade marks may become more important as enabling effectively identical materials to be identified with differing manufacturing sources. For the moment, however, there is little activity in these areas.

Computers

The rise of the digital personal computer is a phenomenon which is now widely recognised as being symptomatic of the 'information revolution'. The machines themselves and their uses are shot through with intellectual property considerations, perhaps most importantly ones relating to copyright, since copying, particularly digital copying, is something which computers carry out with great speed and accuracy. Indeed, once anything is reduced to digital form, it is possible to create a physical copy far more exact than any mechanical copying method could produce. With the advent of computer programs capable of handling vast quantities of data and storage devices capable of storing it, the material with which computers deal has moved from being text and number-based to being 'graphics-based' and, more recently, to adding sound as well, leading to the current generation of 'multi-media' computers, ie ones which combine both sound and graphics in an interrelated and interactive way.

Two major copyright areas emerge immediately: the first is the copyright in computer programs themselves. Although some early decisions showed a certain wariness or disinclination on the part of the judiciary to equate writing a computer program with writing a novel, it seemed to become rapidly accepted that both activities required the application of skill and labour to produce an original work and as countries have revised their copyright laws over recent years, there has been a tendency, for the avoidance of any doubt, to write in explicitly that copyright covers computer programs. Secondly, there has been a realisation that the language in which a copyright work is expressed is essentially irrelevant and thus it is of no consequence whether an original program is written in a higher or lower level language, or even in machine code. In any of these cases, copying is easy to achieve and, usually, easy to detect.

The distinction is often drawn between software (which runs a computer) and data (on which the computer carries out operations). Although the distinctions are not hard and fast, it is a useful practical distinction. However, as far as copyright law is concerned, there is no particular distinction to be drawn between a computer program and a stored computer text or image. In each case, if creating the original text or image took skill or labour, there will be an underlying copyright which will be infringed by unauthorised copying.

The practicalities of authorisation are substantial, if not to say nightmarish. The traditional approach to using other people's material almost invariably involved identifying some physical product, such as a print or book, which would have associated with it some clue as to the originator and therefore as to the then copyright owner. Nowadays, the ability to download graphics images from numerous web sites on the Internet, coupled with the ability to scan in printed images from books or other printed media, exacerbates what is already a difficult situation. It is not for nothing that a recent European Union Green Paper in connection with copyright referred to 'The Challenge of Technology' as a major impetus to copyright law development and revision, but there are few easy answers to the numerous questions which arise.

Any computer system requires, in addition to software and data, an actual computer, ie the hardware. In this respect, the three classical registered intellectual property rights are all important ways for the manufacturer or originator to try to protect their own business. Thus, the physical way in which a computer is manufactured, as well as individual components such as microcircuits, transducers and the like, are all fit subject matter for patent protection, and inventions in these fields are all clearly protectable. What was not at all clear until recently (though the current situation is not much improved) was the ability to protect software by way of patents. Indeed, the protection of software 'as such' is still proscribed by many patent laws, but what has emerged as clearly patentable subject matter is a computer or other like complex piece of electronic equipment programmed to operate in a particular way. Put another way, the fact that something requires a computer program to make it work does not translate into a ban on patentability of that thing.

The particular design of computer equipment, for example monitors, keyboards, printers and scanners, is an area to which substantial attention is paid by manufacturers since design can serve to attract and distinguish, and accordingly promote sales. This is particularly so where intending purchasers may well have sufficient aesthetic sensitivity to prefer one design over another while being wholly unable, on a technical basis, to decide which of two pieces of equipment actually performs better its intended task. The value of design in this area is accordingly substantial.

Even more, the distinguishing power of a trade mark can very materially enhance repeat business. In a market with product offerings which are not easy to distinguish in technical terms to the lay purchaser, the power of a strong and respected trade mark to secure the purchase can be material. It is perhaps mostly neatly summed up in the possibly apocryphal slogan 'No one ever got fired for buying IBM'.

The application of a highly distinctive trade mark to software products can also be of immense value since, in the same way as many people cannot distinguish one personal computer from another in terms of performance (though the distinction between prices is clear), so they will have difficulty in distinguishing one word processing or accounts software package from another. It should be said that some operators in the software industry have displayed a remarkable lack of invention in naming software products, which has undoubtedly led to confusion on the part of purchasers, but there are conspicuous examples of those who adopt highly distinctive branding and imaginative product naming.

Broadcasting

At first sight, the only material intellectual property right which would seem to be connected with broadcasting is that of copyright. Sound and video recordings possess copyright and broadcasting, save with permission, is an act of copyright infringement. Of course, nowadays the difficulty with broadcasting is that, at the receiving end, someone can make a copy. It is clear that in many jurisdictions, that act of copying is saved from being actionable only by virtue of the fact that it is done for private purposes. The theoretical approach is clear and understandable and the practice is obviously unstoppable. Where the broadcasters and, indeed, other copyright owners become concerned is where the recording actually causes economic detriment. This problem is likely to increase in future rather than decrease, for example with the increasing popularity of 'pay per view' programming. The 'Holy Grail' of copy protection systems is still being sought by numerous crusaders.

As with radio broadcasting, concern has long been expressed by the phonographic industry that off air recording of popular music was severely diminishing revenues. Attempts to meet this legitimate concern have resulted in the concept of a 'blank tape levy' and to a levy on recording and/or copying machines, but none of these proposed solutions is essentially anything more than a pragmatic approach to meeting concern. A new approach to paying for copying seems to be needed, but progress towards it seems to be slow.

Broadcasting also gives rise to substantial international considerations since once material is being transmitted through the ether, it is no respecter of national boundaries. International attempts have been made to regulate the position, most notably the Rome Convention on satellite broadcasting, but they are under stress and there is little doubt that the problems of securing an adequate return to the programme creators will be with us for decades, if not forever.

One general attempt to match the desires of copyright holders to secure a return commensurate with the use made of their copyright works and the desire of broadcasters to be able to broadcast such works, particularly musical works, has emerged in the form of so-called 'copyright collecting societies'. These are organisations which monitor broadcasting and which have agreements with broadcasters and others enabling broadcast to take place of material effectively 'administered' by the society in return for payment. These have tended to emerge as national institutions and have fulfilled a very satisfactory role in providing the centralised mechanism of collecting performance royalties and paying the copyright owners. However, with increasing internationalisation of broadcasting, their task becomes more difficult, and to this must be added the problem of massive expansion of the amount of broadcasting which occurs. Where there were a handful of radio channels and a smaller number of television channels a few decades ago, there are now numerous local broadcast radio stations and a bewildering variety of television satellites and satellite channels. The advent of computer-based systems has, naturally, materially assisted the efficiency of the whole operation, but the sheer volume of broadcasting can tend to overwhelm attempts at comprehensive monitoring. No doubt, however, free market forces will continue to shape activity in this area, while technology may be expected to assist monitoring.

Film

As in broadcasting, the interaction between the film industry and intellectual property law is predominantly in the area of copyright. A cinematograph film (or its parallel, the video recording) is, of course, a work requiring application of skill and labour to produce it, and one accordingly which gives rise to copyright in the film or video recording itself. That copyright is to be seen as separate from usually a number of copyrights which underlie it, for example in the original story such as a novel, an adaptation made for the purpose of turning the novel into a script and/or screenplay, and sometimes also a translation. Film makers may thus need to secure copyright clearance from a number of sources before the film can be made and distributed.

Copyright law also covers the screening or public showing of a film and the industry has developed extensive licensing and distribution arrangements reflecting this.

Film production and distribution companies are naturally concerned to protect their image and this may be done via trade mark protection. The sequence which precedes the opening of a feature film almost invariably shows, often in animated form, the trade mark of the production or distribution company, and the graphic imagery of searchlights pointing skywards by a stylised imposing building and that of a man striking an enormous gong are no doubt as well known to readers as that of a roaring lion surrounded by a heraldic frame.

Franchising

Over recent decades, a way of doing business has been developed in which an original successful 'business formula' can be developed by individuals by licensing others to operate in the same way. This is particularly effective as a means of growing effectively a very large business without the central major capital investment otherwise required; franchisees provide the capital for their own individual operations.

What binds the franchisor and franchisee together into a coherent operation is the identity of the business, and this is protected by a mix of contractual arrangements enabling strict control to be exercised as to how the franchisee operates, and trade mark protection for the central identity. The franchisee is a licensee or permitted user of the mark or marks in question. Registration of the mark or marks is important since once a particular business formula has been shown to be successful, imitators may emerge, and the strength of a franchised operation usually resides in the confidence of the customer that he will secure essentially the same service or product from any franchisee within the system.

In this connection, copyright can have a part to play as well as trade mark law, particularly if the franchise operation is one which relies on written contracts between the individual franchisee and its customers, for example in the fields of pawnbroking or television rental. The terms and conditions of the transaction between the customer and the franchisee will almost certainly be standardised by the franchisor and the need for a copyist to generate his own written contractual material is a barrier to entry into the field, albeit not an insuperable one.

Finally, many franchise operations require the would-be franchisee to undergo a period of training which is essentially the communication of know-how and, indeed, show-how from franchisor to franchisee. While many aspects of a franchise operation may not be difficult to copy, because they are effectively published as soon as the business starts up, there may well be areas of information which can be kept confidential, for example the ingredients, recipes and processing conditions to produce a foodstuff recognisably the same in Brisbane, Bombay, Beijing and Baltimore.

Conclusion

Any particular business or commercial activity will involve the use (and sometimes the creation) of a variety of intellectual property rights. Care should be taken to be aware of what rights are used, to secure a clear line of authority from the rights' owners if separate from the business, and to take such steps as may be appropriate to protect the business against copying by appropriate development of intellectual property rights, either in the capacity of an owner of those rights or in that of a licensee.

PART 2

PRINCIPLES OF TAXATION

9 Individuals and partnerships

Individuals: general principles

Individuals, resident and domiciled in the UK are subject to income tax on the whole of their income arising worldwide, whether remitted to the UK or not (TA 1988, ss 18, 19). A non-resident is normally taxable only on income arising in the UK and a non-UK domiciliary is normally liable to income tax on income arising in the UK and remittances of income arising overseas (TA 1988, ss 19, 65).

An individual, both resident and ordinarily resident in the UK, is also liable to capital gains tax on any chargeable gains (TCGA 1992, s 2). A non-UK domiciliary is only liable to capital gains tax on disposals of assets situated in the UK, or remittances of gains from overseas assets sold at a profit (TCGA 1992, s 12). Individuals neither resident nor ordinarily resident in the UK are not liable to capital gains tax even on assets situated in the UK, except where UK assets have been used for a trade or business carried on in the UK (TCGA 1992, s 10).

UK domiciliaries wherever resident are liable to inheritance tax on worldwide assets on death and on certain gifts (IHTA 1984, ss 1–4). A non-UK domiciliary is only liable to inheritance tax in respect of UK assets (IHTA 1984, s 6). In certain cases a non-UK domiciliary may be deemed to be domiciled in the UK for inheritance tax purposes but not for income tax or capital gains tax (IHTA 1984, s 267).

An individual may also be subject to tax on certain deemed income or gains under various anti-avoidance provisions, designed to prevent the avoidance of tax through, in particular, the use of non-resident trusts and companies and the diversion of income to children.

Personal allowances

The rates of personal allowances for 1997/98 which are available are as follows:

		£
Personal allowance (TA 1988, s 257)		4,045
Married couple's allowance (TA 1988, s 257A)		
given at 15 per cent		1,850
Age allowance (TA 1988, s 257)		
65–74	single	5,220
	married (each)	3,185

73

		£
75 or over single		5,400
married (each)		3,225
Single parent (TA 1988, s 259)		
given at 15 per cent		1,830
Widow's bereavement (TA 1988, s 262)		
given at 15 per cent		1,830
Blind person's (TA 1988, s 265)		1,830

Self-assessment

The mechanism for taxing individuals changed in 1996/97 to a system of self-assessment. Under this system the taxpayer will normally be sent a tax return at the beginning of the tax year, in April, but if he does not receive a tax return and has income subject to tax he must, within six months of the end of the tax year, notify the Revenue of his liability to tax under TMA 1970, s 7 and the Revenue will then send him the appropriate tax return for completion. It is not necessary to notify the Revenue where the taxpayer's only income is remuneration or benefits already taxed under PAYE, or untaxed income taken into account in his PAYE coding, or has been subject to deduction of tax at source and the individual is not liable to tax at higher rates.

Tax returns

Taxpayers who do receive a tax return will receive a core return plus supplementary pages tailored to their needs for example, if they have income from employment, self-employment, are a partner, have income from property, income from trusts, income from abroad or are non-resident, or have capital gains. The tax return has to be submitted by 31 January following the end of the tax year unless the return has been issued late by the Revenue. The taxpayer will normally be expected to calculate his tax liability but may submit the return by the 30 September following the end of the tax year and request the Revenue to calculate the tax for him. In cases where there are small amounts of other income or minor underpayments of up to £1,000 the Revenue will code out the underpayment and collect the outstanding tax under the PAYE system during the following fiscal year, provided that the return is submitted by 30 September.

The standard tax return includes claims for reliefs and allowances which must normally be claimed in the tax return although, where the information is not available at the time, for example, in respect of pension premiums carried back to an earlier period, a claim outside the return may be made. Under self-assessment the Revenue may make corrections if the mistake is obvious under TMA 1970, s 9(4)(*b*). If the correction is not obvious the return has to be sent back to the taxpayer for re-submission and is not treated as a proper return. Once a return has been submitted and accepted and the calculation of tax due confirmed as correct, the return will be accepted unless it becomes the subject of an enquiry.

Revenue enquiries

The Revenue have 12 months from the filing date to enquire into a tax return, which may be a general enquiry to test the veracity of the information supplied by the taxpayer. A general enquiry of this nature at district level will normally involve the production of the underlying books and records, and a meeting between the Revenue and the taxpayer and his agent, if any. Most cases for enquiry will be chosen following the Revenue's risk assessment of cases most likely to be incorrect, or may be chosen at random by the Revenue's central computer. The majority of enquiry cases will be chosen following a risk assessment and only a small proportion of returns, something like one in 1,000, will be subject to random enquiry.

In addition to general enquiries the Revenue may raise aspect enquiries where they are not seeking confirmation of the correctness of the taxpayer's records, but are querying the tax treatment of certain items or asking for additional information.

Under self-assessment the taxpayer has a statutory requirement to keep the records used to complete his tax return for a minimum period of 12 months following the filing date or until an enquiry is completed, if later; if the taxpayer is in business, the period becomes five years.

Payment

Tax not deducted at source is due for payment in two equal interim instalments, on 31 January in the tax year and 31 July following the tax year, with any balance being payable on 31 January following the end of the tax year, which is also the last date for submission of the tax return and the date of payment of the first instalment of tax for the following year.

Where 80 per cent or more of the tax due for the year is collected under PAYE or deducted at source, interim payments are not required. Nor are interim payments required in respect of capital gains.

The amount of the interim payments are based on the final tax liability for the preceding year, half that liability due for each of the two interim instalments. A claim may be made to reduce the interim instalment where there are good grounds for believing that it would be excessive, for example because of a downturn in business or loss claims.

There are fixed financial penalties or tax-geared penalties for failure to deliver tax returns as required and interest is payable on tax paid late. A 5 per cent surcharge is also levied if the final instalment is not paid by 28 February and a further 5 per cent surcharge is due if a tax is more than six months late, ie not paid by 31 July following 31 January on which it was due.

Estimates and amendments

Where information is not available to complete a tax return, the taxable income must be estimated to the best of the taxpayer's ability and the attention of the Revenue drawn to the fact that this is a provisional estimate. This will be superseded by an amended self-assessment when the correct figure is known. A reasonably reliable estimate does not have to be drawn to the Revenue's attention but a figure that is little more than a guess should be identified as such and the reason why the figure is not more accurate explained.

Once a return has been submitted and the enquiry period is over it becomes final unless the Revenue can make a discovery under TMA 1970, s 29. A discovery may be made where there is evidence of the taxpayer's fraud or neglect or where, on the basis of the information available to him, an officer of the Board could not reasonably have been expected to have recognised that tax had been underpaid. Where a self-assessment is reopened on discovery it will be superseded by an amended self-assessment once a position has been agreed with the Revenue.

In some cases the figures in the tax return will depend on subjective opinions such as the value of unquoted shares and in these cases the fact and basis of the valuation should be disclosed to the Revenue. Valuations of property will normally be referred to the district valuer and valuation of unquoted shares and intellectual property referred to the Shares Valuation Division.

Electronic lodgement service

Under self-assessment, agents are able to register with the Inland Revenue and submit taxpayers' returns electronically, which has the advantage of avoiding transcription errors and enabling the agent to receive electronically a copy of the taxpayers' statements, which would normally be sent direct to the taxpayer, showing the amount of tax currently due and the future instalments so far as ascertained.

Partnerships

Under self-assessment partnerships are not a taxable entity, but a nominated partner is responsible for submitting the partnership tax return to the Inland Revenue, and preparing a partnership statement showing the allocation of the taxable profit among the partners. Each individual partner is then responsible for returning his share of the partnership profits in accordance with the information on the partnership statement, and to pay the tax on his share of the partnership profits. Clearly, this means that if there is a Revenue enquiry into the partnership this automatically extends to an enquiry into each individual partner, at least as an aspect enquiry, on his partnership income.

Accounts and computations

Under self-assessment it is not necessary to submit accounts and computations or taxed income vouchers even where a repayment is due, except in the case of labour only sub-contractors, unless specifically requested in the course of a Revenue enquiry. In many cases, however, it will be appropriate to submit accounts and computations and such other information as the taxpayer considers necessary for the proper understanding of the tax return and to refer to the accompanying documents in the white space on the tax return. The reason for this is both to enable the Revenue to have the information necessary to confirm the return in the first instance, rather than to have to go through the formality of opening a formal enquiry, and to ensure that once the enquiry period is over the Revenue would not be able to make a discovery, as they would already have the appropriate information. The main reason why the Revenue do not consider that accounts and computations are normally required is because the returns for partnerships and the self-employed contain an analysis of the accounts in a standardised format, together with a summary, computation and capital allowances adjustments. This should be sufficient to calculate the tax due, and also give the Revenue a basis for computerised risk assessment in the future.

Post-transaction rulings

A post-transaction ruling from the Revenue confirming the tax treatment in advance of submission of the return is to become available. This facility is likely to be of most benefit to unrepresented taxpayers. In the case of capital gains involving the agreement of valuations it will be possible, once the transaction has been completed, to submit details to the Revenue for submission to the Shares Valuation Division in order to commence the valuation enquiries at the earliest possible moment. In simple cases this will enable agreement to be reached prior to submission of the return or, in more complex cases, at least get the valuation discussion under way as soon as the transaction has been completed, rather than waiting for the Revenue to refer it to the Shares Valuation Division in the course of a formal enquiry at some later date.

Repayment claiming

Small repayment claims remain outside self-assessment and repayment claim forms, together with the appropriate vouchers to cover the tax repayment, will be submitted by taxpayers as previously. The Revenue may also make targeted review enquiries outside the self-assessment system to employees to check that the correct code number is being applied for PAYE purposes.

An overpayment of tax may be reclaimed on submission of the appropriate return or information to the Inland Revenue, together with repayment supplement from the date of payment or, in the case of tax deducted at source, the deemed date of payment, which is 31 January after the end of the tax year.

Residence

Residence and ordinary residence are not defined by the Taxes Acts. In *Levene v IRC* (1928) 13 TC 486 the dictionary definition of place of usual abode was followed. Ordinary residence has been contrasted with casual or occasional residence (*Lysaght v IRC* (1928) 13 TC 511, *Thomson v Minister of National Revenue (Canada)* 1946 SCR 209), and may be treated as meaning that in the normal course of his life the taxpayer had been resident in the UK. Actual cases relating to residence show that where there is some business or permanent tie in the UK, the taxpayer tends to be treated as resident, subject to the specific exemptions contained in TA 1988, ss 334–336 although the purpose of the visit will not outweigh the time spent (*Lord Inchiquin v IRC* (1948) 31 TC 125). A house available for use in the UK, by a visitor to the UK for some temporary purpose only, may be ignored in determining residence (TA 1988, s 336).

Staying in hotels implies non-residence (*IRC v Zorab* (1926) 11 TC 289 and *IRC v Brown* (1926) 11 TC 292). Living in a yacht anchored in the UK (*Brown v Burt* (1911) 5 TC 667) and use of a hunting lodge (*Loewenstein v De Salis* (1926) 10 TC 424) has resulted in residence. Temporary visits abroad do not cause UK residence to be lost (*IRC v Combe* (1932) 17 TC 405) nor do temporary visits to the UK give rise to residence (*Withers v Wynyard* (1938) 21 TC 724).

The Revenue practice relating to residence is set out in Revenue booklet IR20 (recently revised) and SP3/81. If no place of abode is maintained in the UK the taxpayer is resident for any tax year in which visits to the UK total 183 days or if visits are habitual and substantial, ie on average three months a year for four years. If the visits are habitual and substantial ordinary residence may also be claimed. Ordinary residence and residence may still be claimed where the absence abroad amounts to less than three years and the taxpayer visits the UK for three months in a tax year. The three-year period is reduced where there is a full-time occupation overseas and the taxpayer has been abroad for a complete tax year (subject to permitted visits to the UK). As to visits extended because of exceptional circumstances, see SP2/91 and FA 1991, s 46.

If a place of abode is maintained in the UK (which is not to be ignored under TA 1988, s 336 *above*, or under TA 1988, s 335, because of a full-time employment overseas or being engaged full-time in a trade or profession outside the UK), the taxpayer who is normally resident in the UK, may be resident for any year in which he is physically present in the UK for however short a length of time and ordinarily resident if the visits are habitual and substantial.

Under Extra-Statutory Concessions (ESC) A11 and D2 a taxpayer coming to the UK is treated as resident in the UK in the year of arrival only from the date on which he arrives, and a taxpayer leaving the UK is treated as resident in the year of emigration only up until the date of his departure, although the concession is not applied where there is a tax avoidance motive (*R v IRC, ex p Fulford-Dobson* [1987] STC 344).

However, a full year's personal allowances are given in each case against the income for the resident period (*Fry v Burma Corporation, Ltd* (1930) 15 TC 113). A non-resident may be liable to tax on UK income not taxed at source at lower, basic and higher rates (*Brooke v IRC* (1917) 7 TC 261), provided that the Revenue can collect the tax.

For capital gains tax purposes, Extra-Statutory Concession D2 (1992) does not exempt capital gains realised before arrival where the individual has been either resident or ordinarily resident in the UK at any time in the 36-month period immediately before arrival. Similarly, on leaving the UK capital gains realised after departure but before the end of the tax year (ie in the split period) remain technically chargeable to capital gains tax, as do gains which relate to assets used by a trade, business, profession or vocation carried on by the taxpayer through a UK branch or agency.

Temporary absence from the UK does not make a Commonwealth or Irish citizen non-resident for tax purposes (TA 1988, s 334), but see *Reed v Clark* [1985] STC 323, which held in the circumstances of the case that an absence for a complete fiscal year was not an absence for some temporary purpose.

A person with a full-time employment outside the UK has his residence for tax purposes determined without regard as to whether he maintains a place of abode in the UK for his use. Similar provisions apply if a trade, profession or vocation is carried on entirely outside the UK. Incidental duties in the UK are ignored (TA 1988, s 335, *Robson v Dixon* (1972) 48 TC 527 and SP/A 10).

A temporary visitor to the UK is not liable to tax under Schedule D, Cases IV or V on remittances, unless he has spent six months in the UK in any tax year (TA 1988, s 336). The six-month period in TA 1988, s 336 is calculated exactly (*Wilkie v IRC* (1951) 32 TC 495). See, however, Inland Revenue IR 20, para 8, which generally ignores days of arrival and departure.

As with residence, there is no statutory definition of ordinary residence and it was held in the case of *Lysaght v IRC, above,* to be the converse of casual or occasional residence. It may therefore be treated as meaning in the normal course of events the taxpayer is resident for substantial periods of time in the UK. For example, in *Kinloch v IRC* (1929) 14 TC 736 it was held that a widow who lived mainly in hotels, and had spent substantial periods in the UK to visit her son at school, was ordinarily resident. See also *Peel v IRC* (1927) 13 TC 443; *Miesegaes v IRC* (1957) 37 TC 493; *Reid v IRC* (1926) 10 TC 673 and *Elmhirst v IRC* (1937) 21 TC 381; also *R v Barnet London Borough Council, ex p Shah* (1980) *The Times,* 21 July and *Cicutti v Suffolk County Council* (1980) *The Times,* 30 July. For the Revenue practice on ordinary residence see SP 3/81.

Dual residence

Because the UK, in common with many other countries, will treat a taxpayer as resident in cases where he is habitually in the country for periods of less than 183 days (the UK only requires 91 days on average over a four-year period for ordinary residence) it will be appreciated that it is perfectly possible for a taxpayer to be resident in two or more countries in the course of a single tax year, and thus become dual resident. This means that he may be liable to tax in both countries, perhaps on his worldwide income in both countries. This problem is frequently overcome under a double taxation treaty as a bilateral agreement between the two countries in question, under which the taxpayer is regarded as fiscally resident in one country but not the other. This is frequently known as a tie-breaker clause and residence under such a provision depends on the country in which the taxpayer has the permanent home, if in both countries, where his centre of vital interests (ie his social and economic interests) is; and if in both countries, in the country of which he is a national, unless he is a national of both countries or neither in which case the Revenue authorities of both countries have to sort out his fiscal residence. This is one of the few cases where nationality has a bearing on UK taxation. The double taxation treaty may also provide that income is taxable only in the country in which the taxpayer is resident or in which the income arises, which is particularly common in the case of rents from immovable property. The UK does not give an exemption to income that is subject to foreign tax under a treaty or local domestic law but will give a credit for UK income tax or capital gains tax on the same income or gain under TA 1988, s 788 where there is a double taxation treaty, or s 790 where there is no treaty and the relief is given unilaterally. An international treaty overrules UK domestic legislation (*Australian Mutual Provident Society v IRC* (1947) 28 TC 388).

Domicile

An individual's domicile determines the system of private international law by which he is governed in matters relating to marriage and divorce, the division of his estate on death and the legitimacy of his children. So far as the UK is concerned, it is possible to be domiciled in England and Wales, Scotland or Northern Ireland as there are three separate systems of law within the UK. For tax purposes a reference to UK domicile or non-UK domicile is generally accepted to mean domicile within one of these three jurisdictions. A person is normally domiciled in the country in which he is considered to have his permanent home, although it is possible to be domiciled in a country in which he does not actually have such a home. No person can be without a domicile, and unlike residence it is only possible to have one domicile at any one time for any one purpose. An existing domicile is presumed to continue until it is proved that a new domicile has been acquired, and most importantly, the onus of proof lies with whoever seeks to allege the change of domicile.

Every individual acquires at birth a domicile of origin, which in the case of a legitimate child, where the father is alive at the date of birth, is the country in which the father was domiciled at that time. If the father has died or the child is illegitimate, the domicile of origin is the country in which his mother was domiciled at the time of his birth. In these days when a large number of couples live together and have children without getting married, it may no longer be presumed that a child is legitimate, if it ever could have been (*Udny v Udny* (1869) LR1 Sc and Div 441, *Re Grove* (1888) 40 Ch D 216).

Any independent person can acquire a domicile of choice, which displaces the domicile of origin, by residing in a country with the intention of remaining there permanently or indefinitely (*Attorney-General v Pottinger* (1861) 6 H and N 733; *Waddington v Waddington* (1920) 36 TLR 359; *Cramer v Cramer* (1987) 1 FLR 116). If a domicile of choice is abandoned, either a new domicile of choice is acquired or the domicile of origin revives. To give up a domicile of choice requires both leaving the country of choice and giving up the intention of remaining there permanently or indefinitely (*Thiele v Thiele* (1920) 150 LTJ 387).

A domicile of choice is basically the country in which an individual intends to make his permanent home, but it is not possible to claim a domicile of choice without actually living in the country claimed (*IRC v Duchess of Portland* [1982] STC 149; *Plummer v IRC* [1987] STC 698).

The domicile of a child under 16 is a dependent one and would usually follow any change in the father's domicile. A minor may acquire an independent domicile of choice at the age of 16 or earlier marriage.

A woman already married on 1 January 1974 would have acquired her husband's domicile on marriage as a domicile of dependence, now regarded as one of choice, but under the Domicile and Matrimonial Proceedings Act 1973 a woman who marries after that date retains an independent domicile. A married woman with a dependent domicile can by her actions now establish an independent domicile of choice, but her domicile of origin does not automatically revert, even on divorce (*Faye v IRC* (1961) 40 TC 103), or on her husband's death (*Re Wallach dec'd, Weinschenk v Treasury Solicitor* (1949) 28 ATC 486; *IRC v Duchess of Portland* [1982] STC 149). A wife who is an American citizen is deemed to have married after 1 January 1974 under article 4(4) of the UK–USA double taxation treaty (SI 1980 No 568).

As domicile is very much a matter of fact and of intention (*Earl of Iveagh v Revenue Comrs*. Supreme Court (1930) IR 431), mere length of stay in the UK would not be sufficient to establish a UK domicile. In *Winans v A-G* [1904] AC 287 and *Bowie (or Ramsay) v Liverpool Royal Infirmary* [1930] AC 588, residence for nearly 40 years did not establish a change of domicile. Similarly in the more recent cases of *Buswell v IRC* [1974] STC 266 and *IRC v Bullock* [1976] STC 409 a foreign domicile of origin was not overruled by residence in the UK for a considerable period, in the face of the taxpayer's avowed intention not to change his domicile. In *Steiner v IRC* [1973] STC 547, *Re Lawton* (1958) 37 ATC 216, and *Re Furse (dec'd), Furse v IRC* [1980] STC 596, however, a change of domicile was on the facts of each case upheld. It is difficult to throw off a UK domicile of origin (*IRC v Cohen* (1937) 21 TC 301) and if a foreign domicile of choice is obtained, a return to live in the UK would usually resurrect the domicile of origin (*Fielden v IRC* (1965) 42 TC 501).

IHTA 1984, s 267 provides that for inheritance tax purposes a person is deemed to be UK-domiciled for three years following the acquisition of a foreign domicile or if resident in the UK for 17 out of the previous 20 fiscal years.

Remittance basis

If a sizeable proportion of the work is done overseas it may well be desirable for a non-UK domiciliary to enter into a foreign partnership within TA 1988, s 112 under which the income is taxable under Schedule D, Case V; or to enter into a contract of employment with a non-resident company, in which case the remuneration would be dealt with under Schedule E. This would be particularly appropriate in the case of a non-UK domiciled individual because in respect of income taxed under Schedule D, Cases I and II, a non-UK domiciled individual has no advantage under UK tax law compared with a person domiciled in the UK being taxed on his worldwide profits, whereas remuneration from a non-resident company or partnership for services performed wholly abroad would be taxed only on remittances to the UK and not on the income arising (TA 1988, ss 19(1), 192, 65(4), 112).

Remittances in a fiscal year following that in which the recipient ceased to be a partner would be tax-free in the UK as there would be no source of income to tax. There can therefore be advantages in alternating periods of overseas activities through a series of partnerships and employments and remitting only during a fiscal year following that in which the source ceased. However, a UK domiciled and resident partner of a foreign partnership would be assessed to tax on the arising basis on his share of the profits of the foreign partnership. Remittances from a ceased employment remain taxable under TA 1988, s 19(4A).

Assessments on a remittance basis include not only direct remittances to the UK but also constructive remittances, such as the satisfaction of a debt incurred in the UK under TA 1988, s 65(5)–(9). A cheque drawn on an American bank account was held to be a constructive remittance when sold to a UK bank (*Thomson v Moyse* (1960) 39 TC 291), as was a loan enjoyed in the UK (*Harmel v Wright* (1973) 49 TC 149). Remittances of the proceeds of foreign securities could be a remittance of capital if the securities were acquired before the taxpayer became resident in the UK (*Kneen v Martin* (1934) 19 TC 33), but not if purchased out of foreign income while the taxpayer was resident in the UK (*Walsh v Randall* (1940) 23 TC 55). It is arguable that remittance of a physical asset is not a remittance of income, for the purposes of Schedule D, but the benefit from its use in the UK could be under Schedule E.

If a non-UK domiciled individual is assessable on a remittance basis, it is important to ensure that, so far as possible, remittances to the UK are out of capital. This means that a taxpayer may require several bank accounts. The account containing his capital prior to becoming resident in the UK may be freely remitted. An account containing the proceeds of disposals of overseas investments could be remitted, but any chargeable gains element would be taxable on the remittance basis under TCGA 1992, s 12(1). However, the effective rate of tax applicable to capital gains is usually less, as a result of indexation allowance and rebasing, than that applicable to income and, therefore, a remittance from such an account should normally be made in preference to a remittance of income, assessable under Schedule D, Case V or Schedule E.

Gifts overseas

A non-domiciled individual taxable on the remittance basis could make gifts overseas of funds from his foreign bank accounts to his wife, family and friends. An overseas bank account into which the gift can pass thereby avoids falling into the constructive remittance problems previously mentioned (*Carter v Sharon* (1936) 20 TC 229). If, for example, a wife bought an expensive coat or otherwise spent the money so that her husband received no benefit, or if the children paid for their own school fees, it is considered that these would not be constructive remittances.

Where the individual is not UK-domiciled for either income tax or inheritance tax purposes, the gifts mentioned can be made free of inheritance tax. However, if the person is notionally domiciled in the UK for inheritance tax purposes under IHTA 1984, s 267, he would need to take advantage of the potentially exempt transfer provisions or other inheritance tax exemptions.

If a non-domiciled partner makes a gift from his (Jersey) bank account to his UK partners by transferring funds to their own (Jersey) bank accounts, such a gift would be excluded property for inheritance tax purposes. However, it would be necessary to ensure that the UK partners had not made a transfer of assets to the foreign partnership, or otherwise TA 1988, s 739 could cause the gifts to be assessable as income.

Employees

Employees, directors and other office holders are subject to tax under Schedule E (TA 1988, s 18(1)). Case I of Schedule E applies to an employee resident and ordinarily resident in the UK who is taxable on his worldwide earnings, subject to a deduction of 100 per cent of those earnings arising outside the UK during a period of absence of at least one year, under TA 1988, s 193 (*see* p 260 *below*). If the employee is non-UK domiciled and the earnings arise from overseas duties with a non-UK resident employer the income is only taxed if remitted to the UK at any time, whether during the currency of the employment or not (TA 1988, s 19(4A)). These are known as foreign emoluments, assessable under Schedule E, Case III.

A non-resident who is employed part time in the UK is taxable on the income arising from those duties under Schedule E, Case II unless the income is taxed only in the country of residence under a double taxation treaty.

Benefits in kind

In addition to being liable to tax under TA 1988, s 131, on all salaries, fees, wages, perquisites and profits whatsoever, an employee is taxable on gains from share options under TA 1988, ss 135, 136, 137 and 140, on non-cash vouchers under TA 1988, s 141, on credit tokens under TA 1988, s 142, on cash vouchers under TA 1988, s 143, and on tax paid on behalf of the employee by the employer not reimbursed within 30 days under TA 1988, s 144A. Living accommodation is taxable on the annual value of the accommodation under TA 1988, s 145 with an additional charge under TA 1988, s 146 where the cost of the accommodation exceeds £75,000. Termination payments are taxable under TA 1988, s 148, subject to an exemption for the first £30,000 and foreign service payments under TA 1988, s 188. Sick pay, maternity pay, income support and job-seekers allowances are taxable under TA 1988, ss 149–151A inclusive.

Directors and employees paid at a rate of £8,500 per annum or more, inclusive of expenses and benefits, are subject to tax on expenses under TA 1988, s 153, subject to a deduction for those expenses wholly exclusively and necessarily incurred in the performance of the duties of the employment including travelling expenses other than travel between home and the place of the employment under TA 1988, s 198. Travelling expenses reimbursed by the employer, including related subsistence, is allowable under FA 1997, s 62, introducing amendments to TA 1988, ss 198 and 198A.

Employees are also taxable on benefits in kind, normally on the cost to the employer under TA 1988, s 154, except where the benefit is taxable in accordance with particular rules such as the benefit from the private use of a car or van, taxable under TA 1988, s 157, Sched 6 and s 159AA and Sched 6A, on 35 per cent of the list price of the car or a flat £500 for a van. These are subject to amendments where the business travel is greater than 18,000 miles in a year or less than 2,500 miles (TA 1988, Sched 6, para 2), where the car is unavailable for part of the year or is more than four years old at the end of the year or where payments are made for the use of the car. Corresponding adjustments are available for the use of a van. TA 1988, s 55 exempts benefits taxed elsewhere and also allowable benefits such as car parking, canteen meals etc. A crèche provided by an employer does not, within appropriate limits, give rise to a benefit in view of TA 1988, s 155A and there are specific rules for benefits which consist of the use of an asset other than a car or van, which is normally 20 per cent of its market value under TA 1988, s 156(6). Car fuel is taxed on the basis of a scale charge under TA 1988, s 158 which depends on the size of the car, but pooled cars and vans are excluded from a taxable benefit under 1988, ss 159 and 159AB. Mobile telephones are caught by TA 1988, s 159A and beneficial loans by TA 1988, s 160 subject to *de minimis* exemptions for, eg, season ticket loans (TA 1988, s 161). Beneficial share arrangements for employees are caught under TA 1988, s 162 although there are approved share option schemes and profit sharing schemes with beneficial tax treatment provided for under TA 1988, ss 185–187 and Sched 9. Where the employee is provided with living accommodation not only is the benefit of the accommodation taxed but also any expenses incurred by the employer under TA 1988, s 163. Directors' tax paid by the employer is a benefit under TA 1988, s 164 and a scholarship for the child of an employee is caught by TA 1988, s 165.

P11Ds

The way the benefit provisions work is that the employer, or provider of the benefit if it is a third party, has to complete a form P11D for the director or higher paid employee, which has to be submitted to the Revenue by 6 July following the end of the fiscal year to which it relates. This form gives particulars of all benefits provided for the employee and all expenses reimbursed unless these are covered by a dispensation negotiated with the Inland Revenue under the authority of TA 1988, s 166. In addition to benefits excluded because of a dispensation as non-taxable, the employer can agree to pay the tax direct in respect of minor benefits under a PAYE settlement agreement under SI 1993 No 744 and SP5/96. Formal incentive schemes can also be covered by a taxed award scheme which is particularly useful for third party benefits where it is not intended that the beneficiary should suffer a tax charge (see SP5/96, para 17).

A copy of the form P11D or the information returnable thereon has to be given to the employee by 6 July following the year end, which he in turn will use to return the taxable benefits and expenses less the claim for allowable expenses under TA 1988, ss 198 and 198A on the Schedule E employment supplementary pages of his tax return.

Allowances

Tax-free payments may be made to employees of up to £4,000 per annum for 1996/97, under the profit related pay scheme in TA 1988, ss 171–184 (although the scheme is being phased out following FA 1997, s 61).

Other specific allowances for Schedule E include lump sum benefits on retirement from a pension fund under TA 1988, s 189, job release scheme allowances under TA 1988, s 191, removal expenses and benefits under TA 1988, s 191A and Sched 11A up to various allowable limits. Employer-financed house loss indemnity schemes are protected by TA 1988, s 191B and allowances for expenses in connection with foreign emoluments as given by TA 1988, s 192. Relief for foreign travelling expenses, including fares of the employee's family and dependants, is given by TA 1988, ss 193–195 and Sched 12, while foreign pensions qualify for a 10 per cent deduction under TA 1988, s 196. Statutory protection for payments under the fixed profit car scheme are given by TA 1988, ss 197B–197F. The car parking exemption is given by TA 1988, s 197A and sporting and recreational facilities by TA 1988, s 197G. There is a *de minimis* exemption for incidental overnight expenses given by TA 1988, s 200A, work-related training by TA 1988, ss 200B to 200D, and fees and subscriptions to professional bodies etc by TA 1988, s 201. Directors liability insurance is protected by TA 1988, s 201AA and the expenses of employed entertainers by TA 1988, s 201A (*see* Chapter 25). The payroll deduction scheme for donations to charity is governed by TA 1988, s 202.

No deduction is available for business entertaining in view of TA 1988, s 577. These are, however, normally disallowed on the employer in the corporation tax computation rather than on the employee under Schedule E. The exception is where the employee is given a round sum entertaining allowance which is taxable on the employee and tax deductible to the employer.

PAYE

In addition to providing a copy of the P11D or the information provided thereon the employer must also provide the employee with the annual certificate of pay and tax deducted on form P60 by 31 May following the end of a tax year under the Income Tax (Employments) Regulations 1993 (SI 1993 No 744), reg 39. The employee should therefore have the information required to complete the Schedule E employment supplementary pages using separate pages for each employment.

Tax under Schedule E is assessed on the amount received in the fiscal year, under TA 1988, s 202A, irrespective of the period during which it was earned, unless it is received prior to the commencement of the employment in which case it is treated as having been received in the year of assessment in which the employment commences under TA 1988, s 19(4A)(*a*) or the employment has ceased, in which case it is treated as having been received in the last year of assessment during which the employment was held (TA 1988, s 19(4A)(*b*)). The time at which income is received is the time it is actually paid to the employee or credited to an account on which he can draw under TA 1988, s 202B. The PAYE system is governed by TA 1988, ss 203–206 inclusive and the Income Tax (Employments) Regulations 1993 (SI No 744) and PAYE settlement agreements by TA 1988, s 206A. The payment by the employer of an employee's liability is a payment to the employee (*Hartland v Diggines* (1926) 10 TC 247).

Emoluments

Income is taxed under Schedule E on the emoluments of an office or employment under TA 1988, s 19(1) which includes payments for a future employment (*Shilton v Wilmshurst* (1991) STC 88) but must relate to a reward for services past, present or future (*Hochstrasser v Mayes* (1959) 38 TC 673). If the payment does not relate to the employment it is not taxable under Schedule E (*Mairs v Haughey* (1993) STC 569 and *Pritchard v Arundale* (1971) 47 TC 680). Whether income is properly taxable under Schedule E as income from an employment, or Schedule D as self-employed, is sometimes unclear and the point is dealt with further in Chapter 25.

Self-employed

Self-employed individuals are taxable under Schedule D, Case I on trading income or under Schedule D, Case II on income from any profession or vocation (TA 1988, s 18(3)).

For most practical purposes there is no distinction between these two cases of Schedule D. The introduction of self-assessment led to a major change in the basis of tax and profits of the self-employed. Businesses which commenced prior to 6 April 1994 were taxable on the preceding year basis of assessment, that is on the basis of the adjusted profits for the accounting period ending in the fiscal year of assessment prior to that in respect of which they were taxed. The accounts for the year ended 30 April 1994 or 31 March 1995 will both end in the fiscal year 1994/95 and both be assessed for 1995/96. In order to move on to the preceding year basis of assessment, in the opening years profits were taxed more than once; in the first year on the basis of the adjusted profits for the period from commencement to the following 5 April; in the second year for the first 12 months of trading, and in the third year the first 12 months of trading or, if available, the profits for the accounting year ending in the second fiscal year, and thereafter on the basis of the accounting year ending in the preceding fiscal year. The taxpayer had an option to have the first three fiscal years assessed on the basis of the actual profits in each fiscal year. On cessation in 1996/97 or earlier years the assessment would be on the adjusted profits for the period from 6 April to the date of cessation. As the profits of the year prior to cessation would have been assessed on the preceding year basis it will be obvious that profits fell out of assessment. The Revenue had the option to assess the penultimate of the anti-penultimate fiscal years on the basis of the actual adjusted profits for those years, which merely moved the period for which profits fell out of assessment. By careful timing these rules were open to manipulation and substantial profits could legitimately escape tax.

Where a business commences on or after 6 April 1994 it is subject to taxation on the current year basis ie on the adjusted profits of the accounting period ending in the fiscal year for which they are taxed.

The rules setting out the basis of assessment for Schedule D are contained in TA 1988, ss 60–63A which, confusingly, reuse the same section numbers for the current year basis of assessment as were used for the preceding year basis of assessment.

Current year basis

Under the current year basis of assessment, profits for the first year of assessment are assessed from the date of commencement to the following 5 April, as under the old basis (TA 1988, s 61). However, profits for the second year of assessment depend on whether there is a 12-month accounting period ending in the year, in which case the assessment is on the profits for that period (TA 1988, s 60(3)(a)). If there is not a 12-month accounting period ending in the second fiscal year, the assessment is on the basis of the profits for the first 12 months from commencement under TA 1988, s 61(2)(a). Where there is no accounting period ending in the second year of assessment but a change of accounting date in the third year, the change of accounting date is deemed to have taken place 12 months before the actual change under TA 1988, s 62, which may give a deemed accounting date in the second fiscal year. If this is less than 12 months from commencement the assessment will still be on the profits for the 12 months from that date (TA 1988, s 61(2)(b)). Where there is a change in accounting date less than 12 months from commencement, in the second year of assessment, the profits will still be on the profits for the first 12 months (TA 1988, s 61(2)(b)). If the change of accounting date is more than 12 months from commencement the assessment for the second year is based on the profits to the new accounting date under TA 1988, s 60(3)(*a*).

If there is no accounting date in either of the first or the second year, because the first set of accounts is for a long period, the assessable profits for the second fiscal year is on the default basis, ie the fiscal year itself (TA 1988, s 60(1)). In the third year of assessment if there is a 12-month accounting period ending in the third year, that forms the basis of assessment under TA 1988, s 60(3)(*a*). If it was an accounting period of at least 12 months ending in the second fiscal year, the basis period for the third fiscal year is 12 months from the end of the previous basis period (TA 1988, s 60(3)(*b*)). In the fourth and subsequent fiscal years the basis period continues to be the period of 12 months after the end of the basis period for the preceding year of assessment, so long as accounts are made up for a 12-month period (TA 1988, s 60(3)(*b*)).

Where there is a change of accounting period the new accounting date will normally apply for tax purposes provided that the new accounting date does not exceed a period of 18 months, notice of the change has been given to the Revenue, there has been no previous accounting date change in the preceding five years of assessment, or if there has been such a change the Revenue is satisfied that the change is made for *bona fide* commercial reasons (TA 1988, s 62A). If there is an invalid change it will be ignored for the year in which the change takes place, but in a subsequent year it will normally become effective provided that the appropriate notice is given to the Revenue, that the change is to apply for tax purposes (TA 1988, s 62(3) and (4)). Where a change in accounting date skips a fiscal year, for example where accounts are made up for a 13-month period from 1 April in one year to 30 April in the following year, the accounting date is deemed to have changed 12 months prior to the actual date of change (TA 1988, s 60(1)). If the accounting period to the new accounting date or deemed accounting date is for less than 12 months the assessment is on the profits for the 12-month period ending on the new date (TA 1988, s 62(2)(*a*)). If the accounting period is for more than 12 months to the new accounting date, the whole of the period is assessable for the fiscal year in which it ends. If there are two accounting dates ending in the same fiscal year these are amalgamated under TA 1988, s 60(5) and the basis period would be the extended period covering both sets of accounts under TA 1988, s 62(2), (3). In the year in which the business ceases the assessment is from the end of the basis period ending in the preceding fiscal year to the date of cessation under TA 1988, s 63(*b*).

It will be appreciated that under these rules the same profits may be taxed in more than one year of assessment. To the extent that the profits are doubly charged they are overlap profits and the period taxed more than once becomes an overlap period. The overlap profits of an overlap period may be carried forward until relieved. They may be partially relieved on a change of accounting date which has resulted in the assessment of profits of more than 12 months in the fiscal year, under TA 1988, s 63A(1). The proportion of the overlap profits relieved is obtained by applying the formula in TA 1988, s 63A(2), which effectively relieves the overlap profits for the overlap period proportionately to the extent that the change of accounting date results in an accounting period of more than 12 months.

The balance of the overlap profits of an overlap period are relieved on cessation of the business under TA 1988, s 63A(3). If a loss-making period is included in the basis period for two successive fiscal years it is only included in the first such period and treated as nil in the second period, under TA 1988, s 63A(4). If the overlap relief against the profits for the final period results in there being a loss in that period this is relievable in the normal way for loss relief or as a terminal loss.

Transitional provisions

It will be appreciated that a change from the preceding year basis of assessment to the current year basis of assessment requires transitional provisions in order to protect the Revenue from manipulation of the profits that would otherwise fall out of assessment. These transitional provisions are in FA 1994, Sched 20, paras 1–3.

The transitional year is 1996/97. Where there is an accounting date in 1996/97 the basis period for that year is the 12-month period ending with the latest accounting date falling in the year ie the primary basis period under FA 1994, Sched 20, para 1(2)(*a*). If as a result of the exercise of the taxpayers' option on commencement under the preceding year basis of assessment to have the second and third year of assessment taxed on an actual basis, the profits for 1995/96 are assessed on an actual basis, 1996/97 is also on the basis of the profits of the fiscal year (FA 1994, Sched 20, para 2(3)). This would also apply where there is no accounting period ending in 1996/97 (FA 1994, Sched 20, para 1(2)(*b*)). In all other cases the assessment for 1996/97 is on the appropriate percentage of the profits for the primary basis period, that is the accounting year ending in 1996/97 and for the relevant period, which is the period beginning with the end of the basis period for 1995/96 computed under the old rules, and ends with the beginning of the primary basis period computed under the new rules. The appropriate percentage is 365 divided by the total number of days in the basis period (FA 1994, Sched 20, para 1(2)). In the majority of cases where there has been no change of accounting date the relevant period will be the year ending with the beginning of the primary basis period and the appropriate percentage will be half the aggregate of the profits for the two years ending with the normal accounting date in 1996/97.

For 1997/98 and future years the basis period will be the accounting period ending in the fiscal year for both old and new businesses. However, for old businesses, there is a further transitional overlap relief for the proportion of the basis period in 1997/98 that falls prior to 6 April 1997. This compensates for the multiple assessments on the opening years under the old preceding year basis of assessment.

This transitional overlap relief can be utilised in the same way as any other overlap, on cessation or on a change of accounting date resulting in a long period. The relief is given by FA 1994, Sched 20, para 2(4).

If the cessation takes place prior to 6 April 1998 the Revenue have an option to apply the old cessation rules to a pre-6 April 1994 business under FA 1994, Sched 20, para 3(2). If the cessation takes place in 1998/99 the Revenue have the option of substituting for the transitional year profits the actual profits for the fiscal year 1996/97, under FA 1994, Sched 20, para 3(3) and (4).

Transitional anti-avoidance

The complexity of these rules as further exacerbated by anti-avoidance provisions to prevent the exploitation of the transitional provisions by artificially extending the transitional period by a change of accounting date (unless it is to a date closer to 5 April) or by moving profits into the transitional period, where they will only be partly taxed, either by accelerating income or deferring deductible expenses. This exploitation of the transitional averaging provisions is countered by FA 1995, Sched 22, paras 1 and 2 and 14–17. In addition to taxing the profits diverted into the transitional period there is also a penalty of 25 per cent of the tax sought to be saved, unless the taxpayer admits to having contravened the transitional provisions under FA 1995, Sched 22, para 13, which at least avoids the penalty. There are escape provisions for transactions entered into for exclusively *bona fide* commercial reasons or where they fall below the *de minimis* limits set by FA 1995, Sched 22, para 1(3), under the Income Tax (Schedule 22 to the Finance Act 1995) (Prescribed Amounts) Regulations 1997 (SI 1997 No 1158).

The Revenue were concerned that taxpayers, as well as exploiting the transitional averaging provisions, would exploit the transitional overlap provisions by pushing profits into the transitional overlap period; accordingly anti-avoidance provisions are introduced by FA 1995, Sched 22, para 3 to bring into charge to tax the amount by which the profits of the transitional overlap period have been artificially increased, subject to the same 25 per cent penalty and *de minimis* provisions as the transitional averaging anti-avoidance provisions.

Adjusted accounts

The starting point for the assessable profits under Schedule D, Case I or II is the accounting profit computed in accordance with generally accepted accounting principles (*Heather v P-E Consulting Group* (1973) 48 TC 293; *Threlfall v Jones, Gallagher v Jones* (1993) STC 537; *Odeon Associated Theatres Limited v Jones* (1971) 48 TC 257; *Johnston v Britannia Airways Limited* (1994) STC 763). Profits are normally computed on a full accruals basis although the Revenue will accept a cash or bills delivered basis for a professional business, if consistently applied under SP A27. The accounts, however, require to be adjusted for tax purposes as certain income may have to be excluded, because it is taxed under some other provision, or expenses properly deducted for accounting purposes are not allowable for tax purposes as a result of statutory provisions or case law. The general rules as to deductions not allowable for tax purposes are contained in TA 1988, s 74 and include expenses not wholly and exclusively incurred for the purposes of the trade, profession or vocation, private expenditure, capital payments, excessive interest, patent royalties under TA 1988, s 74(1)(*p*) etc. The incidental costs of obtaining loan finance are specifically allowed under TA 1988, s 77 as are expenses in connection with foreign trades and travelling by TA 1988, ss 80 and 81; interest paid to non-residents may be disallowed in whole or part under TA 1988, s 82. Patent and trade mark fees and expenses are specifically allowed under TA 1988, s 83. Relief for certain pre-trading expenditure is given by TA 1988, s 401. Business entertaining expenses are specifically excluded by TA 1988, s 577.

Expenses incurred partly for business and partly for private purposes may be wholly disallowed as not being wholly and exclusively for the purpose of the trade (*Mallalieu v Drummond* (1983) STC 665). On the other hand, it may be possible to apportion expenditure, for example, the cost of heating a house partly used for business purposes, on some just and reasonable basis, and to allow the deduction of the business proportion (*Copeman v William J Flood & Sons Limited* (1941) 24 TC 53).

Capital expenditure is disallowed; this has been described as expenditure made not only once for all but with a view to bringing into existence an asset or advantage for the enduring benefit of a trade (*Atherton v British Insulated and Helsby Cables Limited* (1925) 10 TC 77).

Capital allowances

The prohibition of a deduction for capital expenditure extends to the depreciation provision for the diminution in value of capital assets, normally debited in a profit and loss account. The effect of this disallowance is partly countered by allowing capital allowances on certain defined items of capital expenditure. From 1994/95, in respect of businesses commencing on or after 6 April 1994, and from 1997/98 in respect of businesses commencing prior to that date, capital allowances are given as a trading expense (FA 1994, s 211(2) and CAA 1990, s 140). Capital allowances are available on industrial buildings and structures (CAA 1990, ss 1–21), machinery and plant, (CAA 1990, ss 22–62), including special provisions for ships, expensive motor cars, short life assets, long life assets, leased assets and inexpensive cars and fixtures. Relief is also available for mineral extraction under CAA 1990, s 63, partnerships using the property of a partner under CAA 1990, s 65, building alterations connected with the installation of machinery or plant under CAA 1990, s 66, expenditure on thermal insulation under CAA 1990, s 67, computer software under CAA 1990, s 67A; expenditure relating to films, tapes and disks is however normally treated as a trading expense and not eligible for capital allowances under CAA 1990, s 68, whereas allowances for expenditure on fire safety and safety at sports grounds and security is given by CAA 1990, ss 69–72. Expenditure is given on certain scientific research expenditure by CAA 1990, ss 136–139; dwelling houses let on assured tenancies are covered by CAA 1990, ss 84–97; mineral extraction allowances by CAA 1990, ss 98–121; agricultural and forestry buildings allowances by CAA 1990, ss 122–131, and dredging by CAA 1990, ss 134 and 135.

Under the preceding year basis of assessment there were, in the opening and closing years of a business, separate basis periods for capital allowances which ensured that expenditure whenever incurred fell into only one basis period but that all such expenditure was included. These provisions are unnecessary under the current year basis where capital allowances are treated as an expense. The rate of capital allowances is given on the basis of a 12-month period and if the basis period is for a longer or shorter period the rate of writing down allowance is adjusted accordingly. Where, however, there is an overlap of two periods of account the period common to both is deemed to fall in the first period of account only for capital allowance purposes under CAA 1990, s 160(6).

Under the transitional provisions any unused capital allowances carried forward under CAA 1990, s 140(4), which have not been relieved in 1996/97 or earlier periods, are treated as due in the first period of account ending after 5 April 1997, under FA 1994, Sched 20, para 9. The effect of this is that if the allowances are not relieved in 1997/98 they would be included in the figure of losses carried forward under TA 1988, s 385. The transitional overlap relief for part of the 1997/98 basis period which falls prior to 6 April 1997 is calculated prior to capital allowances under FA 1994, Sched 20, para 2(4A).

Loss relief

Whenever trading activities of a business result in a loss, the adjustment of the figures for tax purposes is exactly the same as where there is a profit, except that disallowable items such as depreciation reduce the loss rather than increase the profits. Capital allowances treated as a trading expense, as they are in all cases from 1997/98, increase the loss. For businesses commencing prior to 6 April 1994 capital allowances are normally given as a separate allowance up to and including 1996/97 but are then added to losses for loss relief purposes under TA 1988, s 383. Effectively, therefore, loss relief applies to loss as increased by capital allowances.

Under self-assessment, losses are calculated by reference to the loss in the accounting period ending in the fiscal year and may be set against the total income either of that year, ie set against other income, or against the total income of the preceding fiscal year, ie carrying the loss back one year (TA 1988, s 380(1)). For pre-6 April 1994 businesses, losses up to and including 1996/97 were strictly calculated by reference to the loss arising in the fiscal year, apportioning results over the fiscal year on a time basis, although in practice, loss relief was often given on the basis of the loss for the accounting period ending in the fiscal year which was treated as the loss for the fiscal year, as under the current year basis of assessment.

A claim to set off losses must be made by 31 January following the end of the year of assessment in which the loss arises. The taxpayer may elect whether to set off the loss, or carry it back, but he cannot claim part of the loss in each year except to the extent that the loss exceeds the income available for relief in the chosen year. Loss relief for a loss arising in the current year takes precedence over a loss arising in a succeeding year carried back (TA 1988, s 380(2)). A loss arising in 1995/96 can be set against total income either for that year or 1996/97 under FA 1994, s 209(7). A loss arising in the first four fiscal years of a trade may be carried back and set against the total income of the three preceding years, using up the earliest available income first under TA 1988, s 381. Where a loss appears in a computation for a second time, for example under a change of accounting date, it is only given in the first year for which it is available and treated as nil in the second year (TA 1988, s 382(4)).

Where losses are not set against other income they may be carried forward under CA 1985 and set against the first available profits from the same trade.

A loss arising in the last 12 months of trading may be set against total income for the final year and any surplus against total income for the preceding three years against the latest year first (TA 1988, ss 388 and 389).

A capital loss on unquoted shares, as computed for capital gains tax purposes, may, where the shares have originally been subscribed for rather than acquired from an existing shareholder, be relieved for income tax purposes against total income under TA 1988, s 574. Farming losses may be subject to a restriction under TA 1988, s 397.

Annual payments

Annual payments are payments made under a legal obligation (*Drummond v Collins* (1915) 6 TC 525; *Dealler v Bruce* (1934) 19 TC 9). The payments must be recurring

(*Moss Empires Ltd v IRC* (1937) 21 TC 264) over a period exceeding 12 months (*Whitworth Park Coal Co Ltd v IRC* (1959) 38 TC 531). They must be pure income profit of the recipient taxable under Schedule D, Case III on the gross amount received, with no expenses deductible against them (*IRC v London Corporation (as conservators of Epping Forest)* (1953) 34 TC 293). They must be income not capital receipts of the payee (*Campbell v IRC* (1970) 45 TC 427). In some cases it is necessary to divide a payment between its capital and income elements (*IRC v Church Commissioners for England* (1976) STC 339; *IRC v British Salmson Aero Engines Ltd* (1938) 22 TC 29; *Brodies Will Trustees v IRC* (1933) 17 TC 432; *Ramsay v IRC* (1935) 20 TC 79; *Vestey v IRC* (1961) 40 TC 112).

TA 1988, s 74(1)(*m*) specifically excludes as an allowable expense, any annuity or other annual payment (other than interest) payable out of the profits or gains and TA 1988, s 74(1)(*p*), excludes a deduction for any royalty or other sum paid in respect of the user of a patent.

An annual payment which is unrelieved as a trading expense may be relieved as a charge on income under TA 1988, s 348(1) including, under TA 1988, s 348(2)(*a*), any royalty or other sum paid in respect of the user or patent. In order to obtain relief for an annual payment as a charge on income the payer deducts income tax at the basic rate from the payment and therefore if he were due to pay, say, £1,000 to the licensor he would in fact pay £770 where the basic rate of tax is 23 per cent. He therefore retains in his own hands £230. Provided that his tax payable for the year of assessment in which the payment is made consists of at least £230 payable at the basic rate he does not pay over to the Revenue the amount deducted from the royalty payment, which compensates him for the lack of any deduction for the payment. In the words of TA 1988, s 348, the annual payment is paid wholly out of profits or gains brought in to charge to income tax. It is worth noting that there is no compulsion to deduct tax at the basic rate, but the licensee is entitled to deduct, and only by making such a deduction can he obtain tax relief. It will be appreciated that if, as in the example, he pays tax on his total income without basic rate relief for the royalty paid but deducts tax from the actual royalty, he is in the same net position as he would have been if he had paid the gross royalty and claimed the amount as an expense for tax purposes provided, of course, that he is only liable to tax at the basic rate. Relief for higher rates is given, despite the annual payment not being a trading expense, by treating it as a deduction from the payer's total income under TA 1988, s 385(6)(*b*) and therefore deductible when calculating the higher rate taxes payable.

As a charge on income the deduction is made in respect of the fiscal year in which the annual payment is paid, irrespective of the period to which it relates, (TA 1988, s 835). The somewhat convoluted method of giving relief for annual payments ensures that the payee suffers tax at least at the basic rate and the Revenue therefore only has to collect by direct assessment any higher or additional rate tax on the payee. It will be appreciated that the system falls down to the extent that the payer does not have a basic rate liability sufficient to cover the tax deducted from the annual payment. In such cases, TA 1988, ss 349 and 350 come into play and the payer has forthwith to notify the Revenue of the payment and pay the shortfall in tax to the Revenue following the issue of an assessment under TA 1988, s 350(1).

To the extent that the annual payment is dealt with under TA 1988, ss 349 and 350 rather than TA 1988, s 348, relief is not obtained at the basic rate or at the higher rates by the payer. However, if the annual payment is incurred wholly and exclusively for the purposes of a trade, profession or vocation carried on by the payer, the unrelieved amount may be treated, under TA 1988, s 387, as though it were a loss sustained in the trade, profession or vocation and therefore carried forward against future profits of the same trade, profession or vocation under TA 1988, s 385 or on the transfer of a trade to a company in exchange for shares, against income from the company under TA 1988, s 386.

Failure to deduct tax

If the payer fails to deduct tax from an annual payment the Revenue can none the less assess the recipient (*Glamorgan Quarter Sessions v Wilson* (1910) TC 537; *Grosvenor Place Estates Ltd v Roberts* (1960) 39 TC 433).

If the licensee who is entitled to deduct tax from a royalty payment fails to do so he cannot recover the tax from future payments (*Shrewsbury v Shrewsbury* (1907) 23 TLR 224) unless there is an error of fact, eg, whether the payment is a royalty payment or some other payment. If there has been an honest mistake of fact, the tax not deducted could be deducted from future payments (*Re Musgrave, Machell v Parry* [1916] 2 Ch 417, *Turvey v Dentons* (1923) Ltd (1952) 31 ATC 470). Money paid under a mistake of law, ie the payer did not realise that he should have deducted tax, cannot normally be recovered, (*Barclays Bank Ltd v W J Simms Son & Cooke (Southern) Ltd* [1980] QB 677).

TA 1988, s 4(2)(*a*) specifies that if a royalty or other annual payment is made out of profits or gains brought into charge to tax under TA 1988, s 348 the rate of tax to be deducted is that for the fiscal year in which the amount becomes due for payment, irrespective of whether it is paid on time or not. If on the other hand the payment is not made out of profits or gains brought into charge to tax, and is therefore dealt with under TA 1988, ss 349, 350, the rate of tax to be deducted is that for the fiscal year in which the amount is finally paid, irrespective of when it was due for payment (TA 1988, s 4(2)(*b*)). (See *Re Sebright, Public Trustee v Sebright* (1944) 23 ATC 190; *Regal (Hastings) Ltd v Gulliver* (1944) 24 ATC 297).

Pure income profits

This usually turns on the question as to whether the payment is 'pure income profit' in the hands of the recipient or whether the recipient has assumed reciprocal obligations involving him in expenditure such as would diminish his income from the payments. The relevant principles are stated in such cases as *IRC v National Book League* (1957) 37 TC 455; *Earl Howe v IRC* (1919) 7 TC 289 and *Campbell v IRC* (1968) 45 TC 427. If the payment is considered to be an annual payment, then the question of deduction of income tax is relevant.

In the *National Book League* case, Vaisey J said of the covenanted subscriptions (at p 468):

> But the fact remains that these covenanted payments were not ordinary typical covenanted subscriptions to a charity. I think they were payments to the incorporated body, the League, in return for which the subscriber got some substantial advantage, so that these payments cannot be described as pure income payments when they reached the hands of the League and those who conducted its affairs.

Similarly, Lord Justice Morris stated (at p 475):

> The question arises whether the payments can be said to be pure gifts to the charity. In the terms of a phrase which has been used, can the payments be said to be pure income profit in the hand of the charity? If the payments were made in such circumstances that the League was obliged to afford to the covenantors such amenities and such benefits of membership as would at any particular time be offered to all members, and if those amenities and benefits were appreciable and not negligible, then I do not think that the payments were pure income profit in the hands of the charity.

In *Campbell v IRC*, Lord Donovan stated (at p 446):

> The truth is, in my opinion, that one cannot resolve the problem whether a payment is an annual payment within Case III simply by asking the questions 'Must the payee give or do something in return?' or 'Did the payer make some counter-stipulation or receive some counter-benefit?' or 'Was it pure bounty on his part?' Such questions come more easily to the mind perhaps where, as here, payment to a charity is involved. But there is no warrant in the Income Tax Acts for applying a special test in the case of charities. The test must be applicable to all annual payments; and the problem must continue to be resolved, in my opinion, on the lines laid down by Scrutton LJ in Earl Howe's case. One must determine, in the light of all the relevant facts, whether the payment is a taxable receipt in the hands of the recipient without any deduction for expenses or the like—whether it is, in other words 'pure income' or 'pure profit income' in his hands, as those expressions have been used in the decided cases. If so, it will be an annual payment under Case III. If, on the other hand, it is simply gross revenue in the recipient's hands, out of which a taxable income will emerge only after his outgoings have been deducted, then the payment is not such an annual payment. This, of course, has been said often enough before, but the judgement under review makes it necessary, I think, to say it again. The test makes it necessary to decide each case on its own facts. If goods and services are supplied in return for the payments in question, no doubt it will normally be found that this is done continuously or periodically during the time that the sums are payable, though there may be exceptions to this situation.

Income from UK land

Income from real property in the UK is taxable under Schedule A. The rules were substantially modified from 1995/96 onwards prior to the introduction of self-assessment. The previous rules and transitional arrangements are outside the scope of this book. Income tax is now charged under Schedule A on income from land and property, as if it were income of a business under TA 1988, s 15, (income tax version). Rules for taxation of income from real estate are totally different for companies although the same section numbers are used, which can lead to substantial confusion. Although the income is calculated as if it arose from a business under Schedule D, Case I, which means that for example interest and capital allowances are allowed as trading expenses, the income does not qualify as trading income for loss relief, which is therefore ring fenced (TA 1988, s 379A) and may be offset only against future rental income, nor does the rental business qualify for capital gains tax relief such as retirement relief or roll over relief on replacement of business assets.

Furnished holiday lettings, although taxed under Schedule A, are treated more like a trade in that losses may be set against total income, and the capital gains tax reliefs available for a trade apply. Because the Schedule D, Case I rules apply, income and expenses are calculated on an accruals basis, not on the cash basis, property by property, which was the position prior to 1995/96. Where property is let on a favourable rent below the full market value, there is no requirement to bring in a notional rent, except in the case of single estate elections. There may, however, be a disallowance of part of the expenses, to the extent that they exceed the income on property let out at an under value, on the grounds that the excess expenditure is not incurred wholly and exclusively for the purpose of the letting business. Apart from this, there is no need to deal with properties on an individual basis, and rents and expenses of a number or properties may be pooled. It is only properties within the UK that are within Schedule A, rental from overseas real estate being assessed under Schedule D, Case V.

It is not uncommon to run into difficulties in agreeing allowable travelling expenses in connection with the supervision of property as the Revenue take a fairly strict line and need to be convinced that the travelling expenses are allowable and that the taxpayer's home is the base from which those expenses are computed, following *Horton v Young* (1971) 47 TC 60.

Furnished lettings are taxed within Schedule A in the same way as for unfurnished property except that there is an allowance for wear and tear which is 10 per cent of the rent less council tax, water rates and other services normally borne by the tenants (Extra-Statutory Concession B47).

There is an exception to the rule that, except in the case of furnished holiday lettings, losses cannot be offset against total income which applies where the losses arise from excess capital allowances or agricultural expenses (TA 1988, s 279A(2), (3) and (8), (9), (10)). Any Schedule A losses brought forward under the old rules are treated as if they were expenses arising in 1995/96 under FA 1995, Sched 6, para 19(2) and (3). Property income is taxed under Schedule A on a fiscal year basis, except in the case of partnership income or income from subletting business premises brought into the Schedule D, Case I profits by concession.

Joint ownership of the property does not necessarily amount to a partnership and each co-owner is assessed on his share of the rents less expenses.

In the case of landed estates it is possible to have in force a single estate election, if it has continuously been so held since 1962/63, under TA 1988, s 26. In this case the annual value, ie the deemed gross rateable value is brought in, as the minimum income for parts of the estate which are owner-occupied or let on a nominal rent. The costs of running the entire estate may then be set against the entire estate income, without any disallowance of expenses relating to the unlet portion. Any excess of expenses on the estate over the estate income however is ring fenced and can only be carried forward against future income from the estate.

Casual letting of a room in the taxpayer's home may be covered under the rent-a-room relief provisions in F(No 2)A 1992, Sched 10.

Income from investments

Interest and discounts

Interest and discounts are taxed under Schedule E, Case III on the income arising in the fiscal year for sources of income arising on or after 6 April 1994 and for previously held sources from 6 April 1997 (TA 1988, s 64). There are transitional provisions for pre-6 April 1994 sources under FA 1994, Sched 20, para 4, basically providing that the income of the transitional period will be on half the income for the two years ending on 5 April 1997, where the income has previously been assessed under the pre-self-assessment rules on the basis of the income arising in the preceding fiscal year.

Strictly speaking, each deposit on an interest-bearing account creates a new source of income (*Hart v Sangster* (1957) 37 TC 231) and the Revenue will apply the strict basis where it appears that the transitional rules are being manipulated. There are also specific anti-avoidance provisions under FA 1995, Sched 22, para 9, which applies a penalty, subject to *de minimis* levels, where the transitional rules have been exploited.

As with rental income, taxed under Schedule A, partnerships are taxed on untaxed interest by reference to the accounting year ending in the fiscal year not by reference to the income arising in the fiscal year.

Taxed investment income

Income from Government securities, debentures, deposit interest from banks and building societies normally has tax deducted at source at the lower rate of 20 per cent for 1997/98 (TA 1988, s 1A) which is taxable on the recipient under Schedule D, Case III, under TA 1988, s 18(1) or if arising from overseas securities or possessions under Schedule D, Cases IV or V. Dividends from UK companies are taxable under Schedule F under TA 1988, s 20 and are deemed to have suffered tax at the lower rate of the total of the dividend and tax credit. Non-interest income from annual payments, such as patent royalties, are still subject to tax deducted at the basic rate of 23 per cent for 1997/98.

Where the taxpayer is not liable to tax at the higher rates the amount suffered by deduction exhausts his liability. A higher rate taxpayer however, is liable to tax on the total of the amounts receivable in the tax year and the credits relating thereto, as it is part of his total income under TA 1988, s 836. Under self-assessment the tax payable for 1997/98 and future years is payable in two instalments based on the preceding year's income, less the credit for the tax deducted at source, with the balance being payable on 31 January after the end of the fiscal year. The interim payments are dealt with by TMA 1970, s 59A and the final payment of income tax and capital gains tax by TMA 1970, s 59B. The payments on account in the transitional year 1996/97 are governed by FA 1995, Sched 21.

Foreign securities and possessions

Income from foreign securities and possessions is taxed under Schedule D, Cases IV and V under TA 1988, s 65. The income is taxed on the amount arising in the current fiscal year where the source first arose on or after 6 April 1994. Where the source arose prior to that date it would have been assessed on the preceding year basis, which continues to apply up to and including 1995/96. 1996/97 is the transitional year, taxed on the average of the income for the two years ended on 5 April 1997. The income is calculated on the amount arising and, in the case of foreign trades and professions, the income is calculated as if it arose under Schedule

D, Case I or II on the income arising in the accounting period ending in the fiscal year. Interest payable is deductible from income from foreign investment properties under TA 1988, s 353(1) and FA 1995, s 41. Income from an overseas partnership is also taxable under Schedule D, Case V to a non-UK domiciliary (TA 1988, s 112(1A)). A trade controlled from the UK is charged under Schedule D, Case I (*Ogilvy v Kitton* (1908) 5 TC 338), but if controlled abroad, for example through a resident manager, under Schedule D, Case V (*Colquhoun v Brooks* (1889) 2 TC 490).

Where the income is taxed under Schedule D, Cases IV or V in the bands of a non-UK domiciliary the amount taxable is the amount remitted to the UK, unless in connection with income from property in the Republic of Ireland which remains taxable on an arising basis under TA 1988, s 68. The remittance basis is given by TA 1988, s 65(4)–(9). As with interest, there are anti-avoidance provisions designed to prevent the exploitation of the transitional rules applying on the change from the preceding to the current year of assessment basis, which are contained in FA 1995, Sched 22, para 10. The concentration of remittances by a non-domiciliary into the transitional year is not regarded as anti-avoidance even though only one half of the remittances would be taxable.

In the case of overseas let property the furnished holiday lettings rules have no application, nor do the Schedule D, Case I rules relating to overseas travelling expenses which are disapplied by FA 1995, s 41(2). Each property is treated as a separate business up to and including 1996/97 (FA 1995, s 41(6)) but from 1997/98 the income will be pooled. As the Schedule A rules are now applied to overseas properties the anti-avoidance provisions, such as those relating to premiums on leases, which apply for Schedule A also apply to properties abroad (FA 1995, s 41(4)).

The only relief for losses on overseas lettings was under Extra-Statutory Concession B25 which allowed them to be carried forward and set against future income of the same property. This remains the position up until 1996/97 but any remaining deficit may be carried forward and set against rental income from the same property in 1997/98 and against the pooled income in 1998/99 and subsequent years (FA 1995, s 41(8)). Even where overseas properties are pooled for tax purposes it may be necessary to calculate the profit or loss for each property individually where foreign tax is payable in order to apply the correct double tax credit, following *Yates v GCA International Ltd* (1991) STC 157, see SAT 1 (1995) 9.160.

Casual profits

The sweep-up provision taxing profits or gains not otherwise brought into charge for tax is Schedule D, Case VI (TA 1988, s 69), which is computed on the income arising in the fiscal year except in the case of partnerships where it is by reference to the accounting period ending in the fiscal year. In theory Schedule D, Case VI has always been assessed on a current year basis but in practice, the Revenue have allowed the preceding fiscal year basis and even the accounting year ending in the preceding fiscal year. Transitional provisions in such cases are then applied along Schedule D, Case 1 lines subject to the strict basis applying, if necessary, to prevent the anti-avoidance provisions being exploited.

National insurance

National insurance contributions are largely outside the scope of this book but the amounts levied can be substantial. Employees are subject to Class I contributions of up to 10 per cent of their earnings, up to £465 per week and the employer is subject to contributions of 10 per cent of the gross earnings without limit. A self-employed individual is taxed at a flat rate of £6.15 per week for 1997/98 once above the small exemption of £3,480 and is also liable to tax at 6 per cent of the annual profits between £7,010 and £24,180. Those not in employment may pay a voluntary contribution of £6.05 per week.

Capital gains tax

Capital gains tax is payable on chargeable gains of taxpayers resident or ordinarily resident in the UK, in the year in which the disposal takes place (TCGA 1992, s 2(1)). Non-residents are normally taxable on chargeable gains in respect of assets in the UK used for the purposes of a trade, branch or agency carried on in the UK (TCGA 1992, s 10(1)). Non-UK domiciliaries are only taxable on chargeable gains remitted to the UK on non-UK assets (TCGA 1992, s 12). The situs of assets for capital gains tax purposes is given by TCGA 1992, s 275 for example, an interest in land is where the land is situated, an interest in shares is where the principal register is situated, if registered, or where the shares certificates are physically held if bearer shares, goodwill is situated where the trade or business or profession is carried on. Patents, trade marks and registered designs are situated where they are registered, and if registered on more than one register where each register is situated, and rights or licenses to use a patent or trade mark or registered design are situated in the UK if those rights are exercisable in the UK (TCGA 1992, s 275(h)); copyright, design right and franchises and rights or licenses to use in the copyright, work or design in which design right subsist are situated in the UK if those rights are exercisable in the UK (TCGA 1992, s 275(j)).

There is a *de minimis* exemption for capital gains tax of £6,500 for 1997/98 (TCGA 1992, s 3 and SI 1996 No 2957), but otherwise, capital gains are subject to tax at the income tax rate as if the gains were the highest amounts of the taxpayer's income in the fiscal year (TCGA 1992, s 4). For self-assessment purposes interim payments are not required for capital gains tax and the tax is therefore due on 31 January following the end of the fiscal year in which the gain arose.

There are complex anti-avoidance provisions enabling gains of non-resident companies to be apportioned to the shareholders, under TCGA 1992, s 13, and value shifting where rights of shares are amended, under TCGA 1992, ss 29–34.

Chargeable gains and losses

Chargeable gains are calculated on the excess of the consideration proceeds less disposal costs over the base cost plus acquisition costs (TCGA 1992, ss 37 and 38), unless the consideration has been taxed as income (TCGA 1992, s 27(1)), or the costs have been allowed for income tax purposes as deductible expenses or capital allowances (TCGA 1992, ss 39–41). The base value of assets held on 31 March 1982 will normally be the market value at that date (TCGA 1992, s 35), and the base cost may be increased by reference to indexation in accordance with the increase in the retail prices index between the date of acquisition of the asset or 31 March 1982 if later, and the date of disposal (TCGA 1992, ss 53–57).

Where the disposal is a transaction between connected parties or not at arm's length, the market value may be substituted for the proceeds, if any, under TCGA 1992, ss 17 and 18. There are anti-avoidance provisions to prevent the mitigation of capital gains tax by transferring assets in a series of transactions under TCGA 1992, ss 19 and 20. The disposal proceeds in particular cases where an asset is lost or destroyed are dealt with by TCGA 1992, ss 21–28 and part disposals and assets derived from other assets by TCGA 1992, ss 42 and 43.

Where the asset is a wasting asset, ie has a predictable useful life of less than 50 years, the base cost less any residual or scrap value is written off over the predictable life (TCGA 1992, ss 44 and 46), except where the asset has qualified for capital allowances (TCGA 1992, s 47), or is a tangible moveable wasting asset, which is exempt from capital gains tax under TCGA 1992, s 45. Cases with less than 50 years to run are depreciated on a curved line basis under TCGA 1992, Sched 8.

Losses are calculated in the same way as profits, but a loss on a non-UK asset of a non-domiciliary is not an allowable loss (TCGA 1992, s 16). Capital gains tax losses can only be set against chargeable gains in the same, or subsequent years. Trading losses can however be set against capital gains in the same year to the extent that they exceed any taxable income, under FA 1991, s 72.

Indexation can be used to reduce a chargeable gain to zero but cannot create an allowable loss (TCGA 1992, s 53(2A)). Losses may be carried forward indefinitely to set against future gains but, under self-assessment, TCGA 1992, s 16(2A) provides that losses for 1996/97 onwards must be claimed and relieved before any losses for earlier years, and have to be quantified. It has not been necessary, nor indeed possible (*Tod v South Essex Motors (Basildon) Limited* 1988 STC 392) to quantify capital losses of earlier periods except where necessary to compute the net chargeable gain.

In the first instance, in a capital gains tax computation, consideration due after the time of disposal is brought in at its full value and there is no deduction for any contingent liabilities. If however, the consideration does not materialise or a contingent liability crystallises, an appropriate adjustment is made (TCGA 1992, ss 48 and 49).

Transfers between husband and wife

Transfers between husband and wife living together are exempt from capital gains tax (TCGA 1992, s 58) and partnership gains are taxable proportionately on the partners personally, not on the firm (TCGA 1992, s 59). Death is not a chargeable event for capital gains tax purposes and therefore assets passing on death receive a capital gains tax-free uplift to the probate value at the date of death (TCGA 1992, s 62). There are rules for the identification of shares, and shares acquired since 6 April 1982 constitute a pool of shares but those acquired between 6 April 1965, when capital gains tax was introduced, and 5 April 1982, are treated as a separate pool (TCGA 1992, ss 104–114). Gilt-edged securities and qualifying corporate bonds are exempt from capital gains tax (TCGA 1992, ss 115–117B).

Re-structuring of companies

There are complex rules relating to the reorganisation or reconstruction of companies with the broad effect that where shares or securities are received in exchange for shares previously held, the gain will be deferred, which is usually known as 'roll-over' on a paper for paper transaction, though any cash element will be immediately chargeable to capital gains tax (TCGA 1992, ss 126–140B).

The appropriate amount in cash treated as income under the stock dividend provisions of TA 1988, ss 249–251 is deemed to be additional expenditure on the shares for capital gains tax purposes under TCGA 1992, s 141, as if it were a payment on a rights issue under TCGA 1992, s 128. As under these rules the recipient of a stock dividend has on imputation tax credit, the use of a stock dividend could significantly reduce the capital gains tax otherwise payable.

Options are treated as assets for capital gains tax purposes but, may be absorbed into the principal asset if exercised (TCGA 1992, ss 143–149A). Specific capital gains tax exemption is given to investments qualifying under the business expansion scheme or the enterprise investment scheme, personal equity plans, and venture capital trusts, under TCGA 1992, ss 150–151B.

Roll-over relief

Certain classes of assets such as land and buildings, fixed plant and machinery, ships and aircraft, goodwill, and certain agricultural quotas, as defined by TCGA 1992, s 155, qualify for roll-over relief under the rules relating to replacement of business assets in TCGA 1992, ss 152–160. Relief is only available to the extent that an amount equal to the whole of the proceeds on disposal is reinvested in qualifying assets within a window of opportunity commencing one year prior to and ending three years after the disposals. Any proceeds not reinvested remain chargeable. These provisions may be contrasted with reinvestment relief under TCGA 1992, ss 164A–164N, under which any chargeable gain made by an individual on an actual disposal, as opposed to a deemed disposal, may be rolled over into a qualifying investment to the extent that the gain is actually reinvested in qualifying unquoted shares. Under these rules the chargeable gain can be rolled over by reinvesting an amount equal to the gain, not the whole of the proceeds. The rules are complex with many anti-avoidance provisions.

It should be noted that intellectual property is not a qualifying asset for roll-over relief for business asset rules.

Roll-over relief may be available on the transfer of a business to a company in exchange for shares under TCGA 1992, s 62 or as a gift of business assets under TCGA 1992, s 165. The gift relief is restricted if the donee is non-resident or a foreign controlled company, or dual resident trust, or if the donee ceases to be UK-resident (TCGA 1992, ss 166–169).

Retirement relief

One of the most valuable capital gains tax relief is in respect of retirement which is available to any individual who has obtained the age of 50, whether he retires or not, or who retires on ill-health grounds below the age of 50, and who makes a disposal of the whole or part of a business. Relief is given by TCGA 1992, ss 163, 164 and Sched 6. The first £250,000 of chargeable gains are exempt from capital gains tax as is half the excess of chargeable gains over £250,000 up to £1m so that gains on the first £1m from the disposal of business assets are subject to a maximum capital gains tax charge of £150,000 (TCGA 1992, Sched 6, para 13).

Other provisions

An individual's main residence is exempt from capital gains tax under TCGA 1992, ss 222–226. There are other exemptions or holdover reliefs in respect of charities (TCGA 1992, ss 256 and 257), works of art (TCGA 1992, s 258), chattels (TCGA 1992, s 262), cars (TCGA 1992, s 263) and gifts on which inheritance tax is chargeable (TCGA 1992, ss 260–261).

There are also provisions relating to the valuation of assets, double taxation relief, delayed remittances on foreign assets etc, under TCGA 1992, ss 272–291.

Partnerships

Old partnerships

Old partnerships, ie those which commenced business prior to 6 April 1994, are, up to 5 April 1997, assessed to tax as a separate entity even though in England and Wales a partnership has no separate legal existence, though it does in Scotland. The amount of tax payable was arrived at by allocating the partnership profits to the partners and calculating the tax payable on them as individuals on the amount of the partnership profits, as adjusted for tax purposes, allocated to them. The liability however, was that of the firm with each partner being jointly and severally liable for the whole of the tax payable. If a partner joined or left the partnership, there was an automatic cessation, subject to a unanimous election by the partners including those leaving or joining, or their personal representatives, for the business to be treated as continuing under TA 1988, s 113(2). An old partnership continues to be taxed as a separate entity up to and including 1996/97. Profits were calculated on the basis of Schedule D, Case I or II on the profits of the accounting year ending in the preceding fiscal year. The special rules for opening and closing years were broadly similar to their rules for sole traders described earlier on in this chapter. Similar transitional provisions are applied in 1996/97 to average the partnership profits as apply to a sole trader and there are similar transitional overlap provisions.

Similar anti-avoidance provisions apply to partnerships in 1996/97 as apply to sole traders, although there is an additional anti-avoidance provision covering the privatisation of interest. The Revenue were concerned that partnership borrowings would be repaid in the transitional period and replaced by borrowings by the partners individually. This would increase the partnership profits which would be reduced on averaging, and the interest payable by the individual partners would be allowed in full as a charge on income under TA 1988, s 353. Any additional interest claimed in this way is likely to be lost under the transitional anti-avoidance provisions of FA 1995, Sched 22, para 2 in relation to transitional averaging and by FA 1995, Sched 22, para 5 in relation to transitional overlap. The normal transitional overlap anti-avoidance provisions which applied to sole traders and partners are specifically extended to retiring partners under FA 1995, Sched 22, para 4 and to partners in foreign partnerships taxed under Schedule D, Case V by FA 1995, Sched 22, para 8.

An old partnership normally would have been assessed to tax on other income such as rents under Schedule A, deposit interest under Schedule D, Case III and income from overseas securities and possessions, including overseas partnerships under Schedule D, Cases IV and V by reference to the income arising in the fiscal year. Income from dividends assessable under Schedule F would also be taxed by reference to the income arising in the fiscal year. In practice in many cases, other income of the partnership was taxed by reference to the income arising in the preceding fiscal year rather than on the strict statutory basis. In such cases, the principles applying to the transitional provisions for Schedule D, Case I, are applied in practice.

Because the partnership is subject to assessment in 1996/97 the tax on partnership income is due in two instalments on 1 January and 1 July 1997. In many cases the figures would not be available and tax would become payable on estimated assessments with the assessment being revised when the figures are finally agreed. Interest would be charged or paid in respect of tax under or overpaid.

Self-assessment by partners

Although the partnership remains taxable as a separate entity in 1996/97 the individual partners are required to self-assess in that year, on their share of the partnership income. This is done by each partner self-assessing on the basis of his share of the adjusted partnership profit for 1996/97 and taking credit for his share of the tax payable by the firm in completing his individual payments on account and final liability for 1996/97. This means that the partnership needs to prepare a partnership return showing the partnership's taxable income for 1996/97 and a partnership statement allocating that income among the various partners. The usual penalties for non-compliance for an individual are applied to each partner in a partnership.

New partnerships are those commencing to trade on or after 6 April 1994 or which have a partnership change after that date without a continuation election being made in respect of the change. New partnerships are dealt with under the current year basis of assessment throughout. New partnerships are not a taxable entity for tax purposes and each partner is responsible for his own tax on his own share of the partnership profits (TA 1988, s 111(1)).

The partnership is however, treated as a notional individual for the purposes of the calculation of its profits chargeable to tax under TA 1988, s 111(2). The nominated partner will therefore have to lodge a partnership return containing details of the partnership income and a partnership statement allocating that income among the individual partners.

Each partner is treated as if he were carrying on a separate trade, the amounts of the profits of which were his share of the partnership profits (TA 1988, s 111(3)). The effect of this is that commencement and cessation provisions do not apply to the partnership, but a partner joining the partnership is deemed to have commenced his notional sole trade and a partner leaving will be deemed to have ceased his notional sole trade which in turn means that the individual partners will have overlap relief on commencement and overlap relief on cessation in the same way as a sole trader carrying on an actual trade. The anti-avoidance provisions which apply to sole traders ceasing in 1997/98 and 1998/99 do not apply to a partner leaving the partnership, unless the partnership trade actually ceases. This is because the transitional cessation provisions in FA 1994, Sched 20, para 3(3), require a cessation and, under TA 1988, s 111(2), the partnership is treated as an individual, and that deemed individual will not have ceased to trade merely because a partner has ceased, in view of the amended TA 1988, s 113(2).

Partnership taxed income and chargeable gains are allocated to the partners entitled to receive such income and gains in the fiscal year, but other partnership income including rental income taxable under Schedule A, untaxed interest taxable under Schedule D, Case III, income from foreign securities taxable under Schedule D, Case IV, foreign possessions under Schedule D, Case V, or miscellaneous income taxable under Schedule D, Case VI are all calculated by reference to the accounting period ending in the fiscal year, as if it were income of a deemed second trade. The income has to be returned and is taxed in accordance with the rules applicable to the type of income, the deeming provisions only applying to allocate the income among the partners in the appropriate fiscal year. The deeming also applies to the consequent adjustments for overlaps and overlap relief on a partner joining or leaving the partnership, but does not convert the investment income into trading income for any other purpose (TA 1988, s 111(7)–(9)).

The change of accounting date rules are applied at the partnership level by TA 1988, s 111(5) and (6) to avoid individual partners having different accounting dates other than in the years in which they join or leave the partnership.

Non-resident partner

Where a partnership contains a non-resident partner, TA 1988, s 111(2) provides that for the purpose of his tax liability the partnership is deemed to be a non-resident individual and therefore a separate partnership tax return would have to be prepared calculating the tax payable on this basis, ie by reference to the profits arising in the UK and excluding any non-UK profits and gains, for the purposes of allocation among the non-resident partners. The UK-resident partners would continue to have their allocation on the basis of the partnership's worldwide income.

Partnership carried on outside UK

Where the partnership is carried on wholly or partly outside the UK and the control and management is situated abroad, a non-UK domiciled partner is taxable on his share of non-UK profits under Schedule D, Case V (TA 1988, s 112(1A)). In the case of such a partnership the profits would be computed along UK lines on the worldwide income for any UK resident and domiciled partners, and a separate computation restricted to the UK profits, if any, for the non-UK domiciled partners. An appropriate partnership statement would be required allocating profit among each class of partner. Non-domiciled partners would then be taxable on their share of profits arising in the UK and on any remittances of the overseas profits taxable under Schedule D, Case V.

Corporate partner

Where there is a corporate partner in the partnership, TA 1988, ss 114–116 require the profits to be computed along corporation tax lines for the partnership for allocation through a separate partnership statement to the corporate partners.

Limited partnership

Limited partnerships are taxed in exactly the same way as ordinary partnerships except that there is a restriction on loss relief which cannot exceed the limited partners paid-up capital (TA 1988, ss 117 and 118). Because in Scotland a partnership is a separate legal entity, Scottish limited partnerships are sometimes used to provide an entity with a separate legal existence which is transparent for UK tax purposes.

Inheritance tax

Inheritance tax is charged on the value transferred by a chargeable transfer by an individual, after 26 March 1974, which is not a potentially exempt transfer (IHTA 1984, ss 1 and 2). The measure of a transfer of value is the reduction in the transferor's estate as a result of the transfer (IHTA 1984, s 3). A transfer by an individual on or after 18 March 1986 is a potentially exempt transfer under IHTA 1984, s 3A if it is to an individual, or an interest in possession or accumulation and maintenance trust. Transfers on death under IHTA 1984, s 4 are charged at the full rate of 40 per cent on the excess of the chargeable transfers, including potentially exempt transfers made within seven years prior to death, over the exemption of £215,000 on cumulative chargeable transfers, applicable from 5 April 1997 (IHTA 1984, Sched 1). Tapering relief for gifts is given by IHTA 1984, s 7 and lifetime transfers are charged at half the rate of tax applicable on death, for example on a gift into a discretionary trust.

Taxpayer's estate

A taxpayer's estate for inheritance tax purposes includes not only all assets worldwide, beneficially owned by him, but also the assets of a trust in which he is a life tenant (IHTA 1984, s 5) and assets given away where he has retained an interest in the property (FA 1986, s 102 and Sched 20). Excluded property under IHTA 1984, s 6 includes property situated outside the UK, beneficially held by a non-UK domiciled individual who is not deemed to be UK domiciled under IHTA 1984, s 267. There are no specific situs rules for inheritance tax purposes, so the normal rules apply, for example bearer securities are situated in the country in which the documents are kept (*Winans and another v Attorney-General (No 2)* [1910] AC 27). Certain gilt-edged securities are excluded property in the hands of non-domiciliaries. Because the life tenant of an interest in possession trust is deemed to own the capital of the trust for inheritance tax purposes under IHTA 1984, s 5, the reversionary interest therein is excluded property under IHTA 1984, s 48. There are specific exclusions from inheritance tax for dispositions not intended to confer gratuitous benefit on the recipient or for the maintenance of the taxpayer's family, for retirement benefits, for the benefit of employees, waivers of remuneration and dividend, the granting of tenancies of agricultural property and written variations affecting the disposition of a deceased's estate, under IHTA 1984, ss 10–17. Transfers between spouses are exempt subject to a limit of £55,000 to a non-UK domiciled spouse by a UK domiciled spouse (IHTA 1984, s 18). There is an annual exemption of up to £3,000 (IHTA 1984, s 19), relief for small gifts (IHTA 1984, s 20), normal expenditure out of income (IHTA 1984, s 21), gifts in consideration of marriage (IHTA 1984, s 22), gifts to charities, political parties, housing associations, for national purposes, public benefit and into employee trusts, under IHTA 1984, ss 23–29A.

Conditionally exempt transfers

There is a conditionally exempt transfer regime covering historic houses, works of art, etc, under IHTA 1984, ss 30–35. Allocation of exemptions is dealt with by IHTA 1984, ss 36–42 and trusts by IHTA 1984, ss 43–48. Trusts are divided into those where there is an interest in possession, where all the trust property is treated as that of the life tenant under IHTA 1984, ss 49–57A, which includes a charge to tax on the termination of an interest in possession during the life tenant's life under IHTA 1984, s 52, which is not a potentially exempt transfer.

Discretionary trusts

Discretionary trusts are dealt with by IHTA 1984, ss 58–93. An inheritance tax charge may arise on the settlor on creating the trust in the first instance and thereafter on the tenth anniversary of the creation of the trust with a *pro-rata* charge on any additions to the trust fund. The ten-year charge is basically 30 per cent of the normal lifetime rate, which itself is 50 per cent of the standard rate of 40 per cent. The effective rate of the ten-year charge is therefore a maximum of 6 per cent of the value of the assets in the trust (IHTA 1984, ss 64 and 66). There is also a charge under IHTA 1984, s 65 on assets leaving a discretionary trust, calculated on the reduction in value of the trust assets as a result of the distribution. Accumulation and maintenance trusts have specific benefits under IHTA 1984, s 71. Not only is the transfer into an accumulation and maintenance settlement a potentially exempt transfer so far as the settlor is concerned, but there is no ten-yearly charge, nor is there a charge on distribution to a beneficiary. In order to qualify, beneficiaries have to acquire an interest in possession at age 25 at latest, but this may be an interest only in the income of the trust not necessarily the trust capital. There are various relieving provisions available for charitable trusts, employee trusts, disabled person trusts and maintenance funds for historic buildings.

Close companies

Transfers by close companies can be apportioned through and subject to inheritance tax as if they were transfers by the shareholders, under IHTA 1984, ss 94–102.

Reliefs

There are some important inheritance tax reliefs, including business property relief for assets used in a business which includes intellectual property used for the purposes of the trade, or licensed as part of a business. The relief is available on a disposal of the business or an interest in a business, unquoted shares, which includes those on the alternative investment market, all at 100 per cent. Listed securities giving the transferor control, land or building, plant or machinery used for the purpose of a business carried on by a partnership in which the transferor was a partner, or for a business carried on by a settlement qualifies for a 50 per cent relief (IHTA 1984, ss 103–105). The value of the business is the net value of the business assets including goodwill, after deducting any liabilities incurred for business purposes (*Finch and others v IRC* (1983) STC 157). There are various restrictions on minimum periods of ownership, replacement assets and an exclusion for excepted assets which are basically investment assets not used in the business (IHTA 1984, ss 106–112). There are one or two traps to emphasise, in particular that relevant business property consists of a business or interest in a business not business assets in isolation (IHTA 1984, s 105(1)(*a*)). Where there are contracts for sale such as buy/sell agreements, these are treated as an entitlement to cash not business assets, under IHTA 1984, s 113 and SP12/80. Where assets have been transferred within seven years of death, relief is only available where the donee has retained the assets or replacement assets, under IHTA 1984, ss 113A and 113B. A broadly similar relief is available for agricultural property under IHTA 1984, ss 115–124B, but not both on the same asset (IHTA 1984, s 114).

There are other reliefs for such things as woodlands (IHTA 1984, ss 125 and 130), quick succession relief (IHTA 1984, s 141), alterations to the disposition of a deceased's estate (IHTA 1984, ss 142–147), avoidable transfers (IHTA 1984, s 150), pension schemes, and in particular the cash entitlement under a pension scheme which may be paid direct to the beneficiaries without passing through the estate, under IHTA 1984, ss 151–153. Double taxation relief is available for inheritance tax under IHTA 1984, ss 158 and 159 either by treaty or unilaterally. Property is to be valued on the basis of a disposal in the open market, at arm's length, with no deduction for flooding the market (IHTA 1984, s 160). For valuation purposes, assets of the transferor must be aggregated with those of his spouse and any property which has been settled on a charity and held by the charity within five years of the transfer. This is known as related property under IHTA 1984, s 161.

In the case of unquoted shares and securities, IHTA 1984, s 168 provides that the market value is on the basis of a sale in the open market on the assumption that there is available to any prospective purchaser all the information which a prudent, prospective purchaser might reasonably require for a purchase from a willing vendor by private treaty at arm's length (IHTA 1984, s 168). A lease for life is treated as an interest in possession and therefore the lessee is deemed to own the entire property (IHTA 1984, s 170). Changes occurring on death such as the receipt of insurance policy proceeds are included in the estate at death under IHTA 1984, s 171. There are allowances for funeral expenses, expenses incurred abroad, income tax and unpaid inheritance tax, future payments due on the transfer of assets and sales of related property assets under IHTA 1984, ss 172–176. The sale proceeds can effectively be substituted for the probate value where shares are sold within a year of death under IHTA 1984, ss 178–189 or where land is sold within three years of death under IHTA 1984, ss 190–198. Adjustments have to be made for reinvestment.

Other provisions

There are provisions dealing with the liability to tax by the transferor, his personal representatives, trustees of settled property, etc under IHTA 1984, ss 199–214 and the administration and collection provisions are covered by IHTA 1984, ss 215–261. In particular, where the asset disposed of is land, shares or securities which gave the transferor control of the company or amounted to at least 20 per cent of his estate, or unlisted shares or securities where immediate payment of tax will create hardship, or represent at least 10 per cent of the nominal value of the issued share capital, or commercial woodlands, inheritance tax may all be paid by equal annual instalments over ten years under IHTA 1984, ss 227–229. Interest is only due on overdue instalments in such circumstances under IHTA 1984, s 234. There are various anti-avoidance provisions relating to future payments, annuities purchased in conjunction with a life policy, transfers reported late, more than one chargeable transfer on one day under IHTA 1984, ss 262–266. Non-UK domiciliaries are deemed to be domiciled in the UK if they were domiciled in the UK within the three years immediately preceding the transfer, or were resident in the UK in at least 17 out of the previous 20 fiscal years under IHTA 1984, s 267. Associated operations may be aggregated under IHTA 1984, s 268 and treated as if they were a single disposal.

10   Companies and trusts

Companies and corporation tax

Background

Until 1965 income tax applied to all entities whether they were individuals, trusts, unincorporated associations or incorporated bodies. Corporation tax was introduced in 1965 and applied to all bodies corporate who were resident in the United Kingdom.

'Bodies corporate' includes unincorporated bodies such as clubs and associations as well as the more familiar limited and unlimited companies. It does not include partnerships or trusts.

The residence qualification for corporation tax is important. A body corporate that is resident outside the United Kingdom is not liable to corporation tax. Instead, such bodies are liable to income tax to the extent that the income is taxable at all. For example, foreign companies with rental income in the UK pay income tax under Schedule A and not corporation tax. The distinction is important principally because of the rate of tax, but also, in respect of the regulations, returns and general compliance which differ as between income tax and corporation tax.

Although residence is a question of fact, a company will none the less be deemed to be resident in the United Kingdom if it was incorporated there, unless it is also resident in a treaty country such that under the double tax treaty in question, it is considered more resident in the other country. In such circumstances the company will be treated as resident in that other country.

Structure of corporation tax

The basic schedular system is carried over from income tax to corporation tax, albeit that there is no separate assessment for the Schedules and cases. Instead, there is one taxable amount being the total of all the various amounts computed under the schedular and case system. There are special rules which principally affect trading losses, retainable charges and the deduction of tax at source.

Chargeable gains are not separately chargeable to corporation tax but are added in to the total amount chargeable to corporation tax. In consequence, the amount on which corporation tax is chargeable is the sum of income computed under the schedular and case system as modified for corporation tax, and chargeable gains computed in accordance with the Capital Gains Tax Act 1983.

Chargeable gains are computed in the same way as for individuals and net chargeable gains after losses are added to the income and profits charged. There is no equivalent annual exemption for companies and net chargeable gains simply form part of the overall corporation tax assessment. Capital losses may be offset only against capital profits.

Rate of tax

Companies pay tax at a flat 33 per cent on the total assessable profit, traditionally referred to as the chargeable amount.

Companies with a turnover of less than £250,000 are defined as small companies and pay tax at the lower rate of 23 per cent. Profits falling within the range of £250,000 to £1,250,000 are taxable at an overall intermediate rate, and companies with profits in excess of £1,250,000 will pay tax at a full 33 per cent. An alternative way of defining this is that the first £250,000 of profits are taxable tax at 23 per cent; the next £1m at 67 per cent; and any excess over £1,250,000 at 33 per cent.

The rate for small companies is subject to an anti-abuse provision which allocates the £250,000 and £1,250,000 limits between the number of associated companies— broadly companies under common control or which are in a parent subsidiary relationship. In arriving at the number of associated companies, it is possible to ignore dormant companies which carry on no activities and which do not either pay or receive dividends from their associated companies.

Investment companies are not permitted to use the small company rate unless their income is predominantly rental income.

Losses

Trading losses for corporation tax can be offset against the total profits, including chargeable gains, of the year or of the preceding year. Otherwise trading losses can be carried forward against future trading profits only, but without time limit. Trading losses may also be grouped for relief if there is an appropriate group relationship.

Relief for other income losses largely follows the income tax rules restricting relief to that particular source of income only.

Capital gains tax losses, computed in the same way as for personal capital gains tax, can be offset only against capital gains of the same company in the same year; any unused capital losses can be carried forward indefinitely in the same company. There is no group relief in respect of capital losses.

Charges on income

Those costs which are not specifically deductible under the various schedules and cases but which constitute annual charges are deducted from the total profits liable to corporation tax including capital gains. Such charges generally relate to annual interest, normally in respect of bank borrowings or loan stock interest, as well as gift aid, charitable deeds of covenant and patent royalties.

Trading companies

Charges, where not relieved against profits and gains of the year, can be carried back against the chargeable amount for the previous year or added to any unrelieved trading losses for the year and carried forward for offset against future trading profits only. To the extent that the charges relate to non-trading activities, they cannot be carried either backwards or forwards.

Special rules apply to investment companies which incur costs which are not properly deductible under any of the appropriate Schedules and cases and consequently would otherwise not rank for relief at all. Such costs are treated as management expenses and relieved against profits and gains of the year or carried back to the previous year, or added to the management expenses of the subsequent year for relief in the same fashion.

It is important to note that an investment company is one defined as carrying on activities wholly or mainly in the making of investments. There is therefore a category of company which is neither a trading company nor an investment company and which may have a number of costs which simply do not qualify for relief as being neither management expenses on the one hand nor permitted deductions under the various Schedules and cases or for capital gains tax purposes.

Groups of companies

In recognition of the close association that companies within a group have with each other, important concessions are made in respect of both income and capital gains.

For income, losses and excess charges of one company may be offset against another in the same 75 per cent group. For capital gains tax purposes transactions between companies within the same 75 per cent group do not give rise to a capital gains tax gain or loss, and the acquiring company effectively stands in the shoes of the disposing company in respect of the original base cost of the asset. There is, however, no group relief in respect of capital gains tax and it is therefore common to transfer assets into group to the company that has capital gains tax losses in order that gains on disposal outside the group can be crystallised in the company which has capital gains tax losses, thereby achieving relief for the losses.

Deduction of tax at source

Unlike individuals, who may retain tax deducted at source and thus obtain basic rate relief, companies are obliged to retain tax at source and pay it over to the Inland Revenue on a quarterly basis using Form CT61. Every quarter, therefore, companies return and pay over to the Inland Revenue the tax they have deducted from retainable charges (usually interest and patent royalties) after taking credit for any tax deducted from their income by other companies. Thus, a net amount of tax is paid over. To the extent that tax suffered on income exceeds tax deducted on payments, an amount is refundable. However, any refund is made only to the extent that previous payments have been made to the Inland Revenue in the tax year. Any unclaimed excess may be deducted from net tax payable on the corporation tax assessment. Consequently, if net tax is being suffered, relief will be available only on the tax payment date, ie nine months after the year end.

Dividends and advance corporation tax

The special feature of corporation tax is the treatment of dividends. The UK adopts an imputation system and not a straight classical 'deduction of tax at source' system. Dividends are declared by a company net of tax out of net taxable profits. A company is however required to pay over to the Inland Revenue one-quarter of the net dividend as advance corporation tax ('ACT'). This broadly equates to a 20 per cent deduction of tax at source. The sum of the net dividend and the ACT is termed a 'chargeable payment'. Dividends received from other UK resident companies will have had ACT deducted in their turn and this gross amount is referred to as 'franked investment income'. One-fifth of net franked payments, ie franked payments less franked investment income, is paid over quarterly on Form CT61. To the extent that in any quarter franked investment income exceeds franked payments, one-fifth of the difference may be reclaimed on Form CT61 but only to the extent that ACT has been paid in the tax year.

If franked investment income for the year exceeds franked payments, the surplus franked investment income may be carried forward indefinitely or else surrendered to a company within the 75 per cent group for offset against that company's franked payments for the year. Such surrender may be made only with the corporation tax computation, and relief therefore occurs only on the tax payment date, ie after the year end.

Companies which pay dividends and do not receive franked investment income pay advance corporation tax on the dividends which they pay which is then credited against their ultimate corporation tax liability. Timing is, however, important. Relief is given in respect of corporation tax liability for a period in respect of dividends paid in that period. Consequently, a dividend must be paid before the year end for the ACT associated with that dividend to be credited against the liability for the period. Furthermore, there is a maximum amount which can be offset against the corporation tax liability. This maximum is equal to the ACT which would have been paid on a notional gross dividend equal to the taxable profits. For companies paying tax at the small companies rate, no balancing amount of corporation tax (mainstream corporation tax) would be payable as the whole liability would have been extinguished by ACT if profits were fully distributed. However, for companies paying tax at the full rate of corporation tax there will always be a balance of tax representing the difference of rate, ie 31 per cent less 21 per cent.

Dividend receipts

It is a feature of corporation tax that companies within its scope do not pay tax on franked investment income (dividends from UK resident companies). This income is outwith the scope of tax. Instead, the franked investment income may be used to frank the payment of dividends, thereby reducing the amount of ACT due when a dividend is paid.

Individuals, trusts and other persons who are not companies within the scope of corporation tax are entitled to a tax credit in respect of a dividend. The tax credit amounts to 20 per cent of the 'gross' dividend (ie the dividend plus the tax credit). As this proportion is 20 per cent it discharges any liability at the lower rate of 20 per cent and gives rise to repayable credits if the income tax liability is less than that percentage. Where tax liability is at the basic rate of 23 per cent, the credit is treated as extinguishing that liability, even though it is repayable at the rate of only 20 per cent. With effect from Budget Day in 1997, pension funds are no longer able to reclaim this credit even though they are tax-exempt bodies. Individuals and charities can continue to recover this credit until 5 April 1999.

Corporation tax payments and accounting periods

Corporation tax is payable in respect of accounting periods which have event-specific commencements and terminations. An accounting period begins when a company is incorporated; when a company begins to trade; immediately after the end of the previous accounting period; or 12 months after the beginning of the previous accounting period. An accounting period ends when a company ceases to trade, or 12 months after it began. In consequence, an accounting period cannot exceed 12 months, and if accounts are made up for, say, an 18-month period this will, for corporation tax, be treated as a 12-month period followed by a six-month period, ie two separate accounting periods of different lengths.

The rate of tax is determined by the tax year, which is defined as a period from 1 April to the subsequent 31 March. Accounting periods (however short) which straddle 31 March will therefore fall in two financial years and may have two different tax rates requiring apportionment or allocation of profits, income and gains.

Corporation tax is due nine months after the end of the accounting period. An 18-month accounting period therefore has two tax payment dates, one nine months after the expiry of the first 12-month period and one nine months after the expiry of the second six-month period.

Under 'pay and file', tax is payable nine months after the year end whether or not accounts are submitted but accounts must be submitted within 12 months of the end of the period of account. Consequently, with, say, an 18-month accounting period the accounts need not be submitted until 12 months from the end of the 18 months, whereas tax payment dates are determined by the end of the strict accounting periods. The submission of accounts must be accompanied by a tax return (Form CT200) which incorporates a signed declaration by the taxpaying company or its agent.

Trusts

Trusts are recognised as separate bodies and pay tax at their own rate which is assessable on the trustees, who are personally liable.

Income tax

For income tax purposes trusts pay tax at a rate dependent upon whether or not they are discretionary and accumulation trusts on the one hand or any other kind of trust (principally life interest trusts) on the other. The former category will pay tax at the rate applicable to trusts, currently 34 per cent, while the latter will pay tax at the basic or lower rate of tax, as appropriate to the type of income being taxed.

Whatever the kind of tax, when the beneficiary receives an income distribution, tax will be treated as deducted from that income at 34 per cent, in the case of a discretionary or accumulation trust, and at a computed rate derived from the mix of dividend income and other income, in respect of life interest trusts.

Discretionary and accumulation trusts   Broadly, the gross income of the trust is computed and the trust's administration expenses properly chargeable to revenue are also computed. Relief is given for the trust's administration expenses by deducting the expenses from the net savings income within s 1A (income subject to tax deduction at source) and income taxed at source (principally taxed interest and net dividends) before grossing up at 100/80 and applying a 14 per cent (34 per cent less 20 per cent rate). From this tax payable are deducted any tax deducted at source and tax credits.

Example

In the year ended 5 April 1998 the Harum Discretionary Trust had the following income and expenses:

	£
Property rents (Schedule A)	40,000
UK dividends (including tax credits of £1,000)	5,000
Taxed interest (tax deducted at source £700)	3,500
	£48,500
Trust administration expenses—proportion chargeable to revenue	1,350
Overdraft interest	1,050
	£2,400

The tax liability of the trust for 1997/98 is as follows:

	£	£
Schedule A: £40,000 at 34%		13,600
Taxed interest (net)	2,800	
Net dividends	4,000	
Deduct: Expenses	(2,400)	
	£4,400	
£4,400 grossed at 100/80 = £5,500 @ 14% (34% less 20%)		770
Tax payable by assessment		14,370
Add: Tax deducted at source		700
Tax credits		1,000
Total tax borne		£16,070

Notes

(a)   Expenses (including in this example the overdraft interest) are set first against income falling within s 1A (savings income). The effect is that the expenses, grossed up at 20 per cent, save tax at 14 per cent (the difference between the 20 per cent rate applicable to savings income and the rate applicable to trusts).

(b)   The net revenue available for distribution to the beneficiaries at the trustees' discretion will be £30,030 (£48,500 less £16,070 less £2,400).

Any income distribution to the beneficiary is treated as having tax deducted at a flat rate of 34 per cent which is treated as his gross income, and tax credits can be recovered in line with tax deducted at source from other income.

A 19-year-old student is one of the beneficiaries to whom the trustees can pay the settlement income. The trustees make a payment of £3,000 to him on 31 January 1998. He has no other income in the year 1997/98 and is unmarried.

	£
Net income	3,000.00
Tax @ 34/66	1,545.45
Gross income	£4,545.45

He can claim a tax repayment for 1997/98 of:

Total income	4,545.00
Deduct: Personal allowance	4,045.00
	£500.00
Tax thereon at 20% (within lower rate band)	100.00
Tax accounted for by trustees	1,545.45
Repayment due	£1,445.45

The mechanism for tax relief on expenses is to offset them first against net income within s 1A, ie against income which is taxed at 20 per cent. This deduction, grossed up, effectively gives relief at 14 per cent (the difference between the 34 per cent rate applicable to trusts and the 20 per cent rate applicable to savings income). If the expenses exceed savings income or if there is no savings income the expenses will be deducted from other income and will save tax at only 10 per cent, being the difference between the rate applicable to trusts and the basic rate of tax.

Other trusts (life interest trusts)   Life interest trusts pay tax at the lower rate applicable to savings (without limitation) on savings income and at the basic rate on other income. There is no relief to the trustees in respect of trust expenses chargeable to revenue. In consequence, tax will be assessable at the basic rate on income received gross.

Strictly, the lower rate of tax of 20 per cent does not apply to trusts but the 20 per cent rate applicable to savings does.

Example

The Wonga settlement is a life interest settlement which has the following income and expenses in the year 1997/98:

	£	£
Property income		500
Taxed investment income (tax deducted at source £300)		1,500
Dividends	800	
Add: Tax credits	200	
		1,000
		£3,000
Expenses chargeable to revenue		£400

A is sole life tenant of the Wonga settlement and therefore receives all the settlement income. A's income for 1997/98 from the Wonga settlement is as follows:

	£	£
Trust dividend and interest income (gross)	2,500	
Other trust income		500
Deduct: Lower rate tax (20%)	(500)	
Basic rate tax (23%)		(115)
	2,000	385
Deduct expenses (Note (b))	400	

	£	£
Net income entitlement	£1,600	£385
Grossed-up amounts: £1,600 × $\frac{100}{80}$	£2,000	
£385 × $\frac{100}{77}$		£500
Tax deducted	£400	£115

Notes

(a)   This income falls to be included in A's return even if it is not actually paid to him, as he is absolutely entitled to it. He will receive a tax certificate (Form R185E) from the trust agents, showing two figures for gross income (£2,000 and £500), tax deducted (£400 and £115) and net income (£1,600 and £385).

(b)   The trust expenses are deducted from income falling within s 1A (savings income) in priority to other income.

(c)   That part of A's trust income which is represented by savings income (£1,600 net) is treated in A's hands as if it were savings income received directly by A. It is thus chargeable at the lower rate only, the liability being satisfied by the 20 per cent tax credit, except to the extent, if any, that it exceeds his basic rate limit.

Discretionary and accumulation trusts: particular features   Income received by a trust which is to be accumulated, or payable at the discretion of the trustees or some other person is, for 1993/94 and subsequent years, taxed at the rate applicable to trusts rather than at the basic or lower rate. The rate applicable to trusts is 34 per cent, or such other rates as Parliament may determine. For 1996/97 it was also 34 per cent, and for 1993/94, 1994/95 and 1995/96 it was 35 per cent, being defined for those years as the sum of the basic and additional rates for the year. Before 1993/94, income was charged separately at the basic and additional rates. The special charge does not apply where:

(a)   the trust is exempt as a charity;
(b)   the income arises from property held for the purpose of certain retirement benefit or personal pension schemes; or
(c)   the income is income of any person other than the trustees or treated as income of a settlor.

As regards (c), for 1995/96 onwards, the position is considered before the income is distributed, so that income paid to the settlor's unmarried minor children does not fall within the exemption. The trustees may offset management expenses against trust income for the purpose of determining income chargeable at the rate applicable to trusts (before 1993/94, for determining income chargeable at the additional rate), although income so relieved remains subject to basic or lower rate tax.

The tax assessable on the trustees will be £115 (£500 at 23 per cent). The expenses are not deductible in arriving at the tax payable by the trustees.

Tax relief in respect of expenses is given by deduction for the whole expense from savings income in preference to other income. In consequence, relief will be obtained at the 20 per cent rate against savings income rather than at the 23 per cent rate in respect of other trust income. Computations must therefore be done in respect of savings income at the 20 per cent rate and for other income at the 23 per cent rate to arrive at the net income entitlement which is then grossed up at either 20 per cent or 23 per cent and tax deducted.

The beneficiary is treated as having received all the net income of the trust whether or not it is actually paid to him and the certificate of tax deduction (Form R185E) will show the two different streams of income gross and the tax deducted in net income.

The beneficiary will then be assessed on the savings income only at the lower rate as if it were dividend income, and on the other income as gross income at its marginal rate of tax with credit for the tax deducted of 23 per cent.

Tax return   Trusts are within the scope of self-assessment, as it applies to individuals. The normal time limits for the submission of the SA9 return will apply, ie 31 January following the end of the year of assessment.

Capital gains tax

The taxation of capital gains in trusts is, by comparison with the income tax treatment, relatively straightforward. Discretionary and accumulation trusts pay tax on capital gains at the rate applicable to trusts (34 per cent) whereas life interest trusts pay tax at the basic rate (currently 21 per cent). The computation of the gain itself follows ordinary capital gains tax principles in that the base cost, cost of sale and indexation are deducted from sale proceeds in order to arrive at the gain. Trusts benefit from the capital gains tax annual exemption but only to the extent of 50 per cent of the exemption available to individuals. Furthermore, this exemption has to be shared by all 'connected trusts', subject to a minimum exemption of £200.

Anti-avoidance provisions deem trust gains to be those of the settlor if the settlor or his spouse are beneficiaries of the trust in the year of the gain or if a beneficiary is the unmarried minor child of the settlor.

Holdover relief   Holdover relief is applicable in respect of any transfer either into or out of a discretionary settlement as inheritance tax will be payable on the transfer, albeit that this may be only at the nil rate.

Holdover relief will be claimable in respect of a life interest trust only if the asset itself qualifies for the relief, as transfers in or out of a life interest trust are normally potentially exempt transfers.

Foreign trusts

This is a highly complicated area, full of anti-avoidance legislation, and should be approached with great care. None the less, basic principles are followed.

Foreign trustees are not UK persons and as such will bear tax only on UK income. Overseas trustees are technically liable to the rate applicable to trusts if they are discretionary or accumulation trusts. Non-resident trustees are outwith the scope of capital gains tax due to their non-residence.

UK dividends received by non-resident trusts do not give rise to a credit which can be carried through to an income beneficiary of the trust unless the offshore trust makes full returns and pays all its tax as if it were a UK trust. Under Extra-Statutory Concession C18 pre-March 1991 overseas trusts enjoy a special privilege (are 'golden trusts') in that they do not fall within the capital gains tax anti-avoidance legislation which was then enacted. Golden trusts defer the payment of capital gains tax until a distribution is made to a UK-resident ordinarily resident individual, at which time the deferred gain is attributed to that distribution and becomes assessable on the beneficiary. A levy is charged in respect of this deferment, but if the gain can be locked up for a sufficient period of time the cost of the levy is outweighed by the benefit of the deferral of the gain. Gains on post-March 1991 offshore settlements in which the settlor or his family can benefit have any capital gain assessed directly on the settlor.

In respect of inheritance tax, if the overseas settlement is created by a non-domiciled settlor in respect of non-UK property, the settlement will be an excluded property settlement irrespective of any change in the settlor's domicile. In order to retain the offshore nature of the settlement assets, an offshore company should be inserted beneath the trust to hold any UK assets as this will retain the excluded property character of the settlement.

Inheritance tax

Accumulation and discretionary trusts are treated as separate taxable persons and therefore have their own inheritance tax 'clock'. Transfers out of such settlements therefore are transfers of value subject to inheritance tax. The computational rules in respect of transfers from such trusts both within the first ten years and subsequently are complicated and outwith the scope of this brief overview. However, it should be noted that accumulation and discretionary trusts cannot make potentially exempt transfers and that they are subject to an additional ten-yearly charge (effectively an internal gift on which inheritance tax is payable). This ten-yearly charge is the reference by which any distributions out of the settlement in the subsequent ten years are computed.

Life interest trusts, in comparison, are not treated as separate persons for inheritance tax. Instead, the assets are deemed to belong to the life tenant and are aggregated with his estate for all purposes. Any tax payable by virtue of transfers involving a life interest trust is payable by the trustees out of the trust assets even though computed by reference to the life tenant's personal inheritance tax circumstances. Potentially exempt transfers may be made and there is no ten-yearly charge.

11 Value added tax

Introduction

Value added tax ('VAT') is the tax on the supply or deemed supply of goods and services unless those goods and services are exempt. The tax is charged on the supplier who has an obligation to register if his turnover exceeds the registration threshold. The VAT charge (output tax) is accounted for by the supplier to Customs and Excise, either quarterly or monthly depending on his circumstances.

To the extent that a recipient of a VATable supply uses the supply for his business to make VATable supplies in his turn, he may recover the VAT he has incurred (input tax) by set-off against any VAT output tax he may owe in any return period, or by direct repayment if his input tax exceeds his output tax. If input tax is not attributable to the making of taxable supplies (because the supplies made are either exempt or outwith the scope of VAT), such input tax will not be recoverable.

Apart from those clearly identifiable supplies, 'supply' includes anything done for a consideration. There is a specific exclusion that the supply of money itself (in return for a supply) does not itself constitute a supply. However, in any barter-type transaction there will be cross-supplies in the same way as there is for direct tax.

The distinction between supplies of goods and supplies of services is largely concerned with the time and place of supply. There are also important differences in connection with the international supply of goods and services.

The supply of goods is defined as any transfer of property or possession in goods, the supply of power, heat, refrigeration or ventilation or the grant of a major interest (freehold or lease exceeding 21 years) in land. The supply of goods also includes transfer of own goods between EC member states and there are a number of deemed or self-supplies which are supplies of goods. The supply of services is defined as anything which is not a supply of goods and consequently covers a huge range of supplies.

Place of supply of goods

The place of supply of goods not involving their removal from or to the United Kingdom is the UK if the goods are there and outside the UK if they are not there. Goods supplied as part of an installation or assembly are treated as supplied where they are assembled.

Goods and services supplied under other circumstances are supplied in the UK if the goods enter the UK by or under the direction of the supplier or if they are acquired in the UK by an unregistered person from a supplier in another EU state. Further tiers of rules apply in increasingly uncommon circumstances.

A supply within a country not involving the goods passing over any border is a straightforward matter involving the charging of VAT by the supplier and its payment to Customs and Excise and the recovery of the VAT input charge from Customs and Excise by the recipient. Where goods cross the border, however, different rules apply.

Exports out of or into the European Union

Supplies of goods involving an export where the goods physically move across a border out of or into the EU are zero-rated provided that the zero-rating conditions (principally involving the removal of the goods outside the EU within the time limit, such that the goods are not delivered, collected or used by any UK person including the customer in the interim) are satisfied. The importer will deal with any import duty, etc when importing the goods into the country of destination. It is, of course, possible for the supplier to export the goods to himself in a foreign country, dealing with the importation into that country on his own account before making an onward sale to his customer in that country. This would make him liable to whatever sales, tax, etc might be applicable in that country.

With the abolition of border controls cross-border movements of goods within the EU have to be dealt with on a self-assessed basis. The terminology is amended to refer to 'dispatches' in substitution for 'exports' and 'acquisitions' in substitution for 'imports'. Generally, the dispatch of goods from a supplier in one EU state to a recipient in another is treated as outwith the scope of VAT for the supplier and as an acquisition by the recipient. The recipient must charge himself his own country's VAT and then recover it if it is in respect of an onward taxable supply by him. The effect, in the case of fully taxable persons, will be that the VAT by the recipient is both charged by him and recovered by him on the same VAT return, ie merely a set of book entries. This applies also to the movement of goods across a border without change in ownership. Consequently, a UK importer taking goods to France for his own business would make a dispatch in the UK outwith the scope of VAT and have to charge himself French TVA with appropriate recovery, quite possibly incurring a liability to register in France in respect of the transaction. It should be noted that the dispatch may be treated as outwith the scope of VAT only if the supplier quotes his customer VAT registration number on the VAT invoice.

Goods are acquired and become liable to VAT on acquisition when they have crossed an EU border into the acquirer's EU state. It is important to determine the person making the acquisition and this will often depend on when and where title passes. This is particularly noticeable in triangular trade where, for example, goods are supplied from supplier A to customer C in another EU state but have been invoiced to an intermediate supplier, B, in a third member state, who reinvoices to customer C. While the goods may pass from the supplier's EU state to the member's EU state, crossing only one border, the change in ownership from A to B and then to C gives B a potential liability to register for VAT in C's state to account for VAT on their acquisition and their subsequent onward supply to C. All EU states have agreed in these circumstances that, provided that B is not registered in C's state, the acquisition and onward supply by B is completely ignored and this supply is treated in its simplest form as a dispatch by A and an acquisition by C. This simplification procedure is at B's option and is compulsory on all parties once he so opts. Notification must be made to HM Customs and Excise and the proper procedures complied with.

Place of supply of services

Services have different places of supply depending upon the type of service. Supplies in relation to land are considered to be supplied where the land is physically situated; supplies in connection with the services listed in Sched 5 to the VATA 1994 are treated as supplied where received; supplies relating to cultural, artistic, sporting, scientific, education or entertainment services or relating to exhibitions, conferences and meetings are supplied where physically carried out; and any other supplies follow the basic rule. That is that the place of supply of services is treated as being where the supplier belongs, which in turn means where he has his place of business or, if more than one, where he has the place of business most concerned with the making of a particular supply.

The counterpart to import and acquisition VAT is the reverse charge on services received (VATA 1994, s 8). This, however, applies only to those services listed in Sched 5 to the VATA 1994, which, under para 1, include transfer and assignments of copyright, patents, licences, trade marks and similar rights.

The receipt of such services from outside the EU causes the recipient to charge himself VAT at his own country's rate and pay it over to Customs, while at the same time allowing him to recover the VAT input tax, if appropriate, on the same VAT return. It is, therefore, in the case of a fully taxable trader, a book entry. The reverse charge of itself, if sufficiently large, can cause a trader to register where otherwise he would not have an obligation to do so.

The receipt of reverse charge services from another EU state is treated as neither a supply of goods nor a supply of services if the EU recipient would use the supply for any EU business, whether or not it is a business which makes taxable (rather than exempt) supplies. Although not obligatory, it is common and recommended practice to quote the recipient's VAT registration number on the supplier's invoice. There is no equivalent to the simplification involving triangular supplies of goods.

The importation by an EU trader of goods from outside the EU and its onward supply to an EU trader in another EU state will involve the rules of import and supplies of goods followed by the rules on intra-EU supplies of goods. The person importing the goods into the EU is important, so that if it is the person making the supply from outside the EU he will need to register for VAT in the country of importation and be responsible for VAT on the onward supply.

Time of supply

The time of a supply is the earlier of the date of an invoice for the supply, the completion of the supply or the receipt of cash in respect of the supply, VATA 1994, s 6. The receipt of part of the cash triggers the VAT liability only on that part of the cash received, rather than the whole of the supply.

Rate of VAT

VAT is chargeable upon all supplies of goods and services by way of business (or, under EU law, in the pursuance of an economic activity). That specific profit-making motive is required. Those transactions which are not by way of business are outwith the scope of VAT. A business may make some supplies which are outwith the scope of VAT because they are not in pursuance of the business, or indeed any business carried on by that person.

If a supply is within the charge to VAT it is chargeable at a zero rate if within Sched 5 to the VATA 1994 or, failing this, it is an exempt supply if it is within Sched 6 to the VATA 1994 and is otherwise a standard-rated supply chargeable to VAT at 17½ per cent. This is a precise order of precedence.

Recovery of VAT in general

The recovery of VAT input tax is possible only if it relates to specific taxable supplies or is in pursuance of a taxable activity. There is furthermore a category of supplies which relates to neither goods or services and is outwith the scope of VAT but which nonetheless ranks for VAT input tax credit particularly cross-border EU supplies. If, however, a business is an exempt business, ie making exempt supplies only, it will not be able to recover any VAT. Most exempt businesses, however, are not wholly exempt but are partially exempt and this requires an allocation of input tax between the exempt and the non-exempt (taxable) parts. Non-recoverable VAT input tax (exempt input tax) may nevertheless be recovered if it comes within the *de minimis* limits (less than £600 per month, on average, and where exempt supplies are less than 50 per cent of the output of the business). Certain otherwise exempt supplies are treated as not exempt for partial exemption purposes, including, for example, bank interest received by a business. On recoverable input tax (exempt input tax etc).

VATable persons

VAT is a tax on persons and not on particular supplies, so that every business carried on by a VAT-registered person must be aggregated for one VAT return. A business consultant who is also a portrait photographer would have one VAT registration in respect of both his businesses. VAT recognises the individual, the partnership and the company and they must be separately registered. Furthermore, partnerships with a different partnership composition are treated as separate partnerships even if there is only one partner different between them. Anti-avoidance provisions exist to counteract the fragmentation of a business between VATable persons with a view to avoiding VAT registration.

There is a special relieving provision under which companies forming a group, or even those under common control, can share a VAT registration such that all transactions within the group are deemed to occur within the same VATable entity. One company is chosen as the representative member and all supplies are deemed to be made by or to the representative member. The same concept is applied, with interesting regional variations, in other EU states. Complex anti-avoidance provisions arise in respect of companies leaving or joining such a VAT group.

VAT on intellectual property

Collection of VAT

Only businesses which are registered for VAT have to charge VAT on taxable supplies made. Anyone who makes taxable supplies is eligible to register for VAT, but it is not obligatory for any business which has a turnover of less than £48,000 per year.

VAT registered businesses which make only taxable supplies add VAT at either 17.5 per cent (5 per cent for domestic fuel) or 0 per cent on the provision of goods or services. Likewise, such businesses will also pay VAT on expenses incurred. Each business which is registered for VAT is obliged to make either a monthly or quarterly return to Customs and Excise. On these returns, the business will enter all VAT charged on its supplies (output tax) and at the same time declare the level of VAT incurred on expenses (input tax). The difference between these figures will be the amount payable.

There are certain items of expenditure on which VAT cannot be recovered, including the purchase of motor cars, business entertainment costs and non-business items such as personal expenditure.

VAT on expenditure can be recovered only if it is attributable to a taxable supply. It therefore follows that a business which makes entirely exempt supplies cannot recover any VAT because all expenditure will be attributable to those supplies. Similarly any business which makes both taxable and exempt supplies will suffer an appropriate restriction in the recovery of VAT.

Treatment of intellectual property

Intellectual property transactions are supplies of services by virtue of VATA 1994, s 5(2)(*b*):

> anything which is not a supply of goods but is done for a consideration (including, if so done, the granting, assignment or surrender of any right) is a supply of services.

If, therefore, a UK-registered business grants a patent licence to another UK business in return for a royalty or lump sum, VAT at the standard rate is payable on the gross, pre VAT amount even though the payer may deduct income tax at the basic rate on making the payment. This applies whether or not a royalty is described as a gross royalty from which tax is to be deducted by the payer, or as a free of tax or net royalty which has to be grossed up to arrive at the gross equivalent.

Example

Anxious Antony Ltd pays UK patent royalties and is due to pay £10,000 (gross) on 17 September 1997. The amount due he pays is as follows:

	£
Gross royalty	10,000
VAT @ 17.5%	1,750
	11,750
Less: tax deducted at 23% × £10,000	2,300
Cheque to licensor	9,450
Being: net royalty	7,700
VAT on gross royalty	1,750
	9,450

The £2,300 deducted will be accounted for on Form CT 61(Z) for the period to 30 September 1997.

If the royalty paid by one UK business to another registered UK business is in connection with a foreign patent, VAT is still payable even though there may be no requirement to deduct income tax.

12 Valuation

Introduction

It is apparent that intellectual property is not, as such, of any intrinsic value although the article or work that it protects may well be. As a right to prohibit other people from exploiting an invention, a written work, photograph, painting, computer program, trade mark, logo, know-how or secret process the protection given to intellectual property concentrates on its economic value. This protection shows its value in the additional profits earned by the manufacturer or publisher as a result of the monopoly given to them over the exploitation of the property. However, as intellectual property is normally assignable or licensable the proprietor of the intellectual property can turn it to account by way of a fee or royalty for the licence to use the property or a lump sum paid on the assignment of the property in whole or part.

There may be a number of reasons why it is necessary for commercial purposes to value intellectual property, for example, on an assignment of the interest, on entering into a licensing or franchising agreement, on a take-over or merger or sale of a company owning intellectual property, for the purposes of revaluation to justify borrowings, or to resist a take-over, or in connection with divorce proceedings.

It may also be necessary to value intellectual property for fiscal purposes either as part of the process of valuing shares or on an assignment of the intellectual property rights in circumstances giving rise to a charge to income tax, capital gains tax, inheritance tax or stamp duty.

The first stage in any fiscal valuation is to determine precisely what rights are being valued (*Borland's Trustee v Steel Brothers & Co Ltd* [1901] 1 Ch 279; *Short v Treasury Commissioners* [1948] 1 KB 116). In the first instance this means that it must be assumed that the rights are capable of assignment in that it has to be assumed that the assignee acquires a valid title to the intellectual property and thereafter holds that property subject to any rights or restrictions attached thereto (*Re Crossman* (1936) 15 ATC 94).

Market value

For fiscal purposes the valuation is usually at the market value, ie the price which the property might reasonably be expected to fetch if sold in the open market at that time (IHTA 1984, s 160, TCGA 1992, s 272).

> The term 'open market' includes a sale by auction but is not confined to that (*IRC v Clay* and *IRC v Buchanan* [1914] 3 KB 466 at 471).

> A value ascertained by a reference to the amount obtainable in an open market shows an intention to include every possible purchaser. The offer is to the open market as distinguished from an offer to a limited class only, such as the members of the family. The market is not necessarily an auction sale. The (phrase) means such amount as the (property) might be expected to realise if offered under conditions enabling every person desirous of purchasing to come in and make an offer, and if the proper steps were taken to advertise the property and let all likely purchasers know that the (property) is in the market for sale (*ibid* p 475).

The phrase 'open market' means the market in which the property in question would normally be dealt (*Salomon v Customs and Excise Commissioners* [1966] 3 All ER 871; *Glass v IRC* [1915] SC 449).

The importance of looking at the precise statutory and contractual terms setting out the rights to the intellectual property have to be considered. In the stamp duty case of *Stanyforth v IRC* [1930] AC 339 at 334 it was stated with regard to a sale in the open market:

> at such a sale the property would have to be put up with all its incidents, including provisions for defesance, either in whole or in part, powers vested in persons not controlled by the vendor to create charges taking precedence of the propery sold and so forth. I really fail to understand, with all respect to those who have taken a different view, how the most drastic power of destroying the property to be sold vested in the persons over whom the purchasers could have no control could properly be disregarded.

In *Duke of Buccleuch v IRC* [1967] 1 AC 506 at 524 it was stated:

> There was some argument about the meaning of 'in the open market'. Originally no doubt when one wanted to sell a particular item of property one took it to a market where buyers of that kind of property congregated. Then the owner received offers and accepted what he thought was the best offer he was likely to get. And for some kinds of property this is still done. But this phrase must also be applied to other kinds of property where that is impossible. In my view the phrase requires that the seller must take, or be supposed to have taken, such steps as are reasonable to attract as much competition as possible for the particular piece of property which is to be sold. Sometimes this will be by sale by auction, sometimes otherwise. I suppose that the biggest open market is the Stock Exchange where there is no auction. And there may be two kinds of market commonly used by owners wishing to sell a particular kind of property. For example, it is common knowledge that many owners of houses first publish the fact that they wish to sell and then await offers. They only put the property up for auction as a last resort. I can see no reason for holding that in proper cases the former method could not be regarded as sale in the open market.

And in *Re Lynall, Lynall v IRC* (1971) 47 TC 375 at 411:

> There may be different markets or types of markets for different types of property but (in this case) the market which must be contemplated, whatever its form, must be an open market in which the property is offered for sale to the world at large so that all potential purchasers have an equal opportunity to make an offer as a result of it being openly known what it is that is being offered for sale. Mere private deals on a confidential basis are not equivalent of open market transactions.

Special purchasers

It is clear, therefore, that the open market hypothesis assumes that all potential purchasers are in the market to buy the intellectual property being valued and it is necessary to consider the price that they would pay for such property. However, it could well be that in certain cases the intellectual property has a particular value to an identifiable potential purchaser, usually known as a special purchaser, because of some synergistic value that the property would give him. This could be particularly important, for example, in the case of a patent where the master patent holder is prevented from developing the property in a particular manner because of some subsidiary patent held by another party. The master patent holder cannot develop the invention to its fullest potential without the subsidiary patent, and the subsidiary patent holder cannot exploit his improvement without some agreement with the master patent holder (*Hawkings-Byass v Sassen* [1996] STC (SCD) 319).

In valuing it is therefore necessary to consider whether a special purchaser exists, and if so, whether this is likely to have an effect on the value. If the existence of a special purchaser is known, or can reasonably be inferred, this is likely to affect the price.

> The knowledge of the special need would affect the market price and others would join in competing for the property with a view of obtaining it at a price less than that of which the opinion would be formed that it would be worth the while of the special buyer to purchase (*IRC v Clay, IRC v Buchanan* [1914] 3 KB 466 at 476).

This line of reasoning is confirmed in *Glass v IRC* [1915] SC 449; *Raja Vyricherla, Narayana Gajapatiraju v Revenue Divisional Officer Vizagapatam* [1939] AC 302 and *Robinson Brothers (Brewers) Ltd v Houghton and Chester-le-Street Assessment Committee* [1938] 2 All ER 79. 'All likely purchasers are deemed to be in the market' (*Re Lynall, Lynall v IRC* (1971) 47 TC 375 at 396).

Real sales

An actual arm's length sale of the intellectual property in question is clearly a point that would have some bearing upon its market value for fiscal purposes (*McNamee v IRC* (1954) IR 214) although it would clearly be necessary to consider whether the sale in question was a true arm's length sale in the open market as many real sales do not meet the hypothetical requirements of a fiscal valuation, being sales by private treaty rather than in the open market. Sales subsequent to the date of valuation should not affect the earlier fiscal valuation (*IRC v Marr's Trustees* (1906) 44 SLR 647) although it may of course have some persuasive value.

It is important to remember that the fiscal valuation is on a hypothetical basis.

> It is common ground that (property) must be valued on the basis of a hypothetical sale ... in a hypothetical open market between a hypothetical willing vendor ... and a hypothetical willing purchaser on the hypothesis that no-one is excluded from buying and that the purchaser would ... hold (the property) subject to (the legal and contractual arrangements applying to that intellectual property) (*Re Lynall, Lynall v IRC* (1971) 47 TC 375 at 377 *see also Attorney General v Jameson* (1904) 2 IR 644 and *Re Crossman and Re Paulin* (1936) 15 ATC 94 and *Re Holt* (1953) 32 ATC 402).

It is therefore a statutory fiction and the fact that a sale at the valuation date would be impossible (*Duke of Buccleuch v IRC* [1967] 1 AC 506 at 535), or illegal (*Re Aschrott, Clifton v Strauss* [1927] 1 Ch 313 at 322), is irrelevant. Notional costs of disposal are not deductible (*Duke of Buccleuch v IRC* [1967] 1 AC 506 at 541) although actual costs of disposal would be deductible for most tax purposes (*see* TCGA 1992, s 38).

Optimum lotting

When considering the intellectual property rights to be valued it is necessary to consider how these could best be packaged commercially to realise the maximum price. It may be, for example, that an invention consists of a number of elements, each of which is capable of being patented, thus widening the protection available, or there may have been material improvements to the invention capable of being patented. Similarly, when considering the copyright in a musical work, the performing rights and potential film synchronisation rights have to be considered. The law applicable to fiscal valuation allows for the optimum lotting of the various rights available.

> The value of the property shall be estimated to be the price which it would fetch if sold in the open market. That in my opinion does not necessarily mean the price which it would fetch if sold to a single purchaser. There may be many cases where a sale to a single purchaser cannot realise 'the price which it would fetch if sold in the open market'. Take the case of an owner having property, including a colliery and a drapers shop. It is conceivable that if the colliery and the drapers shop were sold separately the best possible price might be obtained for each. On the other hand a purchaser who was anxious to buy the drapers shop might not wish to be encumbered with the colliery and vice versa and consequently if the owner insisted upon selling the whole property to one purchaser it would not obtain the market price which the act contemplates (*Earl of Ellesmere v IRC* [1918] 2 KB 735).

On the other hand the principle of optimum lotting must not be carried to extremes.

> It is sometimes said that the estate must be supposed to have been realised in such a way that the best possible prices were obtained for its parts. But that cannot be a universal rule. Suppose that the owner of a wholesale business dies possessed of a large quantity of hardware or clothing, or whatever he deals in. It would have been possible by extensive advertising to obtain offers for small lots at something near retail prices. So it would have been possible to realise the stock at much more than wholesale prices. It would not have been reasonable and it would not have been economic, but it would have been possible. Counsel for the respondent did not contend that that would be a proper method of valuation. But that necessarily amounts to an admission that there is no universal rule that the best possible price at the date of death must be taken (*Duke of Buccleuch v IRC* [1967] 1 AC 506 at 526; *see also Smyth v IRC* (1941) IR 643 and *Trustees of Johan Thomas Salvesen v IRC* (1930) 9 ATC 43).

It may be possible to obtain the best price by selling a complete package, for example, the design of a machine could include a number of features protected by patent, copyright drawings, technical know-how and a trade mark licence, and in such cases it is reasonable to assume for valuation purposes that the most attractive package would be put together (*Attorney General of Ceylon v Mackie* [1952] 2 All ER 775).

> The appellant contends that the respondent must be supposed to have taken the course which would get the largest price for the combined holding of management and preference shares and to offer for sale, together with the management shares, the whole or at least the greater part of the preference shares owned by the deceased. In their Lordships' judgment this contention is correct (*ibid* p 777).

Hindsight

Fiscal valuations are usually considered by the Revenue sometime after the transaction has taken place, and, as a result, information is often available which would not have been at the date of valuation. It is clear that documents that were not available at the date of the valuation cannot be admissible as evidence (*Re Lynall, Lynall v IRC* (1971) 47 TC 375 at 383).

> I rule out of consideration the knowledge provided by the passage of time since March 11 1948 that the company's dividend on ordinary shares has not been increased from 5 per cent and that the company has been able to avoid a public issue of ordinary shares by launching an exceedingly successful issue of new preference shares in September 1950 (*Re Holt* (1953) 32 ATC 402 at 410).

On the other hand it is permissible to consider subsequent events to the extent that they may clarify or provide additional information with regard to the information available at the date of the valuation (*Trustees of Johan Thomas Salvesen v IRC* (1930) 9 ATC 43 at 51; *Buckingham v Francis* [1986] 2 All ER 738; *Re Bradberry, National Provincial Bank Ltd v Bradberry and Re Fry, Tasker v Gulliford* [1943] Ch 35).

Willing parties

An open market assumes a sale between a hypothetical willing seller and a hypothetical willing, prudent and cautious buyer.

> It is true that the so called willing vendor is a person who must sell, he cannot simply call off the sale if he does not like the price, but there must be on the other side a willing purchaser so that the condition of the sale must be such as to induce in him a willing frame of mind (*Re Lynall, Lynall v IRC* (1971) 47 TC 375 at 392).
>
> It does not mean a sale by a person willing to sell his property without reserve for any price he can obtain (*IRC v Clay, IRC v Buchanan* [1914] 3 KB 466 at 476; *see also Winter (Sutherland's Trustees) v IRC* (1961) 40 ATC 361 and *Duke of Buccleuch v IRC* [1967] 1 AC 506).

Conversely, the purchaser must be assumed to be a man of prudence (*Trustees of Johan Thomas Salvesen v IRC* (1930) 9 ATC 43 and *Re Holt, Holt v IRC* (1953) 32 ATC 402), who would make diligent enquiries before buying (*Caton's Administration v Couch* [1995] STC (SCD) 34; *Clark v Green* [1995] STC (SCD) 99).

> In estimating the price which might be fetched in the open market for the goodwill of the business it must be assumed that the transaction takes place between a willing seller and a willing purchaser and that the purchaser is a person of reasonable prudence who has informed himself with regard to all the relevant facts such as the history of the business, its present position, its future prospects and the general conditions of the industry, and also that he has access to the accounts of the business for a number of years (*Findlay's Trustees v IRC* (1938) 22 ATC 437).

The fiscal valuation therefore is based on the price at which the hypothetical sale is likely to take place, and although the effect on that price of the existence of any special purchaser has to be considered, the market value ignores the actual identity of both the vendor and purchaser (*Battle v IRC* [1980] STC 86).

Present value

Having arrived at the theoretical framework of the valuation of the intellectual property the problem then becomes one of determining the relevant price at which the hypothetical sale would take place and this in turn is often calculated, in the real market (and equally in the hypothetical market for fiscal valuations) on the basis of the present value of the estimated future income that would be generated by the intellectual property being acquired either directly from royalties or any lump-sum assignments that could be possible, or indirectly from the accretion to profits which would result from the acquisition.

Estimating this future income is, not surprisingly, the most difficult part of the valuation and will depend on the circumstances of each case. Experience within the industry will be of considerable assistance. For example, a drug company may, from its own experience, be able to estimate that a particular drug could be manufactured for a cost of £x per thousand pills and could be sold for £y resulting in a profit of £z per thousand. If the market is estimated at so many million pills per annum for a period of, say, five years before the drug is likely to be replaced by a rival product, the income to be generated can be calculated as a matter of arithmetic and if this income flow is then discounted back to a net present value, using an appropriate rate of discount, the current value of the income stream can be calculated. The present value of the income stream represents the amount that could be paid for the licence of the product subject to the purchaser's required margin.

Example

		£
x	cost per thousand pills	26.00
y	sale price per thousand pills	40.00
z	profit per thousand pills	14.00

Estimated sales

year 1	5 million
year 2	10 million
year 3	15 million
year 4	20 million
year 5	5 million

Estimated profit

		£
year 1	$\dfrac{5,000,000 \times 14.00}{1,000}$	70,000
year 2	$\dfrac{10,000,000 \times 14.00}{1,000}$	140,000
year 3	$\dfrac{15,000,000 \times 14.00}{1,000}$	210,000
year 4	$\dfrac{20,000,000 \times 14.00}{1,000}$	280,000
year 5	$\dfrac{5,000,000 \times 14.00}{1,000}$	70,000

Present value at 15 per cent per annum

	£
year 1	60,869
year 2	105,860
year 3	138,078
year 4	160,090
year 5	34,802
	499,699

	£
Less tax at, say, 33 per cent	164,900
	334,799
Margin required	
say 25 per cent on cost	66,959
	267,840
say	260,000

Any such calculation of course involves a number of assumptions, any one of which may be wrong. For example, in spite of all preparatory testing the drug may have undesirable side effects and its use be severely curtailed or banned. A rival product may appear sooner than anticipated which would reduce the potential sales of the product. Manufacturing techniques in bulk may prove more difficult than anticipated or raw materials scarcer and more expensive. On the other hand the drug may prove highly beneficial in practice and have wider applications than were first thought, demand may greatly exceed forecast and improved manufacturing techniques might enable expensive ingredients to be synthesised, thus reducing the cost of the product. This in turn could lead to governmental interference in the price. It has to be appreciated that every element in the forecast is in many ways no more than a best guess on the basis of experience within the industry.

Industry price multiple

In some industries there is an established market in the sale of intellectual property packages at a multiple of the average historical income over a period. The multiple will depend on the number of rights in the package; the broader the base, the lower the risk. It will also be affected by the volatility of the market and the specific attributes of the intellectual property involved. In such cases it is assumed that past performance may give a useful indication of the likely future income and, for example, a publisher's past catalogue may be saleable on the basis of, say, three-and-a-half to five years' purchase of the net income generated from the product in question for the average of the previous three years (the 'net publisher's share' or NPS). In this case the real calculation is an estimated falling future income from the products in question over a period of years based on the average historical data showing the past performance of the product. Again, there are any number of uncertainties involved in that, for example, an author included in the catalogue may become the subject of a film or television series which would increase sales enormously. Alternatively the product may turn out to be a 'seven-day wonder' and pale into insignificance within a short space of time. This is particularly common in the case of a popular music catalogue although the effect of the continued success of the performing artistes could have a very considerable effect on the value of the catalogue, particularly if further successful recordings are made and extensive touring and live performances given, which could lead to a marked upturn in the anticipated level of sales.

In any commercial deal involving intellectual property, it is much easier if a number of items are involved than if a single patent or copyright work has to be valued. On the basis of experience, a publisher will take into account the fact that a number of authors included in the catalogue would be likely to become the starting point for a film or television series, although he might not be able to identify which ones will in fact so feature. Similarly a music publishing catalogue would include a number of works which would no doubt receive a new lease of life on rerecording, or further exploitation as a result of film synchronisation rights, or the continued success of the original artistes, or others taking up the work. In such cases it would be usual to analyse the income over the various types, eg mechanical royalties, from the sale of recordings, performance royalties, sundry income, print royalties from the sale of sheet music and synchronisation rights. Synchronisation rights tend to be one-off and difficult to predict and may be excluded from a schedule of past income as being a distortion, the prospect of such income being taken into account in an enhanced multiple instead. Again, it is reasonable to build some expectation into a complete catalogue although it may not be possible to identify which particular works will perform better than anticipated or conversely which ones will die much earlier.

Royalty comparisons

In some cases the best approach may be to anticipate the royalty that would have to be paid in order to manufacture or reproduce the item under licence; that rate of royalty may be a fairly common feature of the industry in question, or derived without too much difficulty from comparable situations. This is often called the 'royalty relief method'. On the other hand there may not be any truly comparable licensing agreements covering the type of property under consideration and it may be necessary to consider what an arm's length royalty might be. In order to convert a royalty rate into a present value for the whole intellectual property, it is necessary to estimate not only the royalty rate itself, but the likely production under the hypothetical royalty agreement in order to convert the royalty rate into an income stream, the present value of which can then be calculated using normal discounted cash flow techniques. In order to do this it is necessary not only to calculate the likely levels of production but the timing of that production, which will have an effect on the value.

The effect of taxation on the figures has to be considered and this will depend on whether the valuation is required for the purpose of evaluating a transfer of intellectual property itself, in which case the pre-tax value is normally required in order to calculate the potential gross value and the taxation consequences are then considered by each party. In the case of a valuation of intellectual property which forms part of a calculation of the value of shares in the company owning the property, it may be appropriate to discount the value at which it is brought into the calculation by the potential tax charge which would arise if it were to be disposed of at that figure (*Winter (Sutherland's Trustees) v IRC* (1961) 40 ATC 361).

Example

Grushin Innovative Products Ltd
Valuation of Patent Rights

Instructions
We have been asked to consider the current cost valuation of Grushin's rights under the patents listed on the schedule headed 'Status Report on Patent Applications'. The date of valuation has been taken as 1 July 1997.

Purpose of valuation
The valuation is required for Companies Act purposes in order to establish the value of the patent rights to be included in Grushin's balance sheet. This valuation report has been prepared for internal purposes only. The value will be reported to the company in non-speaking form only.

Basis of valuation
'Current cost valuation' is equivalent to open-market value, which is usually defined as the best price reasonably obtainable in an arm's length transaction in the open market between a willing buyer and a willing seller.

Valuation approach
We consider it reasonable to arrive at the current value of the company's patent rights by estimating the net present value of the future royalties the company could reasonably expect to achieve if it were to license its patent rights to another manufacturer.

Valuation
We have been provided by the company with a forecast of its turnover in the five-year period from 1997 to 2001. At present the company achieves gross margins (after allowing for costs of sale which include manufacturing costs) in the region of 61 per cent. We therefore consider that the company could reasonably expect to receive a royalty on turnover of about one-half of that gross margin, say 30 per cent. In view of the uncertainty involved, however, we would reduce that rate to 20 per cent after the first three years.

As the company is forecasting a considerable increase in turnover over the next five years, arising in part from contracts which have yet to be awarded, we consider it prudent to adopt relatively high discount rates in arriving at the net present value of the assumed royalty income. We would therefore apply a discount rate of 25 per cent over the five years covered by the forecast.

The company's patents will run out by the year 2005. We have therefore added a further four years' turnover to the company's forecast, at the same level of turnover as in 2001, the last year of the company's forecast. We have, nevertheless, increased the discount rate for those final four years to 35 per cent.

On that basis the net present value is as follows:

Year	Turnover	Royalty level		Discount factor		Net present value of royalty
	£m	£m 30%	£m 20%	@ 25%	@ 35%	£m
1997	1.9	.57		.8		.456
1998	5.2	1.56		.64		.998
1999	8.15	2.445		.512		1.251
2000	8.325		1.665	.409		.680
2001	10.2		2.04	.327		.667
2002	10.2		2.04		.164	.334
2003	10.2		2.04		.121	.247
2004	10.2		2.04		.090	.183
2005	10.2		2.04		.066	.134
						4.950
Corporation tax at 31 per cent						1.534
After Corporation tax						3.416
					say	3.4

We therefore put the value of the company's patent rights at £3,400,000

As well as valuing for fiscal purposes an entire piece of intellectual property on its absolute assignment or a partial interest on the grant of a licence for a lump sum or royalty, it may be necessary to consider the acceptability of a commercially agreed royalty rate for tax purposes. Where there is a payment from one UK company to another the Revenue will normally be prepared to treat the payment as deductible as either an expense or annual payment as appropriate, and the income taxable on the recipient. If however the royalty is seen merely as a means of moving profits between companies and not justified by the commercial circumstances the deductibility could be challenged (*Finsbury Securities Ltd v Bishop* (1966) 43 TC 591; *Lupton v FA & AB Ltd* (1971) 47 TC 580; *Thomson v Gurneville Securities Ltd* (1971) 47 TC 633). In a case in Hong Kong in 1996 (*Chen Hsong Machinery Co Ltd v IRC*) (D52/96) before the Board of Review a trade mark was valued on the basis of the capitalised value, using a multiple of five, of a notional royalty of 6 per cent, less 1 per cent for the maintenance of the mark, 5 per cent net, applied to the projected turnover for the forthcoming year.

The valuation of brands, 'trade marks with attitude', in that they carry the magic ingredient of consumer loyalty, is becoming an area of major importance both commercially and in the taxation field, with Revenue authorities requiring, under transfer pricing rules, foreign affiliates to be charged at market rate for the use of brand names. Brand names, protected as trade marks, service marks or under passing-off prohibitions at common law, have an indefinite life, unlike the 20-year life of a patent, and the valuation of the net present value of the brand income stream, real or hypothetical, usually includes an annuity element covering future years beyond which projections can realistically be made. The problem, in practice, is to arrive at a reasonable estimate of the future results of the brand, the proportion of that income which relates to the brand or other intellectual property, and the rate of discount which is appropriate, starting with the risk-free cost of long-term debt and adding in appropriate risk factors, often termed 'beta factors'.

External factors

No valuation can take place in a vacuum, and the general economic and political situation is relevant both to the calculation of the likely levels of future income and to the rate of discount to be applied which is affected by market rates (*Attorney General of Ceylon v Mackie* [1952] 2 All ER 775; *Re Holt* (1953) 32 ATC 402). The state of the industry and industry sector is also important for the same reasons (*Trustees of Johan Thomas Salvesen v IRC* (1930) 9 ATC 43 and *Findlay's Trustees v IRC* (1938) 22 ATC 437).

13 Transfer pricing

Introduction

The rate of royalty payments between connected companies should be at market value because many countries have transfer pricing provisions whereby artificial values can be disregarded and the market value substituted. The main UK provisions are contained in TA 1988, ss 770–773.

The first requirement to enable the Revenue to invoke the transfer pricing provisions of TA 1988, s 770 is that the seller has control over the buyer, or the buyer has control over the seller, or some other person has control over both the buyer and the seller (TA 1988, s 770(1)(*a*) and (2)(*a*)). (In the context of intellectual property TA 1988, s 773(4) provides that licensor and licensee may be substituted for seller and buyer.) 'Control' for this purpose means voting control or control by virtue of powers conferred by the articles of association or other document regulating the powers of a company whereby the company's affairs are conducted in accordance with the wishes of the controller. In the case of a partnership it means the right to a share of more than half the assets or income of the partnership (TA 1988, ss 773(2), 840). 'Control' includes indirect control through a nominee or connected person, ie, spouse, sibling, spouse's sibling, ancestor or lineal descendant (or their spouses), trustee or partner (TA 1988, s 773(3)) In considering the definition of control under TA 1988, s 840, the Revenue argued in *Irving v Tesco Stores (Holdings) Ltd* (1982) STC 881 that control had to be at company meeting level and not merely at board meeting level. In determining control it is not sufficient to look merely at the first named trustee of the trust holding in order to determine whether control may be exercised (*IRC Lithgows Limited* (1960) 39 TC 270). Transfer pricing adjustments cannot apply to a sole trader, as an individual is not a body of persons.

The second requirement is that the price is greater or less than might have been expected in a transaction between independent persons dealing at arm's length (TA 1988, s 770(1)(*b*) and (2)(*b*)). The transfer pricing provisions do not require the Revenue to show any tax avoidance motive in order to substitute an arm's length price for that agreed between the parties; see *Page v Lowther and another* (1983) STC 799, where motive was held to be irrelevant in deciding whether or not TA 1988, s 776 applied to a transaction in land. TA 1988, s 770(3) provides that all necessary adjustments are to be made by assessment, repayment or otherwise where a direction is given which may require adjustment to open assessments (*Glaxo Group Limited and others v IRC* (1996) STC 191). Appeals relating to transfer pricing directions are made to the Special Commissioners under TA 1988, s 772(8).

Transfer pricing provisions do not apply for capital allowance purposes in view of TA 1988, s 773(1). There may, however, be adjustment to market value under anti-avoidance provisions in CA 1990, ss 75–79 or ss 157 and 158.

The transfer pricing provisions in TA 1988, ss 770–773 are explained in the Inland Revenue Manual at IM 4650–4662, and in Chapter 15 of the *International Tax Handbook*.

TA 1988, s 209(4) may apply to treat as a distribution, the difference between the market value and the transfer price where an asset is transferred at an undervalue or a liability at an overvalue unless both companies are resident in the UK.

The Revenue may then make a direction under TA 1988, s 770(3) to substitute for tax purposes the price which would have been applied in a transaction between independent persons dealing at arm's length. Under self-assessment, the Revenue will expect taxpayers to reveal where transfer pricing adjustments are necessary. Draft legislation was published on 9 October 1997 as *Modernisation of the transfer pricing legislation* which will change many of the administrative procedures and detailed rules referred to in this chapter. The Revenue has published notes on the application of TA 1988, s 770 (*The transfer pricing of multinational enterprises*, 26 January 1981) supplemented by *Tax Bulletin*, 25 October 1996, confirming that the Revenue will follow the recommendation in the OECD report *Transfer Pricing Guidelines for Multinational Enterprises and Tax Administrations* published in July 1995. The transfer pricing provisions do not apply where both parties are trading in the UK (TA 1988, s 770(2)(*a*)(ii) and (2)(*b*)(ii)) or to capital allowances (TA 1988, s 773(1)) where the main anti-avoidance provisions are contained in CAA 1990, s 75.

Information powers

The information-gathering powers of the Inland Revenue for transfer pricing purposes are contained in TA 1988, s 772. This gives the Revenue power to issue a notice to any company requiring it to provide within the time specified in the notice (which must be at least 30 days) such particulars including details of relevant documents as may be specified in the notice, of any related transactions which appear to the Revenue to be connected with the transaction in respect of which a direction is possible and to be relevant to determining whether such a direction could or should be given or is relevant in determining the arm's length price (TA 1988, s 772(1)). A notice can only be given where there is the necessary degree of control.

By its nature transfer pricing involves cross-border transactions and therefore the transactions of overseas companies. TA 1988, s 723 gives the Revenue power to require the parent company of an overseas 51 per cent subsidiary or body of persons over which it has control to produce the books, accounts or other documents or records of the overseas subsidiary as well as for the UK parent. The parent company can, under TA 1988, s 772(4), apply to the Revenue not to require the records of the overseas subsidiary on the grounds that the circumstances are such that the requirement ought not to have effect—for example, there may be a statutory requirement in the overseas country that its accounting records be kept in the country of its operation. In such cases the Revenue may overrule the notice and if it refuses to do so the parent company may appeal within 30 days to the Special Commissioners under TA 1988, s 772(5).

A 51 per cent subsidiary is defined as one where more than 50 per cent of its ordinary share capital is owned directly or indirectly by the parent company (TA 1988, s 838(1)(*a*)). The reference to ownership is beneficial ownership and holdings through a chain may be included (TA 1988, s 838(2)–(10)).

The wide-ranging information-gathering powers in TA 1988, s 772 are rarely invoked formally, companies usually instead responding to informal requests for information. See the written answer of June 1990, *Hansard*, Vol 174, Col 143. Penalties for failure to furnish particulars under TA 1988, s 772(1), (3) or (6) are set out in TMA 1970, s 98.

The information-gathering powers of the Revenue extend to the Revenue specifically authorising an Inspector to enter any premises used in connection with the relevant trade in respect of which the transactions being investigated were carried on, and to inspect any books, accounts or other documents or records whatsoever relating to that trade, which he considers it necessary for him to inspect, and to require such books, accounts or other documents or records to be produced to him for inspection (TA 1988, s 772(6), (7)). It will be seen therefore that the Revenue's information-gathering powers under these provisions are draconian. In *Beecham plc v IRC* (1992) STC 935 the UK parent company applied to have notices under TA 1988, s 772 set aside on the grounds that compiling the information required by the notices would be burdensome, oppressive and a waste of time. The Revenue argued that there was no appeal against a Special Commissioner's decision and the notices requiring information were necessary for the settlement of outstanding appeals. The court held that it had jurisdiction and that the question of whether or not the notices were valid was a separate issue which should be heard prior to the substantive appeals.

The very wide powers of the Revenue under TA 1988, s 772 to obtain information are in addition to the normal information-gathering powers in TMA 1970, ss 20A–20B and 21.

Foreign legislation

Consider other countries' transfer pricing rules, for example:
Australia: Part IVA, Division 13, Income Tax Assessment Act.
Belgium—abnormal benefits: Article 24, Code des Impots Sur la Revenu.
France—connected companies: Article 57, Code General de Impots;
—tax havens: Article 238A.
Germany: Aussenstauergesetz.
Netherlands—abuse of legal form: Article 31, Algemene wet inzake rijksbelastingen.
Spain—abuse of legal form/market value: Article 25, Ley General Tributaria.
Switzerland—abuse of Swiss treaties/constructive dividends/abuse of legal form: Federal Decree of 1962, Article 49.
USA—extreme reporting requirements: s 482 Internal Revenue Code (1986);
—super royalties on basis of income ultimately generated: Tax Reform Act 1986, regulations 8552, 1 July 1994; 8632, 19 December 1995; 8670, 9 May 1996.

Unilateral transfer pricing adjustments can give rise to economic double taxation for which no relief is available. The only remedy until recently has been to invoke the competent authority procedure under a double taxation treaty and hope the Revenue authorities of the two countries will agree a common transfer price.

Arbitration Convention

The European Union Arbitration Convention on the elimination of double taxation in connection with the adjustment of profits of associated enterprises (EE90/436) came into force on 1 January 1995 and is applied to the UK by TA 1988, s 815B. This gives some protection against such double taxation arising from different transfer pricing of adjustments in different countries within the European Union.

Theory of international transfer pricing

The theory of international transfer pricing is succinctly described in article 4, para 2 of the Arbitration Convention as follows:

> Where an enterprise of a contracting state carries on business in another contracting state through a permanent establishment situated therein there shall be attributed to that permanent establishment the profits which it might be expected to make if it were a distinct and separate enterprise engaged in the same or similar activities under the same or similar conditions and dealing wholly independently with the enterprise of which it is a permanent establishment.

This statement forms the basis of the comparable arm's length price calculated as if the parties to the transactions were independent persons dealing with each other at arm's length; that is the assumption underlying the Associated Enterprises Article of the OECD Model Double Taxation Convention (article 9(1) of the OECD *Transfer Pricing Report* of 1979).

In the field of intellectual property the problem is quite simply to find a comparable situation where a royalty level has been agreed between arm's length companies in a similar situation. It is very often impossible to find such a situation and it is then necessary to try to determine from first principles what would be a fair royalty in the circumstances. The problem here is that different Revenue authorities have different approaches to this problem which in turn gives rise to the need for the Arbitration Convention. *Tax Bulletin* 25, October 1996, sets out the mutual agreement procedure in the UK double tax conventions and Arbitration Convention.

In the field of international transactions the Inland Revenue are likely to look closely at royalty levels in view of the transfer pricing provisions in TA 1988, s 770 as applied by TA 1988, s 772 and 773. These provisions apply where the royalty payer and recipient are under common control, ie one has control over the other or a third party has control over both, and the royalty level is greater or less than the arm's length price which might have been expected if the parties to the transaction had been independent persons dealing at arm's length. The general provisions in TA 1988, s 770(1) are extended to royalties by TA 1988, s 773(4) which applies to grants and transfers of rights, interests or licences and the giving of business facilities of whatever kind which includes interest on connected loans. In *Ametalco UK v IRC* (1996) STC SCD 399 (SPC94) it was held that the term 'giving of business facilities' under TA 1988, s 773(4) included the provision of interest-free loans within the transfer pricing provision. This Special Commissioners' decision did not however clarify the arm's length price appropriate for an interest-free loan. Arguably it should be the arm's length price which the seller, ie the provider of the loan could have obtained and therefore relate it to the deposit interest which the seller has forgone by making the loans interest free. The Revenue would no doubt argue that the arm's length price is the amount the borrower would have had to pay in arranging a loan, ie the market lending rate. The position is not clear because the transfer pricing rules are cast to apply to trading transactions and are only extended to other transactions by TA 1988, s 773(4). Control is defined through TA 1988, ss 773(2) and 840 as the power to secure by means of voting power or powers given by the articles of association that the affairs of the company are conducted in accordance with the wishes of the person having control.

TA 1988, s 770(2) disapplies the provisions where the payer is resident in the United Kingdom and can claim a trading deduction where the actual price is less than the arm's length price; or where it is greater than the arm's length price and the seller/licensor is resident in the UK and the royalty would be a trading receipt for tax purposes. In practice therefore the provisions are normally applied to cross-border transactions with other countries, particularly where a royalty is paid to a low tax area or tax haven, although they can also be applied to transactions between UK-resident trading and investment companies (IM 4651)

The effect of TA 1988, s 770 is to enable the Inland Revenue to substitute what they deem to be an arm's length price for the price actually agreed and to levy tax accordingly. Unfortunately other countries also have similar provisions and there is no reason to suppose that different Revenue authorities would agree the same arm's length price for the royalty arrangements. It is perfectly possible for example that the Inland Revenue in the UK may regard a royalty of 7½ per cent paid to the USA as excessive and tax the licensee as if he had paid a royalty of only 5 per cent. On the other hand the Internal Revenue Service in the USA may regard a 7½ per cent royalty as being too low and under s 482 of the Internal Revenue Code 1986 amend the royalty received by the licensor for American tax purposes to say 10 per cent. This clearly involves economic double taxation for which no relief is available under the double taxation treaty.

The transfer pricing rules are not the only rules which could affect the deductibility for tax purposes of a trading expense. Management charges paid to a connected party could be disallowed in the absence of evidence to justify the expenses as being wholly incurred for the purposes of the trade (TA 1988, s 74(1)(*a*); *Fragmap Developments Ltd v Cooper* (1967) 44 TC 366; *New Zealand Commissioner of Inland Revenue v Europa Oil (NZ) Ltd* (1970) 49 ATC 282). In a complex case where the arrangements were held to be designed to cheat the public Revenue, the taxpayer's professional advisers were jailed (*R v Charlton and others* [1966] STC 1418).

Interest paid to a non-resident at more than a reasonable commercial rate is disallowed by TA 1988 s 74(*n*) and any annuity or other annual payment which includes in particular patent royalties is disallowed by TA 1988, s 74(1)(*m*).

Business entertaining expenses are disallowed by TA 1988, s 577 and illegal bribes and extortion payments are disallowed by TA 1988, s 577A.

Where transactions take place in goods forming trading stock, for example under a franchising operation, the Revenue can substitute market value for the transaction price on the basis of *Sharkey v Wernher* (1955) TC 275; *Watson Bros v Hornby* (1942) 24 TC 506; *Petrotim Securities Ltd v Ayres* (1963) 41 TC 389; *Skinner v Berry Head Lands Ltd* (1970) 46 TC 377 and *Ridge Securities v IRC* (1963) 44 TC 373. The same principle does not apply to the provision of professional services where the Revenue have no power to substitute the market value (*Mason v Innes* (1967) 44 TC 326).

The capital gains tax legislation contains a number of sections under which bargains not at arm's length are treated as being disposed of for a consideration equal to market value (TCGA 1992, s 17). Transactions between connected persons as defined by TCGA 1992, s 286 are deemed to be bargains not at arm's length and any loss arising from such a transaction is ring-fenced so that it can only be set against gains on other transactions between the same parties (TCGA 1992, s 18), but TCGA 1992, ss 19 and 20 prevent the exploitation of the valuation rules in TCGA 1992, ss 272 and 273 to prevent the reduction in chargeable gains by transferring assets in a series of transactions to reduce the aggregate value. There are also anti-avoidance rules to prevent changes in rights, for example to shares, to move value from one asset to another without a disposal under what are known as value shifting provisions in TCGA 1992, ss 29–34.

The rules relating to distributions, loan relationships and foreign exchange dealt with in Chapter 10 can also have the effect of substituting different figures for tax purposes from those agreed between the parties or for treating what would otherwise be allowable expenses as distributions out of taxed profits. The thin capitalisation rules in TA 1988, s 808A are dealt with in this chapter. Artificially inserted transactions can be ignored for tax purposes, as explained at pp 246–7.

Arm's length price

The provisions apply where the actual sale price is greater or less than the arm's length price, defined as the price which it might have been expected to fetch if the parties to the transaction had been independent persons dealing at arm's length (TA 1988, s 770(1)(*b*)). In such circumstances, if the seller's actual price is less than the arm's length price or the buyer's actual price is greater than the arm's length price, the arm's length price may be substituted for the actual price, on the Revenue giving the appropriate direction. However, there will be no adjustment where the seller's actual price was more than the arm's length price or the buyer's actual price was less than the arm's length price. Nor do the provisions apply to the seller where the actual price is less than the arm's length price but the buyer is carrying on a trade in the UK and the cost would be a deduction in computing profits of the trade (TA 1988, s 770(2)(*a*)) or where the buyer's actual price is greater than the arm's length price but the seller is resident in the UK carrying on a trade such that the actual price would be a trading receipt of the seller (TA 1988, s 770(2)(*b*)). There are special provisions relating to transactions by petroleum companies which are outside the scope of this book (TA 1988, s 770(2)(*c*) and s 771).

OECD guidelines for multinational enterprises and tax administrations

This three-part report, although a discussion draft, is accepted by many Revenue authorities, including the UK Inland Revenue, as a working document to assist in the calculation of arm's length prices for transfer pricing adjustments.

Transfer pricing methods to arrive at the arm's length price

One of the most difficult problems in practice in any transfer pricing adjustment is agreeing an arm's length price for a transaction which does not, and in reality would not, take place between parties at arm's length and this report attempts to set out a basis for arriving at arm's length value which is likely to be fair both to the taxpayers in both countries and to the Revenue authorities of both countries. The report breaks down transfer pricing comparisons into transaction-based methods and profit methods.

Transaction-based methods

There are three transaction-based methods, (a) the comparable uncontrolled prices method (CUP), (b) the resale price method and (c) the cost plus method. An uncontrolled third party transaction may be identified for the purposes of comparison with a connected party transaction if there are no differences between the transactions being compared or between the enterprises undertaking those transactions that could materially affect the price in the open market, or such differences exist but reasonably accurate adjustments can be made to eliminate their effects. The CUP method is the most favoured method.

Comparable uncontrolled prices method (CUP) The main problem with the CUP is finding the comparable transaction, as this information is usually confidential and unlikely to be available to a trader except in the most general terms of published statistics, or where it is available from price lists and published terms of trade from competitors selling similar products. In practice this happens only rarely in a transfer pricing investigation. It may be that the Revenue authorities have information in relation to comparable prices charged by other businesses but this information will normally be held on a confidential basis and cannot be used in evidence to support a transfer pricing adjustment.

In comparing products that are at first sight thought to be comparable it is necessary not only to consider their physical features, such as the materials out of which they are made, their expected quality and reliability and function, but also the extent to which they are readily available, the time at which they are available, the terms and date of delivery, guarantees and warranties, the market at which they are aimed, the terms of payment including transport costs, the back-up support available, such as technical support and technology transfer, the conditions of use and the volume of sales quantities, discounts available and market into which they are sold. The CUP should also take account of the brand name and advertising costs of the product which may be heavily marketed on a worldwide basis, and in practice justify a significant premium over an unbranded competitor.

The trouble with the CUP is that any such comparison is likely to highlight differences rather than similarities and even where finished products are concerned the businesses are normally trying to emphasise to their customers the differences between their product and those of their rivals, rather than the similarities. Obviously there will be cases where there are no material differences or where such differences as there are can be both quantified and adjusted for.

Resale price method Because of the difficulty of finding a CUP, in practice an alternative is to look at the resale price. X in one country may supply goods or services to Y in another country which are incorporated into a product which Y in turn sells to unconnected customers. By deducting from the resale price from Y to the third party, customer Y's reasonable gross margin, it may be possible to arrive at the arm's length price which X ought to have charged Y.

Y's margin will depend on the value which Y adds to the product or service, for example assembling the product or tailoring it for local use, distribution, advertising, guarantees, warranties, servicing etc; Y's costs, which will depend on the value added by Y to the product or service obtained from X, and may include manufacturing and assembly costs, marketing distribution, advertising, financing, administration, testing, stock holding, transportation etc; with an allowance for the risk taken by Y and its financing costs and perhaps the costs of supporting the brand name and exclusive franchise obtained from X.

It will be immediately apparent that a number of these costs are difficult to allocate to specific products and the allowable mark-up is a subjective figure, although it in turn should, where possible, be related to comparable third party transactions with adjustments as necessary.

The cost plus method In many cases controlled subsidiaries, for which transfer pricing adjustments may be appropriate, are not dealing with the end market but are themselves producing goods or services for fellow entities within the multinational group which are incorporated into the final product sold worldwide. In such cases the resale price method will not readily produce an arm's length price and the cost plus method may be appropriate. This seeks to add to the costs incurred by the overseas subsidiary a reasonable margin for the value added by, and profit of, the overseas companies. This on its own is of no help where a major part of the cost arises from the goods or services brought in from controlled enterprises, but in a typical chain transaction in a multinational chain it might provide some guidance, particularly if substantial costs are incurred locally.

In chain transactions it may be possible to look at each company in turn on the basis of its costs plus a reasonable mark-up, and compare that with a resale price method carried down through the chain from the ultimate sale price to arm's length customers. It may, however, in such circumstances be preferable to use one of the profit methods.

Profit methods

Where a lack of suitable comparisons makes a transaction-based method inappropriate, a profit-based method is perhaps the only sensible alternative.

The profit split method In a profit split method the profit arising on the entire transaction within the group of connected enterprises is calculated and apportioned on a rational basis between the various entities, in accordance with their contribution to the overall profit. Although this is a seemingly sensible approach in theory, it is often very difficult to apply in practice. The first requirement is to be able to identify the profit per product and then to apportion it among the entities involved. This basis often uses a functional analysis by reference to the functions supplied by each to the overall product. These would include items such as management, administration and finance, manufacturing, assembling and processing, tasting, research and development, packaging, labelling, warehousing, preserving, storing, distribution, branding, marketing, wholesaling, retailing, transportation, advertising, after sales servicing, warranties and guarantees, ownership of intellectual property and brand names and capital employed by each enterprise. The analysis of risk should take account of the commercial risk to each entity, taking account of parent company guarantees and support, liabilities to third parties, product and environmental liabilities, employee liabilities, financing costs and political and currency risks. Any such functional analysis needs to be evidenced by appropriate contemporary evidence.

The functional analysis may be complicated by set-off where, for example, patent licences are granted by the parent company to the local manufacturer who, in turn, develops the production know-how in the light of manufacturing experience and customer input, which is passed back to the parent company and perhaps ultimately incorporated in further patented developments of the product.

A profit split may have to take account of market penetration strategies whereby products are heavily discounted in a new market in order to obtain a critical market share with a view to increasing profits to acceptable levels in a reasonably short time. If such a strategy is accepted it may be a loss split method for the whole or part of the chain.

As well as functional analysis a contribution analysis may be useful where the profits are allocated on the basis of the relative value of the functions performed by each entity in the chain. The trouble with this approach is that it is likely to be highly subjective and difficult to obtain evidence to confirm the analysis put forward. In some cases market data may be available to support an analysis on this basis.

Residual analysis requires the total profit from the entire transaction to be allocated on the basis of a theoretical margin, dependent on the services provided by each transaction in the chain and comparing this with the overall margin resulting in a residual profit or loss, which itself is allocated to those areas most responsible for the final results. The initial split on a residual analysis may take account of the cash flow projections from the transactions being considered.

Comparable profits method The comparable profit method (CPM) also seeks to arrive at an arm's length price using a functional analysis approach. The return on assets and other financial ratios such as net profit to sales are analysed in order to arrive at a net profit for the connected transaction. Again the problem is finding comparable data that is available in the public domain and to adjust for differences between the transactions under review and the model taken as comparison.

This sort of comparison is only likely to give an acceptable result if data over several years is compared both for the controlled transactions and the chosen comparison.

The rate of return method This method, which is not referred to as such in the OECD 1995 draft report, is a variant of the comparable profits method which looks at the reasonableness of the return on equity or net assets between the connected entities and independent comparable transactions. A return on equity is unlikely to be meaningful given the substantial differences in financing between independent companies and the debt-to-equity ratios which they use. A return on assets employed may be more helpful but has to take into account assets not used directly in the business and other distorting factors, such as inflation and the value of intangible assets.

The problem with comparable profit methods is the difficulty of adjusting adequately for differences between the connected party transactions and the independent comparisons.

Global methods Methods that allocate profit by reference to costs of turnover, labour costs etc, may be easy to calculate but end up by producing a result that is almost entirely arbitrary.

Arm's length range

The problem with trying to identify an arm's length price for transfer pricing purposes is that in most cases it does not exist, because the goods or services under consideration are not available in the same quantity and quality in unconnected transactions. The various methods suggested to try and arrive at the arm's length price necessarily contain a substantial degree of subjective judgement and the OECD report recognises the dangers of chasing a chimera by recognising that there is a range within which a price could be said to be arm's length. There is a danger in any transfer pricing exercise in the Revenue authorities trying to substitute their own commercial judgement for that of the enterprise which they are examining, often with the benefit of hindsight which was not available to those fixing the price for the original transactions. The OECD report warns against this danger and emphasises the requirement to find the arm's length price for the transactions that have actually taken place, not those which the Revenue authorities wish had taken place. There are occasions when the actual transaction can be recast but only where the commercial reality of the transaction is dressed up in a manner which is different from its form, such as where interest is in reality a dividend or distribution of profits.

So far as this book is concerned the main area of interest in transfer pricing is that relating to the licensing of intangibles, not the transfer price to be attached to goods or services, although these may have relevance in, for example, a franchising operation, and the techniques mentioned *above* will normally be the most appropriate, in particular the comparable uncontrolled price method, where feasible.

With regard to services, a distinction has to be drawn between managerial, technical and commercial services which are to the benefit of the paying company's trade, and central management and servicing costs, including the costs of controlling the overall enterprise, and shareholder costs related to the production of group accounts and financial controls to safeguard shareholders' interests. The extent to which such central management costs should be passed down to the overseas subsidiaries is likely to be disputed by the local fiscal authorities and excluded from their transfer pricing calculations. Some of these control costs will actually have a direct benefit reflected in the proper management of the subsidiary and should be allowable. Methods of calculating such costs and apportioning them vary from group to group but a direct cost charge for head office functions of benefit to the subsidiary would normally be acceptable, and an allocation by reference to turnover, profit or other arbitrary basis would often be acceptable provided that it was supported by the contractual arrangements between the parties and applied consistently from year to year in accordance with generally accepted accounting principles.

Intangibles

With regard to intangibles, the OECD report distinguishes between production intangibles such as patents, know-how, designs, models etc, and marketing intangibles such as trade marks, trade names, logos etc. These two categories of intangibles can be further sub-divided between the transfer of particular intangibles such as the sale or licence of intellectual property, or the sale of goods protected by intellectual property, where the value of the patent, for example, is reflected in the price charged for the goods. In such cases where the purchaser has no benefit from the underlying intellectual property, the transaction should be regarded as sale of goods and not a transfer of intellectual property.

The other area of intangible rights coming into transfer pricing calculations is where there are group research and development facilities recharged to group companies benefiting or likely to benefit from the research and development on a cost contribution basis, or directly commissioned research and development contracts where the purchasing company specifically commissions another company in the group, in a different jurisdiction, to develop a particular product or service for the benefit of the commissioning company. In such circumstances the terms of the contract may determine who owns any resultant intellectual property and who has the right to exploit it further and on what terms. Any Revenue authority is obviously likely to be suspicious of arrangements whereby group companies in tax haven jurisdictions are commissioned to develop particular products on behalf of profitable companies and then in turn sub-contract the research and development work to high technology, high cost centres, with the result that the costs of development attract substantial tax relief but the intellectual property ends up owned by the tax haven company which is then in a position to licence worldwide at a royalty rate which reflects the pioneering nature of the invention.

Again, the main problem of applying transfer pricing rules to intangibles is the difficulty of finding comparable royalty rates for what are normally unique situations. The OECD report is very firmly in favour of the concept of the arm's length royalty which would have been paid by the licensee to the licensor, totally rejecting the American concept of the super-royalty under which the compensation receivable by the transferor should be commensurate with the actual income which can be generated from the licensed rights. In one of the few recent cases on the value of trade marks, before the Hong Kong Board of Review, it was held that in the circumstances the use of a notional 5 per cent royalty in the valuation was correct.

It is important to ensure that the licensing of intellectual property is fully recorded in written agreements and the methodology used in calculating the royalty rate is retained in order to justify to an investigating Revenue authority that this is within the range of an acceptable arm's length price. Evidence of royalty rates is difficult to come by as few are in the public domain. It is generally accepted that it is unfair for a Revenue authority to challenge royalty levels on the basis of confidential information available to it, which cannot be produced, as evidence for the dissatisfaction with the rates actually used.

The consideration of appropriate royalty rates is dealt with in more detail in Chapter 12 (*see* pp 130–2) on the valuation of intellectual property. One of the commercial realities that makes the calculation of royalty rates difficult is that the value of the invention may have little direct relevance to the research and development costs spent on it. In the real world much research and development expenditure is inevitably abortive and some of the most valuable inventions have arisen as a by-product from efforts to develop something else entirely. This makes the use of techniques such as cash flow-based net present valuation calculations somewhat suspect.

In the field of marketing related intangibles, the activities of the licensee have to be considered as well as those of the licensor. The licensee's local advertising, for example, may have a beneficial effect on the value of the worldwide trade mark so that the licensee is not merely paying for the use of the trade mark but contributing to its development. In cases where franchising is involved it may be possible to arrive at a useful comparison by comparing the royalty levels for arm's length franchisees in certain territories compared with the levels charged to connected licensees in others. However, even this comparison may be influenced by questions of volume, market penetration, maturity of the market etc, and as in all transfer pricing negotiations, a good deal of judgement is required in considering the relevance which should be attached to any raw data.

Inland Revenue practice

IM 4651 mentions the alternatives to a transfer pricing adjustment, ie a disallowance under TA 1988, s 74; the substitution of market value for sales at undervalue relying on *Sharkey v Wernher* (1955) 36 TC 275, *Petrotim Securities Ltd v Ayres* (1963) 41 TC 389 and *Skinner v Berry Head Lands Ltd* (1970) 46 TC 377; transaction between connected parties under TCGA 1992, s 18; intra-group transfers under TCGA 1992, s 173 and distributions under TA 1988, s 209(4). Also considered is the associated enterprise article of the relevant double taxation agreement and arguments that the non-resident company may, in fact, be resident in the UK. The controlled foreign company legislation (*see* Chapter 14) is also referred to.

IM 4652 explains that the transfer pricing provisions can apply to transactions with branches as if the branch were the company of which it is a part so that, for example, transfer pricing adjustments could apply between the UK branch of an American company and an associated UK or overseas company, but transfer pricing adjustments cannot be made to transactions between a company and its own branch as it is part of the same entity, although the business profits article of the double tax treaty might enable adjustments to be made.

The extension of transfer pricing adjustments under TA 1988, s 770 by TA 1988, s 773(4) to lettings and hiring of property, grants and transfers of rights, interests or licenses and the giving of business facilities of whatever kind is referred to, and it is confirmed that in the Revenue view an interest-free loan is within the transfer pricing provisions, although these rules cannot be extended to impute dividends from overseas subsidiaries to UK-resident parents where none has been paid, although the controlled foreign company rules may apply in such circumstances (*see* Chapter 14).

IM 4654 defines the circumstances in which transfer pricing adjustments apply and the meaning of the various definitions, including sale, which is deemed to take place at the earlier of the time of completion and the time when possession is given, under TA 1988, s 773(2).

The Revenue's information gathering powers are explained in IM 4655 and it is pointed out that these wide-ranging powers only apply to obtaining information from bodies corporate, not other bodies or persons such as partnerships. It is also emphasised that only the Revenue can authorise the information powers. Local inspectors are advised to refer to International Division in appropriate cases. It is suggested that information not available through the information powers in TA 1988, s 772, for example the accounts of overseas members and foreign-owned groups, may be obtained in suitable cases using the exchange of information article in the relevant double taxation agreement.

IM 4656 sets out arm's length pricing methods, in particular the comparable uncontrolled price method, cost plus method, the resale minus method and other approaches such as the functional division of net profit, with the following example:

Example

For example, if company A manufactures a product in the UK and non-resident associate, company B, sells the product overseas, the costs and profits may be capable of adaptation from the accounts or for individual products to the following format:

B's end sale price to third parties	100
Purchase price from A	90
B's gross profit	10
B's added costs	5
A's sale price to B	90
Cost of sales	50
A's gross profit	40
A's added costs	30
A's net profit	10
Total added costs: 30 + 5 =	35
Total profits: 10 + 5 =	15

If, for example, an examination of the trade suggests that the manufacturing and sales functions should be given equal weight, the overall profit can be allocated in proportion to added costs to reflect this.

A's profit would then become:

$$\frac{\text{A's added costs}}{\text{Total added costs}} \times \text{Total profits}$$

$$\frac{30}{35} \times 15 = 12.9$$

and B's profit would be:

$$\frac{5}{35} \times 15 = 2.1$$

The profit and loss statements of the two companies could then be re-written as follows:

Company A	
Sale price to B	92.9
Cost of sales	50.0
Gross profit	42.9
Added costs	30.0
Net profit	12.9
Company B	
End sale price to third parties	100.0
Purchase price from A	92.9
Gross profit	7.1
Added costs	5.0
Net profit	2.1

Reference is made to the OECD publication *Transfer Pricing Guidelines for Multinational Enterprises and Tax Administrations* 1995.

Guidance on the practical selection of cases is given by IM 4657, and the Inspector is reminded that the aim in selecting cases suitable for a transfer pricing enquiry is to pick cases where there appear to be strong grounds for thinking that goods, services, facilities etc are being priced between associated persons in such a way that there is a loss of UK tax. Large and/or complex cases should be referred to International Division. It is also pointed out that all UK associates must be included in the initial review, as without a complete picture the potential of an enquiry cannot be evaluated.

The Inspector is directed towards companies owned by a company in a tax haven or where there are tax haven subsidiaries in the group, although he is reminded that particular income in a high tax rate country may still effectively escape tax. The nature of the trade is also to be considered and in particular patent right or know-how dependent industries are suggested as likely targets. An examination of the UK accounts compared with those of the consolidated group may indicate UK profits lower than expected which require investigation. Sales, distribution and service companies are dealt with in IM 4658.

Intangible rights are dealt with in IM 4659 and as such rights are normally licensed rather than sold outright, the International Division is interested in cases where UK-owned intangible rights are sold outright to an overseas associate, or where tangible assets are purchased by a UK company but intangible assets by an overseas associate. A cross-reference is made to CG 68654 where the brand name has been sold but the vendor will continue to use the name and pay a royalty for its future use. CG 68651 states that CGT(Solihull) would like to be told of any case where a trade mark or brand name is transferred without the associated business. Enquiries into intellectual property based transfer pricing matters are recommended to be referred to International Division.

It is pointed out that payments made for intangible right to associates in tax havens are to be treated with caution as the underlying research and development is unlikely to have been undertaken there, and may have been transferred from elsewhere in the group, and possibly from the UK, at an undervalue. Payments which appear to be excessive are round sums, or where there is an element of double counting ie where completed goods are purchased and a royalty is paid for the intellectual property in those goods.

It is also pointed out that payments due to UK companies in the group may be inadequate although it is accepted that the UK associate may be getting reciprocal benefits to the same or greater value free of charge. Interest-free loans are dealt with by IM 4660. It is recognised that a thinly capitalised overseas subsidiary funded by an interest-free loan from the UK might be being funded through quasi-equity, and therefore imputed interest may be inappropriate depending upon the wording of the associated enterprises article of the double taxation agreement. In the case of an investment the disallowance of part of the loan interest under TA 1988, s 209(2)(*d*) or (*e*)(iii), (iv) or (v) should not be overlooked.

IM 4661 outlines those cases which should be referred to International Division, the most interesting of which is where it is suspected that royalty or other payments to overseas associates may be excessive because of over-compliance with the transfer pricing legislation of another jurisdiction. This emphasises one of the fundamental problems of transfer pricing. Because the whole basis of the system envisages transfers between entities in different jurisdictions, the fiscal authorities of each jurisdiction will have an interest in the resultant transfer price and in many cases their taxpayer is not particularly concerned as to the transfer price finally fixed so long as it is the same in both jurisdictions. This may give rise to a corresponding adjustment claim under the competent authority provisions in a double taxation agreement dealt with at IM 4662. The purpose of a corresponding adjustment claim is to ensure that any transfer pricing adjustment taxed by a foreign jurisdiction is reflected in an adjustment to the UK taxable profits by the other party to the transaction, to avoid economic double taxation. Such claims are dealt with by International Division. Where a company considers it is in a position to make a corresponding adjustment claim it may approach the Inland Revenue who will then take up the transfer pricing adjustment proposed with the other Revenue authority and endeavour to agree a figure acceptable to both authorities. The Revenue does not like undisclosed claims for a deduction in a company's accounts reflecting another country's transfer pricing adjustment as this may deprive the Revenue of the opportunity of challenging the suggested adjustment with the other Revenue authority.

US royalties

The Internal Revenue Service of the USA has gone further than any other Revenue authority in trying to determine a set procedure for arriving at the proper royalty level in a transfer pricing situation. Proposed inter-company transfer pricing and cost-sharing regulations were published under s 482 of the US Internal Revenue Code as amended by the Tax Reform Act of 1986. The American provisions seek to ensure that the royalty level for intangible property be commensurate with the income attributable to that property. These regulations set out a matching transaction method which is the first choice in arriving at the appropriate royalty level. It will be extremely rare to have a totally matching transaction and the second most desirable basis is the comparable adjustable transaction method where it is possible to determine and quantify the differences between an arm's length situation and a controlled transfer price situation. Again, it is often not easy to find suitable examples and it is then necessary to consider an arm's length consideration determined under the comparable profit method. This method requires a comparison of the operating income that results from the consideration actually charged in a controlled transfer with the operating incomes of similar taxpayers that are uncontrolled.

It may also be possible to consider a fourth method where the comparable uncontrolled price method is inapplicable, provided that the end result can be shown to produce a result which falls within the comparable profit range ('comparable profit interval' in the USA).

The American regulations are set out in very considerable detail with the steps to be followed in each case and innumerable examples are given. The whole problem of the American approach, however, when compared with the normal arm's length approach adopted elsewhere, is the requirement that the consideration for intangible property be commensurate with the income attributable to the intangible. In real arm's length situations it is normal to agree a royalty level probably varying with production and covering a period of years. The licensor will, when negotiating the terms of the licensing agreement, obviously take into account the likely value of the intellectual property to the licensee and therefore the royalty level that he might be able to extract. The licensee will similarly have to have consideration for the value of the licence in terms of the profits he is likely to make after payment of the royalty. Once the agreement has been entered into, however, if the licensee is particularly successful in making profits, which would no doubt be partly attributable to the value of the licence, he would not expect the royalty level to vary other than on the basis of production as agreed in the licensing of contract. Conversely, if he is less successful than anticipated and the royalty payable does not leave him with sufficient profit he will scale down production, subject of course to the terms of the agreement.

Very often the licensor will now know the profit generated by the licensee attributable to the intellectual property licensed and the licensee would regard such information as highly confidential. The commercial reality of licensing is therefore in immediate conflict with the American approach which envisages a renegotiation of the deal each year with the benefit of hindsight into what the IRS think it would have been had that information, which did not even exist at the time, been available to the parties. As the assumptions that are required to be made are so far away from the real world it is not surprising that it often results in a 'super-royalty' that would not be acceptable to the Revenue authority of the licensee, with the result that the American parent is taxed on a royalty commensurate with the income deemed to be generated from the intellectual property, while the licensee is allowed to deduct only an arm's length royalty such as would be payable in a real commercial situation between arm's length companies. The economic double taxation that this gives rise to can only be mitigated if the competent authority procedure under a double tax treaty can be successfully invoked and if the two Revenue authorities involved are prepared to agree a compromise transfer price acceptable to both authorities. The multinational company sitting in the middle of this argument will often feel that it does not mind particularly what royalty level is to be used as long as it is the same one for both the licensor and the licensee and is acceptable to both Revenue authorities.

This in turn means that the likelihood of there being economic double taxation is going to increase. Although a number of double taxation agreements with the USA seek to eliminate economic double taxation through the competent authority procedure, experience would suggest that this is a slow and unsatisfactory method of dealing with the problem. Although the USA, for example, will approve an advance pricing agreement between the taxpayer, the IRS and the overseas Revenue authority, this may not be practical in the payer country if, as in the UK, there is no procedure for agreement in advance with the Inland Revenue.

The IRS has put forward a functional analysis approach to fixing royalty levels by asking what was done, what economically significant factors were involved in doing it, who performed each function and what is the measure of economic value of each function performed by each party. In practice these questions may be answered by applying a number of methods: the matching transactions method, the comparable adjustable transaction method and the comparable profit method. The matching transaction method applies where there is an exact comparable in an arm's length situation between the American owner of the intellectual property and a licensee abroad. It will of course be fairly unusual in practice to find an exact comparable in this way and the comparable adjustable transaction method is more likely to be met with in practice. This allows for an inexact comparable.

Under the comparable profit method the total profit arising from the exploitation of the intangible is allocated in accordance with the perceived economic contribution of each party. Where more than one party is involved in the development of the intangible, one is regarded as the developer and the others as assisters, all of whom must be adequately remunerated for their contribution.

The IRS approach is codified in the regulations. If the agreement covers more than one year the fact that it is accepted in one year may not make it acceptable for a subsequent year and the 'commensurate within income' test has to be applied each year. The comparable profit interval used for testing the arm's length consideration for intangibles is based on a three-year period covering the audit year and the previous and subsequent years. Cost sharing arrangements may be approved under which each party contributes to the cost of developing the product in return for a commensurate share in the resulting intellectual property.

In view of the problems arising from this American super-royalty concept it may be preferable to substitute some form of contract manufacturing agreement for a licence agreement under which the overseas subsidiary would manufacture for the American parent which would make the sales and pay a price for the goods based on cost plus a reasonable percentage profit to the overseas manufacturer, say, cost plus 10 per cent.

In practice it is usually a good idea to have as much detail for the transfer price calculation as possible, with projected sales and results of both licensor and licensee and comparable royalty levels charged by third parties where known in circumstances as similar as possible, in order to build up a comprehensive picture of why the royalty level is fixed at the rate agreed and to show that the intention is merely to arrive at a commercial royalty level and not to avoid taxes.

Customs valuations

Customs, duties and VAT on goods and services passing between associated companies may be computed by reference to valuations imposed by the Excise Authorities and not necessarily by reference to the prices agreed between the connected parties or those agreed for direct tax purposes.

Double taxation treaties

Whereas double taxation treaties are designed to prevent double taxation on the same income, they do have relevance to transfer pricing in a number of respects. Although each bilateral treaty has to be examined with care, as there are substantial differences between them, the majority of treaties follow the OECD Model Tax Convention on Income and Capital published by the OECD Committee on fiscal affairs in 1992 with subsequent updates. This in turn is based on 1977 and 1963 and earlier models. There are other model treaties such as the United Nations Model Double Taxation Convention between Developed and Developing Countries published in 1980 by United Nations Publications and the Nordic Convention on Income and Capital published in 1989, as well as the US Model Double Taxation Treaty which the Internal Revenue Service attempts to impose on its treaty partners.

The business profits article (article 7) in the OECD Model Treaty, under para 2, requires each state to attribute to the taxable permanent establishment the profits which it might be expected to make if it were a distinct and separate enterprise engaged in the same or similar activities under the same or similar conditions and dealing wholly independently with the enterprise of which it is a permanent establishment. This requires the allocation of profits to a foreign branch or subsidiary to reflect the arm's length principle and therefore allows for, in effect, transfer pricing adjustments where that principle has not been followed. Both income and expenses have to be allocated in order to arrive at the arm's length profit and in the case of intellectual property rights the OECD commentary suggests that the costs of creation of such rights might be attributable to all parts of the enterprise including permanent establishments who are users of them, and thus allocation would be without any profit mark-up or royalties.

If royalties are charged, article 12 normally allows such royalties to be taxable only in the country of the beneficial recipient. However, article 12(4) allows the royalties paid to be adjusted to the amount which would have been agreed upon by the payer and beneficial owner had the royalty level been fixed at arm's length, where there is a special relationship between the payer and the beneficial owner, or between both of them and some other person, and the royalty paid exceeds the amount which would have been agreed in the absence of such special relationship.

Similar provisions apply for interest under article 11(6) of the Model Convention.

The associated enterprises article (article 9) allows the Revenue authority to adjust profits of an enterprise resident in their state (a) where an enterprise of one contracting state participates directly or indirectly in the management, control or capital of an enterprise in the other contracting state or (b) the same persons participate directly or indirectly in the management, control or capital of an enterprise of the contracting state and (c) conditions are made or imposed between the enterprises which differ from those which would be made between independent enterprises.

The article requires the competent authorities of each state to consult on such adjustments. It is not a requirement of any such adjustment that both fiscal authorities accept the adjustment, although an aggrieved party can require the competent authority to negotiate with its colleagues in the other jurisdiction under the mutual agreement procedure (article 25 of the Model Convention). They cannot however force agreement and within the European Union this has given rise to the Arbitration Convention.

14 Controlled foreign companies

Introduction

The purpose of the controlled foreign company (CFC) legislation is to prevent UK companies avoiding UK tax by diverting profits to offshore tax havens. Until 1979, companies had to repatriate profits under the exchange control legislation; its abolition led to a new look at the definition of company residence for tax purposes, and proposals for the taxation of tax haven profits (first introduced in the USA) and an attack on upstream loans for offshore tax haven subsidiaries to high tax areas. Consultation documents were produced in 1981, and in 1984 the controlled foreign company legislation was enacted. The company residence changes were subsequently modified but the upstream loan legislation was dropped for the time being.

A controlled foreign company is one which is resident outside the UK, is controlled by persons resident in the UK, is subject to a lower level of taxation in the territory in which it is resident, and where the Inland Revenue make a direction that the controlled foreign company provisions will apply. There are proposals to change the CFC rules on the introduction of company self-assessment to require companies to self-assess their CFC income rather than await a direction from the Revenue under TA 1988, s 747(1).

Residence

The question of whether the company is resident outside the UK is dealt with by TA 1988, s 748, which provides that the company is regarded as resident in the territory in which it is liable to tax by reason of its domicile, residence or place of management (TA 1988, s 749(1)). There are tie-breaker provisions where the company might be regarded as resident in more than one territory, with the intention of pinning down a single jurisdiction. It is the place of the company's effective management, which is not the same as the UK residence test of central management and control. The place of effective management, in the Revenue view, is generally understood to be the place where the head office is, not the registered office, but the central directing source where the finance director, sales director and managing director are based, together with the company records and senior administrative staff. The fact that the directors' meetings were held in a different jurisdiction would not move the place of effective management (ITH 348). Where the place of effective management is in two or more territories, it is the territory where the greater amount of the company's assets at the end of the accounting period is situated; if this does not pinpoint one of the territories, it is the territory where it is liable to tax by reason of its domicile residence or place of management in which it has the greater amount of its assets situated at the end of the accounting period; if this still does not identify the territory it may be specified by a direction of the Revenue (TA 1988, s 749(2)). If the company is not liable to tax anywhere it is presumed to be resident in a tax haven. In determining where the greater amount of a company's assets are situated at the end of the accounting period, the market value not the book value of the assets has to be considered.

A UK-resident company that is, for example, UK-resident by reason of incorporation under FA 1988, s 66, may nonetheless be treated as non-resident under FA 1994, s 249 if it would be dual resident under a double tax treaty.

Control

In order to determine whether the company is 'controlled by persons resident in the UK' it is necessary to look at the definition of control in TA 1988, s 416(2) by reason of TA 1988, s 756(3). A person has control of a company if he exercises or is able to exercise, or is entitled to acquire, direct or indirect control over the company's affairs, and in particular if he possesses, or is entitled to acquire, a greater part of the company's share capital or issued share capital or voting power, or which would entitle him to receive a greater part of the amount distributed if the whole of the income of the company were distributed among participants, ignoring any rights as loan creditor, or which would, in the event of the winding-up of the company, or in any other circumstances, entitle him to receive a greater part of the assets of the company available for distribution among the participators. In looking at this wide definition, two or more persons acting together who satisfy the conditions may have control, and future rights are included, as well as present rights (TA 1988, s 416(3) and (4)). Powers of nominees are included as are the rights of any company which the person and his associates control, if the attribution results in the company being treated as under the control of UK residents. The effect of this definition is to require UK residents to have more than 50 per cent control, and therefore a total deadlock company where the holding is precisely 50 per cent is not within the controlled foreign company legislation.

'Loan creditor' has the meaning given to it by TA 1988, s 417(7)–(9) which excludes banks. Connected persons are defined by TA 1988, s 839, ie spouse, brother, brother-in-law, sister, sister-in-law, parent, parent-in-law, grandparent, grandparent-in-law, son, son-in-law, daughter, daughter-in-law, grandson, grandson-in-law, granddaughter, granddaughter-in-law, trustee of a settlement with the settlor and a person connected with the settlor, and a company connected with the settlement and partners. 'Associates' are similarly widely defined by TA 1988, s 783(10) (TA 1988, s 756(2)).

Lower level of taxation

A company is subject to a lower level of taxation where the local tax is less than three-quarters of the corresponding UK tax on those profits, calculated under UK taxation rules, in accordance with TA 1988, Sched 24, on the assumption that a direction were made and ignoring double taxation relief, but deducting income tax deducted at source and corporation tax actually paid and not refunded (TA 1988, s 750). Profits computed in a foreign currency are translated at the rate of the last day of the accounting period (TA 1988, s 750(5)–(8)); the Revenue publish a non-statutory 'white list' of countries which are accepted as not subjecting countries in their jurisdiction to a lower level of taxation and therefore excluding countries resident in such territories from the controlled foreign company legislation. In some cases, countries are only accepted as not falling within the controlled foreign company provisions if they do not fall within specific beneficial provisions in the qualified excluded company list (*see* pp 483–5 *below*).

Specific exclusions

Even though the company may technically be within the controlled foreign company legislation as being a non-resident under the control of persons resident in the UK and subject to a lower level of taxation where it is resident, it may nonetheless escape the consequences of being a controlled foreign company, that is the apportionment of its income to UK-resident shareholders, if it falls within any one of five specific exclusions.

These exclusions apply where the controlled foreign company has paid reasonable dividends, so that the profits are brought into the UK tax net and taxed as income of the recipient shareholders. This is known as the 'acceptable distributions' test.

It is not the intention of the controlled foreign company legislation to 'kill off' genuine overseas trading by British companies merely because that trading happens to take place in a low tax area; accordingly, genuine trading companies within such an area are excluded, as are local holding companies holding and co-ordinating the shares and activities of companies trading in such an area. This is known as the 'exempt activities' test.

Where the controlled foreign company is publicly quoted in its own right, the fact that there are controlling shareholders in the UK does not make it subject to a controlled foreign company apportionment. There would obviously be conflicts if this public quotation test were not available, between the interests of the general public shareholders who might wish the company to develop by re-investing much of its profits, and the UK-controlling shareholders who would need to distribute practically the whole of the profit, in order to avoid a controlled foreign company apportionment and so pay tax on income which they did not receive.

There is also a *de minimus* test where the profits of the controlled foreign company are at such a level that it is not worth going through the distribution procedure for the amount of tax that would be raised.

The fifth exclusion is a motive test, which applies where it can be shown that tax avoidance was not the reason for setting up the structure and running the business in the way in which it is done.

Acceptable distribution policy test

A controlled foreign company follows an acceptable distribution policy (ADP), where a dividend is paid for and during an accounting period, or within 18 months thereafter, which is by reference to a period rather than profits from a particular source such as a distribution of exceptional exchange profits. The dividend must be sufficient to ensure that at least 90 per cent of the company's net chargeable profits are distributed to UK residents (TA 1988, Sched 25, para 2). The normal rules for computing underlying tax on dividends for double taxation relief purposes in TA 1988, s 799 are applied to relate the dividends to the profits of a controlled foreign company. The percentage to be distributed to UK residents is reduced proportionately when there is only one class of shares, some of which are held by non-residents. A more complicated formula is available where there are two classes of shares, one being non-voting fixed rate preference shares, which is designed to ensure that the UK-held proportion of the preference share dividend is received by UK residents and the UK-held proportion of the remaining dividend is also received by UK residents. Any more complex share structure makes it impossible to meet the distribution requirements. It may be necessary to make adjustments to these distribution requirements where the shareholdings held by UK residents at the end of the accounting period do not accurately reflect their interest in the company during the period and to take into account shares held indirectly.

Currently the distribution standard required is 90 per cent of the company's net chargeable profits, taking into account distributions out of profits of earlier accounting periods which have not already been taxed under the controlled foreign company legislation (TA 1988, Sched 25, para 2A). There is a useful article on controlled foreign companies in the Inland Revenue's *Tax Bulletin*, Issue 12, p 138 (*see* pp 486–91 *below*).

The chargeable profits on which the distribution standard has to be applied are those as computed for UK tax if the controlled foreign corporation had been UK-resident, excluding the chargeable gains (TA 1988, s 747(6)). A deduction may be made for the creditable tax, which is the tax for which credit would be given if a CFC distribution were made, but the source rules are disapplied for this purpose so that any foreign tax suffered can be set off. Where a controlled foreign company pays on, as a distribution out of specific profits, dividends received from another controlled foreign company, the dividend is left out of account in determining the profits chargeable to tax for calculating the distribution (TA 1988, Sched 25, para 3). A dividend from a controlled foreign company only counts as having been paid to a UK resident if it is paid up through a chain, if it passes up through a related company in which at least 10 per cent of the voting shares are held directly or indirectly, and is taxable income of the ultimate recipient for corporation tax purposes (TA 1988, Sched 25, para 4).

The acceptable distribution test was originally based on the controlled foreign company's accounting profits, not the profits as adjusted for UK tax purposes and was only 50 per cent in the case of trading companies. Both these provisions were thought to be open to abuse and were changed, although the result is that it may be difficult to meet the distribution requirement if there is any material difference between the controlled foreign company's statutory accounts and the results as computed for UK tax purposes. Further changes to the controlled foreign company legislation to make it compatible for self-assessment are under consideration and may include a reduction in the acceptable distribution requirement to 80 per cent. It is argued that the UK system of corporation tax is extremely complicated and the notional treatment of a controlled foreign company as within the UK tax net, as if it were UK-resident, gives rise to problems of whether or not thin capitalisation rules then apply; and in particular the loan relationship and foreign exchange provisions do not sit happily with the controlled foreign company rules, particularly where the currency of the accounts which has to be used for controlled foreign company calculations is a volatile local currency.

Exempt activities test

In order to pass this test a controlled foreign company must be engaged in activities in the territory in which it is resident and which is deemed to be the low tax area identified under TA 1988, s 749(3) (TA 1988, Sched 25, para 5). It must have a business establishment consisting of permanent premises from which the business is carried on in the territory (TA 1988, Sched 25, para 7) and its business affairs must effectively be controlled and managed from the territory, in which it must employ sufficient personnel to deal with its business such that no major services are provided to the company by persons resident in the UK, unless the controlled foreign company has a UK-resident branch, or the services are merely incidental, or are charged from the UK on an arm's length basis. Employees working wholly or mainly in an active company in the territory or who are employees of a local holding company, as defined by TA 1988, Sched 25, para 6(3), are within this requirement. The main business of the controlled foreign company must not consist of investment, including the holding of securities, patents or copyrights, dealing in securities otherwise than as a broker, leasing, and investment of funds of connected persons (TA 1988, Sched 25, para 9). It is this provision which catches group intellectual property holding companies in tax havens.

The controlled foreign company must not be dealing in goods for delivery to or from the UK or to or from connected or associated persons except for importing goods from the UK for sale in the territory (TA 1988, Sched 25, para 10). If it is engaged in wholesale distributive or financial business, less than 50 per cent of its gross trading receipts from such a business must be derived from connected or associated persons who have an interest in the company (TA 1988, Sched 25, para 6(2)). A wholesale distributive or financial business includes dealing in goods wholesale, shipping or air transport, banking, trust administration, broking of securities, dealing in commodities or financial futures and long term or general insurance business (TA 1988, Sched 25, para 11(1)). A local holding company may pass the exempt activities test, if it is one where at least 90 per cent of its gross income is derived directly from companies which it controls, and which are both resident in the same territory as the holding company and are not themselves holding companies but engaged in exempt activities (TA 1988, Sched 25, para 6(3)). This is extended to include companies not within the definition of a local holding company if at least 90 per cent of its income comes from local holding companies or companies engaged in exempt activities (TA 1988, Sched 25, para 6(4)). A holding company, as defined by TA 1988, Sched 25, para 12, must hold the maximum ordinary shares in its subsidiaries permitted by the territory which caters for those countries which require a local participation. A number of terms are defined by TA 1988, Sched 12, para 11.

Public quotation test

TA 1988, Sched 12, para 13 allows the company to pass this test where, in respect of a particular accounting period, shares controlling more than 35 per cent of the total voting power of the company, excluding fixed rate preference dividends, have been allotted unconditionally to, or acquired unconditionally by, the public, and are beneficially held by them throughout the accounting period. The shares must have been dealt with on a recognised stock exchange in the territory in which the company is resident and listed in the official list of that exchange within 12 months of the end of the accounting period. Where, however, the total percentage of the voting shares held by the company's principal members, ie those holding 5 per cent or more of the voting power, or one of the five persons who possesses the greatest percentage of shares in the company exceeds 85 per cent, it cannot meet the public quotation condition. The shares in a controlled foreign company are deemed to be beneficially held by the public only if they are held by persons other than those connected or associated with the company or are principal members of the company (TA 1988, Sched 25, paras 14 and 15).

De minimus test

This exclusion applies under TA 1988, s 748(1)(*d*) where the chargeable profits of the accounting period do not exceed £20,000 per annum.

Motive test

The motive test under TA 1988, s 748(3) may be passed where it appears to the Revenue that if a transaction or series of transactions achieved a reduction in UK tax, either the reduction was minimal or it was not the main, or one of the main, purposes of the transaction to achieve that reduction and the company did not exist in the accounting period in order to achieve a reduction in UK tax by diversion of profits from the UK. A transaction or series of transactions achieve a reduction in tax if the liability to income tax, corporation tax or capital gains tax would otherwise have been greater or a relief or repayment smaller (TA 1988, Sched 25, paras 16 and 17). If it is the purpose of the CFC or a person who has an interest in the CFC to achieve a reduction in tax, it is one of the main purposes, under TA 1988, Sched 25, para 18. There is a diversion of profits from the UK if, had the controlled foreign company or a company related to it not existed, the receipt would have been received by a UK resident or such receipts would have been greater or reliefs would have been smaller (TA 1988, Sched 25, para 19). The operation of a clearance procedure for the application of the motive test for controlled foreign companies is set out in the Inland Revenue Press Release of 9 November 1994 (*see* pp 479–80 *below*).

Apportionment

Where none of the exclusions apply and the Inland Revenue make the appropriate direction, an amount equivalent to corporation tax on the profits apportioned to a UK-resident company, less the creditable tax of the controlled foreign company, is recoverable as if it were corporation tax (TA 1988, s 747(4)(*a*)). It was held in the Court of Appeal decision in *Bricom Holdings Ltd v IRC* (1997) STC 1179, that a double taxation treaty did not protect against such an apportionment. It is understood that this case will not proceed further. There is a useful article in the Inland Revenue *Tax Bulletin*, Issue 19, October 1995, p 249 (*see* pp 491–3 *below*).

Where profits have been brought into the UK tax net through a controlled foreign company apportionment, they cannot also be brought in under the transfer of assets abroad provisions of TA 1988, s 739 (TA 1988, s 747(4)(*b*)). Apportionment is only made to a UK company where it or its associates are entitled to at least 10 per cent of the controlled foreign company's chargeable profits (TA 1988, s 747(5)). This means that there is no apportionment under the controlled foreign company legislation to an individual or trust shareholder where the anti-avoidance provisions relating to transfers of assets abroad would normally apply to prevent any avoidance of UK tax under TA 1988, ss 739–746. Nor will an apportionment be made to an independent company holding less than 10 per cent in the controlled foreign company.

Chargeable profits

TA 1988, s 747A provides that for all accounting periods beginning after 22 March 1995, a controlled foreign company has to compute its chargeable profits in the currency in which its accounts are made up, if the accounts are required to be kept in a particular currency; and if there are no such requirements the accounts must be those which most closely correspond to the accounts which a company formed under the Companies Act 1985 is required to keep. Amounts computed in foreign currency are translated at the rate for the last day of the accounting period (TA 1988, s 747(4A), (4B)). Chargeable profits are to be computed in accordance with the detailed ruled in TA 1988, Sched 24 (TA 1988, s 747(6)).

Under these provisions, a company is assumed to be resident in the UK, but otherwise to carry on the business it actually does so that, for example, any UK-source income would remain liable to UK tax, and income exempt in the hands of non-residents would become liable to tax. If it is necessary to determine the chargeable profits of a period for which a direction has not been given, and which is not an ADP exempt period, it is assumed that a direction has been made for that period but not any earlier period. An ADP exempt period is an accounting period beginning on or after 28 November 1995 in respect of which a company pursues an acceptable distribution policy (TA 1988, Sched 24, para 1).

The CFC is assumed not to be a close company (TA 1988, Sched 24, para 3), and is assumed to have become UK-resident at the beginning of the first accounting period in respect of which a direction is given, or which is an ADP exempt period, and thereafter continues to be notionally resident until the company ceases to be controlled by UK residents. It is also assumed that for each such accounting period the chargeable profits and corresponding UK tax have been calculated whether or not a direction has been made so that, for example, losses can be carried forward (TA 1988, Sched 24, para 2).

Claims are notionally assumed to have been made to give the maximum relief against corporation tax, unless the company elects otherwise by notice to the Revenue within 60 days (TA 1988, Sched 24, para 4). Advance corporation tax cannot be surrendered to a controlled foreign company, nor may dividends be received gross as group income, nor is group relief available in computing the chargeable profits or corresponding UK tax (TA 1988, Sched 24, paras 5–7).

A transfer of a trade by a UK company is treated as a succession under TA 1988, s 343, but not a transfer of trade to a controlled foreign company (TA 1988, Sched 24, para 8). Where the controlled foreign company has made a loss within six years prior to the first year of direction it can treat the year of loss as the first year of direction and therefore carry the loss forward against the directed profits, on making a claim within 60 days or such longer period as may be allowed (TA 1988, Sched 24, para 9).

Notional capital allowances are given in computing the chargeable profits and corresponding UK tax, on the basis that, in the first accounting period for which a direction is made or which is an ADP exempt period, the assets at the beginning of the period are deemed to have been brought into use at market value at that date and capital allowances calculated as if CAA 1990, s 81 applied. The Revenue, however, may make a direction that an earlier accounting period is the deemed commencement for the purpose of calculating the chargeable profits and corresponding UK tax if the direction was only avoided in the earlier period because the capital allowances which would have been available would have brought the profits within the *de minimis* level of £20,000 per annum or outside the lower level of taxation as defined by TA 1988, s 750, unless the direction would also have been avoided under one of the other exclusions (TA 1988, Sched 24, paras 10–11A).

A CFC in receipt of income from a third country which cannot be remitted either to the UK or to its country of residence may ignore that income until it can be remitted, as under TA 1988, s 584 (TA 1988, Sched 24, para 12). The rules dealing with exchange gains and losses are adapted for a controlled foreign company as if its profits computed in a foreign currency are the relevant currency for the purpose of these rules (TA 1988, Sched 24, paras 13–19).

An accounting period of a controlled foreign company is deemed to begin when it first comes under the control of persons resident in the UK or when it commences to carry on business, or following the end of the preceding accounting period (TA 1988, s 751(1)). Conversely, an accounting period ends when a company ceases to be under the control of UK residents or ceases to be liable to tax in the territory by reason of its domicile, residence or place of management, or becomes or ceases to be dual resident or ceases to have any source of income. In such circumstances the normal consequences of an accounting period ceasing, in TA 1988, s 2, are applied, with the residual power for the Revenue to specify an accounting period of up to 12 months (TA 1988, s 751(2), (25)).

Creditable tax

In addition to apportioning the income of the controlled foreign company to UK residents who are direct or indirect shareholders, the creditable foreign tax is also calculated and apportioned, and may be set against the UK corporation tax liability on the amount apportioned. The creditable tax is defined by TA 1988, s 751(6) as the double taxation relief which would have been available had the company been resident in the UK, plus any credits for income tax that could be set against corporation tax under TA 1988, s 7(2), plus any UK corporation tax borne by the controlled foreign company. Apportionment may be made to those UK companies with at least a 10 per cent interest in the controlled foreign company in accordance with their respective interests. This would normally be by reference to their shareholding but could be by reference to their rights on a winding-up (TA 1988, s 752(1) and (2)). In the case of a non-trading controlled foreign company the Revenue may include a loan creditor as a potential apportionee, having an interest equivalent to the proportion of the company's income expended on redemption, repayment or discharge of the loan (TA 1988, s 752(3)). Normally apportionment will be in accordance with the apportionees' shareholdings, but if there are several apportionees holding shares directly or indirectly the Revenue may choose to apportion to only those holders resident in the UK, whether their interest is direct or indirect (TA 1988, s 752(4)–(8)). Interest held in trust may be treated as held by the beneficiaries. An example of apportionment is given in the Inland Revenue *Tax Bulletin*, Issue 12, August 1994, p 139 (*see* pp 486–91 *below*).

Information powers

The Revenue have wide powers to obtain information in relation to controlled foreign companies and may serve a notice on any company which, alone or with others, appears to have control of a controlled foreign company to make available for inspection any relevant books or accounts. If the notice requires production of books or records of another company, application may be made for the notice not to have effect, for example, because it would be breaking some foreign laws of confidentiality (TA 1988, s 755).

Directions

Notice of a direction under the controlled foreign company legislation must, under TA 1988, s 753, be given to every UK-resident apportionee company with an interest in the CFC, specifying the date on which it was made and the controlled foreign company to which it relates, the accounting period, the chargeable profits and the creditable tax and any reliefs which it is assumed that the company has claimed. It must also, where appropriate, specify the territory in which the controlled foreign company is regarded as resident and specify the rights to appeal. An appeal must be made within 60 days on the grounds that the direction, or any amendment to it, should not have been made, or that the chargeable profits or creditable tax is incorrectly computed, or that the company did not have an interest in the controlled foreign company and the declarations are therefore invalid. Appeal is to the Special Commissioners and then through the courts. Tax on the amount apportioned is assessable and recoverable as if it were ordinary corporation tax for an accounting period in which the CFC's accounting period ends, and an appeal against such an assessment is to the Special Commissioners under TA 1988, s 754. Where the whole of any part of any tax is not paid before the due and payable date, and the Revenue serves a note of liability on another company resident in the UK which is designated the responsible company, and which holds the same interest in the controlled foreign company as was held by the assessable company, the responsible company may be assessed to tax. Interest and penalties apply as for corporation tax. Reliefs may be claimed under TA 1988, Sched 26.

Where the recipient of an apportioned amount of chargeable profits from a controlled foreign company has surplus allowances or losses, it may make a claim to use those allowances to reduce the liability to an amount equal to corporation tax on the apportioned profits. The accounting period to which this applies is the one in which the company is regarded as assessed to an amount equal to corporation tax on the profits apportioned and the appropriate rate means the rate of corporation tax applicable to profits of that accounting period. Losses and reliefs available for set-off against apportioned profits are trading losses carried back, charges on income, management expenses, unrelieved capital allowances, group relief and non-trading deficits on loan relationships. The two-year period for claiming group relief is extended to the end of the accounting period following that in which an assessment to an amount equal to corporation tax on apportioned profits is made. Obviously losses so used cannot also be set against the normal corporation tax liability (TA 1988, Sched 26, para 1). Similarly, if the apportionee has surplus advance corporation tax it may make a claim to reduce the surplus ACT carried forward. The relief is limited to the ACT which would have been payable on a dividend plus the ACT thereon paid at the end of the accounting period, of an amount equal to the chargeable profits apportioned less any losses or capital allowances deducted from those profits (TA 1988, Sched 26, para 2).

Double charges

There is scope for a double charge to taxation where the profits of a controlled foreign company have been apportioned to a shareholder, and the shares are subsequently disposed of, realising a price which includes the profit retained in the controlled foreign company. The controlled foreign company rules do not enforce a distribution as the UK would have no jurisdiction over the foreign company's actual distributions, it merely assesses the UK shareholders to the amount of tax that they would have been liable to had the profits been distributed. To prevent this double charge the company disposing of the shares may claim relief in computing the capital gain for an amount equal to the amount apportioned and brought into charge for an amount equal to corporation tax. There are provisions for part disposals. This relief under TA 1988, Sched 5, para 3, must be claimed within three months of the end of the accounting period in which the disposal of shares took place or, if later, the date the apportionment assessment became final.

A similar double taxation could arise where the controlled foreign company pays a dividend out of profits for which a direction has already been made and chargeable profits apportioned. This is dealt with by giving a notional double tax credit as if the corporation tax charged on the apportioned profits were underlying foreign tax. This, however, could result in an excess credit unrelievable because of TA 1988, ss 796 and 797 and to the extent that this excess credit arises from the corporation tax treated as underlying tax it is referred to as wasted relief. Such wasted relief may then be reclaimed by the apportionee under TA 1988, Sched 26, para 4. This procedure is explained further in the Inland Revenue, *Tax Bulletin*, Issue 12, August 1994, p 138 (*see* pp 486–91 *below*).

The apportionee company may be an indirect shareholder but is nonetheless deemed to have the appropriate holding to qualify for underlying foreign tax. The amount equal to corporation tax on the apportioned chargeable profits is not regarded as underlying tax for the purpose of calculating the gross tax for dividends. Where there are foreign shareholders, so that only part of the chargeable profits are apportioned to UK companies, a similar proportion of the dividend apportioned to

UK shareholders qualifies for notional double tax relief for the amount equal to corporation tax. There are provisions to prevent relief being given twice (TA 1988, Sched 26, paras 5 and 6).

Foreign systems

The UK-controlled foreign company provisions are extensive and complex. At the moment, however, they only apply when the Inland Revenue make an appropriate direction and can often be avoided by making an appropriate distribution. It is also unusual in applying only to create a charge on corporate shareholders with a 10 per cent or greater interest in a controlled foreign company. The first controlled foreign company legislation was the American sub-part F regime introduced in 1962. This was followed some ten years later by Canada and Germany and then by Japan, France, UK, New Zealand, Australia, Sweden, Norway and Denmark, followed in 1995 by Spain, Portugal and Finland, and more recently Brazil and Korea. These systems normally require the routine provision of CFC information either on completion of a return or under self-assessment rules. Of the European controlled foreign company legislation, Finland, Spain and Sweden extend their rules to include entities other than companies such as partnerships and only Denmark and the UK do not apportion profits to non-corporate shareholders. The UK, however, attacks non-corporate shareholders through the transfer of assets, and the anti-avoidance provisions of TA 1988, ss 739–746. The rules in each country differ materially and for example, Denmark, Finland Germany and the UK require more than 50 per cent control to bring in the controlled foreign company rules. Spain and Sweden work on the basis of 50 per cent or more, Portugal 25 per cent and France more than 10 per cent. The UK test of control, however, is the only one which extends to a measuring by reference to assets in a winding-up, all countries measuring control by reference to shares, all but Portugal to votes, and Finland, France, Spain and UK take into account the percentage of profits distributed.

Finland, France, Portugal and the UK operate a territorial system whereby the whole of the income of the tax haven company is apportioned, whereas Denmark, Germany, Sweden and Spain attack specific types of passive income.

Those countries adopting a territorial system do have exemptions for specific trading activities. The definition of a low tax area differs from country to country with Germany regarding anything less than 30 per cent as being low tax while Sweden bases its definition on 15 per cent. The UK 'white list' approach to acceptable jurisdictions is followed by Finland and Sweden whereas other countries such as Denmark, France, Germany and Spain operate a black list of unacceptable tax havens. Spain and Denmark are unusual in apportioning only to shareholders owning 50 per cent or more of the shares.

PART 3

INTELLECTUAL PROPERTY TAXATION

15 Patents

Introduction

There is a considerable body of statue law relating to the taxation of income from patents, introducing forward and backward spreading of the licensor's receipts, the taxation of capital receipts as income and capital allowances for the licensee. There are also provisions relating to the treatment of UK patents as annual payments. This effectively amounts to a withholding tax at the basic rate of tax on payments made to non-resident licensors, subject to double taxation relief. Patent rights are defined by TA 1988, s 533(1) as the right to do or authorise the doing of anything which would, but for that right, be an infringement of a patent.

Annual payments

Patents are frequently exploited by means of a royalty payment from the licensee to the licensor. UK patent royalties, unlike most copyright royalties, are either made out of profits or gains brought into charge to income tax under TA 1988, s 348(2)(*a*) or not out of profits or gains brought into charge to income tax under TA 1988, s 349(1)(*b*).

Deduction of tax at source

Unincorporated licensees As it is a charge on income (*see* pp 92 and 109) the licensee cannot claim the payment of a royalty in respect of a UK patent as a trading expense in view of TA 1988, s 74(1)(*p*). IM 1030 confirms that TA 1988, s 74(1)(*p*) should not be regarded as extending to any royalty paid to a non-resident in respect of the user of a patent abroad. The payer of a royalty in respect of a UK patent does, however, deduct income tax at the basic rate from the payment and therefore if he is due to pay, say, £1,000 to the licensor he would in fact pay £770 where the basic rate of tax is 23 per cent. He therefore retains in his own hands £230. Provided that his tax payable for the year of assessment in which the payment is made consists of at least £230 payable at the basic rate he does not pay over to the Revenue the amount deducted from the royalty payment.

Example

Alexander Yakovlev, a single man, had the following income and expenses in 1997–98:

	£
Salary, Schedule E	5,000
Trading profits, Schedule D	11,000
Rents received	4,000
Patent royalties paid in connection with his trade (gross)	10,000
1998/99 Loss relief set against total income of 1997/98	12,000

	£	
Taxable income:		
Salary		5,000
Profits	11,000	
Less: losses	12,000	
		(1,000)
Rents		4,000
		8,000
Tax payable at 23%		1,840
No higher rate or lower rate liability		
Patent royalties paid—net to licensor		7,700
Held in charge to tax		1,840
Paid to Inland Revenue under TA 1988, s 350, £2,000 @ 23%		460
		10,000
Patent royalties carried forward as excess charges under		
TA 1988, s 387 £10,000 less £8,000 held in charge, ie		2,000

Personal allowances are therefore unused and lost.

In the circumstances Mr Yakovlev decided not to claim tax relief for 1998/99 losses against total income for 1997/98 and the computation became:

	£	£
Salary		5,000
Profits		11,000
Rents		4,000
		20,000
Less: personal allowances		4,045
		15,955
Basic and lower rate tax payable 4,100 @ 20%		820.00
11,855 @ 23%		2,726.65
		3,546.65
No higher rate liability		
Patent royalties paid—net to licensor		7,700
Held in charge to tax		2,300
		10,000
Reconciliation:		
Tax paid		3,546.65
Tax held in charge on royalties		2,300.00
Tax on income		1,246.65

This represents tax on trust income, after allowances of £5,955
(15,955 – 10,000 = 5,955)

Losses carried forward and available to set against profits of same
trade in future years: £12,000

			£
	4,100	@ 20%	820.00
	1,855	@ 23%	426.65
	5,955		1,246,65

Incorporated licensees The above provisions apply only where the licensee is an individual or partnership and therefore subject to income tax. Where the licensee is a company, which is subject to corporation tax, the royalty cannot be paid out of profits or gains brought into charge to income tax (TA 1988, s 7(1)) and therefore the provisions of TA 1988, ss 349, 350 apply. As a result, the licensee company pays the tax deducted at the basic rate from the royalty payment to the Revenue. However, instead of paying the amount deducted under TA 1988, s 350(1) the amount is paid over in accordance with TA 1988, s 350(1) and Sched 16.

As far as the licensee is concerned the royalty paid is not a deduction from its trading profits, in view of TA 1988, s 74(1)(*p*), but is a deduction from its total income subject to corporation tax under TA 1988, s 338(3)(*a*). The relief is given for the royalties paid in the accounting period irrespective of the period to which they relate. The anti-avoidance provision aimed at annual payments such as reverse annuities in TA 1988, s 125 do not apply to patent royalties (IM 4865).

The Revenue may authorise a deduction of tax from royalties at less than the basic rate under double taxation treaties in accordance with the Double Taxation Relief (Taxes on Income) (General) Regulations 1970 (SI 1970 No 488), reg 2(2).

If a company can arrange for the annual payment which it makes to fall due towards the beginning of a *return period* it will maximise the time between withholding the tax from the payment and accounting for it to the Revenue, although it is not usually desirable to postpone payment into the following *accounting period* as this would delay the deduction of the royalty as a charge on income.

Form R185

In order to keep track of the tax deductions on annual payments, TA 1988, s 352 provides that the licensor can request, and indeed compel, the licensee to give him a statement in writing showing the gross amount of the payment, the amount of tax deducted and the net amount paid. Such statements are usually given on Form R185 (AP).

Excess charges

In the case of a company making payments for patent royalties in excess of its total income for the purposes of corporation tax, relief would not be available under TA 1988, s 338 as a charge on income. To the extent that such payments are made wholly and exclusively for the purpose of a trade carried on by the company, such excess charges are treated as if they were a trading expense for the purpose of calculating a trading loss and carried forward against future income from the same trade under TA 1988, s 393(1). This relief is available under TA 1988, s 393(9) and it should be noted that the excess charges are effectively available only for carry forward and cannot be added to losses for the purpose of carry back against the total income of preceding years. The relief is the equivalent of that available to individuals and partners under TA 1988, s 387.

Foreign patents

References to patent royalties in TA 1988, ss 74(1)(*p*), 348–350 refer in the view of the Inland Revenue, to royalties in respect of a UK patent and not in respect of an overseas patent, IM 1030, This interpretation has recently been confirmed by the Financial Institutions Division 4 of the Inland Revenue, except that UK patent for these purposes includes a UK patent granted on an overseas application under the European Patent Convention. The comment in the Revenue *Manuals* at CA 5551, that 'the legislation covers patents granted anywhere in the world except where it specifically refers to a UK patent' refers to the provisions relating to capital allowances and the taxation of capital receipts in TA 1988, ss 520–533 and in particular to TA 1988, s 524(3) which is the only specific reference to a UK patent as defined by TA 1988, s 533(1) for the purposes of those sections. It does not, however, follow that royalties in respect of overseas patents can automatically be paid gross by a UK resident licensee. The payer has to consider whether he is making an annual payment chargeable to tax on the recipient under Case III of Schedule D.

This usually turns on the question as to whether the payment is 'pure income profit' in the hands of the recipient or whether the recipient has assumed reciprocal obligations involving him in expenditure such as would diminish his income from the payments. The relevant principles are dealt with at p 92 *above*.

It often happens that the licensor provides various back-up services together with a licence to exploit the patent such as the use of a trade name, if closely connected with the user of a patent, to have any improvement of the patent made by the licensor during the currency of the agreement and to receive advice or assistance as to how best to use the patent (*Paterson Engineering Co Ltd v Duff* (1943) 25 TC 43, IM 1031). In such a case the royalties would not be pure income profit of the licensor and tax would not have to be deducted by the licensee. If no services were provided by the licensor, the royalties may well be pure income profit.

Even if the royalty were an annual payment it must furthermore be assessable on the recipient under Case III of Schedule D, for deduction of tax to be applicable. The royalty would therefore need to stem from a UK source asset. The possible sources are the patent, the trade and the licensing agreement; probably in that order. Royalties from a foreign payment are unlikely to derive from a UK source asset, unless the source is not the patent itself but is more properly the trade from which the patent has derived or the licensing agreement. If there is no UK trade and no UK agreement, it is difficult to see how a UK source could be involved, and deduction of tax would not therefore be possible.

Royalties received from foreign patents by a UK resident are assessed to tax under Schedule D, Case V in accordance with the normal rules (*see* p 96 *above*). Foreign tax deducted will usually be creditable against any UK tax liability (*see* p 266 *below*).

Non-residents

A non-resident is liable to UK tax in respect of UK patent royalties as income arising in the UK, under Schedule D, Case III limited to the UK tax deducted at source under FA 1995, s 128(1)–(3), unless he was carrying on a trade in the UK taxable under Schedule D, Case I, in which case he would be liable to UK tax on the whole of the profits unless relieved under a double taxation treaty.

The payer would have to deduct tax at the basic rate unless the recipient applies to the UK Revenue for the deduction of tax at a nil or reduced rate under a double taxation treaty, *see* p 266 *below*. The Revenue would then instruct the payer to pay royalties gross or to deduct tax only at a reduced rate, under the Double Taxation Relief (Taxes on Income) (General) Regulations (SI 1970 No 488).

It is interesting to note that UK patent royalties paid by a non-resident to a UK resident licensor would still be paid under deduction of tax at the basic rate and the non-resident should account for the tax so deducted to the Revenue under TA 1988, s 350(1). If the non-resident does not account for the tax so deducted to the Revenue (and in practice he is unlikely to do so) the Revenue must nonetheless give credit for the tax notionally deducted when assessing the UK resident licensor (*Stokes v Bennett* (1953) 34 TC 337), but only where it is evident from the documentation that the sum actually transmitted was the net sum and not the gross sum (*Hume v Asquith* (1968) 45 TC 251).

Patent income

According to the Inland Revenue, in its booklet *Patents and Income Tax*, No 490 (1964) (not since revised for the advent of corporation tax or capital gains tax), expenditure and receipts in respect of patents may be of either an income or a capital nature:

> Royalties or other sums paid in respect of the user of a patent, a term that is regarded as covering broadly payments in respect of past user [ie continued use or enjoyment] or future limited user, restricted as to amount or quantity, where there is no acquisition of a defined portion of the property in the patent are treated as income. There are provisions enabling certain reliefs to be claimed by inventors and others in respect of patent income. Other payments in respect of patents (eg, for outright acquisition; for exclusive user during the whole of the unexpired life; or for the future unlimited user within a defined area or for a term of years) are, in general, treated as capital. With certain exceptions, such payments qualify for Income Tax allowances in the hands of the payer and are taxed as income of the recipient.

This guidance has not been replaced by the Revenue *Manuals* so far published, but is restated at IM 3922 as:

> the expression 'any royalty or other sum in respect of the user of a patent' in ICTA 1988, s 349(1) applies to income payments as distinct from capital payments (see *IRC v British Salmson Aero Engines Ltd* (1938) 22 TC 39 at p 42). Whether a payment is of an income nature or a capital nature depends upon the particular facts of each case, including the contractual relationship between the parties.
>
> A lump sum payment in respect of the past user of a patent, or for the future user to a limited extent (that is, restricted to the amount or quantity), where there is no acquisition of a defined portion of the property in the patent but merely a personal right of user, should be regarded as an income payment. Lump sum payments which are in respect of the acquisition of
>
> (a)   a patent outright by assignment
> (b)   the exclusive user of a patent for the whole of its unexpired life
> (c)   the future unlimited user of a patent for a term of years, should be regarded as capital payments.
>
> The expression 'exclusive user' should be taken as applicable to the sole right to use a patent for a particular country or countries. The expression 'unlimited user' should be taken as applicable to the right to use a patent, without quantitative restriction, for a particular country or countries.

Attempts to argue that the wording of the Letter Patent gave exemption to tax not surprisingly failed in *Kirke v IRC* (1944) 26 TC 208 and *Kirke v Good* (1955) 36 TC 309.

Trading income

In a number of cases it has been held that patent royalties received by a trading company constituted trading income rather than investment income. Such cases include *IRC v Anglo American Asphalt Co Ltd* (1941) 29 TC 7; *IRC v Rolls-Royce Ltd (No 2)* (1944) 29 TC 137; *IRC v Desoutter Bros Ltd* (1945) 29 TC 155; and *IRC v Tootal Broadhurst Lee Co Ltd* (1949) 29 TC 352.

It has also been held that royalties payable in respect of manufacturing in the UK under UK patents were income arising in the UK and therefore liable to UK tax (in the absence of any double tax treaty provisions to the contrary); (*International Combustion Ltd v IRC* (1932) 16 TC 532). The practical effect of this is that the income would be subject to UK income tax at the basic rate under TA 1988, ss 348–350 unless the appropriate rate of withholding tax is reduced under the double taxation treaty between the UK and the country of residence of the licensor.

As income from annual payments is taxable on the recipient under Schedule D, Case III (TA 1988, s 18(3), (3A)) the tax deducted at source, if any, exhausts the UK income tax liability of a non-resident or it is excluded income under FA 1995, s 128(3)(*a*). This does not apply where the recipient is a non-resident trust with a UK resident beneficiary, current or prospective (FA 1995, s 128(5), (6)) in which case it would be liable to the rate applicable to trusts under TA 1988, s 686 (34 per cent for 1997/98, *IRC v Regent Trust Co Ltd* (1980) STC 140), unless the UK beneficiary is a life tenant, who would be liable at the higher rates, if applicable (*Williams v Singer* (1920) 7 TC 387, *Archer-Shee v Baker* (1927) 11 TC 749), or a discretionary beneficiary to whom the income has been distributed who could also have a higher rate liability with a credit for the rate applicable to trusts under TA 1988, s 687. Nor does the exclusion apply to income from a trade carried on in the UK (FA 1995, s 126 and Sched 23). In the case of a non-resident corporate licensor there would be no corporation tax liability in view of TA 1988, s 11(1) in the absence of a branch or agency in the UK.

Investment income

Patent income could be received by a person not carrying on a trade and would be assessed under Schedule D, Case III under TA 1988, s 18(3).

Lump sum receipts treated as capital

As with know-how payments, dealt with in Chapter 18, there have been a number of cases which considered whether lump sums paid to a licensor were correctly taxed as trading receipts or were capital.

In *IRC v British Salmson Aero Engines Ltd* (1938) 22 TC 29 a licence was obtained by a UK company to enable it to construct, use and sell Salmson aero engines. Article 2 of the agreement provided:

> As consideration for the Licence thus granted to them the Licensees shall pay to the Constructors the sum of £25,000 payable as follows:—
>
> £15,000 on the signing of this agreement. £5,000 six months after the signing of this agreement. £5,000 twelve months after the signing of this agreement.
>
> There shall be paid in addition to the foregoing payments and as royalty £2,500 twelve months after the signing of this agreement, and a like sum each twelve months during the following nine years.

The taxpayer argued that the entire amount was a capital sum, whereas the Revenue argued that the entire amount was taxable as income, being a sum paid in respect of the user of a patent under what is now TA 1988, s 348(2)(*a*). In his judgment Sir Wilfrid Greene MR stated:

> The first thing to notice about it is that it is not merely an agreement under which the English Company receives the right to use a patent: under this agreement the English Company is entitled to restrain the patentees themselves from exercising the patent in the territory, and it is entitled to call upon the patentees to take steps to prevent others exercising the invention within the territory. Now those rights are, to my mind, in essence different from the mere right of user. A licensee under a patent is a person who is put into such a position that the patentee disentitles himself to complain of what would otherwise have been an infringement. That is all a patent licence is. On the other hand where the patentee himself undertakes not to exercise the invention, that is something quite different: he is restraining himself by a covenant or contract from exercising his monopoly rights, and, further, if he undertakes to prevent others from infringing his monopoly rights, he is giving an undertaking which also in its nature is quite different from what is given by a patent licence, which, in effect, is an undertaking not to complain of what would otherwise have been an infringement.

The Court of Appeal supported the Special Commissioners' decision that the sums of £15,000, £5,000 and £5,000 represented instalments of a capital sum of £25,000, whereas (p 32):

> As regards the ten further payments of £2,500, we hold that these payments are royalties or other sums paid in respect of the user of a patent.

A case where a lump sum paid for the future use of a patent was regarded as capital is that of *Desoutter Bros Ltd v JR Hanger & Co Ltd and Artificial Limb Makers Ltd* (1936) 15 ATC 49 in which it was held that the payer was not entitled to deduct tax from an instalment of what was a capital sum as though it were a royalty for the user of a patent.

Similarly in the case of *William John Jones v IRC* (1919) 7 TC 310. At p 312 it is stated:

> By Clause 2 of the Indenture the purchase money of £750 was to be paid as to £300 thereof as follows: £100 on the signing of the Agreement, £100 at the expiration of one year and £100 at the expiration of two years from the date thereof and as to the balance of £450 by a royalty of 5 per cent upon the invoiced price of all machines sold by the Purchasers until such royalty should have amounted to £450. In addition the Purchasers were to pay a further royalty to the Vendors of 10 per cent upon all sales of machines and parts thereof constructed under the said inventions for a period of ten years from the date of the Indenture computed on the invoice price.

The Court held that the lump sum of £750 payable by instalments was capital, but that the further royalties of ten per cent were patent royalties taxable as income.

Keep out covenants

In *Murray v Imperial Chemical Industries Ltd* (1967) 44 TC 175, ICI Ltd granted exclusive licences or sub-licences to foreign companies in various countries for the manufacture of terylene fibre. In each licence they covenanted that they would not themselves enter the market for that country. They covenanted to keep out of that country. In return for these keep out covenants they received considerable sums of money from the overseas company. At p 211 Lord Denning MR stated:

> In these circumstances I do not think it would be correct to consider a 'keep-out' covenant as a thing by itself. The essence of the transaction in each case is that ICI granted to the foreign company an exclusive licence to use the patents in the country concerned for the term of the patent, and in return received remuneration in the shape of:
>
> (1)   a royalty on the net invoice value of products sold or utilised (this was for use of the master patents of CPA);
>
> (2)   a royalty of a fixed sum payable each year (this was for use of the ancillary patents of ICI);
>
> (3)   a lump sum payable by instalments over six years (this was said to be for the 'keep-out' covenant).

Lord Denning made repeated reference to the fact that it was an exclusive licence and continued at p 212:

> Applying these criteria in the present case, it is quite clear that the royalties for the master CPA patents and the royalties for the ancillary ICI patents were revenue receipts. That is admitted. So far as the lump sum is concerned, I regard it as a capital receipt, even though it is payable by instalments. I am influenced by the facts:
>
> (1)   that it is part payment for an exclusive licence, which is a capital asset;
>
> (2)   that it is payable in any event irrespective of whether there is any user under the licence even if the licensees were not to use the patents at all, this sum would still be payable;
>
> (3)   that it is agreed to be a capital sum payable by instalments, and not as an annuity or series of annual payments.

In these circumstances I am quite satisfied that the lump sum was a capital receipt and ICI are not taxable upon it.

This was the decision of the Court of Appeal. Such keep out covenants might now be taxable as know-how under TA 1988, s 531(8) (*see* p 213). In *Kirby v Thorn EMI plc* [1987] STC 621, it was held by the Court of Appeal that a non-competition covenant by a parent company on the sale of shares in subsidiaries was not a disposal of an asset, except to the extent that it was a capital sum derived from the exploitation of goodwill within TCGA 1992, s 22. Purchas LJ at p 633 stated:

> The right to trade in the marketplace is a right common to all, as has already been described by Nicholls, LJ. To suggest that it is an incorporeal right within TCGA 1992, s 21 is wholly unjustifiable within the basic concept of an acquisition of an asset with its accretion in value owing to changes in economic circumstances etc, over a period of inflation followed by disposal with a realisation of a chargeable gain. With respect to those who proposed it, I think that this was a fanciful submission and was rightly rejected both by the commissioners and by Knox, J.

In *Margerison v Tyresoles Ltd* (1942) 25 TC 59 the taxpayer agreed not to introduce another tyresoling plant nor to canvass for orders within the licensee's prescribed territory. Although the company retained the right of tyresoling tyres sent direct to its own works by persons within the said territory for their own use, the lump sum payment by the company was regarded as being effectively a capital sum for an exclusive licence or covenant not to compete.

Lump sum receipts treated as income

The mere fact that patent royalties are payable in a lump sum does not mean that they are of necessity capital.

In *Constantinesco v R* (1927) 11 TC 730 an inventor was awarded a lump sum after the First World War in respect of an interrupter gear for aircraft machine guns used during the War. It was held that the payment was taxable as income. In the words of Viscount Cave LC, at p 746:

> The payment was made in respect of the use of the invention over a period of time. The claim put in was a claim as for royalty in respect of the successive uses of the invention. In the case of patented inventions it was the practice of the Commission, as appears from their Report which has been cited on behalf of the Appellant, to take as a basis of their award a fair royalty as between a willing licensor and a willing licensee, and I have little doubt that that basis was accepted in the present case, subject, no doubt, to certain deductions. Lastly, the patent itself, that is the corpus of the patent, was not taken away from the Appellant and his partner but still remains in them. In view of all the facts I am satisfied that the sum awarded is to be treated as profits or gains, and annual profits or gains, within the meaning of the Income Tax Act.

A similar conclusion was arrived at in the case of *Mills v Jones* (1929) 14 TC 769 in respect of a lump sum awarded after the First World War to the inventor of the Mills Bomb. This was held to be a royalty taxed as income for the past use of the patented bombs, in spite of an attempt to differentiate it from the *Constantinesco* case, on the ground that the amount involved some future use of the Mills Bombs. It was argued that further manufacture was unlikely in view of the considerable stocks still left of the 75,132,000 lbs of such bombs produced during the First World War. This contention was doomed to failure when the Commissioners held that the amount of future use included in the payment was negligible.

In *IRC v Rustproof Metal Window Co Ltd* (1947) 29 TC 243 a non-exclusive licence was granted for the manufacture of not more than 75,000 ammunition boxes for a so-called capital sum of £3,000 and a royalty of 3d per box. Both the royalty per box and the £3,000 were held to be income. As Lord Greene MR stated at p 271:

> The fact that parties call the £3,000 a capital sum cannot make it a capital sum if it is not. The word 'capital' is a mere label attached to the £3,000 with an eye, no doubt, to tax considerations. The fact that the agreement separates the £3,000 from the royalties is nothing more than a drafting necessity having regard to the fact that the latter are based on the actual number of boxes treated with the process while the former is paid for the right to apply the process to any number of boxes up to 75,000.
>
> If a patentee negotiating with an intended licensee who wishes to obtain the right to manufacture up to a stated number of articles in accordance with the patent states his terms to be a lump sum down and a royalty of so much per article, I can see no reason why the mere division of the price into those two separate elements should by itself necessarily produce the result that the sum down must be regarded for tax purposes as a capital receipt. Such, however, is the argument, but I cannot accept it.

A complicated case involving lump sum payments was that of *Harry Ferguson (Motors) Ltd v IRC* (1951) 33 TC 15, in which it was argued that lump sums received by the company were for the sale of patents relating to a plough. This argument failed because, in the words of Lord MacDermott CJ at p 44:

> We think that on their true construction the agreements provided for the future exploitation of the plough as a commercial profit-earning enterprise and for a division of the profits of this enterprise between the parties until the Company's share of those profits had reached an agreed total.

As there was no outright sale it was not feasible to argue that the receipts were of capital.

In *Rees Roturbo Development Syndicate v Ducker* (1928) 13 TC 366 it was argued that the outright sale of patents for a lump sum gave rise to a capital receipt. On the facts of the case, however, the Commissioners found that the company's sole business was the exploitation of patents as part of its trade and that the profits on the sale of patents arose in the course of the company's business and were therefore taxable as income. This finding of the Commissioners was supported by the House of Lords.

Where the royalty was paid under a guarantee it was argued, unsuccessfully, in the case of *Wild v Ionides* (1925) 9 TC 392 that the payments amounting to £1,000 a month should be regarded as payments on account of a capital sum. As no evidence was produced which, in the view of Rowlatt J supported this contention, it was doomed to failure and the receipt taxed as income.

Brandwood v Banker (1928) 14 TC 44 was a lovely little case where a manufacturer added to the sale proceeds a sum which he referred to as 'shop rights' which enabled the purchaser of his equipment to use it. He then claimed that these 'shop rights' were an exclusive licence and as such a capital sum.

Ingenious though this argument may have been, it fell on deaf ears and the Court held that the payments for 'shop rights' had to be included with the payments for the machinery in the taxable receipts of the manufacturer's business.

Taxation of capital receipts as income

Although it is still necessary to decide whether a lump sum royalty is capital or income, for example, to see whether or not tax has to be deducted at source, the distinction is not in practice of paramount importance to the recipient, in view of TA 1988, s 533(1) which defines income from patents as (a) any royalty or other sum paid in respect of the user of a patent and (b) any amount on which tax is payable for any chargeable period by virtue of TA 1988, ss 520(6), 523(3) as balancing charges or TA 1988, ss 524 or 525 as receipts from the sale of patent rights (see CA 5551–5553). TA 1988, s 533(2) provides that the grant of a licence in respect of a patent is treated as a sale of part of the patent rights and TA 1988, s 533(3) provides that a licence granted by a person entitled to any patent rights for the whole of the remainder of the term of the patent is treated as a sale of the whole of the patent rights. The use of a patent by the Crown or similar use by a foreign government is treated as use under a licence (TA 1988, s 533(4)). The grant of a right to acquire in the future patent rights in an invention is treated as a sale of patent rights by TA 1988, s 533(6), whether or not the patent is actually granted (CA 5553–5555).

TA 1988, s 532(1) applies the provisions of the CAA 1990 to patents and therefore an exchange of patent rights, for example for shares, is treated as a sale by CAA 1990, s 150(4) (CA 5556), but the arm's length price for connected person transactions in CAA 1990, ss 157, 158 are specifically disapplied by TA 1988, s 532(2) from 31 March 1986 so ESC B17 is no longer needed, except for a disposal to which TA 1988, s 521(6)(*c*)(i) applies (*see* p 179). TA 1988, s 524(1) provides that where a person resident in the UK sells worldwide patent rights for a capital sum he is to be charged to tax under Schedule D, Case VI on one-sixth of the amount received, less any allowable costs of acquisition (the disposal value, as defined by TA 1988, s 521(6) *see* p 179), for the chargeable period in which it is received and a similar amount in each of the next five years. The net capital sum is therefore spread over the period of six years beginning with its receipt.

If the chargeable period is for less than 12 months the amount chargeable in that period is reduced proportionately.

If the capital sum is payable in instalments, the first instalment is spread over the six-year period and any subsequent instalments over the remainder of the initial six-year period (CA 5580–5581).

The recipient, under TA 1988, s 524(2) and (2A) may elect for the purposes of income tax within one year ten months from the end of the fiscal year and in the case of corporation tax within two years of the end of the chargeable period in which the capital sum was received, for the whole of it to be subject to tax under Schedule D, Case VI for the chargeable period in which it is actually received. This he might elect to do if, for example, he had Schedule D, Case VI losses, or if he anticipated that his income would be taxed at higher rates in future periods.

In the case of *Green v Brace* (1960) 39 TC 281 the vendor received a capital sum of £1,000 which he subsequently had to refund with costs and damages on failure to deliver a satisfactory prototype. He was nonetheless held taxable on the original £1,000 received, spread over six years under the provisions of what is now TA 1988, s 524.

Non-residents: capital sums

If a non-resident sells UK patent rights for a capital sum he is taxed on them under Schedule D, Case VI under TA 1988, s 524(3) and the payer must deduct UK income tax at the basic rate under TA 1988, ss 349, 350 which he cannot treat as a trading loss (TA 1988, s 387(3)(*d*)). The recipient may within one year ten months of the end of the year of assessment in which the sum is received, by notice in writing to the Board of Inland Revenue under TA 1988, s 524(10), elect that the capital sum be taxed as to one-sixth in the year of receipt and a further one-sixth in each of the following years under TA 1988, s 524(4) and (5). This does not affect the payer's liability to deduct tax at the basic rate under TA 1988, ss 349, 350. If one-sixth of the tax deducted results in an over-deduction of tax, compared with the recipient's eventual Schedule D, Case VI liability for each year on one-sixth of the income, the excess will be repaid on finalisation of the liability for the year. A UK patent is defined by TA 1988, s 533(1) as a patent granted under the laws of the UK, and in the Revenue view includes a UK patent granted abroad under the European Patent Convention.

If the vendor, although a non-resident company, is within the charge to corporation tax, for example, through having a branch or agency in the UK, it may elect under TA 1988, s 524(6), by written notice to the Board not later than two years after the end of the accounting period in which the capital sum is received, for the sum to be treated as arising rateably in the accounting periods ending not later than six years from the beginning of that in which the amount is received, provided that it remains within the charge to corporation tax.

Costs of acquisition

Where a person in receipt of a capital sum from the sale of patent rights originally acquired those rights for a capital sum, he is liable to tax under Schedule D, Case VI only on the net proceeds, under TA 1988, s 524(7). If he disposes of a further proportion of the rights purchased, any unrelieved balance of the original cost may be deducted (TA 1988, s 524(8)) but this does not affect the purchaser's duty to deduct basic rate income tax on the whole amount (TA 1988, s 524(9), CA 5585–5590).

Effect of death

Where a person who is in receipt of a capital sum from the sale of a patent which is being taxed in instalments under the provisions of TA 1988, s 524, dies, this crystallises the charge on the remaining instalments, which are deemed to be received in the chargeable period in which the death occurs (TA 1988, s 525(1)). Similar provisions apply on the winding-up of a company. In the case of a death, the personal representatives may by notice in writing served on the Inspector of Taxes within 30 days of the additional assessment under TA 1988, s 525(1) elect for the amount chargeable under Schedule D, Case VI to be reallocated equally over the fiscal years beginning with that in which the capital sum was received and ending with that in which the death occurred (TA 1988, s 525(2)).

Under TA 1988, s 525(3) and (4) if the recipient of the capital sum is a partnership it is treated as if it were a company being wound up, except that the additional assessment on the balance of the instalments is apportioned to the partners in their profit sharing ratio immediately prior to the discontinuance, and if any part is apportioned to a deceased partner his personal representatives have the same rights to reallocation as if he were the sole recipient, *as explained above* (CA 5596–5598).

Earned income

Although a capital sum on disposal of a royalty is assessed to tax under Schedule D, Case VI it may nonetheless be treated under TA 1988, s 529(1) as earned income if it is in respect of a patent granted to a person who devised the invention, whether alone or jointly with any other person, except to the extent that the rights were acquired from some co-inventor, which proportion would be treated as investment income (TA 1988, s 529(2)).

Lump sum for previous use

TA 1988, s 524 deals with the spreading of a lump sum capital receipt for the future use of a patented invention. TA 1988, s 527(1) applies where a lump sum royalty or other payment is received for the prior use of a patented invention where the period covered by the use is a period of six complete years or more. In such cases the royalty would normally have been taxed as income and subject to the deduction at source rules under TA 1988, ss 348–350 (*see* pp 92 and 109). The recipient may elect, apparently within the usual six years, to spread the income received and treat it as a royalty receivable in six equal instalments made at yearly intervals, the last of which was paid on the date on which the lump sum payment was in fact made.

TA 1988, s 527(2) provides for a similar election to spread where the period of user is two complete years or more, but less than six complete years, and the period of spread is by reference to so many equal instalments as there are complete years comprised in the period of user.

The reallocation provisions do not extend to the non-resident recipient of a capital sum which is subject to deduction of tax at the basic rate at source under TA 1988, s 349 by reason of TA 1988, s 524(3)(*b*), as described above (TA 1988, s 527(4)). It is interesting to consider whether such provisions could be defeated by the non-discrimination article in a double taxation treaty.

Conclusion

It will be seen from the foregoing that the whole of the proceeds from the exploitation of a patent will be taxable on the recipient as income whether the sale is for a capital sum or not, although the precise manner in which the calculation proceeds will depend on whether it is an income payment of a royalty or a capital payment apportioned over six years under TA 1988, s 524.

Expenses

Under TA 1988, s 526(1) a non-trader's expenses for patent fees may be claimed as expenses in the year in which they are incurred against patent income, any excess being carried forward, if they would have been allowable had he been carrying on a trade. An inventor may claim the costs of devising his invention, if not otherwise allowable, under TA 1988, s 526(2), where a patent is actually granted (CA 5602–5604).

TA 1988, s 83 allows as a trading expense the costs of patent applications in connection with a trade, whether successful or not; these could otherwise be disallowed as giving rise to a capital asset under TA 1988, s 74(1)(*f*) (CA 5600, 5601). It seems that a non-domiciled inventor can claim the costs of worldwide patenting even though he is assessed only on remittances of royalties from non-UK patents under Schedule D, Case V.

Expenses relating to claims before the Royal Commission on Awards to inventors for Crown user of a patent are allowable either under TA 1988, s 526 or as a trading expense under TA 1988, s 83 as appropriate (CA 5605).

Capital allowances

Licensee's capital payment

A licensee paying a royalty for the use of a patent will normally claim a deduction as a charge on income but this relief is not available in respect of capital expenditure on the purchase of patent rights.

Post-31 March 1986 expenditure

The system for giving capital allowances for capital sums spent on the acquisition of patent rights was totally changed in respect of expenditure incurred on or after 1 April 1986 to a broadly similar basis to that applicable to the pool basis used for plant, under the provisions of TA 1988, ss 520, 521. The rate of writing-down allowance is 25 per cent a year on the excess of the qualifying expenditure on patent rights over the disposal value on any sales, reduced proportionately for an accounting period of less than 12 months or in the year of commencement or cessation of a non-incorporated business, TA 1988, s 520(4)(*a*)(i). No allowance is available unless a trade is being carried on, or the income from the exploitation of the rights is otherwise taxable (TA 1988, s 520(2)). Expenditure incurred prior to the commencement of trading is deemed to be incurred on the first day of trading (TA 1988, s 520(3)) unless it had been on-sold prior to commencement.

There is a balancing charge if the disposal value of a patent exceeds the qualifying expenditure (TA 1988, s 520(6)). The qualifying expenditure for a chargeable period is the capital expenditure incurred on the purchase of patent rights during the period plus the written-down value brought forward in respect of an excess of qualifying expenditure over disposal value in earlier periods (TA 1988, s 521(1)).

Example

Fantastic Fiona Ltd commenced business on 1 July 1991 and on 23 November 1991 acquired patent rights for £25,000. On 1 September 1992 further rights were acquired for £12,000 and Fantastic Fiona Ltd granted a sub-licence on 1 December 1992 for a lump sum of £15,000. Accounts were made up for the calendar year.

Patent capital allowances:

	Qualifying expenditure £	Allowances £
6 months to 31/12/91		
Expenditure incurred	25,000	
Writing-down allowance at 25% × 6/12	(3,125)	3,125
Qualifying expenditure carried forward	21,875	
Year to 31/12/92		
Expenditure incurred	12,000	
Disposal value	(15,000)	
	18,875	
Writing-down allowance at 25%	4,719	4,719
Qualifying expenditure carried forward	14,156	
Year to 31/12/93		
Writing-down allowance at 25%	3,539	3,539
Qualifying expenditure carried forward	10,617	

Where the whole or any part of patent rights so acquired are sold, the disposal value is equal to the net sale proceeds, up to a maximum of the capital expenditure originally incurred (TA 1988, s 521(2), (3)). Any excess would be taxed as a capital receipt under the provisions of TA 1988, s 524 (*see* p 175 *above*). Where the patent rights have been transferred between connected persons within TA 1988, s 839, the capital expenditure referred to is that on the original acquisition of the rights (TA 1988, s 521(4)). There is an overriding anti-avoidance provision in TA 1988, s 521(5) where the purchaser and seller are connected within TA 1988, s 839 (TA 1988, s 521(7)) or it appears that the sole or main benefit from the transaction was a capital allowance. Expenditure over and above the seller's disposal value is ignored in such circumstances. The disposal value is normally the net sale proceeds (TA 1988, s 521(6)(*a*)) or if the seller has no disposal value but receives a capital sum taxable under TA 1988, s 524, that sum (TA 1988, s 521(6)(*b*)), or if neither of these applies, the smallest of the open market value, the capital expenditure on acquiring the rights or a connected party's acquisition costs (TA 1988, s 521(6)(*c*)).

A balancing allowance is given on any unallowed expenditure on the permanent discontinuance of the trade (TA 1988, s 520(4)(*b*)) or when the relevant patent rights come to an end without being revived, (TA 1988, s 520(4)(*c*)), ie those rights acquired for a capital sum but not relieved as qualifying expenditure (TA 1988, s 520(5)). Capital allowances are given either against the profits of the trade under TA 1988, s 528(1) or against patent income under TA 1988, s 528(2) (CA 5560–5574).

Pre-1 April 1986 expenditure

Capital expenditure on patents before 1 April 1986 is dealt with under TA 1988, s 522 which provides that where a person incurred capital expenditure on the purchase of patent rights in the course of his trade, or where any income in respect of the rights was liable to tax, he could write off the expenditure as if it were a capital allowance, equally over the writing-down period, which was normally the 17 years beginning with the chargeable period in which the expenditure is incurred.

If, however, the rights were acquired for a period of less than 17 years the writing-down period was the number of complete years in that lesser period, TA 1988, s 522(4). If the rights were not acquired for such limited period but were purchased more than one year after the commencement of the patent, the relief was given over what remained of the first 17 years of the patent. If the patent has been in existence for 17 years the amount paid was relieved in the year in which the expenditure was incurred. If the expenditure was incurred prior to the commencement of the trade it was deemed to have been incurred on the first day of trading unless prior to that date it had been on-sold. Where the writing-down period was less than 12 months the appropriate proportion of the annual deduction was allowed with the overriding proviso that no more than the total cost could eventually be written off.

It should be noted that if the vendor and purchaser of patent rights are under common control, and the capital expenditure was incurred before 1 April 1986, the capital allowances provisions of CAA 1990, s 157, are imported into the provisions by reason of TA 1988, s 532(1)–(3). The provisions apply where:

> the buyer is a body of persons over whom the seller has control or the seller is a body of persons over whom the buyer has control, or both the seller and the buyer are bodies of persons and some other person has control over both of them or the buyer and the seller are connected with each other within the terms of TA 1988, s 839.

References to a body of persons include references to a partnership (CAA 1990, s 157(2)).

The effect of these provisions is that the market value has to be substituted for the actual sale price and the charge on the vendor and allowance to the purchaser calculated accordingly.

It is, however, possible under CAA 1990, s 158 to elect by notice in writing to the Inspector of Taxes to substitute the amount of any capital expenditure remaining unallowed in accordance with TA 1988, s 523 for the market value, in accordance with TA 1988, s 532(3).

It is not possible to elect to substitute the written-down value for the market value if at the time of sale a balancing allowance or charge would fall to be made on a non-resident (CAA 1990, s 158(3)).

These provisions relating to connected persons do not apply to the sale of know-how which is specifically dealt with under TA 1988, s 531(7), nor to sales where the expenditure was originally incurred by the vendor after 31 March 1986 (TA 1988, s 532(2)), which are dealt with under TA 1988, s 521(5) above.

Extra-Statutory Concession B17 (Appendix 5) dealt with cases where patents were sold between persons under common control which would normally have been treated for capital allowance purposes as sold at open market value. The parties could in certain circumstances have elected that the patents should be treated as if sold at the written down value for tax if it were lower (CAA 1990, s 158 and TA 1988, s 532). This right of election did not in terms apply to a patent invented by the seller who would pay tax on the open market value of the patent rights while the purchaser would be given capital allowances on the same amount.

Where, however, an inventor sold the patent rights in his invention to a company which he controlled for a sum less than their open market value in exchange for shares, loan stock, loan account or cash, the assessment on the seller was restricted to the actual price, provided that the purchasing company undertook to restrict its capital allowances claim to that amount. This determined the amount on which the purchaser could claim capital allowances. The change in the basis of allowances means that this concession is not necessary for expenditure incurred after 31 March 1986.

The Revenue does not seek to charge the undervalue to capital gains tax on a sale of rights at less than market value, provided the purchasing company accepted a restriction in the allowable expenditure and subsequent disposal.

Lapsed rights and sale of rights

Under TA 1988, s 523 where the purchaser allows the rights to lapse without them being subsequently revived, or sells all the rights, or so much thereof as he still owns, or sells part of the rights, and the net proceeds of sale exceed the capital expenditure remaining unallowed, he is not entitled to any further writing-down allowance. In the first two cases, where full relief has not been given for the total expenditure, he is entitled to a balancing allowance under TA 1988, s 523(2) amounting to the capital expenditure remaining unallowed less, in the case of a sale, the net proceeds of the sale.

Conversely, if under TA 1988, s 523(3) he sells the rights for more than the expenditure remaining unallowed any allowance previously given would, up to the amount of the sale proceeds, be withdrawn by means of a balancing charge. Any profit over and above the expenditure originally incurred and not withdrawn by means of a balancing charge would be taxed as a capital sum under Schedule D, Case VI in accordance with the provisions of TA 1988, s 524, as explained previously.

Where part of the rights are sold for less than the expenditure remaining unallowed at the time of sale, the net sale proceeds, so far as they consist of capital sums, are deducted from the expenditure remaining unallowed and that amount is divided by the number of complete years of the writing-down period which remain at the beginning of the chargeable period in which the sale occurs. This procedure is repeated for any subsequent sales (TA 1988, s 523(4), CA Appendix 2 parts 57–62, CA 5560).

Method of relief

Under TA 1988, s 528(1) an allowance for capital expenditure on patents is made to a person carrying on a trade in the same way as for other capital allowances in arriving at the taxable profits of the trade. In other cases the allowance must, on a claim being made, be set first of all against any income from patents in the year of assessment, under TA 1988, s 528(2), with the balance being set off against income from patents in the following year of assessment and so on. Similarly with a company, to the extent that the relief is not given against trading profits, it can be deducted from patent income only in the accounting period or future accounting periods (TA 1988, s 528(3)).

A balancing charge would usually be treated as additional income of the trade, but if that had ceased the charge to income tax would be under Schedule D, Case VI, or to corporation tax as income from patents TA 1988, s 528(4) (CA 5775–5777).

Scientific research allowances

Revenue expenditure on scientific research by a person carrying on a trade may be deducted as a trading expense, including sums paid to Scientific Research Associations approved by the Secretary of State for Trade and Industry which are related to the trade, under TA 1988, s 136 (CA 5020–5022).

Capital expenditure on scientific research qualifies for 100 per cent allowance in the period in which the expenditure is incurred where it is on scientific research related to the trade which is directly undertaken by the taxpayer, or on his behalf by someone acting as his agent (*Gaspet Ltd v Elliss* (1987) STC 362, CA 5013).

Relief is also given for pre-trading expenditure under CAA 1990, s 137(1)(*b*). Where, for example, under the VAT Capital Goods Scheme, additional VAT was incurred in relation to the capital expenditure, it is treated as if it were capital expenditure qualifying for the 100 per cent allowance (CAA 1990, s 137(1A), CA 5042). The allowance for pre-trading expenditure is given in the period in which the trade was set up and commenced under CAA 1990, s 137(5). Expenditure on land is specifically disallowed by CAA 1990, s 137(2) and on dwellings by CAA 1990, s 137(3) although where not more than one-quarter of the capital expenditure on a building relates to the dwelling, Scientific Research Allowances may be claimed on the whole of the cost, apart from the land. Apportionment is allowed by CAA 1990, s 137(4).

There is no provision in the Scientific Research Allowance legislation for writing down or balancing allowances so it would normally be advisable to claim the full 100 per cent allowance available. There is no withdrawal of Scientific Research Allowances on assets ceasing to be used for scientific research purposes, but on disposal there could be a balancing charge of the smaller of the sale proceeds, equivalent to the market value on sales between connected persons under CAA 1990, s 157, and the allowances originally given. The destruction of an asset is treated as a disposal and demolition costs also qualify for Scientific Research Allowances under CAA 1990, s 138(5). Where the sale takes place between connected persons they may jointly elect for the acquirer to take over the disponor's written-down value under CAA 1990, s 158, CA 5030–5041. Grants and subsidies are deducted from the expenditure claimed, apart from Regional Development Grants (CAA 1990, s 153, CA 5012).

Scientific research is defined by CAA 1990, s 139(1), as any activities in the fields of natural or applied science for the extension of knowledge (CAA 1990, s 139(1)(*a*)) but it excludes expenditure on acquiring rights such as know-how and patent rights (CAA 1990, s 139(1)(*c*)) but the expenditure must be incurred by a trader and relate to his trade (CAA 1990, ss 139(1)(*d*), and 136 and 137, CA 5001–5010). The appeals procedure as to whether the expenditure qualifies for scientific research allowance is by way of written submission lodged by the Board of Inland Revenue to the Secretary of State for Trade and Industry under CAA 1990, s 139(3), CA 5011.

CAA 1990, s 139(2) prevents expenditure on scientific research qualifying as a deduction in more than one trade and CAA 1990, s 147 prevents scientific research expenditure, on which capital allowances have been claimed, from qualifying for any other capital allowances.

The Scientific Research Allowances may be a useful relief for traders involved in a lot of research and development as it is an accelerated relief compared to the capital allowances available on plant and machinery and may apply to buildings such as laboratories which would probably not qualify for any relief at all under any other provisions.

Employee awards

It is interesting to consider the tax liability of an employee in receipt of an award under PA 1977, ss 40–42.

In normal circumstances an inventor who is employed by a company to invent would be rewarded by a salary, possibly with bonuses, commissions, fringe benefits and other perquisites, all dealt with under the rules of Schedule E.

However, it is possible to apply to the court under PA 1977, s 40, which provides for an additional payment to be made by the employer to the employee where his work has given rise to a patent of outstanding benefit to the employer. The court may award some further payment to the employee if it considers it just to do so bearing in mind the remuneration already paid to the employee.

It is likely that such an award would take the form of a lump sum payment and it is quite likely that employers might make such a further lump sum, over and above the remuneration already paid, by way of out of court settlement.

It is fundamental to such a claim that the patent must be of outstanding benefit to the employer. It is not the work of the inventor that needs to be of outstanding benefit, but the patent resulting therefrom, which may or may not be directly related. On the assumption that the employee is employed to invent and has been properly remunerated, it could presumably be argued that the additional payment, arising as it does from the patent itself, which is the company's property, is not directly related to the employment, the duties of which have already been remunerated. It is in the nature of a windfall profit to the employee as a result of the exceptional value of the patent to the employer. In such circumstances the employment becomes the *causa sine qua non* of the payment but is not the *causa causans*. Following cases such as *Bridges v Bearsley, Bridges v Hewitt* (1957) 37 TC 289 it would follow that the payment, not being directly related to the employment, is not taxable under Schedule E. It is understood that the Revenue might seek to argue that a cash payment of this type could be a benefit within TA 1988, s 154(2) in view of TA 1988, s 168(3), although this argument has yet to be tested in the courts.

If it is not taxable under Schedule E it would appear to be taxable under Schedule D, Case I as patent income, following *Constantinesco v R* (1927) 11 TC 730 and *Mills v Jones* (1929) 14 TC 769 (*see* p 173). It would also appear that any such payment would be a royalty or other sum paid in respect of the user of a patent within TA 1988, s 348(2)(*a*), which means that the employer would deduct tax at the basic rate from the payment in the same way as for any other patent royalty payment.

If the employee were to argue that he was not carrying on the trade of inventor, being already in employment for such activities, the assessment would appear to be under Schedule D, Case VI, being the residual category, but would still be taxed as earned income under TA 1988, s 529. For a one-off payment there would be no difference in the tax liability resulting between a Case I and a Case VI assessment. If, exceptionally, the court were to award a continuing payment it would probably be advantageous to claim Schedule D, Case I treatment.

It is not thought that the amount received by the employee would be a capital sum from the sale of any patent rights under TA 1988, s 524, and would not be taxed as a capital gain in view of TCGA 1992, s 37(1), on the ground that the sum had already been subject to income tax.

In the vast majority of cases it is likely that the employee who produces a patent of outstanding benefit to the employer is an employee of considerable talent and the employer in most cases will see that the employee is properly remunerated, in view of his worth to the company, and such remuneration would be dealt with under the normal provisions of Schedule E. It is therefore likely to be only the exceptional cases that have to be considered for an award under the provisions of the PA 1977, ss 40–42.

Enterprise Investment Scheme: roll-over relief on reinvestment and venture capital trusts

A research and development trade is not excluded from the Enterprise Investment Scheme merely because its income arises from royalties (TA 1988, s 297(5), IM

7000). A similar exemption from exclusion applies for roll-over relief on reinvestment under TCGA 1992, ss 164I(6) and 164N(1) and for venture capital trusts under TA 1988, Sched 28B, paras 4(6) and 5(1).

Capital gains tax

Intellectual property, such as patent rights, represents property which can be transferred and can in certain circumstances result in a chargeable capital gain or an allowable capital loss. This would be subject to the normal capital gains tax provisions, summarised in Chapter 9 (*see* pp 98–101).

Intellectual property does not qualify for rollover relief as it is not a relevant asset under TCGA 1992, s 155, except for know-how treated as goodwill (*see* p 213). It could, however, be a chargeable business asset for retirement relief purposes under TCGA 1992, s 163 and Sched 6 on a disposal after the age of 50 by way of sale or gift of the whole or part of a business or shares or securities in a family company.

Such property could also qualify for holdover relief under TCGA 1992, s 165 on a gift or sale at undervalue of business assets by an individual. This relief is extended by TCGA 1992, s 260 to gifts between UK resident individuals and into or out of UK settlements provided inheritance tax is chargeable on the transfer, albeit at the nil rate. Under these provisions the transferor and transferee can jointly elect for the transferee to take over the transferor's or transferee's base value. Where the transferee is a trustee, only the transferor need elect for the trustee transferee to take over his base value.

Inheritance tax

A transfer other than by arm's length sale under IHTA 1984, s 10 or in the course of business under IHTA 1984, s 12 could be a chargeable transfer for inheritance tax purposes equal to the reduction in the transferor's estate as a result of the transfer (IHTA 1984, s 3—*see* p 104 *above*). It could be a potentially exempt transfer under IHTA 1984, s 3A, if *inter vivos* or involving interest-in-possession, accumulation and maintenance trusts, or other specialist trusts. Intellectual property could be part of a business disposed of for the purposes of business relief under IHTA 1984, ss 103–114 or could be part of the assets of a company where the disposal of shares qualifies for such relief.

There are no specific provisions relating to intellectual property as such, which means that the normal market value rules in IHTA 1984, s 160 apply to the valuation of patent rights, ie the price which they might reasonably be expected to fetch if sold in the open market. The value of patent right is normally calculated on the basis of the capitalised present value of its income-earning ability.

Stamp duty

An exclusive non-revocable licence or assignment for consideration is subject to *ad valorem* duty as a conveyance on sale under Stamp Act 1891, ss 59 and 62 but a revocable assignment or non-exclusive licence is not subject to duty (Sergeant and

Sims, *Stamp Duties and Capital Duty and Capital Reserve Tax*), as explained in Chapter 23.

VAT

Treatment of patents

Patent transactions are supplies of services for VAT purposes, as explained in Chapter 11, by virtue of VATA 1994, s 5(2)(*b*):

> anything which is not a supply of goods but is done for a consideration (including, if so done, the granting, assignment or surrender of any right) is a supply of services.

If, therefore, a UK-registered business grants a patent licence to another UK business in return for a royalty or lump sum, VAT at the standard rate is payable on the gross, pre-VAT amount even though the payer may deduct income tax at the basic rate on making the payment. This applies whether or not a royalty is described as a gross royalty from which tax is to be deducted by the payer, or as a free of tax or net royalty which has to be grossed up to arrive at the gross equivalent.

The Inland Revenue have been advised that tax due on an annual payment within TA 1988, s 348 or 349 should be computed by reference to the full amount of the payment inclusive of VAT. However no objection will be raised if the payer and recipient agree to make and accept a deduction of income tax calculated by reference to the net payment exclusive of VAT, subject to retaining the right to review the situation in the light of actual experience in the operation of VAT (IM 3900).

If the royalty paid by one UK business to another registered UK business is in connection with a foreign patent, VAT is still payable even though there may be no requirement to deduct income tax. VAT may not be payable if the licence was granted by a foreign branch as a result of the place of supply rules in VATA 1994, s 9 and this would apply to both UK and foreign patents.

16 Trade and service marks and designs

Introduction

Unlike patents and copyright there is practically no mention of trade marks, service marks and designs in the Taxes Acts. There are, therefore, no problems of capital being taxed as income, although conversely there are no capital allowances. There is normally no withholding tax in the UK on trade mark, service mark or design royalties, unless they are annual payments.

It is often commercially advantageous to attach a high value to trade marks, service marks and designs to avoid the deduction of tax at source and because, in the case of trade marks and service marks, the life is indefinite.

Income

There is no specific tax legislation dealing with income from trade marks, service marks and designs. This means that if profits are received by a business from exploiting a product which is protected by trade marks, service marks, registered designs or design rights the income would be a trading receipt in the normal course of business included in the profits taxable under Schedule D, Case I under TA 1988, s 60(1), see *Orchard Wine & Spirit Co v Loynes* (1952) 33 TC 97.

Backward spreading

In the particular instances of design rights under Part III of the Copyright, Design and Patents Act 1988 and registered designs under the Registered Designs Act 1949, TA 1988, s 537A permits receipts by the designer or author from the assignment or licence of the rights to be spread. In order to qualify for this relief the designer or author must have been engaged in the creation of the design for a period of more than 12 months. Furthermore, the receipt must either be a lump sum payment, including a non-returnable advance of royalties, or alternatively any other royalty or payment which does not only become receivable more than two years after articles made to the design are first made available for sale or hire (TA 1988, s 537A(4)).

If the period does not exceed 24 months, 50 per cent of the income is treated as received on the day it became receivable and 50 per cent is treated as received 12 months later. If the period exceeds 24 months, one-third of the income is treated as received on the day it became receivable, one-third 12 months earlier and one-third 24 months earlier (TA 1988, s 537A(3)). A claim must be made before 5 April following the expiry of the eighth anniversary of articles made to the design first being made available for sale or hire (TA 1988, s 537A(5), IM 1032, 1033 and 4000–4013). The relief is not available to partnerships or companies for receipts after 5 April 1996, TA 1988, s 534(6A).

Investment income

Trade marks, service marks, registered designs and design rights could be held as an investment other than by a business. In such cases the income is likely to be assessable under Schedule D, Case III in accordance with the provisions of TA 1988, s 18(3).

Expenses

It is specifically provided under TA 1988, s 83 that the fees or expenses incurred in the registration of a design or a trade mark which, under the Trade Marks Act 1994 would include a service mark, or in an extension of the period of copyright in a design or a renewal of the registration of a trade mark may be treated as a trading expense, in spite of the fact that it may give rise to a capital asset which could otherwise be disallowed under TA 1988, s 74(1)(f) (CA 5600–5601, IM 1160).

Royalties

A licence agreement for the use of a design, service mark or trade mark would normally be for a fee or for a recurring royalty which would be taxable as a trading receipt of a business. If on the other hand a royalty is paid for the use of a trade mark, service mark or design where no services are performed by the licensor it could (if of a UK source) be assessed under Schedule D, Case III on the recipient as pure income profit and therefore regarded as an annual payment of the payer and be subject to deduction of tax under the provisions of TA 1988, ss 348–350 in the same way as patent royalties, as discussed under foreign patents on p 168. These provisions apply in respect of a UK or foreign trade mark or design whether the licensor is resident or non-resident.

In the particular instance of design rights and registered designs, royalties paid to an owner whose usual place of abode is outside the United Kingdom, must be subjected to deduction of basic rate tax at source as if they were annual payments, under TA 1988, s 537B. The owner of the rights includes a recipient who whilst entitled to royalties has assigned the design or registered design right (TA 1988, s 537B(2)).

An agent making the payment is entitled to reduce the amount of royalty liable to deduction of tax by any commisson to which he is entitled for services rendered (TA 1988, s 537B(3)). If the commission is unknown, deduction of tax applies to the full royalty, but the agent may later claim a repayment of tax deducted (to be passed on to the royalty recipient) on paper proof of any commission charged (TA 1988, s 537B(4)).

The time of making the payment is defined as being the time when the royalty payment originates, and not when an agent makes the payment to the overseas recipient. These provisions are analogous to TA 1988, s 536 applicable to copyright royalties. *Further commentary may be found on* p 201 (IM 4000–4013).

Lump sums

If the business consists solely of the exploitation of a trade mark or design which is sold for a lump sum, this amount would be capital as being for the total loss of the sub-stratum of the business: see Slesser LJ in *Handley Page v Butterworth* (1935) 19 TC 328, at p 359. It also seems from the same case that an outright sale of one of several designs, service marks or trade marks would be a capital receipt if the capital asset thereupon ceased to be owned (per Romer LJ *ibid*, p 360). If it were a lump sum for a mere licence it would normally be taxed as income but could conceivably be a partial disposal of a capital asset. A disposal or part disposal taxed as a capital receipt would be subject to assessment as a chargeable gain under TCGA 1992, s 21. A mere disposal of a trade mark or design for a single product among many is unlikely to be a capital receipt (*Orchard Wine & Spirit Co v Loynes* (1952) 33 TC 97).

Similar provisions would apply to an unregistered design, as in the case of *Handley Page v Butterworth* which related to the designs of the O-100, O-400 and V-1500 aircraft which were incapable of being registered as designs.

Relief to purchaser

The purchaser of a trade mark, service mark or design, who is not himself the originator, may pay a lump sum for the use of the asset, or a royalty. A lump sum could be regarded as a capital expense rather than as a trading expense and as such would be disallowed under TA 1988, s 74(1)(*f*). There are no provisions for giving tax relief for capital payments on the purchase of a trade mark, service mark or design and the cost could be taken account of only in a capital gains computation on a subsequent disposal. The Revenue will, however, sometimes allow the acquisition costs of a trade mark, service mark or design with a limited commercial life, to be written off over a period as deferred revenue expenditure (*see* p 337). The distinction between deferred revenue expenditure and capital expenditure is vital, because if the expenditure is capital, ie being made not only once and for all, but with a view to bringing into existence an asset or advantage for the enduring benefit of the trade, no allowances are available (*Atherton v British Insulated and Helsby Cables Ltd* (1926) 10 TC 155). Vinelott J, in *RTZ Oil and Gas Ltd v Elliss* [1987] STC 512 stated, at p 541:

> It is elementary that although it may be necessary in order to give a true and fair view of the profits earned by a trade in a given year to make an allowance for the depreciation of a wasting asset on which capital has been expended no such allowance can be made in ascertaining the taxable profits for that year. The disallowance has always been founded in cases within Case 1 of Sch D on that part of rule 3 of the Rules applicable to that Case which is now reproduced (though modified so far as concerns the deduction of interest on capital) in [TA 1970] s 130(*f*) [(TA 1988, s 74(*f*)] (see, in particular, *Alianza Co Ltd v Bell* (1906) 5 TC 172).

And on p 546 Vinelott J stated:

> The legislature has not left the allowance of depreciation to be determined in accordance with accountancy principles and practice. Instead, it has imposed a general prohibition and has, since 1886, dealt with the question whether a depreciation allowance should be made in a particular case by a separate, detailed and frequently amended code. The question whether that code should not be further amended to permit the deduction claimed in the instant case is one which must be determined by the legislature and not by the court.

Royalties paid

If a royalty were paid for the use of the trade mark, service mark or design it would normally be treated as a trading expense wholly and exclusively incurred for the purposes of the trade and therefore allowable under TA 1988, s 74 (IM 1032). If, exceptionally, the royalty were paid under deduction of tax as an annual payment or under TA 1988, s 537B, taxable on the licensor as investment income under Schedule D, Case III, it would be treated as a charge on income under TA 1988, ss 348–350.

In the case of an individual or partnership the charge, to the extent that it exceeded total income and was therefore subject to deduction of tax under TA 1988, ss 349, 350, would be subject to carry forward as a trading loss under TA 1988, s 387 as an excess charge incurred for trading purposes. In the case of a company the charge would be allowable under TA 1988, s 338 against total income and excess charges would be carried forward under TA 1988, s 393(9) as a trading loss offsettable against future trading profits from the same trade.

There have been no cases on the treatment of trade mark, service mark and design royalties as annual payments but the basic provisions seem analogous to royalties for secret processes and in *Delage v Nugget Polish Co Ltd* (1905) 21 TLR 454 it was held that such royalties were annual payments subject to deduction of tax at source when taxable on the recipient. It is arguable that this case incorrectly attributed the royalties as arising from a UK source. Under current law if the source were not UK, Schedule D, Case III would not be in point and deduction would not be possible.

Dealing and investment

If the trade mark, service mark or design were purchased other than for the buyer's trade, it could be acquired in the course of a trade of exploiting trade marks, service marks and designs. In this case, the sale proceeds less the cost would be taxed under Schedule D, Case I. No spreading under TA 1988, s 537A would be available as the seller would not be the designer. Alternatively, the property may be held as an investment to exploit in return for royalties or licence fees which would be taxable under Schedule D, Case III in accordance with TA 1988, s 18(3).

In the latter case the complete assignment of the trade mark or design for a capital sum would give rise to a chargeable gain in the normal way.

Stamp duty

A trade mark or design is property in the same way as a patent and similar provisions apply: *see* Chapter 23.

VAT

The VAT rules for the assignment or licence of trade marks and designs are exactly the same as for patents: *see* Chapter 11.

17   Copyright

Introduction

Over the years there has been a great deal of litigation on the taxation of copyright income and there are special provisions in the Taxes Acts relating to the spreading of income in certain cases. Copyright royalties, unlike UK patent royalties, are not automatically within the deduction of tax legislation, but there is a limited withholding tax for copyright owners whose usual place of abode is abroad.

The taxation of income deriving from copyright material depends to a large extent on the taxation position of the person entitled to the royalties. Although design right under CDPA 1988, Part III is in many ways analogous to copyright it is not within the definition of copyright for tax purposes and the taxation treatment is dealt with in Chapter 19.

Professional income

Income from the activities of a professional author, dramatist, composer etc are normally taxable as professional income under Schedule D, Case II (IM 2690–2701). The manner in which copyright income becomes payable to the originator of the copyright material was considered in the leading cases of *Purchase v Stainer's Executors* (1951) 32 TC 367 and *Carson v Cheyney's Executor* (1958) 38 TC 240. In the *Cheyney* case, at p 257, Viscount Simonds commented with regard to Peter Cheyney:

> He was accordingly assessed during his lifetime under Case II of Schedule D in respect of the royalties so received by him after deducting therefrom all proper and allowable expenses of carrying on his profession. There is no doubt that he was rightly so assessed, and the learned Attorney-General very properly admitted that he could not lawfully have been assessed under any other Case or any other Schedule. It must be recorded also that he was consistently assessed upon a form of receipts basis, being credited with royalties upon the day when they fell due for payment, and no account being taken of the present value of royalties due at a future date.

This is the manner in which royalties are in practice assessed to tax on authors, composers and other producers of copyright material.

The point at issue in both *Purchase v Stainer's Executors* and *Carson v Cheyney's Executor* was that copyright continued after the death of the author, which gave rise to royalties which would nowadays be caught under the post-cessation receipts provisions of TA 1988, ss 103–110. Prior to the introduction of these provisions such income was tax free unless the Revenue could show that the income arose from property, ie, from the copyright itself and was therefore taxable under

Schedule D, Cases III or VI. This argument was decisively rejected in the House of Lords both with regard to the activities of Leslie Howard Stainer as an actor and film producer and for Peter Cheyney as an author. In *Carson v Cheyney's Executor* at p 260, Viscount Simonds said:

> I doubt not that in a proper context royalties may be described as income of an investment, as in *IRC v Sangster* (1919) 12 TC 208, nor that, as in *Jarvis v Curtis Brown Ltd* (1929) 14 TC 744 copyright royalties may be merged in the receipts of a trade.

Lord Morton of Henryton stated (at p 261) that so far as the author was concerned:

> As Jenkins LJ, put it in delivering the judgment of the Court of Appeal [at p 254]: 'It', that is the copyright, 'was brought in to existence by his professional activity in the writing of books and by nothing else, and it was just as much part of his profession to turn his literary labours to account by licensing the copyright he had created to publishers as it was to write the books in which the copyright subsisted.'
> If the sums in question had the quality of professional earnings during the author's lifetime, I cannot see that his death in any way changed their quality.

Lord Reid, in *Carson v Cheyney's Executor* at p 264, commented:

> I shall consider the present case on the footing . . . that the sums assessed were instalments of fees payable under contracts obtained by Mr Cheyney in exploiting his copyright in books written by him by licensing publishers to publish or translate them. But I must add that even so there is an essential difference between that case and the case of a person who buys a copyright from the author and then proceeds to exploit it by granting licences to publishers. Where the author exploits his own copyright by granting licences to publishers, the fees which he receives are admittedly part of his professional earnings and are not taxable as annual payments under Case III, at least during his lifetime. But where the author sells his copyright, the price which he receives is part of his professional earnings and the fees which the purchaser gets from granting licences to publishers are from the beginning taxable as annual payments to him irrespective of whether the author is still practising his profession. They are no part of the author's professional earnings.

Also, on p 266, Lord Reid commented:

> To my mind, if a person receives as part of his remuneration an asset which yields income, that income is not the fruit of his professional activity any more than it would be if that person had received his remuneration in money and had then used that money to buy that asset. From the moment when the asset comes into his hands the source of any income which it yields is that asset and not his professional activities. There would be no question of the income falling under Case II during his life and then being taxable under some other Case after his death. The receipt by a professional man of income yielded by an asset which has been transferred to him is not a method of gaining professional income, whether or not the asset came to him as professional remuneration. But for an author exploitation of his copyright is a method of gaining professional income.

So far as the author is concerned therefore copyright royalties are taxed under Schedule D, Case II as income of the profession.

Acquired copyright royalties

The case of *Hume v Asquith* (1968) 45 TC 251 illustrates the difference between royalties which would have been treated as part of the author's professional income and royalties arising to third parties as a result of their ownership of copyrights. The case concerned the works of the late Sir James Barrie. The first set of royalties considered were royalties under agreements which had been entered into by Sir James Barrie during his own lifetime, which then passed by will to Lady Cynthia Asquith and by assignment to her son, Mr Asquith, the taxpayer in the case. Pennycuick J, confirmed the Commissioners' finding that these royalties were not taxable as they were post-cessation receipts of the profession. They would now be taxed under TA 1988, ss 103–110.

The second set of royalties were royalties under an agreement whereby Lady Cynthia Asquith assigned to Samuel French Ltd the sole and exclusive right of representation by amateur performers, as mentioned in the contract. As a result, these royalties were annual payments taxable under Schedule D, Case III on the recipient under TA 1988, s 18(3) and should have been paid under deduction of tax under the provisions of what are now TA 1988, ss 348–350.

Also considered in the case were contracts under which amounts were paid from an American company and it was held that these also arose from an agreement entered into by Lady Asquith as copyright owner and as a result the income was assessable under Schedule D, Case III or Case V. Although the point was not decided in the case, as the agreement was with a foreign company apparently under a foreign contract, presumably Case V was the correct head of charge (IM 2693). A deduction is usually given for any agent's commission payable. Such income is not earned income of the acquirer (IM 2694).

Post-cessation receipts

It seems that an author who merely ceases to write is still assessed under Schedule D, Case II on royalties received, except in exceptional cases where there is a long gap between the physical cessation of writing and the republication of a work. In such cases the income could be taxed as a post-cessation receipt (IM 2697 and 1750–1759). Similarly, income received after death by the author's executors would also be taxed as a post-cessation receipt. The author would usually have been assessed on a cash basis on royalties actually received and would therefore be assessed under TA 1988, ss 103(2)(b) and 104(1) on post-cessation receipts. Such income would be treated as earned income, if received by the original author, in view of TA 1988, s 107. Although the assessment is under Schedule D, Case VI, expenses are allowable as if the profession had continued, under TA 1988, s 105.

There are two important exemptions from the post-cessation receipt charge. Under TA 1988, ss 103(3)(a) and 104(3) sums received by a non-resident in respect of income arising directly or indirectly from outside the UK eg, on non-UK sales, are not taxed as post-cessation receipts.

Under TA 1988, ss 103(3)(b) and 104(3) a lump sum paid to the personal representatives of an author, on assignment in whole or part of the copyright, is not taxed as a post-cessation receipt. There could be a capital gains tax charge on any excess of the sale proceeds over the probate value.

It is possible to elect under TA 1988, s 108 to carry back post-cessation receipts and tax them as if received on the last day of the accounting period ending with cessation. It is interesting to consider whether, if an author was non-resident at that time but subsequently returned to the UK, this could result in all future royalties being tax free, either as being deemed to arise when the author was not liable to UK tax, under TA 1988, s 108, or because in the year of discontinuance there was no profession charged to tax under Schedule D, Case II and therefore the provisions of TA 1988, ss 103–110 have no application.

There is an exemption under TA 1988, s 109 for part of the post-cessation receipts for an author born before 6 April 1917 engaged in his profession on 18 March 1968.

Post-cessation expenses

If post-cessation expenses, paid on or after 29 November 1994 and within seven years of discontinuance cannot be set against post-cessation receipts under TA 1988, s 105, relief may possibly be claimed under TA 1988, s 109A, for damages for defective work and legal costs, insurance against such liabilities and debt collection, reduced by any unpaid expenses for which relief has been claimed on the renewals basis. Relief may be claimed against total income and then capital gains of the fiscal year of payment made within one year ten months from the end of that year. It is unclear whether damages for libel could fall within these provisions.

Assignment of copyright

One result of assessing an author to tax under Schedule D, Case II is that the copyright in his works, although capable of assignment, does not have to be brought into the author's accounts at the market value at the time of assignment. This arises from the decision in *Mason v Innes* (1967) 44 TC 326.

The Revenue argued that following the Schedule D, Case I decison of *Sharkey v Wernher* (1956) 36 TC 275 the copyright in a book which had been written by the taxpayer and given to his father was taxable at the market value. It was held that the author's copyright was not stock in trade and, therefore, that the decision in *Sharkey v Wernher* had no application. The principles were very clearly laid down in the judgment of Lord Denning MR at p 339:

> I start with the elementary principle of income tax law that a man cannot be taxed on profits that he might have, but has not, made: *Sharkey v Wernher* (1956) 36 TC 275. At first sight that elementary principle seems to cover this case. Mr Hammond Innes did not receive anything from 'The Doomed Oasis'. But in the case of a trader there is an exception to that principle. I take for simplicity the trade of a grocer. He makes out his accounts on an 'earnings basis'. He brings in the value of his stock-in-trade at the beginning and end of the year; he brings in his purchases and sales; the debts owned by him and to him; and so arrives at his profit or loss. If such a trader appropriates to himself part of his stock-in-trade, such as tins of beans, and uses them for his own purposes, he must bring them into his accounts at their market value. A trader who supplies himself is accountable for the market value. That is established by *Sharkey v Wernher* itself. Now, suppose that such a trader does not supply himself with tins of beans, but gives them away to a friend or relative. Again he has to bring them in at their market value. That was established by *Petrotim Securities Ltd v Ayres* (1964) 41 TC 389. Mr Monroe, on behalf of the Crown, contends that that exception is not confined to traders. It extends, he says, to professional men, such as authors, artists, barristers and many others. These professional men do not keep accounts on an 'earnings basis'. They keep them on a 'cash basis', by which I mean that on one side of the account they enter the actual money they expend and on the other side the actual money they receive. They have no stock-in-trade to bring into the accounts. They do not bring in debts owing by or to them, nor work in progress. They enter only expenses on the one side and receipts on the other. Mr Monroe contended that liability to tax does not and should not depend on the way in which a man keeps his accounts. There is no difference in principle, he says, between a trader and a professional man. And he stated his proposition quite generally in this way: the appropriation of an asset, which has been produced in the ordinary course of a trade or profession, to the

trader's or professional man's own purposes amounts to a realisation of that asset or the receipt of its value, and he must bring it into account.

I cannot accept Mr Monroe's proposition. Suppose an artist paints a picture of his mother and gives it to her. He does not receive a penny for it. Is he to pay tax on the value of it? It is unthinkable. Suppose he paints a picture which he does not like when he has finished it and destroys it. Is he liable to pay tax on the value of it? Clearly not. These instances—and they could be extended endlessly—show that the proposition in *Sharkey v Wernher* does not apply to professional men.

It appears that the Revenue does not normally argue that, as the value of the copyright assigned has not been charged to income tax as income within TCGA 1992, s 37, there should be a deemed disposal at market value under TCGA 1992, s 17 for capital gains tax purposes, but it is likely to raise the argument where the recipient sells the copyright for a lump sum or legal avoidance is suspected (IM 2698 and 2699). Where such an argument is raised the assignor and assignee, if individuals, might claim for the assignee to take over the nil base value of a business asset of the assignor under TCGA 1992, s 165.

Future copyright

CDPA 1988, s 91 (*see* Appendix 1) enables the copyright in works not yet created to be assigned so that when written the copyright vests in the assignee *ab initio*. The value of copyright in a work yet to be written cannot be great and if assigned to, say, a child's maintenance and accumulation settlement the capital gains tax and inheritance tax should be negligible and there would be no income tax liability, following *Mason v Innes, above*. This can be a useful means of transferring wealth free of tax if the work subsequently written turns out to have considerable value (*see* p 230). It is likely that the Revenue would disallow any expenses specifically relating to a work in which the copyright had been assigned, such as research expenses, unless it can be shown that these related to the profession as a whole. Whether this is likely to be a serious problem depends on the circumstances of the case.

Income of assignee

The case of *Mason v Innes* does not deal with the taxation liability of the assignee and it is to be presumed that an assessment under Schedule D, Case III was accepted. It will be appreciated that the post-cessation receipts provisions would not apply to the income arising from the book where the copyright had been given away and there is a very interesting paragraph in the case of *Hume v Asquith* (*see* p 191), where Pennycuick J states, at p 266:

An aspect of this matter which was much pressed by Counsel for the Crown has given me considerable perplexity. That is the position which arises where a professional man, having entered into a royalty contract, and while still carrying on his profession, proceeds to assign the benefit of that royalty contract. In such a case it seems clear—at first sight, to say no more—that the royalties could not be treated as part of the professional income of the person who has made the disposition, because they are no longer his income. On the other hand, it appears that, representing as they do uncollected income owing to the person carrying on the profession, they could equally not be taxed in the hands of the assignee. That is a very strange and anomalous position. On the other hand, a comparable position appears to arise in the simple case where, whilst still carrying on his profession, a person who is charged to tax on the basis of receipts assigns uncollected fees of a non-recurrent nature due to him. I do not know what the practice is in such a case, but the anomaly is not specific to the case of royalties or other income of a recurring nature, and I do not think that the existence of this anomaly, common to recurrent and non-recurrent payments, is a justification for attributing to the recurrent payments a character which they would not otherwise have possessed.

It should be pointed out, however, that under TA 1988, s 59(1) income tax under Schedule D shall be charged on, and paid by, the persons receiving or entitled to the income in respect of which the tax is directed by the Income Tax Acts to be charged. Perhaps on this basis the income which would escape tax under Schedule D, Case II as not having been received by the author could nonetheless be assessed on the recipient under these provisions, although to do so would appear to be contrary to *Purchase v Stainer's Executors* and *Carson v Cheyney's Executor*.

However, it seems that if the income is not assessed on the assignee it would be a capital amount received by him, as defined by TA 1988, s 777(13), and as such could be assessed on the assignor under TA 1988, s 775(2) as earned income under Schedule D, Case VI, if one of the main objects was the avoidance of tax.

Capital receipts

Authors have on a number of occasions tried to argue that a lump sum received from granting various rights in connection with their work is not part of their professional income assessable under Schedule D, Case II, but is a capital receipt. This argument has met with little success in the courts (IM 2691).

Exceptionally, the taxpayer was successful in the case of *Beare v Carter* (1940) 23 TC 353. In the course of his judgment MacNaghten J at p 356, stated:

That copyright is property and that a price paid for an out-and-out purchase of copyright is capital are propositions which are not disputed by the Crown. On the other hand royalties are income, and that is not disputed by the Respondent.

The line to be drawn between the payments which are capital and those which are income is by no means clear and distinct; and even if it were clear and distinct there would still be border-line cases. The question in every case is a question of fact depending upon the circumstances of the particular case under consideration.

The Commissioners had found that the lump sum of £150 to publish a further edition of a book was a capital receipt. As a point of principle this clearly caused the Revenue considerable concern, but although the taxpayer won it was made clear by MacNaghten J at p 358, that:

For the reasons I am about to give, I apprehend there is no question of principle in this case at all, and that it is only a question whether on the particular facts of this case there was no evidence which could support the decision of the Commissioners. There is this justification, I think, for the view that there was a question of principle, because, if the facts were that this was merely a lump sum payment for permission to publish so many copies of the work, then I apprehend that on the authority of the cases that were cited to me there is no doubt the decision of the Commissioners would be wrong.

The Judge confirmed the Commissioners' decision that the licence for the sixth edition of the book was in the nature of a capital transaction in as much as the long-retired author sold a part of the rights he had in the book.

Film rights and outright sales

The Judge's comments in *Beare v Carter* that it was not a question of principle is supported by further cases on authors attempting to argue that a lump sum received was capital. In the case of *Billam v Griffith* (1941) 23 TC 757 the sale of film rights of a play was held to be part of the Schedule D, Case II receipts of the author. In this case Lawrence J stated, at p 762:

> When such a vocation is carried on, and it is an ordinary incident of the disposition of plays either to realise them by means of royalties or by outright sale, it seems to me that it is really the realisation of what may be regarded as the circulating capital of the dramatist, his brain being his fixed capital, and his circulating capital being the plays which, no doubt, may for certain purposes be regarded as property but, at the same time, may be realised in the course of the business which he carries on.

It is not easy to reconcile this judgment with that in *Nethersole v Withers* (1948) 28 TC 501, in which income from the sale of film rights was held to be capital. The main distinction seems to be that in *Billam v Griffiths* the author was held still to be carrying on his profession, even though he had only ever written one successful play, whereas in the case of *Nethersole v Withers*, Miss Nethersole had given up her Schedule D profession many years previously and the alternative was between a Schedule D, Case VI charge or a receipt of capital. This view seems to be accepted by the Revenue (IM 2691). The court drew a distinction between the partial assignment of copyright and a licence to use copyright material. As Viscount Simon stated, at p 517:

> It is not disputed that the present case is a case of assignment; the Respondent, under the relevant agreement, made a partial assignment of her copyright and ceased to be the owner of the portion assigned, receiving a sum of money in exchange. This amounts to a sale of property by a person who is not engaged in the trade or profession of dealing in such property, and the proceeds of such a sale is, for Income Tax purposes, a sum in the nature of untaxable capital and not in the nature of taxable revenue.

In *Glasson v Rougier* (1944) 26 TC 86 Georgette Heyer (Mrs Rougier) sold her copyright in various works for a lump sum and it was held by MacNaghten J (at p 90) that:

> Whatever Mrs Rougier receives, whether by way of royalty or by payment for the sale of her copyright, each and all are profits earned by her in her vocation which must, in accordance with the Income Tax Acts, be included in the assessment.

Again the case was distinguished from *Beare v Carter*, where the author had only ever written one book and was not at the time of the lump sum receipt carrying on the profession of an author.

Similarly in *MacKenzie v Arnold* (1952) 33 TC 363 the court held that the sale of copyright by Sir Compton MacKenzie for a lump sum was nonetheless a receipt of his profession as author. A similar decision was arrived at in the case of *Household v Grimshaw* (1953) 34 TC 366 in respect of a lump sum received by an author on cancellation of an agreement to write a film script.

In *Howson v Monsell* (1950) 31 TC 529, concerning the film rights of books written by Margaret Irwin (Mrs Monsell), it was held that the amounts received for the sale of film rights should be assessed under Schedule D, Case II. In the words of Danckwerts J (at p 534):

It is plain that Mrs Monsell received these sums by reason of the fact that she was carrying on the vocation of writer or authoress of historical books and that the receipt by her was plainly in the course of carrying on that vocation.

When a professional author sold his working papers to a university the receipts were taxable under Schedule D, Case II as part of the exploitation by an author of anything produced in the course of his profession (*Professor Wain's Executors v Cameron* (1995) STC 555).

The principle which clearly emerges is that the sale of copyright for a lump sum by somebody not currently carrying on the profession of author may be capital, whereas a similar sale by an author currently carrying on his profession is part of his Schedule D, Case II receipts.

Normally the income received by an author will be assessed under Schedule D, Case II even if, as in *Billam v Griffiths*, there is only one successful work.

Publishing and casual receipts

However, on occasions the activities of the author are inconsistent with the mere exercise of his profession.

In *IRC v Maxse* (1919) 21 TC 41 it was held that an author and publisher could divide his remuneration into two sources of income, that of publishing assessed as a trade under Schedule D, Case I and that of author assessed as income from a profession under Schedule D, Case II. In the case of *Hobbs v Hussey* (1942) 24 TC 153 a series of newspaper articles which were the sole literary activity of the taxpayer gave rise to profits assessed under Schedule D, Case VI because, in the words of Lawrence J at p 156:

Does then the fact that the present transaction involved the sale of the copyright in the Appellant's series of articles, constitute the profits therefrom capital; or is such a sale merely subsidiary to what was in its essence a performance of services by the Appellant? In my opinion, the true nature of the transaction was the performance of services.

In the case of *Housden v Marshall* (1958) 38 TC 233 the taxpayer did not himself write articles but provided information for articles ghosted by a newspaper journalist. The payment was held assessable under Schedule D, Case VI (IM 2691).

In *Alloway v Phillips* [1979] STC 452, the wife of one of the 'Great Train Robbers' supplied information to a UK newspaper for use in articles published in the newspaper (IM 1702). As in *Hobbs v Hussey*, the profit was assessed under Schedule D, Case VI. The case was complicated by the fact that the taxpayer was resident in Canada at the relevant time, but it was held that the income was UK source income arising from a UK contract and therefore was included within the definition of any property whatever in the UK under TA 1988, s 18(1)(*a*)(iii) and therefore still taxable.

Another case where material was provided for the use of an author was that of *Earl Haig Trustees v IRC* (1939) 22 TC 725. In this case the trustees of the late Earl Haig arranged for a biography of him to be written, using material from his diaries. The profits were shared between the author and the trustees. The trustees clearly could not have been assessed under Schedule D, Case II as their sole activity was making the diaries available to the biographer. The Revenue attempted to assess the trustees under Schedule D, Case VI, but the court held that by making the diaries available to the biographer they had in fact made a partial realisation of one of the assets of the estate, as the diaries could not in future be again made available in the same manner. As a result the amount received by the trustees was a capital sum, even though received in instalments. At that time such an amount was tax free, although it would now be subject to capital gains tax as a disposal of rights.

In the case of *Lawrence and Others v IRC* (1940) 23 TC 333 certain royalties accrued to a trust from the publication of Colonel TE Lawrence's writings and the charity was held to be assessed to tax on the copyright royalties under Schedule D, Case VI. Such amounts were nonetheless annual payments and so would be exempt from income tax to a charity if the income were allocated for charitable purposes only.

Casual authors

In practice the Revenue taxes an occasional author, such as a politician writing his memoirs, under Schedule D, Case VI on royalties when received. The advantage of such treatment is that a lump sum received on an absolute assignment of the copyright, as opposed to a lump sum advance or grant of a licence, would give rise to a capital gains tax liability rather than, as in the case of a professional author, be included as part of professional income (*Leeming v Jones* (1930) 15 TC 333, IM 2691). Such income will normally be earned income if received by the originator of of the work (IM 2694).

The disadvantage is that it may be difficult to obtain relief for travel and research costs other than in the year the royalties are received on the ground that such expenses were capital. It might be desirable to obtain an advance on royalties in such circumstances, although, in general, the Revenue will allow reasonable expenses to be claimed (IM 2692).

It would appear that if an author claimed to carry on a profession as author, and made a profit, the Revenue would find it difficult to refuse Schedule D, Case II treatment. If the author consistently made losses the Revenue would refuse relief under TA 1988, s 384(1) and (9) unless it was shown that the profession was being carried on on a commercial basis with a view to the realisation of profits.

Spreading provisions

An author is taxed under the usual provisions of Schedule D, Case II on the royalties or lump sums received during the period of the accounts less the expenses incurred during the same period. There are, however, certain additional statutory provisions contained in TA 1988, ss 534–537 which apply only to copyright and artists' receipts.

Backward spreading

TA 1988, s 534 enables an author assessed under Schedule D, Case II or VI who has spent more than 12 months on a work to spread sums received from the assignment in whole or part of copyright or from the grant of a licence for a lump sum or royalties. The period of spread depends on the period during which he was engaged in making the work. If this does not exceed two years then half the income is deemed to have been received at the time of the actual receipt and the remaining half 12 months beforehand (IM 2695–2697).

Under TA 1988, s 534(3) if the period in which the author was engaged in making the work exceeded two years one-third of the income may be treated as received on the date it was actually received, one-third 12 months previously and one-third 12 months before that date.

The backward spreading of a payment of or on account of royalties earned applies only to amounts receivable within two years of first publication (TA 1988, s 534(4)(*b*)).

This contrasts with the backward spreading of a non-returnable lump sum payment, including a non-returnable advance on royalties, which may be spread backwards whenever received under TA 1988, s 534(4)(*a*), provided that a forward spread claim has not been made under TA 1988, s 535 (TA 1988, s 534(6)).

The claim for backward spreading of royalties may be made under TA 1988, s 534(5A) at any time not later than one year from 31 January following the year of assessment in which the payment is receivable.

These provisions apply not only to writers of books but to the author of any literary, dramatic or artistic work and the date of first publication means the first occasion on which the work, or a reproduction of it, is published, performed or exhibited. The relief is not available to partnerships or companies for receipts after 5 April 1996, TA 1988, s 534(6A).

Forward spreading

It is not possible to claim the backward spreading relief under TA 1988, s 534 and in respect of the same payment forward spreading under TA 1988, s 535 (TA 1988, s 535(9)).

TA 1988, s 535(1) provides that where copyright or an interest therein is assigned or a licence granted for a period of at least two years for a lump sum payment, which term includes a non-returnable advance on royalties, the author may claim to spread the lump sum forward. This forward spreading provision is available only where the assignment or grant of a licence is made more than ten years after first publication of the work, on making a claim within one year ten months from the end of the fiscal year in which it is receivable (TA 1988, s 535(8A), IM 2695–2697). A lump sum for these purposes would normally include a non-returnable, recoupable advance.

Under TA 1988, s 535(2) if the copyright is assigned or licensed for a period of six years or more, one-sixth of the lump sum is treated as being receivable on the date in which the lump sum was actually receivable and the remaining five-sixths is treated as having been receivable in five equal annual instalments on each anniversary of the date when the lump sum actually became receivable. Where the period of assignment or licence is less than six years the lump sum is spread over the number of whole years for which it is licensed (TA 1988, s 535(3)). If, therefore, copyright was licensed for three and a half years, one-third of the lump sum would be taxed by reference to the date of receivability and one-third would be treated as being receivable on each of the following two anniversaries of the date of receivability.

Under TA 1988, s 535(4) where the author dies the amount of the lump sum being carried forward is treated as arising on the last anniversary of the date of receivability prior to death. Up until 1995/96 this was subject to an election under TA 1988, s 535(5) to recompute the period of spread as if the copyright had been licensed for a period ending with the death. Such election had to be made by the personal representatives within two years of death. This election was abolished from 1996/97 onwards by FA 1995, s 115(10).

Similarly if the author's profession is discontinued any amount of the lump sum being carried forward will be treated under TA 1988, s 535(6) as received on the last anniversary of the date of actual receivability prior to the date of discontinuance. This was also, up until 1995/96, subject to the author's right to elect within two years to recompute the period of spread as if the licence were for a period ending with the day before discontinuance, but this right was abolished by FA 1995, s 115(10) from 1996/97 onwards.

If, exceptionally, the lump sum is assessable to tax under Schedule D, Case VI either for a casual author not carrying on a profession or under the post-cessation receipts provisions of TA 1988, ss 103–110, the spreading provisions apply only to the net amount after deduction of any expenses claimable against the receipt. The normal provisions under Schedule D, Case II tax the income when received and allow the expenses of a continuing profession to fall in the period in which they are actually incurred. TA 1988, s 535(8), however, requires the expenses to be deducted from a lump sum taxable under Schedule D, Case VI before allowing spread over the appropriate period.

It would appear from these provisions that if the lump sum was receivable immediately prior to discontinuance the period of spread would be reduced under TA 1988, s 535(6), as explained above, but that if the lump sum were received after the discontinuance and therefore taxed as a post-cessation receipt the net amount could be spread over the full period of six years. This seems somewhat anomalous. The normal time limit of six years is extended and any adjustments necessary, for example, arising in a recomputation on death under TA 1988, s 535(4), would be in time if made within one year of the determination of the claim (TA 1988, s 535(10)). The relief is not available to partnerships or companies for receipts after 5 April 1996, TA 1988, s 534(6A).

Artists

Artists, sculptors and others who receive a commission or fee for the creation of a work of art and who were engaged on the making of the work of art in question for more than 12 months, or were making a series of works of art for an exhibition over a period of more than 12 months, may claim backward spreading relief under TA 1988, s 538. This is very similar to the relief for authors under TA 1988, s 534 (IM 2695–2697).

Under TA 1988, s 538(2) if the period during which he was engaged on the work or works exceeds 12 months but does not exceed 24 months, one-half of the fee is treated as receivable on the date it actually became receivable and the remaining half is treated as having become receivable 12 months previously.

If the period involved was in excess of two years, one-third of the fee is treated as receivable on the date it actually became receivable, one-third 12 months previously and one-third 12 months before that. The relief is not available to partnerships or companies for receipts after 5 April 1996, TA 1988, s 534(6A).

Deduction of tax at source

United Kingdom patent royalties are subject to deduction of tax at source under the provisions of TA 1988, s 348(2)(*a*). Copyright royalties, however, are subject to deduction of tax at source under the general provisions of TA 1988, s 348(1) only if they are chargeable to tax on the recipient as pure income profit under Schedule D, Case III. As has been seen, most royalties are taxable under Schedule D, Case II on the recipient and are therefore paid gross. Only royalties arising from copyright held as an investment would normally be within Schedule D, Case III.

Non-residents

However, if the copyright owner's usual place of abode is outside the UK copyright royalties may come under the provisions of TA 1988, s 536(1).

Under these provisions income tax at the basic rate has to be deducted under TA 1988, ss 349, 350 on any copyright royalties paid to the owner of a copyright whose usual place of abode is not within the UK.

The owner of a copyright, in this connection, means the person entitled to some or all of the royalties, except that it is not extended to cinematograph films or video recordings, including the soundtrack not separately exploited. The Revenue view is that this exemption applies to the owner of the copyright in the film or video and not to the copyright in the screenplay or music held by the author or composer (IM 4000, TA 1988, s 536(2)).

There is also an exception under TA 1988, s 536(2) for copyright royalties paid in respect of copies which have been exported from the UK for distribution outside the UK which are therefore not subject to deduction of tax at source (IM 4004).

Where the publisher merely acts as the author's agent in arranging publication and sales, at the author's expense, any payments to the author are not copyright royalties at all, but the publisher may be taxable as agent of the author carrying on a trade in the UK under FA 1995, s 126, and be his UK representative for self-assessment purposes (IM 4002).

The agent's commission may be deducted before calculating the amount on which tax is to be withheld (TA 1988, s 536(3) and (4)). This can be done only where the payer has proof of the commission payable to a UK agent.

These withholding tax provisions only apply to royalties and advances on account of royalties, not to lump sums payable on assignment of copyright (*IRC v Longmans Green & Co Ltd* (1932) 17 TC 272, IM 4001). They may also be affected by double taxation treaties providing for a reduced rate or zero rate of withholding tax, in which case FICO International Division, on receipt of a competent claim for relief from the recipient, will usually authorise the payer to pay the reduced rate or not to deduct tax at all. Computer software licences authorising the user to copy programs for his own use are usually outwith these withholding arrangements (IM 4001).

It is not possible to enter into an agreement to avoid the deduction of tax under these provisions. The time of payment, under TA 1988, s 536(5), is deemed to be when the publisher originates the payment, not the date of payment by the agent to the copyright holder. The provision is to be compared with TA 1988, s 43, relating to the payment of rents to a non-resident, where it is the payer to the non-resident who has the liability to deduct tax at the basic rate, which is rather more satisfactory in practice.

It is arguable that TA 1988, s 536 is merely a machinery section giving effect to TA 1988, ss 348, 349, and is not a charging section. Consequently the section would apply only where a UK source was involved and support for this exists in TA 1988, s 536(2), the exception for royalties for foreign copies as well as the Hansard statement (*below*). Thus the mere payment of copyright royalties to the owner whose place of abode is outside the UK is insufficient to require deduction of tax: location of the source in the UK is a requisite for deduction of tax at source—TA 1988, s 536 is not a withholding tax section, ie it relates to sales of books or music or performances of plays etc, within the UK only (IM 4003).

Note that the withholding tax procedures apply to copyright owners whose usual place of abode is outside the UK, rather than to those who are not resident or not ordinarily resident in the UK for tax purposes. It would not be difficult to imagine the case of a person whose usual place of abode was outside the UK, but who was regarded as resident in the UK because, for example, he spends on average four months a year in the UK (IM 4005). Tax is withheld by the payer whether the payment is made direct to the overseas recipient or to his bank or agent (IM 4006).

The tax deducted is accounted for to the Revenue under TA 1988, ss 349, 350, which means that the amount deducted is immediately paid over and is not treated as an annual payment out of profits or gains brought into charge to tax under TA 1988, s 348, as described at p 109 for patent royalties (IM 4007).

Non-resident authors

It is interesting to note under TA 1988, s 536 that, in spite of appearances, the provisions do not apply to authors exercising their profession whose normal place of abode is outside the UK. The argument appears to be that so far as an author is concerned the source of his income is his profession, which is outside the UK, rather than the UK copyright as an independent asset. This interpretation was confirmed in a Parliamentary written answer on 10 November 1969 (Hansard, Vol 791, col 31):

> *Overseas British National (publication fees)* Mr Ashton asked the Chancellor of the Exchequer what steps he takes to recover tax on fees paid to British nationals living abroad by publishers in this country.
>
> Mr Roy Jenkins: Section 391, Taxes Act 1970 [TA 1988, s 536] requires any person making such payments to deduct income tax at the (basic) rate and to pay it over to the Inland Revenue. I am advised that this does not apply to payments made to those who are authors by profession, nor does it apply if the recipient is living in a country with which we have a Double Taxation Agreement requiring us to exempt such payments.

This arrangement is only obliquely referred to in the *Inspectors' Manual* which states at IM 4001: 'Where it is claimed that tax should not be deducted from a payment within (a) or (b) above, on the grounds that the recipient is a professional author, composer etc., the fact should be reported to BP3 (Literary and Artistic Profits).'

It is interesting to note that the original rules relating to the deduction of tax from royalties paid to a copyright owner whose usual place of abode was abroad were considered in the case of *Rye and Eyre v IRC* (1935) 19 TC 164. Under the provisions of FA 1927, s 26 it was provided that where such a payment was made by or through any person, 'that person shall forthwith deliver to the Commissioners of Inland Revenue for the use of the Special Commissioners an account of the payment', and it was held that the agents of the author were liable to deduct tax on payment to him.

In *IRC v Longmans Green & Co Ltd* (1932) 17 TC 272 the UK publishers paid a lump sum non-returnable advance to a French author and were held accountable to tax at the basic rate on the whole amount. The court rejected an argument that the advance was in fact a capital payment for the partial assignment of copyright and not a payment on account of royalties within the meaning of what is now TA 1988, s 536(1).

On the facts of the case, Finlay J held (at p 280):

> I have come to the conclusion, though not without hesitation, for I think the case near the line on this point, that this was a licence and not a complete assignment of the copyright. I think it is obvious that between a partial assignment of copyright and a licence the line may run extremely fine, and I think this does run rather fine; but, construing the agreement in the light of the authorities, and each agreement has to be construed in the light of its own facts, I think that the correct view here is that this was not an assignment of the copyright but rather a licence to do certain specific things—not, of course, to translate into every language, but to translate into one particular language, namely, English.

He contrasted this, at p 283, with the situation which could have arisen:

> It may well be, indeed I think for myself that it would be, that, if for 500,000 francs or any other sum, the right of translation—what I may call the unlimited right of translation, that is, the right of translating and the right of publishing any number of the expensive edition and any cheap editions that the publishers might be minded to publish—if, so to speak, the whole thing, the whole English rights of translation and publication had been transferred and transferred for a lump sum, I think that it probably would be right to say that that sum would not be assessable as a royalty.

As has been seen, such a lump sum would for a UK-resident author be part of his normal Schedule D, Case II profits, but for someone whose usual place of abode was outside the UK a lump sum for the assignment of part of the copyright would not be within the deduction of tax provisions.

It is difficult to reconcile this case with the Revenue practice confirmed by the Hansard statement quoted above.

The case of *IRC v Longmans Green & Co Ltd* is also interesting because it is one of the instances where the case was taken as a point of principle and the Revenue picked up the bill for the costs of both sides in spite of being the victorious party. In the words of EJ Macgillivray, for the Crown at p 284:

> The Commissioners do not ask for the costs of this appeal. It is an unusual case, because here the Respondents are being assessed in a representative capacity and, although they have made provision for the payment of tax, they are not in a position to recover the costs of this appeal as against the French author. In these unusual circumstances the Commissioners have agreed that they shall pay the publisher their costs of this appeal in any event.

Realisation of investments

Most of the cases so far considered concern payments in respect of copyright to authors or those who have contributed directly to the work in question. One case in which the copyright was treated as a pure investment was the case of *Shiner v*

Lindblom (1960) 39 TC 367. In this case Ronald Shiner acquired an option for the film rights of Noel Streatfield's book *Aunt Clare* which was converted into a film in which Mr Shiner starred. The Commissioners held as a question of fact that it was Mr Shiner's intention upon acquiring the option for the copyright of the book *Aunt Clare* to use it as an investment. They then held, somewhat surprisingly, that the profit from the sale of the film rights was part of Mr Shiner's professional income as an actor, which was clearly insupportable and dismissed by Danckwerts J. The Revenue also contended that the purchase and resale of the film rights constituted an adventure in the nature of trade assessable under Schedule D, Case I. This was also dismissed by the learned Judge (p 373):

> As regards the other point, whether it was a transaction in the nature of trade, it seems to be that a conclusion can be reached on the facts which have been found by the Commissioners. It is quite plain that he had no other transactions of this nature and they have found that he acquired it as an investment and had no intention of realising it; he was not, in other words, trading in copyright or anything of that sort. It was something which he had acquired. He received an offer which was favourable and he decided to realise the investment.

The result was, at the time, a tax free capital profit which would now be subject to capital gains tax.

Prizes and grants

A prize or gift won by or given to the originator of intellectual property is unlikely to be taxable (*Simpson v John Reynolds & Co (Insurances) Ltd* [1975] STC 271; *Moore v Griffiths* (1972) 48 TC 338; *Reed v Seymour* (1927) 11 TC 625). This would normally apply in whatever way the income is taxed, although if in excess of £25,000 and to an employee he could be taxable under the golden handshake provision of TA 1988, ss 148, 188 and Sched 11 (*Ellis v Lucas* (1966) 43 TC 276; *Walker v Carnaby Harrower, Barham & Pykett* (1969) 46 TC 561). It would normally be argued that a prize was not a reward for services (*Ball v Johnson* (1971) 47 TC 155), unless part of normal remuneration (*Moorhouse v Dooland* (1954) 36 TC 1; *Davis v Harrison* (1927) 11 TC 707; *Corbett v Duff* (1941) 23 TC 763; *Cooper v Blakiston* (1908) 5 TC 347). *See below* for Arts Council awards and bursaries.

A grant or subsidy directly relating to the business however is likely to be taxable (*IRC v Falkirk Ice Rink Ltd* [1975] STC 434; *Smart v Lincolnshire Sugar Co Ltd* (1937) 20 TC 643; *Temperley v Smith* (1956) 37 TC 18; *Duff v Williamson* (1973) STC 434; *McGowan v Brown and Cousins* (1977) STC 342). If, therefore, an author wrote a piece specifically for a competition, the prize money, if he won, would be taxable.

It is understood that the author Andrew Boyle, who won the Whitbread Award, successfully resisted a Revenue attempt to tax it as income, before the Special Commissioners. However, the Revenue may challenge other cases, although it seems to accept the Booker Prize as tax free, as an unsolicited mark of honour for outstanding achievement. Awards may also, depending on the circumstances, possibly be taxable under Schedule E as emoluments, as casual profits under Schedule D, Case VI or exceptionally as annual payments under Schedule D,

Case III. Awards to students may be exempt from tax as scholarship income under TA 1988, s 331 (IM 2691a).

Arts Council awards and bursaries

The Arts Council, on 10 September 1979, published a press release setting out the taxation treatment of awards and grants, which the Revenue follow (IM 2691 B):

The Arts Council and the Inland Revenue have now agreed this note on the tax treatment of awards and bursaries which the Council makes to artists, writers, photographers, musicians and the performing artists. Such awards and bursaries form a small but important part of the Arts Council's budget.

Since the Arts Council has been introducing new types of awards there have been some difficulties in the application of the understanding reached between the Arts Council and the Inland Revenue in 1968. These notes are intended to clarify the treatment of the awards, etc. for tax purposes. They do not impinge on the rights of appeal against an assessment to tax on any individual recipient of an award or bursary.

Awards and bursaries made by the Arts Council fall to be treated for tax purposes in the following categories:

Category A awards and bursaries which are chargeable to tax

1. Direct or indirect musical, design or choreographic commissions and direct or indirect commissions of sculpture and paintings for public sites.

2. The Royalty Supplement Guarantee Scheme.

3. The Contract Writers' Scheme.

4. Jazz bursaries.

5. Translators' grants.

6. Photographic awards and bursaries.

7. Film and video awards and bursaries.

8. Performance Art awards.

9. Arts Publishing grants.

10. Grants to assist with a specific project or projects (such as the writing of a book) or to meet specific professional expenses such as a contribution towards copying expenses made to a composer, or to an artist's studio expenses.

Category B awards and bursaries which are not chargeable to tax

1. Bursaries to trainee directors.

2. In-service bursaries for theatre directors.

3. Bursaries for associate directors.

4. Bursaries to people attending full-time courses in arts administration (the practical training course).

5. In-service bursaries to theatre designers and bursaries to trainees on the theatre designers' scheme.

6. In-service bursaries for administrators.

7. Bursaries for actors and actresses.

8. Bursaries for technicians and stage managers.

9. Bursaries made to students attending the City University arts administration courses.

10. Awards, known as the Buying Time Awards, made, not to assist with a specific project or professional expenses, but to maintain the recipient to enable him to take time off to develop his personal talents. These at present include the following awards and bursaries known as the Theatre Writing Bursaries, Awards and Bursaries to composers. Awards and Bursaries to painters, sculptors and print makers, Literature Awards and Bursaries.

It will be open to the Arts Council to make both a grant in Category A10 and an award in Category B10 to an individual and accordingly, in such a case, part only of the sum received by the individual concerned will be treated as taxable. However, it is agreed in relation to these cases that if the expenditure incurred by the individual in connection with the matters covered by the A10 grant and the B10 award exceeds the amount of the A10 grant the excess up to and including the amount of the B10 award will be regarded as covered by the B10 award, and to this extent will not be allowable as a deduction in arriving at his or her taxable profits. The remainder of any of the expenditure will be subject to the normal Schedule D expenses rules. The arrangements noted herein will be followed by the Inland Revenue, whilst the law remains as it is, in cases involving awards both for future assessments and in settlement of appeals now open. The Arts Council will, in making future awards, inform the recipient of the category applicable for tax purposes.

Public lending right

For income and corporation tax purposes public lending right payments are treated under TA 1988, s 537 as copyright payments for the purposes of the return of payments under TMA 1970, s 16 and for forward and backward spreading under TA 1988, ss 534 and 535 (IM 2700). They are also treated as copyright royalties for the purposes of TA 1988, s 536 for the deduction of tax on payments to copyright holders whose usual place of abode is abroad, and for post cessation receipts purposes where TA 1988, s 103(3)(*b*) excludes a lump sum paid to the personal representatives of the author of a literary, dramatic, musical or artistic work as consideration for the assignment, or partial assignment, of the copyright. They are also included in the definition of copyright for the purposes of TA 1988, s 821 where tax has been under deducted from payments to non-UK copyright holders under TA 1988, s 821(3)(*a*).

Public lending right receipts will normally be included as part of the author's professional income for Schedule D purposes.

Leasing

In certain cases, in particular relating to computer software, the user may have unrestricted right to use the copyright material for his own use on payment of a fee. In other words he effectively leases the software and in many cases the contract is set out in the form of a lease agreement. As the payment is not related to user but to time it is not a royalty per Jenkins LJ in *Carson v Cheyney's Executor* (1958) 38 TC 240, and the withholding tax provisions of TA 1988, s 536 and other provisions relating to copyright royalties would have no effect.

Purchase of copyright

Capital allowances

There are no specific provisions giving capital allowances on the purchase of copyright except for computer software (*see below*) and it is doubtful whether copyright work is within the definition of plant as originally defined in *Yarmouth v France* (1887) 19 QBD 647. In many cases this is not a problem because the acquirer is carrying on a trade of publishing or otherwise exploiting copyright and the cost of copyright purchases is written off as a trading expense or carried forward at the lower of cost or market value as part of the publisher's stock in trade.

In the case of an investor acquiring copyright material as a capital acquisition there is a possibility that an original manuscript may be plant. This could follow from *Munby v Furlong* [1977] STC 232 which held that books could be plant, and would be consistent with the treatment of cinematograph films and record master tapes as plant (*see* Inland Revenue statement of practice SP9/79 10 August 1979 in Appendix 6), prior to CAA 1990, s 68.

Wallpaper designs however, which are clearly copyright, were held not to be plant in the case of *McVeigh v Arthur Sanderson & Sons Ltd* (1968) 45 TC 273, but the cost of the printing blocks must include something for the cost of the designs. It should be emphasised in this case that Cross J regarded himself bound by the decision in *Daphne v Shaw* (1926) 11 TC 256, although this has largely been overruled by *Munby v Furlong, above.*

Deferred revenue expenditure

Where copyright material is not stock in trade it may, nevertheless, be deferred revenue expenditure if it has a short life of say, less than two years, on analogy with video tapes for rental and computer software, if the correct accounting treatment is to write off the expenditure over its life (*see* Chapters 26 and 27).

Capital taxes

Copyright, as intellectual property, is subject to capital gains tax and inheritance tax in the same way as patents: *see* Chapter 15. On 25 February 1983 Mr Nicholas Ridley confirmed 'the value of a copyright for capital transfer tax (inheritance tax) is the price the property might reasonably be expected to fetch if sold in the open market at the time of the transfer' (Hansard Vol 37, Col 570). In practice copyright is rarely sold in isolation but any such sale would be on the basis of the discounted present value of a conservative estimate of the likely future royalties. Copyright would usually become a wasting asset under TCGA 1992, s 44 only after the author's death when the remaining life was less than 50 years.

Books, manuscripts, pictures, photographs, documents and sculptures protected by copyright are also tangible moveable property for capital gains tax purposes. This means that disposal proceeds of up to £6,000 would be exempt under TCGA 1992, s 262 and any loss on a sale for less than £6,000 would be restricted on the basis of a deemed sale price of £6,000. In the case of a gain, marginal relief is given by deducting from the gain the excess of the gain over five-thirds of the excess of the consideration over £6,000.

Example

	£
Sale proceeds	7,200
Cost	400
Gain	6,800

Marginal relief	
Sale proceeds	7,200
Less:	
Deemed cost	6,000
Excess	1,200
5/3 excess	2,000
Gain as calculated	6,800
Relief £6,800 – £2,000	4,800
Revised gain	2,000

In other words the gain is the lower of the normal gain or five-thirds of the excess of the sale proceeds over £6,000.

Such tangible property could in the view of the Treasury be of national, scientific or artistic importance and thus qualify for capital gains tax exemption under TCGA 1992, s 258 if the transfer was or could have been exempt from inheritance tax as a conditionally exempt transfer under IHTA 1984, s 30 on an undertaking given under IHTA 1984, s 31 or TCGA 1992, s 258(3). The undertaking requires the property to be made available to the public and kept in the UK. On a subsequent sale or breach of undertaking where the exemption is not available there could be both a capital gains tax and an inheritance tax charge under TCGA 1992, s 258(5) and IHTA 1984, ss 32 and 33.

Stamp duty

Copyright is property in the same way as a patent and similar provisions apply for stamp duty: *see* Chapter 23.

VAT

The VAT provisions relating to patents apply similarly to copyright: *see* Chapter 11.

For VAT purposes public lending right payments are different from royalty payments and cannot be treated in the same way. Public lending right is outside the scope for VAT and should not be declared on the VAT return form. Public lending right payment is not a royalty but derives from the author receiving a share of a subsidy or grant.

The public lending right registrar is not registered for VAT and no VAT is chargeable to him on public lending right payments. Monies distributed by the registrar under the Public Lending Right Act 1979 do not constitute considerations of a supply to the registrar and therefore no VAT is chargeable on the monies solely distributed. In case of difficulty authors' local VAT officers should be asked to refer to VAT Administration Directorate (VAH2) quoting reference TL 1158/82 which confirms that no VAT is chargeable on public lending right monies.

Copyright royalties are often paid to authors and others whose taxable outputs are below the registration limit and who do not have to register for VAT. In such cases the royalties would be paid without any addition for VAT. Most publishers also operate a self-billing system whereby an invoice is not raised by the author but the royalties are accounted for by the publisher who produces a statement which acts as if it were an invoice from the author. This means that if the author is registered for VAT the publisher adds VAT at the standard rate to the royalties due and if the author is not so registered the publisher merely pays over the basic royalty. For a self-billed invoice to count as a tax invoice, the self-billing arrangement must have been cleared by HM Customs & Excise under Value Added Tax (General) Regulations 1985 (SI 1985 No 886).

18   Know-how and show-how

Introduction

Although the sale of know-how has for many years normally been assessed as a trading receipt, special provisions are included in the Taxes Acts to tax as income those few receipts which would otherwise be capital. Show-how is the provision of services rather than a transfer of intellectual property and there are no special taxation provisions to consider.

Definitions

'Know-how' is defined for tax purposes by TA 1988, s 533(7) as:

> any industrial information and techniques likely to assist in the manufacture or processing of goods or materials, or in the working of a mine, oil well or other source of mineral deposits (including the searching for, discovery, or testing of deposits or the winning of access thereto), or in the carrying out of any agricultural, forestry or fishing operations.

This is a wide definition and would include many payments normally referred to as know-how fees and could also include designs for manufactured products and secret processes. It does not, however, include commercial know-how which is becoming of greater commercial significance. In this chapter 'know-how' refers to all know-how, and 'industrial know-how' to that within TA 1988, s 533(7). 'Show-how' is the term often applied to agreements for the provision of technical assistance and training.

Income

Know-how is often licensed in return for royalties and as these are not patent royalties they would be taxed in the same way as royalties for trade marks and designs (*see* p 187).

Show-how fees are rather different in that show-how is, strictly, the provision of services rather than an assignment or licence of intellectual property. This means that the show-how fees would normally be taxed as trading income of the recipient and allowed as a trading expense of the payer. This would apply whether there is a single payment or lump sum fee or whether the payment is spread over a period, even if it is calculated on a royalty basis.

A know-how royalty for the use of a secret process for 40 years was exceptionally treated as an annual payment taxable on the licensor and as a charge on income of the licensee in the case of *Delage v Nugget Polish Co Ltd* (1905) 21 TLR 454 (*see above*, p 189). Normally the services to be provided by the licensor prevent the receipt from being 'pure income profit' and therefore know-how royalties are not normally annual payments.

Lump sums

Case law

Know-how may be sold for a lump sum and it is then necessary to determine whether this is taxable as a trading receipt or not (CA 6015–6022). The leading case on the topic is that of *Jeffrey v Rolls-Royce Ltd* (1962) 40 TC 443. In this case it was held that the disposal of rights to manufacture certain aircraft engines for a lump sum payment, including the provision of all technical assistance, gave rise to a trading receipt on the ground that it was merely a way of turning the company's expertise into income. As Lord Radcliffe said on p 492:

> I cannot accept the contention that by each of these agreements the Company sold a part of that capital asset and received a price for it. There is nothing in the Case to indicate that that capital asset was in any way diminished by carrying out these agreements. The whole of its knowledge and experience remained available to the Company for manufacturing and further research and development, and there is nothing to show that its value in any way diminished.

The case was distinguished from that of *Evans Medical Supplies Ltd v Moriarty* (1957) 37 TC 540, under which the sale of know-how was held to be a capital receipt. The distinction was, in the words of Lord Radcliffe in the *Rolls-Royce* case, at p 492:

> In that case [*Evans Medical Supplies*] it was held that the company parted with a capital asset and received for it a capital sum. For one thing, it lost its Burmese market. And, further, it was said to be obvious that the capital value of the secret processes must have been greatly diminished by their disclosure to the Burmese Government. Every case of this kind must be decided on its own facts.

The *Rolls-Royce* decision was followed in the case of *Musker v English Electric Co Ltd* (1964) 41 TC 556. Attempts by the company to distinguish the sale of its know-how from that in the *Rolls-Royce* case were rejected by the House of Lords.

The basic distinction is that where the know-how remains with the vendor for further exploitation it is a trading receipt. If on the other hand the disposal is of part of the company's assets so that the information once imparted cannot again be utilised commercially the receipt would be one of capital following *Evans Medical Supplies Ltd v Moriarty*.

The principle in the *Rolls-Royce* case was also followed in *Coalite & Chemical Products Ltd v Treeby* (1971) 48 TC 171.

The case of *John & E Sturge Ltd v Hessel* [1975] STC 573 not only confirmed that the sale of know-how was, in the circumstances, a trading receipt, but also that the receipt was taxable when it was earned, that is when, under the agreement, the services to be rendered were rendered.

In an early case on the topic of know-how, *British Dyestuffs Corporation (Blackley) Ltd v IRC* (1924) 12 TC 586, it was argued that a payment for know-how was a capital receipt in spite of the fact that it was payable by ten annual instalments, each of £25,000.

In the words of Banks LJ at p 596, it was stated:

> I do not myself think that the method of payment adopted in carrying through a transaction between a company, such as this, and a licensee is very much guide to the true nature of the transaction. The real question is, looking at this matter, is the transaction in substance a parting by the Company with part of its property for a purchase price, or is it a method of trading by which it acquires this particular sum of money as part of the profits and gains of that trade?

The amount was held to be a trading receipt in that case.

Apart from the case of *Evans Medical Supplies Ltd v Moriarty*, already referred to above, the only other case where a sale of know-how was held to be capital was that of *Wolf Electric Tools Ltd v Wilson* (1968) 45 TC 326. In that case the company was forced either to abandon its exports to India or to set up local manufacture through a company in which it held a minority interest. It chose the latter course. It was held that the transfer of know-how to the new company in exchange for the minority interest was not a disposal of know-how for the value of the shares in the new company, but was an alteration in the company's structure. In the words of Pennycuick J at p 340:

> In a case such as the present, the effect of the whole arrangement—and I must look at the whole arrangement—is that the trader receives a new capital asset, namely, the shares in the foreign company, in exchange for that which he previously had, namely, his connection or goodwill in the foreign country. That is a transaction of a wholly capital nature.

In *Thomsons (Carron) Ltd v IRC* (1976) STC 317, the sale of know-how in exchange for shares in the acquirer was still a revenue receipt of the vendor.

Statutory provisions

Attempts to argue that the sale of industrial know-how is a capital receipt in respect of amounts received after 19 March 1968 would be largely abortive in view of the provisions of what is now TA 1988, s 531(1). This states:

> (1) Subject to subsection (7) below, where, after 19 March 1968, a person disposes of know-how which has been used in a trade carried on by him, and continues to carry on the trade after the disposal, the amount or value of any consideration received by him for the disposal shall—
>
>   (a) if it is received in respect of the disposal of know-how after 31 March 1986, so far as it is not brought into account as disposal value under section 530(5), nor is chargeable to tax as a revenue or income receipt;
>
>   (b) in any other case, so far as it is not chargeable to tax as a revenue or income receipt, be treated for all purposes as a trading receipt.

There are no provisions for spreading the receipt over a period (CA 6019).

Common control One of the exceptions to these provisions is that under TA 1988, s 531(7) the treatment as an automatic trading receipt does not apply where the buyer is a body of persons over whom the seller has control, or the seller is a body of persons over whom the buyer has control, or both the seller and the buyer are bodies of persons and some other person has control over both of them, and for this purpose 'body of persons' includes partnerships. In such cases the sale of industrial know-how, together with the trade or part of the trade, is deemed to be a sale of goodwill giving rise to a capital gains tax charge. The sale of know-how by itself would normally be a trading receipt (CA 6032).

Disposal of know-how and goodwill If, however, the industrial know-how is sold, together with the trade or part of a trade, any consideration received is treated under TA 1988, s 531(2) as a payment for goodwill and therefore a capital sum taxed as a chargeable gain under TCGA 1992, s 21 (CA 6025 and 6026).

Except in the case of transactions between persons under common control under TA 1988, s 531(7), it is possible under TA 1988, s 531(3) to elect that the sale of industrial know-how will be treated as a trading receipt, even if on the disposal of a trade, where a joint election is made by the transferee and the transferor and given to the Inspector of Taxes within two years of the disposal. Nor is it to be treated as a capital transaction, in spite of being linked with the disposal of a trade, where the transferor was previously carrying on a business wholly outside the UK. It could be advantageous for example, where there are unused trading losses brought forward, to treat know-how proceeds as a revenue receipt rather than a capital receipt.

Non-trading know-how Where the industrial know-how disposed of has not been used for the purpose of a trade the receipt of a capital sum would be taxed under Schedule D, Case VI, with a deduction for the cost of the know-how if not otherwise relieved (TA 1988, s 531(5)). If such a sum is received by the devisor of the industrial know-how the income assessed under Schedule D, Case VI will be treated as earned income under TA 1988, s 531(6) (CA 6020–6022).

Restrictive covenants It is not possible to avoid the statutory provisions in relation to industrial know-how receipts by entering into restrictive covenants rather than some form of licence agreement or assignment, as any receipts from such a covenant would be taxable under TA 1988, s 531(8) as a know-how receipt (CA 6030).

Planning aspects

It might be possible in suitable circumstances to sell the know-how to a subsidiary company for a capital sum in which case the provisions of TA 1988, s 531(7), mentioned above, would apply. If this were a disposal of know-how there would be a capital gain, but as this would be an intra-group transaction within TCGA 1992, s 171 there would be no immediate corporation tax liability on the chargeable gain.

If the shares in the subsidiary company were then sold to an intended purchaser of the know-how there would be a chargeable gain if the shares were sold at a profit. If, however, the shares had been issued at par for the full value of the know-how there would be no gain on the disposal of the shares themselves. There would, however, be a deemed disposal of the know-how itself, which would crystallise on the company leaving the group under TCGA 1992, s 178, if the transfer to the subsidiary had taken place within the previous six years. This would nonetheless be a capital gain rather than a trading receipt and could therefore be preferable.

Allowance to purchaser

The net expenditure on industrial know-how incurred after 31 March 1986 if not allowable as a trading expense, qualifies for a writing-down allowance of 25 per cent a year; this is proportionately reduced if the trade has been carried on for only part of a tax year of if the chargeable period is for less than one year (TA 1988, s 530(1), (2)(*a*) and (8)). In the period to cessation a balancing allowance is made for the whole of the unallowed balance of expenditure (TA 1988, s 530(2)(*b*)). If the disposal value exceeds the qualifying expenditure, there is a balancing charge on the excess (TA 1988, s 530(3)).

Qualifying expenditure is the expenditure during the period plus any previous qualifying expenditure remaining unrelieved (TA 1988, s 530(4)) which effectively gives a writing-down allowance of 25 per cent a year on a reducing balance basis. The capital allowances rules applicable to plant and machinery, including the pool basis and balancing allowances and charges are largely applied by TA 1988, ss 530 and 532 except for the control sales rules in CAA 1990, ss 157 and 158 which are disapplied by TA 1988, s 532(5) and replaced by TA 1988, s 531(7) above (CA 6038).

When industrial know-how is disposed of, the whole of the net proceeds will be brought into account: there is no limit by reference to the original cost of the know-how (TA 1988, s 530(5), (CA 6040–6048)). For the purposes of capital allowances on industrial know-how expenditure, deemed know-how, such as expenditure in relation to restrictive covenants does not qualify for writing-down allowances, although it would normally be capital expenditure (*Associated Portland Cement Manufacturers Ltd v IRC* (1945) 27 TC 103, CA 6030). Industrial know-how acquired by a holding company for use by its operating subsidiaries should qualify for relief against management charges received (CA 6007).

A trader who incurred capital expenditure on industrial know-how before 1 April 1986 is entitled to write off the cost evenly over six years beginning with the year in which expenditure was incurred (TA 1988, s 530(6)). Any expenditure remaining unallowed on discontinuance is allowed in that period. Pre-trading expenditure is deemed to be incurred on commencement of the trade (TA 1988, s 530(7)).

Commercial know-how

Commercial know-how, outwith the definition in TA 1988, s 533(7), does not qualify for capital allowances and, if capital expenditure, could only be relieved in a computation for chargeable gains on outright sale, which is unlikely to be of much assistance. Revenue expenditure can be written off immediately or over a short period as deferred revenue expenditure (*see* Chapter 26, p 334, CA 6005–6008). The Revenue accept that both lump sum and recurring payments to acquire know-how for the purposes of a trade are normally revenue payments (CA 6010).

Divers

Divers and diving supervisors employed in the UK are deemed by TA 1988, s 314 to be carrying on a trade. Certain training courses qualify for relief as acquisition of industrial know-how (CA 6033).

Stamp duty

Neither know-how nor show-how are regarded as property for stamp duty purposes and therefore no *ad valorem* duty is payable in respect of any agreement, assignment or licence. If an agreement covers both know-how and the sale of goodwill these elements should be clearly separated, as the goodwill transfer would be subject to the full *ad valorem* duty.

VAT

The provision of know-how is regarded as a service in the same way as any other assignment or transfer of intellectual property and the VAT position is the same as for patents (*see* Chapter 11).

Double taxation

Occasionally, show-how fees may be treated as royalties under double tax treaties and subject to withholding tax in the overseas country.

Article 11 of the 1973 agreement with Jamaica (SI 1973 No 1329), for example, states:

Management fees

(1) Management fees arising in one of the territories and paid to a resident of the other territory may be taxed in that other territory.

(2) Management fees may also be taxed in the territory in which they arise and according to the law of that territory; but where the management fees are paid to a resident of the other territory who is subject to tax there in respect thereof the tax so charged in the territory in which those management fees arise shall not exceed 12 per cent of the gross amount thereof.

(3) The term 'management fees' as used in this Article means payments of any kind to any person other than to an employee of the person making the payments, for or in respect of, the provision of industrial or commercial advice, or management or technical services, or similar services or facilities, or hire of plant or equipment but it does not include payments for independent personal services mentioned in Article 19.

(4) The provisions of paragraphs (1) and (2) of this Article shall not apply if the recipient of the management fees, being a resident of one of the territories, has in the other territory in which the management fees arise a permanent establishment with which the management fees are effectively connected. In such a case the provisions of Article 5 shall apply.

(5) If a resident of one of the territories who receives management fees which arise in the other territory and who is subject to tax in respect thereof in the first mentioned territory so elects for any year of assessment, or financial year, the tax chargeable in respect of those management fees in the territory in which they arise shall be calculated as if he had a permanent establishment in that territory and as if those management fees were taxable in accordance with Article 5 as industrial or commercial profits attributable to that permanent establishment.

(6) Management fees shall be deemed to arise in one of the territories when the payer is the Government of that territory or a political sub-division thereof, a local authority or a resident of that territory. Where, however, the person paying the management fees, whether he is a resident of one of the territories or not, has in one of the territories a permanent establishment in connection with which the obligation to pay the management

fees was incurred and the management fees are borne by the permanent establishment, then the management fees shall be deemed to arise in that territory.

(7)   Where, owing to a special relationship between the payer and the recipient or between both of them and some other person, the amount of the management fees paid, having regard to the advice, services or use of which they are paid, exceed the amount which would have been agreed upon by the payer and the recipient in the absence of such relationship, the provisions of this Article shall apply only to the last-mentioned amount. In that case the excess part of the payments shall remain taxable according to the law of each territory, due regard being had to the other provisions of this Agreement.

19   Merchandising and endorsement

Introduction

The intellectual property aspects of character merchandising are often a mixture of design or trade mark and copyright and there are no special taxation provisions relating to this subject. Similarly, endorsement by a famous person of a product or service may be protected by the individual's copyright in his own commissioned photographs and tangible likenesses and signature, but will often involve services to be rendered, such as publicity photographs or public appearances, as well as a licence for copyright material. It may be possible to protect a 'name and likeness' by registering a photograph or a trade mark or invoking the protection of the passing off or defamation laws. Again, there are no special taxation provisions relating to endorsement.

Merchandising

Character merchandising, that is, the portrayal of fictional characters created by an author or artist on toys and other manufactured articles, has in recent times become a common means of commercially exploiting such characters. The portrayal of a character such as Noddy or Paddington Bear on a child's toy without permission of the author or copyright holder would be in breach of copyright. It is therefore common practice to license the producers of such articles to enable them to portray the character on such goods, or to make model representations of the character.

Income

The income received would normally be trading income of the recipient taxed under Schedule D, Case I and an allowable expense of the payer under TA 1988, s 74. The licence fee is not a patent royalty and not normally an annual payment and would not therefore be subject to deduction of tax at source under TA 1988, ss 348–350. Exceptionally, the copyright owner may be holding it as an investment so that the licence income would be taxed under Schedule D, Case III in accordance with TA 1988, s 18(3)(*a*) and treated as a charge on income of the payer, who would have to deduct tax at source under the provisions of TA 1988, ss 348–350, or have his normal place of abode outside the UK bringing in the provisions of TA 1988, s 536, as explained in Chapter 17.

The leading case on the subject of character merchandising is *Noddy Subsidiary Rights Company Ltd v IRC* (1966) 43 TC 458. In this case it was held that the company carrying on the merchandising activities, that is, granting licences to manufacturers, was carrying on a trade.

The comments of Pennycuick J at p 475 are of particular interest:

> It seems to me that, where a person owns an item of property and grants licences under it, those activities may or may not, according to the particular circumstances, amount to a trade. A number of examples were suggested in argument. I think it is better not to refer to those particular examples in case they arise in any actual case. It seems to me that where you have this position, that a person owns an asset of any kind, whether physical or not, and grants licences under it the activities which he carries on in connection with the grant of those licences may amount to a trade and then Case I of Schedule D applies. On the other hand, at the other end of the scale, the activities may amount to the mere holding of an investment, so that the receipt of income is in the nature of pure income profit and then Case III of Schedule D applies. There may be intermediate cases in which Case VI of Schedule D might apply.

Later in the same judgment (at p 476) Pennycuick J stated:

> The activities admittedly go beyond investment in the ordinary sense, and it is plain that this Company did not carry on the business of an investment company in the ordinary sense, in contradistinction to the statutory sense under the section which I have read. I can myself see no reason for denying to its activities the title of a trade and placing them in the residuary category of Case VI of Schedule D.

In the majority of cases it is likely that the activities of the copyright holder, in obtaining merchandising agreements and monitoring them, would amount to trading and the income would therefore be assessable under Schedule D, Case I.

Merchandising income is within the income caught by the foreign entertainers rules if related to performance in the UK by non-resident performers, often referred to as venue merchandising (*see* p 323) Income Tax (Entertainers and Sportsmen) Regulations 1987 (SI 1987 No 530) reg 3(2), FEU 50 para A3).

Endorsement fees

Closely allied to character merchandising is the practice of endorsement of various articles or services by well-known 'personalities' who either claim to use such goods or services and find them satisfactory or merely recommend their purchase, without making it clear whether they have personally taken advantage of the goods or services in question. In either event they are likely to receive for the endorsement a fee or royalty, possibly related to the amount of goods or services sold as a result of the endorsement, which would, it is submitted, constitute a receipt of the person's trade or profession, taxable under Schedule D, Cases I or II. If, as frequently happens, the services of the person have been sub-contracted to a company in return for a salary, the endorsement fees would be the income of the company and the salary paid would normally be an allowable expense of the company and taxable on the person under Schedule E in his capacity as employee.

So far as the payer of the endorsement fee is concerned, this would be an ordinary trading expense allowable under TA 1988, s 74 as a payment of a similar nature to advertising.

It is conceivable that the Revenue could argue that endorsement fees should be taxed under Schedule D, Case VI, but it is suggested that the correct treatment would normally be under Schedule D, Cases I or II.

A relatively common practice is for the advertiser to supply the celebrity with goods and to take publicity photographs after which the goods are handed over to the celebrity. It may be argued that these are gifts to the celebrity and not endorsement fees and in the circumstances could be tax free. There have been several cases where, for example, a room has been refurnished and redecorated in a celebrity's house at the expense of the advertiser, and the Revenue has accepted that no taxation liability results.

On the other hand, the mere payment for endorsement services in kind would not escape taxation and the endorser would be taxable on the realisable value, if any, of such goods or services received (*Temperley v Smith* (1956) 37 TC 18).

Endorsement fees are within the foreign entertainers rules for non-UK residents if related to activities in the UK (*see* p 323) (Income Tax (Entertainers and Sportsmen) Regulations 1987 (SI 1987 No 530) reg 3(2), FEU 50 para A5).

Stamp duty

Merchandising agreements are in reality an assignment or licence of copyright and subject to stamp duty in the same way as other copyright agreements (*see* Chapter 23). Endorsement fees would not amount to a conveyance of property and should not be liable to stamp duty.

VAT

Merchandising agreements would be subject to VAT in the same way as patent agreements. Endorsement fees would be subject to VAT if paid to a registered or registrable business, in the same way as show-how fees (*see* Chapter 11).

PART 4

TAX PLANNING

20 Tax planning—general principles and non-corporates

Introduction

As with other sources of income, the tax planning of intellectual property should concentrate on maximising the after-tax profits rather than the saving of tax as an end in itself.

The actual manner in which income from intellectual property can be taxed and the statutory provisions enabling it to be spread have already be considered in some detail: the purpose of this chapter is to show how these rules may be used to the best advantage of the taxpayer.

It is essential in modern tax planning to ensure that any arrangements entered into can be justified commercially and are not merely inserted for a tax saving that it is hoped will result. This follows a series of judgments including in particular the dissenting judgment of Eveleigh LJ in *Floor v Davis* [1978] STC 436 and the House of Lords judgments in *Ramsay (WT) Ltd v IRC* [1982] AC 300, *Eilbeck v Rawling* [1981] STC 174, *IRC v Burmah Oil Co Ltd* [1982] STC 30, *Furniss v Dawson* [1984] STC 153, *Craven v White* [1988] STC 476, *Bayliss v Gregory* [1988] STC 476, *News International plc v Shepherd* [1989] STC 617, *Ingram v IRC* [1985] STC 835, *Cairns v MacDiarmid* [1983] STC 178, *Young v Phillips* [1984] STC 520, *Magnovox Electronics Co Ltd (In liquidation) v Hall* [1986] STC 561 and *IRC v McGuckian* [1997] STC 908. However, the mere fact that tax avoidance was a motive in the transaction does not enable it to be disregarded for tax purposes if it otherwise serves a commercial purpose (*Ensign Tankers (Leasing) Ltd v Stokes* [1992] STC 226; *New Zealand Commissioner of Inland Revenue v Challenge Corporation Ltd* [1986] STC 548, a case noted for an attempt by Lord Templeman to draw a distinction between tax avoidance, where a taxpayer seeks to avoid a liability to tax by entering into an arrangement without actually incurring the expenditure or loss, and tax mitigation, where a taxpayer obtains a tax advantage by reducing his income or by incurring expenditure in circumstances in which the taxing statutes afford a reduction in tax liability). *In Furniss v Dawson* Lord Fraser stated at p 155:

> The true principle of the decision in *Ramsay* was that the fiscal consequences of a pre-ordained series of transactions intended to operate as such are generally to be ascertained by considering the result of the series as a whole and not by dissecting the scheme and considering each individual transaction separately.

Lord Scarman commented at p 156:

I add a few observations only because I am aware, and the legal profession (and others) must understand, that the law in this area is at an early stage of development. Speeches in your Lordships' House and judgments in the appellate Courts of the United Kingdom are concerned more to chart a way forward between principles accepted and not to be rejected than to attempt anything so ambitious as to determine finally the limit beyond which the safe channel of acceptable tax avoidance shelves into the dangerous shallows of unacceptable tax evasion. The law will develop from case to case. Lord Wilberforce in *Ramsay* referred to 'the emerging principle' of the law. What has been established with certainty by the House in *Ramsay* is that the determination of what does and what does not constitute unacceptable tax evasion is a subject suited to development by judicial process. The best chart that we have for the way forward appears to me, with great respect to all engaged in the map-making process, to be the words of my noble and learned friend Lord Diplock in *IRC v Burmah Oil Co Ltd* [1982] STC 30 which my noble and learned friend Lord Brightman quotes in his speech. These words leave space in the law for the principle annunciated by Lord Tomlin in *IRC v Duke of Westminster* (1936) 19 TC 490 at 520 that every man is entitled if he can to order his affairs so as to diminish the burden of tax. The limits within which this principle is to operate remain to be probed and determined judicially. Difficult though the task may be for judges, it is one which is beyond the power of the blunt instrument of legislation. Whatever a statute may provide, it has to be interpreted and applied by the Courts: and ultimately it will prove to be in this area of judge made law that our elusive journey's end will be found.

Lord Bridge commented at p 158:

Of course, the judiciary must never lose sight of the basic premise expressed in the celebrated dictum of Lord Tomlin in *IRC v Duke of Westmister* (1936) 19 TC 490 at 520 that: 'Every man is entitled if he can to order his affairs so that the tax attaching under the appropriate Acts is less than it otherwise would be.' Just a year earlier Learned Hand J giving the judgment of the United States Circuit Court (2nd Circuit) in *Helvering v Gregory* (1931) 69 F2d 809, had said the same thing in different words: 'anyone may so arrange his affairs that his tax shall be as low as possible; he is not bound to choose that pattern that will best pay the Treasury'. Yet, whilst starting from this common principle the Federal Courts of the United States and the English Courts have developed, quite independently of any statutory differences, very different techniques for the scrutiny of tax avoidance schemes to test their validity.

The extent to which the speeches of the majority in the *Westminster* case still tend to dominate the thinking in this field of the English judiciary is well shown by the judgments in the Courts below in the instant case. In particular the *Westminster* case seems still to be accepted as establishing that the only ground on which it can be legitimate to draw a distinction between the substance and the form of transactions in considering their tax consequences is that the transactions are shams in the sense that they are not what, on their face, they purport to be. The strong dislike expressed by the majority of the *Westminster* case for what Lord Tomlin described as 'The doctrine that the Court may ignore the legal position and regard what is called the "substance of the matter"' is not the least surprising when one remembers that the only transaction in question was the Duke's covenant in favour of his gardener and the *bona fides* of that transaction was never for a moment impugned.

When one moves, however, from a single transaction to a series of inter-dependent transactions designed to produce a given result, it is, in my opinion, perfectly legitimate to draw a distinction between the substance and the form of the composite transaction without in any way suggesting that any of the single transactions which make up the whole are other than genuine. This has been the approach of the United States Federal Courts enabling them to develop a doctrine whereby the tax consequences of the composite transaction are dependent on its substance, not its form. I shall not attempt to review the American authorities, nor do I propose a wholesale importation of the American doctrine in all its ramifications into English law. But I do suggest that the distinction between form and substance is one which can usefully be drawn in determining the tax consequences of composite transactions and one which will help to free the Courts from the shackles which have so long been thought to be imposed on them by the *Westminster* case.

Lord Brightman in *Furniss v Dawson* at p 164 quoted Lord Diplock in the *Burmah* case as follows:

It would be disingenuous to suggest and dangerous on the part of those who advise on elaborate tax avoidance schemes to assume that *Ramsay's* case did not mark a significant change in the approach adopted by this House in its judical role to a preordained series of transactions (whether or not they include the achievement of a legitimate commercial end) into which there are inserted steps that have no commercial purpose apart from the avoidance of a liability to tax which in the absence of those particular steps would have been payable.

He continued at p 166:

In a pre-planned tax saving scheme, no distinction is to be drawn for fiscal purposes, because none exists in reality, between (i) a series of steps which are followed through by virtue of an arrangement which falls short of a binding contract, and (ii) a like series of steps which are followed through because the participants are contractually bound to take each step *seriatim*. In a contractual case the fiscal consequences will naturally fall to be assessed in the light of the contractually agreed results. For example, equitable interests may pass when the contract for sale is signed. In many cases equity will regard that as done which is contracted to be done. *Ramsay* says that the fiscal result is to be no different if the several steps are pre-ordained rather than pre-contracted ...

The formulation by Lord Diplock in *Burmah* expresses the limitations of the *Ramsay* principle. First, there must be a pre-ordained series of transactions; or, if one likes, one single composite transaction. This composite transaction may or may not include the achievement of a legitimate commerical (ie business) end ... Secondly there must be steps inserted which have no commercial (business) *purpose* apart from the avoidance of a liability to tax—not 'no business *effect*'. If those two ingredients exist, the inserted steps are to be disregarded for fiscal purposes. The Court must then look at the end result. Precisely how the end result will be taxed will depend on the terms of the taxing statute sought to be applied.

The judgment in *Furniss v Dawson* does not, however, put an end to strategic tax planning, as the House of Lords confirmed in *Craven v White, IRC v Bowater Property Developments Ltd* (1986) 130 SJ 15 and *Baylis v Gregory* [1988] STC 476, in which Lord Oliver, at p 507, said:

As the law currently stands, the essentials emerging from *Dawson* appear to me to be four in number: (1) that the series of transactions was, at the time when the intermediate transaction was entered into it, pre-ordained in order to produce a given result; (2) that that transaction had no other purpose than tax mitigation; (3) that there was at that time no practical likelihood that the pre-planned events would not take place in the order ordained, so that the intermediate transaction was not even contemplated practically as having an independent life, and (4) that the pre-ordained events did in fact take place. In these circumstances the court can be justified in linking the beginning with the end so as to make a single composite whole to which the fiscal results of the single composite whole are to be applied ...

There is a real and not merely a metaphysical distinction between something that is done as a preparatory step towards a possible but uncertain contemplated future action and something which is done as an integral and interdependent part of a transaction already agreed and, effectively, pre-destined to take place. In the latter case, to link the end to the beginning involves no more than recognising the reality of what is effectively a single operation *ab initio*. In the former it involves quite a different process, *viz* that of imputing to the parties, *ex post facto*, an obligation (either contractual or quasi contractual) which did not exist at the material time but which is to be attributed from the occurrence or juxtaposition of events which subsequently took place. That cannot be extracted from *Dawson* as it stands nor can it be justified by any rational extension of the *Ramsay* approach. It involves the invocation of a different principle altogether, that is to say, the reconstruction of events into something that they were not, either in fact or in intention, not because they in fact constituted a single composite whole but because, and only because, one or more of them was motivated by a desire to avoid or minimise tax.

Lord Gaffat, at p 511, said:

Before the Court of Appeal, the Crown appears to have submitted that at least some kinds of 'strategic tax planning' might be caught by the principle—a submission which was, in my opinion, rightly rejected by that court.

And Lord Jauncey, at p 521, tried to be helpful:

> If it were appropriate to prepare a formula defining 'composite transaction' in the light of the passages in the speeches in *Ramsay, Burmah* and *Dawson* to which I have referred I should be tempted to suggest the following:
>
> 'A step in a linear transaction which has no business purpose apart from the avoidance or deferment of tax liability will be treated as forming part of a pre-ordained series of transactions or of a composite transaction if it was taken at a time when negotiations or arrangements for carrying through as a continuous process of a subsequent transaction which actually takes place had reached a stage when there was no real likelihood that such subsequent transaction would not take place and if thereafter such negotiations or arrangements were carried through to completion without genuine interruption.'
>
> However, I am conscious that this may well constitute too rigid an approach to the problems and I therefore put it forward as a tentative guide rather than as a definitive exercise.

Schedule D, Cases I and II

The exploitation of intellectual property can give rise to assessment as a trade under Schedule D, Case I. If the trade is carried on in the UK or controlled from the UK, the assessment is in the UK (*Ogilvie v Kitton* (1908) 5 TC 338) and the assessment is on the worldwide income (*London Bank of Mexico v Apthorpe* (1891) 3 TC 143).

If the income is received by a company, the company will be liable to corporation tax on the income arising, less the expenses wholly and exclusively incurred for the purposes of the trade. As the income is assessed on a current year basis, it is only necessary to ensure that the expenses are not incurred before the trade is commenced, although expenditure incurred no more than seven years before the commencement of trade is deemed to have been incurred on the first day of trading under TA 1988, s 401. In the case of an individual or partnership, the pre-trading expenses provision yield a potentially relievable loss in the first period rather than an expense (TA 1988, s 401(1)).

Although it is possible for an individual or partnership to be assessed under Schedule D, Case I, it is more likely that the assessment would be under Schedule D, Case II as income from a profession or vocation. From a practical viewpoint there is usually no distinction between a Case I or Case II assessment, but *see* TA 1988, s 775.

Again, the assessment under Schedule D, Case II for a business controlled from the UK would be on the worldwide income (*Davies v Braithwaite* (1933) 18 TC 198).

Current year basis

As explained in Chapter 9, individuals and partnerships are assessed under the current year basis, in all cases from 1997/98 or earlier. The tax planning opportunities available under the preceding year basis have ceased to exist. However it is usually still advantageous in terms of deferral of tax to make up accounts to a date ending early in the fiscal year, say 30 April, rather than late in the year, say 31 March or 5 April. It also allows, at the cost of some complexity, the maximum period in which to prepare accounts and still meet the filing date requirements.

Investment income

If the assessment is under Schedule D, Case III, eg royalties from intellectual property held as an investment, the assessment under TA 1988, s 64 is normally made on the basis of the income received in the fiscal year. Each source of income under Schedule D, Case III is computed separately in order to arrive at the total assessment for the year (*Grainger v Mrs Maxwell's Executors* (1925) 10 TC 139).

If tax has been deducted from the income, it is treated as if it were a payment on account of the recipient's own liability (TA 1988, s 348(1)(*d*)).

A non-UK domiciled individual is taxed under Schedule D, Case III in the same manner as one domiciled in the UK. Income received by a company taxed under Schedule D, Case III is taxed on a current year basis in the same way as any other income assessed under Schedule D (TA 1988, s 70(1)).

Where income such as patent royalties has been received under deduction of tax the assessment is on a fiscal year basis. If for any reason tax has not been deducted by the payer this does not prevent it being collected from the recipient (*Grosvenor Place Estates Ltd v Roberts* (1960) 39 TC 433). Alternatively the Revenue could collect from the payer, who in turn could recover from the recipient, if he could show that the money had been paid in full owing to a mistake of fact, for example, as to whether the payment constituted a patent royalty (*Turvey v Dentons (1923) Ltd* [1953] 1 QB 218).

It is widely accepted that the remittance basis is a limitation of the arising basis and if this is so the cumulative assessments on a particular source during a period of residence in the UK cannot exceed the cumulative assessment on a (theoretical) arising basis.

Losses

One of the cardinal principles of tax planning is to make the best possible use of tax losses which may arise.

Trading losses

Under self-assessment, losses of an accounting year ending in a fiscal year may be set against the total income of the preceding fiscal year effectively preserving the one year carry-back under the pre-self-assessment rules (TA 1988, s 380(1)). The loss is computed in the same way as a profit by reference to the accounting year ending in the fiscal year, not by reference to apportionment of the loss over the fiscal year (TA 1988, s 382(3)). It is not possible to claim relief for the same loss twice nor make a partial claim for loss relief except to the extent that the loss exceeds available income against which it can be offset. The claim must be made within one year of the filing date, ie one year, ten months after the end of the fiscal year in which the loss arises.

Alternatively, relief for the loss may be claimed against total income for the fiscal year in which the loss arises with any balance in excess of available income carried back for one year (TA 1988, s 380(2)). Where the loss arises in the first four fiscal years of trading it may be carried back and set off against total income for the three preceding fiscal years utilising the earliest available income first (TA 1988, s 381).

Losses arising in the first couple of years of a trade or in a period where there is a change of accounting date can be quite complex to compute, as can losses in the transitional period from the old preceding year basis of assessment to the current year basis applicable for self-assessment.

To the extent that trading losses are not set off against total income they may be carried forward and set off against profits of the same trade under TA 1988, s 385. Under self-assessment, as capital allowances are treated as expenses from 1997/98 they will automatically be included in the computation of any loss, and the special rules which used to apply under TA 1988, s 383 are no longer needed.

Losses arising from a subscription of shares in an unquoted company may qualify for relief under TA 1988, s 574 and be set against total income for the year in which the loss arises.

A terminal loss arising in the last 12 months of trading may be carried back and set against the total income for the year of termination and the three preceding fiscal years under TA 1988, ss 388 and 389. The set off is against the most recent year first.

When planning loss relief claims it is important to bear in mind the time value of money, the potential loss of personal allowances and the rates of tax at which the losses will be relieved. It is often necessary to compute the available permutations for relief available, in terms of tax, in order to make the most appropriate claim.

Casual losses

Where income is assessable under Schedule D, Case VI, but a loss arises, it may be set against any Schedule D, Case VI income in the year of loss or carried forward against future Case VI losses (TA 1988, s 392).

Excess charges on income incurred for trading purposes, other than capital sums paid in respect of patent rights or copyright royalties paid to a person whose normal place of abode is outside the UK, may be carried forward against future income of the trade under TA 1988, s 387. Excess trading interest may be added to a loss carried forward or to a terminal loss under TA 1988, s 390 and losses in respect of a trade carried on abroad where profits would be assessable under Schedule D, Case V are relieved under TA 1988, s 391 the same way as UK trading losses.

Post-cessation receipts

In most cases of intellectual property the income is brought into account when received or when ascertained and can continue to arise for many years after the trade or profession has itself ceased. Such profits were at one time tax-free, as for example in *Purchase v Stainer's Executors* (1951) 32 TC 367 (*see* pp 190–191). However, such income arising after the cessation of the trade or profession would now be taxable under Schedule D, Case VI as post-cessation receipts under the provisions of TA 1988, ss 103–110 (*see* p 192).

If the profits had been assessed on the earnings basis, including accrued expenses and income earned but not actually received, there would be an assessment under TA 1988, s 103 on any amounts not included in the earnings basis calculation. There are exceptions for sums received from outside the UK by a non-resident or his agent under TA 1988, s 103(3)(*a*), for example, from overseas sales of works published in the UK and from the sale of stock and work in progress under TA 1988, s 103(3)(*c*), which would not normally apply to intellectual property. There is also an exception for a lump sum paid to the personal representatives of an author of a literary, dramatic, musical or artistic work as consideration for the assignment by them wholly or partially of the copyright in the work under TA 1988, s 103(3)(*b*).

It will be seen, therefore, that most sums arising after the cessation (such as royalties receivable) will be taxable under these provisions. The exception for a lump sum receipt on the assignment of copyright by personal representatives would be a disposal for capital gains tax purposes, with the probate value being the base cost under TCGA 1992, s 62.

If the assessment has been on the conventional basis, that is on the income actually received, TA 1988, s 104 will charge to tax under Schedule D, Case VI post-cessation receipts which would have been included in an earnings basis had that basis applied, apart from lump sums on the assignment of copyright by personal representatives (TA 1988, s 104(3)). In strictness, therefore, in the field of intellectual property, royalties due but not paid at the date of death would normally be taxable under TA 1988, s 104 but royalties accruing after death would be assessed under TA 1988, s 103. Similar provisions would apply on a cessation for any other purpose.

In practice there is usually no distinction between an assessment under TA 1988, s 103 or 104 and there is merely a Schedule D, Case VI assessment on receipts not already included in the accounts.

TA 1988, s 105 allows as a deduction such expenses as would have been allowed had the business continued and TA 1988, s 110(2) confirms that on, for example, a change of partners the notional cessation rules also apply. However, TA 1988, s 106 states that if there is a sale of the business and post-cessation receipts are receivable by the purchaser the sale proceeds are taxable and the subsequent income is included in the purchaser's normal receipts. Similarly, on a notional discontinuance following a change in partnership there is no post-cessation receipt charge if the post-cessation income is credited to the continuing partners. The only post-cessation receipts charge would be on any amounts credited to the outgoing partners not otherwise brought into taxable income.

However, it is arguable where, for example, copyrights are transferred for a nominal consideration from an individual or partnership being assessed under the post-cessation receipt provisions to a connected company, that the market value of the copyright should be taxed as a post-cessation receipt under TA 1988, s 106(1). The company would be taxable on the subsequent royalties received and there would be effective double taxation unless the decision in *Mason v Innes* (1967) 44 TC 326 could be extended to a Schedule D, Case VI post-cessation receipt, which is unlikely.

In spite of the assessment being under Schedule D, Case VI, TA 1988, s 107 makes it clear that it is taxable as earned income. TA 1988, s 108 gives the taxpayer the right to elect within two years from the date of a post-cessation receipt assessment to carry back the amount chargeable and have it assessed as if it were received on the last day of trading. This right is restricted to post-cessation income of six years following the discontinuance. If this election is made no claim may be made under TA 1988, s 105 setting expenses against the income carried back.

The post-cessation receipts provisions do not apply for Schedule D, Case V purposes (*see* p 263).

Schedule D, Case VI

An assessment under Schedule D, Case VI is on the actual income arising in the fiscal year under TA 1988, s 69. In the absence of legislation to the contrary (for example, post-cessation receipts under TA 1988, s 107; patent income under TA 1988, s 529; know-how under TA 1988, s 531(5); or a capital sum derived from personal activities under TA 1988, s 775(2)) the assessment would be as unearned income. The assessment extends to income of a non-resident arising in the UK, as in *Alloway v Phillips* [1980] STC 490.

It will normally be preferable to claim to be trading or carrying on a profession in the UK if the income is otherwise likely to be caught under Schedule D, Case VI, as a Schedule D, Cases I or II assessment is likely to be beneficial, except for a casual author who may sell his copyright for a capital sum which would be taxed as a capital gain.

Capital gains

If a capital sum received from intellectual property is taxable as a capital gain, which, as has been seen, would be the exception rather than the rule, the assessment would be calculated in the normal way, that is, on the net sale proceeds less the cost of the asset, if any, or if higher the 31 March 1982 value (TCGA 1992, s 35) and any enhancement expenditure allowable under TCGA 1992, s 38 and indexation since 31 March 1982 under TCGA 1992, s 55. If there is a part disposal only the appropriate part of the cost can be deducted, applying the

$$\frac{A}{A + B}$$

formula under TCGA 1992, s 42. In this fraction A is the consideration received and B is the market value of the property retained.

If the asset was held at 6 April 1965 the gain would be apportioned under TCGA 1992, Sched 2, para 16 by applying to the gain the fraction

$$\frac{T}{P + T}$$

In this formula T is the period from 6 April 1965 to the time of disposal and P is the period of ownership prior to 6 April 1965. Alternatively, it is possible within two years of the end of the year of assessment or accounting period in which the disposal took place to elect to substitute for the base value the market value at 6 April 1965 under TCGA 1992, Sched 2, para 17. It is possible to elect for rebasing as if all assets had been sold and reacquired at market value on 31 March 1982, under TCGA 1992, s 35.

The case of *Mason v Innes* (1967) 44 TC 326, where an author gave away the copyright in one of his works, has been discussed (*see* p 193). Although such a disposal is free of income tax under the decision, there could be a capital gains tax disposal, in view of the wide definition of assets for capital gains tax purposes under TCGA 1992, s 21. Normally an assignment of copyright by an author for cash would not be subject to capital gains tax, as there would be an income tax liability and the exemption of TCGA 1992, s 37(1) would therefore apply.

It would seem that this capital gains tax problem can be overcome by an author assigning the copyright in a work yet to be written which can be done under the provisions of CDPA 1988, s 91. It would be argued that at the time of the transfer no substantial asset existed for capital gains tax purposes and that there was no material reduction in the estate for inheritance tax.

Schedule E

TA 1988, s 19(1) provides that income from an office or employment is to be assessed to tax under Schedule E under one of three cases. Schedule E, Case I applies to a person who is resident and ordinarily resident in the UK in respect of his worldwide remuneration, except for foreign emoluments which are within Case III. Case II applies to a person who is non-resident or, if resident, not ordinarily resident and is limited to the remuneration arising from an office or employment the duties of which are carried out in the UK. Under Schedule E, Case III, a non-UK domiciled individual who is resident in the UK and is in receipt of remuneration from a non-resident employer in respect of work done entirely outside the UK is assessed to tax on remittances to the UK under TA 1988, ss 19(1), 192.

Arising basis

From 6 April 1989, remuneration is assessed to tax under Schedule E in the year in which it is received rather than the year in which it was earned (TA 1988, s 202A) whether or not the source still exists, which overrules *Bray v Best* [1989] STC 159 and prevents avoidance of tax on the remittance basis where remitted after the end of the fiscal year in which the source ceased. Under TA 1988, s 202B earnings are treated as received at the earliest of actual payment, entitlement to payment, crediting to a director's current account, or on determination or at the end of the current period of account if determined during that period.

Remuneration under Schedule E is based on the emoluments from the employment, which includes all salaries, fees, wages, perquisites and profits whatsoever (TA 1988, s 131(1), TA 1970, s 183(1)). It has been held in cases such as *Tennant v Smith* (1892) 3 TC 158, *Wilkins v Rogerson* (1960) 39 TC 344 and *Heaton v Bell* (1969) 46 TC 211 that a perquisite is, in the absence of specific provisions to the contrary, taxable only if it is convertible into money or money's worth. Such specific provisions are to be found in TA 1988, s 142 in relation to vouchers including season tickets and purchases by company credit card, TA 1988, s 143 for cash vouchers, and TA 1988, ss 145 and 146 in respect of living accommodation.

Remuneration under Schedule E is normally subject to deduction of tax at source under the PAYE regulations introduced by TA 1988, s 203. In respect of directors and higher paid employees, commonly called P11D employees, TA 1988, ss 153–168 introduced special provisions for the taxation of fringe benefits and expenses (subject to a claim for those expenses wholly, exclusively and necessarily incurred for the purpose of the employment under TA 1988, s 198). It is not intended here to deal with the taxation of fringe benefits, which is a subject in itself, referred to briefly in Chapter 9, but it should be pointed out that one of the advantages of a Schedule E employment is the ability to have certain fringe benefits favourably taxed, for example, cars provided by an employer.

Two other areas of the Schedule E legislation require special consideration for tax planning purposes: 'golden handshakes' and top-slicing relief.

'Golden handshakes'

If an employment ceases it may be worthwhile giving the employee a compensation for loss of office or *ex gratia* payment on retirement. Such payments are basically taxable under Schedule E in accordance with TA 1988, s 148. TA 1988, s 188(4),(5), however, exempt such payments up to £30,000 and s 188(1) exempts payments such as compensation for personal injury or death, restrictive covenants which would be subject under TA 1988, s 313 to higher rate taxes and retirement payments under approved superannuation schemes. There are special provisions relating to foreign service, under TA 1988, s 188(3).

Inducement payments

The case of *Pritchard v Arundale* (1971) 47 TC 680 is a useful case in which a capital payment in the form of shares was made to a self-employed individual to induce him to give up his self-employed status and become an employee. Such an inducement payment was held to be tax-free. The Revenue attempt to tax such a payment, this time to higher rates under TA 1988, s 313, was defeated in *Vaughan-Neil v IRC* [1979] STC 644, although they were successful in assessing under Schedule E a payment to induce a change of employment in *Glantre Engineering Ltd v Goodhand* [1983] STC 1 and *Shilton v Wilmshurst* [1991] STC 88.

Pension schemes

Another advantage of a Schedule E source of income is the ability to provide for a pension under the occupational pension scheme provisions of TA 1988, ss 590–612. Under these provisions it is possible to provide for a pension, on reaching normal retirement age, of 2/3 of the final salary after 20 years' service and to provide a widow's pension of 4/9 of the final salary. However, the final salary cannot exceed £84,000 for 1997/98 (TA 1988, s 590C and Retirement Benefits Schemes (Indexation of Earnings Cap) Order 1996 (SI 1996 No 2951)) indexed to the date of retirement by the movement in the Retail Prices Index. This service can have taken place before the commencement of the pension scheme (known as past service) which makes it possible, though not usually desirable, to postpone setting up the scheme until just before retirement is due.

It is also possible to provide death-in-service life cover of four times final salary and to commute part of the pension on reaching normal retirement age for up to 2.25 times residual pension (equivalent to 1½ times final salary) after 20 years' service (subject to a round maximum of £150,000). It is possible to set up such a pension scheme for an individual employee, even if he is a controlling director of the employing company. The normal retirement age would usually be between the ages of 50 and 75 but in the case of certain individuals, such as pop stars, it would often be possible to arrange for a materially lower retirement age, such as 40, although the pension would probably be restricted.

The premiums paid to the trustees of the pension fund would be allowable for tax as a deduction in the company's accounts in the year of payment, if it were an ordinary annual contribution, and spread over a period of up to four years if it were a special contribution in excess of £25,000. The employee does not have to contribute but it is sometimes helpful to increase the salary by 17.65 per cent and have an employee contribution of the maximum of 15 per cent on the revised salary, which preserves the *status quo* so far as the employee's net income is concerned, but increases the base salary for the final salary calculations. This is an additional National Insurance cost (secondary and possibly primary) on the incremental salary.

The lump sum death-in-service cover can be paid to a nominated individual free of inheritance tax, except in limited cases of death at age 75 or over. It is possible to pay post-retirement increases that keep pace with the level of inflation as measured by the Retail Prices Index, but it is not possible to fund for such payments in advance at an anticipated level of post-retirement increases in excess of 5.3 per cent, compound, for new schemes.

Old schemes

Pension schemes set up before 14 March 1989 enjoyed a less restrictive régime. Transitional provisions enable employees in their old schemes who were scheme members at the time of the old rules (or in the case of 17 March 1987–14 March 1989 schemes prior to 30 June 1989) to continue to benefit from the old rules.

Pension schemes set up between 17 March 1987 and 14 March 1989 differed in that there was no maximum final salary and that the normal retirement age range was 60–75 years. There was, however, a restriction on the lump sum commutation of £150,000.

Pension schemes set up prior to 17 March 1987 again had no maximum final salary and had a normal retirement age range of 60–75 years. There was, however, no restriction on the lump sum commutation and a full pension could be provided after ten years' service.

Small self-administered schemes A pension fund is free of tax on its investment income and chargeable gains except that, from 2 July 1997, it cannot recover payable tax credits on dividends as a result of TA 1988, s 231A. The attraction of a payment fully deductible for tax purposes which is invested in full in a tax-free fund and which gives rise to the ability to commute part of the pension entitlement for a tax-free lump sum and to obtain a pension taxable as earned income makes an occupational pension scheme extremely attractive. This attraction can, in suitable cases, be increased by the use of a small self-administered pension scheme approved by the Pension Schemes Office under IR12. Such a scheme is allowed to reinvest up to half of the fund value (but only 25 per cent of fund value excluding transfers-in, in the first two years of establishment) by loan back on commercial terms to the employing company. As far as the company is concerned, therefore, the cash flow is effectively similar to a payment of corporation tax and it might be possible to afford a higher premium than would be possible for an ordinary insured scheme. Such a scheme can also in suitable cases acquire property let on commercial terms to the employing company or third parties.

It can be quite tax-efficient for the creator of intellectual property to be employed by a company at a salary suitable for his day-to-day requirements with contributions being paid by the company to a self-administered pension scheme out of the surplus income.

Unfunded pensions   The type of pensions that have been considered so far are those which are funded for in advance with an insurance company or other pension scheme. There is no reason why pensions should not be paid by a company or partnership to a former employee or partner out of the continuing profits of the business. In the case of a pension to a former employee this would be a deductible expense of the company and taxed under Schedule E as earned income of the pensioner. If a company enters into an agreement to pay a pension out of continuing profits it is important that this is not included in the employee's service contract, except with the approval of the Pension Schemes Office of the Inland Revenue, as otherwise there could be a Schedule E charge on the notional premiums that would have been required to fund the pension through an insurance company arrangement (TA 1988, s 595).

If at a later date the company decides that it wishes to pay a lump sum to an insurance company so that future pension liabilities will be paid by the insurance company, the cost of relieving itself of the obligation to pay the pension is a trading expense, following *Hancock v General Reversionary and Investment Co Ltd* (1918) 7 TC 358. In practice, a *Hancock* scheme is often agreed with the Pension Schemes Office and some degree of spread of the lump sum payment is involved.

A pension may be paid to the wife or dependants of a former employee in the same way as to the employee himself.

Unapproved schemes   Following the capping introduced by FA 1989, high earning employers in new schemes can no longer fund for a pension commensurate with their earnings. The Chancellor in his Budget speech suggested the use of unapproved pension schemes which would presumably not be bound by Pension Schemes Office regulations and might perhaps be useful in their flexibility.

The taxation of unapproved schemes is simple. There is no tax relief on contributions by the employee and although the employer's contribution is allowed, it is taxable as an emolument of the employee but usually not liable to National Insurance contributions until 6 April 1999. The fund itself has no tax exemption and pays tax as a life interest trust at basic rate as to both income and capital gains. On retirement any lump sum is tax-free, but the pension itself is taxed as earned income. In practice the entire fund is usually taken as a lump sum.

The advantages of these funded unapproved retirement benefit schemes (FURBS) are the lack of National Insurance and the reduced rate of taxation (trust rate only). It is possible effectively to transfer personal investments into FURBS thereby reducing the rate of tax borne by that investment. This is achieved by the employer making a contribution to FURBS equal to the value of investment to be transferred, and then the FURBS acquiring the investment for cash. Clearly, there will be tax liabilities—namely the income tax charge on the FURBS benefit in kind and also any capital gains tax on the disposal into the FURBS.

Partnership pensions   In the case of a pension paid to a former partner or proprietor of a business or to his surviving spouse or dependants the payment will be allowed as a charge on income of the paying partners. If the pension meets the requirements of TA 1988, s 628, that is, that it is paid under a partnership agreement or some variation thereof to a former partner, his widow or dependants, on retirement because of old age, infirmity or death the payment may be treated as earned income of the recipient up to a maximum amount. This maximum is 50 per cent of the average of the partner's share in profits for the best three out of the seven years ending with the retirement or death. It is now possible to index-link these limits, and the pension itself, in accordance with the increase in the General Index of Retail Prices over the preceding calendar year and a partner ceasing to be a member before 1974/75, still in receipt of a pension, is for this purpose deemed to have retired in 1974/75. If any part of the pension is assessable as earned income on the recipient that amount is treated as a deduction from the earned income of the paying partners and not a deduction from their investment income.

Keyman insurance   Employers sometimes insure the life of key employees against accidental death during the course of the employment. If the employee is unrelated to the proprietors of the business and is in an arm's length employment, the company is allowed to pay to the employee's dependants free of inheritance tax any amount up to the amount recovered under such keyman insurance policy. In a keyman policy the proceeds are payable to the company in the first instance. The premiums may normally be claimed as a deduction for tax purposes in which case if the employee is killed the proceeds of the insurance would be a taxable receipt. On the other hand, the Revenue will normally disallow the premiums in computing the company's corporation tax liability if the life insured has a proprietorial interest in the business and in that case would not assess to tax the amounts received from the insurance company if the employee is killed.

State pensions schemes   The government introduced a State Earnings Related Pension Scheme under the Social Security Pensions Act 1975 with effect from April 1978 and many companies had to consider whether or not to contract out of the state scheme. This scheme has been amended and it is now envisaged that a single person's earnings related pension would be 25 per cent of the average yearly earnings falling between the lower earnings limit and the upper earnings limit after 40 years.

The figures for the flat-rate pension at the upper and lower earnings limits will be reviewed periodically but the employee will not be able to include the best 20 years of his earnings up to the upper earnings limit as was originally planned. Instead he will be limited to the average of 40 years' earnings. The state pension would continue for a widow or widower (subject, in respect of the widower, to both husband and wife being over the respective retirement age when the wife dies).

There are no provisions to enable any of the state pension to be commuted for a capital sum. It is now possible for individuals to contract out of the earnings related part of the state scheme (*see* p 239).

Personal pensions—general

TA 1988, ss 630–655 introduced a revised form of pension arrangement for self-employed persons and employees not in an occupational scheme to replace the retirement annuity provisions. Under this scheme employees and the self-employed are encouraged to set up their own tax-effective pension plans thus relieving the state from part of the financial burden of providing benefits. In addition the employee will be able to take the pension scheme with him when he changes his employer and his accrued pension benefits will be preserved. A particular feature of the scheme is that the employer may contribute to his employee's scheme. Contributions by an employer to an approved personal pension scheme are not taxable as emoluments of the employment under Schedule E.

Along with insurance companies and friendly societies, banks, building societies and unit trusts are able to market these policies although the pension at retirement must be bought (if necessary through the open-market cash option) from an insurance company or friendly society.

The pension fund operated by the pension provider is tax-free in the same way a an occupational pension scheme, and the policyholder is therefore making an extremely tax-efficient investment in that he is getting tax relief on the premiums paid and investing the gross premium in a tax-exempt fund. This enables a very much better fund to be built up than would be possible with any other form of investment.

The pension payable under a personal pension scheme is taxed as earned income of the annuitant and cannot be divided between the capital and income proportion in the same way as a purchased annuity taxed under TA 1988, s 656. It is, however, possible to use a commuted capital sum to purchase such an annuity.

Unlike occupational pension schemes, where it is possible to pay additional premiums to take account of past service, with a personal pension policy it is essential to commence paying premiums as soon as possible otherwise it may not be possible to build up sufficient investment to provide a reasonable pension.

All policies should have an open-market option clause so that on retirement the underlying annuity fund may be reinvested for the benefit of the pensioner with another company offering better annuity rates.

Relief by deduction from contributions Regulations introduced by statutory instrument allow the payment of personal pension scheme contributions under deduction of tax at the basic rate. The system is described as PITAS—pension income tax relief at source. The pension scheme administrator will recover the tax that was deducted from the Revenue. Power is taken for the necessary provision of information and for the necessary administrative arrangements. These regulations apply only to employees, leaving the self-employed to claim their tax relief as previously through their annual tax return which will also be the method for employees to claim higher rate tax relief.

Transitional provisions The retirement annuity scheme provisions continue to apply for schemes entered into prior to 1 July 1988 where the first premium was paid before that date. However, the maximum allowable premiums that may be claimed under a personal pension scheme will be reduced by any qualifying premiums paid in the year under a retirement annuity contract. Where an election is made to back-date a contribution, or part thereof, the payment is to be treated as the payment of a qualifying retirement annuity premium. Similarly, unused relief under the retirement annuity scheme provisions may be carried forward for the purposes of making later contributions under an approved personal pension plan.

The personal pension plans provisions from 1 July 1988 to 17 March 1989 likewise continue to apply.

Personal pension plans

These plans are similar to retirement annuity contracts being money purchase plans in that the policyholder (and or his employer) contributes premiums to an insurance company which invests the monies received within a tax-free fund designated for the individual, the proceeds from which are ultimately used to purchase an immediate annuity. As with occupational pension schemes, the pension is taxed as earned income. The new arrangements took effect from 1 July 1988.

Approval Personal pension plans, as for occupational pension schemes, have to be approved by the Board of Inland Revenue and they must therefore satisfy many conditions. In order to simplify matters the Revenue has prepared model scheme documentation. For example one important condition requires that the scheme must accept transfer payments.

Pension age The pension must commence between the ages of 50 and 75, although the lower age of 50 may be reduced where infirmity prevents the member carrying on his occupation or where such persons customarily retire before that age, which often applies in the case of sportsmen and entertainers.

The pension must be payable for the life of the member but may also be guaranteed for a period not exceeding ten years. The pension must not be capable of assignment or surrender except that a guaranteed annuity may be disposed of by will or on intestacy.

Commutation A tax-free lump sum may be commuted but must not exceed 25 per cent of the total value of the fund when paid. Depending on the age of retirement, it may be preferable to commute the maximum amount possible and to use that sum to purchase an immediate annuity, which will then be divided into a tax-free return of capital and an income element which is taxed as investment income (TA 1988, s 656).

The scheme may provide a lump sum payable on the death of a member but only if he dies before attaining the age of 75.

Pension On reaching normal retirement age the policyholder has an option to take a pension which will continue for his remaining life or a reduced pension on a joint lives basis which will continue for the life of his surviving spouse. Alternatively, it is possible to guarantee the pension for a period of up to ten years certain and if the policyholder dies within this period, the pension continues to be paid to his estate for the remainder of the guarantee period where it is taxed as investment income.

Most life companies, within the Revenue limits for approval, adapt the benefits to suit the particular wishes of the proposed annuitant. The permutations are numerous. It is, for example, possible to elect for a lower pension on normal retirement age in order that this may escalate by, up to say, 8 per cent per annum compound up to the maximum pension escalated up to RPI increases. It is not normally worthwhile opting for an increased pension as it is necessary to live considerably longer than the actuarial life expectancy in order to show a profit on an escalating personal pension plan. This is one disadvantage compared with an occupational pension scheme which can provide rather more realistic post-retirement increases.

Death before retirement   In addition to any death-in-service life cover, policies will usually provide for a return of the premiums with interest, or in the case of unit-linked policies a return of the fund.

Dependants' benefits   Up to 5 per cent of the net relevant earnings may be used for family income cover or lump sum cover in the event of the annuitant dying before retirement. If a normal life policy were entered into on a term assurance or family income basis, no tax relief would be obtainable; however, under a personal pension contract (or under a TA 1988, s 621 contract effected prior to 1 July 1988), the full premium qualifies for relief. As the life cover premium falls within the overall allowable premium the lower pension factor must be considered in the overall planning strategy.

Benefits may also include a residual pension for the spouse of the deceased annuitant, but because of prohibitive funding costs such pensions tend to be rare and it is more common for the policyholder to provide for a lump sum on his death before age 75.

Death-in-service payments arising from a personal pension policy may be made to the individual's widow or widower or one or more of his dependants as well as to his own estate. Dependants are not specifically defined for this purpose. Such provision does enable a death-in-service lump sum to be left direct to, for example, children free of inheritance tax in the same way as lump-sum payments from an occupational pension scheme.

It is possible to provide for the death-in-service benefits to take the form of a reducing-term cover with a lump sum being paid at annual or more frequent intervals for the balance of the term up to, say, age 65.

Contracting-out   It is possible for Schedule E employees not in a company scheme providing pension benefits to use a personal pension to contract out of the State Earnings Related Pension Scheme (SERPS). If this is done the policy becomes an 'appropriate personal pension'. The pension provider (insurance company etc) then claims from the DSS the NIC rebates available for contracting-out. These are based on 'middle band earnings' (between £2,808 pa and £21,060 pa for 1992/93 tax year) and total 5.8 per cent of these earnings.

There was an additional 'bribe' of 2 per cent of those earnings payable for a maximum of six years from the 1987/88 tax year if the policyholder has not been contracted out for more than two years before taking out an appropriate personal pension scheme.

A late addition to the 1988 Finance Act introduced 'rebate only personal pensions' (ROPPs). These give employees who are in a contracted-in company pension scheme the option to contract out of SERPS personally. The ROPP, however, can only accept the NIC rebates available (including the bribe if appropriate) with no further contribution from the employer or employee. A great advantage of the ROPP is that the benefit available at retirement date need not to be taken into account when applying the maximum benefit test.

Contracting-out means the loss of the SERPS benefit at retirement date. This benefit was substantially reduced by the Social Security Act 1986 but the reductions start to take effect only from the year 2000. Taking this into account, it is generally agreed that males under age 45 and females under age 40 should seriously consider contracting-out. The decision, however, is dependent not just on age but also pension scheme growth and should take into account all other pension arrangements the individual may have. Failure to observe these factors led to widespread misselling of personal pensions to individuals in inflation-proofed final salary schemes, which was clearly inappropriate.

Premium limits

Relief for approved personal pension scheme contributions is given by set-off against earnings for the year of assessment in which the payment is made.

The percentage of net relevant earnings allowed as a contribution is based on age at the beginning of the year of assessment:

Age range	Percentage
up to 35	17½
36–45	20
46–50	25
51–55	30
56–60	35
61 or more	40

It is important to note that there is an earnings cap of £84,000 for 1997/98 which has the effect that sums in excess of this are *not* net relevant earnings; no premiums may be paid in respect of this excess.

No more than 5 per cent of net relevant earnings may be allocated to provide death before retirement life cover. The maximum allowable premiums are reduced by the amount of any contributions made by the employer in the fiscal year. A DSS 'bribe' for opting out of SERPS is, however, ignored.

'Relevant earnings' means income *chargeable to tax* under Schedule E from an office or employment, income from property which is attached to or forms part of the member's emoluments, or income chargeable under Schedule D derived from

carrying on or exercising a trade, profession or vocation (either as an individual or as a partner acting personally in a partnership) and income from patent rights owned by the original inventor and treated as earned income under TA 1988, s 529. Relevant earnings therefore include benefits-in-kind to the extent taxable, including income from Lloyd's underwriting by a non-working name.

Earnings from a pensionable employment are excluded. Relevant earnings do not include amounts taxable under Schedule E from options, share incentive schemes, or lump sums on termination of employment, nor do the emoluments of a 'controlling director' of an investment company qualify.

'Net relevant earnings'   are 'relevant earnings' less certain deductions, notably charges on income (other than annual interest) incurred for business purposes; necessary expenses of the employment; and deductions in respect of losses or capital allowances derived from activities the profits or gains from which would have been relevant earnings.

Carry-back of contributions   A contribution, or part thereof, under an approved personal pension plan may be carried back and treated as paid in the immediately preceding fiscal year or, if there were no relevant earnings in that preceding year, in the year before that. The relevant earnings of Lloyd's underwriters or persons receiving commission calculated by reference to the profits of a Lloyd's underwriting business may, up to the amount of unused relief attributable to those earnings, treat the payment as being made three fiscal years prior to the year in which it was actually made up until 1993 account, 1994 account is self-assessed on a current year basis for 1997/98.

An election to carry back premiums must be made not later than 31 January after the end of the year of assessment in which the contributions are actually paid. Where a premium is related back it is necessary to give the relief in the tax year in which the premium is actually paid but by reference to the tax rates in the year to which it is carried back. It should be noted that premiums in excess of the percentage limits cannot be carried forward.

The provisions described under which premiums may be related back, although not particularly generous, are of some use, particularly in the case of individuals who are partners. Problems can arise, for example, in a partnership where the assessable profits are agreed but the allocation among the individual partners cannot be ascertained because of changes in profit-sharing ratios.

Unused relief   The difference between the appropriate percentage of net relevant earnings and the premiums actually paid in any fiscal year may be carried forward and used where a premium is paid in excess of the allowable amount within the following six years, the relief being given in the year in which the excess is paid. Excess relief for an earlier year is used up before excess relief for a later year on a first in, first out basis.

If, exceptionally, an assessment becomes final and conclusive more than six years after the end of the year of assessment, for example, as a result of an additional assessment arising in a back duty case, and there is further unused relief, an additional premium may be made within six months of the assessment becoming final and conclusive (or of an offer accepted into a back duty settlement) to absorb the unused relief as a deduction from income in the year of payment provided that the maximum allowable premiums are paid for that year.

Types of policy

A personal pension policy does not have to be an annual contract and may be a single premium policy which gives no continuing commitment to pay further premiums. The insurance company, therefore, deducts its expenses from the premium and the balance is thereupon invested to provide a lump sum at pension age. An annual premium contract has to be viewed with some care. As the term implies, an annual premium contract is a commitment to continue making premiums and should not be entered into unless those premiums are likely to be kept up. However, modern policies allow considerable flexibility and reduced payments are often permissible as is the missing out of one year's (or several years') premiums.

An annual premium contract is often what is known as 'front-end loaded', which means that the majority of the first (and sometimes the second) premium is absorbed almost entirely by the insurance company's expenses for the whole period of the contract. Thereafter, the whole of the premium is invested and the overall charges in a front-end loaded annual premium contract may be lower than on a series of single premium contracts provided many years' premiums are paid. Annual premium contracts may be paid annually or at more frequent intervals as the policyholder requires, although a charge is often (indirectly) made for quarterly or monthly premiums to cover additional administrative costs.

Although the rules for granting tax relief are fairly flexible, difficulties can arise where earnings fluctuate or where the business experiences difficult times, so that premiums contracted for on an annual basis exceed the relief due. This can cause problems, and it may be advisable that annual premium contracts are kept on the low side and for additional pension rights to be acquired through separate single premium policies with the same life company or other life companies as circumstances permit. It is, of course, unwise to put all one's eggs in the same basket anyway and a company leading the field in insurance and investment rates at a given time may not be so competitive some 20 years later.

Unit-linked policies   Schemes may be broadly divided into two categories, the conventional insurance company with reversionary bonuses and the managed fund schemes where the policy is linked to a unit trust or some specialist fund investing in equities, gilt-edged securities, properties or whatever. Which type of investment will ultimately produce the best pension is something that it is not possible to foretell as it really depends on the future investment performance of the various fund managers. Past performance, although a guide as to the capabilities of the fund managers, might not be matched in the future due to the vagaries of the stock markets or a change in the management team.

With a unit-linked policy it is often possible to switch between funds and on approaching retirement age it may be sensible to switch from, say, an equity-linked fund to a fixed-interest-linked fund if the equity market is standing at a reasonably high level. Otherwise, on the retirement date the value of the fund may have fallen due to the stock market being at a particularly low level, in which case the purchased pension would be less than was originally anticipated.

One of the main disadvantages of a personal pension fund is that it is an inflexible investment since it may be used only for the primary purpose of producing a pension and cannot, for example, be used as security for a loan or encashed prior to retirement, unlike an endowment policy. There is a minor exception to this rule in that some insurance companies and banks will lend on an interest-only basis to professional partners and partnerships on the assumption that the partners pay premiums on suitable personal pension policies. However, lenders are becoming much more flexible and personal pension policies may well become common security/collateral for loans.

Pre-14 March 1989 personal pension plans

Personal pension plans started on 1 July 1988 and plans taken out between that date and 14 March 1989 enjoyed a slightly more liberal régime. The two main differences are as follows:

Premium limit   A different table applies to give the maximum percentage of net relevant earnings which may be paid by way of premium dependent upon age at the beginning of the year of assessment. Although the table is *less* advantageous, there is *no* limit on net relevant earning so that larger premiums may be contributed.

Age range	Percentage
up to 50	17½
51–55	20
56–60	22½
61 or more	27½

Commutation   The maximum lump sum which may be taken is £150,000 per policy, or 25 per cent of the fund, whichever is the smaller.

Self-invested schemes   Schemes are available for partnerships where special units are issued to the partners for the premiums paid. The partners then take over the management of those units and invest them in approved investments which could include, for example, property let to the partnership on commercial terms, and loans to the partners on security or indirectly.

Retirement annuity policies (RAPs)

Up until 1 July 1988 personal pension plans did not exist and instead a régime of retirement annuity policies subsisted.

Since 1 July 1988 it has *not* been possible to take out a retirement annuity policy. RAPs were available to the self-employed or those in non-pensionable employment under very similar rules to personal pension plans. Retirement annuity policies continue and their 'old' rules still apply which can in certain circumstances be advantageous.

In order to continue making premium payments to RAPs after 1 July 1988, the policy would have had to have been either an annual policy, or alternatively a type of single premium policy which specifically permitted further premiums. The later single premium policies tended to be of this type.

Retirement annuity policies are money purchase policies in that the policyholder pays a premium to an insurance company (there are no entirely self-administered retirement annuity policies, although self-invested schemes exist) which invests the premium within a tax-free fund designated for the individual, and uses the proceeds to pay an immediate annuity which would be taxed entirely as earned income upon reaching pension age, whether retirement takes place or not. The salient differences between RAPs and personal plans are:

Legislation

Retirement annuity policies, also known as self-employed deferred annuities, are governed by the provisions of TA 1988, ss 619–629, as amended.

Premium limit   The percentage of net relevant earnings allowed as a contribution is based on age at the beginning of the year of assessment;

Age range	Percentage
up to 50	17½
51–55	20
56–60	22½
61 or more	27½

Net relevant earnings   Net relevant earnings are calculated post-17 March 1989. It should be noted that these percentage limits are less than the equivalent personal pension plan limits but there is no earnings cap for RAPs so that much larger premiums may be contributed.

Pension age   The normal pension age for a self-employed deferred annuity is somewhere between 60 and 75. It is not possible to extend the period beyond age 75, but in cases of ill health or in certain professions where the normal retirement age would be below 60 it is possible to have an earlier retirement date.

Older RAPs required the pension to take the form of an annuity form the insurance company to which the premiums were paid, but newer policies now allow a market value option. The annuity is usually taxed as earned income of the recipient.

Dependants' benefits   It is possible to take advantage of the provisions of TA 1988, s 621 to provide benefits for dependants in a very similar way to personal pension plans.

Commutation　On reaching normal retirement age the policyholder can commute part of his pension for a lump sum. This is such an amount as does not exceed three times the pension remaining after commutation. There is no limit on premiums or the fund at retirement and in consequence the lump sum may be very large. As the lump sum is tax-free the continuation of RAPs, rather than personal pension plans with their earnings cap, can be very worthwhile. Furthermore, the formula for the lump sum gives a larger lump sum than the simple 25 per cent of fund method used for personal pension plans. It is vital, however, that if the open-market option is exercised, the annuity is taken out with a company with which the policyholder had another RAP. If the open-market option is exercised in any other way, the commutation is restricted to 25 per cent of the fund.

Trusts

The use of trusts in the tax planning of intellectual property is no different from their use for holding other assets such as shares or loan stock and any detailed consideration of this highly complex subject would justify a book of considerable length.

So far as intellectual property is concerned it is usually advisable to make any intended transfer to a trust at the earliest possible moment. In the case of patents the trustees themselves may apply for the patent and in the case of copyright it is possible to assign future copyright before a work is written (*see* p 194).

Income tax on trusts

Trusts are liable to income tax at the rate applicable to trusts on accumulated income under TA 1988, s 686, which makes the effective rate of tax on such trust income 34 per cent for 1997/98. Trusts where a life tenant has an interest in possession are liable to tax at the lower or basic rate and the life tenant is liable for any higher rate tax change on the income to which he is entitled (*Archer-Shee v Baker* (1927) 11 TC 749; *Williams v Singer* (1921) 7 TC 387).

The income of a trust for the settlor's minor children is taxed on the settlor under TA 1988, s 660B, unless accumulated.

If a trust is revocable within six years or the settlor retains an interest the income remains that of the settlor for tax purposes under TA 1988, s 660A.

When income is distributed to a beneficiary he is entitled to a credit for basic rate tax paid by the trust and for the additional rate, if paid by the trust on income previously accumulated (TA 1988, s 687).

Capital taxes on trusts

There would usually be a disposal for capital gains tax (which may be held over on a valid election), and a chargeable or potentially exempt transfer for inheritance tax on the creation of a trust and on subsequent distributions to beneficiaries. There may also be deemed disposals on appointment or the termination of an interest in possession, or at ten-year intervals in a discretionary trust.

Children's maintenance and accumulation trusts

Trusts for the benefit of children up to age 25 may be set up by potentially exempt transfers and avoid altogether an inheritance tax charge on termination under IHTA 1984, s 52 and are often used in general family tax planning.

21 Corporate tax planning

Introduction

The principles of tax planning for companies are no different from any other form of tax planning. The aim is to end up with the largest accretion to assets after taxation, and not to regard the saving of taxation as an end in itself. In its most basic form this requires the taxpayer to ensure that it claims the relief to which it is entitled, whether as allowable expenses, charges on income, or allowances for capital expenditure. It must be remembered that not every business expense is deductible for taxation and not all capital expenditure qualifies for capital allowances. The Chartered Institute of Taxation has published a booklet of non-allowable expenditure, usually known as 'tax nothings', which sets out in some detail a surprisingly large number of commercially justifiable expenses which do not qualify for tax relief. Obviously the avoidance of 'tax nothings', so far as possible, is sensible tax planning.

Sometimes, if the problem is recognised, a relatively straightforward change in commercial arrangements might avoid the loss of tax relief. For example, if a franchisee agrees to pay a larger ongoing royalty rather than a substantial up-front payment, it may convert what would otherwise be non-deductible into an allowable expense. In this way, the retailers, Dixons, were able to hive off distribution into a separate company, thereby enabling their warehouse to qualify for industrial buildings allowances which would not have been eligible for such capital allowances if operated by part of the retail trading group (*Sarsfield v Dixons Group plc* and related appeals [1997] STC 283).

Losses inevitably arise even in the best managed businesses and it is important to ensure that tax relief is available for such losses wherever possible. This applies to capital losses as well as trading losses and it takes care and planning to ensure, in any complex group, that losses do not go unrelieved unnecessarily. Similarly, advance corporation tax, which cannot be set against a mainstream loss liability, becomes an unrelieved expense and is to be avoided where possible.

Part of the secret of corporate tax planning is to ensure that the commercial arrangements are such that the profits arise in an entity or jurisdiction where the tax charge is kept to a minimum and losses are crystallised where they can best be relieved.

It is not normally sensible tax planning to seek to shelter a profit which has already arisen by entering into some artificial tax avoidance scheme. At the time of writing the government is considering the introduction of a general anti-avoidance provision which would be designed to defeat artificial avoidance arrangements but, as explained in Chapter 20, the courts have already decided to ignore non-commercial transactions interposed for the avoidance of taxation. A recent comment by Lord Cooke of Thorndon in *IRC v McGuckian* [1997] STC 908 at 920, was:

> My Lords, this approach to the interpretation of taxing Acts does not depend on general anti-avoidance provisions such as are found in Australasia. Rather it is antecedent to or collateral with them. In the *Furniss* case (1984) STC 153 at 156 . . .), Lord Brightman spoke of certain limitations (a pre ordained series of transactions including steps with no commercial or business purpose apart from the avoidance of a liability to tax). The present case does fall within these limitations, but it may be as well to add that, if the ultimate question is always the true bearing of a particular taxing provision on a particular set of facts, the limitations cannot be universals. Always one must go back to the discernible intent of the taxing Act. I suspect that advisers of those bent on tax avoidance, which in the end tends to involve an attempt to cast on other taxpayers more than their fair share of sustaining the national tax base, do not always pay sufficient heed to the theme in the speeches in the *Furniss* case, especially those of Lord Scarman, Lord Roskill and Lord Bridge of Harwich, to the effect that the journey's end may not yet have been found.

Looking for the discernible intent of the taxing Act is clearly a highly purposive interpretation which courts are now applying, in some cases perhaps with excessive enthusiasm; see, for example, *Macniven v Westmoreland Investment Ltd* [1997] STC 1103, where in the court of first instance, borrowing in order to pay interest was held to be an artificial transaction.

Intellectual property holding companies

Some companies find it convenient to set up a separate company to hold and manage all the intellectual property in a group. All patents, trademarks, know-how, copyright, design rights and other intellectual property are held by this holding company and licences are issued to third party users by a single entity which can most easily monitor the collection of royalties, arrange for royalty audits where appropriate and look after the deduction of taxation and relief of charges on income. In practice, the UK intellectual property investment company is not normally a good idea because it could be argued that it was an investment company within TA 1988, s 130 if the intellectual property is exploited as an asset and has been acquired from other companies within the group. This in turn means that intellectual property passing to the company from other group members and the use of intellectual property within the group would be taxed as if the transaction took place at market value under the transfer pricing provisions, as explained in Chapter 13. The disapplication of the arm's length rule for transactions within the UK, in TA 1988, s 770(2), is dependent upon the acquisition being a trading expense and income a trading receipt, which would not apply if the intellectual property holding company were not carrying on a trade. It may, on the facts, be arguable that the exploitation of intellectual property amounts to a trade, but it seems an unnecessary tax risk to run. The commercial objective can be achieved by an intellectual property division which manages the intellectual property on behalf of the group companies without taking title to that property.

Where an intellectual property holding company does make sense is within an international organisation where it may well make sense to own the worldwide intellectual property rights in a low-tax, offshore jurisdiction and route the exploitation of the rights worldwide to minimise withholding taxes, as explained in

Chapter 22 (*see* p 265 *below*), always bearing in mind the controlled foreign company rules explained in Chapter 14.

Research and development

Many companies, in accordance with generally accepted accounting principles, write off research and development expenditure, in the company incurring the expense, in the year in which the expenditure is incurred, although the Statement of Standard Accounting Practice, No 13, para 10, does allow expenditure to be carried forward to be matched against future revenue where there is a clearly defined project and the related expenditure is separately identifiable. Hopefully the expenditure would then be allowed in accordance with the accounting policy in the year in which it is written off, following *Johnston v Britannia Airways Ltd* [1994] STC 763. In this connection the discussion on the allowability of deferred revenue expenditure is explored further in Chapter 26 on Franchising.

In some cases, expenditure on research and development is undoubtedly capital, for example the building of a laboratory or wind tunnel. The relief, which is explained in Chapter 15, pp 181–182, is, however, limited to activities in the field of natural or applied science related to a trade, and a good deal of research and development does not come within this restrictive definition. In such cases it may be sometimes be possible to situate the research centre within a designated enterprise zone, as defined by CAA 1990, s 21(4), so that 100 per cent first-year allowances would be available on buildings or structures, CAA 1990, s 190(1).

It may even be advantageous to situate research and development facilities outside the UK. The Republic of Ireland, for example, will normally treat industrial research and development as a manufacturing activity qualifying for the reduced 10 per cent rate of corporation tax in Ireland, and this will extend to licensing income received from the exploitation of patents arising from research and development carried out there. Such royalties will normally be receivable with a zero or reduced rate withholding tax as a result of Ireland's extensive network of double taxation treaties.

Commissioned research and development

Research and development very often has to take place in a jurisdiction where there are sophisticated research facilities and a pool of highly qualified individuals available to work on the research projects. This normally precludes most tax havens, which are unlikely to have the appropriate facilities for complex research giving rise to valuable patents. If, as a result, a valuable patent arises in a high-tax jurisdiction, it means that it could be expensive to transfer to a tax haven-based intellectual property holding company, as it may have acquired a substantial market value by the time the application for the patent is filed. If the patent was transferred at this value there would be an acceleration of tax, in that the market value on disposal would be immediately taxable whereas the subsequent exploitation would give rise to a tax saving only over a period, as royalties are received from the licensing of the patent.

In order to overcome this problem it might be worth considering whether the offshore intellectual property holding company should commission the research and development leading to a likely patentable product, from a company in a high-tax jurisdiction, on the basis of a pre-agreed fee or costs plus a reasonable percentage. It would be difficult to argue that these were not commercial arrangements if the high-tax jurisdiction ends up with a taxable profit, even though the commissioning company may then have a very valuable patent which it can license over the years. This sort of arrangement can give rise to a problem where the research is carried on in the USA in view of the American transfer pricing rules which would allocate most of the value of the patent to the area in which the research took place.

Commissioned research and development has its place in proper tax planning where it is anticipated that the product will give rise to a valuable patent, but in practice it is not always easy to identify in advance the research that is likely to give rise to a patentable invention, as many valuable patents arise merely from the ongoing development in the course of manufacture of an existing product. In such cases, however, it is probably more valuable actually to use the patent within the manufacturing process, and make the profit out of the product, rather than to exploit the patent by way of licence. It will, of course, depend on the circumstances and there are no hard and fast rules.

Division or group?

Many companies arrange their affairs so that there is a holding company with a number of subsidiaries creating a group. There may be good commercial reasons for this, in that high-risk activities can be ringfenced within a separate company, although the extent to which this is effective may be limited by banks' demands for cross-guarantees, and the fact that a holding company which allows its subsidiary to go into insolvent liquidation is likely to be unpopular. It is also convenient from a management point of view, and enables senior employees in each activity to be given the status of director. It does, however, have potential problems from a tax point of view in that losses arising in an activity which ceases can be difficult to relieve if there are insufficient current profits elsewhere in the group and capital assets have to be carefully managed to ensure that losses do not arise in part of the group which cannot be set off against profits elsewhere.

As a result, therefore, some companies have a single trading entity which they then organise into various divisions for management purposes. This is certainly easier to manage from a tax point of view and in many cases will have no commercial disadvantages. However, there may be disadvantages of a single company in that if a major part of the activity is closed down the remaining activities could amount to a new trade, which could result in losses brought forward ceasing to be available (*Rolls-Royce Motors Ltd v Bamford* [1976] STC 162). There can also sometimes be advantages in splitting up activities into separate companies, (see *Sarsfield v Dixons Group plc* [1977] STC 283). Each case must be considered on its merits, taking into account both the commercial and taxation considerations.

Group and consortium relief

Group relief enables losses arising in one company in a group to be surrendered against profits arising in another company, in the same accounting period.

A group consists of one company and at least one 75 per cent subsidiary, under TA 1988, s 413(3)(*a*). A 75 per cent subsidiary is defined by TA 1988, s 838 as a company where not less than 75 per cent of its ordinary share capital is owned directly or indirectly by the other company. The parent company also has to be entitled to not less than 75 per cent of any profits available for distribution to equity shareholders, and to not less than 75 per cent of the assets available for distribution to equity holders on a winding up, under TA 1988, s 413(7). Indirect ownership is calculated by multiplying through the percentage holding, so that a 90 per cent subsidiary of a 90 per cent subsidiary, of a parent company would be a 75 per cent subsidiary being indirectly 81 per cent owned. An 80 per cent subsidiary of a 90 per cent subsidiary, however, would only be 72 per cent indirectly owned, and not therefore within the group for group relief purposes, even though it would be under the control of the parent company for commercial purposes. As group relief is available only within a 75 per cent group it is important to identify any companies which are not within the definition. A group relationship has to exist only for the accounting period, not when the claim is actually made (*A W Chapman Ltd v Hennessey* [1982] STC 214). A company in liquidation ceases to be within the beneficial ownership of the company owning its shares, and is therefore outside the group (*IRC v Olive Mill Spinners Ltd* [1963] 41 TC 77). Group relief is also denied by TA 1988, s 410 if arrangements are in place under which the company may cease to be a member of the group (*see Pilkington Brothers Ltd v IRC* [1982] STC 103 and *Shepherd v Law Land plc* [1990] STC 795). Dual resident investment companies are also prevented from claiming group relief by TA 1988, s 404.

Where a company is within a 75 per cent group, as defined for group relief, the tax loss in an accounting period may, under TA 1988, s 403 be surrendered and set against the taxable profits of the surrenderee company for the corresponding accounting period. The whole of the loss may be surrendered even where the shareholding is less than 100 per cent, provided that the '75 per cent subsidiary' test is met.

Where group relief is not available it may be possible to claim consortium relief under TA 1988, s 402(3) where a trading company is owned by a consortium, or is a 90 per cent subsidiary of a holding company which is owned by a consortium, or is itself a holding company owned by a consortium. With consortium relief, the surrendering company's loss is surrendered to the other members of the consortium, *pro rata* to their interests in the consortium. Consortium relief is available where not less than 75 per cent of a company's ordinary share capital is owned directly and beneficially by UK resident companies, which each own at least 5 per cent (TA 1988, s 413(6)). As with group relief, shares held as trading stock by a share dealing company are not eligible for a consortium relief claim (TA 1988, s 402(4)).

The losses which can be surrendered are limited to trading losses which would have been eligible for set-off against total profits in the surrendering company, had there been sufficient profits (TA 1988, s 403(1) and (2)) plus capital allowances, (TA 1988, s 403(3)) and excess management charges of an investment company (TA 1988, s 403(4) and (5)). Excess charges on income may also be group relieved under TA 1988, s 403(7). Non-trade charges could be lost, if there is no excess when losses or allowances brought forward are ignored (TA 1988, s 403(8)). Non-trade excess charges of an investment company are therefore lost if they cannot be relieved in the year, as they cannot be carried forward to future years (TA 1988, s 393(9)).

Group relief is given after other reliefs for the year, but before deducting losses or allowances for a subsequent accounting period (TA 1988, s 407). Losses may be group relieved only where the surrendering and claimant companies are both members of the same group throughout the whole of the surrendering company's accounting period, and the claimant company's corresponding accounting period (TA 1988, s 408). Where the accounting periods do not coincide, apportionments are made on a time basis (TA 1988, s 408(2)).

The form of a group relief claim has been prescribed under TMA 1970, s 42(5) which requires a written claim identifying the claimant company, the accounting period of the claimant company for which the relief is claimed, the identity of the surrendering company or companies, the relevant accounting periods of each surrendering company, the amount claimed in respect of each surrendering company, and the total profits of the claimant company claimed to be covered by group relief (STI 1992 754). A claim requires an appropriate signed declaration. A claim for consortium relief must be made within two years from the end of the surrendering company's accounting period and the time limit is strictly applied. There are anti-avoidance provisions to prevent the creation of artificial groups (TA 1988, s 413(7)–(9) and Sched 18). Payments for group relief under an appropriate agreement are ignored for corporation tax purposes under TA 1988, s 402(6).

Loss management

The scope for the management of the relief for losses in a company was materially reduced by F (No 2) A 1997, s 39 in respect of an accounting period ending on or after 2 July 1997. Prior to that date, trading losses could be carried back under TA 1988, s 393A for a period of three years. Where the loss straddles 2 July 1997, the loss is time-apportioned, and the pre-2 July proportion may be carried back three years, under the old rules, but the post-2 July loss may be carried back for only 12 months, except in the case of a terminal loss on the cessation of trading, which can still be carried back three years under TA 1988, s 393A(2B). Similar restrictions are applied to loan interest deficits under FA 1996, Sched 8, para 3, by F (No 2) A 1997, s 40.

Though losses cannot be carried back or group relieved, they may be carried forward under TA 1988, s 393(1). Losses on deals where the profit would be assessed under Schedule D, Case VI are allowed to be set off against any Schedule D, Case VI profits in the same or future periods, under TA 1988, s 396.

F (No 2) A 1997, s 20 prevents relief under TA 1988, s 242 or 243, in respect of accounting periods beginning on or after 2 July 1997, under which trading losses could be set against surplus franked investment income. Relief is still available for the pre-2 July 1997 proportion of an accounting period straddling that date. Where relief has previously been claimed under these provisions the ability to restore the loss and adjust the set-off of ACT has also been curtailed.

Where a business ceases in circumstances such that the loss could be carried forward under TA 1988, s 343 there is no terminal loss, in view of F (No 2) A 1997, s 39(7). Where there is both a change in ownership in a company and, within a three-year period before or after that change, there is a major change in the nature or conduct of the company's trade, the loss cannot be carried forward, under TA 1988, s 768, or backwards under TA 1988, s 768A.

These changes will obviously make it more difficult for a company to ensure that the whole of its allowable tax losses are actually relievable against profits.

ACT management

Where a company makes a qualifying distribution it is required to account for advance corporation tax, unless the distribution is covered by franked investment income under TA 1988, s 241, or there is a group income election in force under s 247. The advance corporation tax paid in relation to the dividend is treated as a payment on account of the company's mainstream corporation tax liability, but has to be paid over to the Inland Revenue with Form CT61, 14 days after the end of the return period, which is normally a calendar quarter. From a cash flow point of view, therefore, it is normally desirable to pay a dividend at the beginning of a return quarter rather than the end, although towards the end of the company's financial year it may be sensible to pay a dividend at the end of the final quarter, as the advance corporation tax may then be set against the corporation tax liability for the accounting period due nine months after the end of the accounting period.

If the dividend is not paid until the beginning of the first quarter in the following period, although payment of the ACT is deferred for three months, relief for the ACT against the mainstream corporation tax liability is deferred for 12 months (TA 1988, Sched 13).

Advance corporation tax was normally fixed at a rate equivalent to the lower rate of tax on savings income, on the combined total of the distribution and tax credit. Under TA 1988, ss 14(3) and 231(1), the rate of ACT is 25 per cent of the dividend, equivalent to a credit of 20 per cent of the combination of the dividend and credit. However, a major change is to be introduced from 6 April 1999 by F (No 2) A 1997, s 30 which will reduce the tax credit to one-ninth of the distribution, which is equivalent to 10 per cent on the total of the distribution and credit, although the amount of the advance corporation tax payable by the company in respect of the distribution remains unchanged. There are corresponding reductions to the rate at which dividend income will be taxed on recipients under F (No 2) A 1997, s 31, with corresponding amendments where the recipients of the dividends are trusts or estates of deceased persons in administration under F (No 2) A 1997, ss 32 and 33, with transitional relief for charities given s 35. Foreign income dividends are also abolished from 6 April 1999 by F (No 2) A 1997, s 36 and Sched 6, although it would appear that this decision may be subject to reconsideration, or the introduction of an alternative to a foreign income dividend. The entitlement of pension funds to payment of tax credits in relation to dividends is removed from 2 July 1997 by F (No 2) A 1997, s 19, introducing TA 1988, s 231A.

Advance corporation tax may be surrendered within a 51 per cent group under TA 1988, s 240. A 51 per cent group is measured by reference to direct and indirect holdings under TA 1988, s 838 in the same way as for group relief, although the proportionate income required is lower. There is no provision for surrendering ACT within a consortium.

A 51 per cent group may elect for dividends to be paid gross under TA 1988, s 247, although dividends can still be paid subject to advance corporation tax, if desired, so that the recipient company is in receipt of franked investment income, which will reduce the ACT which it, in turn, has to pay. This mechanism for moving

ACT around a group is quite important because a company may carry back a surplus of advance corporation tax for six years under TA 1988, s 239(3). It may also surrender advance corporation tax to another company within the group, but that company may set off the surrendered ACT only against its current or future mainstream liability without being able to carry it back under TA 1988, s 240. Managing advance corporation tax within a group can be quite complex, but basically the combination of ACT carried back or surrendered or dividends paid under a group election should enable a properly planned group to keep to a minimum the unutilised advance corporation tax.

The foreign income dividend rules in TA 1988, ss 246A–246Y were introduced to enable dividends arising from foreign source income paid on or after 1 July 1994 to be passed through a UK paying company without increasing the irrecoverable advance corporation tax. Although ACT had to be paid in respect of the dividend in the normal way, it was recoverable on a claim after the end of the accounting period. An international headquarters company in the UK may elect that any dividend that it pays shall be treated as a foreign income dividend, and to the extent that it can be matched with foreign source profits, no ACT is payable under TA 1988, s 246T. An international headquarters company is defined by TA 1988, s 246S.

Where there is a change in ownership in a company, and, within three years either side of the change, there is a major change in the nature or conduct of a trade carried on by the company, TA 1988, ss 245 and 245A, prevent surplus ACT being carried forwards or backwards through the change in ownership. Payments for surrendered ACT, if made, are ignored for tax purposes if pursuant to an appropriate agreement (TA 1988, s 240(8)).

Chargeable gains management

The management of chargeable gains for corporation tax purposes usually involves groups of companies. A capital gains tax group which consists of a company and its 75 per cent subsidiaries as defined in TCGA 1992, s 170. 75 per cent subsidiaries are measured according to ordinary share capital, as defined by TA 1988, ss 832 and 838(1)(*b*). In addition, each subsidiary must be an effective 51 per cent subsidiary of the principal company, measured according to beneficial entitlement to profits and assets available on a winding up. A subsidiary which does not qualify as a member of one group may itself be the principal company of another group, but a company cannot be a member of more than one group for chargeable gains purposes. Non-resident companies are excluded from the group definition and therefore a non-resident holding company may interpose a UK holding company over its UK subsidiaries to create a UK sub-group for managing chargeable gains.

Under TA 1988, s 171 transfers of assets within a group of companies are deemed to take place at such price as gives no gain and no loss to the transferor company (*Innocent v Whaddon Estates Ltd* [1982] STC 115). Where the transferor company held assets on 31 March 1982 the transferee company can benefit from rebasing on a subsequent disposal. As there is no group relief for company capital gains, a loss on an asset sold by one company in a group cannot be transferred to another company in the group to set against a gain in the latter company. This means that the asset itself has to be transferred on a 'no gain, no loss' basis under TCGA 1992, s 171 either from the company with the loss-making asset to the company with the profit-making asset, or *vice versa*, before the disposal of the second asset takes place, and within the same accounting period. If this is done the loss on one asset may be set against the profits of the other asset, reducing the corporation tax on the chargeable gain to a minimum.

Where an asset is transferred within a group, which was trading stock of one group company and a capital asset of the other, it is deemed to have been appropriated at market value under TCGA 1992, ss 173 and 161, subject to an election under TCGA 1992, s 161(3) to treat the asset acquired for trading purposes as acquired for its group base value for chargeable gains purposes, so that any subsequent profit is taxed entirely as a trading profit. Roll-over relief for company chargeable assets is available on a group-wide basis under TCGA 1992, s 175.

The disposal of assets within a group at below market value is a depreciatory transaction and TCGA 1992, s 176 denies relief for a loss arising as a consequence of the transfer. Another important anti-avoidance provision is in relation to companies leaving a group under TCGA 1992, s 178. Where there has been an intra-group transfer of a chargeable asset within the previous six years the transferee company leaving the group is deemed to have made a disposal and reacquisition of the asset at its market value immediately after the original intra-group transfer, although the disposal is treated as arising in the accounting period in which the subsidiary leaves the group (TCGA 1992, s 179).

Where a company ceases to be resident in the UK there is an exit charge under which it is deemed to have sold and immediately reacquired its assets at market value, unless those assets continue to be used for a trade carried on in the UK, and therefore sold subject to a charge to corporation tax on chargeable gains (TCGA 1992, s 185).

There are also anti-avoidance provisions (TCGA 1992, ss 189–191) to prevent companies from making intra-group transfers to deplete their assets, leaving the Revenue with the non-recoverable tax.

Financing—loan relationships

The taxation of interest received and the liability for interest paid by companies was totally recast by the loan relationship rules introduced by FA 1996, ss 80–105 and Scheds 8–15. The intention is to treat all interest and profits and losses on loans made or received as taxable income or allowable expenditure on an accruals basis, except in the case of financial institutions which would deal with capital movement on debts on a 'mark to market' basis. Where a company is carrying on a trade the income receivable or payable is taxed or relieved under Schedule D, Case I. If the company is not carrying on a trade the income is assessable under Schedule D, Case III and any loss allowed as a 'loan relationship deficit', which may be set against the total profits for the same accounting period, group relieved, or carried back for 12 months against Schedule D, Case III loan relationship income, or carried forward indefinitely until set off against similar income (FA 1996, s 83). The loan relationship provisions also apply to corporate bonds and gilt-edged securities held by a company, the taxable income in all cases being the excess of the accrued income over the costs incurred, adjusted for profits or losses on the loans under the computation of debts and credits under FA 1996, s 84, bringing in, for a non-financial institution, accruals on an authorised accounting method under FA 1996, s 85(1)(*a*).

From a tax planning point of view, it is worth noting that two issues of gilts are excluded: 3½ per cent Funding Stock 1999–2004, and 5½ per cent Treasury Stock 2008–2012. Although the interest is taxed on an accruals basis for such investments the profit or loss on sale or redemption would be a tax exempt transaction under TCGA 1992, s 115 and FA 1996, s 96(1). It is also worth noting that convertible securities are excluded from the loan relationship regime where there is a more than negligible likelihood that the securities will be converted into shares and they are not relevant discounted securities, ie, the difference between issue price and the amount payable on redemption must not be greater than 0.5 per cent for each year or more than 15 per cent in total. The interest on such convertible loan stock is dealt with on an accruals basis but not the profit or loss of the investing company (FA 1996, s 92). Securities linked to chargeable assets such as the FT-SE Index are also outside the loan relationships rules in respect of the capital profit or loss, which is dealt with under the chargeable gains regime (FA 1996, s 93). Loans between connected parties must be dealt with on an accruals basis, not on a 'mark to market' basis (FA 1996, ss 87 and 88). Where interest is capitalised and amortised over the life of the loan under FRS 4, the accounting treatment would be followed for tax purposes.

The waiver of a loan is normally treated as a taxable receipt in the borrower's hands, in the accounting period in which the waiver takes place, unless the two parties are connected (FA 1996, Sched 9, paras 5 and 6). The waiver of inter-company balances should be considered carefully because there could be a corporation tax charge as a debt released under TA 1988, s 94 or as a distribution under s 209(2)(*b*).

As interest is dealt with on an accruals basis, credits for foreign withholding tax will also be dealt with on a similar basis (TA 1988, ss 797(3)(*a*), 797A and 807A), or will be treated as an expense under TA 1988, s 811(3).

Although the accruals basis normally applies it should be noted that there are some important exceptions for connected party transactions. In particular, interest paid more than 12 months after the end of the accounting period in which it has been accrued can be deducted only when paid (FA 1996, Sched 9, para 2). Similarly, for a relevant discounted security, the discount will be deducted only on redemption unless the recipient is taxed under the loan relationship rules (para 17) and provided that the discounted security is not held by the participator or an associate in a close company (para 18).

Relevant discounted securities are dealt with by FA 1996, s 102 and Sched 13. There is normally an income tax charge on a non-corporate investor on the transfer or redemption of a deep discount security under Schedule D, Case I or Schedule D, Case VI, depending on whether or not the securities are held as part of a trade. The advantage of deep discount securities in corporate tax planning often arises where the lender is an unconnected party outside the UK, which enables the corporate borrower to obtain tax relief for the accruing interest during the currency of the loan and to repay the loan at the end of its term without any requirement to withhold income tax on the excess of the redemption over the amount borrowed, as this is not interest. Normally, interest paid to a non-resident would, subject to the provisions of the double tax treaty, be subject to withholding tax at the basic rate, under TA 1988, s 349(2)(*c*).

Enterprise zones

Capital allowances for buildings are normally available only for industrial buildings or structures as defined by CAA 1990, s 18 or qualifying hotels under CAA 1990, s 7. Wherever the building or structure is in an enterprise or zone, a 100 per cent initial allowance on the cost of the building or structure is given by CAA 1990, s 1. This does not extend to the cost of the land. The site must have been acquired within ten years of the site first being included in the Enterprise Zone (CAA 1990, s 1(1A)(*b*)), and expenditure must be incurred within 20 years of that date (CAA 1990, s 17A).

Enterprise investment schemes

The Enterprise Investment Scheme, introduced with effect from 1 January 1994, replaced the Business Expansion Scheme and allows an individual to obtain relief if eligible shares are issued to him by a qualifying company in order to raise money for a qualifying business activity. The individual must be a qualifying individual and the money must be employed wholly for that activity within a specified time. The investor need not be UK resident but he must have UK taxable income to benefit from the relief, which amounts to 20 per cent of the amount subscribed (TA 1988, s 289A), up to a maximum of £100,000. Relief is therefore worth up to £20,000 for a higher rate taxpayer.

The company for whose business activity money is raised must be carrying on a qualifying activity or be managing group property. A qualifying business activity is carrying on a qualifying trade, or research and development from which such a trade will be derived, and must be carried on wholly or mainly in the UK.

The provisions are complex and included in TA 1988, ss 289–312. It should be noted that a trade which consists of leasing or receiving royalties is specifically excluded by TA 1988, s 297(2)(*e*), unless the company is engaged in film production or distribution and the royalties and licence fees relate to films, or sound recordings in relation to such films, or merchandising arising from such films, which are excluded from the exclusion by TA 1988, s 297(4) and may therefore count as a qualifying trade. A company is also entitled to receive royalties or licence fees in respect of research and development carried out in the course of a trade under TA 1988, s 297(5).

Leasing

A company can normally claim capital allowances on purchasing plant and machinery and fixtures and fittings whether purchased outright or acquired under a hire purchase contract. In many cases companies had found it beneficial to lease plant and machinery, particularly where the capital allowances would exceed the taxable profits. The leasing company would itself be entitled to claim capital allowances on the equipment and would reflect the value of those allowances in the terms offered for leasing the equipment on a finance lease over the economic life of the equipment. In some cases the lessee would be offered an amount equivalent to the residual value of the equipment at the end of the lease by way of a rebate on lease rental.

The benefit to the lessee of leasing equipment has been severely curtailed by the restrictions to capital allowances for finance lessors in F (No 2) A 1997, ss 44–47. These provide that a finance lessor may claim capital allowances in the year of acquisition for only the balance of the accounting period instead of the full year's writing down allowance, irrespective of the time during the year in which the asset is acquired, which is the normal rule for capital allowances. A finance lessor acquiring the equipment it leases on a hire purchase agreement is entitled to capital allowances only on the hire purchase instalments actually paid in the period, instead of, as is normally the case, the full price of the equipment. These restrictions apply to expenditure incurred on or after 2 July 1997 by the finance lessor although there is transitional relief to 1 July 1998, for expenditure contracted for prior to 2 July 1997. If the lease is part of a 'sale and lease back' refinancing operation, the lessor's qualifying expenditure for capital allowances purposes is restricted to the seller's written down value, on the assumption that he had claimed any capital allowances available. There are no allowances at all where the finance lessor is not at risk for non-payment of rent etc. Relief is also restricted where the lessee is carrying on non-trading activities, such as a local authority.

Where the lessor's expenditure is restricted on a time basis by being bought during the year, the balance of the expenditure in the first allowable period is available for relief in the following period, so the allowances are merely deferred. Effectively, the new provisions, in many cases, will make leasing uneconomic for the lessee, compared with acquisition on hire purchase or borrowing to acquire the equipment.

Reconstructions and amalgamations

Where a company is acquired in exchange for shares or debentures, in a takeover for *bona fide* commercial purposes, the vendor is not deemed to have realised a capital gain but to have acquired the shares in the acquiring company, which he receives in exchange for the shares in the company being sold, at the cost and date of the original shares (TCGA 1992, s 135). The acquisition must be one under which the acquiring company obtains more than a 25 per cent interest as a result of the transaction, or it is a general offer which, if accepted, would give the acquirer more than a 50 per cent interest, or the acquirer already holds or acquires voting control as a result of the transaction.

Similar 'paper for paper' roll-over treatment is given under s 136 of TCGA 1992 where shares or debentures are received in a new company as a result of a scheme reconstruction or amalgamation, such as under s 110 of the Insolvency Act 1986 or a scheme of arrangement under s 425 of the Companies Act 1985, whereby shares in company 'A' are cancelled and new shares are issued to a new company 'B', which issues its shares to the former members of company 'A' *pro rata* to their holdings in the original company.

Similar relief is also given on splitting a company under Statement of Practice 5/85. In each case any cash element would give rise to a proportionate chargeable gain, and the arrangements must not have, as a main purpose, the avoidance of capital gains tax (TCGA 1992, s 137). Clearance may be obtained on application under TCGA 1992, s 138.

Where shares are sold for a consideration that is deferred and unascertainable, usually on an earn-out arrangement, tax may be deferred under TCGA 1992, s 138A by treating the earn-out right as a security in the acquiring company.

Ascertainable deferred consideration has to be brought into account at the time of the initial disposal under TCGA 1992, s 48. Roll-over relief is also available on a transfer of a business within the UK for no consideration other than taking over its liabilities. The assets are deemed to have been disposed of on a 'no gain, no loss' basis as for an intra-group transfer (TCGA 1992, s 139).

Where a company's foreign branch is converted into an overseas company, roll-over relief for chargeable gains is available under TCGA 1992, s 140.

Most reconstructions and amalgamations will also be transactions in securities which could potentially give rise to a tax charge under TA 1988, ss 703 and 704. Again there is a clearance procedure, this time under TA 1988, s 707.

In a demerger where shareholders are given assets such as shares in a subsidiary company, this would normally be treated as a taxable distribution outside a liquidation under TA 1988, s 209. However, certain payments in a demerger may be exempt from being taxed as distributions under the provisions of TA 1988, ss 213–218. A demerger usually consists of a distribution *in specie* by a company to its members, of shares in its 75 per cent subsidiary. An indirect demerger may also be an exempt distribution where a trade or trades are transferred, or shares in the 75 per cent subsidiary are distributed *in specie* to another company, in exchange for the issue of shares by the transferee company to the members of the transferor company, under a Companies Act 1985, s 425 reconstruction.

A demerger is available only where the distributing company, which is demerging, is a trading company or a member of a trading group and the subsidiary being demerged is either a trading company or a holding company of a trading group. There are assets to be excepted and numerous provisions to prevent exploitation in tax avoidance under a demerger.

TCGA 1992, s 192 treats a demerger as a 'paper for paper' reconstruction for capital gains tax purposes.

A company may now purchase its own shares under CA 1985, ss 162–177. Such an acquisition would normally be a distribution to shareholders. If, however, numerous complex conditions are complied with it may be possible to arrange that a purchase of its own shares by the company for the benefit of its trade, or to enable inheritance tax to be paid, may be treated as a capital disposal under TA 1988, ss 219–229. Where the purchase of own shares is treated as a capital transaction under these provisions, the normal capital gains tax rules will apply to the disposal.

22 International tax planning

Introduction

The international dimension of tax planning runs the whole gamut from non-residence and the law of domicile through the complexities of controlled foreign companies (Chapter 14) and other anti-avoidance legislation to profit engineering and the bête noire of transfer pricing, particular American transfer pricing (Chapter 13). These subjects necessarily do not form a cohesive whole and each is sufficiently complex to merit more detailed discussion than can be encompassed in a book of this nature. The overview given in this chapter is a distillation of the salient features of many different matters, and no apologies are made for the inherently piecemeal approach adopted.

Non-residents

Non-residents in receipt of income from intellectual property arising in the UK (ie a UK patent, defined by TA 1988, s 533(1) as a patent granted under the laws of the UK, royalties in respect of UK copyright under the CDPA 1988, or other rights over UK intellectual property) would have income from property in the UK and would therefore be taxable under the provisions of TA 1988, s 18(1)(a)(iii) on the income arising, unless exempt or taxable at a reduced rate under a double taxation agreement (*see* p 265). The deduction of tax at source provisions apply, in effect, a withholding tax at the basic rate of 23 per cent to patent royalties paid to a non-resident, and under TA 1988, s 536 in respect of copyright royalties paid to a person, other than the author, whose usual place of abode is outside the UK. For the rates of withholding tax under the various double taxation agreements between the UK and other countries see Appendix 9.

Overseas rights

A UK resident in receipt of income from overseas intellectual property, such as foreign patent and copyright royalties under foreign agreements, is in receipt of income which would be assessed under Schedule D, Case V as income arising from possessions out of the UK, unless included in the worldwide income of a trade or profession under Schedule D, Cases I or II. Income is also assessed under Schedule D, Case V in the case of a company if the trade is carried on abroad with no control from the UK (*Trustees of Ferguson, deceased v Donovan* [1929] IR 489). Such a state of affairs would be most unusual, although if the intellectual property income is received by a wholly owned foreign subsidiary, dividends therefrom would be assessed under Schedule D, Case V (*Stanley v The Gramophone and Typewriter Ltd* (1908) 5 TC 358).

A further source of income under Schedule D, Case V is that of a UK resident but non-UK domiciled partner in a partnership managed and controlled from overseas.

The actual assessment under Schedule D, Case V is very similar to that under Schedule D, Case III except for persons domiciled outside the UK. The assessment is therefore normally on the income arising in the year of assessment under TA 1988, s 65.

The main difference is that under Schedule D, Case V a non-UK domiciled individual is taxable only on remittances, whereas a domiciled individual is taxable on the income arising whether remitted to the UK or not (*see* pp 263–5).

Overseas earnings

100 per cent deduction

A UK resident and ordinarily resident individual may claim relief under TA 1988, s 193 and Sched 12 if part of the activities of an employment take place overseas during a period in which he remains UK resident throughout. If there is a long period of absence, that is, a qualifying period which consists of at least 365 days, the deduction from the Schedule E earnings is 100 per cent, which makes those earnings effectively free of UK tax. Such a long period of absence may possibly make the remuneration taxable in an overseas country and this aspect should not be overlooked. During the period of absence it is possible to return to the UK for limited periods. The period spent in the UK must not consist of more than 62 consecutive days and the days in the UK must not exceed 1/6 of the total number of days in the relevant period under TA 1988, Sched 12, para 3. This means that if an individual goes abroad, returns to the UK and departs overseas once more it is necessary to measure the relevant period when he again returns to the UK. Each visit to the UK potentially brings an end to the relevant period.

It is sometimes convenient to consider the relevant period as a multidecker ham sandwich. If the period overseas is regarded as the bread and the period in the UK as the ham the relevant period will continue to run so long as the ham does not exceed 1/6 of the total sandwich. For a day to count as a day of absence from the UK it is necessary for the employee to be absent at midnight (TA 1988, Sched 12, para 4). As a safe rule of thumb, if the employee spends less than 62 days on his UK visit and spends abroad six times the number of days he spent in the UK before returning again to the UK, he will have satisfied the test (*Robins v Durkin* [1988] STC 588).

In the field of intellectual property the 'long period of absence' exemption is particularly useful in the case of an author who goes overseas for a period to write or in the case of an artiste who may have an overseas tour or film or recording contract. It may be possible to make them an employee of a company in which they and their family own the majority of the shares and provide them with a service contract whereby the remuneration arising from their activities overseas, as employee of the company, will be paid to them largely by way of salary and bonus. It would, however, be necessary to consider whether this would be suitable for the tax rules of the country being visited, as some countries would look through such an arrangement under lend-a-star provisions (*see* p 317).

As TA 1988, Sched 12, para 2(2) provides that the exemption applies to emoluments from the employment attributable to the period of absence, this should ensure that the 100 per cent exemption applies to the whole of the remuneration arising from that employment even if paid out of royalties received in a later period although the Revenue have been known to resist this argument. It would be relatively unusual for a UK resident inventor to qualify for the 365-day exemption.

It should be noted that it is not necessary to be absent for a complete fiscal year in order to obtain the exemption, and if the period of absence does include a complete fiscal year the relief could be displaced by non-residence (SP 18/91; *Tax Bulletin*, Issue 5, November 1992, p 40).

It should also be noted that it is not necessary for the whole of the long period of absence, or even the majority of it, to be spent actually working.

Foreign partnerships

A UK partnership is not a separate legal entity (apart from a Scottish partnership under Partnership Act 1890, s 4(2)), but its income is computed as if it were a separate entity, and a partnership self-assessment return has to be completed on this basis. However, the profit is then allocated on the partnership statement to individual partners who are responsible for their own taxation on their share of the profits, as explained in Chapter 9.

TA 1988, s 18(1)(*a*)(ii) provides that tax under Schedule D shall be charged in respect of any person residing in the UK from any trade, profession or vocation, whether carried on in the UK or elsewhere. TA 1988, s 18(1)(*a*)(iii) provides that tax shall be charged under Schedule D on any person, whether a British subject or not, although not resident in the UK, from any property whatever in the UK or from any trade, profession or vocation exercised in the UK.

A non-domiciled individual is taxed in the same way as a UK domiciled individual under Schedule D, Case I or II.

Court decision such as *Colquohoun v Brooks* (1889) 2 TC 490, show that it is possible for a UK resident to carry on a trade abroad as a partner and not exercise control and management of the business, and therefore avoid a tax liability under Schedule D, Cases I and II, it being income of a foreign possession assessed under Schedule D, Case V. However, *Ogilvy v Kitton* (1908) 5 TC 338 and *Spiers v Mackinnon* (1929) 14 TC 386 establish that where the head and brains of the business reside in the UK, the profits are assessed under Schedule D, Case I or II. The decision in *Davies v Braithwaite* (1933) 18 TC 198 confirms that the whole of the worldwide profits of a profession carried on by a UK resident is liable to UK tax under Schedule D, Case II. Similarly, a Schedule D, Case D trade carried on partly in the UK and partly abroad by a UK resident is wholly liable to UK tax under Schedule D, Case I following the decision in *London Bank of Mexico v Apthorpe* (1891) 3 TC 143.

The effect of these decisions is that the UK resident partners in a partnership carrying on a business partly in the UK and partly overseas are liable to UK tax on the whole of the overseas income. If the overseas income arises from a permanent establishment in the foreign country it is probable that there will be a foreign tax liability on the overseas profits, which will be credited against the UK tax liability either under the terms of the double taxation treaty with the overseas country or unilaterally in the UK under TA 1988, s 790.

When considering the foreign activities of a UK resident it is important to bear in mind that the double taxation treaties which, following *Ostime v Australian Mutual Provident Society* (1959) 38 TC 492, would overrule the UK legislation, may provide that a dual resident is deemed not to be resident in the UK. For example, a Spanish national with a home in both the UK and Spain and business interests in both countries would probably be deemed, under Article 4(2)(*c*) of the UK/Spain double taxation agreement, to be resident in Spain and not in the UK. Similar provisions are to be found in other recent agreements, for example, those with the Irish Republic and with the USA. There is a body of opinion, however, which argues that where dual residence exists the treaty deeming provision of single residence *only* applies for treaty provision purposes and does not affect the underlying dual residence position, although in practice the Revenue usually regard the treaty residence as applicable for all tax purposes.

A non-resident or deemed non-resident trading in the UK would be taxed under Schedule D, Case I only on profits arising in the UK, following such cases as *Erichsen v Last* (1881) 1 TC 351, 537, 4 TC 422; *Pommery & Greno v Apthorpe* (1886) 2 TC 182; and *Werle & Co Colquhoun* (1888) 2 TC 402 or the appropriate provisions of the treaty.

It will be appreciated that a UK resident may be a partner in a partnership which is managed and controlled outside the UK. TA 1988, s 112(1A) provides that:

Where—

(a)   any persons are carrying on a trade, profession or business in partnership,

(b)   the trade, profession or business is carried on wholly or partly outside the United Kingdom,

(c)   the control and management of the trade, profession or business is situated outside the United Kingdom, and

(d)   any of the partners who is an individual resident in the United Kingdom satisfies the Board that he is not domiciled in the United Kingdom or that, being a Commonwealth citizen or a citizen of the Republic of Ireland, he is not ordinarily resident in the United Kingdom,

section 111 shall have effect in accordance with subsection (1) above as if that partner were not resident in the United Kingdom and, in addition (as respects that partner as an individual who is in fact resident in the United Kingdom), his interest as a partner, so far as it entitles him to a share of any profits or gains arising from the carrying on of the trade, profession or business otherwise than within the United Kingdom, shall be treated for the purposes of Case V of Schedule D as if it were a possession outside the United Kingdom.

TA 1988, s 112(1) limits the Schedule D, Case I assessment on non-UK resident partners to their share of any profits of the foreign partnership arising from activities in the UK which would be assessable in the same way as any other non-resident trading in the UK through a UK branch or agency. The remaining income due to a UK resident and domiciled partner would be taxed under Schedule D, Case I on his share of the worldwide income, while a non-UK domiciled, UK resident partner would be taxed on his share of the UK income under Schedule D, Case I and on his share of the non-UK income overruling *Padmore v IRC* [1989] STC 493.

Control and management

To ensure that the control and management of a foreign partnership is outside the UK it is desirable to have a majority of non-UK resident partners and provisions in the partnership agreement that partnership meetings must be held outside the UK. It is not essential to have a majority in number of non-resident partners, provided that the voting control is such that they control the partnership. See in this respect the case of *Newstead v Frost* [1980] STC 123, in which the UK resident partner had 95 per cent of the profits of the partnership but was still assessed under Schedule D, Case V, as the control and management of the partnership were outside the UK. Where or not both the control and management are outside this country are questions of fact, to be decided by the Commissioners if necessary. Consequently, all communications from the UK to the foreign partnership must be requests and advice and not instructions.

Schedule D, Case V

A Schedule D, Case V assessment on income of a non-UK domiciliary from a foreign partnership is computed along the normal Schedule D, Case V lines on the income remitted to the UK (TA 1988, s 65(4)–(7)).

If goods or services are transferred between a foreign partnership and an associated UK firm under common control TA 1988, s 770 will enable the Board of Inland Revenue to substitute market value for the price charged for such goods or services. Similar transfer pricing provisions are contained in most double taxation agreements and in Article 9 of the OECD model double tax treaty, as explained in Chapter 13.

The post-cessation receipts provisions of TA 1988, ss 103–110 do not apply to Schedule D, Case V income from a foreign partnership and it could apparently be argued that such post-cessation receipts are tax-free on the basis that the source has ceased and remittances from a non-Schedule E ceased source in a tax year after that in which the source ceased are not taxable (*Joffe v Thain* (1955) 36 TC 199).

Remittance basis

If a sizeable proportion of the work is done overseas it may well be desirable for a non-UK domiciliary to enter into a foreign partnership within TA 1988, s 112(1A) under which the income is taxable under Schedule D, Case V or to enter into a contract of employment with a non-resident company, in which case the remuneration would be dealt with under Schedule E. This would be particularly appropriate in the case of a non-UK domiciled individual because in respect of income taxed under Schedule D, Cases I and II, a non-UK domiciled individual has no advantage under UK tax law compared with a person domiciled in the UK, whereas remuneration from a non-resident company or partnership for services performed wholly abroad would be taxed only on remittances to the UK and not on the income arising (TA 1988, ss 19(1), 192, 65(4)).

Remittances in a fiscal year following that in which the recipient ceased to be a partner would be tax-free in the UK as there would be no source of income to tax. There can therefore be advantages in alternating periods of overseas activities through a series of partnerships and employments and remitting only during a fiscal year following that in which the Schedule D source ceased. Remittances from a ceased Schedule E source are treated as emoluments for the year in which the employment ceased under TA 1988, s 19(4A). If however, he was domiciled in the UK, a UK domiciled and resident partner of a foreign partnership would be assessed to tax under Schedule D, Case I or II on the arising basis on his share of the profits of the foreign partnership.

Assessments on a remittance basis include not only direct remittances to the UK but also constructive remittances, such as the satisfaction of a debt incurred in the UK under TA 1988, s 65(5)–(9). A cheque drawn on an American bank account was held to be a constructive remittance when sold to a UK bank (*Thomson v Moyse* (1960) 39 TC 291), as was a loan enjoyed in the UK (*Harmel v Wright* (1973) 49 TC 149). Remittances of the proceeds of foreign securities could be a remittance of capital if the securities were acquired before the taxpayer became resident in the UK (*Kneen v Martin* (1934) 19 TC 33), but not if purchased out of foreign income while the taxpayer was resident in the UK (*Walsh v Randall* (1940) 23 TC 55). It is arguable that remittance of a physical asset is not a remittance of income.

If a non-UK domiciled individual is assessable on a remittance basis, it is important to ensure that, so far as possible, remittances to the UK are out of capital. This means that he may require several bank accounts. The account containing his capital prior to becoming resident in the UK may be freely remitted. An account containing the proceeds of disposals of overseas investments could be remitted, but any chargeable gains element would be taxable on the remittance basis under TCGA 1992, s 12(1). However, the effective rate of tax applicable to capital gains is less as a result of indexation allowance and rebasing than that applicable to income and, therefore, a remittance from such an account should be made in preference to a remittance of income assessable under Schedule D, Case V.

If it is likely to prove necessary to remit part of the overseas income it might be desirable to have two overseas bank accounts for such income, one relating to earned income from the foreign partnership and one relating to investment income. Such bank accounts might well be held in the Channel Islands. Where deposit interest is received it may be possible to close the deposit and interest accounts on 4 April and place the funds on current account with a different bank and place them on deposit on 6 April. Remittances after 6 April from the new account will be remittances of capital so long as the interest is credited to a separate account.

Gifts overseas

A non-domiciled individual taxable on the remittance basis could make gifts overseas of funds from his foreign bank accounts to his wife, family and friends. An overseas bank account into which the gift can pass thereby avoids falling into the constructive remittance problems previously mentioned (*Carter v Sharon* (1936) 20 TC 229). If, for example, the wife bought a fur coat or otherwise spent the money so that her husband received no benefit, or if the children paid for their own school fees, it is considered that these would not be constructive remittances.

For inheritance tax purposes a person who is not domiciled in the UK can be treated as so domiciled under the deemed domicile provisions of IHTA 1984, s 267.

The most likely case is that of an individual who has been resident in the UK in at least 17 out of the previous 20 years.

Where the individual is not UK domiciled for both income tax and inheritance tax purposes the gifts mentioned can be made free of inheritance tax. However, if the person is notionally domiciled here for inheritance tax purposes he would need to take advantage of the potentially exempt transfer provisions or other inheritance tax exemptions.

If a non-domiciled partner makes a gift from his (Jersey) bank account to his UK partners by transferring funds to their own (Jersey) bank accounts, such a gift would be excluded property for inheritance tax purposes. However, it would be necessary to ensure that the UK partners had not made a transfer of assets to the foreign partnership, for otherwise TA 1988, s 739 could cause the gifts to be assessable as income.

The whole question of taxation of income by reference to the existing residence and domicile rules came under review and the Revenue published a consultative paper, although in the event the government decided to make no change to the existing rules. However, a new government may take a different view.

Withholding taxes

In order to see whether the intended benefits of any overseas tax planning are in fact obtainable it is first of all necessary to consider the question of withholding taxes deducted by the countries from which the income is likely to emanate. It could be preferable for a UK resident to have the use of income which could be remitted to the UK with the result that, after credit for foreign taxes paid, the additional UK tax liability on the income would be small or at an acceptable level. On the other hand, it may be possible to set up a more sophisticated arrangement whereby the patent or copyright is owned by an offshore company.

Double taxation relief

Many countries apply a withholding tax on royalty payments to a non-resident of that country, as does the UK, in connection with UK patent royalties and certain copyright royalties. If the recipient of the foreign royalties is resident in the UK, the rate of withholding tax is often reduced or eliminated under the appropriate double taxation treaty between the UK and the country where the royalty arises. It is important to look carefully at the definition of royalty under the particular treaty and to look at the treaty currently in force, as double taxation treaties tend to be undergoing continual revision. It is also necessary to consider the practice of the overseas country.

For example, the American Internal Revenue Service has been known to argue that record royalties are not royalties exempt within the UK/USA Double Tax Treaty but are connected with income from performances in the USA and should be taxed as such. It might be necessary to resist such contentions under the law and practice of the overseas countries.

It should be borne in mind that a double taxation agreement in the UK normally overrules the provisions of the Taxes Act (*Ostime v Australian Mutual Provident Society* (1959) 38 TC 492 and TA 1988, s 788(1)).

Under TA 1988, s 790 if overseas income suffers foreign tax which is not relieved under a double tax treaty, unilateral relief may be given whereby the foreign tax is treated as a credit, that is, as it were a payment on account of the UK tax liability arising on the same income. The relief primarily applies to income tax and corporation tax but is extended to capital gains tax by TCGA 1992, s 277.

TA 1988, s 796 provides that the double taxation relief cannot exceed the UK income tax payable on the overseas income concerned, treating the latter as the top slice of income and ignoring the foreign tax credit; see *Yates v GCA International Ltd* [1991] STC 157 and SP7/91 (Appendix 6). Where there are a number of overseas income sources the UK tax credit appropriate to each is calculated separately by successively treating each source as the top slice of income subject to UK tax, but thereafter excluding that source in the total income computations. Thus, to maximise relief overseas sources should be dealt with in descending order of overseas tax rates with the higher tax rate source being dealt with first. For corporation tax purposes TA 1988, s 797 provides that the double taxation relief credit cannot exceed UK corporation tax on the foreign income. If the foreign income is part of Schedule D, Case I profits an attribution of expenses to this income will be required to arrive at the amount of doubly taxed income.

If dividends are paid out of overseas income TA 1988, s 239 allows the foreign tax credit to be used before the attributable advance corporation tax. As unused double taxation relief cannot be carried forward but surplus ACT can be carried back six years, this change in the order of set-off is helpful.

Foreign tax unrelieved under any double taxation treaty or under the unilateral relief provisions of TA 1988, s 790 can, under TA 1988, s 811, be treated as an expense in computing the profits liable to UK tax (*Harrods (Buenos Aires) Ltd v Taylor-Gooby* (1964) 41 TC 450; *IRC v Dowdall O'Mahoney & Co Ltd* (1952) 33 TC 259). It is obviously preferable to claim foreign tax as a credit against the UK tax payable, rather than as a mere expense in computing the UK tax liability.

Royalties paid by an overseas licensee for the use of UK intellectual property in the overseas country are treated as income from overseas of the UK licensor even though, technically, the source of income is the UK, under Extra-Statutory Concession B8 (1992).

Current rates of withholding tax for royalties received by a UK resident recipient from various overseas countries are listed in Appendix 9.

Profit engineering

It is worth considering a patent owned by a company in the Netherlands Antilles, the shares of which are owned by a Jersey trust. If the company is a Netherlands Antilles corporation the shareholders of which are not residents of the Netherlands Antilles, and the income is derived from outside the Netherlands Antilles, it should be possible to obtain a foreign exchange licence from the bank of the Netherlands Antilles which would make the company an offshore company under articles 8, 14 and 14A of the Profit Tax Law 1940, as amended. The object is to have the income taxed in the Netherlands Antilles at the favourable rate of between 2.4 per cent and 3 per cent, which is guaranteed until the year 2000. The reason why the Netherlands Antilles tended to be chosen is that it is one of the few tax havens with taxation treaties in its own right (with the Netherlands and Denmark—the UK agreement was terminated from 6 April 1989) and it is able through the special relationship with the Netherlands to take advantage of the Dutch double tax treaties.

There is no withholding tax on royalties and no tax on capital gains. The Netherlands has, after the UK, one of the most comprehensive treaty networks in the world. The patented invention, for example, could be licensed to a company in the Netherlands and in turn sub-licensed to the user in, say, Russia. Under the Russian/Dutch double tax treaty the rate of withholding tax on paying a patent licence fee to the Dutch company would be nil. The amount received in Holland would be subject to Dutch tax on the amount of the royalty received less the royalty paid. It is usually possible to negotiate with the Dutch Revenue authorities the amount of profit to be retained in Holland and the amount is usually up to 7 per cent of the royalty.

It is possible, and advisable, to obtain a ruling in advance, which is usually for three years but may normally be extended. The amount to be retained in the Netherlands depends on the amount of royalties received, thus:

Dfl	*Percentage*
0 — 2,000,000	7
2,000,001 — 4,000,000	6
4,000,001 — 6,000,000	5
6,000,001 — 8,000,000	4
8,000,001 — 10,000,000	3
Over 10,000,000	2

Six per cent of film royalties of any amount must usually be retained in the Netherlands.

The agreed percentage of the royalty would be subject to Dutch tax at, say, 42 per cent and the balance would be paid to the Netherlands Antilles where it would be subject to tax at between 2.4 per cent and 3 per cent. The Netherlands Antilles company could then pay a dividend to a trust in Jersey and no withholding tax would be levied. If the beneficiaries of the trust were resident outside Jersey there would be no tax in Jersey on the dividend received.

Example

A royalty is payable to a company in Russia and it is desired to route the royalties to minimise taxation.

	DM
Royalty paid by Russian licensee to BV in Netherlands	100,000
Royalty received by BV (withholding tax nil under treaty)	100,000
Less: royalty paid to parent NV in Netherlands Antilles	93,000
Agreed liable to Dutch tax	7,000
Tax in Netherlands at 36%	2,520
Dividend paid to NV	4,480

(Withholding tax 7.5% under treaty where NV holds 25% or more of shares in BV)

		DM
Royalty received by NV		93,000
Dividend received by NV (4,480 × 92.5)		4,144
		97,144
Tax in Netherlands Antilles at 3%		
less national expenses, effective rate 1.5%		1,457
Dividend paid to Jersey Trust		95,687

No withholding tax

Although the use of the Netherlands intermediate licensing company in this way is well known it might be worthwhile exploring other potential tax havens. For example, the UK Revenue are becoming increasingly conscious of the anti-avoidance provisions in article 12, para 5 of the UK-Dutch double taxation agreement (SI 1980 No 1961) and it may be preferable to route royalties through the Austrian subsidiary of a non-resident Cyprus company relying on article 12 of the UK–Austrian double taxation treaty (SI 1970 No 1947) which has a limitation only if the UK company is more than 50 per cent controlled by Austrian residents. Anti-avoidance measures against cascading royalties of this nature are beginning to be applied, for example, by the IRS in the USA with wide-ranging anti-avoidance measures in the recent American/Dutch anti-avoidance treaty. It is not possible to route royalties from the UK direct to a Cyprus offshore company because such companies are specifically excluded from treaty protection by the protocol to the UK Cyprus treaty for dividends, interest and royalties.

However, it may be worth considering using an independently owned Cyprus resident company which does have treaty protection. Although the profits would be liable to tax in Cyprus only the net profit after paying any outgoing royalties would be subject to tax in Cyprus. There is no Cyprus withholding tax on outgoing royalty payments and the only anti-avoidance restriction in the UK–Cyprus double tax treaty is that the rate of royalties must be commercially justifiable. Therefore a structure such as a Jersey trust owning a British Virgin Islands company which owns the intellectual property rights and licenses these to the independently owned Cyprus resident company. This is a contractual arrangement which ensures receipt of the royalties from the Cyprus company at an appropriate level say 96 per cent of the royalties received by the Cyprus company from the UK licensee. Again this would be on a contractual basis and therefore not dependent on the ownership of the Cyprus company. The Cyprus fisc will usually confirm in advance an acceptable royalty spread at these sort of levels.

The UK itself may be used in this fashion and if it is an independently owned company which is contractually in receipt of royalties from say the USA and is contractually paying out royalties to some other country say the Bahamas both of which are independently owned, the UK company should only be subject to UK tax on the royalty spread. The UK would not charge withholding taxes on intellectual property that did not have a UK source; in other words non-UK patents and royalties from the exploitation outside the UK of material which is subject to copyright outside the UK. It is normally preferable in such circumstances to have the royalties paid into an overseas bank account and paid to the head licensor in the tax haven to emphasise the non-UK source of the income. Provided that the company is still managed and controlled from the UK as UK incorporated it should be eligible for the UK treaty network protection. There may be anti-avoidance provisions where the royalties emanate from say the US or Germany under their legislation and it is obviously important in any form of international tax planning to take account of the liabilities and withholding tax requirement of each jurisdiction involved even though they may like US secondary withholding tax be difficult to enforce against a foreign company. Obviously the proper law of the licensing agreement in such circumstances should not be that of the UK.

The Republic of Ireland is also a popular venue for intermediary licensing companies as many of the Irish double tax treaties do not have limitation of benefit clauses. Again a combination of routing from the final licensee through an Irish company then on to a Cyprus onshore or offshore company and finally through to the tax haven based head licensor can be worth looking at. A Cyprus offshore company is taxed at only 4.25 per cent but is excluded from treaty benefit under treaties with the UK, the USA, France and Canada.

Hungary has also been a popular venue for an intermediary licensing company as it is normally only necessary to leave the small spread of royalties of say 5 per cent which in turn are only subject to a 3 per cent of tax from 1 January 1997. It is important to look carefully at the treaties; for example the Hungarian–Japanese treaty reduces the standard rate of Japanese withholding tax from 20 per cent to 10 per cent except for cultural royalties which are exempt, and include literary, artistic or scientific works, including films or tapes for cinema, television or radio.

The licensing agreement may be for a period that is much shorter than the commercial life of the intellectual property and may be useful for example for the tax haven licensor to sell to the Dutch intermediary company the right to exploit the intellectual property for a period of say five years for a capital sum. The independently owned Dutch company will have taken into account in fixing the price to be paid the fact that the royalty income will be subject to Dutch tax but that Dutch fiscal law allows for the acquisition costs to be depreciated over the life of the licence. If this were for example a five-year licence 20 per cent annum of the original cost would be allowed as a depreciation allowance against the royalties receivable by the Dutch company. This would reduce the Dutch tax to negligible proportions. The lump sum would have been paid without any withholding tax as the Netherlands does not levy a withholding tax on intellectual property payments. This can be a useful mechanism where the royalty stream can be estimated with a reasonable degree of accuracy under the contract and it should prevent many of the anti-avoidance provisions being applied because the Dutch company is the true beneficial owner of the royalty stream by virtue of its licence and does not pay out any further royalties, merely the lump sum for the acquisition of the royalties in the first instance which may in appropriate cases be payable by instalments.

Any such treaty shopping has to take account of anti-avoidance provisions such as those relating to controlled foreign companies (Chapter 14) and transfer pricing (Chapter 13) and offshore trust rules referred to below.

Switzerland, under a decree of the Federal Council in 1962, may limit the rights to Swiss double tax treaty protection where Switzerland is used merely as a conduit. Although it only charges federal tax on intellectual property held by a domiciliary company after notional expenses an effective rate of 9.8 per cent on say 50 per cent of the income is normally acceptable. However the Swiss also require passive profits of this nature to be distributed by way of dividend of at least 25 per cent of the income received which is then subject to a hefty 35 per cent Swiss withholding tax. A solution may be a Swiss resident branch of a Dutch company which will qualify for the Swiss double tax treaty protection and would not be subject to tax in the Netherlands as it was subject to tax in Switzerland at the effective rate of less than 5 per cent and would accrue to the Swiss company as of a right as income of the branch, not by way of dividend.

Film distribution agreement

Although the UK does not levy a withholding tax on film distribution royalties many other countries do. Films can be extremely expensive to make and co-productions are common. It is possible to have a straightforward co-production between companies in two different countries where each is entitled to a proportion of the receipts throughout the world and each party has to consider the withholding taxes likely to be levied on their own share of the income. A more tax efficient structure is very often a split rights deal in which for example overseas distributors acquire the foreign rights of a US film and contribute to the original cost in return for a share of the eventual profit. In these deals each distributor will recover his own costs in the first instance out of the royalties receivable which would reimburse, the original investment, and as each distributor goes into profit he will start paying royalties to the other co-distributors which may be subject to withholding taxes. In such circumstances a jointly owned distribution company in a suitable intermediary licensing country such as the UK, Ireland, Netherlands or Hungary could be used to advantage to reduce the withholding taxes to a minimum. In large co-productions there may be several such intermediary distribution companies covering different territories and taking advantage of their double taxation treaty network. There may also be a general sales company covering those countries where distributors do not participate in the equity of the film.

These joint distribution agreements often require the use of an independent collection account manager to collect the receipts and make the appropriate payments under the agreements. The Netherlands is often used as the jurisdiction of the collection account manager.

Authors

One of the advantages of copyright is that, at least under UK law, it can be transferred before the work to which it relates has been written, and therefore before it has acquired any value. One of the major problems of exploiting intellectual property is ensuring that it ends up legitimately in a suitable low-tax jurisdiction without incurring an enormous tax charge in transferring it to the offshore licensor. In the case of an author it may be appropriate to contract with a company in say Hungary owned by a tax haven company in turn owned by an offshore trust to write a book in return for a salary to be paid by the Hungarian company which would be entitled to the royalties on the eventual sale of the book. As long as the salary was reasonable the author should not become a deemed additional settlor of the trust as in *Crossland v Hawkins* (1961) 39 TC 493 or *Mills v IRC* (1974) STC 130. So long as the Hungarian company is accepted as an offshore company by the Ministry of Finance, which it should in view of the fact that its income will be derived from sources outside Hungary, the rate of tax should be minimal. Under the existing law such income would only be taxed when distributed to beneficiaries and can therefore be accumulated tax-free by the Hungarian company's tax haven trust or parent company.

A variation on this theme is the use of two companies where for example the employment agreement is with an offshore Cyprus company which in turn licenses through a suitable treaty country such as the Republic of Ireland to the UK. The UK–Ireland treaty has no limitation of benefits clause and the Irish company would contractually pay say 98 per cent of the royalties received to the Cyprus company and the Cyprus company would be taxable on 4.25 per cent of its profits after deduction of the salary paid to the author.

There are a number of other suitable combinations such as UK–Austria, Cyprus–Norway, Cyprus–UK, Denmark–Cyprus.

Dividend routeing

Instead of extracting royalties by way of sub-royalties through to a tax haven parent, it may be possible to take advantage of the European Community Parent/Subsidiary Directive to extract profits by way of dividend to a tax haven parent. It seems that at the moment Gibraltar, although in the European Community, is not covered by the directive but that Madeira, being part of Portugal, is, provided that it has a Portuguese tax liability, for example from a branch in Lisbon. In such cases it may be possible to have the Madeira company owning a Dutch subsidiary holding company through which royalties are licensed and to pay the royalty up to Madeira and then extract it by way of a dividend through to a tax haven parent company relying on the parent/subsidiary directive 1990/435/EEC. There should be no withholding tax from Madeira. Rather than paying royalties from the Dutch company to the Madeira company, relying on the lack of Dutch withholding tax on royalties, it may be better to pay by way of dividend in respect of which there should be no withholding tax under the directive.

Loan routeing

A further alternative to royalties routing would be to extract profits from a royalty receiving company by financing it with loans from a tax haven-based finance company funded by means of equity participation. The loan interest, at a proper commercial rate, should be allowed as a deduction from the royalties received. The extent to which this method may be employed may be circumscribed by thin capitalisation or debt/equity rules in the interest paying country. The finance company must serve a proper commercial purpose (*Overseas Containers (Finance) Ltd v Stoker* [1989] STC 364).

Tax havens

The choice of the appropriate tax haven will be dependent upon the countries of residence of the licensor and licensee. A route which reduces the rate of withholding taxes to an acceptable level may involve the use of an intermediate licensing company in, for example, the Netherlands.

It is necessary also to ensure that the tax haven allows the tax-free, or low-tax accumulation of income, and taxes royalties at a low rate if at all. The country must be politically and economically stable and impose no exchange control restrictions on the movement of funds. It must have efficient banking, legal and accounting systems and have good communications. It will be necessary to show that the company is genuinely managed and controlled in the tax haven and is not a mere post box.

There may be tax charges on the existing holder of intellectual property transferring the property to the tax haven and there could be exchange control difficulties. It may be necessary to ensure that the transfer is at full market value. It will be necessary to ensure that the proposed route does not result in the royalties paid ceasing to be deductible by the licensee.

The intermediate licensing company requires a tax treaty which can be used (Switzerland, for example, by the decree of Federal Council in 1962, severely restricts the use of a Swiss company in such a manner). The treaty or national laws should also avoid the imposition of withholding taxes on royalties and dividends to be paid to the tax haven and should not require too high a proportion of royalties received to be retained in the intermediate company.

Switzerland Switzerland may be considered as a suitable venue for a domicilary company to hold intellectual property as it would be exempt from cantonal and municipal income taxes and the rate of federal income tax varies from 3.63 per cent to 9.8 per cent, depending on the ratio of net profits to shareholders' funds. There is also a net worth tax of 0.0825 per cent on shareholders' equity and small cantonal net worth taxes, which are all deductible for federal income tax purposes.

Switzerland has a fairly wide range of treaties but France, Germany and Italy do not reduce their withholding taxes for a Swiss domiciliary company. The 1962 decree of the Federal Council requires the Swiss company to distribute to shareholders as a dividend at least 25 per cent of passive income received, subject to treaty relief, which then becomes subject to a Swiss anticipatory tax of 35 per cent and provides that the Swiss company must not pay more than 50 per cent of such income to its parent company as interest or royalties. Interest-bearing loans may not exceed six times the Swiss company's capital and reserves.

As a result of these restrictions Switzerland is not usually a suitable place for an intermediate licensing company but may be a very useful centre for the receipt of know-how and show-how fees for services performed outside Switzerland. A Swiss branch of a Dutch company can sometimes be useful and a Swiss investment and service company, for example in Neutchatel, may be worth considering in certain cases. Switzerland is also a suitable place for a company holding portfolio investments in quoted companies.

Liechtenstein Holding and domiciliary companies and *anstalts* are exempt from corporate income tax and are subject to a capital tax of 0.1 per cent on capital and reserves subject to a minimum of SF 1,000 pa. There is no charge to tax on a capital gain on the disposal of intellectual property. There is a dividend and interest of withholding tax of 4 per cent which does not apply to *anstalts*. There are no exchange control problems. As there are no double tax treaties (except with Austria) Liechtenstein is of no use for intermediate licensing companies but could be used as an ultimate holder of intellectual property, preferably by an *anstalt*.

Luxembourg Such double tax treaties that Luxembourg has are of little use for royalty routing and the country would therefore be a contender for ultimate holder of intellectual property through a holding company, under the Holding Company Act 1929, which would be subject only to an annual subscription duty of 0.2 per cent of the capital (minimum LFr2,000) or a *société de participation financière* which qualifies for treaty relief and a participation privilege on dividend like a Dutch holding company. There are no exchange control difficulties.

Isle of Man and Channel Islands The absence of suitable double tax treaties means that companies situated here are best used as ultimate holders of intellectual property. The usual income tax rate of 20 per cent for resident companies is reduced to a £450 pa company registration tax in the Isle of Man and £500 pa corporation tax in the Channel Islands in respect of exempt companies, irrespective of the amount of profit. There have been no exchange control restrictions since 23 October 1979 but the Islands were previously effectively with the UK for exchange control purposes and would presumably return were such controls to be reintroduced.

Republic of Ireland Residents in the Republic of Ireland are exempt from Irish tax on patent royalties for patents devised therein under FA 1973, s 34 and Corporation Tax Act 1976, Sched 2, para 35. Individuals solely resident in the Republic are exempt from Irish tax under FA 1969, s 2 in respect of earnings from works of cultural or artistic merit such as books, plays, music, paintings and sculpture. International Financial Service Centres in Dublin are subject to tax at only 10 per cent until 2005 but cannot hold most forms of intellectual property except for certain computer software.

Other havens There are many other areas of the world which could be used in appropriate circumstances. In some cases Denmark may be used instead of the Netherlands for an intermediate licensing company. The UK was for a time used for this purpose with the licence holder in Cyprus but the double tax treaty has been modified to prevent Cyprus being used as a tax haven with the benefit of treaty relief with the UK.

Transfers of assets abroad

A further hurdle to be overcome for a UK taxpayer, other than a quoted public company, is the provisions of TA 1988, s 739: This section is a widely drawn anti-avoidance provision, supplemented by TA 1988, ss 741–746, to prevent ordinarily resident individuals avoiding income tax by transferring assets to non-residents. It applies where there has been a transfer of assets anywhere in the world at any time and as a result income is received, directly or indirectly, by a non-resident or non-domiciled individual, company or trust for the direct or indirect benefit now or in the future of an individual ordinarily resident in the UK. The transfer may or may not be in conjunction with associated operations as defined in TA 1988, s 742(1). A transfer of assets by a company not controlled by the taxpayers was not within this section in *IRC v Pratt* [1982] STC 756. The transfer may have been made before the individual became resident (TA 1988, s 739(1A), overturning *IRC v Willoughby* [1995] STC 143).

The Revenue are empowered to apportion income of the overseas person to the UK resident transferor (or spouse) if he is able to enjoy income as defined in TA 1988, s 742, and tax is assessed under Schedule D, Case VI.

The section does not apply directly to companies, but it is possible to trace a benefit through a company or a trust, although in practice the Revenue would not attempt to apportion income to the shareholders of quoted companies. It is also important to ensure that a beneficiary of the trust is not an additional settlor under the decision in *Mills v IRC* [1974] STC 130 and *Crossland v Hawkins* (1961) 39 TC 493, and that the trust is not liable to challenge as a sham. The section does not apply to the extent that income is apportioned under the 'controlled foreign companies provisions' (*see* TA 1988, ss 747–756).

The UK resident does not have to receive income; a capital sum, which includes a loan or repayment of a loan (other than one wholly repaid before the beginning of the year in which it would be charged) is also caught. A capital sum also includes an amount received by a third person (including jointly with another) by direction or assignment and which would otherwise not constitute a capital sum. There is an escape route under TA 1988, s 741 allowing *bona fide* commercial transactions not designed for the purpose of avoiding taxation or where the avoiding of taxation was not one of the purposes of the transaction.

Cases under this section include *Aykroyd v IRC* (1942) 24 TC 515, *Beatty v IRC* (1940) 23 TC 574, *Beatty's (Admiral Lord) Executors v IRC* (1940) 23 TC 574, *Cottingham's Executors v IRC* (1938) 22 TC 344, *Lee v IRC* (1941) 24 TC 207, *Latilla v IRC* (1943) 25 TC 107, *Howard de Walden (Lord) v IRC* (1941) 25 TC 121, *Ramsden v IRC* 37 TC 619, *Corbett's Executrices v IRC* (1943) 25 TC 305, *Sassoon v IRC* (1943) 25 TC 154, *Philippi v IRC* (1971) 47 TC 75 and *Lord Chetwode v IRC* [1977] STC 64.

Leading cases relating to the wide ambit of this section are:—*Vestey's Exors v IRC, Same v Colquhoun* (1949) 31 TC 1 and *Fynn v IRC* (1957) 37 TC 629; *Vestey v IRC (Nos 1 and 2)* [1980] STC 10 which overruled *Bambridge v IRC* (1955) 36 TC 313 and *Congreve v IRC* (1948) 30 TC 163. *IRC v Schroder* [1983] STC 480 confirmed that the ability to appoint trustees may not mean control over the income.

In *Rahman v Chase Bank (CI) Ltd* (Royal Court of Jersey, 12 February 1990) a widow brought a case attacking her deceased husband's trust on a number of grounds. One of these was that the powers retained by the settlor were so substantial that they breached the Jersey maxim of '*Donner et Retenir ne Vaut*', freely translated being 'to give and to retain is worth nothing'. Interestingly, although the judge held that the trust was in fact in breach of this particular maxim, he also held that the trust was a sham in that:

1.   The trustee did not seek remittance of the entire initial trust fund.

2.   Under the trust deed, responsibility for investment policy lay with the trustees. However, the trustee never exercised that responsibility; rather the trustee left such matters wholly to the settlor who dealt exclusively with a named investment adviser.

3. The settlor unilaterally changed the investment adviser and negotiated the investment adviser's fees on behalf of the trustee.

4. On several occasions funds which had been assigned by the settlor to the trust were diverted by the settlor and used for his own purposes.

5. All payments out of the trust were made upon the settlor's instructions.

6. The trustee acted upon the instructions of the settlor without considering its fiduciary responsibilities.

7. The settlor retained the power to sign on trust accounts opened by the trustees with Geneva banks.

This is obviously an extreme case but it does serve to emphasise that the position of trustees is an onerous one and has to be taken seriously. Settlors are sometimes very domineering individuals and like to have their own way, but the trustee who allows that situation to develop is likely to face an expensive claim at the end of the day. The *Rahman* case merely emphasises the earlier decision of *Bartlett v Barclays Bank Trust Co Ltd* [1980] 1 All ER 139 in which Barclays were held responsible for a loss made by an underlying company owned by the trust, and the court held that they should have exercised their powers to control the situation and prevent losses being made by the underlying company. Trustees have to take a positive control over the trust for which they are responsible and a policy of merely honest inactivity is not good enough.

Liability of non-transferors

The provisions of TA 1988, ss 740 and 744 are a consequence of the House of Lords' decision in *Vestey v IRC (Nos 1 and 2)* [1980] STC 10. Under that decision it was confirmed that the existing rules under TA 1988, s 739 charged to tax those who took part in transfers of assets abroad together with their spouses but did not apply to others who received benefits as a result of those transactions. This section applies in respect of benefits received and relevant income arising after 9 March 1981, but irrespective of when the transfer or any associated operations took place.

This section complements TA 1988, s 739 to catch the recipients leaving that section to catch the other parties to such arrangements and has effect where, as a result of a transfer of assets either alone or in conjunction with associated operations, income becomes payable to a person who is not resident or domiciled in the UK and an individual who is ordinarily resident in the UK and who is not caught by TA 1988, s 739 itself (ie is not the transferor or his spouse) receives a benefit (not otherwise taxable) from those assets which are available for the purpose. The benefit which falls within the 'relevant income' of the tax years up to and including that in which the benefit is received is treated as the income of the individual for the year of the receipt, or, to the extent to which the benefit has exceeded that relevant income, it will be treated as the recipient's income to the extent that it is within the amount of relevant income for the next following tax year, and so on. This provision prevents a benefit being arranged in anticipation of future income arising as a consequence of the transfer of assets abroad, and a further consequence is that payments cannot be made out of accumulated income of a trust whilst relevant income arises to the trust.

'Relevant income' is defined as any income arising in the year to someone who is resident or domiciled outside the UK and which is in consequence of the transfer or the associated operations (as defined in TA 1988, s 742) and which can be directly or indirectly used for providing a benefit to an individual or for enabling a benefit to be provided to him.

Income taxable under these provisions will be charged under Schedule D, Case VI and thereby will be treated as unearned income.

These provisions do not apply to a non-UK domiciled individual, whether resident in this country or not, in respect of benefits received which are not brought into the UK. In the case of a non-UK domiciled individual who is ordinarily resident in this country the application of any benefit arising to him in the form of income from possessions outside the UK towards paying off a debt for money lent in or effectively received in the UK will be subject to tax under Schedule D, Case V on the deemed remittance (TA 1988, s 65) and will not be exempt from income tax under the foregoing provisions.

Under this section if the transfer of assets or associated operations are shown to have been for purposes other than tax avoidance or were *bona fide* commercial transactions not designed to avoid tax these provisions will not apply.

If any benefit has already been charged as a capital payment under FA 1981, ss 80, 81, the amount so charged is treated as his income under this section for a tax year before the year of charge under TA 1988, s 740.

Exemption from the application of TA 1988, ss 739 and 740 is available if the individual can demonstrate to the Board (in writing or otherwise) that the transfer of assets and associated operations were for purposes other than tax avoidance, or were *bona fide* commercial transactions not designed to avoid tax. Commercial motives were established in *Clark v IRC* [1978] STC 614 and *IRC v Kleinwort, Benson Ltd* (1969) 45 TC 369 (TA 1988, s 741).

'Associated operation' for the purposes of TA 1988, ss 739–741 and 'power to enjoy income' (for the purposes of TA 1988, s 739 only) are defined by TA 1988, s 742, as are 'assets' and 'benefit'. References to an individual includes a spouse. The provisions of the sections are extended to the amount that would have been caught in the hands of a non-resident or non-domiciled person by the accrued income provisions of TA 1988, s 714 as though it were 'income payable' to such person.

Bodies incorporated outside the UK, or resident outside the UK under a double taxation agreement, are treated as non-resident even if resident (TA 1988, s 742).

If income assessed under TA 1988, s 739 has already borne UK tax at the basic rate, for example as an annual payment made to a non-resident, the charge will be limited to the higher rates. Tax is charged under the provisions of Schedule D, Case VI and the recipient will qualify for the same reliefs as would have been available if the income had actually been received by him. If the income is subsequently received it is ignored for income tax purposes so there is no double charge to UK tax (TA 1988, s 743).

The recipient of a benefit giving rise to a charge under TA 1988, s 739, is taxed in the year in which the benefit is received.

A non-UK domiciled individual is not chargeable to tax under TA 1988, s 739. In a case where if the income had in fact been his income he would have been taxed on it by virtue of its being non-domiciled and therefore taxable only if the income was remitted to the UK.

No amount of income is to be taken into account more than once in charging tax under the provisions of TA 1988, ss 739, 740. The Board may choose who is chargeable where the choice exists and apportion income in a just and reasonable way. Such a decision may be reviewable by the Special Commissioners on an appeal against an assessment (TA 1988, s 744).

Power to obtain information

The Board has power under TA 1988, s 745 to serve a notice in writing on any person to furnish them with such particulars as they think necessary for the purposes of deciding whether there is a charge under TA 1988, ss 739 and 740 whether or not in the opinion of the person receiving the notice any liability arises. A solicitor is compelled to give only the name and address of his client and of the transferees, transferors, non-trading companies incorporated or resident outside the UK, or resident outside the UK under a double taxation agreement, which would be close companies if in the UK, or settlors in the transactions covered by the notice.

Banks do not have to furnish particulars of ordinary banking transactions unless acting for the same customer in the formation of non-resident companies (with a similar exclusion for trading and non-close companies) or trusts etc.

Nevertheless the provisions of this section are extremely wide and attempts to resist such notices were defeated in *Royal Bank of Canada v IRC* (1971) 47 TC 565, *Clinch v IRC* (1973) 49 TC 52 and *Mankowitz v Special Commissioners* (1971) 46 TC 707 (TA 1988, s 745).

These provisions are, at the time of writing, under review.

Gains of non-resident settlements

Gains of non-resident trustees are allocated to beneficiaries in accordance with TCGA 1992, s 87.

It is first necessary to calculate the capital gains made by the trustee as if they were resident in the UK. The gains are calculated on a cumulative basis from 6 April 1981 and the total, less any amount already treated as a gain of the beneficiaries either under this section or TCGA 1992, s 89 (migrant settlements), is regarded as the trust gain for the year and is apportioned to beneficiaries in proportion to any capital sums they have received from the trust since 10 March 1981, except to the extent that it has been taken into account in allocating previous capital gains among beneficiaries. Gains chargeable on the settlor under TCGA 1992, s 86 and Sched 5 are excluded.

The gain apportioned to a beneficiary cannot exceed the capital distribution to him and a gain apportioned to a non-UK domiciled beneficiary is not taxed.

In order for the section to apply a settlor must have been domiciled and either resident or ordinarily resident in the UK in the year of the gain or when the settlement was made. A trust arising on death is deemed to be made at the date of death.

See *Re Weston's Settlement* (1968) 47 ATC 324 on the emigration of a trust.

As to increased tax where gains are received more than one year after the tax year in which they arose see TCGA 1992, s 91.

The trustees of a dual resident settlement who are treated as resident both in the UK and in some other territory giving rise to relief under a double tax treaty in a year in which the settlor is domiciled and resident or ordinarily resident in the UK are within the gains of non-residential settlement provisions of TCGA 1992, s 87 as if the settlement were non-resident by virtue of TCGA 1992, s 88.

If a UK resident settlement becomes non-resident or dual resident for a year or more any capital payments to beneficiaries in the resident period are disregarded unless made in anticipation of a disposal by the trustees in the non-resident or treaty-protected period under TCGA 1992, s 89.

If a trust is thereafter repatriated to the UK any trust gains in the non-resident or treaty-protected period which have not been apportioned to beneficiaries will be chargeable to them in proportion to capital payments subsequently received by them subject to the limitation of the gain not exceeding the amount of the capital payment and there being no charge on a non-domiciled beneficiary.

There is an anti-avoidance provision to prevent the non-resident trust provisions in TCGA 1992, ss 87 and 89 being circumvented by transferring assets between trusts. The provisions do not apply so far as the transfer is made for consideration in money or money's worth under TCGA 1992, s 90.

Supplementary charge

The provisions of TCGA 1992, s 91 include a supplementary charge for beneficiaries of non-resident settlements who receive capital payments made on or after 6 April 1991 from the trustees or who are beneficiaries of dual resident trusts, unless the settlor is non-domiciled or the beneficiary is non-resident or non-domiciled.

Where a capital payment is matched with a chargeable gain which arose before the immediately preceding year of assessment, the tax payable is increased at the rate of 10 per cent a year as if it were interest. Notional interest is therefore calculated on the period from 1 December in the tax year following that in which the gain arises to 30 November in the tax year following that in which the capital payment is made, subject to a maximum of six years. The minimum period is two years, so the minimum charge is 20 per cent. As gains arising in 1990–91 or earlier are all allocated to 1990–91 the notional interest charge arises if such gains were not distributed to beneficiaries by 5 April 1992.

The tax and notional interest cannot exceed the amount of the capital payment and the rate of interest may be varied by Treasury order. At an effective 40 per cent rate of capital gains tax the effective maximum charge is 64 per cent.

Payments by and to companies

Capital payments received from a qualifying company controlled by the trustees are taxed as if received from the trustees as are payments received by non-resident qualifying companies. A receipt by a non-resident company controlled by a UK resident is treated as capital payment received by him. If the company is controlled by two or more persons, taking each one separately, the capital payment is apportioned equally to as many UK residents as control the company under TCGA 1992, s 96.

If the company is controlled by two or more persons together the capital payment is apportioned among the participators on a just and reasonable basis, but a participator receiving less than ¹⁄₂₀ of the payment actually received by the company is ignored. A qualifying company is a close company or would be if it were resident in the UK, and is controlled by the trustees if it is controlled by them under TA 1988, s 416 (close company control by reference to capital, income or assets). For this purpose it is possible to include with the trustees the settlor or a person connected with him. These provisions apply to capital payments received on or after 19 March 1991.

Capital payment is defined as any payment made otherwise than as income and includes a transfer to bare trustees and indirect payments. Although a loan is a capital payment it is regarded as such only to the extent that benefit is conferred thereby. A loan on normal commercial terms would not give rise to a capital gains tax charge as arm's length transactions are specifically excluded from the definition of capital payments.

Capital payments received from trustees include those received indirectly under TCGA 1992, s 96 unless they are already treated as being received by a beneficiary, ie the recipient becomes a deemed beneficiary but not so as to treat the trustees themselves as beneficiaries on appointments or advances. The very wide information gathering provisions of TA 1988, s 745 are extended to non-resident and repatriated trusts by virtue of TCGA 1992, s 98.

Gains accruing to a non-resident company may be apportioned under TCGA 1992, s 13 to non-resident shareholders, who are thereby treated as having a proportion of the gain accruing to them under TCGA 1992, s 13(10).

A disposal of an interest in settled property is not exempt under TCGA 1992, s 76 if the trustees are non-resident unless the disponor thereby becomes absolutely entitled as against the trustees, in which case there would already be a capital gains tax charge by the combination of TCGA 1992, ss 71(1) and 87.

Trustees ceasing to be resident in UK

If trustees become neither resident nor ordinarily resident in the UK on or after 19 March 1991, and as a result cease to be within the capital gains tax charge, they are deemed to have disposed of the trust assets and immediately reacquired them at their market value at that time (TCGA 1992, s 80).

This exit charge excludes assets used in a trade carried on in the UK through a branch or agency, which are already subject to capital gains tax under TCGA 1992, s 10. It similarly excludes assets specified in a double taxation agreement which would not have been liable to UK capital gains tax if the assets had been sold before the trustees ceased to be resident in the UK. Roll-over relief under TCGA 1992, s 152 is not available on the deemed disposal and reacquisition, unless the new assets are UK assets used for a trade carried on in the UK through a branch or agency.

Where the emigration of the trust is caused by the death of a trustee and within six months of the trustees again becoming resident and ordinarily resident in the UK, the exit charge on the emigration of the trust is restricted to any assets which are either disposed of during the period of non-residence, or are protected by a double taxation agreement after the repatriation of the trust (TCGA 1992, s 81).

Conversely, where the trustees become resident and ordinarily resident in the UK, as a result of a trustee's death, any exit charge on re-exportation of the trust is restricted to assets acquired during the period of UK residence under the hold-over provisions relating to gifts of business assets (TCGA 1992, s 165) or gifts subject to inheritance tax (TCGA 1992, s 260).

Where the exit charge arises on the emigration of the trust and the capital gains tax is not paid within six months of the due date, the Board may, within a period of three years beginning when the tax is finally determined, serve on the past trustees a notice (TCGA 1992, s 82).

If the trustees remain resident in the UK but become eligible to exemption from capital gains tax under a double tax treaty because, for example, they are also resident abroad (dual resident), there is a deemed disposal and reacquisition of the treaty-protected trust assets at market value on becoming eligible for the treaty protection if this is on or after 19 March 1991 (TCGA 1992, s 83).

Roll-over relief under TCGA 1992, s 152 is not available where on or after 19 March 1991 the new assets are acquired by dual resident trustees entitled to treaty protection in respect of those assets (TCGA 1992, s 84).

A person is chargeable to capital gains tax on the disposal of an interest in a non-resident trust under TCGA 1992, s 138. Where this has previously been the subject of an exit charge on emigration, during his period as a beneficiary he is deemed to have disposed of and immediately reacquired his interest in the trust at the time of the emigration to avoid what would otherwise be a double charge. The effect of TCGA 1992, s 85 is that the gain in the trust up to the point of emigration is subject to the exit charge and from that date on the gain on the disposal of interest in the settlement is charged on the beneficiary disposing of it under TCGA 1992, s 138.

Alternatively, if before the trustees became non-resident they become dual resident and subject to treaty protection within TCGA 1992, s 83, the beneficiary shall be treated as having disposed of and immediately reacquired his interest in the settlement at the time the trustees became eligible for treaty protection. Thus the gain up to that date would be caught under s 83, and the subsequent gain caught on the beneficiary on the disposal of the interest in the settled property under TCGA 1992, s 138.

Where TCGA 1992, s 87 applies, which charges gains of non-resident settlements on beneficiaries, the gain is reduced by the amount already charged on the settlor under TCGA 1992, s 86 and Sched 5.

The right to recovery by the settlor who has an interest in a UK resident trust in TCGA 1992, s 78, if he pays the tax, is amended to ensure that the gains so charged and recovered are deemed to be the highest part but one of his gains, the highest part being those gains attributed to him from a non-resident trust under TCGA 1992, Sched 5.

Capital gains tax charge on settlor

TCGA 1992, Sched 5 applies to charge certain settlors to tax on gains of a non-resident trust as if the gains were made by the settlor. It applies where the settlement is a qualifying settlement and the trustees are not resident or ordinarily resident in the UK during any part of the year or, while resident, are regarded as resident other than in the UK under a double tax treaty.

The settlor must be domiciled in the UK at some time in the year, and resident in the UK for any part of the year or ordinarily resident during the year. The settlor must have an interest in the settlement.

If the disposal of property originating from the settlor would have given rise to a chargeable gain and the trust been resident, there would be a charge to tax provided that the exceptions to the charge do not apply.

The gains of a UK resident trust may be attributed to a settlor under TCGA 1992, s 77 if he or his spouse are beneficiaries.

The gain that would have accrued to the trust had it been resident or the treaty inapplicable is treated as the settlor's gain and is subject to the maximum amount of capital gains tax as if it had been his own highest gain.

The settlor has an interest in a settlement if property comprised in the settlement could be applied to the benefit of a defined person under any circumstances, or income could be paid to such a beneficiary or he could benefit directly or indirectly from the property comprised in the settlement. Relevant property or income is that originating from the settlor.

A defined person is the settlor, his spouse, any child of the settlor or his spouse (but not grandchildren) and any spouse of the child, or any company controlled by such persons or associated with such a company. Control for this purpose is defined by TA 1988, s 416 (the close company definition), and a child includes a stepchild.

A settlor does not have an interest in a settlement if that interest arises only on the bankruptcy of the beneficiary or his making an assignment or charge of the property, or the death of the parties to a marriage including the children under a marriage settlement or the death of a beneficiary under the age of 25 who would become entitled to the property on attaining that age. Former spouses may be ignored for these provisions.

Where the settlor is charged to capital gains tax under these provisions he has a right to recover the tax from the trustees and for this purpose may require the inspector to give him a certificate specifying the amount of the gains concerned and the amount of tax paid. It is questionable whether a UK Finance Act can give a settlor a right to recover money from overseas trustees in respect of a settlement of which he is not a beneficiary, and it could well be that such a payment could be in breach of trust.

Property originates from a settlor if it is provided by him or can be traced back to such property. Income originating from a person includes income from property originating from the person or income provided by him. Reciprocal arrangements are included.

A settlement created on or after 19 March 1991 is a qualifying settlement for the year in which it is created and subsequent years.

A pre-19 March 1991 settlement becomes a qualifying settlement only if any one of four conditions become satisfied in which case it is a qualifying settlement for the year in which any of those conditions becomes satisfied and subsequent years of assessment.

Condition 1. Property is provided directly or indirectly for the purposes of the settlement otherwise than under a transaction entered into at arm's length, or in pursuance of a liability incurred before 19 March 1991. However, the provision of property is ignored if it is only to meet the expenses of the settlement which are not covered by its income.

Condition 2. The trustees become neither resident nor ordinarily resident in the UK or are deemed so to become under the provisions of a double taxation treaty.

Condition 3. The terms of the settlement have been varied on or after 19 March 1991 to include an additional beneficiary, ie one who is neither already a named beneficiary nor within an existing discretionary class.

Condition 4. The settlor or his spouse, or any child of the settlor or his spouse, or the spouse of any child or a company controlled by such persons or associated with it, enjoys a benefit from the settlement for the first time; and it is not one who would be capable of enjoying a benefit, looking only at the terms of the settlement before 19 March 1991.

Controlled and associated companies are defined as for close company purposes under TA 1988, ss 416, 417 (by reference to capital, income or assets) but ignoring the rights of a non-participator's associates. 'Child' includes a stepchild.

An inspector may serve a notice requiring information from any person who either is or has been a trustee, beneficiary or settlor, requring him to provide information in connection with the settlement provided that at least 28 days' notice is given.

Limbo trusts

It would seem that many of the anti-avoidance provisions can sometimes be overcome by carrying out overseas activities through what is usually known as a 'limbo trust'.

A limbo trust is one where there is a non-resident, non-domiciled settlor of funds on non-resident trustees for non-resident beneficiaries with an exclusion of anybody ordinarily resident in the UK from being a beneficiary. There is, however, power to appoint additional beneficiaries at the trustees' discretion, with the ultimate intention that a current UK resident would become at some stage not ordinarily resident and become appointed a beneficiary of the trust. This could be the original creator of the intellectual property or a member of his family or other nominated individual as required. There would normally be a non-resident, non-domiciled protector of the trust to ensure that the trustees carried out the required activities.

The trustees would normally incorporate a company in a suitable tax haven, for example, Jersey or Bermuda (although the Netherlands Antilles would often be preferred in the case of intellectual property.) Profits would be accumulated free of tax until such time as it became appropriate to appoint a beneficiary. The anti-avoidance provisions are widely drafted and a limbo trust has to be operated carefully to ensure that, for example, no benefit is passed to a beneficiary while still ordinarily resident in the UK.

General anti-avoidance provisions

A number of countries have general anti-avoidance sections in their tax legislation which are intended to prevent legal avoidance of taxation. It has been announced that the UK is shortly to introduce such a provision, but no further details are available at the time of writing.

23 Stamp duty

Introduction

Stamp duty is chargeable in respect of specific heads of charge on instruments. It is a tax on documents: oral undocumented transactions are therefore not subject to stamp duty. 'Instrument' is an undefined term but includes every written document (Stamp Act 1891, s 122(1)). Stamp duty is payable either on an *ad valorem* basis or at a fixed rate, depending upon the heading of charge. Although *ad valorem* duty includes bearer instruments, clearance services, depository receipts, leases and exchange of partition in respect of freehold land, the most common heading is that of conveyance or transfer of sale for which the rate is 50 pence for every £100 or part thereof in respect of stock and marketable securities and up to £2 for every £100 or part thereof otherwise. Fixed duties are basically a sweep-up for anything which is not subject to an *ad valorem* duty but which is liable to stamp duty. The most common is the miscellaneous conveyance or transfer duty of 50 pence.

Even if falling within one of the heads of charge, a substantial list of exempt duties removes transactions from the scope of stamp duty. The most common are the exemptions in respect of transactions between associated companies under FA 1930, s 27 as amended by FA 1995, s 149, and on gift under FA 1985, s 82. Certain documents are also not chargeable because they do not amount to a conveyance or transfer. In particular, an agreement for sale is not chargeable to *ad valorem* duty provided that it does not relate to an equitable interest in property or an interest in property comprising goods, stock or marketable security or property in the UK, except land. For example, a written agreement for the sale of stock and fixed assets of a business is outwith the scope of SA 1891, s 59. Provided that completion occurs by physical delivery, there will be no stampable instrument.

The main basis for stamp duty is the conveyance or sale, chargeable at the appropriate rate. It should be noted that the duty is expressed to be £*x* per £100 or part thereof, rather than a straight percentage. Furthermore F(No 2)A 1997, s 49, amending FA 1963, s 55, has increased the rate of stamp duty in respect of property other than marketable securities to £1.50 for each £100 in excess of £250,000 and £2 per £100 in respect of consideration in excess of £500,000.

Consideration

If the consideration is in sterling, matters are relatively straightforward. Foreign currency should be converted at the rate of exchange applying at the date of instrument of transfer.

Consideration in kind is valued at market value. Where stock and marketable securities are involved the market value is defined by SA 1891, s 55(1) as the average price of the stock or security on the day. Listed securities specifically are valued at the capital gains tax value (usually quarter-up).

There is a special relief in respect of periodical payments. If the payments are for a definite period of less than 20 years than the consideration is the total of the payments. If the consideration is for a definite period greater than 20 years or is for an indefinite period (excluding reference to life) the value is the total payable during the first 20 years of the instrument. Any payment in respect of a life or lives is the total value of the payments due in the first 12 years of the instrument.

If the consideration is unascertainable at the date of the instrument then *ad valorem* duty is not chargeable unless there is an upper or lower payment quoted in the agreement, in which case the higher of the two figures is taken as the value.

Special rules apply to land where, if there is unascertainable consideration, the consideration is taken to be the market value of the property immediately before the instrument is executed (FA 1994, s 242).

Intellectual property

An exclusive non-recoverable licence or assignment for consideration is subject to *ad valorem* duty as a conveyance or sale under SA 1891, ss 59 and 62 but a revocable assignment or non-exclusive licence is not subject to duty.

Agreement for the sale of goodwill was property stampable under SA 1891, s 59 (*Eastern National Omnibus Co v IRC* [1939] 1 KB 161).

The definition of property for stamp duty purposes include patents, copyrights and trade marks (*Leather Cloth Co v American Leather Cloth Co* (1865) 11 HL Cas 523), but not know-how (*Handley Page v Butterworth* (1935) 19 TC 328).

A non-exclusive licence is not a conveyance on transfer (*Taylor v Caldwell* (1863) 3 B&S 826; *Jones v IRC* [1895] 1 QB 484; *Winter Garden Theatre (London) Ltd v Millennium Productions Ltd* [1948] AC 173; *Street v Mountford* [1985] AC 809).

Where both stamp duty and VAT are chargeable, stamp duty is charged on the VAT inclusive price (*Glenrothes DC v IRC* [1994] STC 74, SP 11/91).

Stamp duty, if payable, is levied on any lump sum together with the amount of future royalties, if ascertainable, payable within 20 years of the assignment or licence under SA 1891, s 56 (*Underground Electric Railways Co of London Ltd v IRC* [1906] AC 21; *Glyn Mills Currie & Co v IRC* [1916] 1 KB 306 and *LM Tenancies 1 plc v IRC* [1996] STC 880) charged at 1½ or 2 per cent where the consideration is in excess of £60,000. Where only the minimum payment is shown on the document it is that amount which is subject to duty (*Underground Electric Railways Co of London Ltd v IRC* [1906] AC 21; *Coventry City Council v IRC* [1978] STC 151). If a basic consideration is obtainable from the document that amount is subject to duty (*ITA and Associated Rediffusion v IRC* [1961] AC 427). Where the quantum of royalties is wholly unascertainable it is arguable that no stamp duty is payable as there is no consideration which can be ascertained from the document.

Exempt instruments

Stamp duty is not payable on transfers which fall within the Stamp Duty (Exempt Instruments) Regulations 1987 (SI 1987 No 516) and are as follows:

A. The vesting of property subject to a trust in the trustees of the trust on the appointment of a new trustee, or in the continuing trustees on the retirement of a trustee.

B. The conveyance or transfer of property the subject of a specific device or legacy to the beneficiary named in the will (or his nominee).

C. The conveyance or transfer of property which forms part of an intestate's estate to the person entitled on intestacy (or his nominee).

D. The appropriation of property within section 84(4) of the Finance Act 1895 (death: appropriation in satisfaction of a general legacy of money) or section 84(5) or (7) of that Act (death: appropriation in satisfaction of any interest of surviving spouse and in Scotland also of an interest of issue).

E. The conveyance or transfer of property which forms part of the residuary estate of a testator to a beneficiary (or his nominee) entitled solely by virtue of his entitlement under the will.

F. The conveyance or transfer of property out of a settlement in or towards satisfaction of a beneficiary's interest, not being an interest acquired for money or money's worth, being a conveyance or transfer constituting a distribution of property, in accordance with the provisions of the settlement.

G. The conveyance or transfer of property on and in consideration only of marriage to a party to the marriage (or his nominee) or to trustees to be held on the terms of a settlement made in consideration only of the marriage.

H. The conveyance or transfer of property within section 83(1) of the Finance Act 1895 (transfers in connection with divorce etc).

I. The conveyance or transfer by the liquidator of property which formed part of the assets of the company in liquidation to a shareholder of that company (or his nominee) in or towards satisfaction of the shareholder's rights on a winding-up.

J. The grant in fee simple of an easement in or over land for no consideration in money or money's worth.

K. The grant of a servitude for no consideration in money or money's worth.

L. The conveyance or transfer of property operating as a voluntary disposition *inter vivos* for no consideration in money or money's worth nor any consideration referred to in section 57 of the Stamp Act 1891 (conveyance in consideration of a debt etc).

M. The conveyance or transfer of property by an instrument within section 84(1) of the Finance Act 1895 (death: varying disposition).

24 Package deals

Introduction

The most important point to bear in mind when entering into a licensing agreement is to achieve the desired commercial result, which in turn means taking into account the taxation situations of both the licensor and licensee to ensure that each is treated in the most favourable way possible. It may well be that the taxation aspirations of both parties are incompatible, in which case a compromise is usually possible.

Manufacturing agreements

In practice, if a business enters into an agreement with another business for the licensed production of a complex piece of equipment it would often be necessary to provide not only the basic permission to enter into production, but also to supply drawings and technical expertise. It may be necessary to provide moulds, tools or jigs, to supervise the installation and commissioning of machinery and to train the licensee's staff to use it. There may also be permission to use a trade mark or registered design.

It will be appreciated that such a situation would involve patent licences, agreements for the provision of copyright drawings, know-how and show-how agreements and licensed use of trade marks and registered designs, as well as the provision of tangible supplies (which is outside the scope of this book).

In respect of deals between unconnected parties, a lot of hard commercial bargaining would be necessary to arrive at the amounts payable, but there is probably a degree of flexibility in the manner in which the total payment would be apportioned amongst the various headings.

In deciding the allocation of the various payments it is necessary to consider both the commercial and the taxation positions of both the licensor and the licensee to arrive at the optimum solution. As to some extent the optimum solutions for the licensor and licensee are contradictory, some degree of compromise is essential.

Licensor's position

As far as the licensor is concerned, if he is resident in the UK, he would like commercially to receive as much as possible in advance, or 'up front', as it is normally phrased, and would not want the income to be reduced by tax deductions withheld by the licensee. On the other hand, the licensor is unlikely to wish to sell outright any of the intellectual property and it is therefore unlikely that any of the proceeds would be treated as a capital receipt.

The licensor would therefore usually like to receive a lump sum payment for know-how, with a royalty for the use of a trade mark, design right and industrial copyright and drawings. These amounts would all be taxable when receivable and not subject to deduction of tax at source. The licensor would clearly like to reduce the license payment in respect of the patent to the minimum and would no doubt accept a modest royalty spread over the life of the licensed production under this head.

So long as there is no exclusive licence there is no stamp duty problem but if, exceptionally, the licence is to be exclusive it would reduce the stamp duty to have the maximum amount under the heading of know-how and show-how with the minimum related to the intellectual property aspects. As far as VAT is concerned, the royalties and fees are likely to be subject to tax at the standard rate.

The licensor would also like to apply a fairly high proportion of the royalties payable to trade marks, as these do not have a limited life, and then to patents, which have a limited life of 20 years under PA 1977 or 16 years for some earlier patents, rather than design right which has a limited life of ten or 15 years from the date of first manufacture of the designed article. Although industrial copyright still exists, preventing copying of the drawing as a drawing, there is no longer protection under copyright in the manufacture of the designed article. In the USA, in particular, there is some doubt as to whether the anti-trust laws would permit the artificial extension of the life of a patent by subsequent licensing of trade mark and industrial copyright, but this sort of arrangement is more likely to be effective if the agreement *ab initio* extends for a period beyond the life of the patent and if a large proportion of the fees are related to other forms of intellectual property.

It must always be borne in mind that the Revenue may challenge the allocation of payments under licensing agreements, as for example in *Paterson Engineering Co Ltd v Duff* (1943) 25 TC 43. It is unlikely to make such a challenge, however, if the agreements entered into between arm's length parties specifically allocate the headings under which payments are made, provided that they are not obviously totally artificial.

It is worth noting the comments in the *Paterson Engineering* case of MacNaghten J at p 50:

> In these circumstances, it is plain that as far as the first agreement is concerned, the case must go back to the General Commissioners to determine whether any part of that so-called 'royalty' is paid in respect of something other than 'the user of a patent'. That is a question of fact for them to determine. If they are satisfied that the whole of the 'royalty' payable under the first agreement was paid in respect of the user of a patent, then so far as that agreement is concerned, the assessment for the year 1939–40 will stand. If, on the other hand, they think that part of the £2,000 was a sum paid in respect of something other than the user of a patent, then they will allow that sum as a deduction from the assessment.
>
> Mr Donovan, for the Appellants, urged very strongly that, although he was entitled to have the case sent back to the Commissioners for them to ascertain what part, if any, of the royalty payable under the first agreement was paid in respect of something other than the user of a patent, the Court was bound by the provisions which the parties had inserted in their second agreement of 1st January, 1938, to hold that £100 and no more was paid under that agreement in respect of the user of a patent. I cannot accept that view.
>
> Mr Donovan was good enough to tabulate under ten heads the various benefits which, in his view, the Appellants obtained under these agreements with the American company, the first of

which is: The exclusive right to manufacture and sell in allotted territory the patented equipment, systems and processes for water treatment, ie, the right to use patents in respect of which the American company gives the licence to the Appellants to make use of. That undoubtedly is a payment in respect of the user of a patent. There is no dispute about that. Amongst the ten benefits tabulated by Mr Donovan is the right to use in the allotted territory all existing or future trade marks, trade names or designs. The exercise of that right, on the face of it, has nothing to do with the user of a patent, yet it may be that the use of a trade name is so closely connected with the use of a particular patent that a Court charged with the duty of ascertaining the facts might come to the conclusion that the sum paid for the right to use the trade name was merely incidental to the right to use the patent. It all depends upon the facts. I was asked to give some assistance to the General Commissioners as to how they should proceed to determine this question. On consideration, I do not think it is possible to give them any further assistance than this: If it is established before them that a part of the payments made by the Appellants is in fact paid in respect of something other than the user of a patent, then they should allow such part to be deducted from the assessment. The words 'a sum paid in respect of the user of a patent' are rather vague; but, as it seems to me, if construed in a narrow sense they would cover not only the right to use the patent but also such rights as might only be considered as incidental thereto, such as the right to have any improvement of the patent made by the grantors during the currency of the agreement and the right to advice or assistance as to how best to avail themselves of the patent.

Now that it is decided (so far as this Court is concerned) that these payments are not payments that come within Rule 3(*l*), it may be that the Inspector of Taxes and the Appellants will be able to arrive at a decision satisfactory to both; but unless they are able to, then it will be for the General Commissioners to do their best to determine this question of fact.

A licensor could well wish to assign part of his patent for a lump sum which would be spread over the following six years for tax purposes, which would mean that he has the use of the money for a considerable period before the tax on it becomes payable. However, this is difficult to achieve in most cases in practice as the licensee is likely to resist strongly the payment of a capital sum on the assignment of a patent on which he would only be able to claim capital allowances at 25 per cent per annum on the reducing balance.

Licensee's position

As far as the licensee is concerned, he would like from a commercial point of view to have royalties paid over the period of production without a large payment 'up front'. He would also like royalties paid in respect of patent licences on which he has to account for tax as annual payments to be paid at the beginning of his quarterly accounting periods for accounting to the Revenue for the tax deduction, as this only has to be paid over within 14 days of the end of each quarter and therefore the tax withheld could be used to improve his cash flow in the meantime. On the other hand, the licensee will get tax relief only in respect of royalties actually paid during the accounting period and may wish to pre-pay royalties due immediately after the end of his accounting period in order to bring the tax relief forward one year by means of a payment before the year end.

The licensee would not normally mind technical assistance fees, which would be paid gross and provided for in the accounts on an accruals basis.

The licensee would, however, like to have payments for technical assistance spread over a period of the contract so that he can claim these as a revenue expense, following *British Sugar Manufacturers Ltd v Harris* (1937) 21 TC 528.

Know-how charges paid as a lump sum would be an allowable expense of the licensee allowed at 25 per cent per annum on the reducing balance, and therefore not particularly attractive. The licensee would rather pay such fees as a royalty related to production even if he has to pay a non-returnable but recoupable advance of royalties, which would be a revenue expense rather than a lump sum of like amount dealt with under TA 1988, s 531. As far as the licensee is concerned, the worst of all possible worlds is a capital payment on the assignment of patents subject only to capital allowances at 25 per cent per annum.

A non-resident licensee would not normally wish to pay VAT and therefore any amount of the licence production consideration allocated to the provision of show-how or technical assistance in the UK, which would be liable to VAT, should be kept down to an absolute minimum. For stamp duty purposes the licensee would normally wish to avoid an exclusive licence other than of know-how.

Common control

If the licensor and the licensee are under common control it may still be necessary to arrive at the market value of the goods and services provided, as the licensee would be able to claim deductions only if the payments were no more than the market value (following the case of *Petrotim Securities Ltd v Ayres* (1963) 41 TC 389). If the licensor and licensee were in different countries it would be necessary to consider the transfer pricing provisions contained in most double taxation treaties and in the domestic legislation of many countries. In the UK the legislation is contained in TA 1988, s 770.

Publishing deals

If a book is produced there may be a number of agreements dealing with various rights for the publication of hardback editions, book club editions, paperback editions, film and dramatisation rights, etc, and it is necessary to consider from both the licensor's and the licensee's point of view how these may be structured. These matters are dealt with in rather more detail in Case Study 1 (p 349) and Appendix 1 and it is sufficient to point out that as far as the publisher is concerned he will claim as a trading expense all payments made to authors, whether for the assignment of copyright or for the grant of a licence.

As far as the author is concerned, he may like a lump sum receipt not only from a cash flow point of view but also in order to take advantage of the backward spreading or forward spreading provisions which might be available (*as described at* p 198). The spreading provisions could apply on the assignment or partial assignment of copyright; a lump sum advance of royalties could also be spread but would normally be treated as income in the year of receipt. Copyright deals are usually simpler to structure from a tax planning point of view than licensing agreements within the manufacturing industry.

Ethical drugs

The main problem with ethical drugs is the very considerable amount of research and development expenditure needed to produce an effective drug, and the substantial cost and period of time required to test the drug both in the laboratory and in clinical trials before it can be actually marketed. On the assumption that the drug company is carrying on an existing trade, it will be ploughing back a large proportion of profits into research and development for future drugs. A lot of this expenditure will consist of ordinary trading expenses allowed under TA 1988, s 74(1). To the extent that expenditure might be disallowed as being too remote for the existing trade or represent capital expenditure, it may qualify for scientific research expenses, as explained in Chapter 15 (*see* p 181). In some cases the effective exploitation of the drug will require the acquisition of patent licences which may require capital expenditure or the payment of royalties, the tax treatment of which is also explained in Chapter 15. To the extent that know-how is acquired, as opposed to developed, relief for expenditure should be allowable as the acquisition of industrial know-how, *see* Chapter 18.

Marketing costs of ethical drugs tend to be very substantial and the promotion of the trade mark of a new drug is likely to be expensive. Any expenditure will, however, normally be trading expenditure, although the Revenue have been known to argue that the initial cost of advertising a new product gives rise to capital expenditure, for which no relief is available. In most cases it should be possible to resist this argument.

Where other manufacturers are licensed to produce the drug there may be lump sums received to cover know-how and licensing the patent, as well as a trade mark licence to use the proprietary name. It has to be considered whether such lump sums have to be treated as capital receipts or, as would usually be the case, income of the vendor, although they may be capital expenditure of the purchaser. Capital expenditure on the acquisition of a trade mark licence may be a capital receipt for the purchaser on which no allowances are available unless he can claim it as deferred revenue expenditure. Where royalties are concerned, it has to be considered whether tax is required to be deducted at source and whether any steps can be taken to mitigate withholding taxes on cross-border licensing, as explained in Chapter 22.

Where licensing and research and development are carried on within a multinational group it may be necessary to consider the controlled foreign company and transfer pricing provisions explained in Chapters 14 and 13 respectively.

Costs of research and development are often so high that joint ventures seem to become more common, which from a tax planning point of view can be both a complication and an opportunity, as explained in Case Study 6 (*see* p 401).

Broadcasting

The taxation of performers and behind-the-microphone workers is dealt with in Chapter 25.

Obviously, the broadcasting company is usually carrying on a trade, and the profits of that trade would be computed on the basis of usual accounting principles, and taxed accordingly. The particular areas of interest so far as this book is concerned are where the broadcasting company plays recordings on its programmes and the mechanism for paying the owners of the various rights for that broadcast. This is usually done by the broadcasting company paying a fee to the Performing Right Society Ltd (PRS) in the UK which allocates the amount received, normally on a quarterly basis, and distributes it equally to the publisher and composer of each record each time it is played on the air. Phonographic Performance Ltd (PPL) also collects a fee which is usually split three ways between the company producing the recording, the featured artistes and the session musicians, if any, who are usually paid through the Musicians' Union. Video Performance Ltd (VPL) also collects similar royalties in connection with videos shown on television; it is an associated company of Phonographic Performance Ltd. Publishing income on the sale of a recording is collected through the Mechanical Copyright Protection Society Ltd (MCPS).

These societies have their overseas equivalents in most of the important countries in the world so that wherever a recording is played on air the income should be accounted for to the performers and copyright holders.

It is obviously very difficult to ensure that the correct recipient is actually credited with the appropriate income collected by the collection societies, and in some cases they are unable to identify the correct recipients. In such cases the societies tend to accumulate the excess income for a period and then distribute it to the main payees in proportion to their allocated income. These additional monies are usually known in the trade as 'black box receipts'.

Recording agreements

When a record company enters into an agreement with an artiste, or group of artistes, the terms of the agreement vary considerably but there is usually a royalty due to the composer, which may be split with a lyricist, and a publishing agreement under which the record company usually becomes the publisher, although a number of successful artistes do take control of their own publishing. The artistes' royalty on the production of the recording is often allocated among one or more artistes in accordance with the agreement, and in some cases this could include the producer.

Because the record company will usually sell records on a worldwide basis through licensed manufacture with its overseas affiliates, there may be difficulties with withholding taxes. Royalty agreements typically have some vague provisions enabling the record company to deduct withholding taxes from royalties payable to the recipients. In practice, what often happens is that the record company suffers a withholding tax on royalties received from its overseas affiliates and licensees, and deducts an equivalent percentage from the royalties accountable to the performers or composers. In such circumstances the record company itself ought to be in a position to obtain credit for the tax deducted from its overseas affiliates and licensees in respect of any withholding taxes that remain irreducible under the appropriate double taxation treaties. Only if a withholding tax cannot otherwise be credited should it be deducted from the amount due to the recipients. The recipient will be unable to obtain credit for withholding taxes in respect of royalties due from overseas territories through the record company's sub-licensing, as they will have no direct contract with the payer of the royalties, and can only claim the cost as an expense. In certain cases the performer may have a direct contract with the overseas record company, in which case the withholding tax would be properly deducted, subject to any reduction under a double taxation treaty, and credit should then be available to the artistes.

Films and record masters

CAA 1990, s 68 (FA 1982, s 72) attacked the exploitation of the first year allowance by foreign companies through transactions involving films, tapes and discs. It removed the allowance and replaced it with a revenue write-off over the income-producing life of the asset. The new provision replaced the Inland Revenue practice published in statement of practice SP 9/79 (Appendix 6) dealing with 'films and similar assets', in which it was agreed by the Inland Revenue that provided that the master-print of the film is retained by the production company and has an anticipated potential life of not less than two years, it would qualify as 'plant' for capital allowance purposes and would be eligible for first year allowances. The statement of practice also applied to other types of expenditure on similar assets, such as master copies of records and tapes (IM 3300–3304).

This practice was ended from 10 March 1992 except for certain qualifying films completed or acquired prior to 10 March 1992, but not records or tapes, which continued to attract capital allowances. The phasing out of the 100 per cent first year allowance, however, by FA 1984, Sched 12 removed much of this benefit (IM 3327). A 'qualifying film' is a film certified under the Films Act 1985, including a television film. These provisions would not affect the position of a production company treating a film as trading stock, which is not common practice.

In other cases capital expenditure incurred after 9 March 1982 on either the production or acquisition of an original master film, tape or disc, or of any rights therein, is to be regarded as revenue expenditure (CAA 1990, s 68(1), (2)). As a corollary, where expenditure is to be treated as revenue expenditure any sums received from either the disposal of the film etc or from any interest or rights, including insurance etc receipts and receipts arising from an interest or right created by the disposal, are to be treated as revenue receipts whether or not they would be so treated under normal tax rules (CAA 1990, s 68(8)).

Where a film is not trading stock of a trade (CAA 1990, s 68(7)) in computing taxable profits or gains the expenditure, both capital and revenue, on the film is to be allocated to those periods for which accounts of the trade or business are made up or, in the absence of such accounts, the periods taken for the purpose of assessing the income for tax purposes. The allocation is usually made by means of the 'income matching method' (IM 3305–3308, CAA 1990, s 68(3), (4)) on a just and reasonable basis having regard to:

(1)   the balance of unallocated expenditure at the beginning of the period;

(2)   the proportion of the expenditure equal to:

$$\frac{\text{the estimated value of the film realised in the period}}{\text{that value and the estimated remaining value at the end of the period}}$$

(3)   the requirement to allocate the expenditure over the time during which the value of the film, etc is *expected* to be realised.

Example

	Period 1	*Period 2*	*Period 3*	*Period 4*
Expenditure	1,200,000	—	—	—
Receipts	—	4,000,000	11,000,000	1,000,000
Allocation of expenditure factors:				
(a) balance of expenditure at beginning period	=	1,200,000	900,00	75,000
(b) allowable proportion of expenditure	=	4,000,000 / 16,000,000	11,000,000 / 12,000,000	1,000,000 / 1,000,000
(c) expenditure spreads over revenue 'life' of film				
Allocation of expenditure		£300,000	£825,000	£75,000

A claim may be made under CAA 1990, s 68(5) and (6) for an additional amount equal to the excess of the income brought into account over the expenditure allocated to that period, up to the amount of the unallowed expenditure on a claim being submitted within one year and ten months of the end of the fiscal year or two years of the end of a company's accounting period (CAA 1990, s 68(5A)). This is known as the 'cost recovery method' and the calculation may be short-circuited in practice to writing off the expenditure incurred against the income to date. A loss may arise where the expenditure incurred and not written off exceeds the anticipated future income and may be claimed when it becomes apparent that the film etc will fail to recover costs (IM 3309). The cost recovery method, but not the income matching method, may be used by a finance lessor (IM 3310). Television films generating advertising revenue may be written off by reference to the income generation likely, effectively as deferred revenue expenditure (IM 3311). These provisions are further explained in the Inland Revenue statement of practice SP 1/93 issued on 11 January 1993 (Appendix 6).

From 10 March 1992 preproduction costs of developing prospective qualifying films are allowed as incurred under F(No 2)A 1992, ss 41–43 and expenditure on a film will be written off at a flat rate of 33⅓ per cent per annum from completion of the film, on making a claim under CAA 1990, s 68(9), SM 3325–3336. The Inland Revenue press release of 2 July 1997 stated that:

(1)   At present the costs of producing or acquiring a British qualifying film can be written off either as the film generates income or at a flat rate of 33⅓ per cent per year starting when the film is completed.

(2)   The government has decided to improve the flat-rate relief for British qualifying films costing £15 million or less to make. In these cases, the new rules will allow 100 per cent write-off for production or most acquisition costs when the film is completed.

(3)   The new rules will apply to production costs incurred after Budget Day or acquisition expenditure on films completed and acquired after Budget Day, including films begun before that date. The relief will be time limited to costs incurred during the three years from Budget Day, 2 July 1997 (F(No 2)A 1997, s 48).

Film production is not excluded from Enterprise Investment Scheme relief merely because it generates royalties (TA 1988, ss 297(4) and 298(5), IM 7000) nor from roll-over relief on reinvestment (TCGA 1992, ss 164I(5) and 164N(1)) or venture capital trust relief under TA 1988, Sched 28B, paras 4(5) and 5(1).

Video tapes for rental

The Revenue, in Issue 19 of the *Tax Bulletin* (October 1995), confirmed that video tapes loaned out to users could, if their economic life exceeded two years, be treated as short-life assets for capital allowances, or accounted for on the renewals basis or, where the life is two years or less, written off as deferred revenue expenditure by valuing the tapes at the accounting date on the basis of writing off the cost less realisable value over their economic life on a straight line basis or by reference to anticipated income stream.

Backward spreading

TA 1988, s 534 enables an author assessed under Schedule D, Case II or VI who has spent more than 12 months on a work to spread sums received from the assignment in whole or part of copyright or from the grant of a licence for a lump sum or royalties. The period of spread depends on the period during which he was engaged in making the work. If this does not exceed two years then half the income is deemed to have been received at the time of the actual receipt and the remaining half 12 months beforehand (IM 2695–2697).

Under TA 1988, s 534(3) if the period in which the author was engaged in making the work exceeded two years one-third of the income may be treated as received on the date it was actually received, one-third 12 months previously and one-third 12 months before that date.

The backward spreading of a payment of or on account of royalties earned applies only to amounts receivable within two years of first publication (TA 1988, s 534(4)(*b*)).

This contrasts with the backward spreading of a non-returnable lump sum payment, including a non-returnable advance on royalties, which may be spread backwards whenever received under TA 1988, s 534(4)(*a*), provided that a forward spread claim has not been made under TA 1988, s 535.

The claim for backward spreading of royalties may be made under TA 1988, s 534(5) at any time not later than the 5 April following the expiration of eight years after the work's first publication.

These provisions apply not only to writers of books but to the author of any literary, dramatic or artistic work and the date of first publication means the first occasion on which the work, or a reproduction of it, is published, performed or exhibited.

The literary and artistic spreading provisions in TA 1988, ss 534, 535, 537, 537A and 538 are disapplied for companies and partnerships by TA 1988, s 534(6A) in respect of sums receivable on or after 6 April 1996.

Forward spreading

It is not possible to claim the backward spreading relief under TA 1988, s 534 and in respect of the same payment forward spreading under TA 1988, s 535 (TA 1988, s 535(9)).

TA 1988 s 535(1) provides that where copyright or an interest therein is assigned or a licence granted for a period of at least two years for a lump sum payment, which term includes a non-returnable advance on royalties, the author may claim to spread the lump sum forward. This forward spreading provision is available only where the assignment or grant of a licence is made more than ten years after first publication of the work, on making a claim within one year and ten months from the end of the fiscal year in which it is receivable (TA 1988, s 535(8A), IM 2695–2697). A lump sum for these purposes would usually include a non-returnable, recoupable advance.

Under TA 1988, s 535(2) if the copyright is assigned or licensed for a period of six years or more, one-sixth of the lump sum is treated as being receivable on the date on which the lump sum was actually receivable and the remaining five-sixths is treated as having been receivable in five equal annual instalments on each anniversary of the date when the lump sum actually became receivable. Where the period of assignment or licence is less than six years the lump sum is spread over the number of whole years for which it is licensed (TA 1988, s 535(3)). If, therefore, copyright was licensed for three-and-a-half years one-third of the lump sum would be taxed by reference to the date of receivability and one-third would be treated as being receivable on each of the following two anniversaries of the date of receivability.

PART 5

SPECIFIC TAXATION APPLICATIONS

25 Entertainers and sportsmen

Introduction

A further class of individual who may be in receipt of royalties is the public performer, musician, actor or artiste. Such royalties from the sale of records, tapes or films are not copyright royalties but recording or performing royalties, often known as artistes' royalties. Performances giving rise to such royalties are protected under CDPA 1988, Part II. Although this income is not strictly from intellectual property, the taxation of such performers is so intimately connected with copyright that it warrants inclusion in this book. Sportsmen are often taxed under the same provisions as entertainers and the distinction, in practice, is becoming blurred, largely through the influence of television, and therefore, in this edition, sportsmen are also included within the term 'performer' except where the context dictates otherwise. Specific provisions relating to sportsmen are also referred to.

Normally a person in receipt of such royalties will be exercising a profession and any royalties received would be part of the Schedule D, Case II income, as for example the singer Miss Lillian Braithwaite in *Davies v Braithwaite* (1933) 18 TC 198.

However, the performer may be paid a salary assessable under Schedule E, as was the dancer in the case of *Fall v Hitchen* [1973] STC 66, or may even be carrying on a trade of, for example, running a dance band, as was Joe Loss in *Loss v IRC* [1945] 2 All ER 683.

It is therefore necessary to consider whether any amounts received by a performer are part of his taxable income, be it assessed under Schedule E, Schedule D, Case I or Schedule D, Case II.

Schedule E or D

It is important to distinguish between a contract of *service*, as in *Fall v Hitchen* *(above)*, *Bhadra v Ellam* [1988] STC 239, *Sidey v Phillips* [1987] STC 87, *Walls v Sinnett* [1987] STC 236 and *Mitchell & Edon v Ross* (1961) 40 TC 11, which is an employment within Schedule E, and a contract *for services*, which is dealt with under Schedule D as part of the trade or profession (*Edwards v Clinch* [1980] STC 438, *Davies v Braithwaite* (1933) 18 TC 198). The distinction is also important for National Insurance purposes. In *Market Investigations Ltd v Minister of Social Security* [1968] 3 All ER 732 Cooke J said at p 737:

> The observations of Lord Wright, of Denning, LJ, and of the judges of the Supreme Court in the USA suggest that the fundamental test to be applied is this: 'Is the person who has engaged

himself to perform these services performing them as a person in business on his own account'. If the answer to that question is 'yes', then the contract is a contract for services. If the answer is 'no', then the contract is a contract of service. No exhaustive list has been compiled and perhaps no exhaustive list can be compiled of considerations which are relevant in determining that question, nor can strict rules be laid down as to the relative weight which the various considerations should carry in particular cases. The most that can be said is that control will no doubt always have to be considered, although it can no longer be regarded as the sole determining factor; and that factors, which may be of importance, are such matters as whether the man performing the services provides his own equipment, whether he hires his own helpers, what degree of financial risk he takes, what degree of responsibility for investment and management he has, and whether and how far he has an opportunity of profiting from sound management in the performance of his task.

This judgment was quoted with approval in *Fall v Hitchen* and in *Global Plant Ltd v Secretary of State for Social Services* [1972] 1 QB 139.

Recent cases concerning playing in orchestras have held that in the particular circumstances the players were self-employed (*Midland Sinfonia Concert Society Ltd v Secretary of State for Social Services* [1981] ICR 454; *Addison v London Philharmonic Orchestra Ltd* [1981] ICR 261).

In the case of *Ferguson v John Dawson & Partners (Contractors) Ltd* [1976] 1 WLR 1213, Mr Ferguson was taken on as a self-employed member of the lump on a building site. He sustained injuries in the course of his occupation and it was necessary to determine whether he was self-employed, in which case it was his own fault, or whether he was an employee, in which case the employer had a responsibility for his safety which it had failed to observe. It was held that because the company was responsible for directing Mr Ferguson's activities and for providing him with tools and equipment as required that he was in reality an employee and not the supplier of independent services. He was therefore employed in reality under a contract of service and not a contract for services.

Unusually, in *Barnett v Brabyn* [1996] STC 716, the taxpayer argued unsuccessfully that he was an employee, not self-employed, and that therefore he was not liable for tax as his 'employer' should have deducted it under PAYE. Lightman J in his judgement stated:

> The badges of a contract of employment relied on by Mr. Way are that:—(1) Mr. Barnett worked only for LTV and no one else; (2) Mr. Barnett was paid originally weekly and later monthly and took only one week's holiday during the twenty five months he worked for LTV; (3) Mr. Barnett was paid for his one week's holiday; (4) when he wanted a haircut during working hours, he sought and obtained permission; (5) Mr. Barnett never submitted invoices to LTV; and (6) LTV gave Mr. Barnett the equivalent of three months' income by three equal post dated monthly cheques on his leaving as compensation for any outstanding loss or claim.
>
> I think that these factors might in an ordinary case carry some weight indicative of his status as an employee. But the weight is very much reduced as regards (1) and (2) by the fact that Mr. Barnett insisted on the contractual right to work as much or as little as he liked: and his later decision during the period of his engagement to work full time cannot affect the character of the contract which (in the absence of any suggestion of an agreed variation) must be determined once and for all when the contract was made. As regards (3), (4), (5) and (6), their significance must be very much affected by the family relationship between Mr. Barnett and LTV and the absence of evidence from Mr. Barnett as to whether any (if so what) discussions or agreement there were pursuant to which the payments referred to in (3) and (6) were made.
>
> Mr. Way further relies as badges of a contract of employment on the existence or non existence of factors found relevant in other cases. Thus e.g. he says that Mr. Barnett (1) had no skill or experience in the work he had to perform, did not engage his own helper, invest capital or provide his own machinery or tools or price his own job—all found to be badges of a contract of employment of a mason working on a building site in Lee Ting Sang v. Chung Chi-Keung [1990]

2 AC 374; (2) took no financial risk and had no opportunity of profiting from sound management—factors found to be relevant in case of a part time interviewer held to be an employee in Market Investigations Ltd. v. Minister of Social Security [1969] 2 QB 173; and (3) had no office or business bank account or prospect by efficiency of achieving a profit—factors found to be badges of a consultant in Hall v. Lorimer supra. I do not find this approach helpful. Factors relevant in one situation may be irrelevant or of no weight in another. I do not find any of these factors of any substantial weight in this case.

Three factors in this case in favour of Mr. Barnett being an independent contractor far outweigh any relied upon by Mr. Way. The first is (in the language of the Commissioners) that Mr. Barnett 'did have the right to control his input to LTV timewise', to enable him to exploit other interests. The second is the clear agreement that Mr. Barnett should be an independent contractor. Such an agreement cannot contradict the effect of a contract as a whole and must be disregarded if inconsistent with the substantive terms or general effect of the contract as a whole: see Narich Pty v. Commissioner of Pay-roll Tax (Privy Council) (1984) ICR 286, quoted 1983 STI 545. But when the terms and general effect of the contract as a whole are consistent with either relationship, the parties' label may be decisive: see Massey v. Crown Life Insurance Co. supra. The third is the cogent factor of the previous determinations all made on this basis.

It would appear from these cases that there are five main elements in a contract of employment.

First, the employer must have control over the manner in which the employee carries out his services and as such the employer is responsible for the actions of the employee.

Secondly, the employer is entitled to exploit the products or services produced by the employee by supplying them to third parties. In the literary and entertainment field it is not unusual to find that an employee is given a power of veto over the manner in which or by whom his activities may be exploited, and although it is not necessarily fatal to an employment contract to have such a veto it is nonetheless an indication of a self-employed rather than employee status. Similarly, any provision that the employee indemnify the employer would be an indication of a self-employed status and if the employment is through a company, which ostensibly has the rights to provide the services of the employee, it is not uncommon to find that the third party consumer of such services requires an inducement letter from the employee direct. This type of letter is one in which the employee confirms that the appropriate company has the rights to his services and should it cease to have these rights he would ensure that any subsequent employer who had the rights to his services would provide them to the third party. Any such letter requires careful drafting as it could negate the employment and put the so-called employee in direct contractual relationship with the third party and therefore in a self-employed rather than employee status. It is important to ensure therefore that the inducement letter is confirmatory of intention and that the third party's rights are primarily against the employer company.

It is also common, and often desirable, for the originator of copyright work to ensure that the ownership of the copyright remains with him and does not pass automatically to the employer. This is again an indication that the contract is for services and not a service contract as under common law the products of the employee would belong to the employer. This problem can usually be solved in practice by the employee granting the employer an exclusive licence to the copyright work during the period of the employment, or as one of the terms of the contract of employment having a right to acquire copyrights at the termination of the employment for a nominal sum. It is important to have the right to acquire the copyright material under the contract of service as otherwise any transfer of the copyrights to the employee on termination would be taxable as remuneration on the market value of copyrights.

Thirdly, the employment contract would normally require the exclusive services of the employee, although again it is not unusual to have dual contracts with separate employers where the services are split on a territorial basis so that activities in the UK are for one employer and those outside the UK or in specified territories are for another employer. It is possible to have different employments for different services although a multiplicity of so-called employments would give rise to a potential argument that the so-called employee was in reality freelance and providing his services via different companies. It is also possible to have both an employment and a self-employed activity, although this could increase the difficulty of ensuring the *bona fides* of the employment. See *Mitchell & Edon v Ross* (1961) 40 TC 11.

Fourthly, an employment contract will provide for remuneration and reimbursement of expenses to be paid to the employee who should be in a position where he is entitled to the remuneration whatever the success his employer may have in marketing the product of his labours. Normally such remuneration would be a fixed sum paid on a monthly basis. The provision of a bonus, perhaps related to the employer's receipts as a result of the employee's activities, could also be paid, although such a provision is regarded in the USA as an indication of a contract for services rather than an employment.

Fifthly, the employment would normally be for a fixed period of time although it would not be unusual for it to continue indefinitely thereafter. A common period for a service contract would be three or five years. A service agreement should normally contain clear provisions as to how it may be terminated, for example, by giving six months' notice, or for a fundamental breach by either the employer or employee.

A leading case, involving a freelance television vision mixer, went to the Court of Appeal as *Hall (Inspector of Taxes) v Lorimer* [1994] STC 23. It concerned the case of Mr Ian Lorimer and whether his activities were as an employee carrying on a series of employments taxable under Schedule E or in business on his own account and properly assessed under Schedule D, Case I.

The facts were relatively simple, with Mr Lorimer joining Molinare Ltd as an electrician on 2 February 1981 and in 1983 changing his job within the company to that of vision mixer which required a nine-month period of training from Molinare's one and only vision mixer. On 31 January 1985 Mr Lorimer decided to go freelance and left Molinare's employment. A vision mixer is a type of editor who is required to have a sense of timing, a feeling for mood, anticipation and music, and dexterity in operating equipment. In a live show he has only one chance to get it right. He may have four cameras operated by four individual cameramen providing shots of an event from different positions. These shots come up on screen in front of the vision mixer. It is his function to select the one which at any moment he thinks is the most interesting for the viewer. The vision mixer works closely with the director responsible for the production. Obviously, with pre-recorded shows there is less opportunity for the vision mixer to show his skill, but it is still a very important function. A vision mixer does not use his own equipment, which is very expensive. The cost of a fully equipped outside broadcast vehicle can be £3 million.

Mr Lorimer set about getting work from his office at home where his wife assisted with the paperwork. He prepared his c.v. and proceeded by writing, telephoning or visiting potential customers and in this he was successful. He built up a client list of 22 companies using his services in the first 14 months and subsequently maintained his list of contacts at about this level, although the identity of the clients varied, with 14 new clients acquired in 1986–87, nine in the following year and eight in 1988–89 which was the last year under appeal. He obtained work for well over 800 days in the four years and two months from 2 February 1985 to 5 April 1989. Mr Lorimer was registered for VAT and accepted as being in business on his own account by Customs and Excise who made the usual control visits. He paid retirement annuity policy premiums and had sickness insurance in case he was unable to work through illness. For a time Mr Lorimer used an agent but gave this up as he found he was merely being introduced to his own contacts. In a small number of cases, six in fact, he was double booked and persuaded his customers to accept a substitute for whom he paid and in respect of which he made a small profit on the differential between what he charged the customer and what he paid the substitute.

The contracts entered into by Mr Lorimer with the television companies tended to be fairly informal but normally with written confirmation of telephone bookings followed by invoices from Mr Lorimer in varying degrees of detail. On occasions clients refused to pay the fee plus VAT and instead paid a net amount after deducting tax and National Insurance for fear that the Revenue would not approve Mr Lorimer as being in business on his own account.

Mr Lorimer was for much of the time a member of the Association of Cinematograph Television and Allied Technicians but he charged more than the normal union rates of pay and worked the period of time necessary to complete the job in hand.

The Commissioner's decision in this case is very important because Mummery J merely had to decide whether, following *Edwards (Inspector of Taxes) v Bairstow* (1956) 36 TC 207, the Commissioner's decision was within the band of possible reasonable decisions and not whether on the evidence he would have reached the same conclusion as the Special Commissioner.

The Special Commissioner considered Cooke J's admirable summary of the fine distinction between a number of casual employments and a series of contracts for services in *Market Investigations Ltd v Minister of Social Security* [1969] 3 All ER 732 and agreed that the fundamental test to be applied was whether or not the person who engaged himself to perform the services was performing them as a person in business on his own account. It is very interesting to note that the courts have been prepared to look to other jurisdictions such as the USA for guidance on matters of difficulty where the legal system is basically the same (*USA v Silk* (1946) 331 US 704).

In the *Market Investigations* case the interviewer was held to be carrying on a part-time employment in view of the high degree of control exercised over her activities. The Special Commissioner looked at *Davies (Inspector of Taxes) v Braithwaite* (1931) 18 TC 198 in which it was held that an actress was exercising her profession and not engaged in a series of part-time employments, contrasted with the case of *Fall (Inspector of Taxes) v Hitchen* [1973] STC 66 which concerned a professional ballet dancer engaged by Sadlers Wells under a contract which amounted to an employment agreement. He also looked at *O'Kelly v Trust House Forte plc* [1984] QB 90 where casual catering staff were held not to be employees and finally held that the activities of Mr Lorimer bore the hallmarks of a man who is in business on his own account and that they outweighed substantially such factors as may have been thought to militate against that conclusion.

Mummery J in his judgment pointed out that it would be possible to have a mixture of Schedule E employments and Schedule D contracts for services as in the case of the barrister whose lecturing activities were held to be employment income (*Sidey v Phillips* [1987] STC 87). Also in *Mitchell & Edon v Ross* (1961) 40 TC 11 it was agreed by both sides that there was no material difference between the various contracts and they were all either Schedule E or Schedule D.

Mummery J also referred to *Ready Mixed Concrete (South East) Ltd v Minister of Pensions and National Insurance* [1968] 2 QB 497 which had also been referred to by the Commissioner and *Lee Ting Sang v Chung Chi-Keung* [1990] 2 AC 374 having further judicial approval to Cooke J's dictum in the *Market Investigations* case, ie did Mr Lorimer perform his services as a person in business on his own account? The Crown presented a formidable argument that Mr Lorimer was not in business on his own account because he did not provide or pay for any of the equipment; he did not, except on the few occasions when the production company consented to the use of a substitute, engage any staff to help him in his vision mixing work. The production company controlled his time, the place and duration of each engagement and the premises where the vision mixing was to be done. The taxpayer had no say or latitude in those matters. The production company had control over the detailed planning of the programme and the taxpayer was subject to what the director wished to achieve and to the scripted directions. The taxpayer ran no financial business risk. He had not invested any capital in the productions. He had no stake in their success or failure. He had no responsibility for investment in the programme making or work or in the management of it. He had no opportunity for profit in the performance of the work, apart from the few occasions on which he hired a substitute, and his reward was not a profit from the running of the business established on his own account, but payment for the provision of his own personal skills to the production company. The risk he ran in not working for one production company under a long-term contract was that of any employee who chooses to work on a casual basis. He ran the risk of being unable to find employment or being unemployed and unpaid. Mr Lorimer's business was clearly not that of vision mixing as he did not have the premises, equipment or means to carry on such a business, so the business could only be of providing to others for reward his services as a vision mixer. But on the authority of *Humberstone v Northern Timber Mills* (1949) 79 CLR 389:

> The essence of a contract of service is a supply of the work and skill of a man.

Mummery J was not persuaded by this analytical approach and quoted with approval Vinelott J in *Walls v Sinnett (Inspector of Taxes)* [1987] STC 236:

> The facts as a whole must be looked at and a factor which may be compelling in one case, in the light of the facts of that case, may not be compelling in the context of another case.

Nor could Mummery J be persuaded that the Special Commissioner had erred in law; he had asked himself the right question and considered in conscientious detail the essential elements of the relationship—control, duration of engagements, number of engagements, provision of equipment, capital, hiring of staff, risk of profit and loss and so on. He applied the right test and came to a decision which was not open to the judge to upset. The Court of Appeal agreed with the learned judge.

This case is useful not only as a summary of the factors relevant to determining whether there is a contract of employment or a contract for services, but also to emphasise the importance of the Special Commissioners as the final arbiter on questions of fact.

In *Ferguson v John Dawson & Partners (Contractors) Ltd* [1976] 1 WLR 1213 at p 1221 Megaw LJ stated:

> Mr Murray accepted that he was responsible for 'hiring and firing'. In other words, as between the defendants and the workmen, including the plaintiff, he could dismiss them. There would be no question of his being able to determine a contract between the defendants and a sub-contractor. He could move men from site to site, if he was so minded, and in support of the existence of that contractual right on behalf of the defendants he gave instances of having done so. If tools were required for the work, it was for the defendants to provide them. Again, as confirmation of that contractual obligation Mr Murray gave evidence of instances where the plaintiff had required tools for the work which he had been required to do, and the defendants had provided them. It was for Mr Murray to tell the workmen, including the plaintiff, what particular work they were to do: 'I tell him what to take and what to do.' The centurion in St Matthew's Gospel says to the man under him: ' "Do this," and he doeth it.' The man under him is a servant, not an independent contractor. All these things are in relation to the contractual relationships existing. 'I tell him what to do,' and he does it on Mr Murray's instructions because, when legal analysis has to be applied, it is a term of the contract that the plaintiff shall carry out the defendant's instructions what to do when they tell him to do it. The men, including the plaintiff, were employed on an hourly basis. The money paid to them would be correctly described as 'a wage'.
>
> In my judgement, on the tests laid down in the authorities, all of this indicates beyond doubt that the reality of the relationship was of employer and employee—a contract of service. I do not propose to lengthen this judgment by examining afresh the criteria, so fully discussed in so many cases. The judge, as I have already said, based himself on the judgment of MacKenna J in *Ready Mixed Concrete (South East) Ltd v Minister of Pensions and National Insurance* [1968] 2 QB 497. Another judgment which I have found very helpful is that of Cooke J in *Market Investigations Ltd v Minister of Social Security* [1969] 2 QB 173.

and at p 1225:

> As a matter of law I can see no reason why a general labourer should not offer his labour on some such terms as these: 'I do not mind what you ask me to do or where and when you ask me to do it but you must understand that I am not going to call you master and I will not be your servant.' Many men offer their labour on some such terms as these; the jobbing gardener is familiar to us all, as are self-employed farm workers to East Anglian farmers. When working they allow themselves to be controlled by those with whom they made a bargain. In most cases when the bargain is made nothing is said about control, but it is accepted by both parties as an implied term that the hirer will exercise control. This does not mean either in fact or, in my opinion, in law that the hired man becomes a servant.

In a written answer of 21 January 1982 Mr Nicholas Ridley stated:

> I have taken steps so that, in due course and in all districts, club musicians will be brought within PAYE where appropriate.
> (Hansard, Vol 16, Col 228.)

It should be noted that an employer is required to deduct tax under the Pay As You Earn system (TA 1988, s 203 and Income Tax (Employment) Regulations 1973 (SI 1973 No 334) as amended). This applies if the employer has a trading presence in the UK (*Clark v Oceanic Contractors Inc* [1983] STC 35).

The Inland Revenue has published a leaflet (IR56) setting out in general terms the indicia of employment and self-employment as follows:

If you can answer 'yes' to the following questions, you are probably **an employee**:
- Do you have to do the work that you have agreed to undertake yourself (that is, you are not allowed to send a substitute or hire other people to do it)?
- Can someone tell you what to do, and when and how to do it?
- Does someone provide you with holiday time, sick pay or a pension? (Though a lot of employees don't get any of these.)
- Are you paid so much an hour, a week or a month? Can you get overtime pay? (Though many employees are paid by commission or on a piece-work basis.)
- Are you expected to work set hours, or a given number of hours a week or month?
- Do you work wholly or mainly for one business? (But remember that many employees work for more than one employer.)
- Are you expected to work at the premises of the person you are working for, or at a place or places they decide? (But remember that a self-employed person, such as a plumber, may by the nature of his job have to work at the premises of the person who engages him.)

If you can answer 'yes' to the following questions, it will usually mean that you are **self-employed**:
- Are you ultimately responsible for how the business is run? Do you risk your own capital in the business? Are you responsible for bearing losses as well as taking profits?
- Do you yourself control what you do, whether you do it, how do you do it, and when and where you do it? (Though many employees have considerable independence.)
- Do you provide the major items of equipment you need to do your job (not just the small tools which many employees provide for themselves)?
- Are you free to hire other people, on terms of your own choice, to do the work that you have agreed to undertake? (But remember that an employee may also be authorised to delegate work or to engage others on behalf of his employer.)
- Do you have to correct unsatisfactory work in your own time and at your own expense?

Revenue guidance

The Revenue published guidance on whether a worker was employed or self-employed in *Tax Bulletin*, Issue 28, page 406, in the context of the construction industry. The rules, however, have general application and the relevant extracts are set out below:

Employment status

There is no statutory definition of 'employment'. However, the question of employment status has come before the Courts on many occasions over the years. The approach taken by the Courts has been to identify the factors which help to determine if a particular contract amounts to employment or self-employment. It is important to note, though, that the contract does not necessarily have to be in writing. It can be written, or oral, or it may be implied by the way in which the parties deal with each other. It may even be a combination of all three.

The relevant factors are:

Control—It is a feature of employment that the engager has the right to tell the worker what to do, or where or when to do it, or how it is to be done. The extent of control may vary from one case to another—a contractor will probably exercise more control over an unskilled labourer than over a skilled craftsman. However, a working relationship which involves no control at all is unlikely to be an employment (Ready Mixed Concrete (South East) Ltd v Minister of Pensions and National Insurance (1968) 2 QB 497).

The right to get a substitute or helper to do the job—Personal service is an essential element of a contract of employment. A person who has the freedom to choose whether to do the job himself or hire somebody else to do it for him, or who can hire someone else to provide substantial help, is probably self-employed (Australian Mutual Provident Society v Chaplin (1978) 18 ALR 385).

Provision of equipment—A self-employed contractor generally provides whatever equipment is needed to do the job (though in many trades, such as carpentry, it is common for employees, as well as self-employed workers, to provide their own hand tools). Provision by the engager of the major items of equipment and/or the materials necessary to do the job will point towards employment (Ready Mixed Concrete (South East) Ltd v Minister of Pensions and National Insurance).

Financial risk—An individual who risks his own money by, for example, buying assets and bearing their running costs and paying for overheads and large quantities of materials, is almost certainly self-employed. Financial risk could also take the form of quoting a fixed price for a job, with the consequent risk of bearing the additional costs if the job overruns. However, this will not necessarily mean that the worker is self-employed unless there is a real risk of financial loss (Market Investigations Ltd v The Minister of Social Security (1968) 2 QB 173).

Basis of payment—Employees tend to be paid a fixed wage or salary by the week or month and often qualify for additional payments such as overtime, long service bonus or profit share. Independent contractors, on the other hand, tend to be paid a fixed sum for a particular job. Payment 'by the piece' (where the worker is paid according to the amount of work actually done) can be a feature of both employment and self-employment (see Example 2 below).

Opportunity to profit from sound management—A person whose profit or loss depends on his capacity to reduce overheads and organise his work effectively may well be self-employed (Market Investigations Ltd v The Minister of Social Security). People who are paid by the job will often be in this position.

Right of dismissal—A right to terminate an engagement by giving notice of a specified length is a common feature of employment. It is less common in a contract for services, which usually ends only on completion of the task, or if the terms of the contract are breached.

Employee benefits—Employees are often entitled to sick pay, holiday pay, pensions, expenses and so on. However, the *absence* of those features does not necessarily mean that the worker is self-employed—especially in the case of short term engagements (see Example 1).

Length of engagement—Long periods working for one contractor may be typical of an employment but are not conclusive. It is still necessary to consider all the terms and conditions of each engagement. Regular working for the same contractor may indicate that there is a single and continuing contract of employment (Nethermere (St Neots) Ltd v Gardiner (1984) ICR 612). See also Question 5 below.

Personal factors—In deciding a person's employment status it may sometimes be necessary to take into account factors which are personal to the worker and which have little to do with the terms of the particular engagement being considered. For example, if a skilled craftsman works for a number of contractors throughout the year and has a business-like approach to obtaining his engagements (perhaps involving expenditure on office accommodation, office equipment, etc) this will point towards self-employment (Hall v Lorimer 66 TC 349). Personal factors will usually carry less weight in the case of an unskilled worker, where other factors such as the high level of control exercised by the contractor are likely to be conclusive of employment.

Intention—It is the reality of the relationship that matters. It is not enough to call a person 'self-employed' if all the terms and conditions of the engagement point towards employment. However, if other factors are neutral the intention of the parties will then be the decisive factor in deciding employment status (Massey v Crown Life Insurance Co (1978) ICR 590).

Approach to be adopted

Given the list of factors mentioned above it is tempting to try to determine a person's employment status by adding up the number of factors pointing towards employment and comparing that result with the number pointing towards self-employment. **The Courts have specifically rejected that approach.** In Hall v Lorimer 66 TC 349 Mummery J made the following comment which was quoted with approval by Nolan LJ in the Court of Appeal:

'In order to decide whether a person carries on business on his own account it is necessary to consider many different aspects of that person's work activity. This is not a mechanical exercise of running through a check list to see whether they are present in, or absent from, a given situation. . . . It is a matter of evaluation of the overall effect, which is not necessarily the same as the sum total of all the individual details. Not all details are of equal weight or importance in any given situation. The details may also vary in importance from one situation to another.'

When the detailed facts have been established the right approach is to stand back and look at the picture as a whole, to see if the overall effect is that of a person in business on his own account or a person working as an employee in somebody else's business. If the evidence is evenly balanced the intention of the parties may then decide the issue (Massey v Crown Life Insurance Co).

The question of when an employment exists is also explored at some length in SE 541–704 (not reproduced).

Actors

The Revenue usually accept that actors are self-employed for tax purposes (IM 1810–1812, SE 7332–7335 following Special Commissioner decisions involving Mr McCowan and Mr West in 1993, before such proceedings were formally reported).

This is so even though the standard Musicians' Union and British Actors' Equity Association standard contracts are currently accepted as employment contracts for National Insurance purposes, subject to Class 1 contributions and entitling the performer to benefits when unemployed.

The Revenue tried to make most actors into Schedule E employees from 6 April 1990, subject to those with already established self-employed status who were given reserved Schedule D status under ESC A75, but the Revenue view changed following the Special Commissioner's decisions in *McCowan* and *West* referred to above (SE 7335).

There are, of course, many exceptions and the engagements may be sufficiently lengthy to amount to employments taxed under Schedule E, as in *Fall v Hitchen* [1973] STC 66, where the taxpayer was employed as a dancer in the chorus at Sadlers Wells. Where an actor is employed, he may still have to pay agents' fees and fees of up to 17.5 per cent are deductible as wholly, exclusively and necessarily incurred in the performance of the employment (TA 1988, s 201A, ICAEW TR 796, 25 June 1990, SE 7347).

Theatrical non-performing workers

People such as stage managers, designers, directors and choreographers may be either self-employed or employees depending on the terms and circumstances of their engagements. Other workers are likely to be employees but there is no hard and fast rule (SE 7351–7354).

Musicians

The rules for actors generally apply to musicians. The status as employee or as self-employed will depend on the contractual arrangements. Those on first call or guaranteed contracts and those with mutually owned orchestras such as the London Philharmonic are self-employed (SE 7363 and 7364).

Film and television workers

The Revenue have set up special units for such workers at LP 10 (Film Industry Unit), and LP 12 (Television and Radio Unit). Front-of-camera or microphone performers are dealt with as actors, as above. Behind camera etc workers are either employed or self-employed depending on their grades and activities. The Revenue have published Guidelines in respect of freelancers in these activities, effective from 1 July 1996 (Appendix 12).

Agency workers

Workers supplied through agencies may be taxed under Schedule E as employees of the agency (TA 1988, s 134). These rules do not apply to actors, singers, musicians or other entertainers or to models (TA 1988, s 134(5), SE 717–738 (not reproduced)), unless working outside their profession, for example, as demonstrators (SE 7206 (not reproduced)).

Sportsmen

Team players, such as footballers and cricketers, are usually employees of a club and taxed under Schedule E. They may also be in receipt of indorsements or merchandising income or even record royalties which are earned outwith their employment duties and therefore taxable as receipts of a separate trade under Schedule D, Case I or as annual profits or gains under Schedule D, Case VI (IM 1822–1825 and 1828).

Benefit years In some sports, notably cricket, it is common for exceptional players to have a benefit year in which a benefit committee, independent of the cricketer or the club which employs him, raises money to give to him at the end of the year. Provided that there is no entitlement to this income under his contract of employment (*Moorhouse v Dooland* (1955) 36 TC 1, SE 1181, *Cooper v Blokiston* (1908) 5 TC 347, *Davis v Harrison* (1927) 11 TC 707, *Corbett v Duff* (1941) 23 TC 763) the gift should be tax-free (*Reed v Seymour* (1927) 11 TC 625). It is important that the benefit committee itself does not carry on a trade which would be taxable.

An unsolicited gift to a footballer for winning the World Cup was also held to be tax-free in *Moore v Griffiths* (1972) 48 TC 338. This has to be distinguished from a share of a transfer fee as an inducement from a past on future employer which was held to be taxable in *Shilton v Wilmshurst* [1991] STC 88.

Athletes

Athletics in the UK is usually under the auspices of the British Amateur Athletic Board which runs bare trusts for athletes to preserve their amateur status under the International Amateur Athletic Association.

Income paid into the general fund is that of the athlete even though it can be withdrawn only for approved expenses. Interest on the fund is retained by the BAAB and is not income of the athlete. Merely because an athlete obtains income, including subventions, grants, sponsorship, endorsement fees, and appearance, participation or performance fees, does not necessarily mean that he is carrying on a trade on a commercial basis. He may merely be receiving a contribution to the expenses of his hobby, or a receipt taxable under. Schedule D, Case VI. However, an athlete may be carrying on a trade, even though retaining amateur status.

The BAAB also runs individual funds for more commercially successful athletes, which are bare trusts the income of which belongs to the athlete. An athlete who qualifies for an individual fund is likely to be carrying on a trade.

Because the BAAB funds are bare trusts the income is that of the athlete when received by the BAAB, not when withdrawn by the athlete (IMI 820a–1829). The usual Schedule D expenses rules apply (TA 1988, s 74(1)(*a*)) and duality of purpose may disallow expenses on clothes (*Mallalieu v Drummond* [1983] STC 665), and medical expenses (*Norman v Golder* (1944) 26 TC 293, *Prince v Mapp* (1969) 46 TC 169).

Receipts paid in kind are taxable at their encashable value (*Gold Coast Selection Trust Ltd v Humphrey* (1948) 30 TC 209, *Temperley v Smith* (1956) 37 TC 18).

An athlete may be an employee of a service company, and taxable under Schedule E, if the company is contractually entitled to the income from the third party provider.

National Insurance

An employee in employed earners' employment is liable to pay primary Class 1 earnings-related contributions and the employer is liable to pay Class 1 secondary contributions. A non-resident employer does not usually have to pay secondary contributions although primary contributions are payable by a UK employee. On taking up employment overseas the employee is liable for primary contributions for the first 52 weeks overseas if the employer has a place of business in the UK. He may retain liability to contribute only to the DSS and not to his country of employment if there are reciprocal arrangements with the country of residence.

A self-employed individual pays Class 2 flat-rate contributions and Class 4 earnings-related contributions unless he is non-resident for at least 26 out of 52 weeks.

There is an annual maximum for contributions so far as the employee or self-employed individual is concerned and where it is anticipated that total contributions for the year will exceed these maxima, deferment of contributions under Classes 2 and 4 (and Class 1 if several employments are held) may be applied for on Form CF 351. Any excess contributions paid for a year may be reclaimed from the DSS on Form CF 28F.

Some taxpayers dealt with as self-employed under Schedule D, Cases I or II, such as actors and musicians, are treated as employed for National Insurance purposes and pay Class 1 contributions and have to claim exemption from Classes 2 and 4. They may claim income support benefit if unemployed which is brought in as income in the Schedule D computation, or alternatively as Schedule E income if the Schedule D assessment is final (*PAYE Procedures Manual*, 9662).

Restrictive covenants

In the case of *Higgs v Olivier* (1952) 33 TC 136 Sir Laurence Olivier was paid a lump sum under a restrictive covenant for undertaking not to act in, produce or direct any film for any other person for a period of 18 months. Sir Laurence had previously acted in a film entitled *Henry V* for which he had been fully remunerated and the restrictive covenant was with the makers of the same film. The Commissioners (at p 139):

found it impossible to say that the sum of £15,000 under the deed came to the Respondent as part of the income from his vocation. On the contrary, it came to him for refraining from carrying on his vocation, and in our opinion was a capital receipt.

The High Court and the Court of Appeal supported the Commissioners in this.

It should be noted that had Sir Laurence been assessed under Schedule E the receipt under the restrictive covenant would have been caught by the provisions of TA 1988, s 313.

Date royalties taxable

Traditionally, royalties have normally been brought into the accounts of the recipient when received from the publisher or other paying agent. This method of accounting is normally adopted because the author or artiste is entitled to royalties on the basis of sales, less returns to the publisher, and this information is available only to the publisher, although the author or artiste may have rights of auditing the publisher's records to confirm that the correct royalties have been accounted for. In the case of an individual unincorporated author or artiste a cash receipts basis is approved in accordance with Statement of Practice SP/A27, except for the opening years when the sums involved are normally not particularly large and a cash basis is unlikely to be challenged by the Revenue.

However, in the case of an incorporated recipient of royalties arising from the exploitation of the services of an author or artiste the Revenue may argue that the royalties should be included on an accruals basis rather than on a receipts basis. On the basis of TA 1988, s 60 which provides that income taxed under Schedule D, Cases I–VI is on the full amount of any profits, gains or income arising in the period, which in the Revenue's view means all sums reported as payable to the recipient by the publisher covering the period up to the end of the accounting date, even if not reported until after the end of the accounting period, and even if not payable until a later date. The technical justification for this treatment is that the royalties will have been earned in that the sales, less returns, will have taken place even though the information would not at the accounting date be available to the recipient. A case cited in support of this contention is *IRC v Gardner Mountain & D'Ambrumenil Ltd* (1947) 29 TC 69. This case concerned Lloyd's underwriting commissions. Further support of the principle is drawn from the case of *JP Hall & Co Ltd v IRC* (1921) 12 TC 382.

One of the problems of such a treatment of royalties is that the publisher itself may well be sub-contracting sales in various parts of the world to sub-publishers and agents and royalty collection societies so that the publisher at any particular accounting date of the recipient would be unaware of all royalties in respect of sales less returns that have taken place anywhere in the world and which, on the Revenue basis, should theoretically be included in the accounts. The Revenue get over this problem by the prudence basis of accounting and accept that the recipient has only to deal with the amounts reported by the publisher immediately after the accounting date and payable normally three or six months thereafter.

The Revenue suggest that there should be some transitional provisions on changing from a receipts to an accruals basis of royalty reporting on some form of extra-statutory but reasonable averaging basis.

A further problem arises in the case of blocked royalties where the amount has been reported by the publisher to the recipient but has not been paid because the publisher himself has not been paid, owing perhaps to exchange control restrictions on the country of origin of the royalty. In these circumstances the Revenue would accept that the royalty is not taxable until received or until the author or artiste enjoys the benefit of the royalty by, for example, spending the proceeds made available to him in the country where the royalty arises.

The Revenue's view that royalties payable to a company should be accounted for on an accruals basis is by no means universally accepted; the argument being that provided that the accounts are prepared in accordance with proper accounting principles they should form the starting point in the determination of the profits for tax purposes. *See, for example, Whimster & Co v IRC* (1925) 12 TC 813; *Duple Motor Bodies Ltd v Ostime* (1961) 39 TC 537; *Odeon Associated Theatres Ltd v Jones* (1971) 48 TC 257; and *BSC Footwear Ltd v Ridgway* (1971) 47 TC 495. Only exceptionally, as in *Willingale v International Commercial Bank Ltd* [1978] STC 75, is the accounting profit departed from for tax purposes.

In order for the Revenue to succeed in adjusting accounts prepared on a cash accounting basis to an accruals basis the Revenue would have to show that cash accounting of royalties received was not in accordance with proper accounting principles, or that an adjustment was required by statutory or judicial authority.

It is a fundamental principle of accounting that profits should not be anticipated but should be recognised only when realised or when the amount which will ultimately be recognised can be ascertained with reasonable accuracy. This is under Statement of Accounting Practice No 2. It is suggested that if at the end of the accounting date the recipient of royalties cannot ascertain the amount due from the payer because the latter has not yet accounted to the recipient, the accounts of the recipient should not include amounts ultimately received even though they may relate back to a period covered by the accounts. It is argued that the accountability by the payer is not equivalent to ascertainment of the amount receivable by the payee and the payee should not be required to hold his accounts open until the amount due from the payer at the next payment date is ascertained. There appears to be no statutory or judicial authority which covers the point and in fact *Willingale v International Commercial Bank Ltd* [1978] STC 75 is authority for adjusting profits shown in the accounts on an accruals basis to the amounts actually realised at the accounting date. Further support for the receipts basis is found in *Robertson v IRC* [1997] STC (SCD) 282.

The judicial authority relied upon by the Revenue of *IRC v Gardner Mountain & D'Ambrumenil Ltd* related to insurance commission for services rendered and depended on the construction of the contract under which the commission was payable and whether or not the services had been rendered in the year. As it was held that the services had been rendered the commission was due and therefore treated as earned in the year for tax purposes. A licence agreement under which a publisher pays a royalty for what would otherwise be an infringement of copyright is rather different from a contract under which specific services have to be performed.

The other case relied on by the Revenue, that of *JP Hall & Co Ltd v IRC*, related to the profit on a contract, the payment of which was due on delivery, and it was held that for tax purposes the profit should be included in the period in which the delivery was made, and not that in which the contract was entered into. As this delayed the taxable profit it would not appear to provide much support for the Revenue's contention that the profit should be brought forward in the accounts of the recipient of a royalty.

Where royalties are paid for services rendered rather than for copyright, for example, the artiste's royalties paid to the performers of a recording, there is rather more substance to the Revenue's case that the services would have been performed during the recording and mixing and therefore all royalties relating to sales of the recording, less returns, in the accounting period should be included in the recipient's accounts for that period. However, the practical problem is that the recipient has no means of knowing what these royalties are to be and there seems no logical justification for holding the accounts open just to include the amount receivable from the immediate payer without including the amounts ultimately payable from all the various sub-publishers throughout the world. This would clearly require keeping the accounts open for a two- or three-year period and is impractical.

Therefore, coming back to the normal prudent basis of accounting it is suggested that accounts produced by the recipient of royalties on the basis of royalties ascertained as due to be paid and not blocked at the accounting year end are accounts prepared in accordance with proper principles of accounting and should form the basis of the taxation computations.

Simpler accounts for small businesses

On 7 November 1989 the Inland Revenue produced a press release as follows:

> Detailed accounts will no longer be needed from up to one million smaller businesses. Announcing this today in a written reply to a parliamentary question [HC Written Answer, 7 November 1989, Vol. 159 col. 525] the Financial Secretary to the Treasury, Mr Peter Lilley, MP said—
>
> 'As from next April detailed tax accounts will no longer be needed from many small businesses. Taxpayers will still need to keep accurate business records, but three line accounts will be accepted with tax returns. This relaxation could simplify dealing with tax for up to a million smaller businesses'.
>
> At present, all businesses are expected to send in accounts consisting of a profit and loss account and sometimes a balance sheet. Traders have to itemise their income and expenditure for the year, for example rent, purchases of trading stock, travelling expenses, fuel, telephone etc.
>
> From next year small businesses need only state their total turnover, total business purchases and expenses, and the resultant net profit. These simplified accounts will be accepted from individuals and partnerships who are trading with a total annual turnover of under £15,000, and also from people with rent from property where the gross income is less than £15,000 (£10,000 prior to 5 April 1992 increased by press release 1 November 1991).
>
> Taxpayers can send in the new simpler accounts with tax returns they will get next year asking them to report income for the year ended 5 April 1990.
>
> Taxpayers will still need to keep accurate business records so that they can submit correct three line accounts. The Revenue will continue to investigate business accounts and records for all sizes of business where it has reason to believe that profits may have been understated.
>
> The Revenue will be publishing more information about the new rules, to help taxpayers, including a range of leaflets, next April. Staff in local tax offices will also be able to help taxpayers with specific enquiries then.

The three-line accounts, where applicable, enable the taxpayer to avoid submitting details of his income and expenses under the standard accounts information in the self-assessment tax return. It is only necessary to return the turnover, total expenses and net profit.

Advance royalties

In *Taylor v Dawson* (1938) 22 TC 189 a singer was paid an advance of royalties of £1,500 which, somewhat surprisingly, the Commissioners held to be a loan in spite of the wording of the agreement that (p 193) it:

> shall be treated and taken in account as payments by the company on account and in advance of the royalties due under the provisions of this agreement.

The Commissioners were, however, duly overruled by MacNaghten J, who had no hesitation in holding that the construction of the agreement was a question of law. As an advance of royalties the payment was part of the recipient's Schedule D, Case II profits. Advances are not usually returnable and are therefore taxed when received, even if recoupable out of future sales. However, it is understood that the Revenue will, exceptionally, sometimes tax advance recoupable royalties when earned by sales and not when the advance is actually received. A returnable advance may be merely a loan, depending on the terms of the agreement. An advance which requires services to be performed, for example, the production of a recording, would normally become a recoupable non-returnable advance only when the recording is delivered and would be returnable prior to that date if, for example, the recording was never completed, and would be taxed on delivery of the recording, not when the advance was received. See also *Smart v Lincolnshire Sugar Co Ltd* (1937) 20 TC 643.

Investment income

In the case of *Mitchell v Rosay* (1954) 35 TC 496 Madame Rosay acquired the rights to exploit a film which she so did for a percentage of the gross receipts. Although she had herself taken part in the film the profit she made was not part of her professional activities and therefore was not included in any Schedule D, Case II activity. Nor was she trading in the exploitation of films, so that the profit could not be assessed under Schedule D, Case I. The film was exploited by licensing a film distributor for a share of the gross receipts and it was held that these were income assessable under Schedule D, Case III as annual payments. Sir Raymond Evershed MR quoted with approval (at p 504) the following extract from the judgment of Jenkins LJ in *Purchase v Stainer's Executors* (1951) 32 TC 367, 401:

> It is I think reasonably plain that periodical payments in respect of a contractual right to a share in the receipts or profits of the distribution of a film acquired otherwise than in the course of a trade, profession or vocation falling within Cases I or II of Schedule D would be taxable under Case III as falling within the words 'Any . . . annual payment . . . payable either as a charge on any property of the person paying the same . . . or as a personal debt or obligation by virtue of any contract . . .' See *Asher v London Film Productions Ltd* [1944] 1 KB 133.

Angels

Acting as the backer for a film or stage production (usually known as an Angel) can be done as a trading activity giving rise to a Schedule D, Case I assessment. In the absence of a trade, however, the assessment, in practice, is under Schedule D, Case VI as an annual profit or gain not falling under any other case of Schedule D (IM 3155). Assessments were made under Schedule D, Case III until 1972 on the basis of Jenkins LJ's comments in *Purchase v Stainer's Executors* (1951) 32 TC 367, at p 401 (*quoted above*) and *Mitchell v Rosay* (1954) 35 TC 496. This means that tax at the basic rate must be deducted on payments of income in excess of the original investment, to non-residents by companies under TA 1988, s 349 and in appropriate cases by unincorporated payers where the period of investment exceeds 12 months, as annual payments under TA 1988, ss 348, 349. The true Case is still Case III even through, in all other respects, the income is assessed under Schedule D, Case VI. Losses were treated as capital losses for capital gains tax, although Mr Nicholas Ridley on 1 March 1983 (Hansard, Vol 38, Col 101) confirmed that relief would now normally be given by set-off or carry-forward against Case VI income under TA 1988, s 392; he did, however, point out that 'whether relief is due will depend on the particular facts of a case'. No one appears to have objected to the change in Revenue treatment from Case III to Case VI.

The unsuccessful backer of a film in *Lunt v Wellesley* (1945) 27 TC 78 was in business as an artistic film producer and the expenses he incurred, including certain guarantee payments for the film, were deductible from his Schedule D, Case II income.

Compensation

The case of *John Mills Productions Ltd (in liquidation) v Mathias* (1967) 44 TC 441 concerned a company which was in being to exploit the services of the actor John Mills. The company received £50,000 compensation for the cancellation of a contract from J Arthur Rank Productions Ltd and promptly went into liquidation. A new company was formed to exploit Mr Mills' services. It was argued unsuccessfully that the compensation received of £50,000 was capital compensation for the loss of the company's substratum, its main income having previously come from Rank. This contention was rejected and the amount judged liable to tax in the company's hands under Schedule D, Case I.

In *John and Others v James and Others* [1986] STC 352 it was held that damages for breach of duty under a fiduciary relationship between a manager and Elton John, songwriter and performer, should be paid gross without deduction of tax, either UK or foreign, following *Bartlett v Barclays Bank Trust Co Ltd* [1980] Ch 515 and distinguishing *British Transport Commission v Gourley* [1956] AC 185.

Inducement payments

In some cases it may be possible to make a lump-sum payment, tax free, to induce someone to give up their current status. Examples that have been through the courts include a fee to a rugby player to give up amateur status (*Jarrold v Boustead* (1964) 41 TC 701), shares allotted to a chartered accountant for giving up his practice (*Pritchard v Arundale* (1971) 47 TC 680), and a fee paid to a barrister on giving up his profession (*Vaughan-Neil v IRC* [1979] STC 644). An inducement fee to persuade someone to join a club or business, is not, however, tax-free (*Riley v Coglan* (1967) 44 TC 481), nor is a payment to persuade someone to give up an existing employment and take on another (*Glantre Engineering Ltd v Goodhand* [1983] STC 1) even when paid by a person other than the prospective employer (*Shilton v Wilmshurst* [1991] STC 88).

Capital receipts

An entertainer, unlike an author, has a reasonable chance of having a capital receipt, for example, on the sale of film rights acquired as an investment, taxed as a capital gain instead of part of his professional earnings (*Shiner v Lindblom* (1960) 39 TC 367).

Expenses

Self-employed entertainers, like other people carrying on a trade or profession, are entitled to deduct those expenses incurred wholly and exclusively for the purpose of their business under TA 1988, s 74. Duality of purpose will result in a disallowance (*Prince v Mapp* (1969) 46 TC 169; *Murgatroyd v Evans-Jackson* (1966) 43 TC 581; *Norman v Golder* (1944) 26 TC 293; *Caillebotte v Quinn* [1975] STC 265; *Bowden v Russell & Russell* (1965) 42 TC 301), unless the reason for incurring the expense was the business and any private benefit is incidental to the business purpose (*Bentleys, Stokes & Lowless v Beeson* (1952) 33 TC 491; *Edwards v Warmsley, Henshall & Co* (1967) 44 TC 431). In practice, the Revenue will often allow apportionment of expenses where there is a genuine business reason.

Entertaining expenses are specifically disallowed in most cases under TA 1988, s 577.

A list of allowable expenses for an entertainer could include:
Accompanist, session musicians and supporting artistes' fees
Accountancy fees
Agent's fees and commission
Bank interest and charges
Capital allowances on cost of equipment, car, instruments etc.
Chiropody and physiotherapy (for dancers)
Cleaning and repair or replacement of professional clothes and props
Cosmetic surgery/dentistry (part)
Cosmetics
Direct costs
Gratuities
Hairdressing
Hire of rehearsal halls, studio and facilities
Hire of television, video, hi-fi etc
Insurance of clothes, instruments, public liability etc
Laundry and cleaning
Legal fees for contracts, protecting copyright etc
Postage and stationery
Professional coaching
Professional journals
Publicity and photographs
Records and books, scores etc

Repairs and tuning instruments
Research assistance and materials, typing and editorial costs
Royalty audit costs
Secretarial assistance
Subscriptions
Subsistence
Tax compliance fees
Telephone and fax
Theatre, concert or cinema tickets for agent, manager etc
Touring expenses
Travel and car expenses, including taxis and chauffeured cars
Union dues
Use of rooms as office at home (proportion of light, heat, insurance, cleaning, power, decorating etc)
VAT irrecoverable on business expenses
Visits to theatre or cinema

Returns

It should be noted that payments to entertainers have to be notified to the Revenue under TMA 1970, s 16 if a notice is required by an Inspector of Taxes. The usual notice is the return Form 46R1 and includes all payments in respect of copyright (*see* Appendix 4).

Lend-a-Star companies

It is by no means unusual for a performer, or for that matter an actor, composer or artiste, to enter into an agreement with a company whereby he is an employee of the company and draws a salary assessed to tax under Schedule E. The company then carries on a trade of exploiting the services of its employee and the fees, royalties or other lump sums received by the company are part of its income taxed under Schedule D. This sort of arrangement, if properly set up and run, is perfectly effective in the UK, although it tends to be regarded as a sham in some other countries, in particular the USA under its 'Lend-a-Star' provisions. The arrangements may fall within the specific anti-avoidance provisions of TA 1988, s 775 but they can also have other implications, as illustrated in the case of *Crossland v Hawkins* (1961) 39 TC 493. In this case Jack Hawkins was employed by a company the shares of which were owned by trustees of his father-in-law's trust in favour of his (Mr Hawkins') children. When dividends were paid by the company to the trustees and then to the children it was held that the income so distributed was taxable on Mr Hawkins as an additional settlor of the trust. In the words of Pearce LJ at p 507:

> The proposals were clearly proposals for achieving the result that has been achieved, namely, a family settlement financed by dividends produced by Mr Hawkins' contract to sell his services to the company at an inadequate and uncommercial rate. Had the proposals been of any other nature, the Case must inevitably have so stated. The foundation of those proposals was his earning power, and they needed not merely his assent but his active participation. He personally entered into the contract to serve for an inadequate remuneration. He was himself a director of the

company when the shares were allotted to the trustees, when the large profit was made by the company's use of the contract and when the dividend was declared. And above all he himself created the source of the company's profit by acting in the film 'Fortune is a Woman'. The mere fact that he did not concern himself with some of the steps in the legal machinery involved does not make it any the less his arrangement within the Section.

The definition of 'settlement' referred to is in TA 1988, s 670 and includes any disposition, trust, covenant, agreement, arrangement or transfer of assets. As a result of his being a settlor, the income of the child remained that of the parent under TA 1988, s 660B. This case was followed in that of *IRC v Mills* [1974] STC 130, which was very similar to *Crossland v Hawkins*, except that the employee of the company, Miss Hayley Mills, was then aged 14 and the settlor of a trust for her absolute benefit on attaining the age of 25 was her father, John Mills. The House of Lords resisted the contention that a minor was not capable of being a settlor and entering into an arrangement such as would constitute a settlement as defined by TA 1988, s 681(4) (which definition is the same as in TA 1988, s 670 with the omission of the reference to transfer of assets).

An extremely complex case involving the taxation of income of a performer was the case involving Miss Julie Christie, *Black Nominees Ltd v Nicol* [1975] STC 372. This involved an incredibly complex series of transactions whereby Black Nominees Ltd, as trustees for a discretionary trust of which Miss Christie was a beneficiary, obtained large sums ostensibly as repayment of a 'loan' of £475,000. Templeman J was unimpressed by the complexity of the scheme. At p 278:

> Once Cymbeline agreed to purchase the interest of Black Nominees [the taxpayer company] under the first settlement, each participant at the meeting required to receive and pay £475,000, each participant received £475,000 and each participant paid away £475,000. No one began the meeting with £475,000 and no one left the meeting with £475,000 or with any asset remotely near that value. I assume that Knowsley were in a position to lend £475,000 when they arrived, but they departed without leaving any such sum on loan to anyone. In effect, £475,000 passed by Knowsley drafts from Knowsley to Univats to Cymbeline to Black Nominees to Swanlack to Woods to Downer to Univats and back to Knowsley, pursuant to documents which divided the profits from the Christie rights between the financiers and Black Nominees in the proportions of roughly 32 and 1/2 per cent and 67 and 1/2 per cent.

At p 284:

> Tax is charged under Case VI in respect of annual profits or gains not falling under any other Case or under any other Schedule. In my judgment, the moneys received by Black Nominees in consequence of the transactions entered into in December 1965 fit within this description. If it were not the trick with the £475,000, no one would suggest that the moneys received by Black Nominees were capital. Once the trick is exposed the moneys are seen to be what they are: namely, annual profits or gains. They escape any other Case or Schedule and fall into Case VI.

It should be noted that this case was not taken beyond the High Court.

IRS rulings

The Internal Revenue Service in the USA will tax an individual on his net earnings in the USA. The income will normally suffer withholding tax of 30 per cent on the gross receipts and at the end of the year a return is filed and any over-deduction repaid or additional tax paid.

If the individual is the employee of a company in which he has no direct or indirect interest or involvement he will be liable to tax in the USA as an employee and subject to graduated wage withholding taxes.

It is often desirable to ensure that earnings are paid over in a year in which the individual is non-resident in the USA so that only 30 per cent withholding tax is deducted from such earnings.

If, however, an employee is employed by a company in which he has an interest or where the circumstances are such that he is deemed to be self-employed under the 'Lend-a-Star' Rulings 74–330 and 331 he will be taxed in the USA as if he were self-employed, or, if the company is deemed to be a sham, as an employee entitled to the income of the company (*see* Appendix 7). The UK/USA double taxation treaty is no help in such cases, in view of Article 17(2) which specifically allows such treatment. The IRS will deem an employee to be self-employed if:

(1) The company cannot control the time, place and method of providing the services of the employee.

(2) The employee has an exclusive long-term contract with the company.

(3) The employee is furthering the business of the company.

(4) The employee has a right to veto arrangements made by the company.

(5) The company is not responsible for arranging venue, costumes, scripts and supporting services.

(6) The employee's salary is based on net receipts of the company.

(7) The company does not bear the risk of failure or reap the rewards of success.

In such cases the company's income will be subject to withholding tax at 30 per cent.

If the IRS looks through a company as a sham, there are even more unfortunate consequences in the USA in that the tax is withheld from the company at the individual's rates.

From the double taxation point of view, the trouble is that the company is eligible for the foreign tax credit against its UK corporation tax liability. If, however, the company pays most of its income to the employee it is unlikely to have sufficient UK liability to absorb the credit and there is no mechanism whereby the excess credit may be set against the employee's personal tax liability. In other words, the IRS looks through the company but the UK Revenue does not.

It may be preferable nowadays to perform services in a personal capacity as full credit for the American tax deducted will be given. It is often possible to obtain specific rulings from the IRS to limit the withholding tax to the net, rather than the gross, receipts by using an independent American resident company to promote a tour or similar operation in the USA.

Other countries besides the USA have the equivalent of 'Lend-a-Star' Rulings, eg, Germany and France.

This subject can be extremely complex in practice and a full discussion of the problem is outside the scope of this work.

Company partnerships

One final case has to be considered relating to income received by a performer. This is the case of *Newstead v Frost* [1980] STC 123. In this case David Frost entered into a partnership agreement with a Bahamian company, Leander Productions Ltd. The partnership was known as Leander Enterprises. The business of the partnership was to act as television and film consultants and advisers, and amongst other things to use and exploit the services of producers or directors, writers and artistes. David Frost was to participate as to 95 per cent in the profits of the partnership and 99 per cent in the capital assets of the partnership. However, the partnership was to be carried on outside the UK. It was not a sham and actually carried on business from the Bahamas. As a result, the partnership was a non-resident partnership within TA 1988, s 112 and therefore David Frost's share was assessable to tax under Schedule D, Case V. At that time income under Schedule D, Case V was assessable only on the basis of remittances to the UK.

Alternative assessments

It will be seen from the foregoing analysis of the case law that a performing artiste may, in the same way as an author, be taxed under various heads on income arising. The normal assessment would be under Schedule D, Case II as arising from the exercise of a profession or vocation. If these activities arise overseas through a non-resident partnership the assessment is under Schedule D, Case V. If the artiste is an employee of a company which exploits his services the company would be assessed under Schedule D, Case I and the employee under Schedule E. Exceptionally, the income arising may be assessed under Schedule D, Case III if related to the exploitation of copyright held as an investment, or under Schedule D, Case VI if the income cannot be brought within any other head of charge. It is, of course, possible that a capital profit could be made, for example, by someone purchasing film rights for a capital sum to hold as an investment and subsequently selling the entire rights at a profit. Such a profit would be subject to capital gains tax under TCGA 1992, s 21.

Anti-Constellation provisions

An important provision that has to be considered in connection with the taxation of income from intellectual property is TA 1988, s 775 which is headed 'Sale by individual of income derived from his personal activities' (IM 4680–4688).

The section applies where an individual (or, presumably, a number of individuals in partnership) makes arrangements to exploit his earning capacity with a view to mitigating his tax liability and as a result a capital amount is received by the taxpayer or any other person. A capital amount is extremely widely defined by TA 1988, s 777(13) as any amount in money's or money's worth which, apart from the principal sections, does not fall to be included in any computation of income for the purposes of the Taxes Acts (IM 4683 and IM 4684).

The classic situation that the section was aimed at is that of Constellation Investments Ltd, which was a company formed to exploit the services of performers, writers and other individuals of talent. Such people would sell a right to their future income for a capital sum. As a result of TA 1988, s 775(2) any such capital sum would now be assessed to tax as earned income under Schedule D, Case VI. The section is sufficiently widely drawn to cover any form of capital sum received by any party, not necessarily the individual, except for the sale of a business or partnership or shares in a company so far as it is attributable to the business as a going concern, ie, goodwill. The section will therefore catch the traditional situation of, for example, an author who contracts to write for a company in which he owns the shares. If in due course the income not drawn out in the form of remuneration is accumulated in the company and the shares subsequently sold, or the company put into liquidation, the capital amount received could be assessed under TA 1988, s 775. There are provisions to charge capital sums indirectly derived from the individual's activities, for example, in the form of shares, and the section applies to all persons whether resident in the UK or not, provided that the occupation of the individual is carried on wholly or partly in the UK (TA 1988, s 775(9)). Tax must be deducted from a capital sum paid to a non-resident and accounted for to the Revenue under TA 1988, s 349(1) and IM 4685.

There are three requirements which have to be met before the section applies to a person carrying on such personal activities (IM 4681 and 4682).

(1) There must be transactions or arrangements to exploit the earning capacity of an individual in any occupation by putting some other person in a position to enjoy the rewards derived from the individual's activities (TA 1988, s 775(1)(*a*)). 'Individual' almost certainly includes individuals acting together, eg, a pop group. 'Occupation' includes profession or vocation but not a trade, which means that the distinction between Schedule D, Cases I and II becomes of considerable importance for a change. It also includes an office or employment under Schedule E. 'Income' specifically includes any receipts from copyright or any other right deriving its value from the activities, including past activities of the individual, eg, patents obtained by an inventor (TA 1988, s 775(3)).

(2) A capital amount must be obtained for the individual or any other person (TA 1988, s 775(1)(*b*)). 'Capital amount' means any amount which does not fall to be included in any computation of income (TA 1988, s 777(13)). It has been suggested that where income has been diverted, say, to an overseas partnership, it is possible, by making a UK resident a partner for, say, 5 per cent of the profit, to ensure that the whole of the income is included in a computation for UK tax and therefore is not a capital amount, even though 95 per cent is not actually taxed as accruing to the non-resident partner under TA 1988, ss 112 and 115(5), subject to a charge for activities in the UK under TA 1988, s 775(9) as explained above.

It is possible to trace a capital amount from the individual's activities through any number of intermediaries (TA 1988, s 775(5)). Income from a foreign partnership or employment assessed on a non-domiciled individual on a remittance basis under TA 1988, s 65(4) or TA 1988, s 192(2) and TA 1988, ss 19(1), 192(1) is not thought to be within the definition of a capital amount, although the point is not entirely free from doubt.

(3)   Finally, one of the main objects of the transaction or arrangements must be the avoidance or reduction of liability to income tax (TA 1988, s 775(1)(*c*)). This question of motive is hard to prove but if it can be demonstrated that there are good commercial reasons for the arrangements the section should not bite. In deciding motive the powers of a company, partnership or trust are not conclusive (TA 1988, s 777(4)).

Although there have as yet been no cases on TA 1988, s 775, a similar motive test in TA 1988, s 703(1) has been considered in *IRC v Kleinwort, Benson Ltd* (1968) 45 TC 369; *IRC v Brebner* (1967) 43 TC 705; *IRC v Goodwin* [1976] STC 28; and *Clark v IRC* [1978] STC 614. The taxpayers argued that the transactions were in the ordinary course of business, to resist a take-over, to prevent loss of control and to buy a farm, respectively, and all were successful. In *Hasloch v IRC* (1971) 47 TC 50 the court upheld the Special Commissioners' finding of fact that the avoidance of taxation was a main object of the transaction.

Exemptions

The sale of goodwill of a business or of shares in a company which will carry on as a going concern is not caught by the section in view of TA 1988, s 775(4), but the going concern value must not be attributable to the prospective income from the individual's activities for which he will not receive adequate reward in an income form. This would mean that a recording artiste selling a company for a value based on prospective future record royalty income from past records would not be within the exemption, but it might be possible for an employing company to cease the employment, set up a new trade of, say, share or property dealing, with the accumulated income and sell the shares which would reflect the value of the new business as a going concern.

A capital sum received in the form of shares is not taxed until the shares are realised (TA 1988, s 775(5)) so it could be possible to transfer a profession to a company and use the company assets to pay remuneration and pension contributions so that value is extracted before the shares are sold.

There are provisions in TA 1988, s 777(8) enabling the Revenue to recover tax from whoever received the capital sum if the individual assessed is unable to exercise his right of recovery within six months of the payable date. Such sums are not charged to capital gains tax as they are liable to income tax (TA 1988, s 777(12)).

The Revenue has power to obtain information under TA 1988, s 778, which is exercised by the Revenue though the Special Investigations Section, which deals with cases under these provisions (IM 4686–4688).

Non-resident entertainers and sportsmen

An entertainer or sportsman carrying on a relevant activity in the UK, who is not resident in the UK in the tax year in which the activity is performed, is within the provisions of TA 1988, ss 555–558 and the detailed regulations contained in the Income Tax (Entertainers and Sportsmen) Regulations 1987 (SI 1987 No 530).

Such a visiting sportsman or entertainer is liable to have tax at the basic rate deducted from payments made to him including loans or transfers.

An entertainer is defined as an individual who performs whether alone or with others (SI 1987 No 530, reg 2) and includes both live and recorded performances. The Revenue Guidance Notes FEU 50 at para A6 mentions, as examples of entertainers and sportsmen, athletes, golfers, cricketers, footballers, tennis players, boxers, snooker players, motor racing drivers, jockeys, ice skaters, contestants in chess tournaments, pop stars, musicians, conductors, dancers, actors, TV and radio personalities, variety artistes. The person may appear alone or with others in teams, choirs, bands, orchestras, opera companies, ballet companies, troupes, circuses etc. Models are not currently included in the list, but in the age of the 'supermodel' earning large fees it is likely that the Revenue will at some stage seek to argue that they are entertainers in their own right, not merely showing off clothes. Payments for ancillary services on an arm's length basis or in respect of recording royalties are excluded (SI 1987 No 530, reg 3) but the provisions extend to any other activities 'in his character as entertainer' including appearance fees, whether live or recorded. They also extend, in the view of the Revenue, to income from merchandising, although it would seem doubtful whether this can properly be described as income received as an entertainer (SI 1987 No 530, reg 6). There is a *de minimis* provision in that payments of no more than £1,000 may be made without deduction of tax although obviously connected payments have to be aggregated for this purpose (SI 1987 No 530, reg 4).

The entertainer is treated as carrying on a trade in the UK separate from any other activities, assessed on a current year basis with provision for losses and expenses (TA 1988, s 556(1)).

Payments to connected parties such as overseas companies employing the entertainer are treated as if they were made direct to the entertainer (SI 1987 No 530, reg 7) and credit is given to the entertainer for the tax deducted at source (SI 1987 No 530, reg 12).

The person making payments has to make quarterly returns to the Revenue and pay over the tax deducted within 14 days of the end of the quarter (SI 1987 No 530, regs 4 and 10).

Reduced withholding agreements

Where a payment is to be made subject to deduction of tax it is possible for the entertainer or the payer or recipient to apply to the Revenue for a reduced withholding agreement (SI 1987 No 530, reg 5). The purpose of the reduced withholding agreement is to enable account to be taken of expenses which have to be met out of the fees; in order to obtain an agreement it is necessary to supply the Revenue with a detailed budget, preferably before the tour commences, and agree a level of deduction from the gross payments which would equate to the entertainers' correct UK tax liability on the net income after all allowable expenses.

The problem with such a reduced withholding agreement is that it is entirely at the discretion of the Revenue and they are likely to insist that marginal income such as that from merchandising is included, and will look closely at the expenses. It is unlikely in practice to be helpful to argue that the tour is unlikely to make a profit at all, even if that is the case. This suggests that the prime purpose of the tour is to promote the group's recordings, rather than to make money out of the tour itself; as a result the Revenue would disallow the expenses of the tour as not wholly and exclusively related to the tour itself but related to promotional activity for the group's recordings, and therefore disallowable on the duality of purpose reasoning. In practice a good deal of haggling over the tour budget is common; experience suggests that the final result is likely to be reasonable.

Double taxation agreements

Most double taxation agreements have an 'artistes and athletes' article which enables the visiting entertainer to be taxed under the domestic legislation. The Revenue argue that these provisions enable payments made indirectly to the entertainer, for example, to a company employing him, to be treated as made to the entertainer (TA 1988, s 556(2)) and therefore there is no need to rely on what is normally paragraph 2 of a typical 'artistes and athletes' article along the lines of the OECD Model Convention. This means that even if there is not a paragraph 2 equivalent extending to indirect payments, the Revenue argue that the UK provisions treat indirect payments as paid direct to the entertainer and therefore have to be treated for double taxation agreement purposes as if they were paid direct.

Whether this line of argument is correct or whether it is possible to argue that a double taxation agreement with a simple artistes and athletes article, which does not extend to indirect payments, could overrule the UK legislation has yet to be tested.

Benefits and apportionment

Payments in kind have to be valued at the cost to the provider and are then treated as a net amount which is grossed up to arrive at the tax to be deducted at source (SI 1987 No 530, reg 17).

Where a tour covers more than one country it is necessary to apportion expenses which relate to the entire tour to the deemed separate trade in the UK on some basis that is just and reasonable (SI 1987 No 530, reg 16), for example, on the number of days performed in the UK compared with the total number of days performed.

The withholding tax may be set against the finally agreed UK tax liability and repaid where appropriate in accordance with the regulations. The obligation to deduct tax may be affected by the provision of any relevant double taxation agreement.

The relevant activities are treated as part of a trade, profession or vocation exercised within the UK except where it is performed in the course of an office or employment (TA 1988, s 556). A payment made to a third party is treated as made to the entertainer or sportsman if a connection of the prescribed kind exists. Regulations enable credit to be obtained for expenses incurred by the third party and to prevent the third party also being taxed on the same income. The assessment is to be made on a current year basis and regulations provide for losses and expenses. The activities in the UK are treated as a separate trade carried on in the UK (TA 1988, s 557). Payment is regarded as the gross amount before deducting the withholding tax. Detailed valuation rules are made in regulations for payments in kind (TA 1988, s 558). Secrecy obligations will not prevent the Board disclosing information to payers to enable them to operate the withholding tax correctly.

The Foreign Entertainers Unit has been set up to administer the new scheme. The address is: Royal House, 2nd Floor, Prince's Gate, 2–6 Homer Road, Solihull, West Midlands, B91 3WG (tel: 0121 606 2861).

VAT

Where a supply of services consists of cultural, artistic, sporting, scientific, educational or entertainment services, services relating to exhibitions, conferences or meetings and services ancillary to, including those organising any supply related thereto, it is treated as made where the services are physically carried out, ie the country in which the performance takes place (SI 1992 No 3121, art 15(*a*)). This means that if an entertainer or sportsman or a company employing him is likely to be in receipt of a sum in excess of the VAT threshold (£48,000 from 27 November 1996; £49,000 from 1 December 1997) (VATA 1994, Schedule 1, para 1(1)) (SI 1996 No 2950, arts 1 and 2, IRPR 2 July 1997), he will be liable to register for VAT as providing services in the UK. The VAT threshold in the UK is substantially higher than in other European countries and VAT rates in Europe on performance services vary from 6 per cent in Belgium to 25 per cent in Denmark.

Once registered for VAT in the UK the entertainer or his employer should charge VAT at the standard rate of 17.5 per cent and will be able to claim input tax for VAT charged on goods and services received, such as legal and accounting fees.

Example

Skip Skyways, a Dutch resident singer, agrees to appear in the UK for five nights for a fee of £50,000. Skip has to register and submits an invoice for £50,000 plus VAT at 17.5 per cent of £8,750, ie £58,750.

The fact that the entertainer is obliged to charge VAT on his services should cause no real problems in that the recipient of the services of the entertainer (ie the promoter) will almost certainly be VAT registered and be able to recover any VAT charged.

It is possible, however, for the entertainer to shift the obligation to account for VAT to the recipient of his services provided that the recipient is VAT registered (VATA 1994, Sched 5, para 9). In this way VAT registration of the entertainer can be avoided although, by using this method, recovery of VAT on expenses incurred within the UK becomes more difficult. Recovery can still be made but it is necessary to make a separate application to the UK authorities and a repayment is not normally made for at least a period of six months (VATA 1994, s 39; SI 1995 No 2518, regs 173–197). The tax shift alternative is also available in most other European Union countries.

If an entertainer decides to register for VAT in the country where he provides performances, it is normally necessary to appoint a fiscal representative. This can be anyone established in the country of the performance, but that representative will be jointly and severally liable for any VAT debts of the entertainer.

In the UK only, it is possible to register as an 'overseas business' and in this way it is not always necessary to appoint a fiscal representative (VATA 1994, s 48(1)). It is still usually necessary, however, to authorise someone within the UK to complete and sign the VAT return forms on behalf of the entertainer.

Apart from the performer's services, ancillary services provided by the road crew, sound and lighting engineers etc are usually regarded as part of the performance services and take place where the performance is held (SI 1992 No 3121, art 15(*c*)). Services of intermediaries (booking agents/management) are not subject to UK VAT provided that the recipient of the service (eg the performer) is not registered within the UK, but is registered elsewhere in the European Union or has no business establishment anywhere within the European Union (SI 1992 No 3121, art 13).

If the performer does have a registration within the UK any services provided by intermediaries will be subject to UK VAT at the standard rate.

Where a supply consists of a transfer or assignment of copyrights, licences, trade marks and similar rights, the requirement to account for VAT normally falls upon the transferee unless the performer and the transferee are VAT registered in the same country (VATA 1994, Sched 5, para 1). Where no VAT is charged, the transferee is obliged to account for VAT in his own country but can recover that VAT at the same time, subject to normal rules (VATA 1994, s 8(1)).

26   Franchising

Advantage to franchisor

Franchising is an arrangement under which a product or service has been established and the proprietors determine that they are unable to exploit it to its maximum potential on their own. Commonly they lack the capital and expertise to develop the product or service to its maximum potential or there are local considerations such as language, infrastructure or legal requirements which require the involvement of local participation to run the business effectively (IM 2400–2403). The advantage to the franchisor in such an arrangement is that he will maximise the return on the initial development by taking a profit for exploitation in areas where it is not practical to exploit the product or service on his own, and therefore take a profit that would otherwise be unobtainable. It also enables the development to be exploited in a wider area than it would otherwise be possible, and spread marketing and advertising costs over a wide market. Very often the product or service is a way of manufacturing or distributing a product or providing a service which will often involve the exploitation by the franchisee of the franchisor's name and logo, which is likely to qualify for trade mark protection, and the provision of know-how, in its widest sense of knowledge of how the product or service may best be exploited, without necessarily falling within the limited definition of know-how for tax purposes under TA 1988, s 533(7), as explained in Chapter 18. This knowledge may be protected as a secret process and under the laws relating to passing off, as well as under the trade mark provisions, and there may well be written instruction manuals for the guidance of the franchisee which would be protected by copyright. It is quite common for franchising arrangements to include the providing of computer programs for assisting and monitoring the development of the franchisees' businesses.

Where a product is involved it may be protected by patents or registered design or design rights but this is not commonly an important element in a franchising operation.

Advantage to franchisee

The advantage to the franchisee is that the franchising arrangement enables him to cut down the learning curve in running a successful business in that he can move immediately into the provision of a product or service that has an established market in the franchisor's territory, which is likely to be of similar relevance to the franchisee's territory. The franchisee also acquires access to a branded product with an established reputation which can be marketed further for the mutual benefit of both the franchisee and the franchisor.

Disadvantage to franchisor

The disadvantage of franchising for the franchisor is that the ability to expand the business is necessarily curtailed by having to avoid competition with the franchisees, while continuing to exploit and develop the product or service. A further disadvantage is the resources that have to be put into monitoring the franchisees' performance to make sure that the product or service supplied meets the franchisor's standards. Clearly as each franchisee is, for a fee, riding on the back of the franchisor the reputation of both is interdependent and a rogue franchisee could quickly have an adverse impact on the reputation of the franchisor's product or service. It is easy to underestimate the resources required to ensure the proper performance of the franchisee.

It is also possible to have a franchisee who may meet the quality requirements of the franchisor but who still fails to develop the product or service to its full potential in his territory, thus inhibiting the worldwide growth and profit potential for the franchisor.

Disadvantage to franchisee

The main disadvantage as far as the franchisee is concerned is that his time, energy and resources are being put into the development of a product or service in his territory, which is building up the franchisor's reputation and profit potential rather than that of the franchisee. It is not unknown for franchisees to be a lot more successful in their territory than the original franchisor, and feel resentment to the extent that they believe they are now carrying the franchisor, whatever the original arrangement may have been.

Agreements

A well-drafted franchising agreement will often overcome many of the potential disadvantages of franchising and give the franchisor powers to ensure that the franchisee meets the appropriate quality requirements and achieves pre-agreed performance targets, and sets out with clarity the rights and duties of the franchisee and franchisor, which may include a compulsory dispute resolution procedure such as arbitration in the event of disagreement. In the UK, the Chartered Institute of Arbitrators and the British Franchise Association have established rules for a specific arbitration scheme which provides an inexpensive and informal method of resolving disputes between franchisors and franchisees, which the parties cannot resolve amicably between themselves.

Code of conduct

The British Franchise Association also publishes a code of ethical conduct based on the European code of ethics for franchising produced by the European Franchise Federation.

These provide a definition of franchising including the wide definition of know-how as a body of known practical information resulting from experience and testing by the franchisor, which is secret, substantial and identified in the franchise agreement. It is also made clear that franchising takes place between independent organisations and it sets out the rights and duties of both parties, including the franchisor's commitment to continuing commercial and technical assistance.

The guiding principles require the franchisor to have himself operated the business concept, with success, for a reasonable period; to grant rights to use the name and trade mark, and to provide the franchisee with initial training and ongoing commercial and technical assistance throughout the franchise period. The duties of the franchisee are to use his best endeavours to ensure the growth of the franchise business and the maintenance of a common identity and reputation throughout the franchise network, to protect the confidentiality of information supplied by the franchisor and to provide performance and financial information relating to the franchisee's operations. The necessity in a franchise arrangement for fair play between the parties is emphasised.

In recruiting potential franchisees, the franchisor should disclose all material facts and ensure that his advertising is not misleading, subject to a requirement on the potential franchisee to keep secret all confidential information. Franchisees should be chosen who appear to have the financial and management skills necessary for the successful implementation of the franchise.

The franchise agreement should certainly comply with the national laws and international law but also with the code of ethics and the mutual requirement of the franchisee and franchisor to protect and develop the commercial reputation of the franchise network. In the case of cross-border franchising the agreement should be officially translated into the franchisee's own language and copies of the signed agreement should be given to both parties. The agreement should also set out clearly the rights and obligations of the franchisor and the franchisee in respect of the goods and services specified in the franchise agreement. The financial obligations of the franchisee should be set out as should the minimum period of the agreement, which should be sufficient to enable the franchisee to recoup his initial investment. The renewal terms of the agreement, if any, should be identified and the ability of the franchisee to sell or assign the franchise business should be explained together with any pre-emption rights for the franchisor. The franchisor's ownership of the intellectual property and the franchisee's rights to use this during the period of the franchise agreement, and the giving up of those rights on the termination of the agreement, should be clearly laid out in the agreement.

For further information on legal and commercial aspects of franchising, see *Franchising* by Martin Mendelsohm and Robin Bynoe (FT Law & Tax, 1995).

The franchisor's tax position

Analysis of agreement

A franchise agreement may relate to the sale of goods or the provision of services and, in intellectual property terms, may combine the use of a trade mark, trade name and logo, an established market presentation and co-ordinated advertising campaign and business systems procedures which effectively amount to a combination of know-how and show-how. The products themselves may be patented or protected under the registered design or design right provisions and literature will be copyright. As has been explained earlier in this book it might be necessary to analyse payments by the franchisee to the franchisor into their constituent components by reference to the market value of the goods and services provided, in order to apply the appropriate tax rules to the particular elements, as in *Paterson Engineering Co Limited v Duff* (1943) 25 TC 43. In practice the franchise agreement is usually a single, all be it comprehensive, document giving the franchisee a bundle of rights within the franchise territory in which he has the exclusive right to exploit the business (without contravening the Restrictive Trade Practices Act 1976, articles 85 and 86 of the Treaty of Rome 1960 or other non competition legislation). In many cases the payment to the franchisor is incorporated in the agreement for the exclusive supply of products or raw materials and it would be unusual for the Revenue to dissect such a payment to extract the intellectual property element, if any. The franchisor will be carrying on a trade and the receipts will be inflated by the enhanced sales as a result of the franchise agreement. Expenses recharged to the franchisee will also enhance the taxable trading profit of the franchisor. Under the normal accruals basis of accounting, receipts due from the franchisee will be brought into account by the franchisor over the period during which they were earned; any potential under-recovery as a result of the franchisee's inability to pay would be covered by a bad debt provision in the normal way.

Initial lump sums

It is not unusual for a franchise agreement to require the franchisee to make an initial lump sum payment to the franchisor and it has to be considered whether any part of this lump sum is a capital receipt for the sale of goodwill. In most circumstances the case law relating to the sale of know-how for a lump sum will be in point. As explained in Chapter 18, cases such as *Jeffrey v Rolls Royce Ltd* (1962) 4 TC 443; *Musker v English Electric Co Limited* (1964) 41 TC 556; *Coalite and Chemical Products v Treeby* (1971) 48 TC 171; *Thomsons (Carron) Ltd v IRC* (1976) STC 317, *John & E Sturge Ltd v Hessel* (1975) STC 573 suggest that in a majority of cases there is no diminution in the franchisor's goodwill as a result of the franchise agreement, and that any lump sum allocated to the acquisition of the franchisor's goodwill by the franchisee will nonetheless be a trading receipt of the franchisor. The fact that the lump sum is payable by instalments is irrelevant (*British Dyestuffs Corporation (Blackley) Ltd v IRC* (1924) 12 TC 586). Circumstances in which a lump sum payment by the franchisee for goodwill would give rise to a capital receipt, and a chargeable capital gain by the franchisor, taxable under TCGA 1992, s 21, will be limited to those cases where part of the franchisor's existing goodwill is given up in return for the receipt from the franchisee. This could arise if, for example, the franchisee takes over the franchisor's operation in an established territory, as in *Wolf Electric Tools Ltd v Wilson* (1968) 45 TC 326 and *Evans Medical Suppliers Limited v Moriarty* (1957) 37 TC 540 (IM 2401a and 2401b). Initial sums are normally taxable when receivable (IM 2401c).

It is questionable whether a trade mark or brand name disposed of without the underlying business is a disposal of a separate asset, for which roll-over relief is not available under TCGA 1992, s 155, or is a partial disposal of goodwill. CG 68131 merely suggests that such cases should be referred to CGT (Solihull).

Amortisation

Where the franchisor has acquired goodwill by purchase, the cost is normally a capital asset in respect of which no capital allowances are available. It may be that on closer inspection the acquisition relates not so much to goodwill but to the acquisition of intellectual property rights and if so, the ability of the franchisor to amortise the cost for tax purposes will depend on the rights acquired, and is considered under the various chapters related to those rights.

Restrictive covenants

Where, as is common, the franchisee acquires the rights to exploit the product or service within a particular territory this is often accompanied by a covenant from the franchisor not to compete within that territory. If any lump sum is attached to this covenant on a proper analysis of the franchise agreement, it has to be considered whether the amount received for such a keep-out covenant is capital or income. In many cases a covenant of this nature will be a capital receipt following a number of cases discussed in Chapter 16 relating to lump sum receipts from patents, such as *IRC v British Salmson Aero-engines Ltd* (1938) 22 TC 29; *Murray v Imperial Chemical Industries Ltd* (1967) 44 TC 175; *Kirby v Thorn EMI Plc* (1987) STC 621 and *Margerison v Tyresoles Ltd* (1942) 25 TC 59; *Higgs v Olivier* (1952) 33 TC 136.

The Revenue view on restrictive covenants is that if it leads to the complete cessation of the trade, money received is likely to be capital in character. Where the trade is merely interfered with, for instance where only part of a trade ceases, then the receipt is more likely to be revenue (CG 68161) although it may depend on the facts of a particular case.

A restrictive covenant given in connection with a disposal of know-how as defined for tax purposes by TA 1988, s 533(7), is treated as a trading receipt under TA 1988, s 531(8) (*see* p 213).

A keep-out covenant in these circumstances is effectively a capital receipt as a part disposal of goodwill, as was made plain in *Kirby v Thorn EMI Plc* (1987) STC 621 and, as such, taxable as a capital gain either as a part disposal of goodwill under TCGA 1992, s 21 or as a capital sum derived from goodwill under TCGA 1992, s 22 (CG 68200–68204).

Know-how

As explained in Chapter 18, know-how is defined for tax purposes by TA 1988, s 533(7) as being limited to any industrial information and techniques likely to assist in the manufacture or processing of goods or materials etc, which is a much narrower definition than that usually thought of in terms of franchising agreements. Where know-how is within this definition, a sale by the franchisor is treated by TA 1988, s 531(1) as a trading receipt except to the extent that it is the sale of know-how previously purchased and treated as a disposal under TA 1988, s 530(5), or is sold together with the goodwill of the trade, or part of the trade and taxed as a capital sum under TA 1988, s 531(2), in which case it would be taxable as a chargeable gain on the franchisor under TCGA 1992, s 21. A restrictive covenant relating to such know-how would normally be taxed as income under TA 1988, s 531(8) as explained above. Also as explained above, and in Chapter 18, the sale of know-how, not statutorily treated as a capital receipt under TA 1988, s 531 is nonetheless a trading receipt on the grounds that the transfer of the know-how to the franchisee does not of itself reduce the capital base of the franchisor.

Show-how

Show-how is the term often applied in the franchising context to fees received for training the franchisee's staff in the operation of the franchise, and the provision of on-going training and updating of the franchisee's staff. As such this will normally be a trading receipt of the franchisor. It is difficult to envisage a receipt of show-how fees which would be a capital receipt for the franchisor.

Advertising pools

Some franchise agreements provide for a levy on turnover from franchisees to be spent on advertising the product or services covered by the agreement, for the benefit of the franchisor and all the franchisees. The receipt of advertising fees of this nature will normally be a trading receipt of the franchisor and the expenditure an allowable trading expense of the franchisor. The accruals matching concepts of generally accepted accounting practice will normally ensure that the fees received from the franchisees will be matched with the advertising expenditure incurred by the franchisor, even when there is a timing difference between the receipt of the income and the incurring of the expenditure, for example where there are periodic advertising campaigns. See for example *Threlfall v Jones, Gallagher v Jones* (1993) STC 537; *Odeon Associated Theatres Ltd v Jones* (1971) 48 TC 257; Inland Revenue *Tax Bulletin*, February 1995, pp 189–93, *Johnston v Britannia Airways Ltd* (1994) STC 763; *Owen v Southern Railway of Peru Ltd* (1956) 36 TC 602; *IRC v Titaghur Jute Factory Ltd* (1978) STC 166 and *Commissioner of Inland Revenue v Lo & Lo* (1984) STC 366.

A mere provision for future advertising expenses that might be incurred would be insufficient to allow the franchisor an immediate deduction (*Clayton v Newcastle-under-Lyme Corporation* (1888) 2 TC 416; *Edward Collins & Sons Ltd v IRC* (1924) 12 TC 773; *Peter Merchant Ltd v Stedeford* (1948) 30 TC 496).

Royalties

The amounts which a franchisee has to pay a franchisor under the franchise agreement are normally calculated by reference to a percentage of the franchisee's sales either in monetary terms or on the basis of a levy per unit sold. In some cases the agreement requires the franchisee to purchase raw materials from the franchisor. In some cases the franchise agreement requires the franchisee to make payments for specific services, such as staff training and advertising, or contribute to the cost of the franchisor's policing of the franchise operation.

In all cases, ongoing receipts of this nature are likely to be trading profits of the franchisor in return for goods or services supplied. It may, however, be the case that the franchisor includes in the agreement intellectual property rights, the fees of which amount to pure income profit, with the result that the franchisee is making an annual payment relieved as a charge on income, as explained in Chapters 9 and 10.

In such cases the franchisee should withhold tax at the basic rate from the amount paid to the franchisor, who will treat the income as having suffered tax at source. It will normally still be trading income of the franchisor except in the very rare cases where the franchisor does not himself carry on a trade.

Where the franchise agreement includes a licence to the franchisee allowing him to utilise the franchisor's intellectual property, protected by a UK patent, TA 1988, s 348(2)(e) and 349(1)(e) provide that the patent royalty is, in all cases, an annual payment from which the franchisee has to deduct tax. As this will normally only be a small element of the franchise fee, the franchise agreement may itself specify a reasonable element of the total fee which relates to the patent licence, which will be treated as an annual payment, with the balance being related to the other services provided by the franchisor and paid in full without deduction of tax.

A franchisee has to deduct tax from royalties under the franchise agreement where they relate to copyright and the franchisor's usual place of abode is outside the UK, under TA 1988, s 536 as explained in Chapter 17, p 202. Where the franchise agreement provides for trade mark or know-how royalties, there is no withholding tax requirement on such income.

This book is only concerned with the taxation of a UK resident franchisor, as the rules applicable to a non-resident franchisor will depend on those of the country of residence. Where, however, a UK franchisor licenses a non-UK resident franchisee, the local law may require the franchisee to deduct withholding tax from fees paid to the UK resident franchisor if not exempt under a double taxation treaty, in respect of which he will normally be able to claim double taxation relief against the UK tax due on the franchise income, either under an appropriate double taxation treaty entered into under TA 1988, s 788 or by way of unilateral relief under TA 1988, s 790.

There can be a problem arising from the UK treatment of double taxation relief on a source by source basis, where foreign rates of withholding tax are relatively high and there are substantial expenses incurred in the UK in relation to the franchise income, so that the UK tax on the profit is less than the foreign tax suffered. *Yates v GCA International* (1991) STC 157, as explained by SP7/91, means that the foreign tax paid in excess of UK tax due on the franchisor's franchise income cannot be relieved, and can therefore only be claimed as an expense under TA 1988, s 811.

Whether the franchise fees are treated as royalties subject to withholding tax, when paid by the franchisee, will depend on the local rules in the franchisee's country and may be substantially different from the UK rules requiring deduction of tax at source. In particular, in certain countries, the definition of royalty subject to withholding tax includes service charges, which would normally be regarded as a fee for services rendered and outside the scope of any definition of royalties. Where the franchisee is non-resident it is very important to ensure that the franchise agreement recognises the franchisee's liability to withhold tax at source on some or all of the franchise fee payments, and this has to be taken into account both in the agreement itself, in requiring the franchisee to obtain confirmation of tax withheld to substantiate a claim for the tax so deducted to be relieved as a credit or expense by the franchisor in the UK, and commercially to ensure that the franchise agreement leaves the franchisor with sufficient profit, after taking into account both UK and foreign tax, to make the operation worthwhile.

Most of the expenses incurred by the franchisor in connection with the franchising operations will be incurred wholly and exclusively for the purpose of the franchising trade and deductible for tax purposes under TA 1988, s 74, unless the expenditure relates to a capital asset such as goodwill, on which no relief is available, or plant and machinery, industrial buildings, agricultural buildings, hotels or buildings in an enterprise zone for which capital allowances may be available, as explained in Chapters 9 and 10. Where the franchisor's expenditure is on the acquisition of intellectual property rights, relief for the acquisition may be available (as explained in Part 3).

Turn-key operations

In some cases the franchisor, either alone or in conjunction with the franchisee, will identify suitable premises for the franchisee's operations and fit these out with the appropriate decoration, trade marks, signs, equipment and whatever else is necessary for the franchisee to commence business, in return for a fee. This fee would normally be part of the franchisor's trading income and the expenses incurred, allowable expenses of the franchisor's trade. It is unlikely that the franchisor would be regarded as carrying on a separate trade of fitting out premises for franchisees and it will be all part of the franchisor's normal trade. In some cases, however, the franchisor will retain ownership of the premises and/or some or all of the equipment, and recharge these to the franchisee by way of a rent which, may be an exclusive rent or a rent for premises, and operating or finance leases on the equipment. In these cases the premises will remain an asset of the franchisor, and the rent from the premises will be Schedule A property income, while the rent for the use of equipment will be trading income. The franchisor will claim any capital allowances available on the premises or equipment and these will no doubt be reflected in the rental charge to the franchisee. Whether the rental of the equipment will constitute a separate leasing trade carried on by the franchisor or will be subsumed within the franchisor's general trade, will depend on the circumstances. The taxation of this income and the allowances available are explained generally in Chapters 9 and 10.

The franchisee's tax position

In many cases the franchisee's taxation treatment will mirror that of the franchisor, but this is not necessarily the case. Normally the purchase of goods and services from the franchisor will be wholly and exclusively for the purpose of the franchisee's trade and allowable under TA 1988, s 74. However, merely because the payment is treated as a trading receipt of the franchisor does not automatically mean that it is a revenue expense of the franchisee.

Initial payment

It is common in franchise arrangements for the franchisee to be charged an initial sum. In order to determine whether an initial payment is capital or revenue, so far as the franchisee is concerned, it is necessary to consider whether it is in connection with the fixed capital of the business, in which case it is not an allowable revenue deduction (*Beauchamp v FW Woolworth Plc* (1989) STC 510) or whether it relates to circulating capital and is therefore *prima facie* a revenue expense (*Pattison v Marine Midland Ltd* (1984) STC 10). Although it may be fairly obvious, for example the acquisition of premises or plant and machinery from the franchisor is fixed rather than circulating capital, it is not necessarily clear whether the payment for the initial training of the franchisee and its staff, or the right to become a franchisee and use the franchisor's expertise and trade marks for which further fees will be paid, is a payment on capital or revenue account. One of the leading judgments is that of Viscount Cave in *Atherton v British Insulated and Helsby Cables Ltd* (1925) 10 TC 155, in which he decided that expenditure is normally capital if 'made not only once for all but with a view to bringing into existence an asset or advantage for the enduring benefit of the trade'. This is, however, rather more than acquiring the ability to commence or remain in business (*Lawson v Johnson Matthey plc* (1992) STC 466). The expenditure has to be wholly and exclusively for the purpose of the franchisee's trade, which can give rise to problems where the trade will be carried on through a group of associated companies (*Garforth v Tankard Carpets Ltd* (1980) STC 251) although it might be possible to argue that the company incurring the expenditure is doing so wholly and exclusively for its own trade and any benefit to a fellow subsidiary or associated company is incidental (*Vodaphone Cellular Ltd and others v Shaw* (1997) STC 734).

Strick v Regent Oil Co Ltd (1965) 43 TC 1, provides a useful review of the distinction between a revenue and capital expense. In this case the observation of Lord Dunedin in *Vallanbrosa Rubber Co Ltd v Farmer* (1910) 5 TC 529 was quoted with the approval: 'It is not a bad criterion of what is capital expenditure and what is income expenditure to say that capital expenditure is a thing that is going to be spent once and for all and income expenditure is a thing that it is going to recur every year'. Also considered were Dixon J's comments in *Sun Newspapers Ltd v Federal Commissioner of Taxation* (1938) 61 CLR 337, 359 (Australia): 'the distinction between expenditure and out-goings on revenue account and capital account corresponds with the distinction between the business entity, structure or organisation set up or established for the earning of profit and the process by which such an organisation operates to obtain regular returns by means of regular outlay. The difference between the outlay and returns representing profit or loss'. Lord Rhead stated at p 31:

> when one comes to intangible assets there is much more difficulty. To help the conduct of his business a trader obtains a right to do something on someone else's property or an obligation by someone to do, or refrain from doing, something or makes a contract which affects the way in which he conducts his business, or the right or obligation or the effect of the contract may endure for a short or a long period of years. The question then arises whether the sum which he has paid for that advantage is a capital or revenue expense. As long ago as 1914 it was settled in *Usher's Wiltshire Brewery Ltd v Bruce* (1915) 6 TC 399 that in determining profit, a deduction is to be made or not to be made according, as it is or is not, on the facts of the case a proper debit item

to be charged against in-comings of the trade when computing the balance of profits of it . . . One reason at least for refusing to allow a lump sum payment as a debit against in-comings and therefore treating it as a capital outlay is that to allow it as a debit would distort the profit and loss account. Counsel agreed that a taxpayer is always permitted to bring the whole of any item of revenue expenditure into the profit and loss account of the year in which the money was spent. The Counsel for the Crown suggested that the taxpayer might be permitted to spread it over more than one year but certainly the Revenue cannot insist on that. So if the whole of a payment made to cover several years is brought into one year's account the profit for that year will be unduly diminished.

Lord Morris of Borth-y-Gest stated at p 45:

I consider that a tie of the kind now being examined is a capital asset. If a lump sum is paid for such a tie for five years (or for a lesser number of years) it would give a false and unreal picture if the whole sum were debited to the profit and loss account for the first year or for the year in which the payment was made. If it is said to be hard that no part of the lump sum can be a debit in the profit and loss account that is merely to voice a regret that there is no statutory provision which enables periodic allowances to be made. That, however, is not a matter for the Courts.

If regard is had to the language of metaphor which is found in some of the cases, a tie would seem to appertain to the structure of the selling organisation or income earning machine of the appellant. If it is argued that a tie for a shorter period than a year may seem to possess the same nature as a tie for a longer period, I think that it can be said that a tie for a period of less than a year (being a right which, so to speak, evaporates within the year) is so closely linked with the selling operations during the year that it becomes different in nature and does not qualify to attain 'the dignity of a capital asset'. See *Henriksen v Grafton Hotel Ltd* (1942) 24 TC 453. In that case it was held that payments in respect of the monopoly value payable upon the grant of a licence for a period of three years were of a capital nature. Du Parq LJ said that 'the right to trade for three years as a Licensed Victualler must be regarded as attaining the dignity of a capital asset'.

It may be worth noting that Lord Upjohn at p 51 stated 'I only desire to say that I regard the decision in *Henriksen v Grafton Hotel Limited* (1942) 24 TC 453 as a very special case, a decision which, if it can be supported at all, can be justified solely upon its own particular facts within the realm of licensing laws'.

Lord Morris also stated at p 42:

in the *Nchanga* Case (*Commissioner of Taxes v Nchanga Consolidated Copper Mines Ltd* [1964] AC 948) Lord Radcliffe at page 960 said that 'Courts have stressed the importance of observing a demarcation between the cost of creating, acquiring or enlarging the permanent (which does not mean perpetual) structure of which the income is to be the produce or fruit, and the cost of earning that income or performing the income earning operations'.

In *Robert Addie & Sons Collieries Ltd v CIR* (1924) 8 TC 671 at p 676, Lord President Clyde posed the question, 'are the sums in question part of the trader's working expenses, are they expenditure laid out as part of the process of profit earning, or, on the other hand, [are they] capital outlays, [are they] expenditure necessary for the acquisition of property or of rights or a permanent character, the possession of which is a condition of carrying on the trade at all?' Lord Morris also quoted with approval Lord President Clyde in *IRC v Coia* (1959) 38 TC 334 at 339, in a case involving a garage proprietor receiving a money payment for a tie with a petrol company, in which he stated that it was capital 'as a consideration for giving up his freedom of trading and changing the structure of this part of his business'. He also quoted Lord Patrick, p 339, 'he parted with what I regard as a valuable asset of a capital nature, the right to obtain the supplies of fuel oils which were his stock-in-trade from such sources as he might consider most suited to the varying nature of the demands made by his customers'. Lord Macintosh at p 340 said that the tie plainly 'affected the overall structure of Mr Coia's garage business. He became henceforth for a ten-year period tied to the Esso Petroleum Co for all his supplies instead of being at liberty from 1953 onwards to buy and sell all the particular brands of motor fuel which were then on the market'.

In *Tucker (HMIT) v Granada Motorway Services Limited* (1977) STC 353, the House of Lords held as capital, expenditure incurred by Granada for a variation of its lease which, though non-assignable and hence having no balance sheet value, was valuable to its trade, and hence a capital asset. The expenditure was designed to make the lease more advantageous and was therefore undoubtedly a payment of a capital nature.

As will be apparent from these comments, under many franchise agreements it is possible for the Revenue to argue that an initial payment which brings the franchise into being is capital expenditure by the franchisee and not deductible for tax and not falling within any of the classes of assets for which capital allowances are available (IM 2402a).

CG68103 argues that although a franchise is an asset for capital gains tax purposes, being property within the meaning of TCGA 1992, s 21(1) it is not regarded as goodwill and therefore not within any of the classes qualifying for roll-over relief under TCGA 1992, s 155.

The Revenue in CG68105–68107 argue that in the case of a franchise the only form of goodwill that can be increased by the franchisee's efforts is his personal goodwill which is not capable of sale as any improvement to the goodwill of the franchise accrues to the benefit of the franchisor. Therefore any disposal of the franchise is a disposal of the franchise itself not a disposal of goodwill and therefore roll-over relief is not available. A dealership however may, unlike a franchise, develop free goodwill which is capable of sale as such (CG68108). CG68109 quotes *IRC v Earl Fitzwilliam* [1913] 2 KB 593 'as authority for the concept that it is the franchise and not the goodwill that has value'.

Deferred revenue expenditure

It may be possible to argue on the correct analysis of the agreement that expenditure is actually incurred for the purposes of the trade and if the proper accounting treatment is to write off the expenditure either immediately or over a period of years as deferred revenue expenditure, there seems no reason to deny relief for the expenditure as a trading expense of the franchisee merely because it is paid in a lump sum up front (IM 2402b). The matter will probably be put beyond doubt by the franchise agreement providing that any initial payment is for specified revenue services such as training or a non-returnable recoupable advance of franchise fees that will become payable under the agreement once the business commences. This can of course be reflected commercially in the franchise fees agreed.

The question of deferred revenue expenditure is a difficult one. As quoted above, *Strick v Regent Oil Co Ltd* (1965) 43 TC 1, itself refers with approval to the concept of writing off expenditure to profit and loss account over a period of years and if this is consistent with proper accounting principles the tax treatment should follow, on the basis of cases such as *Johnston v Britannia Airways Ltd* (1994) STC 763. The accounting treatment is not, however, conclusive (*EEC Quarries Ltd v Watkis* [1975] STC 175). The fact that Revenue accept the concept of deferred revenue expenditure is confirmed by the now obsolete Statement of Practice on expenditure on producing films and similar assets, SP9/79. This was also applied to computer software in an Inland Revenue Technical Division letter dated 18 November 1980, referred to on pp 557–560 (IM 663b and d) and applies to video tapes for rental in certain cases under *Tax Bulletin*, Issue 19, October 1995, p 249.

If it has to be accepted that part of the initial expenditure relates to capital assets, it is worth considering whether any of the expenditure could qualify as plant, (as discussed under the purchase of copyright, Chapter 17, p 206) to the extent that the initial sum includes a licence for a patent or know-how as restrictively defined for tax purposes by TA 988, s 533(7). Relief for capital expenditure may be available as explained in Chapter 15 on Patents and Chapter 18 on Know-how. There is, however, no corresponding deduction for capital expenditure on the right to use trade marks on copyright material (IM 2402c and 2402d).

CG68101 suggests that the initial payment by the franchisee is normally a capital expense, even though it would normally be a revenue receipt in the hands of the franchisor.

In setting out the contention that the initial fee payable by the franchisee is generally a capital sum the Inland Revenue *Manual* at IM 2402a refers to *Atherton v British Insulated Helsby Cables Ltd* (1925) 10 TC 155, *IRC v Granite City Steamship* (1927) 13 TC 1 and *S Ltd v O'Sullivan* (1972) TL (i) 108. However, IM 2402b recognises that an apportionment of the initial fee may be appropriate dependent on the facts; for example, the agreement may show that the franchisor charged a specific part of the initial fee for a revenue service such as the training of staff (other than the franchisee) and if the charge is justifiable in relation to the actual services provided then apportionment may be appropriate. If, however, the agreement terms are such that no part of the initial lump sum fee is specifically attributed to revenue items, then inspectors should critically examine claims for apportionment. In practice apportionments for which franchisees contend may be made without reference to the franchisor and may be difficult to justify in relation to the services provided. For instance, some franchisors are unwilling to negotiate special terms with individual franchisees and the same lump sum is payable irrespective of the actual services required from the franchisor; for example, the number of staff needing training may be irrelevant. The facts may also show that no part of the initial lump sum fees can be attributed to services of a revenue nature provided by the franchisor because such services are separately charged for in the annual fees.

Where the initial fee is accepted as capital, IM 2402c notes that the trader may seek capital allowances under TA 1988, s 530(2): such claims are not generally acceptable. Agreements vary but typically the franchise fee will be for items which do not satisfy the statutory definition of know-how in TA 1988, s 533(7), although IM 2402b acknowledges that if the franchisee can demonstrate that a reasonable part of the total payment was for the acquisition of industrial know-how then a just and reasonable part apportionment should be negotiated (see also *Tax Bulletin*, 17 June 1995).

Advertising contributions

Where the franchise agreement requires the franchisee to contribute specifically to advertising expenditure incurred, or to be incurred, by the franchisor this should be allowable as a trading expense for the franchisee, being wholly and exclusively incurred for the purpose of the franchisee's trade.

Occasionally the advertising pool will be set up in the form of a trust for the benefit of the franchisees but this could lead to complications and is to be avoided if possible. The accounting treatment will probably be to write off payments to the trust fund when made or accrued over a period when the advertising campaign takes place and is therefore properly regarded as expenditure wholly and exclusively for the purpose of trade. However, it is arguable that the payment is a settlement on the trustees and arguably not expenditure on advertising itself, and therefore not expenditure for the purposes of the trade. The position is best avoided by having the advertising pool under the control of the franchisor with a provision for a refund to the franchisees, if the advertising pool is not expended within an agreed period. In this case any payment to the pool should be an allowable expense when payable and any recovery from the pool a trading receipt of the franchisee when received.

Pre-trading expenditure

In many cases the franchisee will incur the initial expenditure in setting up the franchise and making the arrangements to trade before the trading actually commences, which would be when the services are first provided, or sales take place (*Birmingham and District Cattle By-Products Co Ltd v IRC* (1919) 12 TC 92). In practice this is not a problem because relief for pre-trading expenditure given by TA 1988, s 401 provides that expenditure incurred within the seven years prior to commencement of trade is treated as incurred on the day the trade actually commences.

VAT

There is no direct reference to franchising in the Value Added Tax Acts and the normal VAT rules apply, as explained in Chapter 11. The only cases that appear to have arisen in connection with franchising involve the supply of instruction manuals by the franchisor to the franchisee and whether these can be zero rated as books rather than standard rated. In the *Franchise Development Services Ltd* case (LON/95/2530A July 1996 (14295)) it was held that the franchisor was providing a composite service with a single charge and the instruction manuals and other printed materials did not qualify for zero rating. This was contrasted with the case of *Force One Training Ltd* (LON/95/1594A October 1995 (13619)) where it was held that a company providing instruction was making a separate supply of the course material, which qualified for zero rating.

Franchise fees will normally follow the general rule that what is not a supply of goods is a supply of services.

International considerations

Where the franchisor is not based in the UK, it is necessary to decide whether the franchisor's activities take place entirely outside the UK, in which case there will be no exposure to UK tax, or whether activities which do take place in the UK are limited to visits by the franchisor's personnel to the UK-resident franchisees, where the franchisor would not normally be liable to UK tax unless there was a permanent establishment in the UK, provided that the franchisor was resident in a country where there is a double taxation treaty with the UK. This is considered in more detail in Chapter 22 (International tax planning). If the franchisor does have a branch or subsidiary company in the UK this would be subject to UK tax on its profits and this may involve transfer pricing considerations when considering how much of the franchisor's overall profit arises in the UK (*see* Chapter 13).

Similarly a UK franchisor with overseas franchisees may operate through a branch or subsidiary in overseas jurisdictions to supervise the franchisees, and thereby become liable to overseas taxation, and will have to consider the international tax planning points mentioned in Chapter 22 as well as transfer pricing (Chapter 13) and the controlled foreign companies legislation (Chapter 14). The other main problem arising from cross-border franchising, which has already been mentioned in this chapter and is further discussed in Chapter 22, is the question of withholding taxes and how these may be relieved.

27 Computer software

Introduction

The widespread and rapid development of computer technology has not in general been matched by legislation designed to deal with the taxation of payments generated by the exploitation of computer software. In the UK, the Capital Allowances Act 1990 contains provisions for capital allowances relating to capital expenditure on computer software (*see* p 343 *below*), but there is no precise definition of the term 'computer software' which generally has two related but separate meanings. It can refer simply to the programs that allow computers to operate in the desired way but it can also refer to the program and the accompanying instruction manuals and other materials necessary to make full use of the program. The program itself will be provided to the user in an 'object code' which the computer recognises but it will have been written in a 'source code' which will usually be retained by the owner of the software. The user of the software will thus have to revert to the owner to sort out any problems or develop the program further, as it is usually impossible to deduce the source code from the object code in any useful way. The licensing agreement could well in any event prohibit interference by the user.

There is also some blurring of the distinction between the terms 'software' and 'hardware'. 'Hardware' generally includes the physical parts of the computer system such as the monitor, the computer itself, the disk drive and so on, but some software is permanently stored in the computer circuits or in the CD-ROM.

As the user does not usually 'buy' the software but simply obtains a licence to use it, it is important to separate ownership of the floppy disk, CO-ROM etc on which the program is recorded from the rights in the program itself.

Multimedia

The term 'multimedia' is usually used to describe a product consisting of audio, textual, photographic and moving picture images, often supplied on CD-ROM. From a taxation point of view such products are often based on a series of licences and can be broken down into their constituent parts in order to consider their treatment as capital, revenue, expenditure, royalties or business expenses.

The Internet

Fiscal authorities face a severe problem in the tracking of payments made by credit card for software directly downloaded over the Internet. Although the purchaser might not have great security for his purchase, he can sample software and other media packages, then pay for the full version by credit card. The purchaser may not even be aware of the origin of the software to which he is acquiring a licence. It has been suggested that fiscal authorities will eventually be forced to concede defeat and recognise that tax cannot be recovered where the vendor has no permanent establishment.

The Internet can also be used to order physical goods or services, and the supplier is likely to have a tax liability at the base from which such goods or services are supplied.

Acquisition for distribution

A person acquiring software to sell on as a distributor or retailer will usually obtain a licence to do so from the software owner, who might be the original developer or someone to whom the developer has sold the intellectual property rights over the software. The retailer will make payments, usually described as royalties or licence payments, to the owner. There could be an initial lump sum which might or might not be set off against future payments. The Inland Revenue's *Tax Bulletin* of November 1993 sets out their approach to the treatment of expenditure on computer software in general and in particular whether payments are capital or revenue. The payment of regular amounts by a distributor for the licence to distribute will undoubtedly be classified as revenue. Where a significant initial lump sum is payable by a distributor to the owner, the cost should be written off on a prudent basis over the likely period of its recovery. The payment cannot be treated as a capital asset but as deferred revenue expenditure (*see* p 343 *below*).

Exploitation for own use

The user of software might make an initial payment for his own use of the software in the first year and further annual payments to include maintenance and support in subsequent years, or in the case of packaged software he might make a single payment to a retailer for the licence and a maintenance contract. The *Tax Bulletin* of November 1993 stresses that payments akin to rental are categorised as revenue. Correct accounting practice will determine the time of the deduction.

If a lump sum has been paid, it is necessary to look how the software is used in the trade of the licensee. Generally speaking, the Revenue will accept revenue treatment where software is expected to have a useful life of less than two years. Correct accounting procedure will again determine the timing of the deduction.

The Revenue could argue that, where the software will be a tool of the taxpayer's trade for several years, the initial payment, if significant, should be treated as capital. A software product, however, generally requires regular updating in order not to become obsolete. That being so, it is reasonable to argue that it is more prudent to meet the initial payment as revenue, again taking the deduction on the basis of the accounting treatment. If the purchase of the software is a major expense, however, the Revenue might insist on its being treated as capital, unless the user 'trades up to new versions at intervals which are short enough to give a particular version only a transitory value to that business' (IM 663b).

Capital allowances

If capital treatment is appropriate for expenditure on computer software, the position in the UK regarding capital allowances is dealt with by CAA 1990, s 67A which has effect from 10 March 1992. Before that date there was doubt as to whether or not capital allowances were available to software licensees. Under s 67A, the licensee's software expenditure is now treated as plant or machinery belonging to him.

A short-life asset election under CAA 1990, s 37 can accelerate allowances where the software is scrapped or destroyed before the fourth anniversary of the end of the chargeable period in which it was acquired. This also applies in the unlikely circumstances of a sale of the rights to the software within four years.

Revenue expenditure

Where expenditure is treated as revenue, the accounting treatment is central to the timing of relief. Where payments are made overseas from the UK this is of particular importance to determine whether or not tax should be deducted at source but it is also important for the manner and timing of the deduction against taxable profits. Payments for computer software will in almost all circumstances be treated as usual expenses of the trade rather than as 'annual payments'. 'Annual payments' are, generally speaking, amounts due under legally enforceable agreements representing 'pure income profit' in the hands of the recipient. 'Pure income profit' is profit which is not in return for any other consideration from the recipient.

Royalties

The conclusions of the 1992 OECD report on the tax treatment of software ('Model Tax Convention: Four Related Studies: The Tax Treatment of Software', *Issues in International Taxation*, No 4) appear to have been accepted for all practical purposes by the Inland Revenue with regard to payments for software made in the UK. The report favours limitation of the term 'royalty' to circumstances where there is a limited grant of rights (not amounting to a change in ownership) for the commercial development or exploitation of software. In particular, payments for software for personal or business use and payments for the alienation of all rights attached to software do *not* represent royalties. If, however, an original owner receives payment quantified by user where a third party has developed the software, that payment will usually be given royalty treatment. Where royalty treatment is applicable, UK withholding tax may have to be deducted as copyright royalties to an owner whose usual place of abode is abroad, under TA 1988, s 536, subject to any double taxation treaty relief (*see* p 202 *above*).

Withholding tax

Income payable from overseas to the UK for the use of software is often subject to a significant level of withholding tax which may well exceed the UK tax against which it can be credited. There are various strategies for minimising levels of withholding tax.

If the creation of a permanent establishment in the country producing the income can be avoided and there is a bilateral tax treaty in place, business profits will not be taxed in that country. Article 4 of the OECD Model Treaty sets out in detail the factors which determine whether or not there is a permanent establishment. If there is no treaty in place, local law will have to be considered.

If a permanent establishment cannot be avoided, items that are tax-deductible can be maximised within the limitation imposed by the OECD Model Treaty that the permanent establishment's profits must be calculated on an arm's length basis (*see* p 345 *below*).

If the licence fee is paid direct by an overseas user to an owner in the UK, the local jurisdiction could impose withholding tax. In these circumstances, the precise nature of the payment and any treaty protection available have to be studied. Under the OECD Model Treaty, licence fees for software will usually be treated as commercial income (not royalties—*see* above) and will not usually be subject to withholding tax, but not all countries follow the OECD model. If a particular country does treat licence fees as a royalty and thus subject to withholding tax, consideration can be given to allocation of part of the overall payment to maintenance and support, which would escape withholding tax.

'Treaty shopping'

Many jurisdictions, the USA especially, are taking measures to ensure that bilateral treaties established with other states are not used as stepping stones to create treaty protection where there is no direct treaty between the jurisdiction of the user and that of the owner. 'Treaty shopping' and the use of conduit companies is thus becoming more difficult and may be less likely to provide the answer to the problem than previously, although there is still considerable scope for careful routeing in many cases.

Development expenditure

SSAP 13, *Accounting for Research and Development*, sets out the criteria which are used to decide whether expenditure on research and development should be capitalised as deferred development expenditure which will be written off against anticipated revenues, or should be written off to the profit and loss account when incurred. Pure research expenditure is written off in the year incurred whereas development expenditure can be deferred to later periods if there is a clearly defined project with separately identifiable costs and sufficient funding, which is technically and commercially viable, with costs to be covered by future revenues. Unless, however, development expenditure is recoverable from a customer, most software developers write off development expenditure as it is incurred.

Capitalising development expenditure may prevent its deduction as a revenue deduction for tax purposes, unless it can be classified as deferred revenue expenditure (*see* above) whereas expenditure written off as incurred will usually be deductible on the same basis as that used for accounts purposes. If, however, software has been developed for use in a company's own business the Revenue can argue that expenditure should be treated as capital expenditure even if written off as incurred for accounts purposes. The Revenue's approach is summarised in the November 1993 *Inland Revenue Tax Bulletin*. If the expenditure has a sufficiently enduring nature, which is determined by reference to the function of the software in the trade in question, the Revenue will seek to categorise it as capital and capital allowances should be available (*see* above). If the software is expected to have a useful life of less than two years, revenue treatment will be accepted.

Transfer pricing

UK legislation allows the income from transactions between related parties to be taxed on the basis of the income that would have arisen if the transaction had been carried out at arm's length.

The OECD Transfer Pricing Guidelines for Multinational Enterprises and Tax Administration prefers a transaction-based method for determining an arm's length price. Three such methods are identified: comparison with prices in similar arm's length transactions, which is the preferred method; deduction of an appropriate mark-up from retail prices; and the addition of an appropriate mark-up to a supplier's costs. The allocation of profit by reference to some non-profit-related factor such as turnover or size of workforce is not recommended (*see* Chapter 13).

If a UK company licensing software to a subsidiary outside the UK also licenses software to third parties on a similar basis there is clearly a comparable price which it would be difficult to gainsay. If there are no similar third party arrangements, usual pricing structures within the industry as a whole would have to be considered. There is always a difficulty, however, where there are no directly comparable products.

VAT

The correct VAT treatment of the supply of software depends on:

(a) whether the software is a standard off-the-shelf package or a bespoke package;
(b) whether or not the user is registered for VAT; and
(c) whether the user belongs inside or outside the EU.

The sale of an off-the-shelf package to a user registered for VAT in the EU is treated as a supply of goods and can be zero-rated. If the sale of an off-the-shelf package is to a non-registered user in the EU, UK VAT must be added, except that if the seller arranges delivery and the distance selling threshold is exceeded in any particular country, the seller must register for VAT in that country and add VAT at the local rate.

Sales of bespoke software in the EU are supplies of services and subject to the complicated 'place of supply' rules.

If a UK seller supplies bespoke software, the supply will be outside the scope of UK VAT if the user is in business in another EU state and receives the software for business use. The 'reverse charge' provisions will apply in that case. If, however, the user is in another EU state and receives the software for non-business purposes, UK VAT must be added by the seller.

Supplies of software to non-EU users are zero-rated provided that sufficient evidence is retained of their export.

PART 6

CASE STUDIES

Case study 1:   Peter Roberts, author

Introduction

The purpose of this case study is to consider the taxation planning opportunities of an author resident and domiciled in the UK and the way in which the commercial and taxation considerations are intertwined. The study has been kept as realistic as possible in order to illustrate the planning decisions as they arise and is not to be regarded as an optimum solution, as it is usually only possible with hindsight to decide what the best tax planning would have been had all the subsequent developments been known from the beginning.

The study illustrates, in particular, the use of the copyright spreading provisions, personal service companies, trusts and overseas companies.

The product

Peter Roberts, an author of children's books, wrote a book called *Strompy and the Flying Alligator*. He sent the manuscript to this literary agent who in turn took it to a well-known publisher of children's books. The publisher liked the manuscript and agreed to publish the book. It was decided that the book should be illustrated and the publishers and Peter Roberts agreed to approach Miss Ann Pyke to prepare the illustrations.

An agreement was entered into between Peter Roberts and the publisher whereby he agreed to grant a licence to the publisher to publish a hardback edition of the book in return for a royalty of 12 per cent for the first 5,000 copies and thereafter 15 per cent calculated on the retail selling price of the book in the UK. The publisher originally asked for a complete assignment of copyright but Peter Roberts had in mind to write a series of 'Strompy' books, since he thought that the character might prove popular, and he was therefore unwilling to part with more than a licence to publish.

The publisher was sufficiently enthusiastic about the book to agree to a non-returnable recoupable advance of royalties on the basis of an anticipated sale of 4,000 copies. The book was expected to retail for £14.95 in the hardback edition.

Initial income

Peter Roberts had spent 18 months in writing the first Strompy book and claimed to spread the royalty payment over two years under the provisions of TA 1988, s 534. As a result one-half of the advance of royalties was treated as receivable on the day the publishing agreement was signed and the remaining one-half was treated as having been receivable 12 months previously.

Miss Ann Pyke also entered into an agreement with the publishers whereby she became entitled to a 2½ per cent royalty based on the published price, for her illustrations, with a similar advance payment on the basis of 4,000 copies as a non-returnable recoupable advance. As she had not been engaged on the illustrations for more than 12 months she was not able to claim to spread the advance under the provisions of TA 1988, s 538.

The royalty income for both Peter Roberts and Ann Pyke was taxed under Schedule D, Case II as part of their professional earnings.

Strompy and the Flying Alligator met with a good reception and a reprint was arranged on the basis of a royalty of 15 per cent on all copies for Peter Roberts and 2½ per cent for Ann Pyke. Peter Roberts' agent also started negotiations with a publisher of children's paperbacks for the paperback rights of *Strompy and the Flying Alligator*. The paperback royalties were agreed at 17½ per cent of the published price of £4.95 per copy and as these rights were licensed within two years of first publication it was again possible to spread the non-returnable recoupable advance, this time based on 8,000 copies, over a two-year period under TA 1988, s 534. Ann Pyke's illustrations were again used, this time for a lump sum on partial assignment of the copyright for the purposes of the paperback print for a fee of £7,500 which was again brought into her professional earnings when received.

In the meantime Peter Roberts had written *Strompy Goes Hunting* and *Strompy and the Lost Brontosaurus*. Peter Roberts' original publishers agreed to publish the two new books at six-monthly intervals on the basis of a 20 per cent royalty on the published price of £18.49 on condition that there would be no paperback edition within 12 months of the hardback publication and with a recoupable advance of royalties on the basis of expected sales of 7,500.

A royalty agreement was entered into between the publishers and Ann Pyke for her to produce the illustrations for the two new books on the basis of a fee of £10,000 in addition to a 2½ per cent royalty.

Peter Roberts argued that it was now more than three years since he first started working on the 'Strompy' books and as a result he was able to convince the Inland Revenue that his advance royalties on the new books should be spread equally over three years, receivable on the date of signing the new agreement and the two previous anniversaries. The spreading into three equal parts was under the provisions of TA 1988, s 534.

Again Miss Pyke could not claim spreading relief under TA 1988, s 538 as she had not spent more than 12 months on the new illustrations.

For both Mr Roberts and Miss Pyke the periodic royalties were brought into their accounts when received.

The companies

By this time Peter Roberts was convinced that Strompy would prove successful and he formed a series of companies (*see* diagram on p 352).

He formed Strompy Creations Ltd and entered into a service contract with the company under which he agreed to be employed by the company for a period of five years at a salary of £35,000 pa, and during that period he would write five books incorporating the character of Strompy and would grant the company an exclusive ten-year licence for the UK editions of such books, both hardback and paperback. The shares in Strompy Creations Ltd were owned as to 50 per cent by Peter Roberts, as to 25 per cent by his wife Sandra and as to 25 per cent by his children, Alexander, Rona and Brian, equally.

As well as forming Strompy Creations Ltd he also formed Strompy Films Ltd, Strompy Records Ltd, Strompy Performances Ltd and Strompy Merchandising Ltd. The shareholdings in these four companies were held as to 25 per cent by Peter Roberts, 25 per cent by Sandra and 50 per cent on maintenance and accumulation trusts for their three children.

Peter's shares in these four companies were entitled to any capital appreciation on winding up the company, but had no votes and were not entitled to any dividends. The trust shares were entitled to any dividends declared but had no votes and were not entitled to any surplus on a liquidation. Sandra's shares were entitled to the votes but had no rights as to dividends or to any surplus on winding-up. The purpose of the multiple rights was to reduce the value of the shares so far as possible both at the time of issue and at any future date, while still preserving the possibility of paying a sizeable lump sum to Peter should the opportunity occur.

To these companies he granted a ten-year exclusive licence of the UK rights in respect of films (including television films), records and songs, dramatic rights and rights in manufactured goods and designs, incorporating the character of Strompy. The consideration for the licence was, in each case, £5,000, which was agreed to be a fair market value of the rights at that stage, there being no immediate possibility of commercial exploitation of the Strompy character in such formats. Peter Roberts, however, believed in planning for the future. He had considered an absolute assignment but was advised that this could make it expensive in tax terms to reacquire the rights in his own name should he desire to do so.

The limbo trust

Peter Roberts had a friend living in the Bahamas who agreed to set up a limbo trust (*see* diagram on p 352). It was decided that the beneficiaries of the limbo trust should be the Bahamian settlor's nephew and his wife, with the trustees having the power to appoint additional beneficiaries not ordinarily resident in the UK. A protector was appointed who was resident in the Isle of Man.

It was decided that the trust should be formed in Bermuda with trustees in Bermuda, Guernsey and Hong Kong. The trustees incorporated a company in the Netherlands Antilles called Creative Enterprises NV to whom Peter Roberts assigned the overseas film, recording and dramatic rights arising from 'Strompy' for a fee of £12,500, which again was regarded as the fair market value of those rights at that time. This time it was thought desirable to dispose of the rights absolutely as Peter wished to sever his interest in the rights completely.

The overseas publishing rights were licensed for a fee of £15,000 for a ten-year period to Creative Publishing NV, another company in the Netherlands Antilles owned by the Bermudian limbo trust.

The overseas merchandising rights for portraying the character of Strompy on manufactured goods were licensed for a ten-year term to a Jersey company,

Peter Roberts: trading structure

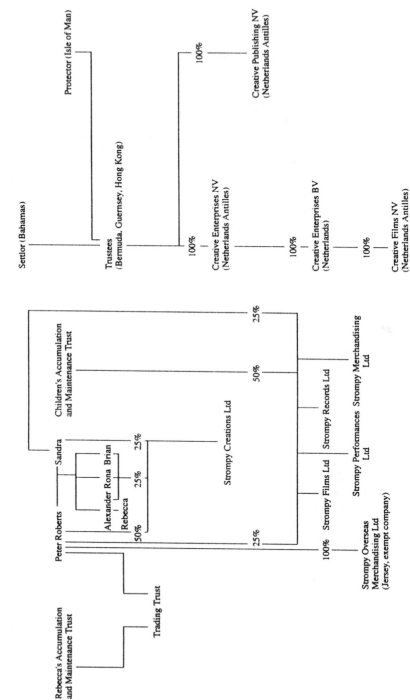

Limbo trust arrangement

Settlor (Bahamas)

Protector (Isle of Man)

Trustees
(Bermuda, Guernsey, Hong Kong)

100%

Creative Enterprises NV
(Netherlands Antilles)

100%

Creative Publishing NV
(Netherlands Antilles)

100%

Creative Enterprises BV
(Netherlands)

100%

Creative Films NV
(Netherlands Antilles)

Peter Roberts: trading structure

Rebecca's Accumulation
and Maintenance Trust

Trading Trust

Peter Roberts — Sandra

Alexander Rona Brian
Rebecca

Children's Accumulation
and Maintenance Trust

50%   25%   25%

50%

25%

100%

25%

50%

25%

Strompy Overseas
Merchandising Ltd
(Jersey, exempt company)

Strompy Films Ltd

Strompy Creations Ltd

Strompy Performances
Ltd

Strompy Records Ltd

Strompy Merchandising
Ltd

Strompy Overseas Merchandising Ltd, the shares of which were owned by Peter Roberts himself and which had two directors resident in the Channel Island of Jersey, as an exempt company for the benefit of non-Jersey residents, to grant licences to overseas manufacturers. As there was no present possibility of such licences being taken up it was agreed that the fair market value of the overseas rights should be fixed at £7,500, which was the amount the Jersey-based company paid to Peter Roberts. All the fees for the assignments and licences were included in Peter Roberts' Schedule D, Case II income as received.

Strompy takes off

The scene was now set for the commercial exploitation of Strompy and Peter Roberts sat down to write *Strompy Goes Sailing, Strompy on the Moon, Strompy on Safari, Strompy Goes to School* and *Strompy in Hospital.*

Strompy Films Ltd entered into negotiations with an established film making company, Kiddikartoon Ltd, for the production of an animated cartoon film for television called *The Adventures of Strompy*, as a joint venture. The film consisted of a number of short episodes based on events in the various Strompy books and was illustrated by a professional cartoon animator using as a basis Ann Pyke's original portrayal of Strompy. Strompy Films Ltd on behalf of the joint venture entered into an agreement with Ann Pyke for the portrayal of Strompy and his friends in any form other than book illustrations for a fee of £25,000.

By this time Ann Pyke had been engaged on portraying Strompy for the various books for a period in excess of three years and therefore claimed under TA 1988, s 538 to spread the receipt of the lump sum of £25,000 over a period of three years. One-third of the £25,000 was therefore deemed to be receivable on the date of the agreement and one-third 12 months previously, with the remaining one-third 12 months before that.

Strompy Films Ltd and Kiddikartoon Ltd granted a licence to the BBC for *The Adventures of Strompy* for one showing and two repeats for the sum of £45,000.

Under the joint venture agreement Kiddikartoon Ltd paid the cartoonist's costs of £25,000 on behalf of the venture and split the balance of £20,000 between Strompy Films Ltd and itself in equal shares. Strompy Films Ltd showed in its accounts a Case I receipt of £10,000 less half the cost of the acquisition of the rights from Ann Pyke of £25,000. The Revenue held, however, that although a royalty paid to Miss Pyke would have been an allowable trading expense, the share of the lump sum of £25,000 although taxable on her as income, would nonetheless be regarded as a capital payment so far as the company was concerned and was therefore a capital sum on which no tax relief was available. An appeal was under consideration.

The television film was licensed to Creative Films NV in the Netherlands Antilles, which in turn licensed the film to Creative Enterprises BV, its immediate parent incorporated in the Netherlands. Creative Enterprises BV licensed the film to China, Japan and a number of European countries, including Holland. The terms agreed were that 94 per cent of the income less expenses received by the Dutch company would be paid over to Creative Films NV as the fee for the sub-licence. The object of the exercise was to obtain the maximum benefit of the double taxation agreements between the Netherlands and other countries outside the UK so that the royalties and licence fees received were not subject to any more than the minimum withholding tax under the various double taxation treaties between the Netherlands and the contracting country. The sub-licence fee paid to the Netherlands Antilles was agreed in advance with the Dutch revenue authorities. Creative Enterprises BV therefore made a small profit in the Netherlands subject to Dutch tax at 35 per cent and a substantial profit accrued to Creative Films NV in the Netherlands Antilles. Creative Films NV paid a dividend to Creative Enterprises BV which was exempt from tax in the Netherlands, under the participation privilege. Creative Enterprises BV in turn paid the same dividend to its parent company, Creative Enterprises NV which was exempt from tax in the Netherlands Antilles. This was subject to Dutch withholding tax of 7½ per cent levied by the Netherlands on dividends to the Netherlands Antilles.

The dividend received by Creative Enterprises NV would not be subject to tax in the Netherlands Antilles as it would already have suffered tax there, having been paid originally from a Netherlands Antilles company, Creative Films NV. Creative Films NV would be liable to tax at 2.4 to 3.0 per cent on its royalties, as a royalty holding company under LVWB 1940, art 14A(1).

The licence fee between Creative Films NV and the producers of the film (Strompy Films Ltd and Kiddikartoon Ltd) was at a relatively modest level as Creative Films NV already had the sole rights to exploit the character of Strompy in film form outside the UK. A substantial profit was therefore accruing in the Netherlands Antilles for the eventual benefit of the limbo trust and, in due course, Peter Roberts or members of his family, if and when they might become not ordinarily resident in the UK and be appointed beneficiaries of the trust.

As a result of the film a number of toys and games were devised by various manufacturers portraying Strompy in the form of soft toys, puppets, jigsaws, scrap books, posters, T-shirts, crockery and various other paraphernalia.

Strompy Merchandising Ltd granted the various licences to UK manufacturers and Strompy Overseas Merchandising Ltd granted overseas licences for the manufacture of such articles.

Selling out

After five years Peter Roberts sold his shares in Strompy Overseas Merchandising Ltd for £300,000 to an arm's length purchaser on the basis of the accumulated profits and likely future profits for the remainder of the ten-year licence term.

The Inland Revenue argued that Peter was in receipt of a capital sum within TA 1988, s 739(3). Peter argued that he had merely disposed of shares in an overseas company and had obtained a capital gain. He argued that TA 1988, s 739 did not apply as the original assignment of the merchandising rights was at a commercial price and therefore was a *bona fide* commercial operation within TA 1988, s 741. The Revenue accepted that the original assignment was for a *bona fide* commercial price but argued that Peter Roberts had not shown that the sale was not designed with the avoidance of tax as a main object and therefore the escape clause of TA 1988, s 741 was not available. It was agreed that the merchandising income would have been part of Peter Roberts' professional income in the absence of the assignment to Strompy Overseas Merchandising Ltd and the income of the company was therefore assessed under TA 1988, s 739 on Peter as part of his professional income for the years in which it arose. The object of setting up the Jersey company was therefore entirely defeated by TA 1988, s 739 and Peter wished that he had followed his accountant's advice and had that company also owned by the limbo trust.

Peter had rather more luck with the UK merchandising company which he sold at the same time because here TA 1988, s 739 had no application, although the Revenue argued that Peter was in receipt of a capital amount under TA 1988, s 775, as defined by TA 1988, s 777(13), and that as the licensing agreement had five years to run the protection of TA 1988, s 775(4) for the sale of goodwill was not available. Peter was able, however, to show both that the original assignment was on commercial terms with the avoidance of tax not being a main reason for the transfer, as it was still within the UK, and that in view of such matters as limited liability there were good commercial reasons for operating through a company. It was therefore accepted that the shareholders received a capital gain.

A Revenue argument that the accumulated income of the company should be assessed on him as settlor of an arrangement following the decision of *Crossland v Hawkins*, and *IRC v Mills* (*see above* at p 318) was defeated on proof that the original assignment had been on proper commercial terms. This, of course, emphasised the advantage of planning the commercial exploitation of Strompy from the earliest possible moment.

Following the success of the film, a musical was developed using the Strompy characters and royalties were paid to Strompy Performances Ltd.

A record of the musical was produced and royalties were paid to Strompy Records Ltd. After five years Strompy Records Ltd was sold for £250,000 to an arm's length purchaser, which gave rise to a capital gain. As the whole of the goodwill was sold with the company TA 1988, s 775 did not apply, in view of TA 1988, s 775(4), and the value did not depend to a material extent on the future income from Peter Roberts' own personal activities.

The beneficiaries' income

When Alexander reached the age of 18 he went to live in Spain for a period and Creative Enterprises NV in the Netherlands Antilles paid a dividend of the equivalent of £200,000 to the Bermudian trust which in turn appointed a Channel Islands resident as an additional beneficiary of the trust and paid him £200,000. The Channel Islands resident in turn paid the sum to Alexander. The Revenue attacked the arrangement under TA 1988, s 740 on the grounds that there had been a transfer of assets, *viz* the assignment of the overseas film rights, and a capital sum had been received by Alexander. However, as Alexander was at the time of payment not ordinarily resident in the UK there was no UK resident to charge. The Revenue could not successfully argue that the payment was in reality to Peter Roberts even if he had been the settlor of the trust, which he argued he was not, in spite of the fact that he was the transferor of the film rights. A claim under TA 1988, s 775 was defeated on the grounds that the sum did not arise from the activities of the individual, Peter Roberts, but from the creation of the film which was a corporate activity involving many people.

The trading trust

At the end of ten years the UK merchandising rights reverted to Peter Roberts and he then entered into a partnership with a trading trust whereby he licensed the Strompy UK merchandising rights to the partnership for a five-year period in return for 65 per cent of the partnership profits. The remaining partnership profits were received by trustees of an accumulation and maintenance settlement for Alexander's daughter, Rebecca and any further children of Alexander. The advantage of the trading trust rather than a company arrangement was that the maximum rate of tax on accumulated income was 35 per cent, being the basic rate of tax and the additional rate. Had the money been received by the company and paid out by way of dividend the effective rate of tax would have been 47 per cent, being corporation tax of 33 per cent in the company's hands and additional rate change of 14 per cent on the accumulated income in the hands of the trustees.

Peter Roberts decided to assign the copyright in a proposed new book *Strompy Underground* to Mrs Lirtl, his mother-in-law who had recently been widowed. It was argued that as there were no rights currently in existence there could be little or no capital gains tax or capital transfer tax on the disposal and there would be no income tax charge on Peter arising from the disposal as a result of *Mason v Innes*. It was accepted that Mrs Lirtl would be liable to tax under Schedule D, Case III on the royalties arising. Although it could possibly be argued, following Pennycuick J's comments in *Hume v Asquith* (1968) 45 TC 251 that the income was tax free (*see above*, pp 194–5), it would not be wise to do so in view of the likely charge under TA 1988, s 775 which would then be raised on Peter Roberts.

The future

Peter Roberts is still writing about Strompy and no doubt his adventures, and his author's tax planning saga, will continue.

Case study 2:   Andrew Rankin, inventor

Introduction

The second case study, like the others, involves a practical commercial and tax structure development rather than an optimum solution, this time for an inventor, and illustrates scientific research allowances, intermediate licensing companies and limbo trusts, sale of goodwill, capital gains, partnerships, patent income spreading, loss claims, capital transfer tax and capital gains tax on gifts.

The product

Andrew Rankin was an engineer employed by a water company who became interested in the development of fuel-saving devices for motor cars. Andrew had a small workshop of his own and produced an elementary prototype of a fuel-saving device which showed encouraging results. Over the next 18 months, he devoted his spare time to the development of the idea and eventually produced a device which consistently showed a 15 per cent fuel-saving when fitted to his Plus 8 Morgan. Andrew consulted a patent agent and after some preliminary searches it was decided that the device was sufficiently different from other fuel-saving inventions to make it patentable. He therefore, through his patent agent, filed the necessary preliminary application for a UK patent. At this stage he realised that to date the device had cost him a great deal of time and a not inconsiderable amount of money; furthermore, commercial exploitation was likely to prove difficult. However, Andrew's great-aunt Matilda had recently died leaving him a sufficiently large sum of money to enable him to rent some premises and commence limited manufacture of the device which he had by this time christened the 'Mizermyle'.

Andrew then left his job to concentrate on the development and sale of his Mizermyle. Andrew was convinced from the start that the device would make his fortune and he therefore consulted his accountant to decide how best to handle the idea.

The company

His accountant suggested that the patent be assigned to a UK company, Mizermyle Ltd, in exchange for shares, as otherwise he would be taxed on his income under Schedule D, Case II as an inventor on the whole of the income arising worldwide, which did not seem a particularly good idea. By transferring the patent in exchange for shares there was no capital gains tax problem as the company merely issued shares at par for the expenses incurred by Andrew to date. TA 1988, s 521(2)–(4) applied so that the par value of the shares was treated as income, but covered by the expenses, and the company could have claimed capital allowances under TA 1988, s 520. Instead, however, the company claimed scientific research allowance on the expenditure, successfully arguing that it was in relation to the development of a prototype, the relief being given in one year under CAA 1990, s 137.

By issuing shares for the expenditure incurred the problem of the valuation of any goodwill attached to the embryo business was avoided, in view of the provisions of TCGA 1990, s 162.

The children's trust

As it was anticipated that the company should prove fairly profitable in the long run Andrew immediately issued further shares to an accumulation and maintenance settlement which he had set up in favour of his children, Jennifer and Stephen. 30 per cent of the shares were then held by the children's trust (*see* diagram on p 360).

Great-aunt Matilda's husband, Colin, decided to spend the remainder of his days in the Algarve and promptly emigrated from the UK. Great-uncle Colin was persuaded to create a limbo trust in Bermuda (No 1) with intended beneficiaries Jennifer and Stephen should they become not ordinarily resident in the UK and he transferred £10,000 to the trustees resident in Bermuda to start the settlement. A Guernsey-resident protector was also appointed.

The trustees incorporated a company in the Netherlands Antilles and subscribed for share capital of $12,000, the balance of the trust fund being placed on deposit.

The Netherlands Antilles company was incorporated in Curacao but managed and controlled from Bermuda. The company was called Rankin Overseas NV. Rankin Overseas NV bought from Andrew the right to patent his invention outside the UK for the sum of £2,000. This modest amount was agreed as the full market value, as at this stage the Mizermyle had yet to be commercially exploited in the UK and the overseas rights were largely based on hope. Nonetheless Rankin Overseas NV borrowed further funds on security of a guarantee given by great-uncle Colin and used the proceeds to patent the Mizermyle in the USA, Canada, France, Germany, Holland, Japan and South Korea.

First year's growth

Mizermyle Ltd in the UK employed a sales representative and Andrew concentrated on the production and development of the device. At the end of the first year of the company's trade he had actually produced some 5,000 units, the vast majority of which had been sold by mail order as his sales representative was having difficulty persuading wholesalers to accept an invention, which sounded about as plausible as the philosopher's stone, from an unknown company.

Andrew, however, had continued to develop the product on behalf of the company and was now regularly achieving a 20 per cent reduction in fuel consumption. He arranged to have the device independently tested by the AA and the RAC Technical Departments which confirmed his findings. Largely as a result of these independent evaluations Andrew's salesman was somewhat overwhelmed to receive an order for 12,000 units from one of the leading independent motor vehicle spares factors. This order was considerably in excess of the first year's entire production and Andrew did not have the financial resources to expand production to the required extent. He approached his bank for a facility of £50,000 to acquire additional premises and machinery, together with the necessary working capital, in order to expand production to 30,000 units pa. The bank manager viewed his request with a somewhat jaundiced eye, having recently had an unfortunate experience with another customer whose brilliant invention was going to produce a fortune, and on which the bank had had to write off £20,000 as a bad debt. The invention had proved a commercial disaster (mainly on the grounds of a total failure to comply with the advertised claims). Andrew did eventually find another bank which was prepared to lend £40,000 on the basis of Andrew's personal guarantee and a second mortgage on his house. Andrew was extremely loath to involve his personal assets in his business ventures, but decided to accept the gamble and duly increased production.

Overseas trading income

After a further two years Mizermyle Ltd had pushed its annual sales to 100,000 and was beginning to export the device. Export sales were made through Rankin Overseas NV as that company had the rights to exploit the invention outside the UK. Although the Mizermyle was sold in the UK with a gross profit of 100 per cent the export prices to Rankin Overseas were at cost plus 50 per cent, thus enabling the overseas company to make a worthwhile profit. Andrew's accountant was somewhat concerned with the provisions of the transfer pricing legislation in the UK under TA 1988, ss 770–773, but came to the conclusion that there was no problem in view of the fact that the beneficial ownership of Mizermyle Ltd in the UK and Rankin Overseas NV were such that they were not under common control and therefore the transfer pricing provisions did not apply.

The real breakthrough came when a Japanese car manufacturer wished to install the device as original equipment in one of its high-volume production cars. Rankin Overseas NV therefore entered into a licence agreement through its new Netherlands subsidiary with the Japanese manufacturer who agreed to pay a royalty of $10 per unit. In order to reduce the rate of Japanese withholding tax on the patent royalties on the Mizermyle, Rankin Overseas NV had formed a wholly owned Dutch subsidiary company, Rankin Netherlands BV, which had in turn sub-licensed the Mizermyle to the Japanese company. It was agreed with the Dutch Revenue authorities that in view of the size of the royalty 4 per cent would be left in Holland and the balance paid by way of licence fee to Rankin Overseas NV. The 4 per cent left in the Netherlands was subject to Dutch Corporation tax at 35 per cent. This enabled the Japanese withholding tax to be reduced to 10 per cent under the Dutch/Japanese Double Tax Treaty whereas it would otherwise have been 20 per cent on a direct payment to Rankin Overseas NV.

Andrew Rankin: trading structure

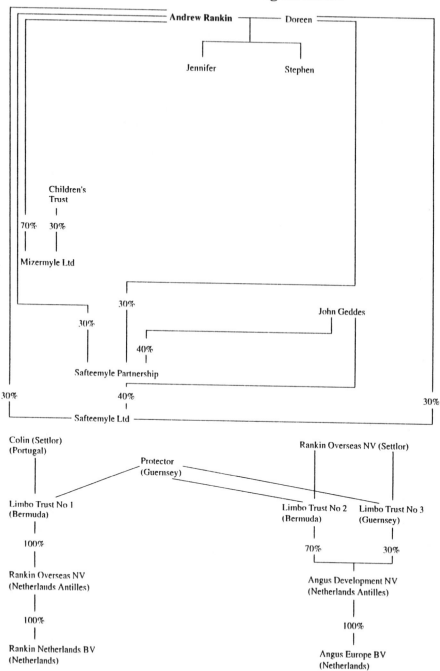

Selling out

Andrew at this stage was beginning to realise that although his family were now very well catered for through Rankin Oversea NV his own position in the UK, although not exactly penurious, was rather less healthy than he would have wished. He realised that he was unlikely to expand significantly the UK production of the Mizermyle unless it was accepted as original equipment by one of the leading UK manufacturers. He entered into discussion with one of the UK manufacturers who showed interest for the possible outright sale of Mizermyle Ltd.

Andrew had under development a new form of anti-skid device which prevented a car's wheels locking under excessive braking in slippery conditions. This invention he had named the 'Safteemyle' and he had provisionally agreed with Rankin Overseas NV to exploit the overseas rights. It was, however, recommended that the new invention be dealt with by its own separate overseas company and Rankin Overseas NV, out of its profits, settled cash on the trustees of another trust in Bermuda (No 2) who used the funds to form a new company, Angus Developments NV, in the Netherlands Antilles. Rankin Overseas NV had the power to settle funds in this manner, which is not uncommon. The overseas rights of the new invention were sold by Andrew for £30,000, being the estimated market value of the rights to the new invention, which although purely in the embryo stage nonetheless had the precedent of the Mizermyle to enhance considerably its commercial appeal.

A wholly owned subsidiary was formed in the Netherlands, Angus Europe BV, to reduce withholding taxes to a minimum in the same way as with Rankin Netherlands BV.

Andrew agreed to sell Mizermyle Ltd to the UK motor manufacturing company for £5,000,000 payable partly in cash and partly in quoted shares and unsecured loan stock of the UK manufacturer. His children's accumulation and maintenance settlement elected to take shares and loan stock and roll over the gain. Andrew elected to take cash for his shares and decided to accept a capital gains tax charge.

Andrew's accountant was concerned that the receipt of a capital sum could possibly fall within the provisions of TA 1988, s 775 and therefore become liable to income tax under Schedule D, Case VI instead of merely being taxed as a capital gain. However, the sale of the shares of Mizermyle Limited included the goodwill of the company and all the UK rights relating to the product, which was where the real value lay; and the personal services of Andrew, who remained with the company on a part-time basis under a five-year service contract, were not a significant part of the deal and therefore the section would not have any application, under TA 1988, s 775(4).

The Safteemyle partnership

When he first started to think about Safteemyle, Andrew realised that certain aspects of the device were outside his professional competence and he approached an engineering friend of his who had considerable experience in dynamics, with a view to the joint development of the idea. His colleague John Geddes was interested and Andrew related the success that he had had with the Mizermyle through arranging things to the best possible advantage from the start; he explained that this was why he had just sold the overseas Safteemyle rights to Angus Developments NV for £30,000. He was, however, prepared to provide for his colleague's family, and in consequence Rankin Overseas NV settled funds on a new limbo trust (No 3), this time in Guernsey, for the benefit of the colleague's children. The new trust acquired 30 per cent of the shares in Angus Developments NV, the company designed to exploit the overseas rights of the Safteemyle, by way of a further issue of shares by the company.

The lump sum of £30,000 which Andrew received from Angus Developments NV was a lump sum on the disposal of patent rights and therefore spread forward over six years under the provisions of TA 1988, s 524. £5,000 was therefore treated as taxable income in the year of receipt and in each of the following five years.

Andrew and John decided to develop the Safteemyle in the UK through a partnership and under the profit-sharing arrangements John was to receive 40 per cent of the overall profits with a minimum profit share of £20,000 pa, but to share in only one per cent of any losses. Andrew and his wife, Doreen, were the remaining partners in the business, which started on 1 January 1994. Doreen kept the books of the partnership and ordered the necessary materials while Andrew and his colleague developed the Safteemyle. It took 18 months to make the Safteemyle work satisfactorily in practice and the partnership therefore showed a loss for the first period, 99 per cent of which was available to Andrew to set against his other income under the provisions of TA 1988, s 380, but he elected to carry back the loss against previous years' income under TA 1988, s 381.

The partnership accounts were made up to 6 April and in the third year the success of the Safteemyle was assured and a large contract entered into with one of the UK manufacturers for a licence to manufacture the product for a volume production car. Andrew and his partners were not willing to sell the business outright and it being the third year of the partnership wished to maximise the income in that year. They therefore agreed to the non-exclusive UK licence of the Safteemyle for a royalty of £1 per unit payable annually on the basis of the production in the preceding calendar year but with a non-returnable but recoupable advance royalty of £800,000 payable in two equal instalments on 3 April 1996 and 3 April 1997. Production in the first three years amounted to 950,000 units and the partnership profits, as adjusted for tax purposes, were as follows:

Commencement 1 April 1994

		£
1 January 1994–5 April 1994	loss	(30,000)
Year ended 5 April 1995	loss	(50,000)
Year ended 5 April 1996	profit	350,000
Year ended 5 April 1997	profit	345,000
Year ended 5 April 1998	profit	100,000
Year ended 5 April 1999	profit	201,500
		916,500

On 6 April 1996, however, Doreen resigned from the partnership and a professional book-keeper was employed to take over her duties and at the same time the business was converted to a company.

The resultant assessments based on these adjusted profits were as follows:

		£	£
1993/94	1 January 1994–5 April 1994 loss actual £30,000		(30,000)
1994/95	Year ended 5 April 1995, actual loss		(50,000)
1995/96	Year ended 5 April 1995, loss already relieved		Nil
1996/97	Year ended 5 April 1996	350,000	
	Year ended 5 April 1997	345,000	
		795,000	
	Transitional averaging		397,500
1997/98	Year ended 5 April 1998		100,000
1998/99	Year ended 5 April 1999		201,500
			619,000

The losses for 1993/94 and 1994/95 are computed an a fiscal year basis under TA 1988, s 380, irrespective of the opening year rules in TA 1988, ss 60, 61. There is no loss relief in 1995/96 since loss relief can be obtained only once.

The Revenue considered whether the profits had been artificially concentrated into the basis periods for the fiscal year 1996/97 which would have enabled them to counter the benefit of the transitional averaging under FA 1994, Sched 20, para 2 under the anti-avoidance provisions in FA 1995, Sched 22, para 1, but it was ultimately accepted that there had been no change in business practice within FA 1995, Sched 22, paras 14–17, as the timing of the advances was negotiated at arm's length with an unconnected party, not to obtain a tax advantage and was not a connected party or self-cancelling transaction. No adjustment was possible on cessation on 6 April 1999, or the anti-avoidance provisions of FA 1994, Sched 20, para 3 only apply to cessations up to and including 5 April 1999. The taxable profits in the partnership were therefore £619,000 compared with the adjusted profits of £916,500.

Although one year (1996/97) produced a high profit and therefore a large income tax assessment this was ameliorated by Doreen's 30 per cent interest in the profits being taxed on her personally. The Revenue at first argued that her contribution to the partnership was insufficient to justify her share of profit, but it was pointed out that the partnership profit share was for the partners themselves to decide and there was no question of having to justify the partners' shares of profit in the same way as for remuneration. Once it was shown that Doreen was actively engaged in the partnership, which she indubitably was, there was no mechanism for the Revenue to avoid assessing her on her share of the income, short of showing that her share of profits was effectively a settlement created by Andrew, which they were unable to do given her contribution to the business over a period of more than five years.

As a result of the careful choice of accounting date and timing of the transfer to the company which gave rise to a cessation in the partnership, one of the substantial years' profits effectively became tax free, without the necessity of using any form of artificial tax avoidance scheme, as a result of the transitional provisions on the change from the preceding year to the current year basis of assessment. This would not have been possible had the business commenced on or after 6 April 1994 and been within the current year basis of assessment from the start.

Safteemyle Ltd

On 10 April 1993 it was decided to transfer the partnership to a limited company. In order to save stamp duty the debtors and creditors would not be transferred, which meant that it would be impossible to claim the capital gains tax roll-over relief under TCGA 1992, s 162.

A company, Safteemyle Ltd, was therefore formed and the goodwill and other trading assets of the partnership sold to the company at cost, the shares previously having been issued for cash at par. This gave rise to a transfer at an undervalue but as the assets were business assets within TCGA 1992, s 165, the capital gains tax charge could be held over. It was argued that even without business property relief there was no inheritance tax on the transfer, as the reduction in the estate resulting from the partial gift of goodwill was balanced by the increase in the estate resulting from the transfer of goodwill to the company, the shares of which constituted part of the transferor's estate.

It was decided that some of the shares should be transferred to a discretionary settlement for Andrew's children, Jennifer and Stephen, but as this would involve a transfer for inheritance tax purposes it was decided to issue deferred shares in the company to the trust. These shares were of a class which carried no rights to participate in dividends or a surplus on liquidation and carried no votes, for a period of 15 years. At the end of the 15-year period, however, the shares would rank *pari passu* with the existing ordinary shares. The issue of the deferred shares was made at market value to avoid allowing value to pass out of the existing shares which would have given rise to an inheritance tax charge under IHTA 1984, s 98 and a capital gains tax charge on the deemed disposal at market value of the existing shares under TCGA 1992, s 29. In view of the lack of rights attaching to the shares for a very considerable period the value for inheritance tax purposes was ultimately agreed with the Shares Valuation Division of the Inland Revenue at £1.50 per share, the price at which they were issued.

Andrew and John started considering further products for Safteemyle Ltd in addition to the Safteemyle.

Case study 3: Brighton Rock, entertainers

Introduction

This case study illustrates the possible treatment of the composing, performing and publishing income of a pop group. It deals with partnerships, employment companies and their shareholdings, pension schemes, small company rates, overseas and UK trusts, foreign earnings, lend-a-star provisions, post-cessation receipts, royalty planning and gifts of future copyright.

The product

Brighton Rock is the name of a pop group formed between Agatha Bentley, Cedric Dawson, Elizabeth Farrow and Gordon Hepplewhite (*see* diagram on p 366). All four were resident and ordinarily resident in the UK. Gordon retained his domicile of origin which was in Guernsey, where his family had lived for generations, but the other three members were all domiciled in England.

Agatha was aged 26 and divorced with a two-year-old daughter, Ingrid. Cedric, aged 28, was married to Jemima, aged 24, and they had two young children, Kathleen and Leslie. Elizabeth, aged 22, was married to the group's manager, Morris and they had two children, Naomi and Ophelia. Gordon, aged 32, was divorced from his wife, Petra, by whom he had two sons, Quentin and Richard, and was now living with Sylvia by whom he had two children, Teresa and Ursula.

The group originally began playing at various gigs as a support band. The group was assessed to taxation as a partnership under Schedule D, Case II on the modest profits then made.

Towards the end of the next year Agatha and Gordon started to write their own songs with some assistance from Morris and from a friend of Agatha's, Vernon Wallace, who was not a member of the group. As some of their own compositions seemed to be having a good reception where they played, the band thought it would be desirable to put together an album, ideally for release during the pre-Christmas period. Vernon then talked to a friend of his, Xavier Yates, who had produced a number of records for which Vernon had written some of the songs and Xavier, having heard the group play, agreed to produce an album for them but pointed out that the suggested timescale was hopelessly unrealistic. Xavier arranged for a company with which he was connected, Zombie Productions Ltd, to publish the record which would be manufactured and distributed by Zombie Records Ltd.

Brighton Rock: dramatis personae

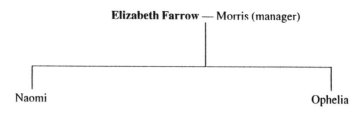

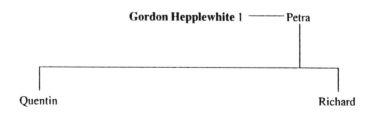

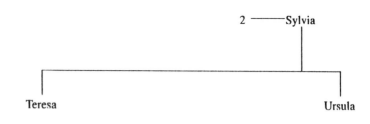

The record was duly produced in the middle of the following year under the title 'Peer West' and was a modest success, reaching 19th position in the UK album charts.

The partnership's income

The group was entitled to an artistes' royalty of 10 per cent of the retail price of records sold in the UK (*see* diagram on p 370). This was a partnership receipt and was included in the Schedule D, Case II income of the partnership.

The composers of the various songs were entitled to a royalty totalling 6.25 per cent of the retail value of the record of which the publishers, Zombie Productions Ltd, took 3 per cent. The producer, Xavier, took one per cent, leaving 2.25 per cent to be divided among the composers of the various songs. It was agreed that the apportionment should be in accordance with the playing time of each track and Agatha and Vernon were each entitled to 0.75 per cent, Gordon 0.5 per cent and Morris 0.25 per cent.

Each of the composers had set up a new business assessed to tax under Schedule D, Case II as a songwriter.

The publisher's and composers' royalties on performances were collected by the Performing Rights Society Ltd to whom the copyright was assigned for collection. Such royalties were payable whenever any track from the record was played on the radio or television or performed in public, either by a live band or discothèque. The publishing and composing royalties were paid by the manufacturer, Zombie Records Ltd, with the artistes' royalties on the sale of records.

The companies

At this stage Morris thought, somewhat belatedly, that it would be a good idea to consider some more sophisticated financial planning for the group and consulted an accountant and a solicitor experienced in the music industry.

One of the main problems of the popular music world is the relative shortness of the earnings period of many performers and the high earnings concentrated into a short period of time, which in the absence of avoiding action would nearly all be taxed at the top rate of tax, 40 per cent.

It was therefore decided to set up a series of companies for each of the group members and for Morris who, as the group's manager, was entitled to 10 per cent of their gross earnings and was therefore likely to receive nearly as much as a performing member of the group (*see* diagram on p 370). Vernon Wallace, the outside writer, and Xavier Yates already had their own companies through which they operated.

Consideration was given to setting up Gordon's company outside the UK but it was thought that it would be preferable to have a UK company which could then pay premiums to fund a pension scheme.

It was decided that the shares in the individuals' companies should be owned as to 70 per cent by the group member and as to 30 per cent by a maintenance and accumulation settlement set up for each of their children, except that Agatha decided to own all the shares in her company personally, on the ground that the financial maintenance of her daughter was a responsibility of her former husband.

Each member of the group then entered into an employment contract with the company under which they undertook to compose and record for the company in return for a salary. There was a territorial limitation in that the contract applied only to work done in the UK.

The partnership remained entitled to the artistes' royalties from the sale of the record 'Peer West' and also continued to receive the income for public performances in the UK. The songwriting royalties for the tracks of 'Peer West' were received by the individuals, except for Vernon and Xavier whose royalties were paid to their own companies.

It was appreciated that the formation of the companies would not enable profits to be built up and the companies then sold for a lump sum subject only to capital gains tax. Such a lump sum would be likely to be caught as a capital amount (TA 1988, ss 777(13) and 775) and the profit would then be liable to tax under Schedule D, Case VI in one year without the benefit of any top-slicing relief. The purpose of the company was to make the profits subject to corporation tax after paying out a reasonable remuneration which would be taxed under Schedule E.

The pension funds

The actual saving between the top rates of personal taxation of 40 per cent and corporation tax at 33 per cent was not enormously attractive but it did enable a small self-administered pension fund to be instituted for the benefit of each of the group members. This in turn enabled a tax deductible ordinary annual contribution, related to the salary drawn to be paid into the pension fund by the company up to the capped earnings limit of £84,000 in 1997/98, under TA 1988, s 592(8)(c) (Retirement Benefit Scheme (Indexation of Earnings Cap) Order 1996 (SI 1996 No 2951), and Retirement Benefit Scheme (Restriction on Discretion to Approve) (Small Self-administered Schemes) Regulations 1991 (SI 1991 No 1614)). This premium would be saved up within a tax free fund for the benefit of the individual group members.

As the funds were self-administered each group member was, as a trustee of the pension fund, able to decide on the investment policy he or she preferred within the tax free structure of the fund, so long as the Pension Schemes Office guidelines were adhered to. The pensioner trustee for the funds was able to agree with the Pensions Schemes Office that in view of the fund members' income coming from the pop music world the normal retirement age would be 40 instead of the more usual retirement age of 60. So far as Morris was concerned, however, as a manager it was not possible to agree a normal retirement age below the age of 60.

The self-administered pension fund enabled the money to be saved up in a tax free environment for the future benefit of the group members when, from age 40 onwards, they would be able to draw a pension taxable as earned income. They would also be able to commute part of this pension entitlement for a tax free lump sum equal to one and a half times the final salary up to the earnings cap based on the number of years the employment had continued.

The children's trusts

It was intended to pay dividends from the companies to the children's maintenance and accumulation settlements, thus transferring some money into the hands of the trustees where, to the extent that it was accumulated, it would suffer tax at the basic rate and the additional rate, totalling 35 per cent. It was appreciated that as the parents were the settlors any income not accumulated but distributed to the children would be taxed as the parents' income. Consideration was given to making friends or grandparents the settlors of the trust, which would then buy the shares in the companies. However, it was thought that the Revenue would argue that the true settlors of the trust funds were in any event the parents and that such an exercise would therefore be pointless.

The small companies' rate

The existence of the partnership meant that the four companies of the group members were associated companies for the small companies' rate and it was therefore decided to look carefully to see whether the partnership could be wound up without adverse tax consequences at a fairly early stage. Any profits left in the companies would then be taxed only at the small companies' rate of 23 per cent rather than the 33 per cent which would apply if profits of more than the lower relevant limit were accumulated within the companies. This limit was £300,000 for the year beginning 1 April 1997. Profits in a single company (with no associated companies) of between this and the upper relevant limit of £1,500,000 for the year beginning 1 April 1997 would be taxed at the marginal small companies' rate of 35.5 per cent. However, the payment of salaries and pension fund contributions would enable the profits to be kept within the small companies' rate for the first period.

Another record

The songwriters in the group were meanwhile working on another record entitled 'Palace Promises' and in view of the success of 'Peer West' Morris was able to negotiate slightly better terms. The group were entitled to an artistes' royalty of 11 per cent of the retail value of the records and publisher Zombie Productions Ltd agreed to split the publishing and composing royalties 70/30 in the writers' favour. All the income from both the latter sources went to the individuals' own companies and was largely paid out by way of remuneration and pension fund contributions.

The overseas companies

Morris now planned for the group to make an overseas tour and, as this involved activities outside the UK, a further company was set up for each individual and consideration given as to whether this should be a non-UK resident company. Setting up an overseas company seemed an attractive solution until the anti-avoidance provisions were looked at in more detail (TA 1988, ss 739 and 740). Under these provisions it seemed that the income of the company could be regarded as the income of the individuals unless there was a good commercial reason for having an overseas company (TA 1988, s 741). Other anti-avoidance provisions would in any event prevent the build-up of a capital sum outside the UK through overseas companies (TA 1988, s 775) and therefore it was decided to form UK

Brighton Rock: structure

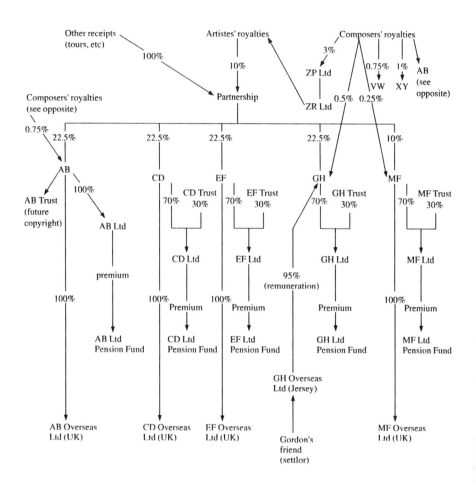

resident companies wholly owned by the group members for the overseas activities, except for Gordon, as in any event it was likely that the majority of the income would at some stage be taken out by way of remuneration or pension contribution.

The purpose of the new companies was to give a separate overseas employment which in turn might enable the remuneration to qualify for a 100 per cent deduction (TA 1988, s 193) as all the duties were performed overseas if the employee were to spend at least 365 days outside the UK. It was accepted that the Revenue had an argument for aggregating the UK and overseas remuneration (TA 1988, Sched 12, para 2) but there was a counter-argument that the remuneration from the overseas activities could be shown to arise overseas.

In view of his non-UK domiciled status, Gordon's company was set up in Jersey as a non-resident company which was beneficially owned by a Guernsey resident and domiciled friend of Gordon's, to forestall any Revenue arguments on transfer of assets abroad (TA 1988, s 739). Gordon, however, had a service agreement with the company whereby he was entitled to 95 per cent of the company's profits as remuneration. As emoluments from a foreign employment with a non-resident company for duties carried out wholly overseas, the remuneration would be taxed only on the full amount of any remittances to the UK (TA 1988, ss 19 and 192).

Gordon accepted the risk that the service agreement itself might constitute a transfer of assets and therefore cause Gordon to be assessed on the profits of the company.

Double taxation

So far as the USA was concerned, however, it was decided that each individual group member would be engaged by the American tour operator, which was a locally managed and controlled American company. The reason for this was that the Internal Revenue Service could tax the earnings of the group members' employing companies as if it were the income of the individual group members personally (UK/USA Double Tax Agreement SI 1980 No 568, article 17). The effect of this, however, was not merely to make the employing companies ineffective from an American tax point of view, but would result in the Internal Revenue Service subjecting the income of the employing company to tax in the USA as if it were the employee's income and to that extent the UK company would have a foreign tax credit. However, if the company then paid out its income in the form of remuneration to the group member, which was the object of the exercise, it would have no UK tax liability against which it could absorb the foreign tax credit. Although the UK Revenue had been known to look through the company in the same way as the Internal Revenue Service and give relief for the American tax against the individual's own UK income from the company, this was concessionary treatment and could not be relied upon. Attempts to resolve this problem with the Technical Division of the Inland Revenue had so far proved unsuccessful. It was therefore decided that each group member's activities in the USA should be in a personal capacity, which would give rise to a Schedule D, Case V assessment in the UK as a professional performing in the USA, as there was no such recording or performing activity being carried on personally in the UK. Gordon claimed the remittance basis as he was not domiciled in the UK (TA 1988, s 65).

In such circumstances there would be no difficulty in obtaining relief for the American tax paid against any UK tax payable personally on that income.

The tour was a modest success and helped considerably in the sale of both 'Peer West' and 'Palace Promises'. The group's third record, 'The Beach', produced following the overseas tour, was an instant success.

By now the group was well established in the UK and was becoming established overseas. Substantial sums of money were flowing into the UK companies. The partnership had outlived its original purpose and was now wound up; the continuing royalty income from 'Peer West' was taxed on the individuals in accordance with their profit shares as post-cessation receipts taxed as earned income on a current year basis (TA 1988, ss 103–110).

Cedric and Elizabeth had decided that there was a possibility of writing a screenplay for a film involving the group while Gordon and Agatha thought it would be desirable to release a new record before the success of 'The Beach' was forgotten. Morris, however, wanted to arrange another overseas tour which would help record sales, particularly in Germany, Japan and the USA. It was decided to combine these activities and to produce the new record outside the UK so that the royalties could legitimately flow to the companies dealing with the overseas activities. For the fourth record, entitled 'Regency Relics', Vernon Wallace was not involved and Agatha and Gordon between them composed all the tracks. The record was actually written and produced in Spain, although still released by Zombie Records Ltd, in the UK and by its subsidiary, Zombie Records Inc, in the USA.

While Agatha and Gordon had been writing the songs for the record, Cedric and Elizabeth had been in Corfu producing a screenplay for the proposed film.

When the record had been produced and released the overseas tour commenced, structured in the same manner as previously. By this time the group had been outside the UK for about eight months and Agatha and Gordon returned to the UK because Agatha was homesick and did not care about money anyway and Gordon was happy with the remittance basis. Elizabeth and Cedric, however, decided to remain outside the UK for a further four months so that they would qualify for the 100 per cent deduction from the earnings paid by their foreign income companies in respect of the overseas activities. As the resultant period exceeded 365 days the 100 per cent deduction would apply not only to the tour receipts, so far as received by the company and paid out by way of remuneration, but also to the income from 'Regency Relics' similarly paid out.

The film

So far as the film was concerned it was decided to set up a traditional royalty strip (*see* p 375). A friend of Agatha's resident and domiciled in Jersey settled $10,000 on a Cayman Islands trust, the beneficiaries of which were charities outside the UK but with power to add additional beneficiaries. The trustees incorporated a company in the Netherlands Antilles called Venah (Holdings) NV which in turn formed a Netherlands subsidiary company Venah BV. Venah (Holdings) NV acquired by way of assignment the screenplay from Cedric and Elizabeth for $100,000 which was thought to be a fair market value. This was a Schedule D, Case II receipt of the two writers but as they had been engaged on the production for less than a year it was not possible to claim the benefit of any of the spreading provisions (TA 1988, s 534). Venah (Holdings) NV also entered into a contract with each of the group members' UK employing companies for their services for a fee of $50,000 each to appear in the film. This was again thought to be a fair market rate for the work involved.

Venah (Holdings) NV sub-contracted the production of the film to a UK company which duly produced the film on its behalf. Venah (Holdings) NV then licensed its Netherlands subsidiary company, Venah BV, which in turn sub-licensed the film to distributors in various countries. The royalties for the showing of the film were largely paid to Venah BV without deduction of any withholding taxes, in view of the double tax agreements between the countries where the film was shown and the Netherlands. It was agreed with the Netherlands Revenue authorities to leave 6 per of the royalty income in the Netherlands where it would be taxed at an effective 40 per cent. The remaining 94 per cent of the income would be paid by way of royalty to Venah (Holdings) NV in the Netherlands Antilles without any Netherlands withholding tax. As Venah (Holdings) NV was not trading in the Netherlands Antilles it was subject to tax at between 2.4 per cent and 3 per cent of its profits which were then distributed by way of dividend to the trustees of the Cayman Islands trust free of all further taxes. By this means the majority of the profits from the film were accumulated in the Cayman Islands for reinvestment. At some future date members of the group expected to become not ordinarily resident in the UK. They could then be made additional beneficiaries of the trust and have a lump sum paid to them which could be free of UK tax. It was thought that in such circumstances the Revenue would not be able to tax the sum under the anti-avoidance provisions (TA 1988, ss 739 and 740) and it was argued that the film royalties were not income arising from the activities of any individual (TA 1988, s 775) which would have made the capital sum taxable in the UK whether or not the individual was then not ordinarily resident.

The royalty income of the group members' own companies was regarded as trading income and not investment income because the entitlement to the income arose from the activities of the company and not from copyrights acquired by purchase. Income arising from the reinvestment of undistributed royalties, however, would be investment income. Thus the majority of such reinvestment took place through the self-administered pension funds rather than in the company itself. This helped to ensure that the companies did not become close investment-holding companies who are not entitled to the small companies' rate (TA 1988, ss 13 and 13A).

Gift of future copyright to trust

When the group came to write the fifth record 'Black Rock', Agatha had decided that it would be a good idea to set up a maintenance and accumulation settlement for her daughter, Ingrid, after all. As her own company was relatively valuable by this time she decided, in view of the capital gains tax implications, not to transfer the shares in her company to the settlement but instead to give the trustees the copyright in the songs she was about to write for the record 'Black Rock'. It was argued that as she had not yet written the songs there could be no reduction in her estate for inheritance tax purposes. It was also argued that as the rights had not been created there could be no material capital gains tax charge. The songwriting activities in the

UK were part of Agatha's own Schedule D, Case II professional income and therefore it was not necessary to bring into her professional receipts any notional income from the copyrights transferred to the settlements. As the income would be accumulated within the trust it would be subject only to tax at the basic rate and additional rate totalling 35 per cent and could in due course be paid out as capital to Ingrid at some stage after she reached her majority. As it was a maintenance and accumulation settlement it was essential that Ingrid became absolutely entitled to the current income of the trust before she reached the age of 25 so that she became entitled to an interest in possession, although it would not be necessary for her to become entitled to the capital at any particular age. Agatha therefore had the trust deed drafted so that Ingrid became entitled to the income of the trust from age 22 and to the capital at age 60 but with wide powers given to the trustees for earlier advancement of the whole or part of the trust capital.

The group then started to plan their future activities.

Brighton Rock: film structure

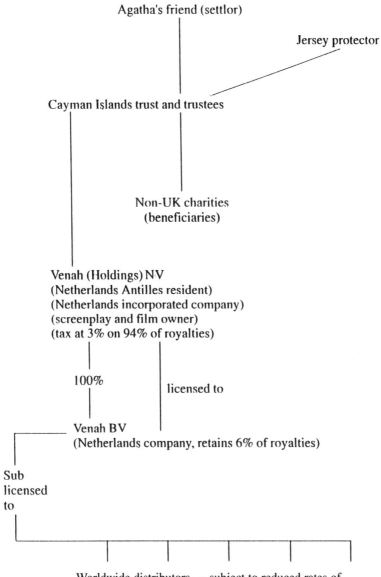

Agatha's friend (settlor)

Jersey protector

Cayman Islands trust and trustees

Non-UK charities
(beneficiaries)

Venah (Holdings) NV
(Netherlands Antilles resident)
(Netherlands incorporated company)
(screenplay and film owner)
(tax at 3% on 94% of royalties)

100%

licensed to

Venah BV
(Netherlands company, retains 6% of royalties)

Sub
licensed
to

Worldwide distributors — subject to reduced rates of
withholding tax under Netherlands double taxation
agreements

Case study 4: Plymouth Sound, entertainers

Introduction

Plymouth Sound are a rock group which has been very successful in the UK and which comprises four members, A, B, C and D, plus their manager, E. All five of them are UK resident and ordinarily resident, the only non-domicile being C, who has retained his domicile of origin in India.

A and C are married with three children and two children respectively, as is E, the manager, who has one child. B and D are unmarried. We understand A's marriage is on the rocks as a result of the groupies luring A from his marital bed and A has asked us to ensure that his tax planning takes account of his forthcoming divorce.

B is the songwriter of the group which now record only their own compositions. E the manager, has recently acquired an interest in a recording studio in the Caribbean and is proposing that their next album is recorded in his Caribbean recording studio.

The group was originally assessed as a partnership, but some time ago they were advised to set up their own employment companies in the UK, including the manager, so that there are currently five UK companies, A Ltd, B Ltd, C Ltd, D Ltd and E Ltd which receive the income generated from existing records.

The group has now become so successful that F, an Austrian corporate promoter, has offered E the opportunity of staging a world tour for Plymouth Sound over a two-year period, ending in the UK but starting in the USA, and taking in Canada, Germany, France, Japan, Australia and New Zealand. F's plan is to commission B, the songwriter, to compose an entirely new album which would be written around the show which G would direct (G is a French director with whom F has worked on previous shows) but F's ideas are to make the show unique in pop-star touring history, bringing the Dutch modern ballet troupe together with Plymouth Sound in a choreographed/rock music show. H, the choreographer, is an hermaphroditic Dutch-man.

Based on the above, you are asked to devise a structure which would receive the income generated from the world tour in the most tax efficient way, and you are also invited to comment on, and improve, the existing arrangements of the group.

Existing arrangements

The partnership

The partnership had been in existence for a relatively short time from 1 June 1994, and had made little money in its first period before it was decided that the companies be formed. It is suggested that the partnership retains its entitlement to royalties from the first record so as to avoid a charge to tax on the present value of the future income. The partnership is taxable on the current year basis throughout, under the self-assessment rules.

The companies

The idea of creating 'slave' companies for each artiste is basically sound. Pop artistes generally have a very short career and if they receive income during a short period at a high level, the marginal income tax rate of 40 per cent will apply. If however a company can receive that income and defer payments to the artistes over a period of years, then the marginal tax rate may be lower, with the smaller companies' corporate tax rate of 25 per cent or the higher 33 per cent being applicable in the meantime. One is also more capable of planning a pension payment through a company and because the income would be coming from the pop music world, the pensioner trustee for the pension funds may be able to agree a normal retirement age of 40 instead of the more usual retirement age of 60, although this would apply only for A, B, C and D, not E.

Plymouth Sound

A	Singer	Married	3 Children	Divorce!
B	Singer	Composer	Single	
C	Singer	Married	2 Children	Non-Domiciled
D	Singer	Single		
E	Manager	Married	1 Child	
F	Promoter	Dutch Corporation		
G	Director	French		
H	Choreographer	Dutch		
I	Dutch Modern Ballet Troupe			

Tour programme:

USA	Japan
Canada	Australia
Germany	New Zealand
France	United Kingdom

Ownership of companies by trusts

At present, A, B, C, D and E all own their own slave companies. Primarily for inheritance tax reasons, it would be helpful at this stage to plan the estate of all five individuals before the world tour is put in place; as far as E is concerned, there could be an element of capital gains tax planning as well since at some stage he may wish to sell his interest in Plymouth Sound.

A, C and E could each create accumulation and maintenance settlements for their children and transfer part of their shares in A Ltd, C Ltd and E Ltd to these trusts. They could also gift shares to the value of their nil rate band on the inheritance tax scale to offshore discretionary trusts which would exclude A and E from benefiting under the trust deed, although C would not have to be so excluded as he has non-domicile status; there may be a small capital gains tax charge in respect of this transfer of shares, but this would be relatively small in relation to the potential tax savings.

C and E may then wish to retain their remaining shares in their own ownership, but for E, he may consider transferring the remainder of the shares into a UK trust of which he is life tenant which would claim hold-over relief for capital gains tax until the shares were eventually sold. A may wish to transfer his remaining shares out of his ownership into the ownership of a UK discretionary trust to prevent his wife from claiming her absolute right in the forthcoming divorce.

B and D, both unmarried, may wish to create offshore discretionary settlements up to the inheritance tax band limit. It is unlikely however that they could plan for a potential capital gain on the sale of their shares, since the companies' income rests solely with the activities of the band members and sale of shares by them would probably be unfeasible. They are therefore more likely to retain the shares in their companies in their own names.

The world tour structure

E and F decide to create a holding company offshore of which they would each own 50 per cent; this 50 per cent interest could prevent control being in either E's or F's hands, thereby blunting some of the anti-avoidance legislation in the UK. In order to enable tax deferral to be achieved, it is essential that the holding company be located in a tax free or low tax jurisdiction. F, who is not taxed on foreign source dividends from a substantial shareholding in a foreign company, wishes to receive dividend income and suggests incorporating a Cyprus offshore company to receive income subject to a low tax rate and distribute it as dividends. E could see no reason why this Cyprus company should not be used as the holding company, although E and the members of the group were unlikely to receive income in the form of dividends from the Cyprus company, but in the form of fees. E and F therefore agreed that Plymouth Sound and E could receive their income from the Cyprus company as fees, waiving their dividend entitlement and allowing all dividends to be paid to F. The Cyprus company would be incorporated as an offshore company, thereby being subject to a tax rate of 4.25 per cent instead of the normal rate of 20/25 per cent.

A Ltd, B Ltd, C Ltd and D Ltd would all contract with CYco (the Cyprus company) to provide the services of A, B, C and D for the world tour. E Ltd would agree to provide the services of E as the financial brain.

CYco would then incorporate two subsidiaries, the first being a Jersey exempt company (Jco) and the second a Netherlands Antilles company (NAco). Jco would contract with B Ltd for the composition of the new album, with A Ltd, B Ltd, C Ltd and D Ltd for the services of A, B, C and D in recording the album, and with the Caribbean recording studio owned by E for recording the album, so that Jco would end up with the entire rights to the music.

NAco would contract with the Dutch Modern Ballet, with G the French director for the show, and H the Dutch hermaphroditic choreographer to provide all of the choreography, design and other similar services, direction, plus the services of the Dutch Modern Ballet Troupe. In order to put together the world tour, NAco, Jco and CYco would have to pool their respective rights and contract either with each other or through a third party so that the tour can take place in each territory. The Dutch promoter F decides to set up a Dutch company, Hco, which will contract with CYco, Jco and NAco for the rights to put on the show, and Hco will then contract

Plymouth Sound: structure

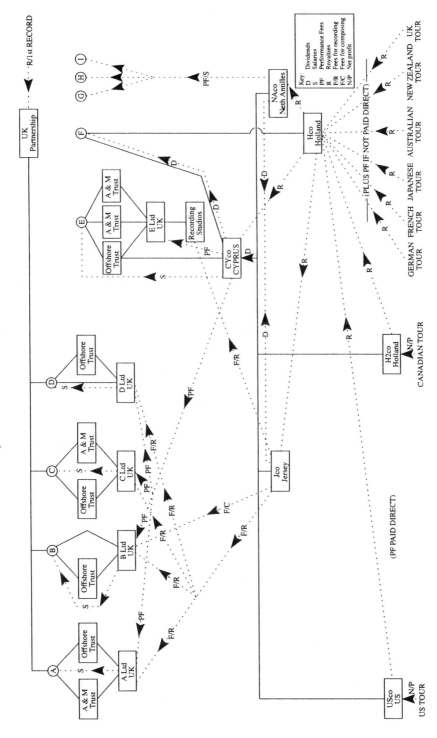

with independent promoters in each of the territories. As far as the rights are concerned, royalties will flow through Hco to Jco and NAco, with fees payable for the services of A, B, C, D, E, G, H and the Dutch Modern Ballet Troupe being paid either direct to the individuals, to their slave companies, or to NAco or CYco depending upon local tax legislation in each territory.

On receipt of royalty income in Hco, an advance tax ruling from the Dutch authorities will require that a spread of 7 per cent remain in Holland to be subject to about 35 per cent tax in respect of the first Dfl 2 m of royalties, falling to 6 per cent for royalties between Dfl 2 and Dfl 4 m, 5 per cent for royalties between Dfl 4 and Dfl 6 m, 4 per cent for royalties between Dfl 6 m and Dfl 8 m, 3 per cent for royalties between Dfl 8 and Dfl 10 m and 2 per cent for royalties in excess of Dfl 10 m. A ruling could also be obtained that in respect of fees paid to Hco for the services of the individuals, Hco would be able to pass these through to CYco or NAco subject only to a 2 per cent retention.

When the fees receivable flow into NAco and CYco, they may be paid out again subject to limited tax charge in the Antilles and Cyprus; similarly royalties may also be paid out either by way of fees or in the case of F, as dividends from Cyprus. The rate of tax in the Antilles will be 2.4 per cent on the first 100,000 guilders of royalty income, rising to 3 per cent in excess of this figure, although favourable rulings can be obtained in the Antilles whereby a percentage of that income may be paid out as expenses, so the effective tax rate can be limited to just 1 per cent of income. Jco, being an exempt company in Jersey which could be managed and controlled by Jersey residents, would not be subject to any tax rate based on income, but merely a flat rate duty of £500 pa.

The royalty income then flowing back to CYco from NAco and Jco would then be subject to a maximum tax rate of 4.25 per cent in Cyprus, although the fees payable to A Ltd, B Ltd, C Ltd, D Ltd and E Ltd (representing E's half share of profits plus the entitlements of A, B, C and D) could be deducted as fees, limiting Cyprus taxation just to F's share. Assuming that A, B, C and D were each entitled to 15 per cent of the net royalty income, 40 per cent would then be split between E and F, leaving F's share of 20 per cent subject only to the 4.25 per cent Cyprus tax rate, ie an overall rate of 0.85 per cent of net income. E can then waive his dividend rights so that F could receive his 20 per cent from Cyprus with no additional Dutch taxation levied.

UK tax objectives

The objectives of A, B, C and D would be to limit their UK personal tax exposure by postponing income receipts from Jco and CYco over a period of time, which would continue long after the tour had ended. Additionally, because all of their activities were going to be abroad until the UK tour (including the recording of the album), they would be able to qualify for 100 per cent deduction under the provisions of TA 1988, s 193 and Sched 12, if their period of absence exceeded 365 days (with an allowance of one sixth of that period being present in the UK without interrupting the 'continuity' of the 365 days period of absence). The absence would not have to be from 5 April in any one year, but could be during the middle of a tax year and could last for say one and a half years with full exemption being given for all income connected with the full period of absence.

E also wishes to benefit from the 100 per cent exemption as he will have to tour with the group, and wonders whether he can avoid the National Insurance surcharge of 10 per cent which will be levied on the remuneration paid by A Ltd, B Ltd, C Ltd and D Ltd to A, B, C and D. Consideration could therefore be given to E limiting his contract with E Ltd to purely UK activities, and entering into a new contract with CYco for all non-UK activities. The 100 per cent exemption would still be given to E, even if his employer is non-UK resident.

The objectives may therefore be summarised as follows:

1. For UK source income to reduce the higher levels of personal income tax by paying salaries over a period of years, with profits in the meantime being subject to lower rates of corporate tax.

2. To provide for pension payments by heavy annual premiums and thereby defer heavy rates of current taxation.

3. To receive non-UK source income subject to low rates of foreign income taxes, whether by direct assessment or by withholding.

4. To avoid UK income tax on income received overseas in respect of employment exercised outside the UK.

Recording and composing the album

B Ltd should contract with B to compose all of the music for the forthcoming album and show, the activities of composition to be performed outside the UK. B will therefore leave the UK, possibly earlier than the rest of the group, and work on his compositions in, say, the Caribbean island where the recording studio is located. His contract of employment with B Ltd will provide for a salary plus bonus to be paid to him.

A, B, C and D will then each have separate contracts with their own slave companies for recording services, again to be performed on the Caribbean island, and again, each contract will provide for a fixed salary plus bonus to be payable. E will arrange for the recording to be carried out on the island, subject to a fee being paid to the recording studio, but the rights will all be in the name of Jco, by means of contracts between A Ltd, B Ltd, C Ltd and D Ltd for the recording and composing services of A, B, C and D.

As stated above, separate contracts will be entered into between A Ltd, B Ltd, C Ltd and D Ltd with CYco for the performing services of A, B, C and D in territories around the world. Where it is necessary, or considered advisable for A, B, C and D to be paid direct (via their slave companies) from a particular territory, CYco will contract with a local promoter to make available the services of A, B, C and D but for payment to be effected direct to A Ltd, B Ltd, C Ltd and D Ltd.

Normal double tax treaty provisions relating to entertainers

Article 14 of the USA/UK double tax treaty provides that income earned by a UK individual who is present in the USA for more than 183 days in a tax year, or who has a fixed base available to him in the USA, will be subject to American tax but only on so much of the income as is attributable to services performed in the USA. This certainly covers the taxation of managers of entertainers, but not entertainers themselves as is described below.

Article 15 covers the salaries of employees and provides that employees of a firm or corporation who are not present in the USA for more than 183 days in a year and whose remuneration is not borne by a fixed base or permanent establishment, will not be subject to American tax. Again, but for the provisions of article 17, an entertainer could be employed by a foreign corporation and shelter under the provisions of article 15.

However, the OECD Model Treaty and the most recent double tax treaties include a provision which is article 17 of the model treaty and is as follows:

1. Notwithstanding the provisions of Article 14 and 15, income derived by a resident of a Contracting State as an entertainer, such as a theatre, motion picture, radio or television artiste, or a musician, or as an athlete, from his personal activities as such exercised in the other Contracting State, may be taxed in that other State.

2. Where income in respect of personal activities exercised by an entertainer or an athlete in his capacity as such accrues not to the entertainer or athlete himself but to another person, that income may, notwithstanding the provisions of Article 7, 14 and 15 be taxed in the Contracting State in which the activities of the entertainer or athlete are exercised.

This provision will be examined in greater detail below as it relates to the USA, Australia, Germany and the other territories covered, but the effect of the provision is to override articles 14 and 15 and permit a foreign country to impose tax on a UK-resident entertainer performing in the foreign country.

It used to be relatively simple to avoid a foreign tax liability since the very old treaties did not contain an article 17, and entertainers could shelter under the provisions of article 14 or 15. Countries then realised that entertainers were not being subject to tax on substantial sums earned during relatively short periods, and therefore introduced an article 17-type provision, but only the first part of the current provision, leaving the opportunity available to employ entertainers through a 'loan-out' company and avoid foreign tax since the company itself is not conducting business activities in that country. Several of these older style treaties have not yet been renegotiated, and there therefore exists considerable opportunity for using these loan-out companies to reduce the overall tax burden of an individual. It must be remembered, however, that the OECD Commentary on the Model Treaty allows countries with special 'look through' rules, such as the UK and the USA, to tax look through companies under article 17(1)-style treaties without the need to rely on article 17(2)-style provisions.

USA tour

In general, all American source income is subject to personal income taxation, whether earned by an American citizen, resident alien, or non-resident alien. Thus, remuneration from any work performed in the USA is basically subject to tax, unless an applicable double tax treaty exempts a non-resident from tax if (*a*) he is present in the USA for less than 183 days in a year; and (*b*) no permanent American establishment is bearing the cost of his salary. However, if the employee is present in the USA for less than 90 days in a year, and his salary does not exceed $3,000 in respect of such employment, no American tax will be levied (regardless of any treaty), provided that the employer does not have a permanent establishment in the USA.

An individual should be treated as a resident of the USA for any calendar year or part of a calendar year if he meets one of the following tests:

1. he is a lawful permanent resident of the USA at any time during a calendar year and has a relevant green card, although residency may be deemed to take effect only from the date when the individual first entered the USA; or

2. he meets the cumulative presence test, ie:

    (a) the number of days the individual is present in the USA during the current tax year; plus

    (b) one third of the days he was present in the preceding tax year; plus

    (c) one sixth of the days the individual was present during the second preceding year;

    exceeds or is equal to a total of 183 days.

Unlike UK rules, any amount of time spent in the USA in a day constitutes presence for that day, even if he was absent at midnight at the end of each day.

An exception to the cumulative presence test is if the individual is present in the USA for less than 31 days in a current year; if (as reserved under treaties) the individual is present in the USA for less than 183 days during a current tax year, and can establish tax residence in a foreign country, provided that the individual does not have a green card; or if the individual is a diplomat, teacher or student and does not intend to reside permanently in the USA.

If an individual is a resident of the USA for three consecutive years then is resident again during one of the subsequent three years, the individual will be subject to American tax for all intermediate years on the same items of income that would be taxed to an American citizen who renounced his citizenship with the intention of avoiding American tax.

Individuals should be aware that classification as a USA resident will not only subject them to worldwide income taxation in the USA, but also affect the status of foreign companies of which they are shareholders under the anti-avoidance rules of Sub-part F.

It is therefore essential that A, B, C, D and E all avoid USA residence if the income of the foreign companies in the structure is to fall outside the scope of American taxation.

Double tax treaties may improve the position generally for non-resident aliens having American source income, but if they are artistes or athletes, a typical article 17 basically still permits the USA to fully tax artistes and athletes for performances rendered in the USA. Even if the payments are not made direct to the individuals but to a company, whether owned as a slave company or otherwise, salaries paid to the individuals by the company will be subject to American taxation. It should be noted that there is a limit in the USA/UK double tax treaty that gross receipts in a tax year of less than US$15,000 will not be subject to tax in the USA, but this tax structure is not predicated in the belief that each musician will earn less than US$15,000 in any jurisdiction.

It should be noted, however, that the artistes and athletes clause of the double tax treaties does not extend to other peripheral members of the tour, even such important individuals as E, the manager and financial brain, G, the French director and H, the Dutch choreographer. Provided that they are employed by non-American corporations and that their salary is not borne by a permanent establishment in the USA and that they keep within the number of days permitted in the USA and do not exceed them, their salaries should be exempt from American tax. If, therefore their salaries were paid by CYco and NAco out of royalty receipts from Hco, no American tax should apply. It is therefore important for royalties to be paid by the local promoter to Hco which, under the terms of the US/Dutch double tax treaty, should be received by Hco without any withholding tax, as Hco is independently owned by a Dutch corporation, which should enable the extensive anti-avoidance provisions in article 26 of the USA/Dutch treaty to be avoided. If there is concern that the IRS may swoop down and confiscate gross receipts under a jeopardy assessment, and if at all possible, the local promoter should be encouraged to pay a lump sum as an advance payment of royalties to Hco.

If the local promoter is not prepared to pay Hco gross royalties but wishes to deduct a withholding tax of 30 per cent and request Hco to reclaim this amount of tax as not being applicable under the double tax treaty provisions, it may be considered advisable for CYco to incorporate its own company in the USA which contracts with Hco and also the local promoter; there is then no obligation on the local promoter to withhold tax on royalties paid to the 'captive' American company, and the American company may then decide that it is perfectly proper to pay gross amounts over to Hco.

The amount of the royalty will have to be justified by reference to the services provided under the royalty arrangement, ie choreography and design of the show itself, rights to the music and services of the entourage, which will include not only the members of Plymouth Sound but also the Dutch Modern Ballet and its choreographer. These royalties should be sufficient to pay all salaries to E, G and H, plus remunerating A, B, C and D for the composing and recording performed outside the USA and therefore not taxable in the USA. However, these payments of salaries to A, B, C and D should be withheld by their slave companies, A Ltd, B Ltd, C Ltd and D Ltd until the year following that in which they are also receiving salaries for performing services in the USA; this is to avoid all salaries being lumped together and being treated as American source income in the year in which performances are rendered. It would not matter even if these amounts were retained by the companies until A, B, C and D returned to the UK after their period of absence, since salaries then paid to A, B, C and D may still be related back to their period of absence if applicable, and obtain the 100 per cent exemption from UK tax. This then leaves the American performing services of A, B, C, D and the Dutch Modern Ballet Troupe to be remunerated, and this should be under a separate contractual arrangement with either the local promoter or the local 'captive' American company. Whether these payments are made to the individuals direct, or to their companies, the Internal Revenue Service is taking the position that the American promoter which sponsors a foreign artist to work in the USA under an H-1 visa is responsible for American withholding taxes because the H-1 visa application certifies that the promoter is the artist's employer. Immigration sends a memo to the IRS regarding each H-1 visa they issue, and the IRS then sends a memo instructing the promoter to withhold income tax, even if the artist is loaned out to the studio by the artist's corporation. In order to avoid substantial withholding in the USA, the artist's loan-out company itself should apply for the H-1 visa, instead of having the promoter applying, so that the IRS is told that the employer is the loan-out company, and the IRS would then instruct the loan-out company to withhold tax. This makes it far easier to ascertain exactly an artist's tax bill by virtue of the salary actually paid to the artist, rather than the fee paid by the local promoter to the artist's loan-out company.

Where the loan-out company can avail itself of a double tax treaty and A Ltd, B Ltd, C Ltd and D Ltd can all fall within the USA/UK double tax treaty provisions, then these companies may retain income and deduct expenditure relating to the artist's services with the result that American tax will be payable only on the net figure paid to the artist.

Canadian tour

In general under the facts and circumstances test of Canadian tax law a person is not resident for Canadian tax purposes unless he is 'ordinarily resident' which would not arise in the case of a visiting entertainer unless he, in fact, 'moves in' to Canada. On the other hand there is a deeming rule under s 250(1) of the Income Tax Act which will treat any person as resident in Canada for the entire tax year (where he is not ordinarily resident) should he 'sojourn' (be physically present) in Canada for 183 days or more.

Aside from concepts of sham which can, of course, have general application to any situation, the only statutory rules with respect to 'loan-out companies' (under ss 18 and 125 of the Act) deal with situations where the relationship between the person who is being seconded or loaned-out and the person to whom the services are being provided would, in the absence of the loan-out corporation, be one of employment not self-employment (or independent contractor status) and thus the individual would have ordinarily been employed by the person to whom the individual's services are being provided indirectly through the loan-out corporation. Inasmuch as most contracts for entertainers and promoters are not contracts of employment these rules should have no application. Where these rules apply they prohibit a deduction by the corporation for any expenses (except salaries).

Non-residents (entertainers included) who are considered to be 'employed' in Canada are subject to regular taxation on the income derived from the services performed in Canada at regular tax rates.

In such case the employer is obliged to withhold taxes according to prescribed withholding tax tables which generally are intended to extract an amount of tax more or less equal to the final tax liability (assuming no other sources of income or loss). Upon filing of a return any overpayment is refunded or deficiency is due.

Where, in the more usual case, the engagement is not one of employment but rather of independent personal services there is again an obligation to pay income tax on net income derived therefrom (after deducting applicable expenses incurred to earn the income) at standard rates of tax normally applicable to a Canadian resident—again, giving rise to standard tax liability.

With regard to withholding tax obligations relative to independent personal services there is the requirement that there be a withholding of 15 per cent (under reg 105 of the Income Tax Regulations and s 153 of the Act) of the gross amount of the fees paid for the services. (In Quebec, there is also a 9 per cent withholding.) This interim withholding tax comprises advance taxes against the final tax liability otherwise determined which will lead either to a refund or additional taxes depending upon the circumstances. Revenue Canada may agree to reduce the withholding tax requirements where it can be shown that the actual liability will be less than the 15 per cent on gross.

In general, where employment income is involved Canada's double tax treaties would not provide exemption from Canadian tax for non-resident performing services in Canada except for minimal amounts. (See, for example, Canada–UK Income Tax Convention, article XIV.)

In the case of independent personal services there are the usual exemptions provided under OECD, article 14-style treaties which exempt tax where a non-resident provides independent personal services without the use of a fixed base. (Nobody really knows what a fixed base means although tax authorities may consider it to be somewhat broader than permanent establishments.) Where such services are provided through a foreign corporation then there are the comparable exemptions of OECD, article 7-style treaties for business profits earned without the use of a permanent establishment.

The problem, of course, is that in most treaties (eg Canada–USA Treaty, article XVI, and comparable provisions of the Canada–UK and most other modern generation treaties) there are special rules for athletes and entertainers which essentially oust all such treaty protection. Furthermore, in treaties such as those with Barbados and Cyprus, there are anti-treaty shopping rules which would render inapplicable any residual exemptions in circumstances involving a third country person.

In the case of A, B, C and D, they must prove themselves to be independent to the local promoter as opposed to being considered an employee of the local promoter. There are four factors which determine whether an individual is an employee or may be considered independent: the first is whether the individual is under the control of a local promoter or can choose how he performs his services; the second is whether the individual has his own 'gear' or is supplied this by the local promoter; the third is whether the individual merely receives a salary irrespective of the profitability of the venture, or, for example, whether he stands to lose anything; and the fourth is whether the individual, together with other individuals, becomes part of a total business, or merely one of the 'products' which that business sells. In the circumstances, it is likely that A, B, C and D would be accepted as independent artists, thereby preserving the independence of A Ltd, B Ltd, C Ltd and D Ltd from the local promoter. In such cases, expenses may normally be deducted by the loan-out companies so that only the net salary payment to the individual artists would be subject to Canadian tax.

In such a situation, the loan-out corporations would apply for a reduced withholding tax at the first level based on its estimated income and expenses, which will include amounts paid to the artist (under Form T4N-NR). Revenue Canada will, however, agree to this only where withholding tax pursuant to reg 102 has been made at the secondary level under Form T4. In these circumstances, all four loan-out companies could request that the local promoter reduce the 15 per cent withholding tax payable to the loan-out companies to the Canadian tax that will ultimately be levied on the salaries paid by the loan-out companies to the four artists; such salaries will contractually be of a small amount.

As far as the other salaries payable to E, G and H are concerned, these should not be subject to Canadian tax if the individuals do not become Canadian residents and they fall within the relevant provisions of the UK, French and Dutch double tax treaties with Canada.

With regard to the royalties to be received by Hco, these would normally be subject to withholding tax of 25 per cent. However, pursuant to the Canadian Income Tax Act, s 212(*d*)(1) and the Canadian/Dutch Double Tax Treaty, Article 12, Canada cannot tax copyright royalties and other like payments made in respect of the production or reproduction of any literary, dramatic, musical or artistic work. If the royalty payments fall within this exemption, then the payments will not be subject to Canadian tax, provided that Hco does not have a permanent establishment in Canada. On the other hand, if the payment is not in respect of a copyright royalty or other like payment made with regard to the production or reproduction of such work, then a Canadian withholding tax of 10 per cent could be imposed under the double tax treaty.

As with the USA, it may be possible to form a captive company to be the intermediary between Hco and the local promoter; this gives greater flexibility in arranging the withholding taxes imposed or otherwise by Canadian domestic and treaty law. However, rather than having a Canadian corporation, it may be advisable to use a treaty country corporation, such as Holland, which company (say H2co) contracts with Hco to promote the tour in Canada. Provided H2co does not have a permanent establishment in Canada within the meaning of the Canada/Dutch double tax treaty, the profits of H2co should not be subject to tax in Canada, always assuming that the local promoter in Canada does not create a permanent establishment for H2co. Without such a permanent establishment, any royalties paid by H2co to Hco may be exempt from Canadian taxation by reason of Canadian domestic law without requiring exemption under the treaty, since royalties paid by one non-resident to another are exempt.

German tour

In Germany only the 'residence' determines whether there is limited or unlimited tax liability: fiscal residence means that a permanent home is available or that there is habitual abode. The German notion of 'residence' is broad, so that a person is considered to be a resident in Germany if he has rooms at his disposal under circumstances where it could be inferred that he will keep and use them (regardless when or for what time period he stays there).

Habitual abode means that someone is present in Germany under circumstances that show that his stay is not only temporary or passing; this is deemed to be the fact if the person stays more than six months regardless of short interruptions.

The limited tax liability (with income derived from German sources) of entertainers, musicians and athletes etc in Germany was enlarged, (subject to reservations in taxation treaties) starting with the fiscal year 1986, to include income of these professionals from Germany not only from personal performance in Germany but also from exploitation of such performance or from income in connection with the aforementioned; it no longer matters who is the recipient of the payments (entertainer, foreign show enterprise or loan-out company), or whether there is one or several (split) contracts as to performance or exploitation. Therefore taxation in such cases is no longer dependent on permanent establishment or a person acting as an agent in Germany.

It has to be noted that the foreign ensemble or loan-out company may become independently taxable apart from the performing entertainer's taxation. In case an ensemble of a foreign company is performing in Germany, using both German resident and non-resident persons, the total income of the foreign company from Germany would be taxable in Germany.

The withholding tax rate is 25 per cent in the case of performance exploitation. The basis for the withholding tax includes VAT at 7 per cent for cultural services and expenses refunded. Deductions for expenses, taxes etc are not allowed, since the rate of 25 per cent already takes these expenses into consideration. The effective rate is therefore 25 per cent of 107 per cent, ie 26.75 per cent which is further increased by the solidarity surcharge of 7 per cent of 26.75 per cent making a rate of 28.76 per cent on payments made by the American company in respect of the German performances.

The promoter who is responsible for the payment has to withhold the tax and is held liable for the tax payment to the tax authorities.

The withholding taxation is final, if there is a German resident promoter; there is—except in the case of a permanent establishment and in cases where there is no German promoter who has to withhold the withholding tax—no system of tax return and assessment.

In case there is no German resident promoter, taxation is not finalised by withholding taxation but a separate tax assessment will take place, which allows business expenses to be deducted.

Double taxation treaties rank before national tax law. The national tax authorities, however, tend to take a position in their favour, so that the practical handling sometimes differs from the result which might arise if the dispute were litigated. Because the German tax authorities hold the German promoter liable for any withholding tax due in Germany, the promoters may—for reasons of their own security—tend to withhold taxes.

Since the foreign enterprise may be subject to limited tax liability and cannot deduct the payments made to the entertainer performing in Germany and the entertainer himself may be taxed, this may lead to 'over-taxation'. The same may be true in cases where there is a withholding tax (no expenses deductible) as to the person performing and the income also is related to a German permanent establishment.

There is for the moment no regulation that avoids this 'over-taxation' except a general 'mitigation' regulation in cases where tax law regulation leads to a result the tax law did not intend. This, however, would require special negotiations with the German tax authorities, and usually only applies where the direct costs exceed half the income.

There is an internal regulation of the fiscal authorities relating to orchestras that do not perform professionally but for cultural reasons; limited taxability is restricted to the foreign enterprise, the persons that perform are not taxed. It remains to be seen in the future, whether such handling will be applied in cases of 'over-taxation' of professional entertainers.

As a consequence of the withholding requirement and in the absence of court decisions for the next years, it is necessary to carefully investigate and structure the legal and business relationship between the parties involved as to type of activity, (separate) agreements for performance in Germany and abroad, or for performance and exploitation and auxiliary services, for obligations of company and performer etc at an early stage (before contracts are signed). As was stated in one court decision, it is up to the parties—at an early stage—to prepare sufficient documentation to avoid disadvantages later on.

In view of the above, it may not be possible to avoid the full 28.76 per cent withholding tax on payments made to A Ltd, B Ltd, C Ltd, D Ltd and even E Ltd, since E's services, as well as those of G and H would clearly be caught under this legislation because they are services rendered in connection with the performances. However, it should be possible to invoke the provisions of the UK, French and Dutch double tax treaties with Germany, whereby the business profits of the corporation would not be subject to tax in Germany in the absence of a permanent establishment, even if the salaries payable to the individuals are taxed in Germany under the new regulations. It would therefore appear sensible to restrict the salaries as much as possible, although of course these may always be open to adjustment if they are not comparable with salaries paid in other jurisdictions.

By maintaining a low level of salaries overall throughout the territories but keeping royalty payments as high as possible, one is able to argue with any particular tax administration that the levels of salaries and royalties are the same in all jurisdictions and are not designed to negotiate the best tax breaks in any one jurisdiction. Royalties paid by the German promoter to Hco should be exempt from the 25 per cent withholding tax in Germany, provided Hco does not have a permanent establishment in Germany.

French tour

An individual is considered to be a tax resident of France if he meets any one of the four following tests:

1. His principal place of abode is in France. This is a physical presence test and in theory it is sufficient for a person to spend more time in France than anywhere else to fall under this definition.

2. His home is located in France. An individual's home is generally speaking to be found where the individual or his family live normally (place of habitual residence). This test enables an individual who never sets foot in France during a tax year but whose family (wife and children) are living there to be considered a tax resident.

3. The individual exercises his principal business or professional activity in France.

4. The individual has the centre of his economic interests in France. For taxation purposes residence may be taken to mean domicile.

The foregoing tests are subject to the provisions contained in French double taxation treaties which take precedence over domestic law.

Until 1990, entertainers and sportsmen performing in France were required to file a tax return in France on a calendar year basis, and pay the income tax together with both the employer's share of social security assessments equal to approximately 35 per cent together with the employee's share of 15 per cent. This 50 per cent social security charge was only assessed on a limited amount of salary, although approximately 18 per cent relating to medical insurance was imposed on all compensation without any ceiling. Certainly, the social security charges could not be imposed on EC resident entertainers and sportsmen who are not residents of France but who pay social security charges in another EC member state or who are resident in those countries where a totalisation agreement with France in respect of social security charges is applicable.

Until 1990, therefore, it was common practice to use foreign loan-out companies resident in say Holland, Cyprus or Austria, which would receive the gross fees due to the entertainers and sportsmen and would then pay the necessary amounts to the individuals who would then file the necessary tax returns on limited salaries.

The 1990 Finance Law brought France into line with other countries and introduced a 15 per cent withholding tax on income earned by resident as well as non-resident authors, artists and athletes. As stated above, the individuals will still have to file a tax return, but the 15 per cent withholding tax on gross receipts would then be creditable against French personal tax on net income; however, any excess of withholding tax over personal tax due will not be reimbursed.

Royalties paid by the French promoter to Hco may again be exempt from tax in France, so that the major part of the income to all interested parties could be paid in the form of royalties.

Japanese tour

Provided that none of the musicians is a Japanese national, and that none will become resident in Japan for more than 183 days, they will be subject to tax only on their Japanese source income. If this income is paid by the local promoter to, say Hco, which, as is the situation in this case study, is not controlled by the musicians, then Hco will not be subject to Japanese tax on its profits in the absence of a permanent establishment (Japan/Dutch Double Tax Treaty, article 18(2)) and therefore the payments made by the Japanese promoter to Hco will not be subject to Japanese withholding tax. In order to obtain the exemption from withholding tax, however, it will be necessary for Hco to execute and present to the Japanese promoter a tax relief application form under the Tax Treaty (Form No 6, Relief from Japanese Tax on Income Derived by an Enterprise Providing Personal Services). If, however, the musicians were to control Hco, either directly or indirectly, all payments made by the Japanese promoter would be subject to withholding tax of 20 per cent.

Any payments made to the musicians while in Japan, whether made by the Japanese promoter or Hco and whether made for expenses or salary, will be subject to the Japanese withholding tax of 20 per cent. Payments made by the Japanese promoter of musicians' expenses however, will not be subject to withholding, if reasonable in amount and made directly by the Japanese promoter to the airline, hotel, restaurant, etc.

However, if payments are made by Hco to the musicians for their services in

Japan, but are made to them when they leave Japan, Hco is not required to withhold the 20 per cent Japanese tax. If Hco itself has also been able to avoid the 20 per cent tax on payments made to it by the local promoter, then the musicians are obliged to file a return and pay this 20 per cent tax before 15 March of the year following the year in which the income was received; they may appoint a tax agent in Japan to do this for them.

Royalties paid by the Japanese promoters to Hco will be subject to a withholding tax, but this will be limited to 10 per cent under the Dutch/Japanese Double Tax Treaty, article 13.

Australian tour

There are in effect four separate tests for determining the residence of an individual and if an individual satisfies any one of them, he will be considered a resident of Australia:

1. if he resides in Australia within the ordinary meaning of that expression;

2. if he is domiciled in Australia, subject to exception where the Revenue is satisfied that the individual's permanent place of abode is outside Australia;

3. if he has actually been in Australia, continuously or intermittently, during more than one half of the relevant year of income, subject to his abode being outside Australia and that he does not intend to take up residence in Australia;

4. if he is an eligible employee for the purpose of the Superannuation Act 1976, or is a spouse or a child under 16 years of age of such a person.

Non-residents are generally taxed in the same manner and by the same process of assessment on their Australian income as applies in the taxation of residents. Non-residents do not enjoy the zero rated first step in the individual tax rates scale. They pay tax on the first dollar of their Australian income. Non-residents are entitled to relief from Australia's Medicare levy (currently 1.7 per cent of taxable income).

Under Australian tax law, every person in Australia holding money due to a non-resident who derives Australian source income is deemed to be the non-resident's agent. (A banker may also be treated as an agent of a non-resident in respect of money held in the non-resident's account).

The non-resident's deemed agent may be required at any time to pay tax due by his overseas 'principal', is authorised and required to withhold sufficient money for the purpose from the money due to the principal, and is personally liable for the tax if he fails to do so.

Despite the apparent width of these provisions, the Commissioner of Taxation takes the view that they are directed at agents carrying on continuous business activities on behalf of a non-resident and that money need not be withheld where the agent is engaged in an isolated transaction unless an assessment has been made and the agent has notice of that fact. However, even in isolated transactions, the Australian agents of visiting entertainers generally adopt the practice of withholding sufficient money to meet their principals' tax liabilities.

A non-resident individual is required to lodge a return of his Australian source income. In the case of an entertainer (deriving all or part of his income from his business or profession) the designated form is 'Form B'.

Returns of or on behalf of non-resident individuals are due on 31 August every year, unless an extension of time is obtained. A return should be lodged on departure from Australia. The return should be lodged at a taxation office in the Australian state where the Australian source income is derived or, if the income is derived from several states, the return should be lodged in the state where the principal Australian records of the non-resident are kept.

Australia has concluded a number of treaties with other countries to avoid double taxation and prevent fiscal evasion. Tax treaties covering all areas of possible double taxation have been made with more than 30 countries including the UK.

The tax treaties have the general effect of reserving taxing rights over certain classes of income to the country of residence of the person deriving the income, and in the case of other income, providing for it to be taxed by the country of origin of that income.

Under the treaties, (including the UK Agreement) the earnings of visiting entertainers may be taxed by the country in which they perform, however short the visit.

UK/Australia Double Tax Treaty, article 13, states that income derived from public entertainers in Australia shall be deemed Australian source income and taxed accordingly. However, there is no article 17(2)-type provision in this treaty, so that UK companies could receive the income of an entertainer performing in Australia. There is no requirement to withhold taxation on payments to a loan-out company, but an entertainer working in Australia must complete the necessary forms prior to performing in Australia, and will then have to submit a tax return to the Australian tax administration. The salary received from the UK company will then be personally assessed on the entertainer by the Australian tax authorities, and double tax treaty relief should then be available in respect of such Australian taxation. As elsewhere, it is important that assessments are made in the names of the entertainers individually rather than in the UK company's names, and receipts from the Australian tax authorities should be obtained in the right form.

It should be noted that provided the UK companies have no permanent establishment in Australia, the amounts received by them in excess of the salaries paid to the artists would not be subject to Australian tax. Although of course there is a UK tax burden, the tax liability at say 33 per cent is considerably lower than the maximum 47 per cent personal tax rate in Australia. Moreover, dividends can then be distributed to the entertainer in years when his tax liability may be lower (or indeed when he may become non-resident for UK tax purposes) so that his overall UK tax rate may be kept at the UK corporate rate.

Income remitted to a tax haven would not escape Australian taxation even if the entertainer was a resident of the tax haven country concerned. Australia is the source of income if the actual physical performance of the services concerned takes place in Australia.

In addition, foreign exchange regulations exist to ensure that money cannot be sent to a tax haven where a proposed transaction involves avoidance or evasion of Australian tax. Where transactions are subject to tax screening, a tax clearance certificate from the Commissioner of Taxation must be produced before a foreign exchange dealer can remit money overseas or give foreign currency.

A, B, C and D could therefore be paid by their slave companies with limited Australian taxation. E can receive his salary without Australian tax being levied, provided he is not a resident of Australia. For this reason, it is often more advantageous to claim the 100 per cent exemption for the 365 day continous period, rather than making E become non-resident throughout the period, since then he may not be able to claim protection under the relevant double tax treaty provision.

Royalties payable from the Australian promoter to Hco would be subject to a withholding tax of 10 per cent under the Australian/Dutch Double Tax Treaty, article 12.

New Zealand tour

All foreign entertainers, no matter where they are domiciled, are subject to New Zealand withholding tax of 20 per cent on gross income. By option they may lodge tax returns and pay tax at the New Zealand rates on net income which is 21.5 per cent on the first $34,200 with the rate being 33 per cent in excess of that figure; it would therefore pay in nearly all cases to opt for the withholding tax of 20 per cent as a final tax bill.

Royalties payable from the New Zealand promoter to Hco would be subject to a withholding tax of 10 per cent under the New Zealand/Dutch Double Tax Treaty, article 12.

Case study 5:   Albert Potcher, bricklayer extraordinary

Introduction

This case study is designed to illustrate the interrelationship between the various types of intellectual property rights applied to industrial manufacture.

The product

Albert Potcher was a bricklayer. He had originally worked for various large construction companies but after a few years found that he enjoyed life much more working as an independent contractor and advertising through the local newspaper. He was self-employed, worked as few or as many hours each week as he wanted to, weather permitting, and generally enjoyed life. What irritated him was that sometimes, despite his best efforts, brickwork shifted. He was constantly at the mercy of people who wanted work done but who tried to economise on the materials. A particular problem in his area was garden retaining walls. He had lots of good contacts with the local landscape gardeners, and was often called on to build retaining walls for terraces. All too often, subsequent ground movement or the activities of the landscape gardeners themselves caused the walls to move, generating dissatisfaction among his customers and the occasional complaint.

Potcher decided something had to be done and turned his mind to whether an improvement could not be achieved by using for such retaining walls bricks which allowed a little more grip both between themselves and with the mortar than that obtained with conventional substantially flat-sided bricks with a frog in one large face. Working away with cold chisel and masonry saw he took some relatively soft bricks (since they were easier to work) and tried changing the shapes, giving them different surface configurations. To his delight he found that there were ways of shaping some of the faces of bricks which gave improved results.

Protecting the idea

Albert was quite excited by his discovery and fortunately the first person he told about it was his accountant, with whom he had, of course, a professional confidential relationship as between client and accountant. His accountant, aware from several past experiences with other clients that secrecy was of the utmost importance in these matters, counselled Albert to tell no-one about the idea before he saw a patent agent. Albert, who trusted his accountant implicitly, duly did so and was received by the patent agent with interest. The agent listened to Albert's description of how the bricks were shaped to give a self-locking action when installed in a certain way and advised Albert that certainly it would seem to be the sort of subject matter for which a patent might be obtained, provided of course that no-one had previously had much the same idea.

Albert asked whether one could find that out but was horrified to learn how much it would cost to do so. The patent agent advised filing a patent application since that was really the only way of getting any protection on the basic idea, if such was available, and it was cheaper to file an application than it was to try to do a search. This seemed good advice and Albert instructed that an application be prepared. The patent agent took down the details and drafted a specification. The agent felt that there were really two slightly separate inventions, one being the shape of the bricks themselves and the other being the way in which they were fitted together, but he wrote descriptions of the article and the method into a single patent application and, having secured Albert's approval of them, filed the written documents at the Patent Office.

This took several weeks, but after that Albert knew that he was at least initially protected, to the extent that he could now go and talk to other people about his idea.

This he did, first to a specialist brickmaker to see if special shaped bricks could be produced to enable a proper test of the idea to be carried out and then to the more reliable of his landscape gardening friends who might be interested. The parties seemed enthusiastic and, although the bricks were obviously going to be more expensive, the area in which they both worked was well populated by people with more money than sense and the landscape gardener thought he could persuade some of them to pay up adequately in return for the promise of a better construction. After a lot of fuss and bother bricks were duly produced and used in three or four different sites. They aroused some interest and unquestionably seemed to work. Of course no-one could be quite sure whether the walls in question would have moved or stayed put anyway, but everybody seemed pleased.

Beginning commercial exploitation

By this time Albert thought he might be on to something and he and the landscape gardeners decided to do a deal. The landscape gardeners would promote the system and try to get orders and in return Albert would supervise the works and have a slice of the profits derived from that particular area of the business. This sounded quite attractive to Albert but he was by no means certain that it was the right way to go. His experience of bricklaying had taught him that bricks were useful in more than building retaining walls in gardens and he wondered whether the potential might not be rather greater. He accordingly approached a civil engineering company of some standing and told them about his ideas. He showed them the patent application, then some eight months old, and they were pleased that he had taken that first step. They said they would like to evaluate the idea but that it would take time and they would let Albert know. Albert communicated this to his patent agent who said that this was all very well but if the idea really was going to take off then it would be desirable to try to secure patent protection on a somewhat broader basis geographically. Albert thought the construction company had been sufficiently enthusiastic to make that a real possibility but he was somewhat daunted by the cost. He therefore went to the contractors and offered them a deal.

He said that he would not try to sell the idea to anyone else within the next 12 months if they would put in some effort to testing the idea on a large scale and additionally put up some money to start securing foreign patent protection. The contractors were keen, particularly since they had just been asked to tender for some very substantial reservoir works where they felt the invention could be advantageously used and in respect of which the cost of patenting was insignificant compared to the potential value of the contract. They therefore advanced some money to Albert which he used for filing, on the basis of his original British application, some applications in other countries, notably North America, Japan, some Commonwealth countries and a European application designating ten countries. The original British application was used just as a basis for claiming priority.

During this time Albert had reserved for himself and his landscape contractor friends the ability to go on buying bricks and using them and they were continuing to operate in that way, and the brickworks themselves were beginning to be interested. The brickmakers in fact wanted to make more of these bricks since they commanded a better margin and it was naturally of assistance in promoting their business as specialist brickmakers to be associated with a new development in bricks. Indeed the brickmakers went so far as to start offering to supply the new sort of brick to third parties which infuriated Albert when he heard about it, and which in turn led to displeasure on the part of the brickmakers when they found Albert wanted to stop them. The brickmakers had never asked Albert for a penny piece in connection with making the moulds or anything like that and effectively told him to get lost. Albert wrote them a letter saying that he had all rights in the new bricks and that he would sue them, whereupon the brickworks instructed their solicitors to enquire gently what the problem was.

At this stage Albert, realising that the brickworks were not terribly happy, started to consider his position more carefully. The brickworks had originally worked from a specimen handmade brick which he had produced for them and Albert's patent agent said that it was by no means certain that there was any copyright in the brick itself. Albert had not done any drawings of the brick so no copyright was to be found there. Albert had heard of registering designs and suggested that, but the patent agent pointed out that by this time the brick had already been manufactured and sold, and indeed used, so the requisite novelty for registering a design no longer existed. There being no special contract between Albert and the brickworks, his position was very weak, so he decided to be conciliatory and point out to the brickworks that, while he had no great wish to stop exploitation of the idea, he did feel that he was entitled to something on all their sales of bricks and, in any case, he had made a patent application and in due course hoped that patents would be granted which would protect him against that sort of activity. The brickworks, unhappy to build up a business which might be liable to attack if Albert ever obtained his patent and in ignorance, of course, of what the patent said (the papers had not yet been published by the Patent Office), decided to do a deal with Albert where they would give him one per cent of the value of any order for the bricks. Albert thought that this was mean but agreed to it.

The brickworks wanted to promote the brick with a little bit of advertising in the trade and wanted a name for it. Albert suggested 'Frogmate', which had a certain allusiveness but was probably registrable. The brickworks asked their solicitors to take the necessary action and applied to register the name in respect of bricks and other non-metallic building materials. This caused further ructions with Albert when he found out about it, since he felt the name was his, but the matter remained unresolved and the brickworks started doing some advertising.

The company

Around this time Albert's accountant, realising that his client might have hit on something which could really make money, suggested that it would be a good idea to set up a little company to exploit the idea and, since there was a little change left over from the money advanced by the contractors, Albert did this. Albert, still annoyed by the actions of the brickworks, called it Frogmate Limited.

After a few months the contractors finished their testing and agreed that the system worked and worked well. Unfortunately, they had not secured the reservoir tender so their enthusiasm was waning. Albert by this time had formed a good working relationship with the people who had actually been doing the testing and they were enthusiastic about the idea so when the contractors finally decided not to go ahead and to write off the expenditure, that left Albert free, or at least freer, to try to exploit the invention.

He was still tied down by the fact that he had only one supplier of the bricks in question, who would clearly never be capable of supplying the enormous quantities of bricks which, by now, Albert had decided that the world needed, so Albert went to see one of the major brickmaking companies. They offered to buy out Albert lock, stock and barrel at that stage but Albert, who was beginning to enjoy wheeling and dealing, rejected that and said he was prepared to do a deal with them provided they would help him disentangle himself from his present brickmakers. This they agreed to do and, furthermore, they agreed to promote the system and pay Frogmate Limited a royalty.

The major brickworks were persuaded by Albert to pay £10,000 as an advance against royalties, which he then used to try to sort out what was going on, on the following basis: first, he transferred all the patent applications which were in his name into that of Frogmate Limited. He then applied to register 'Frogmate' in the name of 'Frogmate Limited' at the Trade Marks Registry, feeling sure that that application would then come into conflict with the earlier application made by the brickmakers and thus that neither party would get anywhere with registering the trade mark for some time. In this respect he was right and eventually the small brickmakers, by then finding themselves being elbowed out, simply faded out of the act. Albert also caused Frogmate Limited to employ one of the contractor's people who had recently been made redundant to try to develop the system a little further. This man, Tom Smith, had been employed in testing the bricks for the contractors. He settled down with Frogmate and improved on the design of the brick and designed some alternative brick types. By virtue of his contract, the property in the new designs was Frogmate's. Albert thought these looked rather good and this time was determined not to lose out on the possibility of getting some early useful protection, so he first of all had drawings made and dated and deposited with his solicitor of each of the new brick types and then he had a set of the drawings sent to his patent agent for considering whether it might not be possible to register the new bricks as designs. The patent agent pointed out that it could be argued that the brick design was purely functional but that nevertheless it did seem to have sufficient features of shape or configuration to make it rather new. Applications were accordingly filed and Albert was very pleased when they all resulted in certificates of registration issuing a few months later. He advised the big brickworks and they agreed, in respect of the modified types, to mark any bricks so produced with the registered design number. Albert wondered about designs overseas and was advised that this was possible but perhaps of questionable value. Anyway, he did nothing about it.

By this time the large brickworks were beginning to sell substantial quantities and received a number of enquiries about the new bricks. Some difficulties were being experienced in the field since people did not know exactly how to manage them, so Albert and the development man settled down and produced a handy guide as to how the bricks could be used. This went out as a brochure from Frogmate Limited, the originators of the bricks, and was widely distributed in the trade. Inevitably, the trade press gave the matter some publicity and one or two unsolicited enquiries started to come into Frogmate from overseas.

Taking the idea abroad

At this stage Albert went to see his accountant again who advised that if the British potential looked good, the overseas potential was probably good also, and suggested to Albert that a basic decision had to be made as to whether to attempt to exploit via the British company or whether an overseas company should be set up under the auspices of an appropriate foreign trust with a view to attempting to generate, and subsequently exploit, business abroad. Albert chose the latter course and his accountant put the necessary wheels in motion. Since the business overseas was very much a hope rather than an actuality, there was little value to be ascribed to the only assets which immediately had to be placed at the disposal of the overseas company, ie, the overseas patents. By this time, Albert was pleased to see that, not without fairly substantial expenditure, Patent Offices round the world were beginning to grant patents on the basis of the applications made. Armed with these patents and wearing his overseas company's hat, Albert set off on an expenses-paid trip to try to drum up business abroad.

He did well in North America, finding several interested parties who were willing to enter into royalty agreements with the overseas company. His greatest surprise came in Japan where an enquirer confided to him after several days of polite negotiation that, although possible exploitation could be arranged in Japan, it was quite impossible to use the trade mark 'Frogmate' in connection with the system, not only because of the difficulties of pronouncing that word in Japan but because of the fact that the mispronounced word could be taken as a pun in somewhat bad taste. However, the Japanese were friendly and letters of intent were exchanged.

Another trade mark

On coming back to the UK, Albert decided that a new name did have to be found and after a fair amount of searching and clearance with Trade Mark Registries via his patent agent the name CYLOCK was settled on. This could be written as a logo with part of the Y intruding into part of the C, thus symbolising in a vague way some of the interlocking features of the brick types which had now been developed. Registration of the trade mark was sought in a number of countries and subsequently secured. Frogmate Limited kept its name but the overseas company changed its name to incorporate the word 'Cylock' and 'Cylock' became the company's main housemark. There were always two elements to the trading arrangements with overseas customers; first, the patent licensing strand and secondly a trade mark licence strand, the latter enabling the arrangements to have, potentially, a very long life.

The business was now running satisfactorily and Albert decided to try to develop other schemes of an analogous nature. He worked himself on developments and collaborated with Tom Smith and third parties, but they never came up with anything quite so good as the original Frogmate idea. In respect of that idea the business had now acquired a momentum of its own and both Albert and Tom were enjoying the benefits of arrangements made via the overseas company and he and Tom made appropriate arrangements for their respective spouses and families. What Albert particularly enjoyed was travelling round the world either doing licensing deals or beavering away with lawyers and other in exploiting the intellectual property.

The competitors

The patents proved surprisingly difficult to obtain in some countries, but early initial successes in obtaining patents in North America acted as a valuable springboard, persuading quite a lot of people outside to take licences rather than fight when they too had started to modify bricks or paving slabs or other constructional units embodying the basic idea underlying the Frogmate bricks. The USA proved a valuable ground for exploitation but not, initially, for Albert. Several small companies set up, obviously wishing to imitate the invention, not doing quite as well but severely under-selling the legitimate licensee, who naturally complained. Albert, working on the assumption that he had a US patent (which he had), promptly sued and unleashed a small army of lawyers all eager to win, but not all working for the same side. Discovery proceedings dragged on with substantial depositions and even though all of the original papers (such as they were) concerning the British company were not directly in question, discovery being against the overseas company which owned the US patents, the piles of paper rapidly grew (as did the lawyers' bills). The counter-claim by the infringers not only asserted patent invalidity but fraud on the US Patent Office and there were various collateral anti-trust claims and unnerving statements in the pleadings about the defendants being entitled to substantial awards of money in their favour from Albert's company because of anti-trust violations. Before too long it became apparent that both parties were dug in for a good fight but also that there was room for everyone to make some money and on appropriate terms the American infringers took licences. Most of the American licensees simply took patent licences rather than sell 'Cylock' bricks but Albert did not mind this because to his mind the Cylock brand bricks which were sold by his main licensee were rather better manufactured and he was jealous of his own reputation in the USA.

Parallel litigation in the UK went well and he secured damages from several parties who had used the system in major construction works without asking for permission first. In Germany, despite valiant efforts, Albert never secured his patent, which was a pity since several German steelmakers had adopted the system for brick linings for furnaces. There was a continuous problem in trying to keep everyone in order in Europe because each one of his licensees thought they were getting a worse deal than the others and kept threatening to invoke Article 85. However, the business was not so substantial as to attract the attention of the Commission on its own account and the various parties were all making satisfactory money out of the arrangements they had and so they never pushed the matter too far.

The outcome

This story ends happily: Albert retired overseas to a house architect-designed and built at great expense using the Cylock brick.

Case study 6: Tanaday, the pill or potion to help you love the sun

The product

Dennis Frankinsop, Professor of Dermatology at Regents College, Oxbridge, discovered that an extract from the Yucca plant caused a reaction in skin cultures which destroyed melanomas caused by skin cancer or even naturally occurring moles, but which discoloured the skin to a pleasing golden brown not unlike the Mediterranean tan of a Swedish nymph besporting herself on the Costa Del Sol. He discovered that this skin discolouration also acted as a block which even in strong sunlight failed to allow the sun's rays to cause any further damage to the skin and therefore had the effect of preventing sunburn.

Sensing the commercial possibilities of this discovery, Professor Frankinsop applied for European patent registration through the UK patent office in the joint names of himself and Regents College. Loot Pharmaceuticals plc, a substantial UK incorporated unquoted company, founded by, and still very much under the control of, Sir Sinbad Loot, became aware of this development and protracted discussions with Professor Frankinsop and the Bursar of Regents College led to an agreement under which they would attempt jointly to develop the Professor's discovery into a commercial product for the benefit of mankind in general and Sir Sinbad in particular.

Loot Pharmaceuticals plc

Sir Sinbad's grandfather, Yefim Lutskii had emigrated in rather a hurry from Russia in 1917 and ended up in Paris where he worked for a small French perfumerie. In the late 1930s, however, Yefim emigrated once more with his family, fearing the generally xenophobic attitudes which appeared to be developing in continental Europe and came to the UK where he changed his name to Loot and founded Loot Cosmetics Ltd. He eventually retired in the early 1960s to California where he died, happily, at the age of 92. A number of Yefim's relations had remained in Russia and a spasmodic and guarded correspondence took place between Yefim and his family members as it was always his desire to return to his native land if ever it were to become free of what he regarded as the Communist totalitarian yoke. His son, Jacques, who had been born in France, took over the reins of Loot Cosmetics on his father's retirement and Loot Cosmetics continued to prosper and diversified by both internal growth and acquisition into the ethical drugs market, changing its name in the process to Loot Pharmaceuticals. In the mid-1980s, Jacques founded a charitable trust in the UK known as the Loot Foundation which he financed by substantial covenants from the company. The Foundation was part of a general restructuring of Jacques Loot's business affairs, during which it was argued on his behalf that he was domiciled in Russia, his father never having acquired a domicile of choice in France where Jacques had spent his entire childhood. Jacques' emigration and business success in England had not prevented him retaining the family desire to return to Russia in the then unlikely event of there being a change in regime. With some reluctance the Inland Revenue accepted his position as retaining a Russian domicile of origin which also determined the domicile of his own children, including Sinbad the eldest son. A structure of overseas trusts and companies was therefore set up to augment and control Loot Pharmaceuticals and its associated companies. The Loot Foundation had financed some university research which, unexpectedly, produced a most useful drug in the treatment of anorexia which was immediately snapped up by one of the rivals to Loot Pharmaceuticals which proceeded to make substantial profits out of the drug. Sinbad's apoplexy at this event was slightly mollified by his own knighthood and the fact that he had now become chief executive of Loot Pharmaceuticals, his father having retired first of all to Spain to enjoy the sunshine and then in 1993 to his native Russia. Unfortunately, Jacques had been killed while exercising his passion for flying in light aircraft, when an overexuberant Russian aerobatics champion attempted a manoeuvre in a Yakovlev 52 at a height which prevented even his consummate skill from achieving it successfully, which resulted in the demise of both of them. However, the non-UK trusts which now controlled the Loot Pharmaceuticals empire ensured that the business continued with no perceivable effect arising from Jacques' untimely death. Sir Sinbad stoutly upheld the family tradition of claiming a Russian domicile of origin and refused to accept any suggestions from the UK Revenue that having been born and educated in the UK and having lived his entire life to date in the UK, it was only reasonable to assume that he had acquired a UK domicile of choice. Sinbad's advisers pointed out that as long as he maintained a definite intention to retire to Russia, the land of his fathers, he would not have acquired the intention to remain in England permanently or indefinitely which was a prerequisite of acquiring an English domicile of choice. The fact that Sir Sinbad had never even been to Russia and that his only property overseas was the family villa in Spain, inherited from Jacques, did not affect the situation.

The joint development agreement

Professor Frankinsop and Regents College were unwilling to enter into any agreement with Loot (Cayman Islands) Ltd for the further development of the Professor's discoveries, but were persuaded that it was perfectly proper for English academics to enter into a joint development agreement with Loot (Ireland) Ltd which had substantial research and development laboratories in the countryside of West Cork, close to Ballydehob. Loot (Ireland) Ltd was commissioned by Loot (Cayman Islands) Ltd to develop the Professor's discoveries in return for the 50 per cent interest in the patent rights which had not been retained by Professor Frankinsop or Regents College (*see* diagram on p 405).

Loot Pharmaceuticals' marketing consultants in the UK were appointed by Loot (Cayman Islands) Ltd to devise an appropriate name and logo for the product which resulted in the name Tanaday and the well-known trade mark of the stylised lettering, with the white marble Grecian goddess T changing colour to the light golden brown of the Y, said to resemble a beautifully tanned Swedish maiden. Under the terms of the commissioning contract, Loot (Cayman Islands) Ltd retained copyright in all the artwork and arranged for the trade mark to be registered in the European Union as a community trade mark and in a number of other countries under the Madrid Protocol or nationally.

The initial manufacturing of the product took place in a new purpose-built factory at Gurteenroe, close to the Irish research facility in order to obtain the benefit of the Irish manufacturing taxation rate of 10 per cent and some extremely persuasive European Union grants. The terms of the assignment of the patent rights from Loot (Ireland) Ltd to Loot (Cayman Islands) Ltd involved a lump sum payment of £2 million which funded the new factory and an ongoing royalty of 8 per cent of the wholesale selling price from any Loot associated company to a third party, which mirrored the terms of the royalty payable jointly to Professor Frankinsop and Regents College. Under the terms of the UK/Irish Double Taxation Treaty, Loot (Ireland) Ltd was able to pay the royalty without deduction of withholding tax in Ireland. The Professor was subject to UK tax on the share of royalties he received, under Schedule D, Case II, as exercising his profession as inventor, as well as under Schedule E on his salary from the college. The college, as a registered charity, was not subject to tax on the royalties received, the funds being ploughed back into other research projects.

Licences and sub-licences

The manufacturing company in Ireland was, for commercial reasons, separate from Loot (Ireland) Ltd and called Tanaday Products Ltd, both companies being wholly owned by Loot Investments Ltd, a Jersey exempt company. Tanaday Products Ltd was able to license other manufacturers to produce the developed product which was available either in the form of a pill which could be taken once a day to ensure 24-hour protection from sunshine or in the form of a spoonful of liquid taken, similarly once a day, neat or mixed in with drinks. A milder formulation called Tanaday Junior was available for young children and babies to ensure protection from the sun from the earliest ages. Because the research and development had taken place in the Republic, Loot (Ireland) Ltd was able to sub-license under the protection of the Irish double tax treaty network to manufacturers in Germany, France, Spain, Italy and the USA, the royalties received being tax-free in Ireland. Patent royalties payable by Tanaday Products Ltd, the Irish manufacturing company, to Loot (Cayman Islands) Ltd were routed through Loot Netherlands BV in order to avoid Irish withholding taxes.

90 per cent of the output of Tanaday Products Ltd was sold to Loot Retailers Ltd, the chain of retail stores in the UK within the Loot Pharmaceuticals empire, and Loot Mail Order Ltd, the UK mail order branch of the group. The Inland Revenue in the UK had expressed dissatisfaction at the high price charged by Tanaday Products Ltd to its UK associated distributors and were seeking information under the provisions of TA 1988, s 773 with a view to issuing a direction under TA 1988, s 770, on the grounds that the transfer pricing between the manufacturer and the distributors was not at arm's length. The remaining 10 per cent of the output of

Tanaday Products was being distributed to overseas agents with a view to test-marketing the product in various countries, pending the conclusion of overseas manufacturing licenses; these sales were at a very much reduced price compared with the sales to the UK. In the overseas markets Tanaday Products was responsible for marketing and spending a lot of money on television and magazine advertisements. However, in the UK Loot Retailers and Loot Mail Order undertook the marketing and advertising of the product, which was the cause of the Revenue enquiries.

Further development of the discovery

Professor Frankinsop had further developed his discovery to concentrate the cancer treatment attributes of his Yucca extract and he was now able to synthesise the active ingredient. This development was taken up by one of the major international drug companies, again on a joint venture basis with the Professor and Regents College, but Loot Pharmaceuticals objected to the patent for the new drug on the grounds that it was in breach of its patents for Tanaday. As neither organisation wished to get involved in a major legal dispute which could become time-consuming and expensive, as well as severely inhibiting the ability of the medical profession to use the new drugs in the treatment of skin cancers, agreement was reached between the organisations under which the international drug manufacturer agreed to pay a royalty to the patent holder, Loot (Cayman Islands) Ltd which resolved the dispute. The Professor and Regents College were naturally entitled to a share of this royalty under the original assignment agreement with Loot (Ireland) Ltd. Loot (Cayman Islands) Ltd also took action against the UK manufacturers of a sun cream called Tan Delight, on the grounds that the logo used reflected the change from white to golden brown in the Tanaday logo and were able to enforce an injunction against the makers of Tan Delight and an order for accounting for profit, being the proceeds of the sale of Tan Delight during the relatively short time it had been on the market prior to the injunction being obtained. This amount was payable to Tanaday (Cayman Islands) Ltd as owner of the worldwide trade marks. As the accounting represented a payment of damages there was no UK withholding tax payable on the amount due.

The research chemists at Loot (Ireland) Ltd also developed from the product a sunburn relief cream for those foolish enough not to use Tanaday prior to their sunbathing. Although neither Professor Frankinsop nor anyone else at Regents College were involved in this development, it was accepted that it relied upon the developments of the master patent for Tanaday and a further licence was entered into between Loot (Ireland) Ltd, Professor Frankinsop and Regents College. Again, patent royalties under this new agreement were payable without deduction of withholding tax under the UK Irish Double Taxation Treaty and also with Loot (Cayman Islands) Ltd as holder of the other 50 per cent of the master patent. Loot (Ireland) Ltd then licensed the manufacturing rights to Tanaday Products Ltd and other manufacturers worldwide. A logo and trade mark for the new product were devised in the style of the original Tanaday logo and registered by Tanaday (Cayman Islands) Ltd which licensed the appropriate manufacturers for the territory under their domain.

Tanaday: trading structure

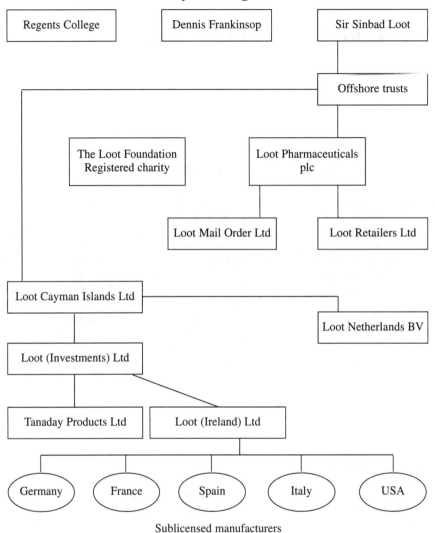

Sublicensed manufacturers

Case study 7: *Gribs by Night*

The product

Eymos Films Inc has entered into a merchandising licence agreement with Valcav Inc, in connection with the names and static visual likenesses of the fictional characters depicted in the live action science-fiction motion picture entitled *Gribs by Night*, excluding the picture dialogue, storylines and plot elements from the picture, except as specifically agreed in writing and in advance by Eymos Films Inc. The proprietary subject matter of the licence specifically includes the characters' names, likenesses (as portrayed by the live talent) and other elements referred to including, if applicable, the names of actors, voice-over artists and other elements, only to the extent of the licensor's ownership or control thereof and only as specifically depicted in and as part of the picture and subject to the actor's approval of the sculpting. The licensee is specifically granted the picture's trade mark and its logo and any derivative live action movie rights, for example books, television, videos, etc during the three-year term commencing on 1 January 1996 and in the territory covered by the licence, *viz* the universe, excluding South America, Australia and New Zealand. The licensee is also granted the right to use footage including the actors' voices in a television commercial subject to the actors' approval. Valcav Inc is licensed to produce action figures of all sizes and materials with and without special features, toy vehicles, play sets scaled to the size of the dolls and figures, dolls of all sizes and materials and fashions and accessories, board games, card games, non-board games including skill under action, playing cards, puzzles, role play and dress up sets including play sets, helmets, weapons, communication devices, etc with pedal or foot-powered ride-ons, ride-on accessories, wind-up toys, activity toys, compounds, play sets, mechanical drawing, audio-visual including projection toys, along with cartridges, software, play microphones and toy cameras, inflatables, bath toys, pre-school toys and collectible figures. The licensee obtains the right to negotiate with third parties for the manufacture and distribution of toys covered by the licence.

Terms of the merchandising licence agreement

Valcav Inc is required to make an advance royalty payment of £150,000 on account of royalties of 8 per cent as a non-returnable, recoupable advance against royalties which are calculated on the net wholesale selling prices of the articles by the licensee and its subsidiaries, affiliates or co-ventures, with no royalties payable on close-out sales at a net selling price of less than 50 per cent of the licensee's usual price to its customers and made in contemplation of the ceasing sales of the articles.

Detailed royalty reports are required, quarterly, including a product sales breakdown by product and style number, article description, unit sales, royalty base price, gross sales and net sales of each and every licensed article. Royalty payments are to be made within 45 days of the end of each calendar quarter. The licensee must deduct any applicable withholding taxes from the licensor's royalties. The licensee must pay and hold the licensor forever harmless from all other taxes, customs, duties, levies, etc which charges may not be deducted from the licensor's royalties.

There is a guarantee under the agreement that the minimum royalties for the three-year period will be £500,000, any shortfall in royalties being payable within 45 days of the expiration of the licence.

The licensee undertakes that the licensed articles are of the highest standard and quality and that the manufacture, distribution, sale promotion and advertisement of the licensed articles comply with all federal, state and local laws and regulations. The licensee also agrees to submit articles for prior approval by the licensor. The licensee acknowledges that the licensor owns and controls the copyrighted works which underly the licence and agrees not to attack the licensor's rights therein or any trade marks based thereon and agrees to co-operate with the licensor in undertaking the registration of any copyright, trade mark, service mark or other intellectual property, registration or filing in connection with the licensed articles.

The licensee has a sell-off period of 120 days on the expiration of the licence to sell off licensed articles which are on hand or in process at the time of the expiration, with accounting 30 days after the end of the sell-off period of any royalties in connection with sales other than close-out sales, at less than 50 per cent of the licensee's usual price.

Three hours before the agreement is due to be signed, Eymos Films Inc requires a further clause in the contract, stating that if withholding taxes are based on the licensor's direct net income the licensee may deduct the required amount from royalties prior to remitting them to the licensor, with a copy of such withholding tax payment prior to deducting it from the royalties and to provide the licensor with the appropriate tax credit forms within 60 days of payment of the withholding tax and to afford all necessary co-operation and support to the licensor in order to get reimbursed or credited. If the licensee does not provide the appropriate tax credit form within 60 days of payment it has to reimburse the licensor for the amounts deducted from the royalties in respect of withholding taxes.

Both Eymos Films Inc and Valcav Inc are quoted American public companies.

Exploitation of the licence

Valcav Inc considers that *Gribs by Night* is likely to be very popular and that the alien beings (ie the Gribs) are likely to appeal to children and that the battle scenes with the humans depicted in the film are likely to give scope for substantial sales in the toy market. Although Valcav Inc has considerable experience in the toy market, it has not previously had experience in creating multi-media games or die-cast metal models and therefore, enters into discussions with EBE plc, a UK quoted company which has considerable experience in both these fields.

Valcav Inc and EBE plc decide to exploit the licence through Vebe Ltd, a company incorporated in the Cayman Islands and jointly owned by both companies (*see* diagram on p 410). Because Vebe Ltd is jointly owned by EBE plc and Valcav

Inc, it is not a controlled foreign company for UK tax purposes nor a controlled foreign corporation for American tax purposes. Under the terms of the joint venture, any sales of product in the USA will be made by Valcav Sales Inc, a wholly owned subsidiary of Valcav Inc. Valcav Sales Inc will buy the licensed articles from product manufacturers and account for the royalty out of its trading profit, the royalty being payable to Valcav Inc which would on pay it to Eymos Films Inc. Similarly, EBE plc in the UK would sell product through its wholly owned subsidiary, EBE (UK) Ltd which in turn would buy direct from product manufacturers.

EBE (UK) Ltd will export products to Europe and Valcav Sales Inc will export products to the remainder of the licensed territory.

Manufacture of licensed articles

Manufacture of licensed articles and games will be undertaken by independent manufacturers in a number of European countries, Hong Kong and the Peoples' Republic of China. The distribution sub-licence between Valcav Inc and Valcav Sales Inc requires payment of a royalty of 10 per cent which may be paid without deduction of any withholding tax as a payment within the USA. The distribution licence with EBE (UK) Ltd requires a royalty of 10 per cent of the wholesale price in respect of sales in Europe which may be paid gross, under the UK/USA Double Taxation Treaty.

Valcav Inc sub-licenses the manufacturing rights to Vebe Ltd for a royalty of 5 per cent. Vebe Ltd contracts with EBE (Multi-Media) Ltd for the design of a multi-media package entitled *Gribs by Night* in return for a fixed fee which it is envisaged will give EBE (Multi-Media) Ltd a net profit of 10 per cent on the contract.

Vebe Ltd licenses the manufacturing of multi-media games and die-cast toys direct to independent manufacturers in Hong Kong. These contracts are supervised by EBE (HK) Ltd, a subsidiary of EBE plc which charges a commercial fee of 2 per cent of the manufacturer's sale price for its services. The manufacturers sell to EBE (UK) Ltd and Valcav Sales Inc and to a distributor in Brazil who has the distribution licence for South America and a distributor in Australia who has the distribution licence for that country and New Zealand. Manufacturers are only allowed to sell to licensed distributors.

The tax position

There are no withholding taxes on royalties paid from Hong Kong to Vebe Ltd. Vebe Ltd also sub-licenses manufacturing of other licensed articles to Vebe NV in the Netherlands Antilles which in turn sub-licenses manufacture to Vebe BV in the Netherlands which manufacturers certain items and sub-licenses to other manufacturers in Germany, France, Belgium and Switzerland. Withholding taxes on royalties received via Vebe BV are kept to a minimum under the Dutch treaties with the sub-licensee manufacturers' countries and there are no withholding taxes on royalties paid from the Netherlands to the Netherlands Antilles. A return on sub-licensing royalties of 7 per cent is retained in Vebe BV as are the Dutch manufacturing profits until paid up by way of dividend, subject to a 7½ per cent withholding tax to Vebe NV where they are taxed at 3 per cent. Vebe Ltd also owns Vebe (Cyprus) Ltd which is licensed for manufacture in the UK. These manufacturing rights are in turn sub-licensed to Vebe Austria which in turn licenses manufacturers of certain articles in the UK. Under the appropriate double taxation treaties with Austria, copyright royalties are not subject to withholding taxes and the anti-avoidance provisions against treaty shopping in the UK/Netherlands Treaty are not applicable to the Austrian Treaty. Vebe Austria suffers a small amount of tax on the spread of royalties left in that country and Vebe (Cyprus) Ltd, as an offshore Cyprus company, pays tax at 4¼ per cent. Trade marks are licensed direct by Vebe Ltd to the UK manufacturers as such royalties may be paid gross without withholding taxes.

Royalties accumulated in Vebe Ltd are retained and lent to EBE plc and Valcav Inc groups at commercial rates of interest.

It is assumed that the manufacturing royalties can be justified commercially as arm's length arrangements, in view of the contractual arrangements entered into by the various parties.

Gribs by Night: trading structure

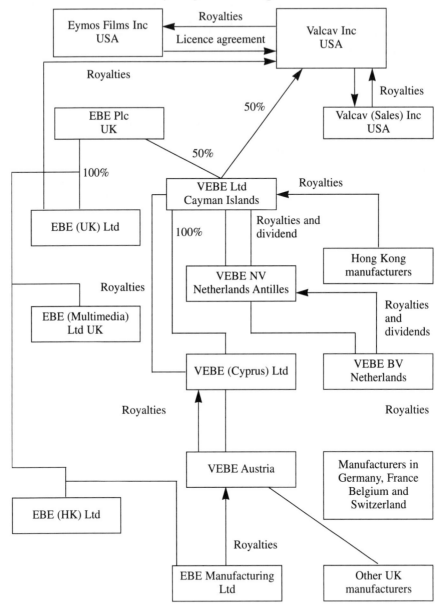

Case study 8: Nuttabun, fast food for the third millennium

The product

Black Hole Developments Ltd, a wholly owned subsidary of Intergalactic Foods plc, has recently developed a new form of bun which it thinks will revolutionise the fast food market. The fundamental property of the bun is that the dough out of which it is made contains all the protein, carbohydrate, sugar, starch, vitamins and other ingredients needed to have the same nutritional value as a three course lunch. The ingredients, however, are based broadly on a mixture of cereals, pulses and nuts with appropriate chemical additives and flavourings.

The bun made from the dough has a very pleasant moist texture and is equally palatable hot or cold and the basic bun is entirely without flavour of any description, which means that the same basic mixture can be used for every flavour of Nuttabun.

The secret of the success of Nuttabun is the development of a flavour injection microwave which is a fully patented process under which a bun is placed in the 'Flavourator' for a period of two seconds, during which the molecules of the Nuttabun are impregnated with the desired flavour.

The Flavourator is capable of impregnating the Nuttabun with any one of 87 different flavours, ranging from salmon and cucumber to beef bourguignon and including trout with almonds, sole walesca and rack of lamb with mint sauce, amongst many others.

The Nuttabun obviously has many advantages over the traditional hamburger or vegeburger, in that whatever the flavour it contains no meat or milk and is suitable for vegetarians and vegans as well as the normally carnivorous members of the populace. It does not require any filling to be cooked separately as it has no filling and this reduces the labour required to run a Nuttabun Express Emporium, the outlet through which Nuttabuns are to be sold to the public. The absence of filling means a corresponding absence of waste, the elimination of dangers of food poisoning and the absence of complaints from customers of the filling running out all over their fingers when trying to eat the delicacy.

The technical success of the Nuttabun depends upon the dough mixture which is a highly complex recipe, the precise formulation of which is the copyright of Black Hole. However, because the formulation is so complex it can only be made in very large, computer controlled production lines with careful pre-processing of the raw materials and precise control over every stage of the mixing phase. The Nuttabun manufacturing process produces golf ball size dough mixtures which grow to hamburger bun size Nuttabuns during the Flavourator process. It is considered that

411

this is the optimum size for Nuttabuns in terms of customer acceptance, as preliminary trials had suggested that leaving the Nuttabun the original golf ball size suggested to customers that they had not truly had the equivalent of a three course meal, while puffing up the Nuttabun to melon or even pumpkin size encouraged customers to share their Nuttabun with friends with the obvious result that everybody ended up hungry. The dough-making process required the development of machinery to extract from the raw materials what was wanted for the production of Nuttabun dough mixture and the successful recovery of any remaining raw materials for conversion into Nuttabake concentrated food for cows and sheep. The marketing department, however, has objected strongly to the use of the name Nuttabake for this material on the grounds of possible confusion, with the potentially unfortunate result of feeding Nuttabuns to the cows or Nuttabake to hungry travellers which, while it would actually cause no real harm to either party, would not improve the marketing image. A number of aspects of this extraction process from the basic raw materials involved the development of new techniques which had been patented worldwide. The name 'Nuttabun', 'Nuttabake', 'Flavourator', and 'Nuttabun Express Emporium' have been registered under the Madrid Protocol and in other countries where trade marks under the Protocol are not yet recognised.

The companies

Black Hole has run a number of trial Nuttabun Express Emporia in railway stations and airports in the UK and abroad and has confirmed public acceptance of the product and appreciation of the speed of service, lack of mess and interesting flavours available. Intergalactic Foods has therefore decided to set up a new company, Nuttabun Express NV, in the Netherlands Antilles to which it has transferred the intellectual property rights developed by Black Hole (*see* diagram on p 415). The rights were transferred for a payment of £10 million to Black Hole which produced a 25 per cent profit on the development expenditure in relation to Nuttabun. Nuttabun Express International BV in the Netherlands has set up a manufacturing plant for the dough mixture in the Republic of Ireland to take advantage of the 10 per cent tax rate applicable to manufacturing business within the Republic. This plant is owned by a local company, Nuttabun Express (Ireland) Ltd. A similar dough manufacturing plant has been set up in California as a joint venture between a wholly owned Delaware subsidiary, Nuttabun Express (USA) Inc and a local American fast food chain, Yukki Super Fast Inc, which was so impressed by the process that it acquired 50 per cent of Nuttabun Express NV.

Franchise outlets

A third manufacturing plant has been set up on the outskirts of Moscow as a joint venture between the wholly owned subsidiary Joint Stock Company Nuttabun Express, and the local Joint Stock Company Cosmonautica, named after Yuri Gagarin. The existing Nuttabun Express outlets within the UK will in future be run by Nuttabun Express Emporia Ltd, a wholly owned subsidiary of Intergalactic Foods plc, but it has been decided to limit the number of directly controlled outlets to 50. It is, in addition, intended to exploit Nuttabuns within the UK through franchise outlets, the terms of which include the franchisee paying a fee of £50,000 to cover the initial training and know-how for the sale of Nuttabuns and running a Nuttabun Express Emporium which will meet the high standards of service and cleanliness demanded by Intergalactic Foods.

The franchisee will also pay a royalty of two pence per Nuttabun for the use of the Nuttabun, Flavourator and Nuttabun Express Emporium trade marks.

A franchisee will also have to buy Nuttabun dough from one of the Nuttabun manufacturing plants and will have to lease the Flavourator from a Dublin Customs House Dock area-based company, Nuttabun Leasing (Ireland) Ltd, a wholly owned subsidiary of Nuttabun Express International BV.

Nuttabun Express NV will also charge a patent royalty for the use of the patented Flavourator process through a series of intermediate licensing companies. Intergalactica SL, a Hungarian non-resident company, has been set up for this purpose as a wholly owned subsidiary of Nuttabun Express NV. Under article 12 of the UK/Hungarian Double Taxation Treaty (SI 1978 No 1056) patent royalties may be paid gross by the UK franchisees to Intergalactica SL which in turn is licensed by an offshore Cyprus company. Intergalactica Cyprus Ltd, a fellow subsidiary of Nuttabun Express NV, will receive a royalty without Hungarian withholding tax which in turn it will pay without withholding tax to Nuttabun Express NV. Profits retained in the Hungarian non-resident company will currently suffer tax at 5.4 per cent and in the Cyprus non-resident company at 4¼ per cent.

Trade mark royalties by UK franchises will be paid direct to Nuttabun Express NV as there are no withholding taxes payable on trade mark royalties from the UK.

The purchase of Nuttabun dough is the purchase of goods by the franchisee from an arm's length supplier and there are no UK tax implications. The initial franchise fee, payable by franchisees, has been considered by the Inland Revenue and regarded in part as a capital payment for commercial know-how for which no allowance is given for tax purposes as it is not a revenue expense and there is no provision for capital allowances on commercial know-how. Reference has been made to the Inland Revenue *Tax Bulletin*, No 8 of August 1993, p 86 and TA 1988, ss 552 and 553. The balance of the franchise initial payment is accepted as an up-front staff training expense which the Revenue will allow to be amortised over three years, following the guidance in *Tax Bulletin* No 17. It has been agreed that of the fee of £50,000, £20,000 should relate to know-how and the balance of £30,000 to staff training, allocable as to £15,000 in year 1 and £7,500 in years 2 and 3.

Other licences and agreements

Nuttabun Express NV has agreed to license a manufacturer of Nuttabun dough in Germany in return for a lump sum know-how payment of £1 million and a royalty on invoiced sales of 5 per cent for the first three years, increasing to 7 per cent for the next four years and 8 per cent thereafter, for a period of 20 years. The licence agreement allows the German manufacturer, Komet AG, the exclusive right to sell Nuttabun dough within Germany, Poland, France, Austria and Switzerland.

Komet AG will also pay a fee for production advice to Black Hole Developments Ltd of DM 500,000 in year 1 and DM 300,000 in years 2 and 3.

Nuttabun Express NV is in negotiation with potential franchisees who wish to open Nuttabun Express Emporia in a number of countries within the EU.

Flavourators are manufactured in Southern China to the exclusive order of Nuttabun Leasing (Ireland) Ltd and may not be sold to any third party, although the manufacturers are seeking a licence to enable them to sell Flavourators in specific areas within the Pacific region.

The production equipment for Nuttabun dough is made to the exclusive order of Nuttabun Express NV and will be leased through Nuttabun Leasing (Ireland) Ltd.

Intergalactic Foods plc is incorporated in the UK but quoted on the London, New York and Tokyo Stock Exchanges and therefore pays foreign income dividends as well as a dividend subject to the normal UK advance corporation tax rules.

The future

The group structure of Intergalactic Foods plc is currently being reviewed, partly as a result of the anticipated success of the revolutionary Nuttabun product, and partly as a result of changes proposed in the UK controlled foreign company legislation which may make the tax deferral enjoyed under the structure difficult to maintain. Currently, Nuttabun Express NV is not a controlled foreign company for UK purposes nor a controlled foreign corporation for US purposes as it is controlled in neither country.

The scientists at Black Hole Developments are currently working on the Slimabun which has half the calorie content of the normal Nuttabun but all the vitamins needed for a healthy diet, the Trencherbun which is aimed specifically at sports people and others engaged in strenuous physical activities and the special small size Kiddibun formulated for children, specially prepared to taste its best with added ketchup.

Nuttabun: trading structure

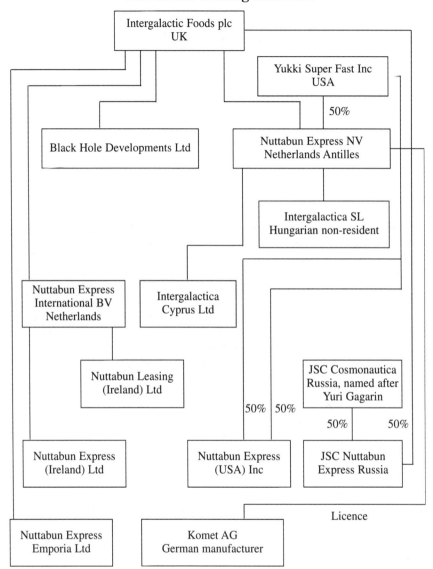

Case study 9:   Transporterplane, economic transport for the 21st century

The product

Transporterplane International Developments plc, a consortium company in which major aeronautical engineering companies in the UK, USA, Germany, France and Spain had varying interests, entered into a joint development agreement with the Chkalov Aero Hydro-Dynamic Institute named after Andrei Alexandrov in the Russian Federation, to develop a vertical take-off and landing amphibious transport aircraft which would be used for long distance travel over the sea, flying at very low level in ground effect in order to conserve fuel when over water. The idea would be develop the Chkalov Institute's expertise in the field of Ekranoplan or wing-in-ground-effect vehicle design and to ally that to the high efficiency engine technology and fly-by wire avionics available within the Transporterplane consortium.

It was important that the vehicle should be able to travel at high speed within ground effect as this would reduce the fuel consumption to one-tenth of that required to fly as an aeroplane. It was, however, necessary to be able to fly as an aeroplane as it was likely for practical purposes that part of each journey would be over land and in order to arrive at the desired final destination, it was appropriate for the vehicle to be able to take off and land vertically. The amphibious capability enabled it to take off or land wherever there was an appropriate stretch of water and the aircraft was therefore ideally suited to be able to deliver goods and cargo at long distances economically, and without the need of major airport or docking facilities at the point of departure or destination.

Applications for patents

An application for a master patent on the concept was challenged on the grounds of lack of innovation. It had been pointed out that the Bartini VVA-14 of the early 1960s had all the major attributes of the Transporterplane in that it was amphibious, able to take off from water and from land, was designed for the provision of lift engines to enable it to take off and land vertically as well as using a runway like a conventional aircraft and was fitted with forward engines to create a wing in ground effect cushion to enable the aircraft to travel at high speed in ground effect, using the forward engines for initial production of the ground effect air cushion and

416

thereafter travelling on the power of the aft mounted engines only. The objectors pointed to the remains of the original VVA-14 currently residing at the Monino Aircraft Museum outside Moscow and a master patent based on the overall concept of the Transporterplane was rejected. However, the Bartini VVA-14 had proved less than 100 per cent successful with the technology available in the 1960s and the new Transporterplane incorporated a number of innovative features which individually were capable of being patented. It also relied on a great deal of know-how from the joint venturers, and the computer-generated drawings for the construction of the vehicle were copyright. Consideration was given to registering the entire design but this was considered to be inappropriate in view of *Handley Page v Butterworth* (1935) 19 TC 328.

Although it proved impossible to arrange a meaningful patent on a number of the more revolutionary attributes of the Transporterplane as they were already in the public domain (despite having previously been regarded as top secret within the old Soviet Union), it was nevertheless possible to patent sufficient of the secondary systems to prevent a competitor copying closely the design and the expertise provided by the Chkalov Institute, and the membership of the consortium was sufficient to ensure a practical, competitive lead based more on know-how and competitive position in the market than any individual aspect of intellectual property.

The consortium company

In view of the very substantial development costs, the consortium members wished to take their share of such costs against the profits of their other activities in their home countries and a UK-based consortium company was formed primarily to co-ordinate the project. Detailed designs and manufacture was spread around members of the consortium as near as possible, in proportion to their share in the overall venture with design leadership for the structure and control systems being with the Chkalov Institute, the avionics being with the German consortium member and the engines with the UK consortium member.

The outcome

Final construction took place in one of the former Soviet military aircraft factories close to the Caspian Sea, which would allow for initial trials in relatively uncluttered waters. The major financing of the project was provided by the members of the consortium. It was decided that it was unlikely that outright sales of Transporter plane would be possible in the near future, except via an international leasing structure, and advice was taken in connection with the leasing arrangements in order to ensure that capital allowances for tax depreciation were available, preferably in more than one territory; and the use of currency swaps and preference share funding would provide an effective fiscal subsidy to the ultimate lease charges, thereby encouraging operators to bring the Transporterplane into service at the earliest possible opportunity.

Case study 10:   Yuri Rakovsky, conductor/composer

Introduction

Yuri Rakovsky, a Russian emigrant, is 30 years old and a brilliant conductor/composer. In the last two years he has conducted a number of leading orchestras. He has also penned (much of it in the air!) three major symphonies and several minor works, although he had not attempted to have them published due to a possessive and secretive trait in his character. He has now been persuaded (by his informal agent, Kurt Hausseman, a mysterious Swiss individual) to publish the symphonies, and two publishing companies have expressed interest in his entire output. The Australian Philharmonic Orchestra is negotiating to play the latest of his symphonies in their 1996 programme.

Yuri has agreed (and has signed up) to a world tour with the Taiwan Free Philharmonic Orchestra. The tour starts in December 1994. Over 50 performances are scheduled in venues in Japan, Germany, France, Spain, UK, Sweden, Australia, Argentina, Mexico, South Africa, Canada and the USA (California). The tour will close in Taiwan in August 1995. The idea is to video major parts of the programme and Hausseman has arranged a Luxembourg company to undertake this work—it is suspected that Hausseman owns the company and Yuri expects to get some of the 'action' on top of royalties due to him.

'Jacko' Records, a major American record company, has offered Yuri a ten-year recording contract, and the intention is to accept it.

Yuri left his Moscow home and place of work in March 1992. He moved briefly to New York and after a major argument over immigration rules moved to Amsterdam in September 1992 where he is now principally residing. He has expressed his intention of moving his principal residence away from Amsterdam but is undecided between Stockholm and Paris. He has personally acquired homes in London, Amsterdam, Nice, New York and Moscow. He has a Greek girlfriend (a very clever water-colourist) who is pregnant with his child. He is also often seen accompanied by the young, beautiful and charismatic new German opera star Uli Schubert and Kurt has suggested there are some very definite musical partnership possibilities here—especially in recording: he has hinted that Yuri may be writing an opera based on the novel *One Day in the Life of Ivan Denisovitch.*

Yuri and Kurt have asked for your assistance in planning his future arrangements to minimise his worldwide tax exposure, maintain personal life-style flexibility and safeguard the confidentiality he demands in his business affairs. What is your advice?

Nationality

It seems that Yuri Rakovsky remains a citizen of the Russian Federation and there are no immediate plans to change this.

Domicile

Yuri clearly has a Russian domicile of origin. There is nothing to suggest that he has as yet decided to live permanently or indefinitely in any particular state and has not thereby obtained a domicile of choice. His domicile or origin will therefore remain, notwithstanding the fact that he is living outside Russia, unless or until this is displaced by a domicile of choice elsewhere.

Residence

Yuri would appear to have accommodation available for his use in London, Amsterdam, Nice, New York and Moscow. He is not currently living in the Russian Federation and therefore it seems unlikely that the Russian tax authorities would have any effective claim to tax him either on the basis of residence, domicile or nationality. The home available for his use in the UK does not create a UK tax problem and he is only likely to be treated as UK tax resident if he spends more than 183 days in the UK in any one year, or more than 90 days on average.

He seems to have been spending most of his time in Amsterdam since September 1992 and is likely to be resident in the Netherlands for Dutch tax purposes.

Although he has a home in Nice it seems that he has not spent more than 183 days in France and is unlikely to be regarded as resident for French tax purposes and would therefore only have a French tax liability on French source income.

He has a home in New York and may have spent more than six months in the USA in 1992 which could have made him a resident alien. It could also affect the residence for 1993 and 1994 if he has spent any material time in the USA in these years.

If as planned he moves his principal place of residence from Amsterdam he might become resident in Sweden under Swedish law. He might also move to Paris and thereby become resident in France with appropriate tax consequences. It might also be worth considering his becoming resident in London in view of the generous UK treatment of non-domiciliaries who, in principle, are only taxable on income originating in the UK and income from abroad remitted to the UK.

It could be worth establishing a peripatetic existence under which Yuri was not resident for tax purposes in any country. Although this is initially attractive, it could mean that the full level of withholding taxes would be levied without the benefit of any double taxation relief.

Sources of income

Yuri is both a conductor and a composer. As a conductor he provides services for which he is likely to obtain performance fees. To the extent that these performances might be recorded and produced as a record, film or video, he would be entitled to what are normally referred to as royalties, that is, performance fees calculated by reference to the sales of product. Radio or TV interviews or live performances would similarly attract fees, with repeat fees on subsequent broadcasts. Where recordings of his performances are played in public or on the air, he would only be entitled to any remuneration if he were the publisher or composer under the rules of most countries' performing rights royalty collection societies, although in some countries the performing rights are also paid to the performers of the recording as well as to the publisher and composer.

There is no indication, nor is it likely, that Yuri is involved in publishing any of his works personally and he will therefore receive the composer's share and in some jurisdictions, also the artiste's share of the performing rights and royalties on the sale of music, and the composer's royalty in respect of performances in which he is not involved.

It appears that a lot of the composing has been outside the Netherlands, or indeed any other state in which he might become resident, which could be important for tax purposes. In some jurisdictions it is important to consider where the works were written and if he were, for example, to become resident in the UK, the fact that these works had been written outside the UK during a period when he was neither resident nor domiciled there should mean that continuing royalties would not be subject to UK tax unless remitted to the UK. If on the other hand he continued to write as a UK resident, he would be taxable on the worldwide income of his profession and royalties would be regarded as part of his professional income. It would be sensible to employ him by a non-resident company for his composing services outside the UK: any remuneration paid from the royalties received by the employing company would be tax-free in the UK unless remitted.

Royalties and performing rights fees would usually be subject to withholding tax from the country of payment unless exempt under a double taxation treaty with the country of residence of the employing company.

If Yuri becomes resident in the UK it might be appropriate to have royalties collected by a UK company to take advantage of the UK double taxation treaties, but for the UK company to contract with an overseas company for the benefit of Yuri's services outside the UK. In many cases royalties paid to the British company would be paid gross or subject to a reduced withholding tax under the appropriate double taxation treaty with the UK, notwithstanding the fact that the majority of the royalties would then be paid out by way of a fee to the non-resident company before being paid through to Yuri as employment income.

The Australian Philharmonic Orchestra will no doubt be negotiating with whichever of the publishing houses is chosen to publish Yuri's works and the fee payable by the APO may well include 'mechanical' and performing rights royalties if the concert of his symphonies is to be recorded. The Australian withholding tax, if any, payable will depend on the country of residence of the publishing house which, in turn, may deduct withholding taxes when accounting to Yuri or his employing company.

World tour

Yuri's income from the world tour is likely to arise from a number of possible sources. There is likely to be a fee as conductor per performance which may be a fixed fee or related to the ticket sales directly or indirectly. If the performance is videoed there would ultimately be royalties from the sale of videos. If the concert is recorded there would be artiste's royalties for the performance. To the extent that the performance is of Yuri's own works, he would be entitled to the composer's proportion of the performing rights fees and the composer's proportion of the publishing royalties for the video and record sales.

It is also quite likely that Yuri will be paid a fee from the orchestra itself for practising with the orchestra in rehearsals, not constituting public performances.

In view of the popular nature of the works there is also a possibility that merchandising material in particular, badges and T-shirts would be produced which would give rise to a fixed fee or more likely a royalty based on sales of merchandise.

From a taxation point of view, it is going to be necessary to consider whether the countries in which the tour operates are likely to charge tax in respect of the performances in their country and, if so, on what basis.

It is probable that every country visited will seek to charge tax whether as a provisional withholding tax, which can be amended to a final figure on submission of the appropriate tax return, or a withholding tax as a final tax. It is also worth considering in the income to which any withholding tax is to be applied. It may be limited to the performance fees or may extend to include other income.

In relation to performances in the UK, if Yuri is not a resident of the UK, there will be entertainers' withholding tax at the basic rate of 25 per cent on payments to members of the Taiwan Free Philharmonic Orchestra and also for performance fees payable to Yuri. In addition, entertainers' withholding tax would be charged on merchandising income due to Yuri and any fees for personal appearances, endorsement, interviews, etc. Recording royalties and composer's royalties would not be subject to the entertainers' withholding tax as such but would be subject to copyright royalty withholding tax as paid to a person whose normal place of abode was outside the UK, to the extent that they are derived from sales in the UK, subject to reduction of withholding tax under a double taxation treaty with Yuri's country of residence. Fees relating to rehearsals or consultancy fees in relation to the running of the orchestra should not be subject to UK tax unless they represent employment income for work done in the UK, in which case they would be taxable as UK employment income and subject to deduction of tax at source under the PAYE scheme.

If Yuri were resident in the UK, it is probable that he should receive performance fees personally in the UK and to be employed by a non-UK company for services in the rest of the world, particularly because he is not UK domiciled. The choice of employment to be used in such circumstances would depend on the proportion of income likely to arise from each venue compared with the time spent in each country. Consideration might be given to using a UK, American or Dutch company specifically to run the world tour.

If a UK company were to be used there would be a liability to UK tax but only on the profits of the company after payment of all fees and remuneration. In some jurisdictions the use of a company in a high tax area with double tax treaties may be preferable to the use of a company in an offshore tax haven and this would be particularly important where there is a double taxation treaty with only a basic entertainers' and sportsmen' clause which would not apply to a non-resident company employing Yuri for his services in the country of the performance. In more recent treaties a tax charge on entertainers' services may apply even where payments are made to an employing company.

If Yuri was tax resident in the UK, another possibility if the tour and related activities were to extend to a period in excess of 12 months, would be for Yuri to be employed and thereby be entitled to 100 per cent foreign earnings deduction.

VAT on the tour

Consideration should be given to the possible advantages of subcontracting the tour to a special purpose company formed in the country of the performance in order to enable VAT paid on expenses to be recovered. Alternatively, it may be possible or desirable to appoint a fiscal representative in a country where VAT is in place or to arrange for the local promoter organising ticket sales to act as fiscal representative or to comply with the VAT requirements by self-supply and recover VAT suffered by direct refund, in which case it is important to make claims on time and to have the appropriate original documentation available. VAT is an area where local advice is essential.

The video

If Kurt Hausseman's Luxembourg company were to video the performance in the UK, it is unlikely that the UK Revenue would regard this as a taxable event in the absence of a permanent establishment of the Luxembourg company in the UK. If Yuri receives royalties from the video, the UK Revenue would seek to apply the foreign entertainers' rules to the income, although these could be difficult to collect if paid direct from the Luxembourg company. It would probably be desirable however, to produce the video elsewhere and consider mixing and finishing and adding additional elements with specific controlled payments being made for each element to contain tax costs.

Jacko Records

Although Jacko Records is an American record company, it no doubt has subsidiaries worldwide and it is worth considering whether the local contract should be with Yuri personally or with a company employing his services and whether there should be a separate recording deal with the American company for American sales and with say, a Dutch subsidiary for sales in the rest of the world. It seems that the works composed by Yuri have been written outside the USA and outside the UK, but it is probable that at least part of the writing has taken place in the Netherlands which has been his base since September 1992. It may be necessary to consider whether any of the writing took place in the USA in case the Internal Revenue Service were to argue that the composer's royalties were a reward for services performed in the USA and taxable as earnings in the USA rather than merely being subject to a withholding tax as royalties arising from the USA. It is similarly worth considering whether a recording should actually be made in the USA or whether they should be recorded in a jurisdiction in which Yuri is not resident.

If Yuri were a resident of the UK it would be desirable for the recordings to be made outside the UK and for Yuri to be employed by a non-resident company for his recording services. This would enable him to take advantage of the remittance basis for earnings of a non-UK domiciliary from a non-resident employer.

Girlfriend

The existence of the pregnant Greek girlfriend may not, at first glance, seem to have any taxation effects but it could influence the country of residence that Yuri is likely to choose in view of a potential paternity suit if he decides not to continue to live with his girlfriend and support their child. It could also have inheritance or estate tax implications in that the child, if acknowledged by Yuri, could acquire forced heirship rights under the provisions of Greek law and be entitled to a substantial portion of Yuri's estate. If this is a real possibility it might be appropriate to consider structuring Yuri so that the rights to his activities are held by companies, in turn owned by appropriate trusts and, if so, consideration should be given to the type of trust that might be appropriate.

Uli

Yuri's increasing interest in Uli is suspected as being not entirely platonic and this could give rise to further problems with the Greek girlfriend and an asset protection trust in a jurisdiction with suitable legislation such as Cyprus is looking increasingly attractive, irrespective of the taxation situation. As far as the opera is concerned, whether this will be written by Yuri in his own capacity or as employee of a suitable company would seem largely dependent on where he is likely to reside for tax purposes. It would also seem that there are considerable possibilities of Yuri conducting for opera recordings in which Uli will star as one of the soloists. Jacko Records are particularly interested in such recordings and wish to produce the records under the proposed recording agreement. There may be an opportunity to establish a commercial partnership between Yuri and Uli Kurt—whatever other partnership interests may be developing.

APPENDICES

Appendix 1   Copyright, Designs and Patents Act 1988

Note Only those sections of the Act which are of particular relevance to tax planning are reproduced here.

Chapter V   Dealings with rights in copyright works

Copyright

90. Assignment and licences

(1) Copyright is transmissible by assignment, by testamentary disposition or by operation of law, as personal or moveable property.

(2) As assignment or other transmission of copyright may be partial, that is, limited so as to apply—

    (*a*)   to one or more, but not all, of the things the copyright owner has the exclusive right to do;

    (*b*)   to part, but not the whole, of the period for which the copyright is to subsist.

(3) An assignment of copyright is not effective unless it is in writing signed by or on behalf of the assignor.

(4) A licence granted by a copyright owner is binding on every successor in title to his interest in the copyright, except a purchaser in good faith for valuable consideration and without notice (actual or constructive) of the licence or a person deriving title from such a purchaser; and references in this Part to doing anything with, or without, the licence of the copyright owner shall be construed accordingly.

91. Prospective ownership of copyright

(1) Where by an agreement made in relation to future copyright, and signed by or on behalf of the prospective owner of the copyright, the prospective owner purports to assign the future copyright (wholly or partially) to another person, then if, on the copyright coming into existence, the assignee or another person claiming under him would be entitled as against all other persons to require the copyright to be vested in him, the copyright shall vest in the assignee or his successor in title by virtue of this subsection.

(2) In this Part—

'future copyright' means copyright which will or may come into existence in respect of a future work or class of works or on the occurrence of a future event; and

'prospective owner' shall be construed accordingly, and includes a person who is prospectively entitled to copyright by virtue of such an agreement as is mentioned in subsection (1).

(3) A licence granted by a prospective owner of copyright is binding on every successor in title to his interest (or prospective interest) in the right, except a purchaser in good faith for valuable consideration and without notice (actual or constructive) of the licence or a person deriving title from such a purchaser; and references in this Part to doing anything with, or without, the licence of the copyright owner shall be construed accordingly.

92. Exclusive licences

(1) In this Part an 'exclusive licence' means a licence in writing signed by or on behalf of the copyright owner authorising the licensee to the exclusion of all other persons, including the person granting the licence, to exercise a right which would otherwise be exercisable exclusively by the copyright owner.

(2) The licensee under an exclusive licence has the same rights against a successor in title who is bound by the licence as he has against the person granting the licence.

93. Copyright to pass under will with unpublished work

Where under a bequest (whether specific or general) a person is entitled, beneficially or otherwise, to—

(a)   an original document or other material thing recording or embodying a literary, dramatic, musical or artistic work which was not published before the death of the testator, or

(b)   an original material thing containing a sound recording or film which was not published before the death of the testator,

the bequest shall, unless a contrary intention is indicated in the testator's will or a codicil to it, be construed as including the copyright in the work in so far as the testator was the owner of the copyright immediately before his death.

Appendix 2   Patents Act 1977

Note Only those sections of the Act which are of particular relevance to tax planning are reproduced here.

Right to employees' inventions

39. (1) Notwithstanding anything in any rule of law, an invention made by an employee shall, as between him and his employer, be taken to belong to his employer for the purposes of this Act and all other purposes if—

(*a*)   it was made in the course of the normal duties of the employee or in the course of duties falling outside his normal duties, but specifically assigned to him, and the circumstances in either case were such that an invention might reasonably be expected to result from the carrying out of his duties; or

(*b*)   the invention was made in the course of the duties of the employee and, at the time of making the invention, because of the nature of his duties and the particular responsibilities arising from the nature of his duties he had a special obligation to further the interests of the employer's undertaking.

(2) Any other invention made by an employee shall, as between him and his employer, be taken for those purposes to belong to the employee.

(3) Where by virtue of this section an invention belongs, as between him and his employer, to an employee, nothing done—

(*a*)   by or on behalf of the employee or any person claiming under him for the purposes of pursuing an application for a patent, or

(*b*)   by any person for the purpose of performing or working the invention,

shall be taken to infringe any copyright or design right to which, as between him and his employer, his employer is entitled in any model or document relating to the invention.

Compensation of employees for certain inventions

40. (1) Where it appears to the court or the comptroller on an application made by an employee within the prescribed period that the employee has made an invention belonging to the employer for which a patent has been granted, that the patent is (having regard among other things to the size and nature of the employer's undertaking) of outstanding benefit to the employer and that by reason of those facts it is just that the employee should be awarded compensation to be paid by the employer, the court or the comptroller may award him such compensation of an amount determined under section 41 below.

(2) Where it appears to the court or the comptroller on an application made by an employee within the prescribed period that—

(*a*)   a patent has been granted for an invention made by and belonging to the employee;

(*b*)   his rights in the invention, or in any patent or application for a patent for the invention, have since the appointed day been assigned to the employer or an exclusive licence under the patent or application has since the appointed day been granted to the employer;

(*c*)   the benefit derived by the employee from the contract of assignment, assignation or grant or any ancillary contract ('the relevant contract') is inadequate in relation to the benefit derived by the employer from the patent; and

(*d*)   by reason of those facts it is just that the employee should be awarded compensation to be paid by the employer in addition to the benefit derived from the relevant contract;

the court or the comptroller may award him such compensation of an amount determined under section 41 below.

(3) Subsections (1) and (2) above shall not apply to the invention of an employee where a relevant collective agreement provides for the payment of compensation in respect of inventions of the same description as that invention to employees of the same description as that employee.

(4) Subsection (2) above shall have effect notwithstanding anything in the relevant contract or any agreement applicable to the invention (other than any such collective agreement).

(5) If it appears to the comptroller on an application under this section that the application involves matters which would more properly be determined by the court, he may decline to deal with it.

(6) In this section—

'the prescribed period', in relation to proceedings before the court, means the period prescribed by rules of court, and

'relevant collective agreement' means a collective agreement within the meaning of the Trade Union and Labour Relations (Consolidation) Act 1992, made by or on behalf of a trade union to which the employee belongs, and by the employer or an employers' association to which the employer belongs which is in force at the time of the making of the invention.

(7) References in this section to an invention belonging to an employer or employee are references to it so belonging as between the employer and the employee.

Amount of compensation

41. (1) An award of compensation to an employee under section 40(1) or (2) above in relation to a patent for an invention shall be such as will secure for the employee a fair share (having regard to all the circumstances) of the benefit which the employer has derived, or may reasonably be expected to derive, from the patent or from the assignment, assignation or grant to a person connected with the employer of the property or any right in the invention or the property in, or any right in or under, an application for that patent.

(2) For the purposes of subsection (1) above the amount of any benefit derived or expected to be derived by an employer from the assignment, assignation or grant of

(*a*) the property in, or any right in or under, a patent for the invention or an application for such a patent; or

(*b*) the property or any right in the invention,

to a person connected with him shall be taken to be the amount which could reasonably be expected to be so derived by the employer if that person had not been connected with him.

(3) Where the Crown or a Research Council in its capacity as employer assigns or grants the property in, or any right in or under, an invention, patent or application for a patent to a body having among its functions that of developing or exploiting inventions resulting from public research and does so for no consideration or only a nominal consideration, any benefit derived from the invention, patent or application by that body shall be treated for the purposes of the foregoing provisions of this section as so derived by the Crown or, as the case may be, Research Council.

In this subsection 'Research Council' means a body which is a Research Council for the purposes of the Science and Technology Act 1965.

(4) In determining the fair share of the benefit to be secured for an employee in respect of a patent for an invention which has always belonged to an employer, the court or the comptroller shall, among other things, take the following matters into account, that is to say—

(*a*) the nature of the employee's duties, his remuneration and the other advantages he derives or has derived from his employment or has derived in relation to the invention under this Act;

(*b*) the effort and skill which the employee has devoted to making the invention;

(*c*) the effort and skill which any other person has devoted to making the invention jointly with the employee concerned, and the advice and other assistance contributed by any other employee who is not a joint inventor of the invention; and

(*d*) the contribution made by the employer to the making, developing and working of the invention by the provision of advice, facilities and other assistance, by the provision of opportunities and by his managerial and commercial skill and activities.

(5) In determining the fair share of the benefit to be secured for an employee in respect of a patent for an invention which originally belonged to him, the court or the comptroller shall, among other things, take the following matters into account, that is to say—

(*a*) any conditions in a licence or licences granted under this Act or otherwise in respect of the invention or the patent;

(*b*) the extent to which the invention was made jointly by the employee with any other person; and

(*c*) the contribution made by the employer to the making, developing and working of the invention as mentioned in subsection (4)(*d*) above.

(6) Any order for the payment of compensation under section 40 above may be an order for the payment of a lump sum or for periodical payment, or both.

(7) Without prejudice to section 32 of the Interpretation Act 1889 (which provides that a statutory power may in general be exercised from time to time), the refusal of the court or the comptroller to make any such order on an application made by an employee under section 40 above shall not prevent a further application being made under that section by him or any successor in title of his.

(8) Where the court or the comptroller has made any such order, the court or he may on the application of either the employer or the employee vary or discharge it or suspend any provision of the order and revive any provision so suspended, and section 40(5) above shall apply to the application as it applies to an application under that section.

(9) In England and Wales any sums awarded by the comptroller under section 40 above shall, if a county court so orders, be recoverable by execution issued from the county court or otherwise as if they were payable under an order of that court.

(10) In Scotland an order made under section 40 above by the comptroller for the payment of any sums may be enforced in like manner as a recorded decree arbitral.

(11) In Northern Ireland an order made under section 40 above by the comptroller for the payment of any sums may be enforced as if it were a money judgment.

Enforceability of contracts relating to employees' inventions

42. (1) This section applies to any contract (whenever made) relating to inventions made by an employee, being a contract entered into by him—

    (*a*)   with the employer (alone or with another); or

    (*b*)   with some other person at the request of the employer or in pursuance of the employee's contract of employment.

(2) Any term in a contract to which this section applies which diminishes the employee's rights in inventions of any description made by him after the appointed day and the date of the contract, or in or under patents for those inventions or applications for such patents, shall be unenforceable against him to the extent that it diminishes his rights in an invention of that description so made, or in or under a patent for such an invention or an application for any such patent.

(3) Subsection (2) above shall not be construed as derogating from any duty of confidentiality owed to his employer by an employee by virtue of any rule of law or otherwise.

(4) This section applies to any arrangement made with a Crown employee by or on behalf of the Crown as his employer as it applies to any contract made between an employee and an employer other than the Crown, and for the purposes of this section 'Crown employee' means a person employed under or for the purposes of a government department or any officer or body exercising on behalf of the Crown functions conferred by any enactment or a person serving in the naval, military or air forces of the Crown.

Supplementary

43. (1) Sections 39 to 42 above shall not apply to an invention made before the appointed day.*

(2) Sections 39 to 42 above shall not apply to an invention made by an employee unless at the time he made the invention one of the following conditions was satisfied in his case, that is to say—

(*a*)　　he was mainly employed in the United Kingdom; or

(*b*)　　he was not mainly employed anywhere or his place of employment could not be determined, but his employer had a place of business in the United Kingdom to which the employee was attached, whether or not he was also attached elsewhere.

(3) In sections 39 to 42 above and this section, except so far as the context otherwise requires, references to the making of an invention by an employee are references to his making it alone or jointly with any other person, but do not include references to his merely contributing advice or other assistance in the making of an invention by another employee.

(4) Any references in sections 39 to 42 above to a patent and to a patent being granted are respectively references to a patent or other protection and to its being granted whether under the law of the United Kingdom or the law in force in any other country or under any treaty or international convention.

(5) For the purposes of sections 40 and 41 above the benefit derived or expected to be derived by an employer from a patent shall, where he dies before any award is made under section 40 above in respect of the patent, include any benefit derived or expected to be derived from the patent by his personal representatives or by any person in whom it was vested by their assent.

(6) Where an employee dies before an award is made under section 40 above in respect of a patented invention made by him, his personal representatives or their successors in title may exercise his right to make or proceed with an application for compensation under subsection (1) or (2) of that section.

(7) In sections 40 and 41 above and this section 'benefit' means benefit in money or money's worth.

(8) Section 533 of the Income and Corporation Taxes Act 1970 (definition of connected persons) shall apply for determining for the purposes of section 41(2) above whether one person is connected with another as it applies for determining that question for the purposes of the Tax Acts.

[*1 June 1978, the day on which PA 1977 entered into force.]

Appendix 3   Treaty of Rome 1960

Note Only those Articles referred to in Part 1 of this book are reproduced here.

Article 36

The provisions of Articles 30 to 34 [which impose obligations on Member States not to introduce any new quantitative restrictions or like measures on imports and exports between Member States and to eliminate over a period of time all such existing measures] shall not preclude prohibitions or restrictions on imports, exports or goods in transit justified on grounds of public morality, public policy or public security; the protection of health and life of humans, animals or plants; the protection of health and life of humans, animals or plants; the protection of national treasures possessing artistic, historic or archaeological value; or the protection of industrial and commercial property. Such prohibitions or restrictions shall not, however, constitute a means of arbitrary discrimination or a disguised restriction on trade between Member States.

Article 85

1. The following shall be prohibited as incompatible with the common market: all agreements between undertakings, decisions by associations of undertakings and concerted practices which may affect trade between Member States and which have as their object or effect the prevention, restriction or distortion of competition within the common market, and in particular those which:

(*a*) directly or indirectly fix purchase or selling prices or any other trading conditions;
(*b*) limit or control production, markets, technical development, or investment;
(*c*) share markets or sources of supply;
(*d*) apply dissimilar conditions to equivalent transactions with other trading parties, thereby placing them at a competitive disadvantage;
(*e*) make the conclusion of contracts subject to acceptance by the other parties of supplementary obligations which, by their nature or according to commercial usage, have no connection with the subject of such contracts.

2. Any agreements or decisions prohibited pursuant to this Article shall be automatically void.

3. The provisions of paragraph 1 may, however, be declared inapplicable in the case of:
— any agreement or category of agreements between undertakings;
— any decision or category of decisions by associations of undertakings;
— any concerted practice or category of concerted practices;
which contributes to improving the production or distribution of goods or to promoting technical or economic progress, while allowing consumers a fair share of the resulting benefit, and which does not:

    (*a*)   impose on the undertakings concerned restrictions which are not indispensable to the attainment of these objectives;

    (*b*)   afford such undertakings the possibility of eliminating competition in respect of a substantial part of the products in question.

Article 86

Any abuse by one or more undertakings of a dominant position within the common market or in a substantial part of it shall be prohibited as incompatible with the common market in so far as it may affect trade between Member States. Such abuse may, in particular, consist in:

    (*a*)   directly or indirectly imposing unfair purchase or selling prices or other unfair trading conditions;

    (*b*)   limiting production, markets or technical development to the prejudice of consumers;

    (*c*)   applying dissimilar conditions to equivalent transactions with other trading parties, thereby placing them at a competitive disadvantage;

    (*d*)   making the conclusion of contracts subject to acceptance by the other parties of supplementary obligations which, by their nature or according to commercial usage, have no connection with the subject of such contracts.

Appendix 4 IR forms 46R and 46R-1: Return of payments to entertainers, etc

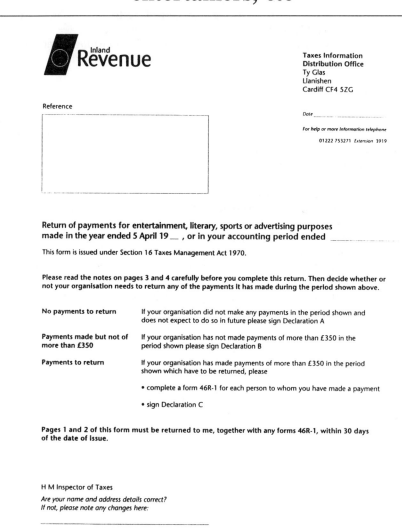

Inland Revenue

Taxes Information
Distribution Office
Ty Glas
Llanishen
Cardiff CF4 5ZG

Reference

Date _____

For help or more Information telephone

01222 753271 *Extension* 3919

Return of payments for entertainment, literary, sports or advertising purposes made in the year ended 5 April 19 ___ , or in your accounting period ended _____

This form is issued under Section 16 Taxes Management Act 1970.

Please read the notes on pages 3 and 4 carefully before you complete this return. Then decide whether or not your organisation needs to return any of the payments It has made during the period shown above.

No payments to return	If your organisation did not make any payments in the period shown and does not expect to do so in future please sign Declaration A
Payments made but not of more than £350	If your organisation has not made payments of more than £350 in the period shown please sign Declaration B
Payments to return	If your organisation has made payments of more than £350 in the period shown which have to be returned, please
	• complete a form 46R-1 for each person to whom you have made a payment
	• sign Declaration C

Pages 1 and 2 of this form must be returned to me, together with any forms 46R-1, within 30 days of the date of Issue.

H M Inspector of Taxes

Are your name and address details correct?
If not, please note any changes here:

_____

_____

_____

_____

46R(1994)   1   21719 1 96 W H Smith Business Supplies W0D7000

Declaration A   No payments made

False statements may lead to prosecution

*No payments have been made which should be returned on forms 46R-1

*No payments are expected to be made in future

Signed _____   Date _____

Name of organisation and position held _____

_____   _____

*Please cross out if the statement does not apply

Declaration B   No payments made of more than £350

False statements may lead to prosecution

Payments have been made but none of more than £350 in the period shown

Signed _____   Date _____

Name of organisation and position held _____

_____

Declaration C   Payments made

False statements may lead to prosecution

To the best of my knowledge and belief the forms 46R-1 now enclosed constitute
a complete and correct return for the year (or period) shown on page 1.

The total number of forms 46R-1 completed for the year (or period) is   [*enter number of forms*]

Signed _____   Date _____

Name of organisation and position held _____

_____

Notes on completing this return form

Payments which you must return

You must make a return if, during the year shown on page 1 of this form, the organisation which you represent made payments within **all three categories** listed below. A fuller definition of payments is given in the note headed 'Types of payment' below.

- Payments to 'persons' for entertainment, literary, advertising, or sports services **provided by** them or for **copyright**. The word 'persons' includes individuals, acts, businesses, companies, and other organisations.

- Payments which were **not liable to tax under the Pay As You Earn (PAYE) Regulations.** This means payments which were not made to employees.

- Payments where the amount paid to any one 'person' was **more than £350 in total** during the period shown on page 1.

Types of payment

You must include the following types of payment:

- any periodical or lump sum payment, for example an advance, for copyright or royalties under a recording contract
- any payments made to persons providing entertainment, for example
  - actors
  - arrangers
  - artistes
  - authors
  - composers
  - dancers
  - designers
  - musicians
  - producers
  - promoters
  - scriptwriters
  - speakers
  - sportsmen
- any other payment for literary, musical, artistic or photographic work or publication. This includes giving information, advice or any other service connected with the work, publication, or contribution
- any payments for pictorial, photographic or written material to be used for an advertisement
- any payments to persons making film or video productions
- any payments for personal appearances, or for using a person's name or likeness for advertising purposes
- any payments to models
- any payment of prizes for sporting events
- any payment of commission to agents

Copyright royalties or other annual payments to persons who normally live abroad

Special tax rules apply to payments of copyright royalties or other annual payments to persons who normally live abroad. If you make these payments and have not been sent a form 11R, please contact us at the address shown on page 1.

Payments which you do not need to enter on this return form

Entertainers and sportsmen who normally live abroad

Special withholding tax provisions apply to entertainers and sportsmen who normally live abroad. If you make payments in these circumstances, you must contact

The Foreign Entertainers Unit
City House
Edmund Street
Birmingham
B3 2JH   Tel: 0121-200 2616

Do **not** include these payments on this return form.

Payments liable to tax under PAYE
You must report payments liable to tax under PAYE to your usual Tax Office. You should **not** include them on this return form.

Please turn over for notes on how to complete forms 46R-1

How to fill in forms 46R-1

Please complete one form 46R-1 for each payee (that is the 'person' who is being paid). The form must show the total amount you have paid to that 'person'.

Form 46R-1

Payee's name
This will be the person or business entitled to receive payment. It may be the performer, if the contract is with him or her, or the promoter who has provided the services of a performer.

Payee's permanent address
Give the business or home address of the payee. Any 'c/o' (care of) address - for example, a bank, other financial institution or agent, other than a theatrical agent - is unacceptable.

Name of artist, production, act or group
If the payee is
- a promoter, or
- an agent, or
- the principal member of a group who in turn pays the other members, or
- a limited company directed by the performers

give the name of the artist, production, act or group. If the payments are for more than one engagement enter 'various'.

Gross amount of payment
Please enter the gross amount paid to the payee. Include any expenses paid to the payee and show whether the payments include or exclude VAT.

Period for which payment made
Usually you enter the income tax year which runs from 6 April in one year to 5 April in the following year. You can enter your own accounting year as long as you make this clear on both forms 46R-1 and 46R.

Description of services
Please make it clear what kind of services are provided. In the film industry, please show the individual grade of the payee.

Description of any other valuable consideration
If you provide the payee with anything apart from money, for example a car or personal wardrobe, please enter the details here. There is more space on the back of the form, or you can attach a separate sheet with a full description of the items supplied.

If you can, please give an estimate of the monetary value. Please also give details of any right to future benefits, for example a share in the proceeds from the distribution of a film.

Payer's name and date
Please enter the name of the organisation you represent in CAPITAL letters, or use a rubber stamp. Enter the date you actually send in the form 46R-1.

Substitute forms 46R-1

You may want to use your own design of form 46R-1. If you do, please send your proposed design to us (at the address shown on page 1) for approval **before you start using it.** Any substitute form must give all the information asked for by the official form. The information can also be supplied on magnetic tape or on disk. Please contact this office for details.

4

Income Tax **Return of payments for services or a copyright**

1. Payee's name _____
and address

_____

_____

2. Stage name _____

3. Name of artist, production, act, _____
group etc *where not payee's name*

_____

4. Gross amount of payments including expenses payments £ _____

Payments include VAT ☐ exclude VAT ☐ '√' one box

For the period from _____ to _____

5. Description of services _____

6. Payee's National Insurance number *where known* _____

7. Description of any other valuable consideration _____

_____

If you need more space please use the back of this form

8. Payer's name _____ date _____

46R-1

A2678/2635L Dd FAL0101229 600M 2/92 TP Gp649

Details of any other valuable consideration

Appendix 5   Extra-statutory concessions

A75. Theatrical entertainers: transition to Schedule E—obsolete

The earnings of theatrical entertainers were, before 6 April 1990, generally taxed under Schedule D. But 'standard contracts', which are widely used for theatrical engagements, are generally contracts of employment and the earnings from them are properly taxable under Schedule E. From 6 April 1990 earnings from engagements under 'standard contracts', which are contracts of employment, and from other contracts of employment, are taxed under Schedule E except where a theatrical entertainer can claim reserved Schedule D status in accordance with the conditions below. In such cases income from theatrical performances, under 'standard contracts' or under any other contract of employment, will continue to be taxed under Schedule D.

Entertainers qualify for reserved Schedule D status where one of the following conditions is satisfied

either

- Schedule D assessments have been made in respect of income from engagements as a theatrical entertainer for at least the three tax years 1986–87, 1987–88 and 1988–89, and an assessment for at least one of those years has been based on accounts or a return of income for that year submitted before 31 May 1989

or

- Schedule D assessments have been made in respect of income from engagements as a theatrical entertainer for at least three of the years 1979–80 to 1988–89 provided that

- there has been a satisfactory history of Schedule D treatment

and

- accounts or returns of income for all relevant years up to and including 1986–87 were submitted before 31 May 1989

and

- the entertainer's last theatrical engagement which started before 6 April 1990 was dealt with under Schedule D (whether or not it ended before that date).

These conditions mean that a theatrical entertainer starting in the profession after 5 April 1987 cannot qualify for reserved Schedule D status.

Entertainers qualifying for reserved Schedule D status will only be assessed under Schedule D so long as they continue to meet their tax obligations satisfactorily, and continue their professional activities without a break. If, following a break, professional activities are resumed, Schedule E treatment will apply to any income from a contract of employment. For the purposes of this concession

- 'standard contract' means a standard contract agreed between theatrical employers and the British Actors Equity Association (Equity)
- 'theatrical entertainer' means an actor, singer, dancer, musician or other theatrical entertainer, and includes stage managers
- 'break' in professional activities means a cessation agreed under the Schedule D rules between the Inland Revenue and the theatrical entertainer.

This concession was announced, in a letter to Associations representing theatrical entertainers and employers, on 25 June 1989.

B8. Double taxation relief: income consisting of royalties and 'know-how' payments—obsolete

Payments made by a person resident in an overseas country to a person carrying on a trade in the United Kingdom as consideration for the use of, or for the privilege of using, in the overseas country any copyright, patent, design, secret process or formula, trade-mark or other like property may in law be payments the source of which is in the United Kingdom, but are nevertheless treated for the purpose of credit (whether under double-taxation agreements or by way of unilateral relief) as income arising outside the United Kingdom except to the extent that they represent consideration for services (other than merely incidental services) rendered in this country by the recipient to the payer.

B17. Capital allowances: sale of invented patent to an associate—obsolete

Patents sold prior to 1 April 1986 between persons under common control are normally treated for capital allowance purposes as sold at open market value, but the parties may in certain circumstances elect that they shall be treated as if sold at the written down value for tax if it is lower (CAA 1968, s 78 and Sch 7 and ICTA 1970, s 387(2) repealed with effect from 1 April 1986). This right of election does not in terms apply to a patent invented by the seller, who would pay tax on the open market value of the patent rights while the purchaser would be given capital allowances on the same amount.

Where, however, an inventor sells the patent rights in his invention to a company which he controls for a sum less than their open market value, the assessment on the seller is restricted to the actual sale price provided that the purchasing company undertakes to restrict its capital allowances claim to that amount.

No capital gains tax liability will be sought in respect of any excess of the market value of the patent right over the consideration actually passing, whether in cash or in shares, provided that the purchasing company accepts that, as a subsequent disposal of the patent right, the allowable expenditure will be restricted to the amount of the actual consideration.

Appendix 6 Statements of practice

SP 9/79* (10 August 1979) Expenditure on producing films and similar assets (FA 1971, s 41)

In the accounts of film production companies the cost of making films is normally treated as deferred revenue expenditure, ie, it is not written off immediately but spread over a period of years starting with the release of the film, on the principle of matching expenditure with receipts to produce a true view of the profit or loss arising from the production of the film. The writing off of the expenditure in the accounts has normally been followed for tax purposes.

It has recently been suggested that, although film production expenditure is not normally capitalised in film companies' accounts, it is nevertheless capital expenditure; that the asset resulting from the expenditure—the master-print of the film—is 'plant' for capital allowances purposes; and that following the case of *McVeigh v Arthur Sanderson and Sons Ltd* (45 TC 273) the whole of such expenditure qualified for 100 per cent first year allowances. On this basis, tax relief for film production expenses would usually be due for the accounting period in which the expenditure is incurred, instead of being deferred and spread over a number of years.

The Inland Revenue has been reviewing the position and agrees that film production expenses can qualify for capital allowances. In future therefore capital allowance claims for film production expenditure will be accepted, provided the master-print of the film can properly be regarded as a capital asset in the business. In practice a master-print would be regarded as meeting this condition if it is retained by the production company and has an anticipated potential life of not less than two years.

Similar considerations apply to some other types of expenditure on producing assets, eg, capital expenditure incurred in producing the master-copy of records and tapes. Capital allowance claims for such expenditure will be allowed on the same basis.

Where a company wishes to continue with an established method of writing off expenditure of this kind in calculating its taxable profits, the Inland Revenue will not normally initiate any change.

This change of practice takes effect from 1 June 1979. Capital allowance claims may therefore be made for any chargeable period (ie accounting period of company or year of assessment for an individual) for which the tax liability had not been finalised before 1 June 1979.

*Note. Although this statement of practice is itself obsolete it is retained because of its reference to deferred revenue expenditure which may be of relevance in other circumstances involving intellectual property.

SP 7/91 (20 July 1991) Double taxation: business profits: unilateral relief

1. TA 1988, s 790 sets out the basis under which relief ('unilateral relief') may be given for foreign tax in the absence of a double taxation agreement. The section sets out the conditions precedent to the granting of relief. So far as business profits are concerned the foreign tax is admissible for relief only if it is a tax which is payable under the law of the foreign territory; a tax which is computed by reference to income arising in the foreign territory; a tax which is charged upon income; and a tax which corresponds to income tax or corporation tax.

2. Hitherto the Revenue have interpreted the conditions so as to exclude from relief a number of foreign taxes having characteristics similar to turnover taxes, that it to say taxes computed by reference to a prescribed proportion of a gross amount of fee or contractual sum from which expenses fall to be deducted in arriving both at the commercial profit and at the amount which, in the UK would be assessable under Case I or II of Schedule D. The taxes excluded from relief were those where the proportion of the gross amount charged to tax prompted the view that the tax could not reasonably be regarded as corresponding to UK income tax or corporation tax charged upon net profits.

3. Following consideration of the point in the High Court (*Yates v GCA International Ltd (formerly Gaffney Cline and Associates Ltd)* [1991] STC 157), the Revenue have decided to change their interpretation. In future the question of whether or not a foreign tax is admissible for unilateral relief under TA 1988, s 790 will be determined by examining the tax within its legislative context in the foreign territory and deciding whether it serves the same function as income and corporation tax serve in the UK in relation to the profits of the business. Turnover taxes, as such, are not therefore affected by the revised interpretation and will continue to be inadmissible for relief. *The revised interpretation will take effect from Wednesday 13 February 1991 when judgment was given in the High Court, and will apply to claims made on or after that date and to earlier claims unsettled at that date.* Taxpayers who would like the Revenue to review a previous decision in respect of a specific foreign tax are invited to address their enquiry to Inland Revenue, International Division, Room 311, Melbourne House, Aldwych, London. WC2B 4LL.

4. It should be noted however that the admissibility of the foreign tax is only one aspect of unilateral relief which can give rise to disputes between the Revenue and the taxpayer. Relief is only available in respect of the foreign tax on income arising in the foreign territory, and according to the facts of the particular case there may be room for argument as to where the income arose and to the amount of the income, having regard to the different principles of law in the foreign territory and in the UK. In the light of the High Court decision the Revenue practice will continue to be to determine questions of this sort by reference to principles of UK tax law. It follows that the charging of foreign tax upon an amount of income will not of itself be sufficient to establish that income of that amount arose in the foreign

territory, and it is necessary to apply principles of UK tax law in order to ascertain the amount of the foreign income. As credit for foreign tax is restricted to the income tax or corporation tax attributable to the foreign income, this last point is one of some importance.

SP 1/93 (11 January 1993) Tax treatment of expenditure on films and certain similar assets

1. Section 68 of the Capital Allowances Act 1990 contains provisions (first enacted in 1982 and 1984) governing the tax treatment of expenditure on the production and acquisition of films, tapes and discs. Sections 41 and 42 of the Finance (No 2) Act 1992 introduced further provisions and section 69 of the same Act introduced consequential amendments to the rules in section 68.

2. This statement updates and combines the earlier Statements of Practice (SP2/83 and SP2/85) on the tax treatment of expenditure on films and similar assets provided by section 68. It also gives guidance (paragraph 26 onwards) on certain procedural and other points arising out of the 1992 provisions.

3. The statement covers the general operation of the provisions. More detailed points arising on particular cases should be settled with the local Inspector of Taxes in the normal way.

Scope and general effect of provisions

4. The provisions of section 68 apply generally to expenditure on the production of the original, master version, of a film or audio product (which may take the form of a negative, tape or disc). The provisions also apply to the acquisition of a master version (or rights in a master version) but not to other rights in the film, tape or disc. They do not apply to expenditure on reproductions (video cassettes, for example).

5. The first effect of section 68 is to treat expenditure on the production or acquisition of a master of a film etc which would otherwise be capital expenditure on the provision of plant (in the form of the master version) as expenditure of a revenue nature. Conversely, capital receipts from the exploitation of master negatives etc (including insurance and compensation monies) are treated as revenue incomings.

6. The section then sets out computational rules as to how such expenditure is to be allowed for tax purposes. Those rules apply to a person carrying on a trade or business which consists of or includes the exploitation of master versions of films etc. The activities of a finance lessor of master versions would amount to the carrying on of a trade so long as it exhibits the necessary degree of organisation, etc.

7. The general rules governing the timing of the deduction of production and acquisition expenditure are described in paragraphs 14 to 25 below. Two write-off methods which broadly follow accountancy practice are available under those rules. These are known as the income matching and cost recovery methods. Cost recovery only applies if a claim is made and serves to supplement the expenditure allocated to a period under the income matching method.

8. Further avenues of relief are available for expenditure on the production or acquisition of 'qualifying' films (ie films certified as meeting certain criteria relating

to their EC and Commonwealth content, including the residence of the film-maker and other participants). An alternative method of relief is also available for 'preliminary' (often termed development or pre-production) expenditure incurred (ie becoming payable) on or after 10 March [1992] on prospective qualifying films. Those rules, which are available at the option of the film-maker, are described in paragraphs 26 to 42 below.

Films held as trading stock

9. Neither the general computational rules nor the alternative rules on production and acquisition expenditure apply to taxpayers who hold the master films etc as trading stock. But a taxpayer who deals in film rights without parting with the master version is not generally to be regarded as falling within that category.

Expenditure covered by computational rules

10. Both the general computational rules set out in section 68 and the alternative rules introduced by sections 41 and 42 Finance (No 2) Act [1992] apply to expenditure which is expenditure of a revenue nature for the purposes of the provisions. For those purposes, expenditure of a revenue nature includes:
   – production or acquisition expenditure which on first principles would have been of a revenue nature (eg royalties paid to acquire film rights to a novel)—but excluding expenditure which is the subject of a specific statutory rule prohibiting relief (eg expenditure on business entertainment) and
   – capital expenditure on production or acquisition which would otherwise have qualified for capital allowances as expenditure on plant, that is the master version. (Examples of such production expenditure in the case of a film include the costs of adapting a story for film purposes, normal production expenses such as wages and salaries, costumes, studio hire and the costs of filming, processing and editing.)

11. Capital expenditure on the provision of assets such as film cameras, lights and sound recording equipment which may be used in the process of production but which are not used up in that process should not be regarded as production expenditure for the purposes of these provisions.

12. Interest on money borrowed to finance production etc may be relieved under the normal rules rather than treated as part of production costs.

Write-off rules

Income matching method

13. Under this method, expenditure is written off over the period during which the value of the film etc is expected to be realised. The amount of expenditure to be allocated to a particular period of account falling within that period is to be 'just and reasonable' having regard to:
   (i) the amount of expenditure remaining unallowed at the beginning of the period of account; and

(ii)   the proportion that the value of the film etc realised in that period bears to the value plus the remaining value as estimated at the end of the period.

14. In the case of a film made of public exhibition, the value of the film realised in a period will be the income earned in that period; and estimated future value will be represented by estimated future income.

15. If the total income from a film could be known precisely at the time of its release, the amount of expenditure to be written off in any period could be arrived at simply by apportioning the total expenditure on the same basis as the flow of income. In practice, however, post-release estimates of total income will tend to fluctuate according to the success or otherwise of a film following its release. That is why it is necessary to introduce the concepts of 'expenditure unallowed' and 'estimated future income'.

16. If a film is less successful than expected, estimates of the total income from the film will be revised downwards from the initial estimate. Where at the end of an accounting period, as a result of such a revision, the estimated future income is less than the amount of expenditure not yet written off, it will be acceptable for the excess to be written off in that accounting period.

17. In estimating the remaining value of the film at a particular accounting date, future income may be discounted at reasonable commercial rates.

18. In the case of feature films, it will normally be necessary to estimate the future income separately for each film. In some cases, however, where the company's records show that the income flow from past productions has followed a fairly regular pattern it will be reasonable to assume that that pattern is likely to apply to current productions, and, in such cases, it may be acceptable to write off expenditure on that same basis. It will be necessary, however, to verify from time to time that the income pattern has not changed.

Advances

19. Under some distribution agreements, non-repayable advances of royalties may be received, and properly brought into account as income earned before a film is completed and released. In such cases, the date from which the value of the film starts to be realised will be the date from which that income is first brought into account and, accordingly, the appropriate proportion of production expenditure should be written off in that period of account.

Finance leases

20. Where a film is made available under a finance lease, the writing off of the cost of acquisition of the lessor, by reference to current income and discounted future income, will not produce a result which is 'just and reasonable'. A finance lease, although involving the acquisition of an asset by the lessor, may be regarded as analogous to a loan of money. The annual rentals can be seen as containing two elements: interest (the income yield) on the outstanding balance, and part repayment of the advance. Viewed in this way, the lease produces higher income in the earlier years, when the rental contains more interest than loan repayment.

21. The expenditure allocated to any period of account should therefore be such as to ensure that the profit from the lease in the period (ie the rentals received less the expenditure allocated) does not fall below the rate of return for that period implicit in the amount of the lease rentals.

Abortive expenditure

22. Where production costs are incurred, or rights are acquired, and a decision is taken not to proceed with the project the expenditure may be charged to revenue for tax purposes at the time that the assets are considered to have no further value.

Television films

23. Where costs are incurred by a television company on the production of, or acquisition of rights in, a film primarily for showing on its own channel, it will not be possible to calculate the rate at which the value of the film is realised by reference to the amount of income earned and estimated future earnings. (Although there may be some income from the granting of exhibition rights on other channels or overseas this exploitation will not normally constitute the primary object of the film's production.) In such cases it will be necessary to have regard to other matters such as the likely number of showings on the company's own channel and the estimated residual value of the film once a showing has taken place.

Short life assets

24. In the case of some assets, for example original master discs for popular music singles where the artist or group is not well known, income from the exploitation rights is likely to arise over a period of only a few weeks or, at most, months after release. Where the costs of production of such assets are relatively small and the predicted life is less than 12 months, there will normally be no objection to writing off the costs when the record or tape is released, if that practice is followed in preparing the accounts.

Cost recovery method

25. A film-maker may claim within two years of the end of any period of account that the expenditure allocated to that period under the income-matching method should be increased so that the total expenditure allocated exactly matches the value realised (typically, outside the field of television films, the income arising) from the film in that period. The effect is that no profit on a film need be brought into account for tax purposes until all the costs of production have been recouped out of the income related to that production. Informal claims to use this method, for example on the face of the computations, are acceptable.

Examples

I   *Income matching method*

A film is in the course of production during year 1 and expenditure of £2.5 million is incurred. The film is completed and released in year 2 after further expenditure of £1.5 million has been incurred. At the end of year 2 the expected total income from the film is £8 million but at the end of year 3 expected total income has fallen to £6 million.

The amounts of income earned are: Year 2   £m3
                                     Year 3   £m2
                                     Year 4   £ml

The expected *future* income is:

At the end of year 2 £m5   (£m8 – £m3)
At the end of year 3 £ml   (£m6 – £m5)
At the end of year 4   negligible

The method of writing off expenditure as income is earned can be expressed by the formula:

$$\frac{\text{expenditure to be allowed}}{\text{in accounting period}} = e \times \frac{a}{a+b}$$

where e   is the total expenditure on producing a film less any amounts already allowed

a   is the gross income from the film in that period

b   is the expected future gross income from the film.

The treatment of income and expenditure for tax purposes is as follows:

Year 1   The production costs of £m2.5 will be carried forward

Year 2   Income: bring into account   £m3
              Expenditure: deduct

              $$£m4 \times \frac{\text{Inc of year £m3}}{\text{Inc of year £m3 + expected future inc £m5}} = £m1.5$$

Year 3   Income: bring into account   £m2
              Expenditure: deduct

              $$(£m4 – £m1.5) \times \frac{£m2}{£m2 + £ml} = £m1.7$$

Year 4   Income: bring into account   £ml
              Expenditure: deduct
              $$(£m4 – (£m1.5 + £m1.7)) \times \frac{£ml}{£ml + nil} = £m0.8$$

If in the above example the income of year 3 were £m0.8 only and the estimated future income at the end of year 3 were £m0.2 only, the amount to be written off in year 3 would be as follows:

As formula:

$$£m2.5 \times \frac{£m0.8}{£m0.8 + £m0.2} = £m2$$

Plus: (to reduce amount carried forward
       to estimated future income)   £m0.3*
                                                                    ———
                                                                    £m2.3
*Expenditure £m4 less allowed (£m1.5 + £m2)   =   £m0.5
 Estimated future income   £m0.2
                                                                    ———
 Difference   £m0.3

II   *Cost recovery method*

This method enables a claim to be made to write off in year 2 a further £m1.5; this is the excess of the £m3 income brought into account over the £m1.5 expenditure allocated under the income matching method.

The figures for year 3 would then be:

Year 3

Income: bring into account	£m2
Expenditure: deduct balance unallowed	
(£m4 – £m3)	= £m1

Alternative rules for preliminary expenditure on prospective 'qualifying' films and expenditure on production or acquisition of qualifying films

26. Under the Films Act 1985 the Secretary of State is empowered to certify films meeting the necessary conditions as qualifying films of tax purposes (see the leaflet FB1 'Evidence of British Nature of a Film' available from Department of National Heritage, 2nd Floor, Grey Core, 151 Buckingham Palace Road, London SW1W 9SS). The effect of certification on the tax rules depends on when the film is completed.

Films completed prior to 10 March 1992

27. Where (at the option of the film producer) such a film was certified as being a qualifying film and in addition that film was expected to have a value realisable over a period of two years or more the special tax rules described in paragraphs 4 to 25 of this statement are automatically disapplied. The most important effect is that capital expenditure on the production or acquisition of the master version of such a film is regarded as expenditure on the provision of plant and thus qualifies for capital allowances.

Films completed on or after 10 March 1992

28. Qualifying films are now no longer automatically excluded from the special tax rules. Instead, for films completed on or after 10 March 1992, an election for exclusion has to be made. Such an election which is irrevocable has to cover all the production or acquisition expenditure on the film concerned. No election is possible if some of the expenditure has been relieved under the special computational rules described above in paras 4 to 25 or under the provisions of sections 41 or 42 Finance (No 2) Act 1992.

29. The election must:

– be made in writing to the claimant's local Inspector of Taxes within two years of the period of account in which the film is completed;

– identify the film and state the amount of expenditure;

– be accompanied by a copy of the Secretary of State's certificate that it is a qualifying film;

– be signed by an individual claimant, by the company secretary in the case of a company or, in the case of a partnership, by the precedent acting partner.

30. Where no election is made in respect of a film which was completed on or after 10 March 1992 and which has been certified as a qualifying film the rules outlined in paragraphs 13 to 25 apply. In addition, under provisions introduced by

sections 41 to 43 Finance (No 2) Act 1992, the film-maker is entitled to adopt alternative bases of writing off expenditure in computing trading profits for a period of account. Different rules apply to preliminary expenditure and other production expenditure. Some features of these rules are described below.

31. In determining whether a film was completed prior to 10 March 1992 the approach described in paragraphs 39 and 40 below will be adopted.

Preliminary expenditure incurred on or after 10 March 1992

32. A claim may be made that preliminary (ie development or pre-production) expenditure meeting the conditions in section 41 be deducted in computing profits for the period of account in which it becomes payable or for a later period.

33. One of those conditions is that expenditure must reasonably be said to have been incurred to enable a decision to be taken whether or not to go ahead with a film. For this purpose it is considered that no decision can be regarded as having been made until all the elements involved, including finance, have been secured. At what point the decision to go ahead is subsequently taken will depend on individual circumstances.

34. Where a film has not been completed at the time when the claim is made it is necessary to consider whether at that time there was a reasonable likelihood that the film if completed would be a qualifying film. This will depend on the plans of the film-maker at the time and in particular whether he was using his best endeavours to ensure that the film would meet the necessary conditions. The fact that a film did not eventually achieve qualifying status would not of itself prevent this test from being satisfied.

35. Although section 41 applies only to taxpayers whose trade consists of or includes the exploitation of films, the availability of relief in respect of preliminary expenditure on a particular film does not depend on ownership of that film. The fact that expenditure is incurred as a contribution towards the preliminary expenditure of another person does not, of itself, prevent relief from being available under section 41.

36. Claims to deduct preliminary expenditure under section 41 must be made in writing within two years of the period of account in which the expenditure becomes payable. They should specify the period for which relief is claimed, the identity of the films concerned, and the amounts incurred on each. Claims should be signed by the person mentioned in paragraph 29 above.

37. Section 41(5) imposes a limit on the amount of expenditure which qualifies for relief under section 46, namely 20 per cent of total budgeted production expenditure as estimated on the first day of principal photography. Exceptionally, cases may arise where the relief already given for preliminary expenditure in previous periods for which the assessments have become final is found (at the date of commencement of principal photography) to exceed 20 per cent of budget. In these circumstances, provided the overclaim was made in good faith and as an alternative to re-opening earlier periods, the Inspector will be prepared to recoup the excess by means of an appropriate reduction in relief for production expenditure costs in the first period of account in which those costs are deducted.

Production and acquisition expenditure—alternative method of write-off

38. Under section 42 a film-maker may (on a claim) deduct one third of the total expenditure on producing a qualifying film (excluding from the total expenditure

already relieved under section 41) in computing profits for the period of account in which the film is completed so long as completion falls on or after 10 March 1992. Where the period of account is of less than 12 months duration, the rate of relief is correspondingly reduced. Similar relief for the balance of unallowed expenditure is available at the same rate for subsequent periods. Thus the whole of the costs of production may be written off by the second anniversary of the end of period of account in which the film is completed (so long as periods are of 12 months duration).

39. The time when a film is completed is defined in section 43(3). In practice a film will normally be regarded as completed at the time when it is ready to be delivered (following completion of editing etc) by the film producer to the distributor even if it is later sent back to the producer for changes. Where the expenditure is incurred on the acquisition of a qualifying film relief is given by reference to the date of acquisition if that is later than the date of completion.

40. The definition of completion includes the condition that the film must be in a state where it could be distributed and exhibited to the general public. Whether or not it is so distributed is not material. In particular, this condition is not regarded as failed merely because the film is not intended or does not in the event go on general release.

41. Claims to write off production expenditure under section 42 must be made within two years of the end of the period of account to which the claims relate. Once made, a claim cannot be withdrawn. Claims should be signed by the person mentioned in paragraph 29 above.

Effect of claims under sections 41 and 42 on subsequent relief under the general rules

42. Relief under the general rules for subsequent periods of account in respect of a qualifying film is not precluded by claims for earlier periods under sections 41 and 42. But, in computing the appropriate deduction for future periods, expenditure relieved under those provisions is excluded just as expenditure deducted for earlier periods under the general rules is excluded.

Appendix 7   US Internal Revenue Service: 'lend-a-star' rulings

Revenue Ruling 74–330

The purpose of this Revenue Ruling is to state the income tax treatment under the Internal Revenue Code of 1954 for a foreign entertainer in the examples described below. These examples involve contracts entered into between a United Kingdom corporation and a United States person for the performance of services by a foreign entertainer and are sometimes referred to as 'single loan-out' arrangements.

Example (1) E, an entertainer who is a resident of the United Kingdom and a nonresident alien of the United States, is the sole shareholder of UKC, a United Kingdom corporation. E executes an exclusive service contract with UKC purportedly as an employee. UKC, as E's agent, negotiates a contract with X, a United States person, for the loan-out of E's services to be performed within the United States. E has a veto over the terms of the contract. X pays UKC under the terms of the loan-out agreement, and E receives payment for his services from his wholly-owned corporation. UKC retains a fee for the services rendered. The amount of E's compensation depends on the size of the payment UKC receives from X. X specifically requires the services of E and no other person. X requires that E sign and guarantee all contracts with UKC. X furnishes E with costumes and E performs his services on X's premises and subject to X's control. In these respects X treats E like an employee of X.

Example (2) The facts are the same as in *Example* (1), except that E owns no stock in UKC. The nominal shareholders of UKC receive only token dividends because almost all the profits of UKC are paid to E in the form of 'salary' and 'bonuses'. Although UKC's agreement with X requires that UKC make certain expenditures, as between E and UKC, E effectively assumes most of the risk of loss of the venture because of his personal guarantee.

Example (3) UKC, a United Kingdom corporation, has numerous entertainers who are residents of the United Kingdom and nonresident aliens of the United States under exclusive long-term contracts to perform only on jobs negotiated by UKC. UKC's sole purpose is to 'loan-out' the services of the entertainers for a consideration. The entertainers own no stock in UKC. UKC enters into a contract with X, a United States person, for the services of E, a resident of the United Kingdom and a nonresident alien of the United States, in the United States. X requires that E sign and guarantee the contract negotiated with UKC. X pays UKC under the terms of the 'loan-out' agreement, and E receives a fixed salary from UKC in accordance with his contract. UKC retains a fee for the services rendered by E. UKC does not perform the function of providing an entertainment program but acts as a booking agent in providing entertainers requested by such persons as X. The salary paid to E is determined in accordance with salaries paid by X to other entertainers of E's stature. E performs services for X and is subject to X's control. In these respects E is treated like any other employee of X. X effectively has the right to discharge E.

Example (4) UKC, a United Kingdom corporation, engaged in the production of motion pictures, has a number of entertainers under exclusive contract to render services for it, or on its behalf in exchange for a fixed salary. The contracts run for a substantial period of time and require the corporation to pay its entertainers a fixed salary. The entertainers, who are residents of the United Kingdom and nonresident aliens of the United States, own no stock in UKC and have retained no veto over loan-out contracts negotiated by that corporation. During a period when UKC's production activities do not require the services of E, an entertainer, his services are loaned-out to X, a United States person, for a fee. During that period E continues to receive his salary from UKC under the terms of his exclusive service contract. E is subject to the control and direction of UKC.

Section 861(*a*)(3) of the Code provides, in part, that compensation for personal services performed in the United States shall be treated as income from sources in the United States unless such services are performed by a nonresident alien individual who is present in the United States for no more than 90 days during the taxable year, who receives in the aggregate no more than $13,000 a year for such services, and who performs services for a nonresident alien individual, foreign partnership, or foreign corporation not engaged in trade or business in the United States.

Section 864 of the Code provides, in effect, that income derived by a nonresident alien from the performance of personal services within the United States under section 861(*a*)(3) is considered effectively connected with the conduct of his trade or business within the United States.

Section 871(*b*) of the Code provides that a nonresident alien individual engaged in trade or business within the United States during the taxable year shall be taxable as provided in section 1 or section 1201(*b*) on his taxable income that is effectively connected with the conduct of a trade or business within the United States.

Section 1441(*a*) of the Code provides for the withholding of tax of the 30 per cent rate on certain income from sources within the United States of nonresident alien individuals.

Section 1441(*c*)(1) of the Code provides that no deduction or withholding shall be required under section 1441(*a*), in the case of any item of income (other than compensation for personal services) that is effectively connected with the conduct of a trade or business within the United States and that is included in the gross income of the recipient under section 871(*b*)(2).

Section 1441(*c*)(4) of the Code provides that under regulations prescribed by the Secretary of the Treasury or his delegate, compensation for personal services may be exempt from withholding under section 1441(*a*).

Section 1.1441–4(*a*)(1) of the Income Tax Regulations provides that no withholding is required under section 1.1441–1 in the case of any item of income if such income is effectively connected with the conduct of a trade or business within the United States by the person entitled to such income, if such income is includible in that person's gross income under section 842, 871(*b*)(2), or 882(*a*)(2) of the Code for the taxable year, and if such person has filed the statement prescribed by section 1.1441–4(*a*)(2).

Section 1.1441–4(*a*)(1) shall apply to income for services performed by a foreign corporation (other than a foreign corporation that has income to which section 543(*a*)(7) applies for the taxable year). Section 1.1441–4(*a*)(1) does not apply to compensation for personal services performed by a nonresident alien individual.

Section 1.1441–4(*b*) of the regulations provides that withholding is not required from salaries, wages, remuneration, or any other compensation for personal services of a nonresident alien individual if such compensation would be subject to withholding under section 3402 of the Code but for the provisions of section 3401(*a*) (other than paragraph (6) thereof) and the regulations thereunder.

Section 3402 of the Code and section 31.3401(*a*)(6)–1(*a*) of the regulations provide that wages paid for services performed by a nonresident alien employee are subject to withholding under section 3402 unless excepted by section 31.3401(*a*)(6)–1(*b*) through (*e*).

Section 31.3401(*a*)(6)–1(*e*) of the regulations provides that no withholding is required if the income is exempt under the Internal Revenue Code, or under an income tax convention, provided the nonresident alien individual files with the employer a statement showing the basis of the exemption. The statement must meet the requirements of that section.

Section 31.3402(*a*)–1(*b*) of the regulations provides that the employer is required to collect the tax by deducting and withholding the amount thereof from the employee's wages as and when paid, either actually or constructively.

Section 882(*a*)(1) of the Code provides that a foreign corporation engaged in a trade or business in the United States during the taxable year shall be taxable as provided in section 11 or section 1201(*a*) on its taxable income that is effectively connected with the conduct of a trade or business within the United States.

Section 1442(*a*) of the Code provides, in part, that in the case of a foreign corporation subject to taxation under subtitle A of the Code, there shall be deducted and withheld at the source in the same manner and on the same items of income as is provided in section 1441 or section 1451 a tax equal to 30 per cent thereof. For the purposes of section 1442(*a*) the reference in section 1441(*c*)(1) to section 871(*b*)(2) shall be treated as referring to section 882(*a*)(2).

Section 882(*a*)(2) provides that in determining taxable income for purposes of section 882(*a*)(1), gross income includes only gross income that is effectively connected with the conduct of a trade or business within the United States.

Article III of the United States–United Kingdom Income Tax Convention (Convention), TD 5569, 1947–2 CB 100, provides, in part, that industrial or commercial profits of an enterprise of one of the Contracting Parties shall be exempt from tax by the other Party unless the enterprise is engaged in a trade or business in the territory of such other Party through a permanent establishment situated therein. Industrial or commercial profits include income derived from furnishing the services of employees or other personnel.

Article XI(1) of the Convention provides that an individual who is a resident of the United Kingdom shall be exempt from United States tax upon compensation for personal (including professional) services performed during the taxable year within the United States if (*a*) he is present within the United States for not more than 183 days during such taxable year, and (*b*) such services are performed for or on behalf of a person resident in the United Kingdom. Services are performed for or on behalf of a resident of the United Kingdom if such services are performed in connection with an employment relationship.

Section 482 of the Code provides that in any case of two or more organizations, trades, businesses (whether or not incorporated, whether or not organised in the United States, and whether or not affiliated) owned or controlled directly or indirectly by the same interests, the Secretary of the Treasury or his delegate may distribute, apportion or allocate gross income, deductions, credits, or allowances between or among such organisations, trades, or businesses if he determines that such distribution, apportionment, or allocation is necessary in order to prevent evasion of taxes or clearly to reflect the income of any of such organisations, trades, or businesses.

At issue in each example is whether the amounts received by E or UKC from X are subject to Federal income tax or withholding or whether all or part of these amounts are exempt from tax under the Convention. As noted above, Article III of the Convention exempts from Federal income tax industrial and commercial profits of a United Kingdom enterprise derived from furnishing the services of its employees in the United States (unless such enterprise has a permanent establishment in the United States). Article XI(1) of the Convention exempts from Federal income tax compensation received by a United Kingdom resident for services performed in the United States as an employee of another resident of the United Kingdom. Thus, whether E is performing services in the United States as an employee of UKC affects the manner in which the respective parties are to be taxed.

For Federal income tax purposes, and for purposes of applying the Convention, an employer–employee relationship depends on an examination of all the facts and circumstances pertaining to the relationships among the parties. In the present context, important factors which indicate an employer-employee relationship between E and UKC are as follows: E is subject to the control and direction of UKC as to time, place, and manner of performance; E has an exclusive personal service contract of substantial duration; E is furthering the regular business of UKC; E may not veto engagements arranged by UKC; UKC is responsible for furnishing E with a place of performance, appropriate costumes, make-up, scripts, musical accompaniment, or the like; E's salary is not based on the net profits derived in respect of his performances; and UKC bears customary business risks in connection with furnishing E's services. Of the foregoing factors, the right to control E in the performance of his services is the most important. An employment relationship does not exist where UKC merely acts as E's agent. *See Bartels v Birmingham*, 332 US 126 (1947), 1947–2 CB 174; *Ringling Bros, Barnum and Bailey Combined Shows, Inc v Higgins* 189 F 2d 865 (2d Circ 1951); *Filipidis v United States*, 71–1 USTC 85, 828 (Md 1970). aff'd *per curiam* 71–2 USTC 87, 830 (4th Cir 1970); section 31 3401(*c*)–1(*b*) of the regulations; and Rev Rul 71–144, 1971–1 CB 285.

On the basis of the foregoing factors, the following conclusions have been reached:

In *Examples* (1) *and* (2) it is held that E, despite the form of the contracts, is not an employee of UKC because E's salary is measured by profits, and UKC does not assume the financial risk of E's performance, does not furnish E with the tools to perform and the place of performance, and does not control the details of E's work. The fact that E retains a veto power over the terms of the entertainment contracts negotiated by UKC is evidence that UKC does not have the right to control the details of E's work. The fact that UKC retains only a fee for its services, and has obligated itself to pay E a salary measured by profits is evidence that E and not UKC assumes the financial risk of payment from X. E is not performing services for or on behalf of UKC. Rather, UKC is merely E's agent.

Although E is not an employee of UKC in *Examples* (1) and (2), UKC does function as E's agent. UKC functions as E's agent because it has consented to find and negotiate employment opportunities for E subject to E's veto. See RESTATEMENT (SECOND) OF AGENCY, section 1(1) (1957).

Since industrial and commercial profits also include income derived by a foreign corporation from furnishing the services of persons other than employees and since UKC does not have a permanent establishment in the United States, the fee retained by UKC in *Examples* (1) and (2) is exempt from Federal income tax under Article III(1) of the Convention.

Although E is not an employee of UKC in *Examples* (1) and (2), he is performing in the United States as an employee of X. Thus, Articles III(1) and XI(1) of the Convention do not exempt his United States source income from Federal income tax.

E, as an employee of X, is taxable under section 871(*b*) of the Code. Therefore, X must withhold on E's salary that it pays to UKC pursuant to section 3402 of the Code, and section 31.3401(*a*)(6)–1(*a*) and 31.3402(*a*)–1(*b*) of the regulations.

In *Example* (3), although E receives a fixed salary from UKC, in performing services for X, E is the employee of X rather than UKC. E is not UKC's employee because UKC has insufficient control over the details of E's work and because the entertainment services that E performs are not part of the regular business of UKC. Moreover, UKC, whose activities consist merely of obtaining performance opportunities (and compensation) for entertainers, is acting only as a booking agent rather than as an employer. In this regard, E's performance of entertainment services in the United States is part of the regular business of X. Moreover, because E is subject to X's control and is treated like any other employee of X, E is an employee of that corporation. *See Linstead v Chesapeake & Ohio R R Co* 276 US 28 (1928), and RESTATEMENT (SECOND) OF AGENCY, section 227 (1957).

Therefore, X must withhold income tax in accordance with section 3402 of the Code on the compensation paid to UKC with respect to E's services, less the compensation retained by UKC as its agency fee.

In *Example* (4) E is an employee of UKC even while on temporary 'loan-out' to X, because of their continuing work relationship, E's continuing receipt of a fixed salary from UKC, and UKC's exercise of sufficient control over E. Therefore, E's salary is exempt from Federal income tax and withholding under Article XI(1) of the Convention.

The fees retained by UKC in *Examples* (3) and (4) are also exempt from Federal income tax and withholding under Article III(1) of the Convention since UKC has no permanent establishment in the United States, E's performance of entertainment services in the United States does not constitute a permanent establishment therein. *See* Rev Rul 67–321, 1967–2 CB 470, which holds that a French corporation does not have a permanent establishment in the United States even though the corporation presented a floor show in the United States.

If in *Examples* (1), (2) or (3) it is determined that E is performing as an independent contractor who is not an employee of X, X must withhold a tax of 30 per cent pursuant to the provisions of section 1441(*a*) and (*c*)(1) of the Code on E's compensation that it pays to UKC. *See* Rev Rul 70–543, 1970–2 CB 172.

If UKC had been determined to be a sham in any of the above examples, its existence would be disregarded for Federal income tax purposes, and all of the income with respect to E's performance of services would be attributable to E. Similarly, if such income were attributable to E under assignment of income principles, E will be regarded as earning the income other than as UKC's employee. *See Richard Rubin*, 56 TC 1155, 1159–60 (1971), aff'd 460 F 2d 1216 (2d Cir 1972). In either event X would be required to withhold a tax, because Articles III(1) and XI(1) of the Convention would not be available to exempt that income from Federal income tax. *See Johansson v United States*, 336 F 2d 809, 812–13 (5th Cir 1964).

In determining whether a corporation is a sham, *see Moline Properties, Inc v Commissioner*, 319 US 436, 438–439 (1943), 1943 CB 1011 and *Floyd Patterson*, TC Memo 1966–329 aff'd, 68–2 USTC 87, 623 (2d Cir 1968).

In determining whether the assignment of income principles apply, thus requiring that income be taxed to the person that earns it, *see Lucas v Earl*, 281 US 111, 114–15 (1930) and *Richard Rubin*.

Section 482 of the Code provides that the Secretary or his delegate may distribute, apportion, or allocate gross income in order to clearly reflect income in an appropriate case where two or more organisations, trades, or businesses are controlled by the same interest. Under the doctrine of assignment of income, or under section 482 where applicable, the income of the entertainer stated in the contracts may be increased in an appropriate case. *See Victor Borge*, 26 TCM 816 (1967), aff'g, mod'g, and rem'g TC, 405 F 2d (2d Cir 1968).

In any situation where the nature of the relationship between the United States person and the entertainer or the entertainer and the foreign corporation is not readily ascertainable the United States person should withhold from the amount paid for services rendered at a rate of 30 per cent, pursuant to sections 1441(*a*) or 1442(*a*) of the Code. The entertainer, foreign corporation, or United States person may apply for a ruling in advance of the transaction regarding exemption or reduction of the tax pursuant to the procedures set forth in Rev Proc 72–3, 1972 CB 698.

Revenue ruling 74–331

The purpose of this Revenue Ruling is to state the income tax treatment under the Internal Revenue Code of 1954 for a foreign entertainer in the examples described below. These examples involve contracts entered into between a Channel Islands corporation, a United Kingdom corporation, and a United States person for the performance of services by a foreign entertainer which are sometimes referred to as 'double loan-out' arrangements.

Example (1) E, an entertainer, who is a resident of the United Kingdom and a nonresident alien of the United States, is the sole shareholder of CIC, a corporation organised in one of the Channel Islands of the United Kingdom. E signs an exclusive service contract with CIC. It is understood that E may veto any arrangements proposed by CIC for the performance of his services. CIC, as agent for E, contracts for the performance of personal services by E with UKC, which may be either a related or unrelated United Kingdom corporation. UKC, as agent for CIC, procures a contract with X, a United States person for E's services. X pays UKC for E's services and, after deducting its agency fee, UKC remits the balance to CIC. CIC deducts an agency fee and pays the balance to E as his compensation.

Example (2) E, a resident of the United Kingdom and a nonresident alien of the United States, is the sole shareholder of CIC, a corporation organized in one of the Channel Islands of the United Kingdom. CIC functions as E's managing agent. E executes an exclusive personal service contract with UKC, an unrelated United Kingdom corporation, to perform services whenever and wherever UKC requires. The contract runs for a substantial period of time and requires UKC to pay E a fixed salary. UKC is generally responsible for providing E with make-up, scripts, and other similar items. E has not imposed restrictions on UKC's 'loan-out' of his services nor has he retained any veto power over such arrangements. UKC negotiates a contract with X, a United States person, for the 'loan-out' of E's services to be performed in the United States. X pays UKC for the services rendered by E. During that period E continues to receive his fixed salary from UKC, and UKC has the right to designate the place and manner in which E is to perform. UKC also pays a fee to CIC for services rendered.

Example (3) E, a resident of the United Kingdom and a nonresident alien of the United States, is the sole shareholder of CIC, a corporation organised in one of the Channel Islands of the United Kingdom. E executes an exclusive personal service contract with CIC for the performance of services whenever and wherever CIC requires. The contract runs for a substantial period of time and requires CIC as E's employer to pay E a fixed salary. E has not imposed restrictions on the 'loan-out' of his services by CIC nor has he retained any veto power over such arrangements. CIC contracts with UKC, a United Kingdom corporation, for the personal services of E. Neither E nor CIC own any shares in or otherwise exercise any control over UKC. UKC, as agent for CIC, negotiates a contract with X, a United States person, for the 'loan-out' of E's services to be performed in the United States. During this period, E continues to receive his fixed salary from CIC. Under the terms of the contract, X pays 1,000x dollars to UKC, and UKC pays the equivalent of 950x dollars to CIC. UKC retains 50x dollars as its fee.

Section 861(*a*)(3) of the Code provides, in part, that compensation for personal services performed in the United States shall be treated as income from sources in the United States unless such services are performed by a nonresident alien individual who is present in the United States for no more than 90 days during the taxable year, who receives in the aggregate no more than $13,000 for such services, and who performs services for a nonresident alien individual, foreign partnership or foreign corporation, not engaged in trade or business in the United States.

Section 864 of the Code provides, in effect, that income derived by a nonresident alien from the performance of personal services within the United States under section 861(*a*)(3) is considered effectively connected with the conduct of a trade or business within the United States.

Section 871(*b*) of the Code provides that a nonresident alien individual engaged in trade or business within the United States during the taxable year shall be taxable as provided in section 1 or section 1201(*b*) on his taxable income that is effectively connected with the conduct of a trade or business within the United States.

Section 1441(*a*) of the Code provides, in general, for the withholding of tax at the 30 per cent rate on certain income from sources within the United States of nonresident alien individuals.

Section 1441(*c*)(1) of the Code provides that no deduction or withholding shall be required under section 1441(*a*) in the case of any item of income (other than compensation for personal services) that is effectively connected with the conduct of a trade or business within the United States and that is included in the gross income of the recipient under section 871(*b*)(2).

Section 1441(*c*)(4) of the Code provides that under regulations prescribed by the Secretary of the Treasury or his delegate, compensation for personal services may be exempt from withholding under section 1441(*a*).

Section 1.1441–4(*a*)(1) of the Income Tax Regulations provides that no withholding is required under section 1.1441–1 in the case of any item of income if such income is effectively connected with the conduct of a trade or business within the United States by a person entitled to such income, if such income is includible in his gross income under sections 842, 871(*b*)(2), or 882(*a*)(2) of the Code for the taxable year, and if such person has filed the statement prescribed by section 1.1441–4(*a*)(2).

Section 1.1441–4(*a*)(1) shall apply to income for services performed by a foreign corporation (other than a foreign corporation that has income to which section 543(*a*)(7) applies for the taxable year). Section 1.1441–4(*a*)(1) does not apply to compensation for personal services performed by a nonresident alien individual.

Section 543(*a*)(7) of the Code provides that certain amounts received under a personal service contract constitute personal holding company income. Section 543(*a*)(7) applies with respect to amounts received for services under a particular contract only if at some time during the taxable year 25 per cent or more in value of the outstanding stock of the corporation is owned, directly or indirectly, by or for the individual who has performed, is to perform, or may be designated (by name or by description) as the one to perform such services.

Section 544 of the Code provides attribution rules for purposes of the 25 per cent ownership requirements.

Section 1.1441–4(*b*) of the regulations provides that withholding is not required from salaries, wages, remuneration, or any other compensation for personal services of a nonresident alien individual if such compensation would be subject to withholding under section 3402 of the Code but for the provisions of section 3401(*a*) (other than paragraph (6) thereof) and the regulations thereunder.

Section 3402 of the Code and section 31.3401(*a*)(6)–1(*a*) of the regulations provide that wages paid for services performed by a nonresident alien individual are subject to withholding under section 3402 unless excepted by section 31.3401(*a*)(6)–1(*b*) through (*e*).

Section 31.3401(*a*)(6)–1(*e*) of the regulations provides that no withholding is required if the wages are exempt under the Internal Revenue Code or under an income tax convention provided the nonresident alien individual files with the employer a statement showing the basis of the exemption. This statement must meet the requirements of that section.

Section 31.3402(*a*)–1(*b*) of the regulations provides that the employer is required to collect the tax by deducting and withholding the amount thereof from the employee's wages as and when paid, either actually or constructively.

Section 882(*a*)(1) of the Code provides that a foreign corporation engaged in a trade or business in the United States during the taxable year shall be taxable as provided in section 11 or section 1201(*a*) on its taxable income that is effectively connected with the conduct of a trade or business within the United States.

Section 1442(*a*) of the Code provides, in part, that in the case of a foreign corporation subject to taxation under subtitle A of the Code, there shall be deducted and withheld at the source in the same manner and on the same items of income as is provided in section 1441 or section 1451 a tax equal to 30 per cent thereof. For the purposes of section 1442(*a*), the reference in section 1441(*c*)(1) to section 871(*b*)(2) shall be treated as referring to section 882(*a*)(2). Section 882(*a*)(2) provides that in determining taxable income for the purposes of section 882(*a*)(1), gross income includes only gross income that is effectively connected with the conduct of a trade or business within the United States.

Section 482 of the Code provides that in the case of two or more organisations, trades, or businesses (whether or not incorporated, whether or not organized in the United States, and whether or not affiliated) owned or controlled directly or indirectly by the same interests the Secretary of the Treasury or his delegate may distribute, apportion or allocate gross income, deductions, credits, or allowances between or among such organisations, trades, or businesses, if he determines that such distribution, apportionment, or allocation is necessary in order to prevent evasion of taxes or clearly to reflect the income of any of such organisations, trades, or businesses.

Article II(1)(*b*) of the United States–United Kingdom Income Tax Convention (Convention), TD 5569, 1947–2 CB 100, defines the term 'United Kingdom' to mean Great Britain and Northern Ireland, excluding the Channel Islands and the Isle of Man.

Article III of the Convention provides, in part, that industrial or commercial profits of an enterprise of one of the Contracting Parties shall be exempt from tax by the other Party unless the enterprise is engaged in a trade or business in the territory of such other Party through a permanent establishment situated therein. Industrial or commercial profits include income derived from furnishing the services of employees or other personnel.

Article XI(1) of the Convention provides that an individual who is a resident of the United Kingdom shall be exempt from United States tax upon compensation for personal (including professional) services performed during the taxable year within the United States if (*a*) he is present within the United States for not more than 183 days during such taxable year, and (*b*) such services are performed for or on behalf of a person resident in the United Kingdom.

Services are performed for or on behalf of a resident of the United Kingdom if such services are performed in connection with an employment relationship.

At issue in each example is whether the amounts received by E, CIC, or UKC from X are subject to Federal income tax or withholding or whether all or part of these amounts are exempt from tax under the Convention. As noted above, Article III of the Convention exempts from Federal income tax industrial and commercial profits of a United Kingdom resident derived from furnishing the services of its employees in the United States (unless such resident has a permanent establishment in the United States). Article XI(1) of the Convention exempts from Federal income tax compensation received by a United Kingdom resident for services performed in the United States as an employee of another resident of the United Kingdom. Thus, whether E is performing services in the United States as an employee of UKC affects the manner in which the respective parties are to be taxed.

For Federal income tax purposes, and for purposes of applying the Convention, an employer–employee relationship depends on an examination of all the facts and circumstances pertaining to the relationships among the parties. In the present context, important factors which indicate an employer–employee relationship between E and CIC or UKC are as follows: E is subject to the control and direction of UKC or CIC as to time, place, and manner of performance; E has an exclusive personal service contract of substantial duration; E is furthering the regular business of UKC; E may not veto engagements arranged by UKC or CIC; UKC or CIC are responsible for furnishing E with appropriate costumes, make-up, scripts, musical accompaniment, or the like; E's salary is not based principally on the net profits derived in respect of his performances; and UKC or CIC bear customary business risks in connection with furnishing E's services. Of the foregoing factors, the right to control E in the performance of his services is the most important. An employment relationship does not exist where CIC or UKC merely act as E's agent. *See Bartels v Birmingham*, 332 US 126 (1947), 1947–2 CB 174; *Ringling Bros Barnum and Bailey Combined Shows, Inc v Higgins*, 189 F 2d 865 (2d Cir 1951); *Filipidis v United States*, 71–1 USTC 87, 828 (Md 1970), aff'd *per curiam*, 71–2 USTC 87, 830 (4th Cir 1971); section 31.3401(*c*)–1(*b*) of the regulations; and Rev Rul 71–144, 1971–1 CB 285.

On the basis of the foregoing factors, the following conclusions have been reached:

In *Example* (1) it is held that E is not an employee of CIC or UKC because neither corporation controls nor has the right to control E in the performance of his services. Moreover, E has the right to veto prospective engagements. In short, CIC is acting merely as E's booking agent and not as his employer. See RESTATE-MENT (SECOND) OF AGENCY, Section 1(1) (1957). In addition, UKC is acting as CIC's agent if CIC has agreed with E to be primarily responsible for UKC's conduct. See, RESTATEMENT (SECOND) of AGENCY, section 5 (1957).

Since UKC is CIC's agent, the fee earned by CIC is not exempt from Federal income tax under Article III(1) of the Convention because the Channel Islands is not covered by that Convention. Thus, X must withhold a tax of 30 per cent on CIC's portion of the compensation that it pays to UKC pursuant to sections 1441(*c*)(1) and 1442(*a*) of the Code. *See* Rev Rul 70–543, 1970–2 CB 173, which pertains to withholding of tax on income effectively connected with the conduct of a trade or business within the United States by a nonresident alien. However, because industrial and commercial profits also include income derived by a foreign corporation from furnishing the services of persons other than employees and because UKC does not have a permanent establishment in the United States, the agency fee retained by UKC is exempt from Federal income tax under Article III(1) of the Convention.

Although E is not an employee of CIC or UKC in *Example* (1), he is performing in the United States as an employee of X. Thus, Articles III(1) and XI(1) of the Convention do not exempt his income from sources within the United States from Federal income tax.

E, as an employee of X, is taxable under section 871(*b*) of the Code. Therefore, X must withhold on E's salary that it pays to UKC pursuant to section 3402, and sections 31.3401(*a*)(6)–1(*a*) and 31.3402(*a*)–1(*b*) of the regulations.

In *Example* (2) it is held that E is an employee of UKC on temporary loan-out to X pursuant to a 'single loan-out' agreement. E is an employee because he receives a fixed salary unrelated to profits, assumes no financial risk, performs pursuant to an exclusive service contract of substantial duration, and performs pursuant to UKC's direction and control. That E cannot veto the contracts negotiated by UKC and thus must perform whenever and wherever UKC requires is evidence of that direction and control.

Thus, in *Example* (2), Article XI(1) of the Convention exempts from Federal income tax the United States source income or (salary) E receives from UKC for performing services in the United States.

Under the provisions of section 864(*b*) and 882(*a*) of the Code, UKC would be subject to United States income tax. However, because E's performance of United States entertainment services in this example does not constitute a permanent establishment of UKC in the United States, Article III(1) of the Convention exempts UKC from paying United States tax on the income it receives from furnishing the services of E to X. See Rev Rul 67–321, 1967–2 CB 470, which holds that a French corporation does not have a permanent establishment in the United States, even though the corporation presents a floor show in the United States.

In *Example* (3) it is held that E is an employee of CIC for the same reasons that E is an employee of UKC in *Example* (2). Moreover, in *Example* (3) UKC functions as CIC's agent. Thus, the fee retained by UKC from the compensation received from X is exempt from Federal income tax under Article III(1) of the Convention.

By virtue of E's performance of entertainment services, CIC is engaged in business in the United States within the meaning of section 864(*b*) of the Code although not through a permanent establishment. Because the Channel Islands is not covered by the Convention and because E controls CIC within the meaning of section 543(*a*)(7), X must withhold a tax of 30 per cent pursuant to sections 1441(*c*)(1) and 1442(*a*) and section 1.1441–4(*a*)(1) of the regulations on the full amount of the compensation, less UKC's fee, that X pays to the latter as CIC's agent.

In addition, E's salary received from CIC is subject to taxation under section 871(*b*) of the Code.

If it is determined in any of the above examples that E is performing as an independent contractor who is not an employee of X, X must withhold a tax of 30 per cent pursuant to the provisions of section 1441(*a*) and (*c*)(1) of the Code on E's compensation that X pays to UKC. *See* Rev Rul 70–543.

If CIC or UKC had been determined to be a sham in any of the examples, its existence would be disregarded for Federal income tax purposes and all of its income with respect to E's performance of services would be attributable to E. Similarly, if such income were attributable to E under assignment of income principles, E would be regarded as earning the income other than as UKC's employee. *See Richard Rubin*, 56 TC 1155 (1971), aff'd, 460 F 2d 1216 (2d Cir 1972). In either event X would be required to withhold a tax under section 1441(*a*) and (*c*)(1) of the Code, or section 3402 (depending on whether E is an independent contractor or employee of X) because Articles III(1) and XI(1) of the Convention would not be available to exempt that income from Federal income tax. See *Johannson v US*, 336 F 2d 809, 812–13 (5th Cir 1964).

In determining whether a corporation is a sham, *see Moline Properties Inc v Commissioner*, 319 US 436, 438–39 (1943), 1943 CB 1101 and *Floyd Patterson*, TC Memo 1966–329, aff'd, 68–2 USTC 87 623 (2d Cir 1968).

In determining whether the assignment of income principles apply, thus requiring that income must be taxed to the person that earns it, *see Lucas v Earl*, 281 US 111, 114–15 (1930) and *Richard Rubin*.

Section 482 of the Code provides that the Secretary or his delegate may distribute, apportion, or allocate gross income in order to clearly reflect income in an appropriate case where two or more organizations, trades, or businesses are controlled by the same interest. Under the doctrine of assignment of income, or under section 482 where applicable, the income of the entertainer stated in the contracts may be increased in an appropriate case. *See Victor Borge* 26 TCM 816 (1967), aff'g, mod'g, and rem'g TC, 405 F 2d (2d Cir 1968).

In any situation where the nature of the relationship between the United States person and the entertainer or the entertainer and the foreign corporation is not readily ascertainable the United States person should withhold from the amount paid for services rendered at a rate of 30 per cent, pursuant to sections 1441(*a*) or 1442(*a*) of the Code. The entertainer, foreign corporation, or United States person may apply for a ruling in advance of the transaction regarding exemption or reduction of the tax pursuant to the procedures set forth in Rev Proc 72–3, 1972 CB 698.

Note: the validity of these rulings has yet to be tested in the courts as they have apparently been cited only in *Boulez v Commissioner* (1981) 76 TC 209.

Appendix 8   Inland Revenue Tax Bulletin extracts

Schedule D Case I: tax treatment of video tapes acquired for rental

(*Source: Inland Revenue* **Tax Bulletin,** *Issue 19, October 1995.*)

We have received a number of enquiries about the correct tax treatment of video tapes used in the rental trade. Practitioners may also be aware of various articles and comments in the accountancy journals and in the trade press. This article summarises our views on the subject.

Introduction

The tax treatment of pre-recorded video tapes will vary between traders because the way that the cost of tapes is written off for tax purposes depends on a number of variable factors, such as how the tape is used in the trade, its useful economic life and, to some extent, the trader's choice.

A video tape acquired primarily for resale at a profit is treated as stock in trade in the normal way.

But most video tapes are acquired for hiring out to produce an income stream while in the trader's ownership. Even if tapes are to be sold at the end of their useful life, they should not be treated as stock but in the way described below.

Useful economic life

The useful economic life of a tape is important in establishing the correct tax treatment of the tape. Useful economic life is not necessarily the same as the physical life of the tape. It depends on the popularity of the tape and so the pattern of demand for it. Typically the useful economic life of a tape will be less than its physical life.

Means of obtaining relief

Relief for the cost of acquiring video tapes for hire may be obtained by way of:
- capital allowances where the tapes are sufficiently durable and have a sufficiently long useful economic life to qualify as plant, or
- valuation basis where the tapes do not qualify for capital allowances, or

- renewals basis (whatever the life of the tapes).

The appropriate basis should be established when trading begins and whatever basis is used, this should then be followed consistently from year to year. Tapes with similar useful economic lives should be grouped together.

Capital allowances

Tapes with a useful economic life of two years or more will qualify as plant. Where that condition is met, capital allowances may be claimed on the tapes that form the original library and replacements and additions to that library. A short life asset election may be made.

Valuation basis

This basis can be used where the facts show that a tape has a useful economic life of two years or less. On this basis the cost of the tape is allowed as a revenue expense. At the end of the accounting period a valuation is made of the tapes held at that date and that becomes the opening valuation for the following period.

The result is similar to treating the tapes as stock in trade, except that the closing value is not measured by reference to the tape's second hand value, but rather by the potential income stream it generates. The effect is to spread the cost of each tape over its economic life to match the cost with the income that arises from it.

Rate of write down on valuation basis

The rate of write down of a tape on valuation basis will normally be on a straight line between the cost of acquisition of the tape and the anticipated disposal proceeds. However, in a particular case the facts may establish that an alternative method is more appropriate.

Renewals basis

Under the renewals basis a deduction is given for the cost of replacing tapes, net of the proceeds of the sale of the tapes replaced. Thus renewals basis does not provide relief for:
- the initial cost of the library,
- additions (and improvements) to the tape library, and
- the cost of replacing a tape on which capital allowances have been given.

For these reasons it is rarely adopted in practice even though it avoids the need for a valuation of tapes at the end of the year.

Example

Consider a trader who buys a batch of newly released 'AA Blockbuster' tapes of a similar nature and a batch of second hand and classic videos, again of a consistent nature, on the first day of a 12 month accounting period. The anticipated useful economic life of the tapes is just less than two years. The tapes are to be disposed of after two years by being scrapped.

Using a straight line write down, a deduction is due for the cost of each batch in the year of acquisition. This is subject to a countervailing valuation at the end of the first year of one half of the difference between the cost of acquisition and the anticipated disposal proceeds.

Alternatively, the trader may be able to establish by reference to the trade's records, that, perhaps, 75% of the new film rentals arise in the first 12 months after acquisition with 24% in the following 6 months and only 1% thereafter. In such a case at the end of the first year a valuation of 25% of the acquisition cost less disposal proceeds would be justified. At the end of the second accounting period the tapes would be valued at the estimated disposal proceeds.

The second-hand and classic films may have a more even rental profile over their useful economic life but, nevertheless, it might be demonstrated by reference to trading records, that they too should be written off at a faster rate than that provided for by the straight line method.

Transfer Pricing: New OECD report: Guidance on Revenue procedures

(Source: Inland Revenue Tax Bulletin, Issue 25, October 1996)

The OECD has recently published new Transfer Pricing Guidelines. In this issue the Inland Revenue sets out its position on those new Guidelines. And we also provide some practical guidance in one area we are often asked about which is of particular importance in the transfer pricing context—the operation of the Mutual Agreement Procedure contained in the United Kingdom's Double Taxation Conventions.

OECD Transfer Pricing Guidelines

In July 1995 the Organisation for Economic Co-operation and Development (OECD) published its report, *Transfer Pricing Guidelines for Multinational Enterprises and Tax Administrations*. This was followed in March this year by publication of the first of what is planned to be a number of releases of supplementary material.

The report is a reflection of the valuable work of the OECD in fostering international consensus in what is one of the foremost areas of importance in the taxation of multinational enterprises, work in which the UK has taken and continues to take, a full and active role. It also reflects considerable valuable input from Member countries' business communities, including the UK's. The Guidelines update the 1979 OECD Report, *Transfer Pricing and Multinational Enterprises*, and, in doing so, provide extended guidance in a number of areas relevant to the conduct of present-day international business. Importantly, the Guidelines emphasise the continuing adherence of OECD members to the application of the arm's length principle in evaluating transfer pricing. The Inland Revenue will be guided by the Guidelines in applying domestic transfer pricing legislation and in seeking to prevent double taxation under the terms of Double Taxation Conventions with OECD Member countries. The Inland Revenue encourages taxpayers to consult the Guidelines when evaluating whether their transfer pricing complies with the arm's length principle.

Copies of the Guidelines can be purchased from HMSO outlets in the UK or directly from: OECD Publications, 2 rue André-Pascal, 75775 Paris Cedex 16 Tel: (33-1) 45 24 81 81 or 45 24 81 67 Fax: (33-1) 49 10 42 76.

The Mutual Agreement Procedure in UK Double Taxation Conventions

Introduction

Chapter IV of the 1995 OECD *Transfer Pricing Guidelines* contains details of administrative approaches to avoiding and resolving transfer pricing disputes. One such approach to which it refers is that provided for under the mutual agreement procedure which is described and authorised by Article 25 of the OECD Model Tax Convention. The Guidelines suggest that it would be helpful if OECD Member countries were to develop and publicise their own domestic rules or procedures for using the mutual agreement procedure so that taxpayers more readily understand the process. This article provides guidance about the UK's practice on the operation of the mutual agreement procedure and the manner in which claims under the relevant Article in the UK's Double Taxation Conventions are handled, with particular reference to transfer pricing and multinational enterprises.

The UK has a large network of Double Taxation Conventions covering in excess of 100 countries. Double Taxation Conventions seek to protect taxpayers from double taxation, provide for the appropriate allocation of taxing rights in relation to profits from cross-border economic activities, and prevent fiscal discrimination by their signatories. The UK seeks to encourage and maintain an international consensus on international tax treatment of cross-border economic activity, and plays an important role in this field through its membership of OECD.

In this respect, the mutual agreement procedure performs an important function, establishing a process by which the competent authorities of treaty partners can consult each other to resolve matters relating to the application of the treaty. In what follows, references to the mutual agreement procedure are to arrangements of the sort which are typically incorporated in the UK's Double Taxation Conventions.

Administration

Claims under the mutual agreement procedure in respect of transfer pricing are dealt with by International Division with the exception of those made by oil companies which are handled by the Oil Taxation Office.

The procedure in most conventions empowers the competent authorities of the two contracting states to consult each other when a taxpayer claims that it is being taxed otherwise than in accordance with the convention, as a result of the actions of one or both of the fiscal authorities. It is a process of consultation, not litigation, between the two competent authorities, to which the taxpayer is not a party as such. But the extent to which the taxpayer is invited to participate informally is at the discretion of the competent authorities.

In the UK the competent authority is the Commissioners of Inland Revenue or their authorised representatives. For claims under the mutual agreement procedure which concern transfer pricing, the Commissioners have authorised to represent them:
- *for matters relating to transfer pricing generally*
  Deputy Director (International Compliance), International Division
- *for matters relating to transfer pricing in the petroleum industry*
  Controller, Oil Taxation Office

A taxpayer may initiate the mutual agreement process by making a claim to the competent authority for the country of which it is a resident or, in some cases, a national. In the UK there is no set form of claim: UK taxpayers may present their claims in writing to the person and at the address set out at the conclusion of this article. A claim should specify the year(s) concerned, the nature of the action giving rise to taxation not in accordance with the convention, and the full names and addresses of the parties to which the procedure relates, including the UK company's tax District and reference number.

Time limits

The 6-year time-limit laid down for making claims in Section 43 Taxes Management Act (TMA) 1970 applies to claims made under the mutual agreement procedure. However, it is recognised that transfer pricing investigations may take many years to resolve and the UK competent authority will therefore accept protective claims. Claimants should, however, bear in mind that other jurisdictions may operate different time limits for claims.

In deciding when to make a claim taxpayers are advised to consider the procedures adopted by different jurisdictions in settling transfer pricing issues. It should be noted that an adjustment made in relation to a transfer pricing issue raised in the UK and settled either by determination of an appeal under Section 54 TMA 1970 or following a case stated to the Courts, may not be varied. However, in such case, the UK competent authority would expect, on request, to take the matter up under the mutual agreement procedure with the appropriate treaty partner with a view to obtaining the partner's agreement to a corresponding adjustment.

Scope for granting relief

The terms of the Article establishing the mutual agreement procedure circumscribe the competent authority's freedom of action. The Article provides no guarantee of relief from double taxation: but the competent authorities *are* enjoined to consult each other and to endeavour to resolve each case with a view to the avoidance of taxation which is not in accordance with the treaty. And in the UK, the mutual agreement procedure has proved itself very effective in doing so.

On considering the case presented to it, the UK competent authority may conclude that the taxation of relevant transactions proposed or applied by a treaty partner does not accord with the provisions of the convention. It may not, for instance, accept that a transfer pricing adjustment complies with the arm's length principle. Where this is so, it is likely that the UK competent authority will take up the matter with its counterpart in the other contracting state. If, following this, the UK remains dissatisfied, there is no obligation on it to grant relief.

However, where there is adequate evidence to satisfy the UK competent authority that an adjustment imposed by a treaty partner is in accordance with the convention and was required in order to comply with the arm's length principle, there will normally be no difficulty in granting a corresponding adjustment.

International Division's experience has shown that it is advantageous for companies involved in transfer pricing investigations to make early claims under the mutual agreement procedure. Where the convention allows this (and the terms of individual conventions do vary) early action by the competent authority can sometimes help to ensure that unrelievable double taxation does not arise from the actions of one fiscal authority. As noted above, the taxpayer is not directly involved in the negotiations between the competent authorities but, as happens in the UK, it may participate indirectly through discussions with the competent authority of its state of residence/nationality.

OECD guidance

In determining whether taxation of relevant transactions will satisfy the arm's length principle and thus result in taxation in accordance with the provisions of a convention, the UK will be guided by the 1995 OECD *Transfer Pricing Guidelines*. The Guidelines represent the consensus view of OECD Member countries on the application of the arm's length principle and are also expected to be influential outside OECD Member countries.

Methods of giving relief

The manner in which relief is granted by the UK depends on the facts and circumstances of the particular case. Relief may be granted either by deduction against UK profits or by tax credit. Following agreement between the competent authorities, the UK company will usually be invited to submit revised computations reflecting the agreed relief.

The UK does not accept that it is permissible for a taxpayer to make, unilaterally, an adjustment through its accounts in order to obtain corresponding relief for an adjustment imposed by another jurisdiction. The only avenue to relief is a claim under the mutual agreement procedure.

Secondary adjustments

Complexities sometimes arise where an overseas jurisdiction makes a secondary adjustment following a transfer pricing settlement. Secondary adjustments may be defined as adjustments that are intended to restore the financial situation of the associated companies which have entered into transactions giving rise to a transfer pricing adjustment to that which would have existed had the transactions been conducted at arm's length. This thus recognises that, while the primary transfer pricing adjustment will adjust the taxable profits of the associated enterprises, it will not rectify the situation that one enterprise actually retains funds that it would not have retained had the transactions in question been undertaken at arm's length. A secondary adjustment seeks to rectify this situation, most commonly by assuming that a constructive dividend, constructive equity contribution or constructive interest-bearing loan has been made in an amount equal to the transfer pricing adjustment. For example, a jurisdiction making a primary adjustment to the income of a subsidiary of a foreign parent may treat the excess profits in the hands of the foreign parent as having been transferred as a dividend, in which case withholding tax may be levied.

A secondary adjustment may, however, itself give rise to double taxation unless a corresponding credit or some other form of relief is provided by the other country for the additional tax liability that may result from a secondary adjustment. The UK will consider the merits of claims to deduct interest relating to the deeming of a constructive loan by a treaty partner following a transfer pricing adjustment. The claim would, however, be subject to the arm's length principle and would be considered in the light of any relevant provisions relating to payments of interest. Where a treaty partner applies a secondary adjustment by deeming a distribution to have been made, the UK neither taxes the deemed distribution nor grants relief for tax suffered on the distribution in the other jurisdiction.

Repatriation of funds

The repatriation of funds to restore the cash position of the associated enterprises to that which would have existed had arm's length terms applied to the transactions giving rise to a transfer pricing adjustment may remove the need for secondary adjustments, and some jurisdictions encourage repatriation and have specific rules governing the procedure. Repatriation of profits to the UK can be made without further tax consequences providing the amount does not exceed the amount of profits reallocated under the transfer pricing adjustment. There is no opposition in principle to the repatriation of profits by a UK enterprise to an overseas enterprise following a transfer pricing adjustment. However, if under the mutual agreement procedure the amount of the transfer pricing adjustment is modified, then the amounts repatriated in excess of the modified transfer pricing adjustment may in certain circumstances be regarded as a distribution. In order to avoid such a result, it is recommended that any repatriation from the UK is only made following agreement of the transfer pricing reallocation as part of the mutual agreement procedure.

Advance pricing agreements

An Advance Pricing Agreement or Arrangement (APA) is an arrangement that agrees an appropriate set of criteria for the determination, in advance, of the transfer pricing of transactions between associated enterprises over a fixed period of time. The UK has no formal mechanism for entering into an APA. Other jurisdictions have legislation establishing such a mechanism and it is becoming more common for UK corporate taxpayers to seek the participation of the UK competent authority in APAs into which their affiliates enter with such other jurisdictions.

The mutual agreement procedure allows the UK to negotiate with a treaty partner where there is difficulty or doubt as to the interpretation or application of the treaty.

This provides authority for the UK to participate in a treaty partner's APA process where those conditions are satisfied with a view to agreeing with the treaty partner how to apply the terms of the treaty, particularly the arm's length principle, to the circumstances of the individual case. The UK considers each case on its merits, but it should be noted that the basis on which the UK enters into bilateral discussions with another fiscal authority is constrained by the terms of the mutual agreement procedure in the relevant convention. Enquiries about APAs should be addressed to the person identified at the end of this article.

Arbitration Convention

An alternative to the mutual agreement procedure under the UK's Double Taxation Conventions, which may be available to resolve transfer pricing disputes, is represented by the Arbitration Convention to which the UK, along with the other member states of the European Union, is a signatory. The Convention came into force on 1 January 1995 for an initial period of five years and provides for independent arbitration to ensure the elimination of the double taxation which could result from transfer pricing adjustments in the signatory states. To date, experience of implementing the provisions of the Arbitration Convention has been negligible.

It is proposed to provide further guidance on the application of the Convention in a future edition of *Tax Bulletin*. In the meantime, enquiries about the Convention, including questions about the possibility of invoking its provisions, or presenting a case, should be addressed to the people named at the end of this article . . .

Further information

Requests for further information on these procedures and claims to relief should be addressed to:

General transfer pricing issues

Daniel O'Mahony
International Division
Melbourne House
Aldwych
London WC2B 4LL
Telephone: 0171 438 6838
Fax: 0171 438 7518

Financial issues

Martin Brooks
International Division
Melbourne House
Aldwych
London WC2B 4LL
Telephone: 0171 438 7758
Fax: 0171 438 7629

APA requests (general and financial transfer pricing issues)

Andrew Hickman
International Division
Melbourne House
Aldwych
London WC2B 4LL
Telephone: 0171 438 6916
Fax: 0171 438 7629

Oil taxation issues

Keith Cartwright
Oil Taxation Office
Melbourne House
Aldwych
London WC2B 4LL
Telephone: 0171 438 6829
Fax: 0171 438 7602

Schedule D Case I: Initial Sum Payable For a Franchise

(*Source: Inland Revenue* **Tax Bulletin,** *Issue 17, June 1995.*)

Various forms of agreement are often described, somewhat loosely, as franchises, (for example licences, dealerships and concessions) but this article is particularly concerned with payments under 'business system franchise agreements'. Under such an agreement, the owner of an established business format (the franchisor) grants to another person (the franchisee) the right to distribute products or perform services using that system.

The terms of agreements vary considerably but, generally, the franchisee gets the use of the system, training and any necessary management back-up for a specified period, of perhaps five to ten years, in return for:

- an initial fee (payable in one sum or in instalments), and
- continuing, usually annual, fees.

Franchisee: treatment of the initial fee

The capital or revenue quality of the initial payment by the franchisee depends upon what it is for. Normally, it is paid wholly or mainly for substantial rights of an enduring nature to initiate or substantially extend a business. To that extent, the initial payment, whether payable in one sum or instalments, is capital, as are any related professional fees. It is immaterial that the expenditure may prove abortive. Nor is the tax treatment of the receipt in the hands of the franchisor relevant.

In some instances, the franchisor also provides, under the terms of the franchise agreement, goods or services of a revenue nature at the outset, for instance, trading stock or services such as the training of staff (other than the franchisee—see below).

Inspectors will accept that an appropriate part of the initial fee is for such revenue items, and hence allowable, where:

- the sum claimed in respect of revenue items fairly reflects the actual goods and services provided, and
- it is clear that those services are not separately charged for in the continuing fees.

Normally, the costs of the initial training of the franchisee are disallowable—see *Tax Bulletin* Issue 11 (August 1991) 'Expenditure on training courses for the proprietors of a business'.

Generally, the annual fee payable by the franchisee will be a revenue expense. [*Atherton v British Insulated Helsby Cables Ltd* (10 TC 155), *CIR v Granite City Steamship Company Ltd* (13 TC 1), *Strick v Regent Oil Co, Ltd*, (43 TC 1) and *S Ltd v O'Sullivan*, (1972) Irish Tax Cases No. 108].

Appendix 9 UK withholding tax on UK patents and most copyright royalties paid to non-UK residents under double taxation agreements

Country	Royalties %	Country	Royalties %
Antigua	0^{10}	Greece	0
Australia	10	Grenada	0
Austria	0^{12}	Guernsey	24
Azerbaijan	10^8	Guyana	10^{10}
Bangladesh	10^{10}	Hungary	0
Barbados	0	Iceland	0^{10}
Belgium	0	India	$20^{2,10}$
Belize	0	Indonesia	10
Bolivia	15^{10}	Ireland	0
Botswana	15	Isle of Man	24
Brunei	0	Israel	0
Bulgaria	0	Italy	8
Burma	0	Ivory Coast	10
Canada	10^4	Jamaica	10
China (People's Rep.)	10^{13}	Japan	10
Cyprus	0	Jersey	24
Czech Republic	0	Kazakhstan	10^{10}
Denmark	0^{10}	Kenya	15
Egypt	15	Kiribati	0
Estonia	$10^{5,10}$	Korea (Rep.)	2/10
Falkland Islands	0	Lesotho	0
Faroe Islands	0	Luxembourg	5
Fiji	15^{11}	Malawi	0^1
Finland	0^{10}	Malaysia	15
France	0^{10}	Malta	10^3
The Gambia	12.5	Mauritius	15
Germany	0	Mexico	10^{10}
Ghana	12.5^{10}	Mongolia	5^{10}

Country	Royalties %	Country	Royalties %
Montserrat	0	Sri Lanka	10^4
Morocco	10	Sudan	10
Namibia	5^4	Swaziland	0
Netherlands	0^{10}	Sweden	0
New Zealand	10	Switzerland	0
Nigeria	12.5^{10}	Thailand	15^9
Norway	0	Trinidad and Tobago	10^{11}
Pakistan	12.5	Tunisia	15
Papua New Guinea	10^{10}	Turkey	10
Philippines	24^6	Tuvalu	0
Poland	10	Uganda	0
Portugal	5	Ukraine	0^{10}
Romania	15^7	United States	0
St. Christopher and Nevis	0	USSR[14]	0
Sierra Leone	0	Uzbekistan	5
Singapore	15	Vietnam	10^{10}
Slovak Republic	0	Yugoslavia[15]	10
Solomon Islands	0	Zambia	10
South Africa	0	Zimbabwe	10
Spain	10^{10}		

1. 25%, if paid to a company controlling more than 50% of voting power of paying company.

2. 15% in general after 6 April 1999. When payer is a government or sub-state, 15%.

3. Anti-abuse provisions in interest article.

4. Nil on literary/artistic copyright royalties.

5. 5% on royalties for patents and industrial or scientific know-how.

6. 15% on royalties where paying enterprise registered with Philippines Board of Investments and engaged in preferred areas of activity.

7. 10% on literary/artistic/scientific copyright royalties.

8. 5% on literary and artistic copyright royalties.

9. 5% on literary/artistic/scientific copyright royalties.

10. Anti-abuse provisions in royalties article.

11. Nil on literary/artistic/scientific copyright royalties.

12. 10% if paid to a company controlling more than half of the voting power of the paying company.

13. 7% on royalties for use of or right to use any industrial, commercial or scientific equipment.

14. The treaty applies to those countries of the CIS which have not yet made their own arrangements with the United Kingdom, being Armenia, Azerbaijan, Belarus, Georgia, Kyrgyzstan, Moldova, Russia, Tajikistan and Turkmenistan.

15. Consequent upon the disintegration of Yugoslavia, the Inland Revenue announced on 19 March 1993 that the United Kingdom–Yugoslavia treaty is to continue in force with Croatia and Slovenia. The position with respect to Bosnia-Hercegovina and the remaining Yugoslav republics is uncertain, but a further statement is expected to be issued in due course.

Appendix 10   Controlled foreign companies

9 November 1994. Inland Revenue

Clearance procedure for non-trading controlled foreign companies

The Inland Revenue have today announced details of a new clearance procedure for companies which might be affected by changes to the controlled foreign companies legislation made by Section 134 Finance Act 1994.

Details

1. This new procedure is intended to help controlled foreign companies to keep down their compliance costs. In future, the Revenue will be prepared to confirm, on the facts provided, that such a company will not be subject to a direction under the controlled foreign companies legislation, because it meets either the 'exempt activities' or 'motive' tests in TA 1988, s 748.

Clearance applications will be considered in respect of non-trading controlled foreign companies for accounting periods ending on or after 30 November 1993. Details of how to make an application and guidance on the information which the Revenue will require can be obtained by writing to International Division 4/2, Room 311, Melbourne House, Aldwych, London WC2B 4LL or by telephoning 0171-438 6945.

Notes for Editors

Controlled foreign company legislation

1. A controlled foreign company is a company which is not resident in the UK but is controlled by individuals or companies who are. It must also be subject to a level of taxation which is less than three-quarters of what it would have paid had it been resident in the UK. UK resident corporate shareholders with a minimum 10 per cent shareholding are chargeable to UK tax on the income of CFCs in which they have an interest. The amount assessable is usually the proportion of the controlled foreign company's income which is equal to the proportion of shares owned. A tax charge can be raised only following the issue of a formal direction by the Board of Inland Revenue. The relevant legislation can be found in TA 1988, Part XVII, Ch IV [ss 747–756] and Scheds 25, 26.

Exclusions

2. No charge is made on most controlled foreign companies' income because of a variety of exclusions within the legislation. There is no charge if any of the following applies:

— the controlled foreign company pursues an acceptable distribution policy, so that the required proportion of its profits finds its way to the United Kingdom;
— the controlled foreign company's activity is specifically exempted (the 'exempt activities' test);
— subject to certain conditions, the controlled foreign company is publicly quoted;
— the controlled foreign company's chargeable profits fall below £20,000 in a full year (chargeable profits are calculated as for UK tax purposes, but exclude capital gains and losses); or
— the arrangements under which the controlled foreign company operates were not made to avoid UK tax (the 'motive' test).

3. The Inland Revenue have also issued a list of those countries in which residence and the carrying on of a business will not trigger a charge under the legislation.

FA 1994, s 134

4. In order to pursue an acceptable distribution policy, trading controlled foreign companies have had to distribute 50 per cent of their accounting profits and non-trading companies 90 per cent. However, some companies exploited the mismatch between the profits shown by their accounts and the profits which would have been chargeable to tax had they been resident in the UK to avoid a charge under the controlled foreign company legislation. To counter this practice, Section 134 Finance Act 1994 changed the measure of profits for non-trading controlled foreign companies from accounting profits to chargeable profits less foreign taxes. In future, non-trading controlled foreign companies will therefore need to calculate what their taxable profits would be if they wish to pursue an acceptable distribution policy.

Clearance procedure

5. The new Inland Revenue clearance procedure has been introduced to give a measure of certainty and save compliance costs for those companies which believe that they would be excluded under the 'exempt activities' or 'motive' tests. It will therefore apply only to non-trading controlled foreign companies.

6. In most cases it should be possible for the Inland Revenue to give an advance ruling about the application of the tests which covers a number of years, provided that all the relevant facts have been accurately disclosed and there is no change in the nature and conduct of the business of the controlled foreign company.

Controlled Foreign Companies: Excluded Countries List

Following consultation the Government confirms the changes to the list of excluded countries, on which views were sought in a Press Release of 26 April 1993.

A complete revised list is attached. For ease of reference all provisions that are either new or revised are [in italics]. The changes apply for all accounting periods ending after 26 April 1993.

Notes for Editors

1. The provisions on Controlled Foreign Companies are contained in Part XVII, Chapter IV of the Income and Corporation Taxes Act 1988. They enable a charge to UK tax to be imposed on certain UK companies with interests in UK controlled companies in low tax areas.
2. The purpose of the excluded countries list is to give an assurance that a company, if it is resident and carrying on a business in a listed country, will be regarded as meeting the conditions for exclusion set out in the legislation itself, subject to any qualification set out in the list for the country concerned.
3. The last fully updated list of excluded countries was published on 8 March 1991.

Controlled foreign companies: list of excluded countries

Covering note

1. This list relates to the provisions on controlled foreign companies contained in Part XVII, Chapter IV of the Income and Corporation Taxes Act 1988. Its purpose is to give an assurance that, if a company is resident and carries on business in one of the countries on the list, it will be regarded as meeting the conditions necessary for exclusion from the charge imposed by the legislation.
2. The list is split into two parts. Any company which is resident and carrying on business (see paragraphs 3 and 4 below) in a country on Pt I of the list will be excluded from the application of the legislation. Where a company is resident and carrying on business in a country which appears on Pt II it will be similarly excluded, provided that it does not benefit from any of the reliefs specified in column 2.
3. For the purposes of this list a company will be treated as resident in a country if, under local law, it is liable to tax there by reason of domicile, residence or place of management. Where a country does not impose tax by reason of one of these criteria, incorporation will be the test used. Thus, a company will be treated as resident in the country under whose laws it is incorporated, if otherwise it would not be resident anywhere for the purposes of this list.
4. A company will be regarded for the purpose of this list as carrying on business in a country if 90 per cent of its commercially quantified income is local source income. For this purpose:

(*a*) 'commercially quantified income' means the profits as determined according to generally-accepted commercial accounting standards, but disregarding any profits or losses of a capital nature; and (*b*) 'local source income' means income which is treated under a country's own laws as accruing in, arising in, or being derived from that country and which is within its charge to tax—ie is actually chargeable there or covered by a specific exemption from the general charge. Income derived from a branch or agency outside a country will not in any event be regarded as local source income of that country.

5. The list will apply by reference to the overseas company's accounting period. No charge will arise if, throughout an accounting period, the company is resident and carrying on business either in a Pt I country or in a Pt II country but not entitled to any of the reliefs specified in column 2.

6. The fact that a company fails to gain exclusion from the charge by virtue of this list does not, of course, necessarily mean that it comes within the charge. A charge can arise only where all the conditions set out in the legislation are present; and where they are all present, the company may escape through satisfying one of the statutory tests for exclusion.

Changes to the list

7. The list will be amended from time to time, as necessary, to reflect tax changes made by the UK or by an overseas country or changes in the way in which the relevant laws are applied, or to reflect indications that the laws are capable of exploitation.

8. Where the need for an amendment arises the Government will give notice of the proposed amendment and invite comments. If, in the light of consultations the list is revised, the change to the list will apply for all accounting periods ending after the date on which the Government gave notice of the proposed amendment to the list.

Part I: Excluded countries

Australia
Austria
Bangladesh
Bolivia
Botswana
Brazil
Canada
China
Colombia
Czech Republic
Denmark
Dominican Republic
Falkland Islands
Fiji
Finland
France
Gambia
Germany
Ghana
Honduras
Hungary
Iceland
India
Indonesia
Ivory Coast
Japan
Korea, Republic of
Lesotho
Malawi
Mexico
New Zealand
Nigeria
Norway
Papua New Guinea
Poland
Romania
Senegal

Sierra Leone	Swaziland
Slovak Republic	Sweden
Solomon Islands	Trinidad and Tobago
South Africa (excluding the Homelands)	Zambia
Spain	Zimbabwe

The following countries have been deleted, in some cases being replaced by entries in Part II: Bulgaria, Italy, Morocco, Soviet Union, Thailand, Western Samoa and Yugoslavia.

Part II: Excluded countries, subject to qualifications

(1) *Country*	(2) *Qualification*
Argentina	Companies obtaining exemption from tax on income from transactions, activities or operations carried on in, or from goods located in, tax free areas in accordance with Law 19640.
Belgium	**1.** Companies which are regarded as foreign sales corporations by the United States and which therefore qualify for reduced Belgian taxation.
	2. Companies approved under Royal Decree No 187 of 30 December 1982 as Co-ordination Centres (as defined by the original Royal Decree or by subsequent amending Laws).
Brunei	Companies qualifying as 'pioneer companies' under the Investment Incentives Enactment 1975.
Bulgaria	*Any company obtaining a tax benefit under Free Zone legislation.*
Chile	Companies obtaining exemption from tax under Law 16,441 of 1 March 1966 on income from property located in the Department of Isla da Pascua or from activities developed therein.
Egypt	Companies outside the scope of Law 157 of 1981, art III because they do not 'operate' in Egypt.
Faroe Islands	Companies deriving interest from Faroese financial institutions from which tax is deducted at source under Law 4 of 26 March 1953.
Greece	**1.** Companies which have profits exempt from tax under Law 3843 of 1958, art 6 (2) (*c*) (profits from the operation of ships under the Greek flag).
	2. Companies having profits exempt from company income tax by virtue of Law 25/1975, art 25 as replaced by Law 814/1978, art 28, or by virtue of Law 89/1967 as supplemented by Law 378/1968 (profits from shipping and associated activities).
Ireland	**1.** Companies obtaining relief or exemption from tax under Finance Act 1980, Chapter VI and as subsequently amended.
	2. Holding companies having income exempted under Finance Act 1985, s 69.

(1) *Country*	(2) *Qualification*
Italy	*Companies operating within the Trieste Free Zone Financial and Insurance Centre.*
Kenya	Companies having income granted exemption from tax under paragraph 11 Schedule 1 of the Income Tax Act 1973.
Luxembourg	**1.** Companies obtaining any special tax benefit under the law of 31 July 1929, decree of 17 December 1938 as amended or Grand Ducal Regulation of 29 July 1977 (holding companies). **2.** Companies carrying on any reinsurance business.
Malaysia	**1.** Companies exempt from tax in accordance with Section 54A of the Income Tax Act 1967 (shipping). **2.** Companies subject to tax at 5 per cent in accordance with Sections 60A and 60B of the Income Tax Act 1967 (inward reinsurance and offshore insurance). **3.** Companies deriving dividends from a company or companies deriving income from one or more of the activities mentioned above. **4.** *Companies obtaining a tax benefit under the offshore legislation relating to the Island of Labuan.*
Malta	**1.** Companies entitled to exemption or relief from tax under Section 11(2) (previously Section 8(2)) of the Income Tax Act. **2.** Companies obtaining exemption from tax under Section 86 of the Merchant Shipping Act 1973. **3.** Companies obtaining exemption or relief from tax under Section 30 of the Malta International Business Activities Act 1988. **4.** Companies obtaining exemption or relief from tax under Section 18 of the Malta Freeports Act 1989.
Morocco	*Companies receiving a tax benefit under legislation relating to offshore financial centres.*
Netherlands	Companies which are regarded as Foreign Sales Corporations (FSCs) by the United States.
Pakistan	Companies deriving royalties, commissions or fees which are exempt from tax under paragraph 139, Part I second Schedule, Income Tax Ordinance 1979.
Philippines	**1.** Companies authorised under Presidential Decree 1034 or 1035, both of 30 September 1976, to operate an Offshore Banking Unit or a Foreign Currency Deposit Unit as defined in those decrees or the regulations thereto. **2.** Companies receiving interest on deposits with a Foreign Currency Deposit Unit, or other interest subject to the reduced rates of tax under Section 24(cc) of the National Internal Revenue.
Portugal	Companies obtaining tax benefits under the legislation relating to free zones in Madeira and the Azores.

(1) *Country*	(2) *Qualification*
Puerto Rico	**1.** *Companies obtaining a tax benefit under any of the Industrial Incentive Acts in respect of income from designated service industries.*
	2. *Companies obtaining a tax benefit under Section 25 of the International Banking Centre Regulatory Act 1989 (international banking entities).*
Singapore	**1.** Any company obtaining tax concessions under Ministry of Finance Regulations pursuant to Sections 43A, C–J of the Income Tax Act.
	2. Companies obtaining exemption from tax on the income of a shipping enterprise in accordance with Section 13A of the Income Tax Act.
	3. Companies obtaining relief from tax in accordance with Sections 45 to 55 (international trade incentives) and 75 to 84 (warehouse and service incentives) of the Income Tax Act.
	4. Companies deriving dividends from a company or companies deriving income from one or more of the activities mentioned above.
Sri Lanka	Companies obtaining relief or exemption from income tax under any of the following provisions of the Inland Revenue Act (No 28 of 1979):
	(*a*) Section 8(*c*) (iv)—foreign currency banking units,
	(*b*) Sections 10(*d*) and 15(*b*)—income derived from approved bank accounts,
	(*c*) Section 10(*e*)—interest of newly resident companies,
	(*d*) Section 15(*cc*)—services rendered outside Sri Lanka,
	(*e*) Section 15(*p*)—re-export of approved products.
Tanzania	Companies relieved or exempted from income tax under Section 15(1) or (1A) of the Income Tax Act 1973.
Thailand	*Companies obtaining a tax benefit under legislation relating to Offshore Banking Units.*
Tunisia	Companies obtaining exemption from or reduction of tax under Law 76–63 of 12 July 1976 (financial and banking institutions dealing with non-residents).
Turkey	Companies obtaining export incentives under Article 8 (4), (6), (7), (8) or (10) of Law 5422 of 3 June 1949.
United States	Domestic International Sales Corporations as defined in Section 992(a) of the Internal Revenue Code 1954.

Controlled foreign companies

(*Source: Inland Revenue* Tax Bulletin, *Issue 12, August 1994.*)

Section 134 Finance Act 1994 changes the measure of profits used in the acceptable distribution policy (ADP) test for non-trading controlled foreign companies (CFCs) from accounting profits to chargeable profits. This article answers various questions that we have been asked about our interpretation of the legislation and how the new rules will operate in practice. It follows consultations with bodies representing companies and their advisers.

What does this mean for trading CFCs?

There is no change to the ADP for trading CFCs (as defined in Section 756(1) of the Taxes Act), which continues to use the accounting profits.

When do the new rules come into effect?

The new rules come into effect for accounting periods ending on or after 30 November 1993.

Can a CFC split its accounting period at 30 November 1993?

Yes. A non-trading CFC can choose to split its accounting period spanning 30 November 1993 into separate accounting periods, so that the old rules apply to the part period up to 30 November and the new rules to the part period after that date. We will accept informal accounts for the part periods for this purpose. They should be made up on the same basis as the accounts for the full period.

Would the anti-avoidance rule for short accounting periods (Paragraph 3(2) Schedule 25) apply to these part periods?

Splitting the accounting period for this purpose would not of itself be regarded as avoidance. But Paragraph 3(2) could be invoked if there was also manipulation of profits between the part periods which resulted in profits being removed from charge.

Can interest paid to a non-resident out of income from the UK be deducted from the chargeable profits?

Yes, where the UK income was paid gross, with a corresponding adjustment where it was paid net to ensure that the tax deducted was not repaid or set against the liability on other income.

Annual interest paid by a CFC, for non-trading purposes, to a person not resident in the UK would normally only be deductible as a charge if it was paid out of foreign income (s 338(4)). If the CFC has both UK and non-UK income then, subject to the CFC indicating to the contrary, the interest would be treated as paid first out of the foreign income.

Where a direction was made under Section 747, we would, in making the just and reasonable apportionment under Section 752(8), apportion annual interest paid out of UK income to the loan creditor, thus reducing the amount apportioned to persons controlling the CFC by that amount. Notwithstanding Section 417(9), which is applied to the CFC provisions by Section 756, we would accept that an overseas bank can be a loan creditor for this purpose.

Where the UK income was received gross by the CFC, the reduction in the amount apportioned to persons controlling the CFC would equal the interest paid.

Where the UK income was received under deduction of UK tax, the reduction would be limited to the amount needed to ensure that the tax charged under the direction, after giving tax credit relief for the tax deducted, equalled the amount which would have been charged under the above rule if in the computation of chargeable profits the interest paid and the income received under deduction of tax had both been reduced by the lesser of the two, with a corresponding reduction in the tax deducted and tax credit relief. Alternatively, the administrative short cut may be followed by agreement with the Revenue of allowing the reduction in full and making the corresponding adjustment to the tax credit relief.

We will follow the same principle for the ADP. We will not make a direction where a distribution is made to the UK which, after giving tax credit relief, would raise 90 per cent of the additional UK tax that would be payable under the above rules if a direction had been made.

Numeric examples of the position where income is received gross and where income is received under deduction of tax are given at the end of the article.

What about interest which may be treated as a distribution under Section 209(2)(e)(iv) or (v)?

This will also be allowed as a reduction to the amount apportioned to persons controlling the CFC where a direction is made, or to the net chargeable profits for the purposes of the ADP, except where the interest is paid as part of arrangements for the indirect payment of an amount from the UK to a person outside the UK which would be treated as a distribution if it was paid directly.

What about short interest?

Short interest which is not otherwise deductible will be treated in the same way, subject to the restrictions explained above for interest paid out of UK income taxed at source. No reduction will be allowed for short interest which is treated as a distribution because of the arrangements described in the previous paragraph.

Can Section 770 apply to the acceptable distribution policy?

Yes, but only where the Board of Inland Revenue makes a direction that Section 770 will apply to the profits of the accounting period. A direction may be made at any time, but would not normally be made more than six years after the end of the period. Where the direction relates to transactions with a CFC or person chargeable to UK tax, the Board will ensure by whatever means appear appropriate that it does not result in double taxation in the UK As there are no provisions for corresponding adjustments for CFCs under double taxation treaties, it is for the CFC to arrange its affairs to avoid international double taxation.

How will the new rules on FOREX apply to CFCs?

This is being reviewed as part of the continuing consultations on the new rules on FOREX. An announcement will be made as soon as possible.

Can additional distributions be made to satisfy the ADP if the computation of net chargeable profits is revised by the Revenue?

Yes. The distributions must be made within 18 months of the end of the accounting period or such further time as the Board may allow. Further time will be allowed where additional distributions are needed to meet the ADP as a result of revisions made to the computation of net chargeable profits by the Revenue.

Can credit be given for tax paid on distributions if a direction is made?

The rules work the other way round, but with a similar effect. Where a direction is made, Schedule 26, paragraph 4 treats tax paid under the direction as underlying tax for distributions made out of the total profits of that accounting period. Unilateral tax credit relief can thereby be given for tax paid under the direction against tax due on the distribution, by repayment if necessary where tax has already been paid on the distribution.

What happens if the distribution has to be made for a different accounting period?

Where a direction is made for an accounting period under Section 747, Schedule 26, paragraph 4 allows tax credit relief to be given against distributions out of the total profits of that accounting period. That allows relief to be given against distributions up to that figure out of the profits of that period. But distributions out of the profits of the accounting period may not be used to satisfy the acceptable distribution policy for a different accounting period under Section 134 Finance Act 1994.

Where the company can show that profits included in the total profits of the accounting period were distributed out of the profits of a different period, tax credit relief would be given for tax paid under the direction as if the distribution was out of the total profits of the accounting period for which the direction was made. This is provided the other condition of Section 134, that the distribution is not used to satisfy the acceptable distribution policy for another accounting period, is also met.

Will I have to make detailed calculations of UK taxable profits every year for every non-trading CFC in the group?

No. The large majority of CFCs are excluded from the direction making power by the excluded countries list, the exempt activities test and the motive test. No computation of UK taxable profits will be required in these cases.

Will the Inland Revenue give an advance ruling on whether a CFC is excluded from the direction making power by the exempt activities test or the motive test?

We are very conscious of the need to avoid introducing unnecessary administrative burdens and to limit compliance costs from this change to the legislation. Accordingly, we are planning to introduce an informal clearance procedure. The details will be announced in a Press Release. In that Press Release, we will set out the procedural steps which companies should follow to obtain advance rulings. We expect that, in many cases, it will be possible to give an advance ruling which covers a number of years, provided that all the relevant facts have been accurately disclosed and there has been no change in the nature and conduct of the business of the CFC.

Will the advance ruling procedure depend on satisfying the motive test?

No. The motive test only needs to be considered where a company has failed all the other exclusions from the CFC provisions. It has been found in practice that the main effect of the motive test is to act as a back-stop when a company is unable to meet one of the other tests solely for reasons other than to achieve a reduction in UK tax or the failure is marginal or due to isolated causes. Outside this narrow band, it has been found that companies which fail the other tests are very unlikely to meet the stringent requirements of the motive test.

Examples showing effect of interest paid to a non-resident out of income from the UK

EXAMPLE 1:
Overseas company issues debt to third parties and lends the proceeds to its UK parent. *The UK parent is not obliged to withhold tax.*
Assumptions:

- Principal of 50,000 lent to UK parent by overseas company at 10 per cent.
- Principal of 50,000 borrowed by overseas company at 9 per cent.
- Overseas company earns other UK source income of 1,500.
- Overseas tax rate of 10 per cent for which relief is due under a double taxation agreement.

QUESTION 1: IS THE COMPANY SUBJECT TO A LOWER LEVEL OF TAXATION?
Overseas tax computation

Interest received from UK parent	5,000
Other income	1,500
Less: Interest paid to third parties	(4,500)
Profits chargeable to overseas tax	2,000
Overseas tax payable (@ 10%)	200

National UK tax computation

Interest received from UK parent	5,000
Other income	1,500
Less: Interest paid to third parties (disallowed by Section 338(4) ICTA 88)	0
Profits chargeable to notional UK tax	6,500
Notional UK tax payable (@ 33%)	2,145

Since overseas tax payable is less than 75 per cent of notional UK tax payable, this company is subject to a lower level of taxation.

QUESTION 2: WHAT PROFITS WILL BE APPORTIONABLE TO THE UK PARENT?

Interest received from UK parent	5,000
Other income	1,500
Less: Interest paid to third parties (apportioned to loan creditors under Section 749(7) ICTA 88	(4,500)
Profits apportioned to UK parent	2,000
UK tax (@ 33%)	660
Less:	
Relief for overseas tax paid	(200)
Additional UK tax payable	(460)

QUESTION 3: WHAT DIVIDEND IS REQUIRED IN ORDER TO MEET THE ACCEPTABLE DISTRIBUTION TEST?

Chargeable profits apportionable to parent	2,000
Less: Overseas tax paid	(200)
Net chargeable profits	1,800
Acceptable distribution (90% of above)	1,620
Additional UK tax payable (1800 @ 33%)	594
Less: Relief for overseas tax paid	(180)
Additional UK tax payable	414

EXAMPLE 2:

Overseas company issues debt to third parties and lends the proceeds to its UK parent. *The UK parent is obliged to withhold tax*

Assumptions:

- Principal of 50,000 lent to UK parent by overseas company at 10 per cent. UK parent withholds tax on interest paid at 25 per cent.
- Principal of 50,000 borrowed by overseas company at 9 per cent.
- Overseas company earns other UK source income of 1,500.
- Overseas tax rate of 10 per cent for which relief is due under a Double Taxation Agreement.

QUESTION 1: IS THE COMPANY SUBJECT TO A LOWER LEVEL OF TAXATION?

Overseas tax computation	
Profits chargeable to overseas tax (as in Example 1, Question 1)	2,000
Overseas tax payable (@ 10%)	200
Notional UK tax computation	
Profits chargeable to notional UK tax (as in Example 1, Question 1)	6,500
Notional UK tax (@ 33%)	2,145
Less: Credit for UK tax withheld	(1,250)
Notional UK tax payable	895

Since overseas tax payable is less than 75 per cent of notional UK tax payable, this company is subject to a lower level of taxation.

QUESTION 2: WHAT PROFITS WILL BE APPORTIONABLE TO THE UK PARENT?

	Formal Method	Short Cut
Interest received from UK parent	5,000	5,000
Other income	1,500	1,500
Less:		
Interest paid to third parties[1]	(1,091)	(4,500)

	Formal Method	Short Cut
Profits apportionable to UK parent	5,409	2,000
Additional UK tax (@ 33%)	1,785	660
Less: Credit for UK tax withheld[2]	(1,250)	(125)
Relief for overseas tax paid	(200)	(200)
Additional UK tax payable	335	335

[1]Restricted to produce correct tax payable (as demonstrated by the short-cut method).
[2]Restricted to tax deducted from the excess of the interest received (5,000) over the interest paid (4,500).

QUESTION 3: WHAT DIVIDEND IS REQUIRED IN ORDER TO MEET THE ACCEPTABLE DISTRIBUTION test?

We would not make a direction if a distribution was made on which the additional UK tax payable was 90 per cent of the additional UK tax which would be payable if a direction was made ie 90 per cent of 335 = 301.

[TA 1988, ss 747–756, Sch 25, para 2A, Sch 26, para 4.]

Controlled foreign companies: holding companies

(*Source: Inland Revenue* Tax Bulletin, *Issue 19, October 1995.*)

Holding companies are able to obtain exclusion from the controlled foreign company legislation in the same way as other companies. In addition, there are special provisions for holding companies within the exempt activities test.

These provisions can be found in Paragraphs 6 and 12 of Schedule 25 Income and Corporation Taxes Act (ICTA) 1988. Broadly, a 'local holding company' is exempted if it derives 90% of its gross income (excluding its own trading income which would qualify under the exempt activities test) directly from subsidiaries resident in the same territory which are engaged in exempt activities but are not themselves holding companies. In addition, Paragraph 6(4) Schedule 25 ICTA 1988 allows a further holding company to qualify under the exempt activities test if it too derives 90% of its gross income from subsidiaries which are local holding companies or pass the exempt activities test. Under these rules, it is possible for only local holding companies and one other holding company within an ownership chain to qualify under the exempt activities test.

Since the introduction of the controlled foreign company legislation the Revenue has consistently stated that it would regard the motive test as satisfied where the main purpose of a holding company is:

- to receive dividends and interest from its overseas subsidiaries as a mere staging post in the course of the process of reinvestment of the profits concerned in the trading operations of the overseas subsidiaries concerned, or
- to hold funds outside the source country for the purpose of reinvestment in that country because of rigorous exchange controls, inflation, exchange fluctuations or political instability and the risk of expropriation.

For a holding company to pass the exempt activities test, its subsidiaries must themselves pursue exempt activities. This means that enquiries relating to the exempt activities test must be undertaken for all subsidiaries, even when they may be covered by, for example, the Excluded Countries List. To save compliance costs in such cases, the Board will now accept that a holding company may be deemed to pass the motive test where its subsidiaries carry on broadly commercial activities along the lines of the Exempt Activities Test.

This will apply where all the other exempt activity conditions apply and 90% of the holding company's gross income arises from trading companies which:

- satisfy the exempt activities test, or
- satisfy the motive test, or
- are not subject to a lower level of taxation, or
- benefit from the excluded country list provisions.

The Revenue has been asked to consider the position of holding companies which would pass the Exempt Activities Test but for the existence of a lower tier non-local holding company. Henceforth, in such circumstances, following detailed discussions with industry representatives, the Revenue will normally accept that a holding company passes the motive test, if at least 90% of its gross income (calculated as for Paragraph 6(3) and (4) of Schedule 25 ICTA 88) consists of:

- income from trading companies and local holding companies, plus
- the income from one or more holding companies which is itself derived from trading companies which pass the exempt activities test or motive test, are excluded under the lower level of taxation test or are covered by the excluded countries list.

For this purpose a holding company will be taken as one falling within the definition in paragraph 12(1) of Schedule 25 ICTA 88, except that the shares or securities held may also include those of holding companies which are not local holding companies but are its 90% subsidiaries.

A holding company may of course pass the motive test for reasons other than those set out in this article.

Since 9 November 1994 there has been a clearance procedure in respect of the application of the exempt activities and motive tests to non-trading controlled foreign companies, for accounting periods ending on or after 30 November 1993. Holding companies may use that procedure to determine whether or not they fall within the guidelines set out in this article. Details may be obtained from:

International Division
(Controlled Foreign Companies)
Room 311,
Melbourne House,
Aldwych,
London, WC2B 4LL.

Example

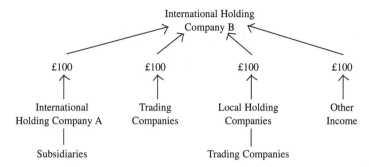

It is assumed that IHCA qualifies under the Exempt Activities Test, but IHCB will not if each of IHCA, the combined trading companies and the combined local holding companies pays up income of £100 to it.

If the income paid up from IHCA is split £90 'trading' (i.e. income from companies which are exempt under the expanded definition) to £10 'non-trading', IHCB has paragraph 6(4) income of £290 to meet the 90% test. It will generally be considered to pass the motive test if its other income is no greater than £22.20. The group is thus in the same position with respect to the 90% test that it would have been had all the income passed through one International Holding Company.

Alternatively, if the income paid up from IHCA is split £95 'trading' to £5 'non-trading', IHCB has income of £295 to meet the 90% test and other income should not exceed £27.80 if it is to meet the motive test.

When calculating the income in subsidiaries for the 90% rule whether it be to satisfy the exempt activities or the motive test, amounts of non-trading income are ignored when they have been derived directly or indirectly from a connected or associated company (Paragraph 12(5) Schedule 25 ICTA 88).

Appendix 11   Payer's guide: foreign entertainers (FEU 50)

Contents

Introduction

Section A

Section B

Section C

Section D

List of forms

Introduction

The 1986 Finance Act introduced a Withholding Tax on payments made for a UK appearance of a non-resident entertainer or sportsman or sportswoman: activity in Britain or Northern Ireland comes within the law.

You, the payer, must take tax off these payments.

This booklet, which is only a guide and does not have any legal force, tells you about

- how the system works
- what you must do as a payer
- the administration of the new scheme, and
- the standard of service you can expect and the steps you can take if you are dissatisfied with the service provided.

You will find the law covering Withholding Tax in Section 555–558 ICTA 1988 and Income Tax Regulations 1987. You can buy a copy of these from HMSO bookshops and other booksellers.

To avoid repetition the term 'entertainer' is used in this booklet to cover both non-resident entertainers and sportsmen and sportswomen. Examples in the booklet assume a basic rate of tax of 25%. The basic rate in force in any particular year can be obtained by telephoning the number shown below.

If this guide does not answer your questions and you need any help please get in touch with:

Foreign Entertainers Unit
Royal House, 2nd Floor
Prince's Gate
2–6 Homer Road
Solihull
West Midlands
B91 3WG
Tel No   0121 606 2861/2862/2863
Fax   0121 606 2865

The Unit was set up to administer the legislation and is part of the Special Compliance Office. Further information on service and complaints can be found in Section D . . . of this booklet.

Section A

A1   How the scheme works

Any payer who makes a payment to any person, which in any way arises directly or indirectly from a UK appearance by a non-resident entertainer must deduct tax at the basic rate.

There are certain exceptions from the scheme. You will find details in A8.

A2   What are payments?

Payments include money (cash, cheques etc.,) and also a loan of money. The list below gives some examples of payments

- appearance fees
- achievement bonus
- exhibition income
- box office percentage
- TV rights
- broadcasting/media fees
- tour income
- tournament winnings
- prize money
- advertising income
- merchandising income
- endorsement fees
- film fees.

The scheme also applies to transfers of assets, for example, an airline ticket provided for an entertainer. Where assets are transferred withholding does not apply to the payment for the acquisition of the asset. But tax should be accounted for on the transfer to the entertainer. See B2.

A3   Does it matter who gets the payments?

The short answer is no!

Payments are within the system no matter who gets them. It does not need to be the entertainer who gets the payment. Any payment to an individual, partnership or company or trust, whether or not they are resident in the UK should have basic rate tax withheld.

A4   What type of appearance is covered?

Any appearance by the entertainer in the UK in his or her character as an entertainer will be within the scheme. The only exception will be where he or she visits the UK as a private individual, for example, on holiday.

To take a simple case, the entertainer appears in his or her recognised profession. This might be an actor performing in the theatre or a golfer competing in the Open Championship.

But the scheme is much wider than this. It also covers promotional activities, advertising and endorsement of goods or services. This may include a photocall, TV or radio interview or other appearances.

The appearance does not have to be in front of an immediate audience. It includes work on film, video, radio and live or recorded television.

A5   What is the link between the payment and the UK appearance?

Any payment which arises directly or indirectly from a UK appearance will be within the scheme. In most cases it will be easy to find the link. For example, a tennis player wins Wimbledon prize money or a pop star is paid for appearing at a concert at Wembley.

The payment does not have to have a direct connection with the UK appearance. Endorsement fees paid to a tennis player using sports equipment in a UK tournament would be linked.

A6   Which entertainers and sportsmen are involved?

This list includes some examples—it is not exhaustive. Athletes, golfers, cricketers, footballers, tennis players, boxers, snooker players, darts players, motor racing drivers, jockeys, ice skaters, contestants in chess tournaments, pop stars, musicians, conductors, dancers, actors, TV and radio personalities, variety artistes. The person may appear alone or with others in teams, choirs, bands, orchestras, opera companies, ballet companies, troupes, circuses.

A7   How do I know whether they are non-resident in the UK?

In most cases it will be obvious.

You may know from the agent or management company, perhaps from the need to get a work permit or clear immigration formalities.

A UK national who is not-resident comes within the scheme so it should not be assumed that withholding applies only to overseas nationals.

If there is any uncertainty about the entertainer's residence position you should get in touch with the Foreign Entertainers Unit. They will advise you.

A8   Which payments are excepted from withholding tax?

If you already deduct tax under the Taxes Acts you do not have to withhold further tax. This will apply, for example, where tax is deducted at source either on copyright royalties (Section 536 ICTA 1988) or under PAYE.

You do not normally have to withhold tax on amounts paid for ancillary services to a person who is resident and ordinarily resident in the UK. This includes, for examples, payments for

- hall hire
- security
- damages/carpentry
- stage hands

- PA equipment
- lighting etc.
- equipment hire
- advertising
- ticket printing
- hire of chairs, barriers or marquee etc.

You do not have to withhold tax on payments to an entertainer for record sales (including black vinyl, pre-recorded music cassettes or compact disc) where the payment is based on the proceeds of sales or is a non-returnable advance on account of future sales.

You do not have to withhold tax if the £1,000 threshold (see A9) is not exceeded.

There are no other exceptions to the scheme

Even if the payments you withhold tax from may not ultimately be assessed on the recipient (for example, because they are protected by a Double Taxation Agreement) you must not exclude these payments from the scheme.

If you are in any doubt at all about which payments are excluded from the scheme please ask the Foreign Entertainers Unit for advice.

A9   How does the £1,000 threshold work?

Do not withhold tax if the total payments to an individual or group, including any connected payments by an associate etc., will be **£1,000 or less** during the tax year. (The tax year runs from 6 April in one year to 5 April in the following year.)

The total payment for this purpose includes not only cash but also expenses paid on behalf of the artiste such as air fares or the cost of any asset transferred to the artiste.

The £1,000 limit is not a total exemption from UK tax; it merely removes the requirement to deduct withholding tax if certain conditions are met. The simplest way to look at the de minimis limit is to consider it solely from each payer's viewpoint in the payment chain. The payer has to take the following into account:-

   (i)   the payments (and grossed up value of expenses met by the payer, e.g. air fares) arising from current activity;
   (ii) the payments (and grossed up expenses) met previously in the same tax year, or which are likely to be made later in the same tax year by him/her;
   (iii) the payments (and grossed up expenses) met by an associate of the payer for past, present or future activity within the same tax year.

If any combination of (i), (ii) and (iii) produces a figure of more than £1,000, then the de minimis limit does not apply and normal procedures must operate. If the total of (i) to (iii) is £1,000 or less, payments may be made gross.

If you are therefore making the first payment and it is less than £1,000 but you know in advance (for example, from the contract) that the total payments for the tax year will be more than £1,000 then you should deduct tax even from the first payment.

If you do not know the total amount of payments for the year then you should deduct tax from each payment

Example

The payer knows in advance that he will be making total payments of £1,200, made in three instalments.

1st payment	=	400
Less tax withheld at 25%	=	100
Net payment to entertainer	=	**300**
2nd payment	=	400
Less tax withheld at 25%	=	100
Net payment to entertainer	=	**300**
3rd payment	=	400
Less tax withheld at 25%	=	100
Net payment to entertainer	=	**300**
Total payments	=	1200
Tax withheld	=	300
Net payments	=	**900**

Section B

B1   What the payer has to do

Each time you make a payment you must deduct tax at basic rate **unless** an arrangement has been made with the Foreign Entertainers Unit (see B6 to B9). The Inland Revenue does not need to make an assessment.

If you do not deduct tax you will be held responsible for the tax due.

B2   How to work out the tax

Where you are paying **money** it is very straightforward to work out the tax.

Assuming the basic rate percentage for the year of payment is 25% deduct this percentage from each payment made. (If Value Added Tax has been charged on the payment only the VAT exclusive figure is liable to withholding.)

Example

Payment	=	5,000
Tax (5,000 × 25%)	=	1,250
Net amount paid to entertainer		**3,750**

The same applies to a loan of money. You should deduct tax from the amount you lend.

Payments to the Inland Revenue of tax withheld should be made in sterling. If you make a payment directly or indirectly to an entertainer in a foreign currency you should calculate the Withholding Tax due using the rate of exchange at the time when the payment is made. The rate of exchange adopted should be shown on your Return form FEU 1.

If the transfer of an asset is involved (for example, a motor car for a 'hole in one' during a golf competition) you must account for the tax as if the asset's cost to you or in connection with providing it was the net amount of the payment.

Example

The car costs you £3,750. You need to work out the gross amount of the payment and deduct tax on that amount. To work out the gross amount you do the following sum.

Net amount of payment $\times \dfrac{25 \text{ (basic rate of tax)}}{75 \text{ (100 less basic rate of tax)}}$

3,750 × 25/75   =   1,250

Add the result to the net payment to get the gross payment.

1,250 + 3,750   =   5,000

Tax (5000 × 25%)   =   1,250

If the payment you make is made out of a payment you have received for the same UK appearance (that is, it is one of a series of payments) then you may 'frank' (treat as paid) your payment to the extent that it has already suffered tax.

Example

Withholding Tax
A engages, via a management company B Ltd, a non-resident entertainer, C, to appear in his theatre in the UK.
B Ltd is resident in the UK and C is the only non-resident entertainer it engages in the quarter. The sequence of payments is:-

A pays £100,000 less £25,000 tax to B Ltd

B Ltd pays £60,000 less £15,000 tax to C

B Ltd is liable to account to the Inland Revenue for £15,000 but as the payment he has received has had £25,000 Withholding Tax deducted from it he can treat the £15,000 as paid.

Entries on B Ltd's return form FEU 1
The amount and income tax columns of B's return for the relevant period should be completed as follows

	Amount	Tax
	60,000	15,000
Less already paid		15,000
Tax payable now		Nil

Evidence of the tax already suffered should be provided with the return using form FEU 2 supplied by A.

You will find details of how the payment is treated in B Ltd's company accounts and of the repayment of tax in certain circumstances at B10.

B3   How do you account for the tax?

You must account for tax withheld within 14 days after the end of the return period during which the payment was made. The return periods for each tax year are

30 June
30 September
31 December
5 April.

B4   Filling in form FEU 1

Complete form FEU 1 as soon as possible after the end of the relevant period and in any case within 14 days of the end of the period. The form itself gives you instructions on completion.

Note the return requires details of payments below the £1,000 threshold (see A9) although no tax has been deducted. Send the completed form FEU 1 and the total Withholding Tax payable to the Accounts Office Shipley within 14 days of the relevant period.

If the return of tax is late you may become liable to interest and/or penalties.

Please note that the return form FEU 1 is due from the payer without the Inland Revenue notifying you. **It is now your responsibility to make a Return.**

New payers should contact Foreign Entertainers Unit who will issue the appropriate Starter Pack.

The Accounts Office Shipley will send you replacement forms FEU 1 before the end of each Return period. If you want to use your own design of form FEU 1 you must submit it to the Foreign Entertainers Unit for approval before you do so.

B5   What record does the payee get of the payment?

Whenever you make a payment you must complete a form FEU 2.
  This form is in 3 parts

Part 1   Send to Accounts Office Shipley along with your form FEU 1 Return.
Part 2   Keep this for your own records.
Part 3   Send this to the payee as a certificate of the payment made and tax withheld.

On no account should you issue a duplicate form FEU 2. If the payee loses the original certificate tell him or her to contact the Foreign Entertainers Unit.

If you are not deducting Withholding Tax because the payment is under the £1,000 threshold (see A8) or no tax is deducted because of an arrangement with the Inland Revenue (see B7 to B9) you do not need to complete a form FEU.2.

B6   Arrangements with the Revenue to limit the amount of tax withheld

An arrangement may be made in writing between the Foreign Entertainers Unit and other interested parties. This arrangement allows the payer to deduct an amount which is less than the basic rate of tax.

For example an arrangement may be made to move responsibility to withhold to a particular point in a payment chain by means of a 'middle man' arrangement (see B11).

In addition it is possible to make an artiste reduced tax payment arrangement so that the payer deducts an amount which corresponds as closely as possible to the entertainer's final liability on the payment. An artiste application can be made by the individual(s) concerned or by anyone authorised to make the application on their behalf, e.g. a payer or agent. However, the application must cover the whole of any current activity in the UK: it cannot be made for part of a UK tour.

If the application is **not** accepted tax must be withheld at the basic rate on all payments.

B7   *Applying for an arrangement*

You and/or the entertainer will have to give the information needed for the Inspector to make a decision on whether or not to grant an arrangement. This includes

- dates of arrival in and departure from the UK
- whether the entertainer is likely to return to the UK again before the next 5 April
- a projection of income with details of dates and venues
- an itemised projection of the expenses which will be incurred
- a copy of any contracts covering appearances.

The application should have sufficient information to show how figures have been arrived at (including the basis for any estimates) and how expenditure common to several countries has been apportioned.

The Inspector will also take into account whether you are making a payment on account of the Withholding Tax due or whether a guarantee has been given.

In some cases, you may be authorised not to deduct any tax from a payment. This would apply, for example, if a pop star prior to a UK tour undertook to pay in advance (or secured by bank guarantee) all the UK tax expected from the tour.

In other cases, you may be authorised to deduct either a reduced rate of tax or a fixed sum from the gross payment. This could apply, for example, where an entertainer has to meet substantial expenditure out of a gross fee thus reducing the expected UK tax liability.

In reaching an agreement the Inspector will make allowances for admissible expenses. What can be allowed depends on the general rules covering expenditure allowable under Case I and II of Schedule D and on the facts of each case. Normally allowances will be made for

- general subsistence expenses
- commission, manager's and agent's fees
- UK travelling
- international air fares to and from the UK where an artiste comes to the UK for an activity and returns directly to his or her home country.

Other expenses may be allowable. What is allowable in each case will need to be agreed with Foreign Entertainers Unit including the proportion of any costs common to several countries.

B8   How do you know that a reduced tax payment has been authorised?

The Foreign Entertainers Unit will authorise you to deduct a reduced amount of tax by sending you a form FEU 4. Even where you have been a party to the agreed arrangement with the Inland Revenue you must wait until you get the form FEU 4.

If you have not received a certificate on form FEU 4 when you come to make the payment you must deduct tax at the basic rate from the gross payment you make.

B9   Action

If you are making a reduced tax payment you must return the details and account for the tax withheld by filling in the return form FEU 1. B3 to B4 tells you about the form FEU 1.

B10   How are payments dealt with in your Schedule D or corporation tax accounts?

If income you receive is attributed to the entertainer under the rules set out in S.556 ICTA 1988 and Regulation 7 Income Tax Regulations 1987 then the tax withheld from the payment you receive will be treated as a payment on account of the entertainer's UK liability.

You will not be charged to UK tax on that income and there will be no repayment of the Withholding Tax to you.

But if

- you are UK resident and
- the income you receive is not attributed to the entertainer under the rules above the payment you receive will be a receipt of your business.

The amount of the assessable income will be the payment received plus the amount of the Withholding Tax which has been deducted. You will be able to claim the gross payment you make as a deduction in your UK Income Tax or Corporation Tax accounts.

'Gross payment' means the payment to the entertainer or intermediary plus the tax accounted for to the Inland Revenue.

If you make the payment in a series of payments as described at B2, that is, a franked payment, you may be entitled to set off tax withheld from payments you receive against your UK tax liabilities or claim a repayment of tax.

Example

A, a UK resident, pays B Ltd, also a UK resident, £100,000 for C's services. C is a non-resident entertainer. C is paid a £60,000 fee by B Ltd.

Withholding Tax

	£	
A pays	100,000	
Less tax at 25%	25,000	paid to Inland Revenue

	£	
	75,000	net to B Ltd
B Ltd pays	60,000	
Less tax at 25%	15,000	(this sum is franked out of the £25,000 already deducted)
	45,000	paid to C

Treatment in the accounts

A is allowed an expense of £100,000 (that is the gross payment shown in his accounts).

B Ltd credits a receipt of £100,000 as income and is allowed an expense of £60,000 in its accounts.

Tax set offs

B Ltd can set the excess Withholding Tax of £10,000 (that is £25,000 less the franked payment of £15,000) against its Income Tax/Corporation Tax liability.

If B Ltd had a tax liability of less than £10,000 it can claim a repayment of the amount by which £10,000 exceeds its Income Tax/Corporation Tax liability.

B11   How do you cope with payment chains?

Some activities may give rise to a chain of payments. For example, money for a concert may flow from a venue to a promoter then to the artiste. Every payer in the chain must deduct tax as required by law.

If a payer higher up the chain has already deducted tax then you must take this into account in deciding how much tax, if any, you need to deduct (see B2 and B10).

Payers can ask for an arrangement (see B6) which moves the withholding point further down the chain so that payments between specified payers can be made without deduction of tax. This can only be done with the Foreign Entertainers Unit's approval.

Example

A concert is arranged at a hall. The venue owners control the box office and pay over the ticket proceeds less a percentage deduction to the concert promoter. He deducts his costs before paying an agreed amount to the artiste.

If the concert promoter makes a 'Middleman' application the Unit may agree to Nil withholding on the venue payments leaving the promoter as the withholding point. The promoter will then have to deduct tax at basic rate on his or her payment or a reduced amount if an artiste's application has been made and agreed in a lower sum.

The Unit will ask for certain information in support of any 'Middleman' application you make, for example, a copy of any contract, dates of appearances, and probably a copy of the budget. If you are submitting a 'Middleman' application for the first time the Unit will be happy to advise you on the procedure and level of information required.

Section C

C1   Assessments

Withholding Tax will be due and payable without the making of an assessment. Any tax paid late may be liable to an interest charge.

If a payer does not deduct Withholding Tax from a payment or does not pay over tax which he/she has deducted, the Inland Revenue may make an assessment to recover the tax due direct from the payer.

An assessment may be made on the payments made in the tax year or for a particular period (see B3). The tax charged in the assessment will be due and payable on or before whichever is the earlier of the normal due date (see B3) or the 14th day after the date of the notice of assessment.

You will see therefore that there is no advantage in delaying payment and waiting for an assessment. The tax will be treated as due at the normal time and interest calculated accordingly.

C2   Appeals

Any appeal against an assessment made to recover Withholding Tax should be made in writing to the Foreign Entertainers Unit. The appeal should be made within 30 days from the date the notice of assessment was issued. Please use form 64-7 (New) to make your appeal.

C3   Interest

Interest may be charged and recovered by the Inland Revenue in any of the following circumstances.
- Withholding Tax paid late. This will apply whether paid late without an assessment or recovered by assessment
- return form FEU 1 submitted late
- an incorrect return having been made.

C4   Penalties

Penalties may be due where the payer fails to make a Return on form FEU 1 or submits an incorrect Return on form FEU 1

C5   Information and inspection

The Foreign Entertainers Unit Inspector will be able, provided due notice is given, to call for information from payers. The information which the Inspector can request is fully set out in Regulation 9 of the Income Tax (Entertainers and Sportsmen) Regulations 1987. Any information requested under this Regulation will only be used for withholding tax purposes. No Self Assessment enquiry into an artiste's return will be made using this Regulation.

Section D

D1   Where can I get help and information?

Any questions which are not answered in this guide may be referred to the Foreign Entertainers Unit. The address, telephone number and fax number of the Unit can be found in the introduction to this booklet. The Unit's staff will try and help you with any practical problems you have in complying with the scheme.

Your professional adviser may also wish to help you deal with practical points arising from the law.

D2   *What service can I expect?*

You can expect to be treated fairly and efficiently by the Foreign Entertainers Unit which will handle each case in accord with the Taxpayer's Charter. This states:

> You are entitled to expect the Inland Revenue
>
> To be fair
> - By settling your tax affairs impartially
> - By expecting you to pay only what is due under the law
> - By treating everyone with equal fairness
>
> To help you
> - To get your tax affairs right
> - To understand your rights and obligations
> - By providing clear leaflets and forms
> - By giving you information and assistance at our enquiry offices
> - By being courteous at all times
>
> To provide an efficient service
> - By settling your tax affairs promptly and accurately
> - By keeping your private affairs strictly confidential
> - By using the information you give us only as allowed by law
> - By keeping to a minimum your costs of complying with the law
> - By keeping our costs down
>
> To be accountable for what we do
> - By setting standards for ourselves and publishing how well we live up to them
>
> If you are not satisfied
> - We will tell you exactly how to complain
> - You can ask for your tax affairs be looked at again
> - You can appeal to an independent tribunal
> - Your MP can refer your complaint to the Ombudsman
>
> In return we need you
> - To be honest
> - To give us accurate information
> - To pay your tax on time

D3   *What can I do if I am not happy with the service I receive?*

Naturally we hope that this question will not arise.

If you have a complaint, first write to the Head of the Foreign Entertainers Unit. His or her name is to be found on correspondence from the Unit or can be obtained by telephoning **0121 606 2861/62/63**. He or she will do everything possible to resolve the problem quickly. Most complaints are settled satisfactorily at this level.

If after this you are still unhappy you can take the matter further by writing to the

> Customer Service Manager
> Inland Revenue
> Special Compliance Office
> Angel Court
> 199 Borough High Street
> London
> SE1 1HZ

If the Customer Service Manager is unable to settle your complaint to your satisfaction you can ask the Revenue Adjudicator to look into it and recommend appropriate action.

The Revenue Adjudicator, whose services are free, is an impartial referee whose recommendations are independent.

The address is

The Revenue Adjudicator's Office
3rd Floor
Haymarket House
28 Haymarket
London SW1Y 4SP
Tel: 0171 930 2292
Fax: 0171 930 2298

At any time you can ask a Member of Parliament to refer a complaint to the independent Parliamentary Commissioner for Administration, commonly known as the Ombudsman, at

Church House
Great Smith Street
London SW1P 3BW
Tel: 0171 276 2130/3000

List of Forms

The forms shown below are those that the **payer** will be involved with

FEU 1	Return of payments made to non-resident entertainers
FEU 1(CS)	Payer's Return continuation sheet
FEU 1(Reminder)	Payer's Return reminder
FEU 2	Foreign Entertainers Unit tax deduction certificate
FEU 4	Payer's notification that basic rate Withholding Tax is not appropriate
FEU 40	Stationery request
FEU 50	Payer's Guide

The forms shown below are those that the **payee** will be involved with

FEU 2	Foreign Entertainers Unit tax deduction certificate
FEU 5	Payee's repayment claim form
FEU 8	Application for Reduced Tax Payment

Appendix 12 Television Industry— Guideline Notes in Respect of Freelancers

1. LIST OF GRADES WITHIN CASE 1 OR 2 OF SCHEDULE D. (See Appendix)

2. '7 DAY RULE'—NB The '7 Day Rule' does not apply to the journalist/reporter grade.

Operation

Where the individual does not come within the general guidelines, you need not deduct tax where he/she is engaged for less than one week, ie, 7 consecutive days or less.

Each engagement should be considered separately for the purposes of the rule.

If a contract at the outset provides for an individual to work a certain number of days each week and these exceed 6 days in total, then the rule does not apply; ie 2 days per week for 6 weeks.

Class I National Insurance Contributions should be deducted on every contract.

Reporting procedures

Payments made under the '7 Day Rule' procedure may be reported under Section 16 Taxes Management Act 1970 completing forms 46R-1. The Return is issued by Taxes Information Distribution Office in Cardiff and details should be sent directly to them.

Class I National Insurance Contribution Returns should be made under the normal procedures or, you may opt to make a Return in list form. A copy is attached. If the list form is chosen, then forms P14 do not have to be completed and a global figure may be entered on forms P35.

NB. This Return must be in the precise format shown as per attached example.

Expenses payments made under the '7 Day Rule'

You need not deduct Class I National Insurance Contributions on any expenses payable under the '7 Day Rule' insofar as they do not exceed your normal Dispensation rates.

The expenses must be added to the total income for reporting purposes under Section 16 to the Taxes Information Distribution Office.

VAT

Where an individual is registered for VAT you should account for this in the normal manner.

3. SPECIAL LETTER OF EXEMPTION

    Where an individual normally has a pattern of work which involves less than '7 day' contracts but on occasions takes on a contract which exceeds this amount, their case may have been reviewed by the Inland Revenue.

    If after this review, the Inland Revenue consider the longer term contracts to have been part of the individual's overall business profits, then a 'Special Letter' will be issued to the individual with a further letter which the individual can produce to you as the 'payer'.

    You will be asked in the letter to telephone this District and quote the unique reference number shown in the letter. You will also be asked the individual's National Insurance Number. This District will then advise you whether the particular contract in question may be paid gross without deduction of Tax or National Insurance Contributions.

4. ADDITIONAL NOTES
    i. *In front of camera*
        The Television Guidelines do not apply to personnel who are engaged in front of camera. Whether such individuals are engaged under contracts of employment or self-employment is a matter for the companies to decide based on the facts of the case.
    ii. *Television grading list*
        Roll Over Contracts—This term applies to contracts where it is stated (written or orally) from the outset of a contract that it will be renewed or there is an expectation of renewal. This expectation can be implied where there is a number of contracts undertaken by an individual over a period of time.
    iii. *Service companies*
        You may pay a service company gross where you are satisfied the Service Company is properly incorporated and you are actually engaging and paying the Service Company not the individual.
    iv. *Partnerships*
        In English Law, a partnership does not exist as a separate legal entity. Therefore, if you are engaging a partner as opposed to an employee of the partnership any fee paid should be dealt with in accordance with the Grading List and '7 Day Rule'.
    v. *Agencies*
        Only bona fide agencies should be paid gross for providing the services of an individual to your company. You are reminded that if you do not keep adequate details in respect of such payments, then should the agency be unable to meet its PAYE responsibilities the Inland Revenue may approach the Television Company for recompense as being mutually obliged with the agency to ensure the proper operation of PAYE.

vi. *NT codes*
Code NT should only be operated when issued by LP12.

vii. *Letters of authority*
Apart from the Special Letters . . . issued by either LP12, LP22 or LP10 showing a specific serial number, companies should not accept letters from any other source. This includes correspondence from other Tax Districts, accountants or individuals. Furthermore, a Schedule D reference number should not be accepted as evidence of self-employment.

viii. *Section 16 returns*
Any gross fee payments made to individuals or for the services of individuals should be returned annually to the:—
Taxes Information Distribution Office (TIDO)
Ty-Glas Road
Llanishen
Cardiff
CF4 5ZG
Tel: 01222 753271

ix. *VAT*
Customs and Excise are in line with the Inland Revenue. Therefore, VAT should be paid on production of a VAT invoice where an individual is covered by the grading list, a Special Letter or the '7 Day Rule'.

Appendix

Television, film and production grading list

This list merges the previously separate TV and Film lists. Most of the grades on the separate lists are on the new list without alteration but there are some where it has been necessary to give additional guidance to ensure this grade stays on the merged list.

These additional qualifications are usually present in the engagements and therefore there should be no practical change.

If exceptionally you are not sure please contact your tax office.

Important notes

1. PAYE need not be operated on payments to non-permanent, casual and freelance workers engaged in one of the grades listed below marked with an asterisk where they are engaged as follows:—
a. for a one-off production, such as a film or single drama/documentary
OR
b. for less than 9 months on a specific strand of programme
OR
c. for less than 9 months on a series
OR
d. for a longer period on a series/programme for which authority has been given by the Revenue.

2.   'Assistants' are excluded unless specifically mentioned in a particular grade.

3.   Premises provided by the company can be either studio, location or other facilities.

4.   Major equipment means items which play an important fundamental role in the work of that grade and are of significant value. It would not include incidental or additional items or small tools.
      * Animal Handler
      * Animation Director
      * Animation Production Co-ordinator
      Animator
      Where providing own facilities and substantial or major equipment.
      * Animatronic Model Designer
      * Art Director
      Assistant Art Director
      Where the work is done on premises other than those provided by the company.
      * Associate Producer (Except when engaged primarily for general research)
      * Auditioner
      Background Artist
      Where the work is done in premises other than those provided by the company.
      Camera Operator/Camera Person/Model Camera (see also *Lighting Director/Lighting Camera Person*)
      Where the individual provides or normally provides substantial or major equipment.
      * Casting Director
      * Chaperone/Tutor
      * Choreographer
      * Composer
      Continuity
      Where script breakdown is an integral part of the engagement.
      Contributor
      Where paid on a per contribution basis.
      Costume Designer/Wardrobe/Assistant Costume Designer
      Where the contract includes:—
      a. the substantial provision of materials OR
      b. facilities away from the studio/premises etc provided by the company.
      * Cricket Scorer and Statistician (in sport)
      * Director
      * Director of Photography
      Dressmaker
      Where the work is done in premises other than those provided by the company.
      Driver
      Where providing own vehicle.
      * Editor

* Fight Arranger
* Film/Photographic Stylist
* First Assistant Director/Senior Floor Manager

Gaffer

Where the contract requires the provision of substantial or major equipment by the Gaffer.

Graphic Artist/Graphic Designer

When engaged for work which is undertaken in premises other than those provided by the company.

Grip

Where the contract requires the provision of substantial or major equipment by the individual.

Hairdresser

Where the contract requires the substantial provision of wigs by the hairdresser or a substantial part of the contract is carried out away from the premises supplied by the company.

Hod/Advance Rigger

Where the contract requires the provision of substantial or major equipment by the Rigger.

Language Assessor

When used occasionally to check the style and delivery on foreign language broadcasts.

Lettering Artist/Designer

Where the work is done in premises other than those provided by the company.

* Lighting Director/Lighting Camera Person (Where responsible for designing lighting or photography.
* Line Producer

Location Manager

Where facilities are provided by the individual.

Make-up Artist

Where the engagement requires the provision of a standard make-up kit by the artist or where the contract is carried out substantially on premises other than those provided by the company.

* Matron

Model Designer/Model Maker

Where the engagement requires the provision of facilities and equipment/materials by the individual.

* Modeller/Sculptor

Musical Arranger/Copyist

Where the work is done in premises other than those provided by the company.

* Musical Associate
* Musical Director
* Musical Score Reader
* Nurse
* Post Production Supervisor
* Producer (including Co-producer and Executive Producer)

Production Accountant

Where the engagement requires the provision of facilities by the individual.

Production Assistant

Where script breakdown is an integral part of the engagement.

* Production Buyer
* Production Designer (Head of Art Department)
* Production Manager
* Production Supervisor

Property Master/Prop Hand

Where the contract requires the provision of substantial props or equipment.

Provider of Occasional Information

eg. tip-offs, racing tips, news and sport.

* Publicist

Scenic Artist/Designer

Where a substantial part of the work is done in premises other than those provided by the company.

Script Reader

Where the work is done on premises other than those provided by the company.

Script Supervisor

Where script breakdown is an integral part of the engagement.

* Script Writer (not Reporting)
* Sculptor/Modeller
* Senior Floor Manager/First Assistant Director
* Senior Special Effects Technician

Set Decorator/Set Dresser

Where the contract requires the design of the set using facilities provided by the individual.

Sound Maintenance Engineer

Where the contract requires the provision of substantial or major equipment by the individual.

Sound Recordist/Mixer

Where the individual provides or normally provides substantial or major equipment.

Special Effects Supervisor

Where the contract includes the provision of equipment by the individual.

Special Effects Wireperson/Wireperson

Where the contract includes the provision of equipment by the individual.

Specialist Researcher

An individual who has an existing profession outside the Industries (eg. University Professor, legal expert) OR with specialist knowledge of the programme subject to be researched and who is engaged for a specific project and is only an occasional contributor.

Stage Manager

Where the contract requires the supply of a substantial number of props by the manager.

Stills Photographer
Where the contract includes the provision of cameras.
Story Board Artist
Where the work is done in premises other than those provided by the
company.
* Story Writer (but not Reporting)
Tracer/Painter
Where the work is done in premises other than those provided by the
company.
Transcript Typist
Where the work is done in premises other than those provided by the
company.
Translator
When engaged for work undertaken in premises other than those
provided by the company.
Transport Manager
Where providing own vehicles.
* Tutor/Chaperone
Video Technician
Where the contract includes the provision of substantial or major
equipment by the individual.
* Warm-up
Wigmaker
When engaged for work undertaken in premises other than those
provided by the company.
Wireperson/Special Effects Wireperson
Where the contract includes the provision of equipment by the individual.
* Writer (but not Reporting)

See Note 1 of 'Important notes' [page 510].

Television and Film Guideline Flowchart—From 1 July 1996

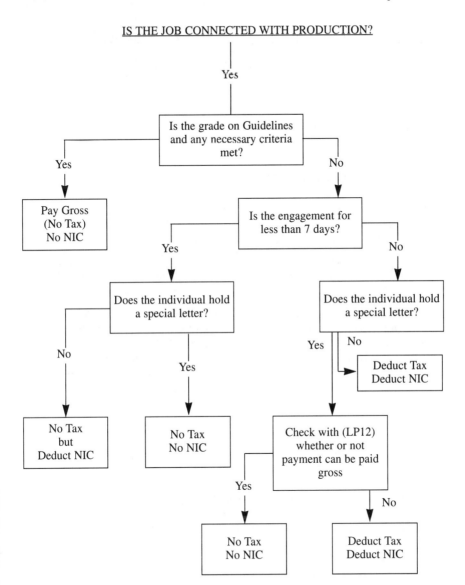

IS THE JOB CONNECTED WITH PRODUCTION?

Yes

Is the grade on Guidelines and any necessary criteria met?

Yes

No

Pay Gross (No Tax) No NIC

Is the engagement for less than 7 days?

Yes

No

Does the individual hold a special letter?

Does the individual hold a special letter?

No

Yes

Yes

No

No Tax but Deduct NIC

No Tax No NIC

Deduct Tax Deduct NIC

Check with (LP12) whether or not payment can be paid gross

Yes

No

No Tax No NIC

Deduct Tax Deduct NIC

Appendix 13   Extracts from Inland Revenue Manuals

Capital Allowances Manual

Part XI—Scientific Research

Introduction, CAA 1990, s 136 to CAA 1990, s 139

5000.   Scientific research allowances are given to a trader:

- who incurs expenditure on 'scientific research related to his trade' (CA 5007),
- *provided* the research is 'directly undertaken by him *or* on his behalf' (CA 5013).

Revenue expenditure on scientific research and payments to approved bodies (*see* CA 5020) are treated as trading expenses (if they would otherwise be disallowed). Capital expenditure **also** qualifies separately for a 100 per cent upfront deduction (*see* CA 5030). There are no writing-down allowances or balancing allowances to provide further relief if the 100 per cent deduction is not taken, or only partly taken; but there are balancing charges which recover excess relief when an asset is sold.

The instructions are laid out as follows:

- who gets allowances: CA 5001
- definition of 'scientific research': CA 5002–5006
- meaning of 'scientific expenditure related to the trade': CA 5007
- separate trade of scientific research: CA 5008
- mixed use: CA 5009
- appeals on meaning of 'scientific research': CA 5011
- grants and subsidies generally deducted: CA 5012
- meaning of research 'directly undertaken by him or on his behalf': CA 5013
- revenue payments: CA 5020–5022
- capital payments: CA 5030
- period for which capital allowance given: CA 5031
- double allowances: CA 5032
- claims for capital allowances: CA 5033
- time when capital expenditure incurred: CA 5034
- how capital allowance given: CA 5035
- balancing adjustments: CA 5036–5039
- destruction of asset and balancing adjustments: CA 5040
- connected person and control sales: election for transfer at written down value: CA 5041

- VAT Capital Goods Scheme: CA 5042.

Only traders are entitled to allowances

5001. Allowances are only given to traders. A person who carries on a profession, vocation etc does not qualify for scientific research allowances. The reason is that the legislation only refers to 'trades' and there are no provisions which (as in the case of machinery and plant) extend 'trade' to include other activities.

Definition of scientific research, CAA 1990, s 139(1)

5002. Scientific research is defined in the statute as 'any activities in the fields of natural or applied science for the extension of knowledge'. Activities are scientific research if they involve:

- the application of new scientific principles in an existing area of research, or
- the application of existing principles in a new area of research.

The application of existing principles in an existing area, however, is not regarded as scientific research, but rather as technological development. The essential test is innovation.

Fundamental research and prototypes

5003. Scientific research includes the development of a piece of fundamental research up to the production stage. Expenditure on the construction of prototypes, pilot plant etc qualifies for scientific research allowances if the prototypes etc are used to test the results of the basic research or the possibility of applying the results of the basic research to manufacture.

Expenditure on prototypes etc constructed to explore purely commercial possibilities does not, however, qualify for scientific research allowances.

—*Oil, gas etc exploration* Certain expenditure on exploring for minerals may qualify for allowances; for example, searching for oil and gas. The Oil Taxation Office may be able to advise in these cases when you have found all the facts.

Approach to claims that 'scientific research' is undertaken

5004. When faced with a claim that activities amount to 'scientific research', ask for an explanation in plain language of the reasons. Do not feel inhibited by a lack of technical knowledge of the subject: those involved in the research ought to be able to translate their activities into language a non-specialist can understand. They may well already need to do this to justify expenditure to the company's management, or to investors or bankers. It is essential to obtain the facts and arguments in writing and, if the case is not straightforward, experience suggests that it is also invaluable to see the research facilities and obtain first-hand explanations of what the research is all about from those doing the work. A site visit—and full notes of what you learn—usually saves time for both sides in the long run. Confining enquiries to correspondence is a recipe for delay because both you and the intermediaries in the agent and client are likely to struggle with the esoteric concepts familiar to the researchers.

Your aim will be to settle the case by agreement where possible but, even so, you will probably find it helpful to keep in mind from the outset the information required for the unusual scientific research appeal procedures: *see* CA 5011 for further guidance.

—*Questions to ask* To focus your enquiries, consider selecting a typical project (or a range of projects) which the taxpayer thinks involve scientific research and asking:

1. What objectives do they set out to achieve in that particular line of research, and what features of the research are new or involve new applications of existing principles?
2. What is the current state of knowledge in the area and how is the research designed to extend that knowledge?
3. To what extent does the work claimed to be scientific research differ from what is being done elsewhere, either privately or by government bodies?
4. What is the background, training and qualifications of the people involved in the project which is claimed to be scientific research? For example, if the project is staffed by sociologists, it is unlikely to be scientific research.
5. To what extent will the results of the work be published (when and where?). The answer may be that commercial confidentiality means the results will not be published. If so, that does not prevent the activities being scientific research; but, if the results are published, this may help establish that the work has broken new ground.
6. Are there any memos, papers etc prepared by the researchers for management or others and can you see them? For example, are there papers setting out the case for expenditure on a project or reporting progress (or the lack of it)?
7. Any other practical questions which seem relevant in the context of the particular case.

—*District is responsible for investigation* When you have full and detailed answers to the questions set out above, you should be able to decide whether the activities amount to scientific research. If appropriate, consider asking a colleague with relevant background or training (such as a science degree) whether they can provide any help. However, the innovative character (CA 5002) of complex and technical research should be capable of explanation in plain language and should not need consideration by experts. **Hence, the District has the main responsibility for**:

- **establishing the facts and arguments, and**
- **considering whether the activities count as 'scientific research'.**

See CA 5011 for further guidance on appeals.

Expenditure on scientific research, CAA 1990, s 139(1)(c)

5005. Expenditure incurred on scientific research is also defined to include:

- expenditure incurred for the prosecution of scientific research, and

- expenditure on the provision of facilities for the prosecution of scientific research; this can include the cost of constructing or buying laboratory buildings and other substantial structures. No allowances are due for the cost of buying land: *see* CA 5006.

Expenditure on scientific research does not include expenditure incurred on the acquisition of rights in, or arising from, scientific research. In other words, SRA is not due for the cost of buying the fruits of someone else's research; for example, for the cost of know-how or patent rights. In such cases allowances may be available separately under the know-how or patents provisions (for which the rate of relief is lower).

Expenditure on facilities or assets used by employees engaged in scientific research is within the definition of expenditure on scientific research.

Expenditure on land or dwellings does not qualify, CAA 1990, s 137(2) & (3)

5006. No allowances are due for expenditure on the acquisition of, or of rights in or over, land or for expenditure on the provision of a dwelling. Hence, you should not give an allowance for the cost of the site of a building, structure or fixed machinery or plant. There is statutory provision for making a 'just apportionment' of expenditure so that allowances can be given on the part of the purchase price paid for qualifying buildings and fixtures—structures and machinery or plant fixed to the land.

Where, however, a dwelling is part of a larger building and the building is used for scientific research, CAA 1990, s 137(3) says that the expenditure on the dwelling is ignored if it is not more than one quarter of the cost of the whole building. *See* CA 5042 for the impact of any additional VAT on the one quarter rule.

Meaning of scientific research 'related to a trade', CAA 1990, s 139(1)(d)

5007. Scientific research 'related to a trade or class of trades' includes:

(i)   any scientific research which may lead to or facilitate an extension of the trade, or of trades of that class: CAA 1990, s 139(1)(*d*)(i); and

(ii) medical research which has a special relation to the welfare of workers employed in that trade or class of trades: CAA 1990, s 139(1)(*d*)(ii). An example would be research into an occupational disease.

Subparagraph (ii) does not include medical research undertaken for the benefit of the community as a whole; but such research may fall within subparagraph (i). For example, medical research undertaken by a drug company for the purpose of its trade.

Separate trade of scientific research

5008. It is possible for a trader to have a trade which consists solely of scientific research. For example, a group of companies may set up a company to carry out scientific research on behalf of the group. In such a case all the assets of the trade are used for, or provide facilities for, scientific research and so expenditure on them qualifies for scientific research allowances unless it is specifically excluded (*see* CA 5006).

Mixed use—part scientific research and part other use, CAA 1990, s 137(4)

5009. If part of an asset is used for scientific research and part is not, only that part of the expenditure on the provision of the asset which relates to the part used for scientific research qualifies for scientific research allowances.

Where an asset is used partly for scientific research and partly for other purposes and no part is used exclusively for one or the other, the expenditure on the asset should be apportioned on a just basis. Give scientific research allowances on the part of the expenditure which relates to the use for scientific research.

CAA 1990, s 139(1)(*e*) defines 'asset' to include part of an asset.

Two or more trades

5010. Do not give allowances on the same expenditure in respect of more than one trade. For example, if the research leads to the setting up of two trades, only make allowances against one of them. CAA 1990, s 139(2) prevents expenditure qualifying for relief (revenue or capital) in relation to more than one trade. This is in addition to the general capital allowances 'double relief' rules in CAA 1990, s 147: *see* CA 5032.

Appeals on meaning of 'scientific research'?, CAA 1990, s 139(3)

5011. Where you cannot reach agreement with the taxpayer, the following issues have to be referred to the Secretary of State (*not* the General or Special Commissioners):

- whether activities constitute scientific research; or
- whether an asset is being used for scientific research.

Any other disputes relating to the relief follow the usual appeal procedures; for example, a dispute about the apportionment of expenditure between land and buildings.

—*Nature of submissions* The Secretary of State's decision is final for matters which are within his or her jurisdiction.

A reference to the Secretary of State is not a routine matter. The Secretary of State acts in a quasi-judicial capacity and deals with cases by way of written submissions. This means that all the facts and arguments will need to be fully set out. And, in accordance with the demands of natural justice, the Secretary of State will want each side to have had ample opportunity to consider the facts and also to consider and comment on the arguments of the other side.

—*Form of submission* The submission of any case to the Secretary of State will usually take the form of a written paper agreed between Revenue and taxpayer which sets out:

1. the agreed facts in a way which non-experts can understand;
2. the taxpayer's contentions;
3. the Revenue's contentions;
4. if appropriate, any further comments by either side on the contentions of the other.

The District is primarily responsible for agreeing the paper but BPD (Capital Allowances) will, after considering the case, arrange for its transmission to the Secretary of State. Do not make direct submissions to the Secretary of State.

—*Direct approach by taxpayer* The legislation provides that any dispute has to be referred to the Secretary of State by the Board of Inland Revenue: CAA 1990, s 139(3). A taxpayer should not, therefore, refer a dispute directly to the Secretary of State; but we would not wish to object if this happens. It may be worth pointing out to the taxpayer or agent who asks about a direct submission that this may be inconvenient for all parties and lead to delays. This is because the Secretary of State will wish to obtain the Revenue's views on the matter, partly in the interests of natural justice and partly because of the statutory requirement in CAA 1990, s 139(3). Then the Secretary of State will wish, in turn, to obtain the taxpayer's comments on the Revenue's views; and so on, until is is clear all the facts have been drawn out and both sides have had every opportunity to present their views.

—*Submissions to BPD (capital allowances)* Where there is a dispute, therefore, you must establish the facts and arguments of both sides as comprehensively as possible. It often happens that this process provides both you and the taxpayer with a fuller understanding of the case and this leads to agreement. Submit the case to BPD (Capital Allowances) when you are satisfied that an agreement cannot be reached and all the facts and arguments have been fully established.

Grants and subsidies are generally deducted, CAA 1990, s 153

5012. Most grants and subsidies towards scientific research expenditure are deducted from the expenditure in order to arrive at the net amount on which relief is due, but there are some exceptions.

No allowances are due for expenditure which is met, or is to be met, directly or indirectly by any of the following:

- the Crown
- any Government
- any public or local authority
- any person other than the person incurring the expenditure.

Expenditure met by any of the following does, however, qualify for allowance:

- a regional development grant made under Part II of the Industrial Development Act 1982
- a regional development grant made under Part I of the Industry Act 1972
- a corresponding Northern Ireland grant . . .

Such grants should not be deducted in the capital allowance computation.

Research undertaken directly by him or on his behalf, Gaspet Ltd v Elliss 60 TC 91

5013. Expenditure (either revenue or capital) incurred by a person on scientific research only qualifies for scientific research allowances if the research is either:

- directly undertaken by him, or
- directly undertaken on his behalf by someone else.

Research is only undertaken on behalf of a person if there is a clear, close and direct link between him and the research undertaken. The relationship between the person claiming the allowances and the person undertaking the research need not be contractual, but if it is not it must be one of agency, or something similar to agency. The fact that research undertaken by someone else is for a trader's benefit, or is in his interest, is not enough to make the expenditure qualify for scientific research allowances (see *Gaspet Ltd v Elliss*, 1987, 60 TC 91).

5014–5019.   . . .

Revenue expenditure and payments

Treatment of revenue expenses, CAA 1990, s 136

5020.   CAA 1990, s 136 deals with revenue expenses. It gives a trader relief for:

(*a*)   revenue expenditure he incurs on scientific research related to his trade which is directly undertaken by him or on his behalf, or

(*b*)   payments which he makes to a scientific research association which has been approved for the purposes of CAA 1990, s 136 and whose object is to undertake scientific research related to the class of trade to which his trade belongs (CA 5021), or

(*c*)   payments which he makes to a university, college research institute or similar institution which has been approved for the purposes of CAA 1990, s 136 and which are to be used for scientific research related to the class of trade to which his trade belongs.

It does not matter whether payments within (b) or (c) above are used by the recipient for revenue or capital purposes.

The relief is not given as an allowance. The relief due is treated as a trading expense and so is deducted in computing the Case I profit or loss. ICTA 1988, s 74 is specifically disapplied. Treat the whole of the expenditure incurred or the sum paid as a trading expense in the accounting period in which it is incurred or paid. See CA 5022 for expenditure incurred before trading starts.

Many revenue expenses within (*a*) to (*c*) above will also qualify as Case I deductions under ordinary principles. The purpose of CAA 1990, s 136 is to remove any doubt which might arise; for example, on the grounds of remoteness from the trade.

Approved research associations etc.

5021. Research associations, universities etc approved for the purposes of CAA 1990, s 136 are set out in List No 1, Part III. These are the bodies within CA 5020 (b) and (c). Approval is given by the Secretary of State for Trade and Industry. If someone enquires about approval tell them to apply directly to the Department of Trade and Industry.

CT 4620 deals with claims by scientific research associations for exemption from tax under ICTA 1988, s 508.

Pre-trading expenditure

5022. There is no relief for pre-trading revenue expenditure unless the general pre-trading rules in ICTA 1988, s 401 apply (*see* IM 940).

5023–5029. . . .

Capital expenditure

Treatment of capital expenditure, CAA 1990, s 137

5030. CAA 1990, s 137 gives 100 per cent allowances for capital expenditure incurred on scientific research. The expenditure which qualifies is:

- capital expenditure incurred by a trader on scientific research related to his trade and directly undertaken by him or on his behalf, and
- capital expenditure incurred by a person on scientific research directly undertaken by him or on his behalf before trading starts provided that person then starts a trade 'connected with that scientific research'.

See CA 5013 for guidance on research undertaken on a trader's behalf.

—*Existing asset begins to be used for scientific research* Allowances are only due where expenditure is incurred on scientific research. No scientific research allowances are due where an asset acquired for ordinary business use later begins to be used for scientific research. The asset may continue to qualify in the ordinary way for other capital allowances, such as machinery or plant allowances or industrial buildings allowances, if they are due.

—*Asset ceases to be used for scientific research* On the other hand, there is no balancing adjustment where an asset has properly qualified for scientific research allowances and later begins to be used for other purposes: CA 5037. The adjustment is made when the taxpayer ceases to own the asset.

—*No writing-down or balancing allowances* There are no scientific research writing-down allowances or balancing allowances. This means that a taxpayer who chooses not to take the full 100 per cent allowance in the first year cannot claim writing-down allowance on the unrelieved expenditure in later years.

Period for which capital allowance given, FA 1994, s 211(2), FA 1994, s 212(2) and FA 1994, s 218

5031. An allowance for capital expenditure is given for the 'relevant chargeable period'. The relevant chargeable period is defined in the old CAA 1990, s 137(5) for Corporation Tax and in the old CAA 1990, s 137(6) and (7) as they stood before changes were made for Income Tax self-assessment in FA 1994.

There is a new CAA 1990, s 137(5) which replaces subsections (5) to (6) as a result of the introduction of Income Tax self-assessment. Self-assessment for income tax applies from the year of assessment 1994–95 for trades which start on or after 6 April 1994 and from the year of assessment 1997–98 for trades which started earlier. The Corporation Tax position is not altered in any way but the Income Tax machinery is changed for cases where self-assessment applies. Note that for Income Tax self-assessment:

- a 'chargeable period' is defined to mean a 'period of account': CAA 1990, s 161(2);

- a 'period of account' is defined in a new version of CAA 1990, s 160.

The tables below summarise the details.

Corporation Tax

When capital expenditure is incurred	Relevant chargeable period
Pre-trading expenditure	The AP in which the trade was set up and commenced
Otherwise	The AP in which the expenditure was incurred

Income Tax before Self-Assessment

When capital expenditure is incurred	Relevant chargeable period
Pre-trading expenditure	The first year of assessment
In the year of assessment in which trading begins	The first year of assessment
In the first 12 months of trading but after the end of the year of assessment in which the trade begins	The second year of assessment
	For example, a trade begins on 1 March 1988: the relevant chargeable period for expenditure incurred in the period 6 April 1988 to 28 February 1989 is 1988–89
More than 12 months after trade begins	The year of assessment in the basis period for which the expenditure is incurred

	There are rules in CAA 1990, s 137(6) like those in CAA 1990, s 160(2) (see CA 210 onwards) to ensure that expenditure is included in one and one only basis year
In the year of assessment in which trade is discontinued	That year of assessment

Income Tax after Self-Assessment

When capital expenditure is incurred	*Relevant chargeable period*
Pre-trading expenditure	The period of account which begins when the trade starts
Otherwise	The period of account in which the expenditure was incurred

Double allowances—from 1989, CAA 1990, s 147

5032. For chargeable periods or basis periods ending on or after 27 July 1989, expenditure does not qualify for SRA if it has qualified for:

- industrial buildings allowance, or
- assured tenancies allowance, or
- mineral extraction allowance, or
- dredging allowance, or
- has been taken into account as qualifying expenditure for the purposes of machinery or plant allowances.

Expenditure which has qualified for SRA does not qualify for any other type of capital allowance. The practical effect for post-1989 expenditure is that the taxpayer can choose which allowance to claim but, once he has claimed one type, he is barred from claiming another.

—Before 1989, CAA 1990, s 148 For chargeable periods or basis periods ending before 27 July 1989 expenditure which qualifies for scientific research allowance cannot also qualify for industrial buildings allowances, machinery and plant capital allowances, mines and oil wells allowances or mineral extraction allowances.

—More than one trade The double allowance rules described above are general capital allowances rules. There is an additional scientific research rule in CAA 1990, s 139(2) which prevents a taxpayer making a claim in respect of the same expenditure for more than one trade; for example, where research leads to two (or more) separate trades: *see* CA 5010.

Claims for capital allowance

5033.   The procedure for claims is essentially the same as for other assets. See CT 10650 onwards for guidance on claims under the Corporation Tax 'Pay and File' system.

Time when capital expenditure incurred

5034.   The definition of the time when expenditure is incurred in CAA 1990, s 159 applies to capital expenditure which qualifies for scientific research allowances (*see* CA 280 onwards).

How capital allowances given

5035.   Allowances for capital expenditure on scientific research are given in taxing the trade. CAA 1990, s 140(2) and (4) apply for Income Tax cases (*see* CA 110 and CA 115) and CAA 1990, s 144 applies for Corporation Tax cases (*see* CA 172).

Balancing adjustments—general

5036.   The balancing adjustment rules only provide for a recovery of excess allowances. They do this by treating the excess as a trading receipt. There are no balancing allowances. Hence, there is no further relief if the trader does not take the full 100 per cent allowance available at the outset.

Balancing adjustments before FAs 1985 and 1989, CAA 1990, s 92

Before the balancing adjustment rules were revised in FA 1985 and FA 1989, the only circumstance in which a balancing adjustment arose was where the asset ceased to be used for scientific research and was then sold or treated as sold on destruction (*see* CA 5040). In such a case the sale proceeds are used to calculate the balancing adjustment (*see* CA 5038). The old rules apply where both the following conditions are met:

—Expenditure incurred before 1 April 1985 and disposal events before 1 April 1989

- the expenditure was incurred before 1 April 1985 or before 1 April 1987 under a contract entered into on or before 19 March 1985; *and*
- the asset ceases to belong to the taxpayer before 1 April 1989.

If either of these conditions is not met, the case is within CA 5037.

Balancing adjustments— CAA 1990, s 138

5037.   The balancing adjustment rules were revised in 1985 and again in 1989. The current rules provide for a balancing adjustment to be made:

—Asset ceases to belong after 31 March 1989 or expenditure incurred on or after 1 April 1985

1. in **all** cases where the asset ceases to belong to the trader after 31 March 1989; in other words, such events are caught regardless of the date the expenditure on the asset was incurred: paragraph 8, Schedule 13, FA 1989;

2. if (1) above does not apply, the asset ceases to belong to the trader and the expenditure on it was incurred on or after 1 April 1985; but expenditure incurred before 1 April 1987 under a pre-20 March 1985 contract is protected (unless (1) applies), in which case CA 5036 applies: FA 1985, s 63.

The cessation of belonging is known as the 'relevant event' and gives rise to a 'disposal value'. The 'disposal value' is used to calculate the balancing adjustment (*see* CA 5038). The table below summarises the definition of 'disposal value'.

—When asset ceases to belong Where an asset ceases to belong to a taxpayer because of a sale, the asset is treated as ceasing to belong to the taxpayer at the *earlier* of:

*   the time of completion; or
*   the time when possession is given: CAA 1990, s 139(4).

This rule for sales applies where the sale was effected, or the contract for sale was entered into, after 26 July 1989 (second subparagraph of CAA 1990, s 139(4)). For sales effected etc. earlier, you take the actual date the asset ceased to belong to the seller. This will normally be the date of completion.

Where the asset is destroyed, CAA 1990, s 138(5) deems the asset to have been sold immediately before destruction: *see* CA 5040. In other cases, such as a gift, you take the time the asset actually ceases to belong to the taxpayer.

—Asset stops being used for research There is no balancing adjustment merely because the asset ceases to be used for scientific research. Close investigation may be required if an asset ceases to be used for research not long after allowances have been given. The object would be to determine whether the original claim failed to make the facts and intentions of the trader clear.

Type of event	*Disposal value to use*
Actual sale at price not less than open market value	The sale proceeds*
Deemed sale (CA 5040)	The deemed sale proceeds*
Any other case (for example, a gift or value sale below open market value)	The open market value*
	* Where an election is possible under CAA 1990, s 158, the tax written down value of the asset: CA 5041

Calculation of balancing adjustments, CAA 1990, s 138(2)

5038.   The balancing adjustment rules bring into charge the smaller of the allowances given and the disposal value. That is, if the cost was £1 m, allowances of £1 m had been given and the asset was sold for £2 m, there is a charge on £1 m. If, instead, the asset was sold for £1/2 m, the charge would be on £1/2 m.

There are no balancing allowances where the trader did not take the full 100 per cent allowance at the outset. There is a separate rule for relieving the cost of demolition: CA 5040.

More precisely, the statute says you compute the recovery of relief by adding the sale proceeds (if CA 5036 applies) or disposal value (if CA 5037 applies) to the allowances given. Then you compare this figure with the cost of the asset. If it is greater than the cost of the asset, you treat the difference as a trading receipt arising at the time of the sale or 'relevant event'. If the sale etc. takes place after the trade has been permanently discontinued, you treat the difference as a trading receipt arising immediately before the trade is discontinued. The amount treated as a trading receipt cannot exceed the allowances given.

No balancing charge arises if one already arises under the industrial buildings or machinery and plant rules: CAA 1990, s 138(6) and (7).

Example of statutory computation

Suppose an asset cost £200 and scientific research allowances of £200 have been given. Later, the asset is sold for £160, its market value. The balancing adjustment is:

Allowances given	200
Add sale proceeds	160
Total	360
Less cost	200
Difference	160

Since the difference of £160 is less than the allowances given, treat the whole of the £160 as a trading receipt. This follows the statutory method. The same answer can be reached more directly by taking the smaller of the sale proceeds and the allowances given.

Disposal before allowances due, CAA 1990, s 138(3)

5039.   The sale or 'relevant event' may take place before the chargeable period for which scientific research allowances would be given. If so, give no scientific research allowances. Instead, if the sale proceeds or disposal value are less than the cost, allow the difference between them in taxing the trade for the chargeable period in which the sale etc. happens.

Destruction of asset and balancing adjustments, CAA 1990, s 138(5)

5040.   Where an asset is destroyed, treat the asset as sold immediately before its destruction. This applies whether the asset was acquired before 1 April 1985 or after. Treat any insurance moneys or other compensation received, plus any money received for the remains of the asset, as sale proceeds.

—*Demolition costs* CAA 1990, s 138(5) also gives relief for the cost of demolishing the asset **provided** it was not used for non-scientific research purposes before demolition; for example, where a research building was later used as ordinary offices, there is no relief for demolition costs. But mere disuse does not prevent relief; that is, where the building is simply left unused.

Where the demolition expenditure qualifies for relief, treat the cost of the demolition as part of the cost of the asset when calculating the balancing adjustment. Note that doing this can only:

- reduce the amount of excess allowances brought back into charge as a trading receipt by the amount of the demolition costs; or
- provide a deduction for the demolition expenses (if there are no sale proceeds or deemed proceeds); or
- some combination of both the above.

The demolition rule does not provide relief for any part of the original cost of the asset for which allowances were not taken at the outset.

—*When to bring in receipt or deduction in destruction case* The receipt or relief is given in the chargeable period in which the asset is treated as sold. Where the trade has ceased before the deemed date of sale, bring in the receipt or deduction for the last chargeable period in which the trade was carried on.

Example of demolition costs

Suppose an asset cost £100 and scientific research allowances of £100 have been given upfront. The asset is later demolished. There are no insurance etc proceeds or sale proceeds and the demolition costs are £20. The balancing adjustment is:

Allowances given	100	
Add: sale proceeds	NIL	
Total	100	
Cost of asset*	120	(* Cost £100 + demolition costs £20)
Difference	20	

The adjusted cost is greater than the allowances given (£100) plus the sale proceeds (nil). So allow the difference of £20 as a deduction in taxing the trade.

Connected person and control sales, CAA 1990, s 157 and CAA 1990, s 158

5041. The legislation in CAA 1990, s 157 and CAA 1990, s 158 about 'connected person' sales, 'control' and 'sole or main benefit' sales applies to disposals of assets which qualify for scientific research allowances. The instructions about CAA 1990, s 157 and CAA 1990, s 158 are at CA 340–378.

Transfer at written down value

Note that an election under CAA 1990, s 158 for a deemed transfer of a scientific research asset at tax written down value was not possible before FA 1993. Then:

FA 1993, s 117, FA 1994, s 119
- FA 1993, s 117 provided the right to elect in respect of disposals after 15 March 1993;
- FA 1994, s 119 retrospectively extended the right to elect to earlier disposals.

The election is still subject to the time limit in CAA 1990, s 158(1); this provides that the election has to be made within two years from the date of the disposal.

VAT capital goods scheme—introduction, FA 1991, s 59 & FA 1991, Sch 14

5042. Normally, VAT presents no special problems for scientific research allowances. Where capital expenditure on an asset qualifies for the 100 per cent allowance, any VAT finally borne by the trader on that asset also qualifies. Where the trader can recover the VAT he has paid, either by offsetting it against VAT he collects or by getting a direct refund from Customs, it is the net expenditure which qualifies for relief.

The situation was complicated a little in 1991 when Customs introduced their Capital Goods Scheme following a Directive from the European Commission. Under this Scheme, additional VAT may be charged for a period of up to ten years after the asset was acquired. There may also be repayments of VAT. Hence, FA 1991 introduced further rules which give scientific research allowances on any additional VAT if the original capital expenditure qualified and, similarly, impose a charge on any recoveries of VAT.

CAA 1990, s 137, which deals with allowances for capital expenditure on scientific research, was amended in two ways by FA 1991.

Allowances for extra VAT

First, any additional VAT incurred by a person qualifies for 100 per cent scientific research allowances if that VAT:

CAA 1990, s 137(1A)
- relates to expenditure on an asset which qualified for scientific research allowances, and
- is incurred while the asset belongs to him.

CAA 1990, s 137(3); FA 1991, Sch 14, paragraph 12 Second, in general, expenditure on a dwelling does not qualify for scientific research allowances. But expenditure on a dwelling which is part of a larger building is ignored if the expenditure on the dwelling is not more than one quarter of the cost of the building (CA 5006). The change made by FA 1991 is that any additional VAT incurred or additional VAT rebates received are disregarded in applying the one quarter test.

Balancing adjustments

CAA 1990, s 138(2A), (3A) & (8); FA 1991, Sch 14, paragraph 13 There is a balancing adjustment under the normal rules where an asset which has qualified for scientific research allowances ceases to belong to a trader: CAA 1990, s 138 (CA 5037). Three new subsections are added to CAA 1990, s 138 which modify the normal rules. Those subsections let us:

- assess any additional VAT rebates received by a trader while the asset belongs to him as trading receipts, and
- take additional VAT incurred and VAT rebates received while the asset belongs to the trader into account in calculating the balancing adjustment when the asset ceases to belong to him.

5043–5499. ...

Part XII—Patents

Layout

5550. There is legislation about patents in ICTA 1988, s 520 to ICTA 1988, s 529 and ICTA 1988, s 532 and ICTA 1988, s 533. The legislation in ICTA 1988, s 522 and ICTA 1988, s 523 applies to expenditure incurred before 1 April 1986. The guidance about this is at Appendix 2 at paragraphs (57) to (62).

The guidance about patents is laid out like this.

Receipts

CA 5580	Capital sum from sale of patent rights
CA 5581	Capital sum received by UK resident
CA 5585	Capital sum received by non-resident
CA 5586	Spreading of capital sum received by non-resident
CA 5587	Payments exempt under DT agreement
CA 5588	Capital sum received by non-resident company
CA 5589	Spreading of capital sum of non-resident company
CA 5590	Capital sum—deductions
CA 5596	Death of an individual
CA 5597	Death of an individual—notice
CA 5598	Partnership discontinuance

Expenses

CA 5600	Grant or maintenance of patent—trader
CA 5601	Renewal of patent
CA 5602	Grant or maintenance of patent—non-trader
CA 5603	Expenses of devising patented invention
CA 5604	How allowance under ICTA 1988, s 526(2) made
CA 5605	Claims before Royal Commission
CA 5610	Royalties—spread back relief
CA 5611	Royalties—spread back relief: payments excluded
CA 5612	Payments for Crown user of patent

Definitions etc.

Scope of legislation

5551.   The word patent is not defined in the legislation. The legislation covers patents granted anywhere in the world except where it specifically refers to a UK patent.

A patent consists of rights conferred by letters patent to the exclusive use and benefits of a particular invention. It will last for a specified period. The period for which a patent lasts is often referred to as the term of the patent.

Basically a patent is a form of protection for an inventor. Once an invention has been patented nobody can use that invention unless they have acquired rights to use the patent or been granted a licence to use the patent.

This lets the inventor control the way in which their invention is used. Once a patent has been granted the inventor can get income by granting rights or a licence to use it.

Example   Galileo invents a thermo nuclear pizza oven and patents it. If Fellini wants to use a thermo nuclear pizza oven in his restaurant he will have to pay Galileo for the right to use Galileo's invention.

Meaning of UK patent, ICTA 1988, s 533(1)

A United Kingdom patent is a patent granted under the laws of the United Kingdom.

Definition of patent rights, ICTA 1988, s 533(1)

5552. There is a definition of patent rights in ICTA 1988, s 533(1). Patent rights are the right to do or authorise the doing of anything which would, but for that right, be an infringement of the patent.

The legislation covers patent rights wherever the patent may have been granted. For example, it covers rights in a US patent.

5553. These are the other definitions which apply to the patents legislation.

Income from patents, ICTA 1988, s 533(1)

Income from patents is defined in ICTA 1988, s 533(1). It is

(*c*) any royalty or other sum paid in respect of the user of a patent, and

(*d*) any balancing charge assessable under ICTA 1988, s 520(6) (CA 5571) or ICTA 1988, s 523(3) (para (62) Appendix 2) or any capital sum assessable under ICTA 1988, s 524 (CA 5580 onwards) or ICTA 1988, s 525 (CA 5596).

Licence, ICTA 1988, s 533(2)

The acquisition of a licence in respect of a patent is treated as a purchase of patent rights. This means that someone who acquires a licence in respect of a patent is treated as if they have bought patent rights and so they can claim capital allowances.

The grant of a licence is treated as a sale of patent rights and the legislation about the sale of patent rights applies.

Exclusive licence, ICTA 1988, s 533(3)

The grant of a licence which gives exclusive rights for the remainder of the term of the patent is treated as a sale of the whole of the patent rights

Use by the Crown or a foreign government, ICTA 1988, s 533(4)

5554. When the Crown or a foreign government uses a patent they are treated as if they are using it under a licence. This means that the legislation about the grant of a licence in ICTA 1988, s 533(2) and (3) (CA 5553) applies and so the Crown or foreign government are treated as if they have bought patent rights. The person who owns the patent is treated as if they had sold rights in the patent to the Crown or foreign government.

Rights in a patent which has not yet been granted—treatment of buyer, ICTA 1988, s 533(5)

5555. A person who obtains a right to acquire patent rights in an invention for which a patent has not yet been granted is treated as if they had bought patent rights. If the patent rights are later acquired the expenditure on the right to acquire them is treated as expenditure on buying them.

Treatment of seller, ICTA 1988, s 533(6)

A person who receives a payment for a right to acquire patent rights is treated as if they had received the proceeds of a sale of patent rights. This happens whether or not a patent is granted.

Application of CAA 1990, ICTA 1988, s 532(1)

5556.   ICTA 1988, s 532(1) says that the legislation about patents in ICTA 1988, s 520 to ICTA 1988, s 529 is to be construed as if it were contained in the Capital Allowances Act 1990 except that the provisions of CAA 1990, s 157 and CAA 1990, s 158 (control sales) do not apply to expenditure incurred on the purchase of patent rights (ICTA 1988, s 532(2)). There are special rules about connected person and sole or main benefit sales of patent rights in ICTA 1988, s 521(5) and (6) (CA 5563).

This means that the legislation in CAA 1990, s 150 (CA 300 onwards) about apportionments etc. applies to the patents legislation and so if patent rights are exchanged for shares, for example, the transaction is treated as a sale.

5557–5559.   . . .

Capital allowances

Background

5560.   A new system of capital allowances was introduced by FA 1985, s 64 for capital expenditure incurred on the acquisition of patent rights. It is very like the capital allowance system for machinery and plant.

Allowances based on pool of qualifying expenditure

Allowances and charges for a chargeable period are based on the qualifying expenditure for that period. The qualifying expenditure for a chargeable period is often referred to as the pool.

Start date

The capital allowance legislation is in ICTA 1988, s 520 and ICTA 1988, s 521. The system introduced by FA 1985 applies to capital expenditure incurred *after 31 March 1986*.

Pre 1 April 1986 expenditure

The legislation about the system of allowances for expenditure incurred before 1 April 1986 is in ICTA 1988, s 522 and ICTA 1988, s 523. There is guidance about it in paragraphs (57) to (62) of Appendix No. 2 (matters no longer current).

Conditions for expenditure to qualify for allowances and charges, ICTA 1988, s 520(1) and (2)

5561. Capital expenditure incurred after 31 March 1986 on the purchase of patent rights qualifies for allowances and charges provided that either of the following conditions is satisfied.

(*a*) The allowances are to be made in taxing the trade under ICTA 1988, s 528(1) (CA 5575)

(*b*) Income receivable from the rights is liable to tax.

Both conditions do not need to be satisfied. One is enough. As soon as one of the conditions is satisfied the expenditure will qualify for capital allowances and there is no need to check the other.

Qualifying expenditure, ICTA 1988, s 521(1)

5562. The qualifying expenditure for a chargeable period is the sum of

- the residue of expenditure at the end of the previous chargeable period, and
- capital expenditure incurred on the purchase of patent rights during the current chargeable period, and
- capital expenditure incurred on the purchase of patent rights during a previous chargeable period which has not been included in qualifying expenditure for a previous chargeable period.

For example, suppose that Jackson

- has a pool of qualifying expenditure carried forward at the end of year four of £10,000
- incurs expenditure of £3,000 on the purchase of patent rights in year five; and
- incurred expenditure of £5,000 on the purchase of patent rights in year three which he did not add to his pool of qualifying expenditure for year three or year four.

Then Jackson's pool of qualifying expenditure for year five is £18,000 (= £10,000 + £3,000 + £5,000).

Patent rights acquired from connected person, ICTA 1988, s 521(5) and (6)

5563. There are special rules in ICTA 1988, s 521(5) and (6) which apply where someone buys patent rights and either

- they are connected with the seller, or
- the sale is a sole or main benefit transaction. A sole or main benefit transaction is one, or one of a series, where the sole or main benefit which might be expected to accrue to the parties is the obtaining of a WDA under ICTA 1988, s 520(4).

The rules are a bit like the rules in CAA 1990, s 75 and CAA 1990, s 76 for connected person sales etc. of machinery or plant (CA 2120–CA 2136).

Where the rules apply the buyer's expenditure qualifying for capital allowances is restricted to the following amounts.

(*a*)   If the seller has a disposal value that disposal value.

(*b*)   If the seller has no disposal value but receives a capital sum chargeable under ICTA 1988, s 524 (*see* CA 5580 onwards) that capital sum.

(*c*)   Or, if neither (a) nor (b) applies, the smallest of
- the open market value of the patent rights
- where capital expenditure was incurred by the seller, that capital expenditure
- where capital expenditure was incurred by anyone connected with the seller their capital expenditure.

5564.   . . .

Disposal values deducted from pool of qualifying expenditure, ICTA 1988, s 521(2)

5565.   If a person sells patent rights in a chargeable period and they incurred capital expenditure on the purchase of those patent rights the sale proceeds are known as disposal value. The disposal value is deducted from the pool of qualifying expenditure for that chargeable period.

If the disposal value is more than the qualifying expenditure in the pool the pool becomes nil and there is a balancing charge (CA 5571).

Disposal value restricted to cost, ICTA 1988, s 521(3)

5566.   In general disposal value cannot exceed the original capital expenditure incurred on buying the patent rights. There is one exception to this. It is described at CA 5567.

There may be a series of sales of patent rights. If there is the total of the disposal values brought to account in the capital allowance computation cannot exceed the original capital expenditure incurred.

For example, suppose that Clapton spends £10,000 on buying patent rights and claims capital allowances. He grants a licence to Cale for £6,000. He has to bring a disposal value of £6,000 to account at that point (CA 5565). If he then grants a licence to Knopfler for £6,000 the disposal value which he has to bring to account is £4,000. The original capital expenditure was £10,000 and £6,000 was treated as disposal value when he granted the licence to Cale. This means that any later disposal value is restricted to £4,000 (= £10,000 – £6,000). The remaining £2,000 he received when he granted the licence to Knopfler is assessed Case VI under ICTA 1988, s 524 (CA 5580).

Disposal value where patent rights acquired from connected person, ICTA 1988, s 521(4)

5567.   Where patent rights are acquired in a connected person transaction or a series of connected person transactions the limit on disposal value is the greatest of the capital expenditure incurred by any of the people involved in those transactions.

Example Crosby, Stills and Nash are connected. Crosby buys patent rights for £11,000.

He sells them to Stills for £10,000 who then sells them to Nash for £9,000.

If Nash sells the rights for £12,000 the limit on his disposal value is £11,000, the amount Crosby paid for the rights. It is not £9,000, the amount Nash paid to Stills for the rights.

Writing down allowances—normal rule, ICTA 1988, s 520(4)(a)(i)

5568. The WDA for a chargeable period is calculated like this. The pool for the chargeable period is calculated (CA 5565). The writing down allowance for the chargeable period is 25 per cent of the balance, that is the balance in the pool after the disposal values have been deducted.

Writing down allowance—chargeable period more or less than a year, ICTA 1988, s 520(4)(a)(ii)

5569. If the chargeable period is more or less than a year the 25 per cent writing down allowance is proportionately increased or reduced.

For example, if the chargeable period is six months, the writing down allowance will be 12.5% because 12.5% is 25% × 6/12.

5570. ...

Balancing charge, ICTA 1988, s 520(6)

5571. If the pool of qualifying expenditure for a chargeable period is less than the disposal value brought to account for that chargeable period the difference is a balancing charge.

Balancing allowance, ICTA 1988, s 520(4)(b) and (c)

5572. There are two situations where a balancing allowance can arise.

1. The taxpayer is a trader and the trade is permanently discontinued.

2. In any other case, the last of the relevant patent rights (CA 5573) come to an end without any of them being revived.

In cases within 1 there is a balancing allowance if the qualifying expenditure is more than the disposal value of any rights disposed of during the chargeable period in which trading ceased. The balancing allowance is the difference between the qualifying expenditure and the disposal value. If the qualifying expenditure is more than the disposal value the difference is a balancing charge (CA 5571).

In cases within 2 the balancing allowance is equal to the qualifying expenditure unallowed. The qualifying expenditure unallowed is the balance in the pool.

Relevant patent rights, ICTA 1988, s 520(5)

5573. The relevant patent rights are patent rights whose purchase price has been included in the pool of qualifying expenditure and which have not been wholly disposed of.

Pre-trading expenditure, ICTA 1988, s 520(3)

5574. If someone incurs expenditure on patent rights for the purposes of a trade they are about to carry on they are treated as if they had incurred that expenditure on the first day of trading unless they sell all of the rights before trading begins.

Method of allowance and charge—traders, ICTA 1988, s 528(1)

5575. Allowances or charges are made to or on a person in taxing their trade if

(a)   they are carrying on a trade whose profits are taxable Case I Schedule D, and
(b)   the patent rights, or the rights out of which the patent rights were granted, which give rise to the capital allowances were used or were to be used for the purposes of the trade in the chargeable period for which the allowance or charge is made.

Method of allowance—non-traders, ICTA 1988, s 528(2) and (3)

5576. Allowances are made to non-traders by discharge or repayment. The allowance must be claimed. The allowance due for a year of assessment is treated like this

- The allowance is deducted from or set off against income from patents for the year for which the allowance is due, and
- any excess is carried forward and set against income from patents in future years.

Balancing charges—non-traders, ICTA 1988, s 528(4)

5577. A balancing charge which is not to be made in taxing the trade is

(a)   assessed Case VI Schedule D in Income Tax cases;
(b)   treated as income from patents in Corporation Tax cases.

5578–5579.   . . .

Receipts

Capital sums received from sale of patent rights, ICTA 1988, s 524(1) and (3)

5580. A capital sum which is received by

(a)   a person resident in the UK from the sale of patent rights, or
(b)   a person who is not resident in the UK from the sale of rights in a UK patent

is chargeable to tax under Case VI Schedule D.

If a capital sum is brought to account as a disposal value, the disposal value cannot exceed the capital expenditure incurred (CA 5565–CA 5566). In such a case it is only the part of the capital sum which is not brought to account as a disposal value which is taxable under ICTA 1988, s 524.

In cases within (a) the patent rights need not be rights in a UK patent. For example, if a person resident in the UK receives a capital sum from the sale of US patent rights they are chargeable on that sum under Case VI Schedule D.

Taxation of capital sum received by UK resident—spread over 6 Years, ICTA 1988, s 524(1)

5581.   A UK resident who receives a capital sum from the sale of patent rights is assessed Case VI Schedule D on one-sixth of the amount received for each of the six chargeable periods which begin with the chargeable period in which the capital sum was received.

If the capital sum is received in instalments, then any instalments received after the first chargeable period are spread over the remainder of the six year period which begins with the chargeable period in which the first payment was received. They are not spread over the six year period which begins with the chargeable period in which they were received.

Example   Jackson is resident in the UK. In 1996–97 he agrees to sell patent rights for £8,000. Under the agreement he receives £6,000 in 1996–97 and £2,000 in 1998–99. He is assessable on £1,000 (= £6,000 ÷ 6) for 1996–97 to 2000–02 and a further £500 (= £2,000 ÷ 4) for 1998–99 to 2001–02.

Taxation as single amount, ICTA 1988, s 524(2)

The taxpayer can choose to have the whole of the capital sum taxed in the chargeable period in which it was received. They do that by giving notice in writing to their Inspector within two years of the end of the chargeable period in which the sum was received.

In the example above Jackson can elect to have the whole of the £6,000 he receives in 1996–97 taxed in 1996–97. The election must be made by the end of 1998–99.

He can also elect by the end of 2000–01 to have the £2,000 he receives in 1998–99 taxed in that year.

5582–5584.   . . .

Taxation of capital sum received by non-resident, ICTA 1988, s 524(3)

5585.   When rights in a UK patent are sold by someone who is not resident in the UK for a capital sum they are assessable under Case VI Schedule D. The buyer should deduct tax when they make the payment and that tax should be collected by making an assessment on the buyer under ICTA 1988, s 349 (but *see* CA 5587).

ICTA 1988, s 387(3)(*d*) stops the buyer treating the ICTA 1988, s 349 assessment as a loss under ICTA 1988, s 387(1).

ICTA 1988, s 524(3) does not apply in some cases where the seller is a non-resident company (*see* CA 5588).

Spreading capital sum received by non-resident, ICTA 1988, s 524(4)

5586.   A non-resident who receives a capital sum from the sale of rights in a UK patent can elect to have the taxation of the payment calculated as if the capital sum were spread over six years beginning with the year in which the capital sum is paid. A non-resident company cannot make an election under ICTA 1988, s 524(3) if it would be chargeable to Corporation Tax on the capital sum. There is guidance about companies at CA 5589.

The election is to be made to the Board by notice in writing within two years of the end of the chargeable period in which the sum is paid. If you receive an election you should refer it to FICO (International). You should also refer any repayment claim in respect of the cost of the rights sold to them.

The spreading election made by the seller has no effect on the amount of tax to be deducted by the buyer. That tax should be collected by making a ICTA 1988, s 349 assessment on the buyer in the way described in CA 5587.

5587.   . . .

Capital sums received by non-resident company, ICTA 1988, s 524(5)

5588.   Where the seller is a company ICTA 1988, s 524(3) (CA 5585) does not apply unless the company would be liable to Corporation Tax on any sale proceeds which were not a capital sum.

Spreading capital sum received by non-resident company, ICTA 1988, s 524(6)

5589.   ICTA 1988, s 524(6) prevents ICTA 1988, s 524(4) (CA 5586) applying where the seller is a non-resident company liable to Corporation Tax on the capital sum it receives from the sale of the patent rights. In such a case the company can make an election like a ICTA 1988, s 524(4) election to have the capital sum taxed over accounting periods which end not later than six years from the beginning of the accounting period in which the capital sum is paid. The election must be made by notice in writing to the Board within two years of the end of the accounting period in which the sum is paid.

Capital sum—deductions from amount chargeable, ICTA 1988, s 524(7) and (8)

5590.   When a capital sum or capital sums are received from the sale of patent rights you should deduct any capital sums paid by the seller when they bought the patent rights.

Example Warren is UK resident. He buys patent rights in 1996 for a capital sum of £5,000. He sells the rights for the following capital sums

part of the rights for £1,000 in 1997;
part in 1998 for £5,500; and
the rest in 1999 for £2,000.

There is no charge under ICTA 1988, s 524 on the first sale because the amount he gets is less than the amount he paid for the rights.

£1,500 (= £1,000 ı £5,500 – £5,000) of the capital sum received in 1998 is taxable under ICTA 1988, s 524(1).

All of the £2,000 he receives in 1999 is taxable under ICTA 1988, s 524(1).

5591–5595. . . .

Death of an individual, ICTA 1988, s 525(1)

5596.   An individual who receives a capital sum which is chargeable over six years under ICTA 1988, s 524 may die before the six years end. In that case no charges under ICTA 1988, s 524 are made for years after the year of death. Amounts which would have been chargeable in years after the year of death are added to the amount chargeable for the year of death.

Company winding up or partnership discontinuance, ICTA 1988, s 525(1) and ICTA 1988, s 525(3)

Similar rules apply where a company is wound up or the trade carried on by a partnership is discontinued.

Example Janis receives a capital sum of £12,000 in *June 1995* which is chargeable under ICTA 1988, s 524. She is chargeable on £2,000 for each of 1995–96 to 2000–01. She dies in January 1998. This means that the last year for which a charge can be made under ICTA 1988, s 524 is 1997–98. The amount chargeable in 1997–98 is £8,000 (= £2,000 for 1997–98 plus £2,000 for each of 1998–99, 1999–2000 and 2000–01).

Death of an individual—notice by personal representatives, ICTA 1988, s 525(2)

5597.   Where an individual dies the personal representatives may give the Inspector notice requiring that the tax payable because of the increased amount charged for the year of death be reduced to the amount which would have been payable if the whole capital sum had been charged in equal amounts over the period beginning with the year in which it was received and ending with the year of death.

The time limit for the giving of notice by the personal representatives is not later than 30 days after notice is served on them of the tax payable under ICTA 1988, s 525(1).

Example In the example in CA 5596 Janis's personal representatives can serve notice on the Inspector requiring the tax payable to be reduced to the amount which would have been payable if the £12,000 had been spread over the years 1995–96 (the year in which the lump sum was received) to 1997–98 (the year of death).

Partnership discontinuance, ICTA 1988, s 525(4)

5598.   Where a trade carried on by a partnership is discontinued and there is an additional amount chargeable under ICTA 1988, s 525(1) (*see* CA 5596) for the year of discontinuance that additional amount is to be apportioned between the partners immediately before the discontinuance. A separate charge is made on each partner. Each partner, or the personal representatives of a partner who has died, can give notice requiring the tax to be reduced just as the personal representatives of an individual who has died can (CA 5577).

5599.   . . .

Expenses

Grant or maintenance of patent or extension of term—trader, ICTA 1988, s 83(a)

5600.   Fees and expenses incurred in obtaining the grant or the extension of the term of a patent for the purposes of a trade are admissible as a deduction in computing the profits of the trade.

Unsuccessful application for patent, ICTA 1988, s 83(b)

Fees and expenses incurred in connection with unsuccessful applications for patents for the purposes of a trade are also allowable.

Renewal of patent

5601.   Fees incurred for the renewal of a patent for the purposes of a trade are allowable. Agents' charges in connection with the renewal of a patent are allowable if the renewal fees are.

Grant or maintenance of patent or extension of term—non-trader, ICTA 1988, s 526(1)

5602.   Where

(*a*)   a non-trader pays any fees or incurs any expenses in connection with the grant or maintenance of a patent and

(*b*)   if those fees or expenses had been paid or incurred for the purposes of a trade they would have been allowable in calculating the profits of the trade (*see* CA 5600)

the non-trader is given an allowance equal to the expenditure incurred.
   The allowance is made for the chargeable period in which the fees or expenses are paid or incurred. It is made by discharge or repayment.

Expenses of devising a patented invention, ICTA 1988, s 526(2)

5603.   Expenses which

(*a*)   are not allowable under any other provision of the Taxes Acts and (*b*)   are incurred by an individual in devising, whether alone or in partnership, an invention for which a patent is granted

qualify for an allowance (*see* CA 5604).
   If no patent is granted there is no allowance due.

How allowance under ICTA 1988, s 526(2) is made

5604.   The allowance is made for the year of assessment in which the expenses are incurred. The allowance is to be made

1.   to a trader as a deduction in charging the profits of the trade where the patent rights were, or were to be, used for the purposes of the trade in the basis period for a year of assessment
2.   in any other case by discharge or repayment against income from patents.

The allowance due may be more than the income for the year. If it is any excess allowances are carried forward and set against trading profits (cases within 1) or patent income (cases within 2) in future years.

Claims before Royal Commission

5605.   An inventor may prosecute a claim before the Royal Commission on Awards to Inventors in respect of Crown user of a patent. If they do that, this is how you should give relief for reasonable expenses incurred in prosecuting the claim.
   If the inventor is a trader and any award granted will be treated as trading income you should treat the expense of the claim before the Royal Commission as a trading expense. This applies where the inventor is using the patent rights for the purposes of their trade and where the inventor is carrying on a trade of dealing in patents. A person who carries on a trade of dealing in patents will create inventions which they patent or acquire patents and then exploit those patents by sale or licence.
   If there is a lump sum award which is a capital sum taxable under ICTA 1988, s 524 (see CA 5580 onwards) you should allow the expense as a deduction in calculating the net proceeds of sale under ICTA 1988, s 524.
   If an award is made to a non-trader for past or limited future user of a patent and tax is deductible under ICTA 1988, s 349 treat the expense as an expense incurred in the maintenance of the patent. You should allow relief under ICTA 1988, s 526(1) (CA 5602). If the award in respect of which the expenses are incurred is not taxable no relief is due for them.
   There is guidance about lump sum awards for Crown user of a patent at IM 3678.

5606–5609.   . . .

Spreading royalties etc.

Royalties—spread back relief, ICTA 1988, s 527(1) and (2)

5610.   A person may receive a royalty or other sum for the user of a patent which lasts for two years or more. If they do they may make a claim for spread back relief to have the tax due on the amount they receive calculated this way.

You assume that the royalty etc. had been received in equal amounts over the number of complete years it covers with the last payment being received on the date that the royalty was paid.

Royalties are normally paid under deduction of tax under ICTA 1988, s 349. There is guidance at RE 2010 about giving spread back relief for patent royalties received under deduction of tax.

The time limit for making the claim is within six years of the end of the year of assessment in which the payment was received.

Example On *31 December 1997* Dylan receives a payment of £3,600 for the user of a patent for the period *1 January 1995 to 31 December 1997*. If he makes a claim for spread back relief the tax due is calculated as if he had received a payment of £1,200 on each of *31 December 1995, 31 December 1996 and 31 December 1997*. The payment was received on *31 December 1997*, which is in *1997–98*. If Dylan wants to claim spread back relief he must claim it by *5 April 2004*.

Royalties—spread back relief: payments excluded, ICTA 1988, s 527(4)

5611.   Spread back relief (CA 5610) is not available where a non-resident sells UK patent rights for a capital sum and ICTA 1988, s 524(3)(b) requires the payment to be made under deduction of tax (CA 5585).

Payments for Crown user of patents

5612.   You may receive details from a Government Department of a lump sum payment they have made to your taxpayer for user of a patent. This is how you should treat lump sum awards for Crown user of patents.

Payments for past user Treat the payment as an aggregated royalty. The paying department will normally deduct tax under ICTA 1988, s 349. If they do not you should make an assessment to collect the tax due. The taxpayer can claim to have the spread back provisions of ICTA 1988, s 527 (CA 5610) applied.

Payments for future user A payment for future user of a patent may be for limited or unlimited user. There is guidance about the meaning of limited and unlimited user of a patent at IM 3922.

If the payment is for limited user it should be dealt with like a payment for past user except that the spread back provisions of ICTA 1988, s 527 are not available.

If the payment is for unlimited user and is a capital payment it is taxable under ICTA 1988, s 524 (CA 5580 onwards).

Payment which covers both past user and future unlimited user In these cases the Department concerned will normally fix the proportion of the payment applicable to past user and deduct tax from it. You should follow the guidance above about payments for past user when you deal with that part.

You should follow the guidance above about payments for future user when you deal with the balance.

There is guidance about expenses incurred in making a claim before the Royal Commission on Awards to Inventors at CA 5605.

5613–5999.   . . .

Capital Allowances Manual

Part XIII—Know-how

General

Outline—capital allowances

6001.   Capital expenditure incurred on the acquisition of know-how for use in a trade carried on, or which is used in a trade set up and commenced thereafter, by the person incurring the expenditure qualifies for writing down allowances (WDAs). The legislation is in Sections 530 to 533 ICTA 1988. It applies to expenditure incurred after *31 March 1986*.

For expenditure incurred before *1 April 1986* there is guidance in paragraphs (55) and (56) of Appendix No. 2 (matters no longer current).

The system of WDAs for know-how is similar to the system of WDAs for machinery or plant. WDAs are based on a pool of qualifying expenditure.

It is possible for balancing allowances and balancing charges to arise as it is with allowances for expenditure on machinery or plant.

There is a balancing charge if the disposal value brought to account is more than the expenditure in the pool. There is one difference from the machinery or plant system. In the know-how system disposal value is not restricted to original cost.

A balancing allowance can only arise on the permanent discontinuance of the trade. It is the amount by which the pool of qualifying expenditure is greater than the disposal value to be brought to account.

The guidance about capital allowances for expenditure on know-how is at CA 6040–6048.

6002–6004.   . . .

Definition of know-how, s 533(7) ICTA 1988

6005.   Know-how is defined in Section 533(7) ICTA 1988. Know-how is industrial information and techniques likely to assist in

- the manufacture or processing of goods or materials, or
- the working of a mine, oil-well or other source of mineral deposits, or
- the carrying out of any agricultural, forestry or fishing operations.

The expression 'industrial information and techniques' is coloured by the words which follow—'likely to assist in the manufacture or processing of goods and materials'. This means that only information relevant to industrial or technical processes is within the definition of know-how.

Commercial know-how

6006.   Commercial know-how includes things like market research, customer lists and sales techniques. It does not assist directly in manufacturing or processing operations. Rather, it is concerned with selling goods or materials once they have been manufactured.

Commercial know-how is not likely to assist in the manufacture of goods or materials or in the working of a mine or in agricultural operations. This means that it is not within the definition of know-how in Section 533(7) ICTA 1988 and so it does not qualify for capital allowances under Section 530.

Know-how acquired by holding company

6007. Where know-how is acquired by a holding company for use in trades carried on by its subsidiary companies, the holding company may qualify for relief as the know-how is also used in its trade of providing management services. The definition in Section 533(7) ICTA 1988 must be satisfied. As in other cases, commercial know-how would not qualify.

Franchise agreement

6008. Sometimes a person who pays for a franchise agreement claims that they have made a payment for know-how and that capital allowances are due. This is unlikely to be the case.

A franchise agreement is essentially a licence to operate a business. Any know-how which is transferred by the franchise agreement is more likely to be commercial know-how than industrial information and techniques. If so it will not qualify for capital allowances.

6009. . . .

Payments

Payments for know-how—normally revenue

6010. Payments made to acquire know-how wholly and exclusively for the purposes of a trade are normally revenue payments and are allowable deductions in computing trading profits under the normal rules of Schedule D. This applies whether the payments are lump sum or recurring.

In other cases payments for know-how may be capital.

A capital payment for know-how will sometimes

- qualify for capital allowances because it is expenditure on the acquisition of know-how (*see* CA 6040 onwards), or
- be treated as a payment for goodwill under Section 531(2) ICTA 1988 (*see* CA 6025). If it is treated as a payment for goodwill no capital allowances are due.

6011–6014. . . .

Receipts

Revenue receipts

6015. Lump sum payments and royalties received in consideration for imparting or disclosing know-how accumulated in the course of a trade are normally trading receipts.

Tax cases‚which support this view are British Dyestuffs Corporation (Blackley) Ltd *v* C.I.R. 12TC586, Jeffrey *v* Rolls Royce Ltd 40TC443, Musker *v* English Electric Co. Ltd 41TC556 and Coalite & Chemical Products Ltd *v* Treeby 48TC171.

The sort of know-how likely to be accumulated in the course of a trade is things like manufacturing techniques, technical knowledge or secret processes.

How to decide whether receipts are capital or revenue

6016.   If you have to decide whether know-how receipts are capital or revenue you should find the case of Jeffrey *v* Rolls Royce Ltd, 1962, 40TC443 useful. In that case the company made agreements with several overseas companies for the sale of know-how relating to aero-engine manufacture. Lump sums received under those agreements were held to be revenue. The House of Lords thought that the repetitive exploitation of know-how was simply an extension of the existing trade carried on by Rolls Royce giving rise to revenue receipts.

Consideration in shares

6017.   A company which acquires know-how may pay for it by issuing shares in itself. A payment for know-how which is in shares may still be treated as a trading receipt (Thomsons (Carron) Ltd *v* C.I.R. 51TC506).

Capital receipts

6018.   A receipt for know-how is capital in the following two cases

(*a*)   know-how is disposed of as one element of a comprehensive arrangement under which a trader effectively gives up an established business in a particular territory (Evans Medical Supplies Ltd *v* Moriarty, 37TC540; Wolf Electric Tools Ltd *v* Wilson, 45TC326);

(*b*)   the receipt is wholly or partly attributable to a covenant against competition (a 'keep-out' covenant) and that covenant is ancillary to the grant of a licence under a patent which is a fixed capital asset of the grantor (Murray *v* Imperial Chemical Industries Ltd, 44TC175).

In cases in (b) above

- there may be Case VI liability under Section 524 ICTA 1988 (*see* CA 5560 onwards)
- the payment may be treated as a know-how receipt within Section 531 ICTA 1988 (*see* CA 6019).

Receipts—continuing trade, s 531(1) ICTA 1988

6019.   If know-how is disposed of in the course of a continuing trade the receipt is normally a trading receipt (*see* CA 6015).

Section 531(1) ICTA 1988 deals with cases where the normal rules for Schedule D do not treat a receipt for know-how as a trading receipt. It does this by treating a receipt for know-how which is not a disposal value under Section 530(5) ICTA 1988 or already chargeable as a revenue receipt as a trading receipt.

The effect of Section 531(1) is that consideration received for the disposal of know-how in a continuing trade is either

(*a*)   treated as a revenue receipt under general law or
(*b*)   brought to account as a disposal value in the capital allowance computation or
(*c*)   if neither (*a*) nor (*b*) applies treated as a trading receipt.

Case VI liability, s 531(4) ICTA 1988

6020.   Section 531(4) ICTA 1988 treats a receipt from a disposal of know-how which is
(*a*)   received *after 31 March 1986* and is not brought to account as a disposal value, and
(*b*)   not chargeable to tax as an income or revenue receipt under general law, nor
(*c*)   treated as a trade receipt under Section 531(1), nor
(*d*)   dealt with as a payment for goodwill under Section 531(2) ICTA 1988

as a profit or gain chargeable under Case VI of Schedule D.

Section 531(4) covers cases like the case where know-how built up by the trading members of a group of companies is exploited by a non-trading holding company.

Case VI liability—deductions, s 531(5) ICTA 1988

6021.   Where the disposal of know-how gives rise to a Case VI charge (*see* CA 6020) on a person any expenditure incurred by that person wholly and exclusively in the acquisition or disposal of the know-how should be deducted in arriving at the amount chargeable Case VI. This does not apply if a deduction can be made for the expenditure under some other provision.

Earned income treatment, s 531(6) ICTA 1988

6022.   Where the taxpayer is an individual who devised the know-how, whether alone or jointly with any other person, the amount of the Case VI assessment should be treated as earned income.

6023–6024. . . .

Miscellaneous

Goodwill treatment, s 531(2) ICTA 1988

6025.   Where know-how is disposed of along with a trade or part of a trade and both parties are in the UK tax net the transaction is treated as a sale and purchase of goodwill (but *see* CA 6026).

The buyer is treated as if they had paid a capital sum for goodwill. This means that the amount they pay will not qualify for WDAs under Section 530 ICTA 1988.

The seller is treated as if they had sold goodwill for a capital sum. This means that they do not have to bring a disposal value to account in the capital allowance computation. Since the sale is treated as a sale of goodwill there may be a capital gain.

When goodwill treatment does not apply, s 531(2) ICTA 1988

6026. The goodwill treatment in CA 6025 does not apply in two cases

(*a*)　to either the buyer or the seller where the buyer and seller jointly elect that it should not apply

(*b*)　to the buyer where the trade was carried on wholly outside the United Kingdom before the acquisition of the know-how.

The election in (*a*) has to be made within two years of the disposal.

Section 531(3) ICTA 1988 does not apply if the sale is a control sale (*see* CA 6032).

Where an election under Section 531(3)(*a*) is made the transaction is not treated as a purchase and sale of goodwill. This means that

(*a*)　the buyer will be entitled to writing down allowances under Section 530 ICTA 1988 if their expenditure on know-how is not otherwise deductible for Income Tax or Corporation Tax purposes, and

(*b*)　the seller should be treated as receiving a trade receipt or, where appropriate (for example, if the whole of the trade has been disposed of), as receiving a profit or gain chargeable under Case VI of Schedule D (*see* CA 6020).

In cases within Section 531(2)(*b*) the payment made by the person acquiring the know-how will normally qualify for writing down allowances under Section 530 ICTA 1988 as expenditure on the acquisition of know-how which is not otherwise deductible for Income Tax or Corporation Tax purposes.

If it is claimed by a seller that Section 531(2) applies to a disposal but

(*a*)　it is not clear that a trade or part of a trade (for example, a branch) has been disposed of, or

(*b*)　there is reason to believe that the buyer may not agree, you should consult BPD (Capital Allowances).

6027–6029. . . .

Keep-out covenants, s 531(8) ICTA 1988

6030. Know-how agreements often contain clauses (commonly described as keep-out covenants) which protect the buyer of the know-how against competition from the seller or from other licensees. The legislation in Section 531(8) ICTA 1988 deals with keep-out covenants.

Where an undertaking which restricts a person's activities is given in connection with a disposal of know-how any consideration received in respect of that undertaking is treated for the purposes of Section 531 ICTA 1988 as consideration received for the disposal of know-how.

The undertaking may be absolute or qualified and may or may not be legally valid. The person whose activities are restricted need not be the person selling the know-how.

Section 531(8) applies to receipts but not to payments. You should deal with any payment made in consideration for a keep-out covenant under the normal Schedule D rules. It will normally be capital expenditure (*see Associated Portland Cement Manufacturers Ltd v CIR*, 1945, 27 TC 103).

Section 531(8) means that any consideration received for a keep-out covenant which is not a revenue receipt under the normal rules of Schedule D or treated as a payment for goodwill under Section 531(2) (CA 6026) will be taxed as a know-how receipt. It will either be treated as a trading receipt under Section 531(1) (CA 6019) or assessed Case VI under Section 531(4) (CA 6020).

A consideration for a keep-out covenant received in connection with a disposal of know-how will be treated as a payment for goodwill where Section 531(2) treats the payment for the know-how as a payment for goodwill.

6031. ...

Control sales, s 531(7) ICTA 1988

6032. Control sales are described at CA 353.

Most of the provisions of Sections 530 and 531 ICTA 1988 do not apply to control sales. The provisions which do apply are

Section 530(2)–(5), (7) and (8)—capital allowances (*see* CA 6040 onwards)

Section 531(2)—goodwill treatment (*see* CA 6025)

Section 531(8)—keep-out covenants (*see* CA 6032)

Section 531(2) ICTA 1988 (*see* CA 6025—goodwill treatment) applies to control sales but Section 531(3) (*see* CA 6026—election to avoid goodwill treatment) does not.

This means that if know-how is sold together with a trade or part of a trade and the sale is a control sale the buyer and seller cannot elect to avoid goodwill treatment.

It also means that in a control sale the buyer cannot avoid goodwill treatment where the trade was carried on outside the UK before the sale.

6033. ...

Divers—courses whose cost qualifies as expenditure on know-how

6034. An agreement was made with the Association of Offshore Diving contractors in January 1983.

Under that agreement the cost of the following courses qualifies for allowances as expenditure on know-how

1. costs of training a diver to the Part I standard of schedule 4 of SI.399—1981, that is basic air diver

2. the costs of training a diver to the Part II standard of schedule 4 of SI.399—1981, that is a mixed gas or bell diver

3.   cost of training a diver by a module from the Part IV to the Part I standard or from the Part III to the Part I standard, of schedule 4 of SI.399—1981 Training costs specifically relating to Part II or Part IV standards only will not qualify

4.   The costs of training a diver through specialised courses using, for instance, NDT techniques for the CSWIP Phase 7 qualification would apply, so long as the trainee diver is already qualified to the Part I or Part II standard of schedule 4 of SI.399—1981 and so long as the diver is carrying on a trade and uses the 'know-how' acquired in the oil/mineral context

The agreement means that the cost of the technical courses listed in the preceding paragraph which a diver undertakes in connection with North Sea oil or gas exploration is treated as expenditure on know-how and qualifies for capital allowances.

Where Section 314 ICTA 1988 treats the diver's activities as a trade the condition in Section 530(1) that the know-how is acquired for use in a trade will be satisfied.

6035–6037. . . .

Application of CAA 1990, s 532(1) ICTA 1988

6038.   Section 532(1) ICTA 1988 says that the know-how legislation in Sections 530 and 531 ICTA 1988 is to be construed as if it were contained in CAA1990.

s 532(5) ICTA 1988

References in CAA1990 to property, its purchase or sale include references to know-how and its acquisition or disposal. This means that the legislation in Section 160 CAA1990 about combined sales (*see* CA 300 onwards) applies to sales of know-how.

The legislation in Sections 157 and 158 CAA1990 about control sales etc. does not apply to sales of know-how. The know-how legislation has its own rules about control sales (*see* CA 6032).

6039. . . .

Capital allowances

6040.   Allowances and charges for a chargeable period are based on the qualifying expenditure for that period. The qualifying expenditure for a chargeable period is often referred to as the pool.

Allowances and charges—expenditure which qualifies, s 530(1) ICTA 1988

6041.   Expenditure incurred by a person on the acquisition of know-how for use in a trade they carry on or for use in a trade which they set up and commence qualifies for allowances and charges if

1.   it is not already deductible for Income Tax or Corporation Tax purposes, and

2.   it is not dealt with as a payment for goodwill (*see* CA 6025).

For example, expenditure which is deductible as a trading expense is in 1. This means that it does not qualify for WDAs as expenditure on the acquisition of know-how because it is already deductible for Income Tax or Corporation Tax purposes.

Definition of pool of qualifying expenditure, s 530(4) ICTA 1988

6042.   The pool of qualifying expenditure for a chargeable period is the aggregate of

(*a*)   capital expenditure incurred on the acquisition of know-how in that chargeable period

(*b*)   capital expenditure on know-how incurred in a previous chargeable period which has not already been included in the pool for an earlier chargeable period

(*c*)   the balance in the pool at the end of the previous chargeable period.

For example, suppose that Dylan is assessable Case I Schedule D and that he

- has a pool of qualifying expenditure carried forward at the end of year 4 of £100,000
- incurred expenditure on the acquisition of know-how of £40,000 in year 3 which was not already deductible for income tax purposes nor added to his pool for year three or year four and
- incurs expenditure of £30,000 on know-how in year five

Then Dylan's pool of qualifying expenditure for year five is £170,000 (= £100,000 + £40,000 + £30,000).

Disposal values deducted from pool, s 530(5) ICTA 1988

6043.   If a person sells know-how in a chargeable period and they acquired that know-how *after 31 March 1986* the sale proceeds are known as disposal value. They are deducted from the pool of qualifying expenditure for that chargeable period.

—*No restriction to cost* In the machinery or plant system of allowances sale proceeds are normally restricted to cost. There is nothing like that legislation in the know-how system. The whole of the net sale proceeds is disposal value even if it is more than cost.

—*Know-how acquired before 1 April 1986* Where the know-how was acquired *before 1 April 1986* the sale proceeds are not treated as disposal value. The guidance at 6015 onwards tells you how to deal with them.

Writing down allowances—normal rule, s 530(2)(a)(i) ICTA 1988

6044.   The WDA for a chargeable period is calculated like this. The pool for the chargeable period is calculated (CA 6042). Disposal values for the chargeable period are deducted from the pool. The writing down allowance for the chargeable period is 25 per cent of the balance, that is of the pool less the disposal values.

Writing down allowances—chargeable period more or less than a year, s 530(2)(a)(ii) ICTA 1988

6045.   If the chargeable period is more or less than a year the 25 per cent writing down allowance is proportionately increased or reduced.

For example, if the chargeable period is six months the writing down allowance will be 12.5 per cent because 12.5 per cent is $25\% \times 6/12$.

Balancing charge, s 530(3)

6046.   If the pool of qualifying expenditure for a chargeable period is less than the disposal value brought to account for that chargeable period the difference is a balancing charge.

Balancing allowance, s 530(2)(b) ICTA 1988

6047.   A balancing allowance can only arise if the trade is permanently discontinued. When the trade is permanently discontinued the qualifying expenditure is compared with the disposal values to be brought to account.

If the qualifying expenditure is more than the disposal values the difference is a balancing allowance.

If the qualifying expenditure is less than the disposal values the difference is a balancing charge (CA 6045).

Pre-trading expenditure, s 530(7)

6048.   Expenditure on know-how incurred before the trade in which it is to be used is set up and commenced is treated as incurred on the day that the trade begins.

Double Taxation Manual

Royalties

216   As with interest Articles, royalties Articles provide that either

(a)   royalties are only taxable in the country of residence of the beneficial owner (in some agreements it is a condition that the recipient of the interest must be subject to tax in his own country on the interest), or

(b)   royalties arising to a resident of one country may be taxed by that country. They may also be taxed by the country in which they arise but at a rate not exceeding a specified percentage if the recipient is the beneficial owner of the royalties (in some agreements it is a condition that the recipient of the interest must be subject to tax in his own country on the interest).

See DT 802 for a note on the meaning of 'subject to tax'.

The definition of royalties for the purposes of the Article is very wide. It includes payment of any kind for the use of, or the right to use, any copyright of literary, artistic or scientific work, any patent, trademark, plan, secret formula or process, design or models, or for information concerning industrial commercial or scientific experience. The last phrase includes payments for 'know-how'. Some agreements specifically include payments for the use of, or the right to use, cinematograph films and films or tapes for radio or television broadcasting. Payments for the use of, or the right to use, industrial, commercial, or scientific equipment are also included in the definition in many agreements; where they are not included such payments fall within the terms of the business profits Article and will not be taxable in the source country unless they form part of the income of a permanent establishment there.

In a few agreements the definition of royalties is extended to cover technical and management fees, but where the taxation of such fees is specifically dealt with in a double taxation agreement, it is normally the subject of a separate Article (see DT 217).

Royalties Articles contain provisions similar to those in the dividend and interest Articles relating to

(a) the deeming of royalties to arise in the country of which the payer is a resident with special rules for permanent establishments, and
(b) royalties 'effectively connected' with a permanent establishment or fixed base which the recipient has in the other country, and
(c) royalties paid where there is a special relationship between the payer and the recipient.

DT 214 discusses the concept of 'effectively connected' income. In the context of royalties it should be noted that a royalty may be 'effectively connected' with a permanent establishment if the intellectual property right from which it is derived was acquired out of the funds of the branch. A royalty may also be 'effectively connected' if the branch played an active part in the creation and/or exploitation of the intellectual property right, notwithstanding that the right may not be regarded as an asset of the branch.

Claims to exemption from, or to a reduced rate of, United Kingdom tax by residents of the other country are made to FICO (International), Nottingham who may authorise the payer not to deduct tax or to deduct tax at the rate specified in the article (see DT 1820). ICTA 1988, s 349 (patent royalties) and ICTA 1988, s 536 (copyright royalties paid to non-residents) are the only provisions in United Kingdom domestic law which provide for deduction of United Kingdom tax at source from payments which are included in the definition of royalties.

Inspectors' Manual

Computer software

Deductions: Computer software

663a. Following the enactment of CAA 1990, s 67A, capital allowances became available for capital expenditure on 'a right to use or otherwise deal with' computer software for the purposes of the trade. *See* IM 663b below for guidance on computer software expenditure before 10 March 1992, and IM 663c/IM 663d for expenditure after that date.

The main changes of emphasis after 10 March 1992 are that

- for expenditure on computer software licences after 10 March 1992—on which capital allowances will be available—you should give more critical consideration to whether lump sums paid out for the licences are revenue expenditure
- where a single payment is made to purchase computer hardware plus a licence to use the accompanying software we now take the view that the expenditure should be apportioned except where that exercise will not have significant tax consequences.

In some cases the treatment of expenditure on software will have been agreed under the practice set out in IM 663b (previously in Technical Notes CA 1.4). For agreements in relation to expenditure before 10 March 1992 you may continue to allow deductions in the accounts that arise in consequence. But for expenditure incurred after 10 March 1992, *see* the guidance in IM 663c and the following paragraphs.

In-house software development costs

For in-house computer software expenditure, *see* IM 663e–IM 663m. The guidance in IM 663e–IM 663m should normally be applied to expenditure incurred after 31 December 1996. It may also be convenient to agree the treatment of earlier expenditure by reference to the guidance. But where its application would lead to treatment of software development expenditure which is inconsistent with a previously agreed approach, Inspectors need not insist on applying it to expenditure incurred in 1996 or earlier. Nor need the guidance be applied to post-1996 expenditure in relation to a project the treatment of which was agreed in 1996 or earlier.

Deductions: computer software acquired before 10 March 1992

663b.   Expenditure on computer software incurred **before 10 March 1992** should normally be dealt with as set out in the paragraphs below. If in any particular case you do not consider that this provides a reasonable result, guidance should be sought from Business Profits Division 4 (Schedule D) if the expenditure is claimed as a revenue deduction, or Company Tax Division (Capital Allowances) if capital allowances are claimed.

Software acquired with associated hardware

When software is acquired along with the associated hardware (and the expenditure on acquisition of the system is capital expenditure) you should normally accept that the system as a whole qualifies for capital allowances as plant.

Software acquired separately, revenue expenditure

But when software is acquired separately, you should consider whether the expenditure is revenue or capital. If the expected life of the software is sufficiently short for the expenditure to be regarded as revenue, the timing of the deduction for tax purposes will normally follow correct accounting principles. Whether or not the cost of software can be regarded as revenue expenditure will depend on the circumstances of individual cases, but an expected life of two years or less may be taken as a broad guideline for treating the expenditure as revenue.

Capital expenditure

If the expenditure is capital, it will usually be regarded as qualifying for capital allowances as plant, provided that the software is sufficiently durable to satisfy the 'permanent employment in the trade' test to be regarded as plant. Alternatively, if the expenditure has been amortised in the accounts over a period related to the expected life of the software, this treatment should normally be followed for tax purposes.

Payments for licence to use software

Regular payments for a licence to use software will normally be revenue expenditure, allowable as they are incurred. A lump sum payment for a licence will not, however, necessarily be capital. You should consider the terms of the agreement and the expected life of the software. Because the software will not belong to the licensee, capital allowances are not available for this type of expenditure.

Deductions: computer software expenditure after 10 March 1992

663c. Computer software expenditure after 10 March 1992 should be dealt with along the lines of the article in Tax Bulletin (November 1993), which is reproduced below for convenience:

Text of Tax Bulletin article

SOFTWARE ACQUIRED UNDER LICENCE
This is the way that nearly all off-the-shelf software is acquired nowadays. The treatment of expenditure of this nature depends on the form the consideration for the licence takes.
Regular payments akin to a rental
Payments of this kind are revenue. The timing of deductions will be governed by correct accounting practice which normally requires the rentals to be spread over the useful life of the software in accordance with the fundamental accruals concept in Statement of Standard Accounting Practice No 2. (What is correct accounting practice is ultimately a question of law but the courts are heavily influenced by current generally acceptable practice.)

Lump sum

The first question to be asked here is whether the licence is a capital asset in the trade of the licensee. In broad terms a licence is a capital asset if it has a sufficiently enduring nature. This approach has to be applied by reference to the function of the licensed software **in the context of the licensee's trade**. Very often the expectation will be that the software will function as a tool of the trade for a period of several years. On the other hand, the benefit to be obtained by the licensee in question may be sufficiently transitory to stamp the payment as revenue even though the licence granted is for an indefinite period.

No simple rule of thumb covering every business situation can be successfully devised but, in any event, where software is expected to have a useful economic life of less than two years Inspectors will accept that the expenditure is revenue. In these circumstances the timing of the deduction will depend on the correct accounting treatment in the same way as it does for regular payments.

Where the licensed software functions as a capital asset of the licensee's trade capital allowances on plant and machinery will be due under CAA 1990, s 67A. This will be the case whether or not the software comes in a corporeal medium (such as on 'floppy discs') separate from the licensee's computer hardware. A short life asset election may be made where appropriate. Computer software is not defined for capital allowances purposes and therefore has its normal meaning which is wide and covers both programs and data (for example books stored in digital form).

Equipment acquired as a package

Often computer hardware and the licence to use software are purchased as a package for a single payment. In these circumstances the expenditure between hardware and software should be apportioned. Capital allowances under the ordinary plant and machinery rules will be due on the expenditure attributable to the hardware. The treatment of the balance of the expenditure, attributable to the software licence, will depend on the considerations described above. Where, however, both the hardware and software are acquired on capital account and the expenditure all goes into the general machinery and plant 'pool', apportionment will not in practice be necessary.

SOFTWARE OWNED OUTRIGHT

Most widely marketed software is licensed to users and not sold to them outright. But some, particularly larger, concerns may develop their own software. The treatment of expenditure on software acquired outright follows the same principles as those governing the treatment of licensed software. In particular, where the expenditure concerned (including salaries of in-house computer professionals) is capital or revenue again depends on the economic function of the software in the trade in question as it does for licences acquired for lump sums.

Computer software: regular payments for licences

663d.   Unless it can be shown that periodical payments are instalments of a capital sum (*see below* for what constitutes capital expenditure in this context) such payments are deductible. The timing of relief will follow generally acceptable accounting practice whereby expenditure is charged against profits in accordance with the accruals concept in Statement of Standard Accounting Practice 2 over the shorter of the useful life of the asset or the term of the licence. The central role of accountancy in timing matters was re-affirmed by the Court of Appeal in *Gallagher v Jones* (66 TC 77).

Difficulties are most likely to be encountered where the payment profile under a licence are front-end loaded and it is argued that, for tax at least, the expenditure should not be spread over the shorter of the useful life of the software or the length of the licence.

As the Tax Bulletin article (IM 663c above) notes the treatment of a single payment for a software licence as capital or revenue will depend on the role in economic terms that the software plays in the business concerned. Authority for this approach can be found, for example, in Lord Wilberforce's judgement in *Strick v Regent Oil* (at 43 TC 55C).

Lump sum payments for licences

On this view it would be wrong to place too great an emphasis on the intangible nature of software (as a set of instructions in digital form and therefore as intellectual property). What the software achieves for the business concerned should be the central consideration. For most businesses (apart of course from those dealing in items of this kind) the software functions as a tool of the trade in the same way as the computer hardware itself. Neither can function without the other.

It follows from Lord Wilberforce's approach that decided cases involving expenditure on the acquisition of legal rights (such as *Bolam v Regent Oil Co Ltd*, 37 TC 56) are of very limited relevance. Rather, a lump sum payment for a licence can reasonably be viewed as analogous to a premium for a lease of a tangible capital asset like land. Such a payment is itself capital on the authority of *McTaggart v Strump* (10 TC 17)—*see* IM 678, and IM 602 for discussion of the distinction between capital and revenue generally.

You should not contend that software with an expected useful life of two years or less is capital. But you should not accept that a particular piece of software has such a limited life solely because updates appear at frequent intervals. The issue is whether the business concerned in fact trades up to the new versions at intervals which are short enough to give a particular version only a transitory value to that business.

In selecting for challenge cases where expenditure is charged immediately to revenue, you should bear in mind that the advantage obtained is wholly one of timing.

Software owned outright

The treatment of expenditure on software owned outright (often developed in-house) follows that on licences. In the case of software developed in-house the fact that the expenditure may take the form of such recurring items as salaries paid to computer programmers does not stop it from being capital. In *McVeigh v Arthur Sanderson & Sons Ltd* (45 TC 273) it was clear that part of the salaries of staff engaged in producing wallpaper and fabric designs was attributable to the capital cost of the physical piece of plant (the printing etc blocks). These staff costs are broadly comparable with the salaries of staff producing software. But if the nature of the advantage obtained by the expenditure makes it borderline the recurring nature of the expenditure may tip the balance towards revenue treatment—*see* Lord Wilberforce's comments in *Strick v Regent Oil Co Ltd* (at 43 TC 56C).

In the normal way the ordinary recurring expenditure of a concern's computer services department will not be capital unless some major new project can be identified. Expenditure on salaries etc of staff engaged on making changes to computer systems, which can at most be viewed as piecemeal improvements, is unlikely to be capital.

The treatment of expenditure in a trader's accounts as capital or revenue will be only of marginal relevance to the tax treatment. But where the expenditure is revenue, the accounting treatment will be central to the timing of relief—*see* regular payments for licences above. In particular where expenditure has been capitalised under Statement of Standard Accounting Practice 13 ('Accounting for Research and Development') the contention that a deduction should be given in the tax computation for expenditure as it is incurred should be resisted. Instead you should argue that the Case I deduction should be equal to the charge for the amortised expenditure in the trader's accounts.

In-house software development costs

Further gudance on in-house costs

663e. The basic approach to determining whether expenditure on computer software is capital is set out in IM 663d above. To recap the key points:

- it is necessary to obtain an understanding of the business function or effect of a concern's software rather than the nature of computer programs themselves and how they are written;
- software normally functions as a tool enabling business to be carried on more efficiently;
- the scope, power, longevity of such a tool and its centrality to the functions of the business will all bear on its treatment.

This paragraph and IM 663f to IM 663m below consider in more detail the treatment of costs of developing software to fit a trader's specific needs. This guidance should be applied whether the software is developed by a trader's own employees or whether outside consultants are engaged. There is no presumption that because expenditure on software is incurred in-house it is more likely to be revenue than it would be if the same software was developed for a concern by an independent software house.

See IM 663a last sub-para for the periods to which the guidance in IM 663e to IM 663m should be applied.

Relevance of Accounting Treatment For the role of the commercial accounting treatment of the expenditure in question *see* the general comments in IM 602. That treatment, though not decisive, will remain relevant to the tax position.

The fact that expenditure on in-house software costs has been taken to the balance sheet does not mean that it is necessarily capital for tax purposes but it is a factor in support of capital treatment. If such expenditure turns out to be revenue for tax purposes then it does not follow that a deduction is due in the year it is incurred. *See* IM 605b.

Conversely, the fact that expenditure on in-house software costs has been written off immediately to the profit and loss account does not mean that it is necessarily revenue for tax purposes. Indeed, where the payment is clearly capital by reference to the other relevant factors *ECC Quarries v Watkis* (51 TC 153) is authority for capital treatment even if an immediate write off is the only available accountancy treatment. Nevertheless, in marginal cases it will be relevant and helpful to seek accountancy advice on whether immediate write-off is the only commercially acceptable accounting treatment.

Layout of further guidance

663f. The penultimate sub-paragraph of IM 663d indicates that:

- expenditure on the development of software for a trader's own use may be capital if it is part of a 'major new project', *but*
- expenditure which amounts at most to the piecemeal improvement of a computer system which is already in use will be revenue.

The layout of the further guidance is:

- IM 663g provides some guidance on the general approach and analogies with tangible machinery and plant.
- IM 663h–IM 663i provides guidance on how the task of identifying capital projects should be approached. But Inspectors should bear in mind that whether a project is sufficiently enduring and substantial to be reasonably regarded as a capital matter will always turn on the particular facts and circumstances. This will not only include the characteristics of the project but also its place in the operations of the business in question.
- IM 663j considers what is meant by a 'piecemeal improvement'. Again this is an issue of fact.
- IM 663k–IM 663m addresses the further question of what costs associated with an admittedly capital project may be capital.

General approach—analogies with tangible plant

663g. Clearly analogies can be drawn between a computer software system and a more traditional tangible asset, such as a piece of machinery or plant. To a degree that approach is helpful and indeed is adopted in this guidance. A major computer program may represent a huge investment of intellectual effort and business resources. And it may play a vital and important role in the conduct of the entire business. But the Commissioners and the courts are unlikely to be impressed by attempts to press such analogies too far. They are unlikely to be viewed in the same light as ordinary tangible fixed assets. The classification of computer software is therefore more problematical. *See* for example Lord Reid's comments in *Strick v Regent Oil* at 43 TC 30 and 43 TC 31.

Nowadays many large businesses incur significant expenditure not only on developing new computer systems but also on piecemeal adaptation or improvement of existing systems. It follows that a good deal of expenditure incurred on computer programming etc will be of a revenue nature.

Identifying major new projects

663h.   As a practical matter, a starting point in identifying the major new projects (IM 663g) which *may* be of a capital nature is to ascertain which ones the management of a business itself singled out as of most importance, as evidenced by the way the projects were in fact handled at the time rather than as perceived after the event. In the absence of contemporary documentary evidence (or to supplement it), discussions with the managers of the information technology department within a concern may be helpful—though Inspectors should guard against the too ready acceptance of assertions made after the event and with the benefit of hindsight.

A project not identified in this way is less likely in practice to be capital—for example, when it will operate, and can be approved, at a local branch or divisional level. Typically, the fact that a project is regarded as especially important will be evidenced by a requirement that budgetary approval and authority to proceed has to be obtained at a higher level of management than that for other projects. The degree of detail (for example by way of a formal project plan) required in support of an application to commit funds is also likely to be greater (though Inspectors may occasionally come across a substantial project which is so essential to a concern's future that management see no point in too rigorous control of its costs).

There is likely to be evidence in the form of internal memos, Board project forecasts and selective extracts from Board papers etc which, for example, discuss the case for the project, review its progress and possible changes in it, including the expected cost-benefit results. These could themselves be helpful in identifying capital expenditure—even if the financial accounts do not separately analyse the salaries of staff and other costs between capital and revenue.

The total amount of expenditure required to develop and implement the new system is clearly likely to be relevant here. As a general matter it is not possible to set out any minimum figure below which a project will be revenue. The nature and size of the business in question has to be taken into account. But in the context of a particular business Inspectors should consider whether it might be convenient to agree monetary guidelines for this purpose, based on the overall business plans and expenditure forecasts for particular projects (rather than on annual budgets), subject to periodical review. Projected expenditure on the salaries etc of those involved in developing the new software for the project will often be a convenient more reliable measure of its likely significance than, for example, the costs of the hardware.

Pointers to capital treatment

663i.   It does not follow, however, that projects regarded by the management of a business itself as of particular importance are necessarily capital. It remains necessary to have regard to all the relevant pointers and to consider what light they shed on the key factual issue, namely how important an economic or functional role the software plays in the business in question.

Possible pointers include:

Duration

1. Even an important computer system may have a relatively limited useful life; for example where it has been designed to meet a business need which, though pressing, is of limited duration. Inspectors should always accept that expenditure on software with an expected life of less than two years is revenue (IM 663d, sixth sub-para). That apart, the shorter the expected life the stronger the other capital features will need to be before the project can reasonably be characterised as capital. The project documentation may indicate over how many years the new system is likely to increase business earnings or reduce running costs.

Inspectors should however resist the view that some longer period should be substituted for the two years mentioned above. In particular, they should resist the adoption of a period derived from case law concerned with a different type of asset or advantage, such as the agreement for the exclusive supply of petrol to filling stations in *Bolam v Regent Oil* (37 TC 56) and *Strick v Regent Oil* (43 TC 1). *See* the comments of Lord Templeman in *Beauchamp v Woolworths* (at 61 TC 581) rejecting the attempt to apply to consideration of whether a loan liability was a capital matter a minimum expected life test (of five years or more) derived from the petrol tie cases. Software is in essence a business tool (often central to a trader's ability to run his business) and far removed from the marketing agreements for trading stock at issue in those petrol tie cases.

Functions may be added on to an existing system or it may be adapted in response to competition to provide a more sophisticated customer service or to meet new trade regulations. Nevertheless, it is expected to remain recognisably the same system. So long as it does so its useful life continues. Major systems are difficult and expensive to develop and core computer code may last a long time.

Cost

2. As noted in IM 663g, last sub-paragraph, it is not possible to set out general guidelines concerning costs. But the more expensive a project the more it is likely to be a central tool of the business and the more enduring is likely to be its effect.

In this context it is necessary to have regard to both the absolute cost (to take an extreme example £10m is, without doubt, a significant sum of money to any business) and the cost as a proportion of total business outlays. Again, a project taking up 20 per cent of business administrative costs in a single year is likely to be significant whatever the sum is in absolute terms. See the final part of IM 663h for a practical approach.

For management purposes a project will usually be analysed into stages or modules and costs allocated to each. Inspectors should consider critically any contention that such smaller units themselves amount to independent and relatively insignificant projects. There may be cases where a series of relatively small undertakings are entered into not because they are perceived as contributing to some larger project but for the benefits they offer in isolation. But equally there will be many others where they represent parts of what in essence is a much larger whole.

Associated capital expenditure

3. The case for capital treatment will be stronger where new computer equipment ('hardware') is provided on which to run the software developed under the project. This is especially the case where the new hardware is not merely desirable but necessary for this purpose.

Degree of associated organisational change

4. Similarly the degree of change intended in the way operations are carried out as a result of the project; for example, savings in the number, and changes in the location, of staff used to provide services to customers will have a bearing. The more radical the changes, the more likely the expenditure will be capital. These changes are likely to be most radical when operations previously carried on manually are computerised.

Piecemeal improvement

663j.   Whether expenditure merely represents the piecemeal improvement of an existing computer system or a stage or module within something sufficiently major to constitute capital expenditure will depend on a detailed consideration of all the facts and circumstances. Among the circumstances which have to be borne in mind is the fast-changing nature of the computer software industry and the fact that a computer program does not as such wear out. Against that background it is hard to envisage any repair which does not involve some element of upgrading the system.

The presence of an element of upgrading, therefore, will not necessarily cause the expenditure in question to be capital. Rather, capital treatment will be appropriate in either of two circumstances:

- where the computer system which has been improved is itself a capital asset of the business and that system, viewed as a whole, has been sufficiently improved to make capital treatment appropriate;
- where the work on the system is itself part of a major new project which is capital (IM 663h–IM 663i).

In considering whether an entire system has been improved Inspectors should have regard not so much to any enhancement of the system's specification but to the practical effects on the service it provides to the business. Inspectors need also consider what proportion of the system has been affected by the changes. The smaller the proportion the more radical the improvements need to be before the view that the expenditure is capital is likely to commend itself to the Commissioners or the Courts.

Capital stages of software development

663k.   Having established whether, and if so which, computer software projects are of a capital nature it remains necessary to identify the relevant capital expenditure. Not all expenditure which is in some sense associated with a capital project is itself capital. The question to be asked is *on what* particular expenditure is incurred. In other words it is necessary to establish for what the payment was made. *See* IM 663l for abortive expenditure.

Nature of Case I Test   The Case I test is not one of purpose. Thus expenditure may have too loose an association with a particular capital project to qualify as capital even though it may be intended to promote the capital project.

Stages in System Development In deciding what expenditure is integral to development of the new system it may be useful to identify the stages in the development and implementation of a project:

1. Initial research expenditure and preliminary planning
    Decision to develop

2. Practical test and trial exercises

3. Design and development of full working systems
    Decision to implement

4. Costs associated with implementation (especially staff training and procedural changes)

5. Upgrading, updating and error correction.

First stage Expenditure at the **first** stage will often be divided into an initial feasibility study and, if the decision is to proceed, expenditure on a much more expensive full study. In many cases it will not be possible to show that expenditure at the full study stage, still less the feasibility stage, is **incurred on** the capital asset. Normally it consists of ascertaining the needs of potential users, investigating the possibilities, albeit in some detail, and drawing up specifications. At this stage very little writing of computer programmes would be expected. The purpose of this expenditure may be the development of a software based system but the objective link between the expenditure and the software is too remote to count.

Second and third stages Expenditure at the **second** and **third** stages will normally be capital (even though the expenditure may prove abortive if the decision is subsequently taken not to implement). At this stage the software can be viewed as a business tool which has been successfully created. An exception would be recurring royalties for a licence to use any bought-in software as the base for the in-house project even though the rights obtained under the licence are of a capital nature. Compare the treatment of rents payable for the occupation of premises which are a capital asset of a business.

Fourth stage To the extent that the **fourth** stage, that of implementation, consists of teaching staff how to use the software the costs should be regarded as revenue (just as the costs of teaching staff to use bought-in software or any item of new capital equipment would normally be regarded as revenue).

Fifth stage Costs incurred at the **fifth** stage would normally be regarded as no more than piecemeal improvement and should be allowed (*see* IM 663j).

Consider analogy of Revenue systems In developing a perspective on the treatment of computer software expenditure Inspectors may find it helpful to bear in mind the likely treatment of the Revenue's own computer systems were it necessary to apply tax law to them. Major systems such as COP, CODA, CT Pay and File, which were developed in-house, would clearly be of a capital nature. Even so, most expenditure incurred on 'upgrading' those systems subsequent to 'roll-out' would probably be revenue. Expenditure on creating the small pieces of software which exist to support various minor technical computations required under current tax law would be revenue.

Abortive expenditure

663l. Whether abortive expenditure on computer software is deductible under Case I or II depends on the same criteria as expenditure which had a successful outcome. *See* IM 602a.

Abortive *capital* expenditure on computer software qualifies for machinery and plant allowances (CAA 1990, s 67A and CAA 1990, s 60: CA 1600 onwards).

Thus for all practical purposes there is no scope for arguing that abortive expenditure on software is neither revenue nor qualifies for capital allowances.

Direct and indirect cost of software

663m.   IM 663i offered guidance on categorising expenditure by reference to the stage of the project reached. This paragraph is concerned with different types of in-house expenditure. The principal distinction here is between the **direct costs** of the computer programmers and others involved on a project (whether they are employees or contractors) and **indirect costs**. In the first category are the costs of remuneration, expense payments and benefits, and such associated costs as employer's national insurance contributions. Lump sum payments for licences to use computer programs developed by others would also count as direct costs. The principal items in the second category are the costs of the accommodation occupied by the project team.

Indirect costs a question of fact and degree Subject to IM 663i, direct costs of capital projects are themselves capital—*see* IM 663d. The treatment of indirect costs, typically the accommodation costs of the project team is less straightforward. On perhaps the only occasion when the Courts have been asked to focus in depth on the treatment of overheads (*Duple v Ostime*, 39 TC 537—where the valuation of trading stock was at issue) the House of Lords, faced with competing accounting evidence, came down in favour of their exclusion from the cost of an asset.

At one extreme there may be situations where a project team occupies accommodation specifically acquired for project purposes. In those situations it is reasonably easy to identify the accommodation costs as part of the overall costs of the project.

But in the case of a building not only occupied by a project team but by other staff or contractors and for different purposes at different times the question whether the accommodation costs can reasonably be viewed as part of the costs of a project is likely to be far less easy to resolve involving complex issues from the discipline of cost accountancy.

Inspectors should consider carefully whether, in the absence of clear authority on the point, the amount of indirect costs potentially of a capital nature is sufficiently material to justify the likely expenditure of resources inherent in detailed enquiries.

Where the costs are sufficiently material, it will normally be appropriate to seek to settle the issue on broad lines.

Royalties

Application of ICTA 1988, s 74(p)

1030.   ICTA 1988, s 74(p) should not be regarded as extending to any royalty paid to a non-resident in respect of the user of a patent abroad. (*See* IM 3922 as to the circumstances in which a lump sum payment may fall to be regarded as an 'income' payment.)

Sums 'paid in respect of the use of a patent'

1031.   Sums paid for rights incidental to the user of a patent should normally be regarded as sums 'paid in respect of the user of a patent'

(*a*)   to use a trade name, if closely connected with the user of a patent

(*b*)   to have any improvement of a patent made by the grantor during the currency of the agreement

(*c*)   to receive advice or assistance as to how best to use a patent.

See Paterson Engineering Co. Ltd. v Duff, 25 TC 43.

Copyright royalties

1032.   Copyright royalties and design royalties are admissible as a deduction. *See also* IM 4000 onwards as to copyright royalties paid to persons abroad.

Registered designs and trade marks: payments for user

1033.   A design registered under the Registered Design Act 1949 and the Copyright Design and Patent Act 1988 Part III, is by those Acts made the subject of a copyright. Payments in respect of the user of such a design are therefore not payments in respect of a patent falling within ICTA 1988, s 74(p)

Rights in trade marks registered under the Trade Marks Act 1938 should not be regarded for tax purposes as copyright.

Trade marks and designs

General ICTA 1988, s 83

1160.   Costs incurred in obtaining the registration of a design or a trade or service mark are admissible.

Costs of obtaining the extension of the period of copyright in a design or the renewal of registration of a trade or service mark are admissible whenever incurred.

Schedule D, Case VI

Casual income arising under contracts made in UK or abroad

1702.   Where a contract which gives rise to casual income is made in the United Kingdom, the income may be chargeable under Case VI even where the services are to be performed outside the United Kingdom (*see Alloway v Phillips*, 53 TC 372). Where casual income arises from services performed in the United Kingdom and it is claimed that there is no Case VI liability because the contract was made abroad, the case should be submitted to Business Profits Division 4 (Schedule D—Case VI) for advice before the absence of liability is agreed.

Actors and other entertainers

Schedule of charge

1810.   Actors, ballet dancers, opera singers, musicians and other performers/artists who appear live in the theatre, opera, ballet, or in clubs, or perform in film, video, radio or television productions may be engaged under either contracts for services (Schedule D) or contracts of employment (Schedule E).

There are a number of standard contracts commonly used to engage performers/artists in these industries. These contracts incorporate a comprehensive range of standard terms and are the result of negotiations between bodies representing engagers and performers/artists in the industry. They are often referred to by reference to the union which has negotiated on behalf of the performers, and accordingly there are a range of contracts known for example as standard Musicians Union contracts and standard Equity contracts. The British Actors' Equity Association is the trade union which represents most performing artists other than musicians.

The union have been able to secure a package of measures designed to project their members such as

- minimum rates of pay
- overtime, bank holiday and Sunday premiums
- agreed rates of touring and subsistence allowances
- holiday pay
- agreed disciplinary procedures.

Because these features are more commonly found in an employer/employee relationship, it is natural that an examination of the standard contractual terms may lead to the view that performers/artists so engaged are engaged under contacts of employment. And in the case of *Fall v Hitchen*, 49 TC 433, it was held that a ballet dancer engaged under a standard contract was engaged under a contract of employment and that his pay fell within Schedule E.

However in 1993 two actors, Alec McCowen and Sam West appealed to the Special Commissioners, and successfully argued that their income from standard Equity theatre contracts did not fall within Schedule E. The decisions were given in public and accordingly they can be openly referred to, but they are not binding on other bodies of Commissioners. The Revenue did not pursue these cases to the High Court.

It is clear from these contrasting cases that the terms of the contract may not be decisive by themselves, and in the case of artistic workers, such as theatrical performers/artists, the way in which they generally carry on their profession also needs to be considered.

In *Fall v Hitchen*, Mr Hitchen was engaged for a minimum period of something like six months 'to rehearse, understudy, play and dance as and where required by the Manager'. Both Mr West and Mr McCowen, however, were engaged to play a specific role in a specific play for the run of a play, or a shorter fixed period. And both Mr McCowen and Mr West had a variety of engagements in different media (film, television, radio and theatre), consecutively and sometimes concurrently.

The type of engagement undertaken by Mr McCowen and Mr West is now much more typical of the profession than that undertaken by Mr Hitchen in 1969. These days it is comparatively unusual for a performer/artist to be engaged to play parts as and when cast in a series of different plays or other productions. The typical performer/artist is likely to have a whole series of separate engagements in different media making up his professional working life, commonly interspersed with periods without paid work, between the end of one engagement and the commencement of another.

Other case law supports the view that, for theatrical performers/artists, independence from a particular regular paymaster may indicate that individual contracts are not contracts of employment, even though the prima facie view based on the particular terms of the particular engagement may suggest otherwise.

Accordingly, Schedule D assessment of a performer's/artist's earnings will normally be appropriate. The sort of engagement where Schedule E and PAYE may be appropriate, is more likely to be in circumstances where a performer/artist is engaged for a regular salary to perform in a series of different productions over a period of time, in such roles as may be from time to time stipulated by the engager, with a minimum period notice before termination of the contract, as was Mr Hitchen in *Fall v Hitchen*. This would apply for example to permanent members of some orchestras and permanent members of an opera, ballet or theatre company. Schedule E and PAYE would apply in these cases regardless of the receipt by the performer/artist of other income correctly chargeable under Schedule D.

Procedure

1811. An actor who is assessable under Case II of Schedule D is normally assessed at his place of residence. *See however* AP 2140 as regards the place of assessment of non-resident professional entertainers.

As regards—

(*a*)   the charge to tax under Sections 103–104 ICTA 1988, where the profession of an actor, etc., is discontinued or there is a change of accounting basis, see IM 1750 onwards;

(*b*)   returns of payments to actors etc. are dealt with by the Entertainers Information Unit (EIU) at TIDO, *see* AP 4025.

Expenses

1812.   Actors, dancers, etc., who are engaged under standard contracts (see IM 1810) may incur few expenses in the course of their work. Such contracts usually require the engager to supply the costume, wigs, hairdressing and exceptional makeup necessary for the role. In addition, the engager may provide transport between theatres and rehearsing rooms and between tour venues. Payments may also be made to cover the actor's travelling between home and the theatre.

Surgical, hospital and medical expenses are normally inadmissible deductions in computing profits under Schedule D (*see Norman v Golder*, 26 TC 293). Some actors may, however, be able to show that extra expenditure of this nature has been incurred for professional purposes. In such cases a proportion of the expenditure incurred may be allowed.

Cases of difficulty where agreement cannot be reached on the deduction of surgical, hospital and medical expense should be submitted to Business Profits Division (Literary and Artistic Profits) before appeals are listed for personal hearing.

Athletes

General: athletes not resident in the UK

1820a.   The following guidance concerns athletes resident in the UK. *See* IH 472 for guidance about the application of ICTA 1988, s 555–ICTA 1988, s 558 to non-resident athletes.

General: other sports: employees

Cricketers, footballers, rugby players and the like are employees of the club for which they play. They may, however, receive other income of the kind described below. Inspectors should always consider whether the income is properly assessable under Schedule E before agreeing a computation under Case I or II of Schedule D.

General: other sports: Case I, II and VI

The following guidance deals specifically with athletes. But when dealing with other sportsmen the guidance may help Inspectors considering whether

- there is a trade, profession or vocation as opposed to a purely leisure pursuit or hobby, *see* IM 1821.
- a receipt is from a Case I or II source, *see* IM 1822–IM 1824. And whether a particular expense is an allowable deduction, *see* IM 1825.
- a receipt is assessable Case VI, *see* IM 1828.

Amateur status and athletes' funds

1820b.   In 1982 the International Amateur Athletic Federation (IAAF) amended its rules to permit 'athletes' funds'. In broad terms, amateur athletes could earn income in connection with their athletic activities without forfeiting their amateur status provided the income was paid into funds administered by the athletes' national associations. Withdrawals were permitted for specified expenses, but athletes could forfeit their amateur status if they withdrew money for other purposes.

The regulations for the British Amateur Athletic Board (BAAB) permit two types of fund:

- the general fund
  and
- the individual fund.

The general fund: how it is operated

1820c. The general fund, sometimes known as the athletic fund, is managed for athletes by the BAAB itself. All the athlete's income from grants, participation fees, sponsorship and other athletics-related activities should be paid into the fund.

Athletes may withdraw their money from the fund at any time, but they lose their amateur status if they withdraw money other than to meet certain expenses specified by the IAAF.

The money is held by the BAAB in a general bank account in trust for the athletes, but separate records are kept of each athlete's income and withdrawals.

The general fund a bare trust

Because an athlete can take complete control over the money, a bare trust is created, and, where income paid into the fund is assessable, it is regarded as the income of the athlete for Income Tax purposes.

The general fund: interest arising

Interest arising on the investment of the fund monies is retained by the BAAB and is not therefore assessable on the individual athletes.

Individual funds: how they are operated

1820d. An athlete who has more than a specified amount in the general fund may ask the BAAB to set up an individual trust fund. If an athlete takes this option, an individual trust deed is drawn up and three trustees are appointed, two by the BAAB and one by the athlete. The athlete does not sign the trust deed, but signs a letter acknowledging its terms.

All of the athlete's income from athletics or athletics-related activities should be paid into the individual trust fund. And amateur status will be lost if withdrawals are made other than for expenses specified by the IAAF.

Only a few leading athletes have been in a position to request their own individual funds. As well as having an individual fund, an athlete with more than the specified sum in the general fund may still remain in that fund.

Individual funds: A bare trust

Under the terms of the trust deed an athlete is free to withdraw money at will. Therefore a bare trust is created.

Individual funds: income from a trade or profession

Usually athletes with individual trust funds are carrying on a trade, profession or vocation. If so, the income paid into the funds should be included in the computation of their profits assessable under Case I or II.

Individual funds: investment income and chargeable gains

One of the advantages of an individual trust fund for athletes is that they are able to retain the benefit of any investment income and chargeable gains. Any such income or gains should be assessed on the athletes themselves.

The borderline between a trade or profession and a hobby: amateur status not decisive

1821. That an athlete is described as an amateur is not decisive in considering whether he should be assessed under Case I or II. The leading figures in amateur athletics are likely to be assessable under Case I or II on their earnings.

But the activities of most athletes remain a purely leisure pursuit or hobby, even though money may occasionally be paid into a fund for their benefit. The distinction between a hobby on the one hand and a trade, profession or vocation on the other is very much a question of fact and degree.

Practical approach In one or two years an athlete's earnings may have exceeded the expenses. And, perhaps, the whole of the athlete's time may be devoted substantially to sporting and associated activities. But even the presence of both those pointers is not decisive. Inspectors will need more information before deciding whether the athlete is organising the activities in a business-like manner and with a view to making a profit. In order to consider the badges of trade (*see* IM 120 onwards) Inspectors will need the full facts concerning:

- the nature and scale of the activities and the way they are organised
- competitions and events entered in the relevant period, the athlete's final position in each event and any prizes received
- any subventions (*see* IM 1822), grants or similar receipts from sporting or other organisations, and copies of documents setting out the terms under which they are received
- any attendance or performance fees, and sponsorship or endorsement fees, with copies of the contracts and relevant documentation
- any other income from associated activities including journalism, TV appearances etc
- the terms of any agreement with an agent negotiating contracts with sponsors

etc. This is usually the BAAB but many of the leading athletes engage their own agents.
- the cost and nature of expenses.

Athletes' sources of income

1822. Athletes may receive all the following types of income:

- Subventions.
- Grants and gifts.
- Sponsorship and endorsement fees.
- Appearance, participation and performance fees.

Subventions, grants and gifts

Subventions are gifts or grants to which no commercial strings are attached.

The Sports Aid Foundation grants are the most common. But there may be other public or semi-public sources and occasionally commercial concerns make payments akin to subventions. Most subventions are paid to athletes who cannot earn much from commercial contracts, and they are usually intended to meet specified expenses.

An athlete who receives only subventions is unlikely to be carrying on a trade or exercising a profession or vocation. Where the payment is received from a commercial concern, the facts and documentary evidence may however indicate that the payment is in reality a kind of sponsorship or endorsement fee.

Sponsorship and endorsement fees

Sponsorship, or product endorsement, usually involves the athlete in lending his name to a promotional campaign. This may be through advertisements or through personal visits to retail outlets. The product may not, of course, have any athletic or other sporting connection. The arrangements will normally be contractual, though the form of the contract may vary from a formal written agreement to an informal letter or even a telephone call. Where accounts are under enquiry it will normally be useful to obtain a copy of any written agreements of other documentation.

Athletes are not permitted to wear clothes bearing sponsorship names or logos in competitions, because usually the Athletics Associations have already made agreements with manufacturers that only their kit should be worn.

Appearance, participation and performance fees

In an attempt to attract leading athletes, many competitions organisers offer fairly substantial sums for appearances or participation at meetings. In addition, bonuses may be paid for meritorious performances such as winning or setting records.

Athletes may also receive fees from activities not directly connected with sport, such as writing newspaper articles, making TV appearances and opening supermarkets.

Athletes: service companies

1823.   Some leading athletes have their own companies, which are often described as sports consultancies, providing the services of the athletes. Where the contracts have been made between the sponsor and the service company the income will be assessable on the company. But where the contracts have been made between the sponsor and the athlete the income will be assessable on the individual (not the company), even if the company is entitled to receive the income (for example, because the service agreements says that the athlete must hand over the money).

Athletes: timing of income

1824.   The time at which an athlete's income should be included in his Case I or II computation will involve a consideration of the relevant agreements and all the surrounding circumstances, *see* IM 546 onwards.

It is unusual for any significant delay to arise between the completion of the service and the income becoming payable, but where such delays seem to be arising the position should be investigated. It should not be accepted that the income is not assessable on the athlete until it is withdrawn either from the general fund (IM 1820b) or from an individual fund (IM 1820c).

Athletes: expenses

1825.   Expenses for which the BAAB may permit withdrawals from a fund may not be 'wholly and exclusively laid out or expended for the purposes of the trade, profession or vocation', within the terms of ICTA 1988, s 74(1)(*a*), *see* IM 601. For example, funds may be withdrawn to meet taxation liabilities without loss of amateur status.

Problems may arise with items such as medical expenses or special diets where the purpose of the expenditure may not be exclusively a business one. The Courts have made it clear on several occasions that to satisfy the ICTA 1988, s 74(1)(*a*) test the business purpose must be the sole purpose, even though there may be incidental non-business benefits. The cases of *Norman v Golder*, 26 TC 293, and *Prince v Mapp*, 46 TC 169, should be considered in connection with medical expenses. *Mallalieu v Drummond*, 57 TC 330, may also be useful in showing that the conscious purpose of the taxpayer may not be decisive in considering expenditure which by its nature must have a private purpose.

Athletes: payments in kind

1826.   Some commercial contracts provide for the supply of goods or equipment as well as payment in kind. Such goods or equipment can be brought into the Case I or II computation at their value if sold by the athlete, *see Gold Coast Selection Trust Ltd v Humphrey* 30 TC 209.

Athletes: retirement annuity relief

1827.   Where income from athletics is assessable under Cases I or II, it may be regarded as relevant earnings for retirement annuity relief. A retirement age of 35 may be allowed for athletic appearances and prize money in accordance with ICTA 1988, s 620(4)(c) but the normal provisions will apply to income from sponsorship etc. Any enquiries concerning early retirement should be referred to the Pension Schemes Office (Retirement Annuity Section).

Athletes: Case VI

1828. Case VI may sometimes be considered as an alternative to Cases I or II. It can only apply to income received under an enforceable contract for work done, services rendered or facilities provided, and it cannot apply to voluntary grants given for nothing in return—*Scott v Ricketts*, 44 TC 303.

Athletes: information

1829. The BAAB makes a return each year of income received by amateur athletes who do not have their own individual trust funds, providing the total income received by the athlete in the year exceeds a specified sum. The figures returned include VAT but exclude the BAAB's own commission. The BAAB also provides a list of names of athletes with their own individual trust funds, with the names and addresses of their legal and financial advisers.

This information is distributed to Districts. It should not, however, be assumed that every athlete included in the return is assessable under Case I or II: this will have to be decided by reference to all the relevant facts.

The sum returned by the BAAB may not be all of an athlete's income. Money may be received which is not paid into a trust fund, and some fees may be paid direct to the athletes themselves.

Franchising

General

2400. Various forms of agreement are often described, somewhat loosely, as franchises, for example licences, dealerships and concessions, but IM 2400–2403 is particularly concerned with the tax implications of payments under 'business system franchise agreements'. Under such an agreement the owner of an established business format (the franchisor) grants to another person (the franchisee) the right to distribute products or perform services using that system. A wide variety of activities are the subject of franchise agreements.

The terms of agreements vary considerably but generally the franchisee gets the use of the system and any necessary management back-up for a specified period, of perhaps five to ten years, in return for

- an initial fee (payable in one sum or in instalments) and
- continuing, usually annual, fees.

The continuing fees may be calculated as a percentage of turnover, a mark-up on purchases from the franchisor or a regular fixed payment per outlet.

Before considering the tax treatment of the payer or recipient Inspectors must get a copy of the signed agreement.

Franchisor

Franchisor: initial lump sum fee

2401a.   The initial lump sum fee is not a capital receipt arising from the disposal of goodwill. The franchisor's goodwill remains intact and may even be strengthened by the extension of its reputation through franchising. For further guidance on this point *see* CG 68100 onwards.

Case law

2401b.   There are similarities between the disposal of a business system and a disposal of know-how and occasionally the franchisor may argue that the initial lump sum fees are capital receipts arising from the sale of know-how. Two cases illustrate the relevant principles:

- EVANS MEDICAL SUPPLIES LTD V MORIARTY (37 TC 540). The company traded in Burma through an agency. It agreed to assist the Burmese government in setting up an industry there for an annual fee which was accepted as a revenue receipt and a lump sum which was said to be for the disclosure of secret processes. The lump sum was held to be capital.
- JEFFREY V ROLLS ROYCE LTD (40 TC 443). The company made agreements with several overseas companies for the sale of know-how relating to aero-engine manufacture. Lump sums received under these agreements were held to be revenue.

There is also a useful review of the case law by Goulding J (from 48 TC 178) in *Coalite and Chemical Products Ltd v Treeby* (48 TC 171). The Court of Appeal and House of Lords judgments in the Rolls Royce case are worth detailed consideration. Most of the reasons for treating Rolls Royce's receipts as revenue are equally applicable to franchising receipts, for example

- the transactions were repeated (franchisors usually have offered, or intend to offer, more than one franchise)
- there was a deliberate policy of expansion by granting licences
- benefits other than know-how were provided
- no capital asset diminished in value; know-how can be imparted to others without necessarily diluting its value.

The view of the House of Lords was that the repetitive exploitation of know-how was simply an extension of the existing trade giving rise to revenue receipts. The *Evans Medical* decision was distinguished because it concerned the total loss of the substantial Burmese trade; once the secret processes had been disclosed the trade could never recommence.

For more information concerning know-how *see* IM 505 and CG 68720 onwards.

Franchisor: when receipts should be recognised

2401c.   Before challenging a timing basis adopted in the accounts *see* IM 355 and 540 onwards. Initial sums are generally intended to be consideration for the grant of the franchise and also perhaps, the initial services of the franchisor, whereas the continuing fees are intended to pay for services which may be required in later years. Thus normally such lump sum fees are earned when the initial services are provided. Inspectors should critically review cases where initial sums are spread.

Franchisee

Initial fee

2402a. Generally the annual fee payable will be revenue but the initial payment, whether payable in one sum or instalments, is usually capital, as are any related legal fees. *See* Viscount Cave on page 192 of *Atherton v British Insulated Helsby Cables Ltd* (10 TC 155), and Lord Sands on pages 14 and 15 of *CIR v Granite City Steamship Company Ltd* (13 TC 1). In *S. Ltd v O'Sullivan* (Irish Tax Cases 108), the judge followed Viscount Cave's approach in deciding that a predetermined sum payable in instalments by an Irish company for access to an English company's know-how for a period of 10 years was capital.

For further information about the Capital Gains Tax implications *see* CG 68100 onwards and CG 68600 onwards.

Apportionment of initial payment

2402b. Whether an apportionment is appropriate depends on the facts. The agreement may show that the franchisor charged a specific part of the initial fee for a revenue service such as the training of staff (other than the franchisee). If so, and if the charge is justifiable in relation to the actual services provided, then an apportionment may be appropriate. If, however, the agreement terms are such that no part of the initial lump sum fee is specifically attributed to revenue items then Inspectors should critically examine claims for apportionment.

In practice, apportionments for which franchisees contend may be made without reference to the franchisor and may be difficult to justify in relation to the services provided. For instance, some franchisors are unwilling to negotiate special terms with individual franchisees and the same lump sum is payable irrespective of the actual services required from the franchisor, for example the number of staff needing training may be irrelevant. The facts may also show that no part of the initial lump sum fees can be attributed to services of a revenue nature provided by the franchisor because such services are separately charged for in the annual fees.

Know-how allowances under ICTA 1988, s 530(2)

2402c. Where the initial fee is accepted as capital, the trader may seek capital allowances under ICTA 1988, s 530(2). Such claims are not generally acceptable. Agreements vary, but typically the franchise fee will be for items which do not satisfy the statutory definition of know-how. ICTA 1988, s 533(7) defines 'know-how' to include 'any industrial information and techniques likely to assist in the manufacture or processing of goods or materials . . .'.

As IM 510 indicates, while Inspectors should not take too narrow a view of these words, the definition excludes commercial know-how.

Know-how allowances under ICTA 1988, s 350(2): apportionment

2402d.   A legal mechanism for apportioning consideration to identify the part relating to 'industrial' know-how exists as CAA 1990, s 150 applies to ICTA 1988, s 530 by virtue of ICTA 1988, s 532(1). If, however, what is acquired is essentially a licence to operate a business in a certain manner then even if a small part of the total does appear to relate to 'industrial' know-how generally an apportionment should be resisted for the same reasons as apportionments between capital and revenue are resisted (IM 2402b). But if the franchisee can demonstrate that a reasonable part of the total payment was for the acquisition of 'industrial' know-how then a just and reasonable apportionment should be negotiated. If a reasonable settlement cannot be reached by negotiation Inspectors should consult Business Profits Division 3 Capital Allowances before listing for a contentious hearing.

Accounts examination

Franchisors' Inspectors

2403a.   Inspectors dealing with traders who grant franchises should consider regularly obtaining and disseminating details of new cases.

Franchisees' Inspectors

2403b.   When examining new cases Inspectors should bear in mind that the notes to a franchisee's accounts may not state that a franchise has been acquired. Also the initial payment may not be apparent because it has been allocated between different heads of charge in the profit and loss account or because it is payable in instalments.

When Inspectors identify a new franchisee they should consider contacting the franchisor's Inspector as the franchisor may use a standard agreement where the technical issues have already been clarified.

2404–2409. . . .

Literary, etc., profits

General

2690.   The profits made by an individual resident in the United Kingdom from literary, composing, etc., activities carried on by him (including his profits from the literary, dramatic, film, musical etc copyright in his works) are assessable—

(*a*)   under Case II of Schedule D, if he is exercising the profession of an author, composer etc or

(*b*)   under Case VI, if his activities do not amount to the exercise of a profession. As regards—

  (i) copyright royalties received by a person other than the author, composer, etc., *see* IM 2693

(ii) copyright royalties etc within the scope of ICTA 1988, s 536 received by persons abroad, *see* IM 4000 onwards

(iii) casual income arising under contracts made in the United Kingdom or abroad, *see* IM 1702.

References to copyright in IM 2690–IM 2700 should be treated as including Public Lending Right (IM 2701).

Receipts

2691. Where the liability arises under Case II, the profits are to be computed inclusive of all receipts from copyright and other sources, including lump sums received for the outright assignment of copyright (for example the assignment of copyright as a whole, or of serial rights or of rights in particular editions, or of film, television or radio rights).

Where the liability is under Case VI, the profits should be similarly computed, except that lump sums received for the assignment of copyright only (*see Nethersole v Withers*, 28 TC 501), as distinct from lump sum and similar payments associated with services (*see Hobbs v Hussey*, 24 TC 153, and *Housden v Marshall*, 38 TC 233), should be excluded. In this connection—

(*a*) a lump sum does not include a sum received on account of royalties or an amount arrived at by reference to a minimum or estimated number of copies of a book or performances of a work

(*b*) an assignment, that is a transfer of ownership of a copyright, should be distinguished from a licence which permits the licensee to use copyrighted matter but does not involve any change in the ownership of the copyright

(*c*) a lump sum payment not assessable under Case VI should be considered for Capital Gains Tax liability.

If, in an assignment case, the question of liability under Schedule D turns on whether or not a profession is being exercised, consideration should be given to the taxpayer's activities both before and after the assignment.

Awards and bursaries

2691a. There are many prizes and awards open to authors and other creative artists (one publication list nearly 200 for authors alone) and entering competitions or seeking awards is a normal part of such professions.

Where an award, grant, bursary or prize is received, the determining factor in considering whether or not such an award etc is taxable is the quality of the award in the hands of the recipient. If it comes to the taxpayer as an incident in the exercise of his profession or vocation (including a subsidiary or part-time activity the profits from which are assessed under Case II of Schedule D), it should normally be treated as a professional receipt within Case II of Schedule D (*see Temperley v Smith*, 37 TC 18, *Smart v Lincolnshire Sugar Co. Ltd*, 20 TC 643, *Duff v Williamson*, 49 TC 1, *CIR v Falkirk Ice Rink Ltd*, 51 TC 42, and *McGowan v Brown and Cousins*, 52 TC 8). The facts relating to the award or prize should be considered for each case.

In some cases publishers enter works for competitions and entries direct from the author are not permitted although the permission of the author is usually a part of the entry conditions. To attract liability, it is not essential that the taxpayer should have applied for the award or prize himself; nor does he necessarily have to commit himself to complete a particular piece of work during the currency of the award or to refund the award in the event of failure to complete his programme of work.

Case II of Schedule D is not the only charging section. The facts may show that the award is one of the following—

(*a*)   An emolument of an office or employment under Schedule E (*see* SE 1000–1046). Where an award is made to a person receiving full-time instruction at a university or other establishment and the award does not exceed certain financial limits (*see* SE 1314), exemption may be available under ICTA 1988, s 331 (*see* SE 1310). Such cases are likely to be rare, however, and, in particular, established academics or leading members of professions will be unlikely to qualify since they will not normally be receiving full-time education.

(*b*)   A profit of a casual or occasional nature chargeable under Case VI of Schedule D (*see* (*a*) of IM 1701).

(*c*)   Exceptionally, an annual payment giving rise to liability under Case III of Schedule D.

A literary etc prize which is unsolicited, and which is awarded as a mark of honour, distinction or public esteem in recognition of outstanding achievement in a particular field, including the field in which the recipient operates professionally, is not chargeable to tax. In 1979 the Special Commissioners found for the taxpayer in a case involving a literary award. The case attracted some press publicity as a reporter was admitted to the proceedings. The book was entered for the competition by the publisher without the author's consent. The decision turned very much upon its own facts and, in particular, a finding that the award was unsolicited and did not represent the proceeds of exploitation of the book by the author personally or by his publishers as agents on his behalf.

Case of doubt or difficulty which cannot be resolved on the lines outlined above should be referred to BPD Literary and Artistic Profits.

Arts Council awards

2691b.   The Arts Council of Great Britain, together with the Arts Councils of Scotland, Wales and Northern Ireland, and the Regional and local Arts Councils, provide financial support through a variety of awards, bursaries and grants, to writers, artists, actors and other creative artists. For tax purposes, the awards etc fall within the following categories—

(*a*)   *Awards which are chargeable to tax*
   (i) Payments under the Royalty Supplement Scheme, the Contract Writers Scheme, Jazz Bursaries, Translators' Grants, Photographic Awards and Bursaries, Film and Video Awards and Bursaries, Performance Art Awards, Art Publishing Grants, direct or indirect musical, design or

choreographic *commissions* and direct or indirect *commissions* of sculpture and paintings for public sites.

   (ii) Grants to assist with a specific project or projects (for example the writing of a book) or to meet specific professional expenses (for example a contribution towards a composer's copying expenses or an artist's studio expenses).

(*b*)   *Awards which are not chargeable to tax*

   (i) Training bursaries to trainee directors, associate directors, actors and actresses, technicians and stage managers, students attending the City University Arts Administration Courses, people attending full-time courses in arts administration (the practical training course) and in-service bursaries for the theatre designers scheme.

   (ii) 'Buying Time Awards' to dramatists, authors, composers and artists to maintain the recipient to enable him to take time off to develop and explore his personal talents. These at present include the awards and bursaries known as the—

Theatre Writing Bursaries;

Awards and Bursaries to Composers;

Awards and Bursaries to Painters, Sculptors and Printmakers;

Literature Awards and Bursaries.

The Arts Council of Great Britain (and, it is expected, the other Arts Councils) will indicate to recipients the category into which particular awards fall for tax purposes. Where necessary, a recipient should be asked to provide documentary evidence of his award and, if doubt or difficulty then remains, the case should be referred to BPD Literary and Artistic Profits.

Expenses It is open to the Arts Council to make both a taxable grant under (*a*)(ii) above and a non-taxable award under (*b*)(ii) above to an individual. In such a case, the expenditure incurred by the individual in connection with the matters covered by the taxable grant and the non-taxable award may exceed the amount of the taxable grant. It has been agreed with the Arts Council that in cases where this occurs, such excess expenditure (up to and including the amount of the non-taxable award) should be regarded as covered by the non-taxable award, and to that extent should not be allowed as a deduction in arriving at the individual's taxable profits. The remainder of the expenditure, and any other expenditure incurred by the individual, is subject to the normal Schedule D expenses rules. Similarly, where only a non-taxable award is received, any expenditure incurred in fulfilling the aims or conditions of the award should not be allowed as a deduction to the extent that it can be regarded as covered by the non-taxable award.

Deductions

2692. In computing liabilities under Case II or Case VI (*see* IM 1706), the allowable deductions may include the reasonable expenses of producing the literary etc works and the expenses, including agents' commission, incurred in putting them on the market. Where the assessment is under Case VI, it should be described as, for example 'Literary earnings'.

Royalties received by a person other than the author etc

2693. Copyright royalties received by a person other than the author, composer etc (unless they form part of the receipts of a trade assessable under Case I or represent post-cessation receipts—*see* IM 2697), are to be assessed under—

(*a*)   Case III, if they are derived from a United Kingdom copyright (or, exceptionally, Case VI if they are not pure income)

(*b*)   Case V, if they are derived from a foreign copyright.
     An allowance should be given, where appropriate, for agents' commission.

As regards copyright royalties received by persons abroad, *see* IM 4000 onwards

Earned income

2694.   Income within IM 2690, sub-heads (*a*) and (*b*)—but not income within IM 2693—should normally be regarded as earned income.

Claims to spread lump sum etc, payments for copyright etc

2695.   ICTA 1988, s 534, ICTA 1988, s 535 and ICTA 1988, s 538 provide that certain payments in respect of copyright etc which would normally be assessable as income of a single year, may be spread over a period of years.
     ICTA 1988, s 534 applies where the author of a literary etc work, who has spent more than twelve months on its production, receives as consideration for the assignment of the whole or part of the copyright or for the grant of a licence therein—

(*a*)   a lump sum payment, including an advance on account of royalties which is not returnable or

(*b*)   any payment of, or on account of, royalties or sums payable periodically, which are receivable within two years after first publication of the literary etc work.

He may claim that the payment should be spread back over two years (if the work took between twelve and twenty-four months to produce) or over three years (if the work took more than twenty-four months to produce).
     ICTA 1988, s 535 applies where the author of a literary etc work receives a lump sum payment as consideration for the assignment of the whole or part of the copyright, or for the grant of a licence therein, and—

(*a*)   the copyright is assigned etc for a period of two years or more and

(*b*)   the assignment etc is made not less than ten years after first publication of the work.

The taxpayer may claim that—

(i)   where the copyright is assigned etc for six years or more, the lump sum payment should be spread *forward* over six years

(ii) where the assignment etc is for two or more but less than six years, the payment should be spread *forward* over as many years as there are whole years in the period covered by the assignments etc.

The Section contains special provisions dealing with the case where the author dies, or his profession is permanently discontinued, during the period over which the lump sum payment has been spread. It is also provided that claims under ICTA 1988, s 534 and ICTA 1988, s 535 may not be made in respect of the same payment.

ICTA 1988, s 538 applies to any sum received by a painter, sculpture or other artist for the sale of a painting, sculpture or other work of art, or by way of commission or fee for the creation of the work of art, where—

A)   he was engaged on the making of the work of art for a period of more than twelve months or

B)   he was engaged for a period of more than twelve months in making a number of works of art for an exhibition, and the work is one of them.

In this context, 'work of art' covers all original works of artistic merit but does not extend to works of conventional craftsmanship of a commercial nature. The painter, sculptor or other artist may claim that the payment should be spread back over two years (if the work took between twelve and twenty-four months to produce) or over three years (if the work took more than twenty-four months to produce).

Claims for relief

2696.   The provisions regarding copyright in ICTA 1988, s 534 and ICTA 1988, s 535 apply not only to the author of a literary work, but also to a composer, dramatist, painter or sculptor who receives a lump sum payment for assigning or granting an interest in the copyright of a work which he has produced. Relief may be claimed in respect of post-cessation receipts (*see* IM 2697 and IM 1750 onwards).

The agreement with the publisher of a literary work will normally establish the nature of the payment. An advance which is not reclaimable by the publisher, but may be wholly or partially returned by the author etc if he terminates the agreement, should be regarded as within the Sections.

Where in a claim under ICTA 1988, s 538, an artist states that his works were, or are being, prepared for an exhibition and there are no grounds for doubting it, his claim may be accepted without other evidence that the exhibition was, or is to be, held.

When allowing relief under ICTA 1988, s 534 and ICTA 1988, s 535, the amount to be spread is the gross amount before deduction of expenses, except that where an agent's commission is deducted from the lump sum before it is passed on to the author etc, the net amount *after* deduction of the commission should be spread.

Cases of difficulty should be submitted to BPD Literary and Artistic Profits before an appeal is set down for hearing. Appeals under ICTA 1988, s 534 are heard by the Special Commissioners and under ICTA 1988, s 535 by the General Commissioners.

Post-cessation etc., receipts

2697. The provisions of ICTA 1988, s 103, ICTA 1988, s 110(2) and ICTA 1988, s 106 will apply where copyright royalties and other receipts arising from the carrying on of a literary or artistic profession accrue—

(*a*)   after the death of the author etc or

(*b*)   after his profession has been permanently discontinued.

Detailed instructions on these provisions are contained in IM 1751 onwards. *See also* IM 1754 onwards as regards certain receipts chargeable to tax under ICTA 1988, s 104, where accounts are not prepared on the earnings basis and the profession is discontinued or there is a change of accounting basis.

Gifts of literary, etc., works

2698. The case of *Mason v Innes*, 1967, 44 TC 326, shows that where an individual who carries on a profession—

(*a*)   produces a literary, artistic or other work in the exercise of that profession and

(*b*)   before or after completion of the work, disposes of his rights therein, otherwise than in the course of the profession, by way of gift or for a consideration less than market value,

the decision in *Sharkey v Wernher* (*see* IM 590) cannot be applied to claim tax under Case II of Schedule D on the market value of the gift, or the difference between the market value and the disposal price, as the case may be.

Any such disposition should, however, be considered for Capital Gains Tax liability.

Reports to Head Office

2699. A report should be made to BPD Literary and Artistic Profits or to BP4 Schedule D, as appropriate, in any case where an Inspector is in doubt as to the application of the decision in *Mason v Innes* and, in particular, where—

(*a*)   the rights in the literary, etc., work are immediately sold by the recipient for a lump sum payment (and not, as in Mason *v* Innes, used as a source of income);

(*b*)   legal avoidance is suspected;

(*c*)   it is contended that there is no liability to Capital Gains Tax; or

(*d*)   any attempt is made to extend the application of the decision in *Mason v Innes* to the case of a trader.

2700. ...

Public lending right

2701. The Public Lending Right Act 1979 gave authors the right to payment from a central fund for the use made of their books when borrowed by members of the public from Public Libraries.

To qualify for payment of Public Lending Right (PLR), authors must register their books with the Registrar of PLR. The maximum amount an author can receive in any one year is £6,000 but most receive substantially less.

PLR can be assigned in the same way as copyright and expires at the same time, usually after fifty years from the end of the calendar year in which an author dies.

PLR is treated in the same way as copyright for tax purposes (ICTA 1988, s 537).

2702–2709. ...

Films, tapes and discs (tax treatment after 9 March 1982)

Relief for expenditure on master versions

3300. There are special rules governing the timing of Case I etc. deductions for expenditure on the production or acquisition of the master negative, tape or disc of a film or audio product. These rules were introduced in 1982 and amended in 1984. They are now in CAA 1990, s 68. Further legislation to accelerate relief for expenditure on certain 'qualifying' films was introduced by Sections 41–43, Finance (No 2) Act 1992. Consequential amendments to CAA 1990, s 68 were made by Section 69, of the 1992 Act.

Capital allowances

As an alternative to relief as a Case I deduction expenditure on certain qualifying films may be regarded as expenditure on plant for capital allowances purposes (see IM 3325). In practice this option is only likely to be attractive to most film concerns at high rates of first year allowance.

Statements of practice

On 11 January 1993 the Board issued a Statement of Practice, SP 1/93. This statement offers guidance on the operation of the 1992 provisions and also incorporates two earlier statements of practice, SP 2/83 and SP 2/85 dealing with the 1982 and 1984 legislation. The material parts of the published guidance are reflected in the instructions at IM 3301–3342 below.

Approach in practice

Inspectors should not seek to fine tune the timing of relief for production and acquisition expenditure where a reasonable attempt has been made to comply with the rules described below. Where agreement cannot be reached locally about the tax treatment of expenditure on films etc. and the amounts involved are substantial, advice should be sought from SPI Schedule D before the appeal is listed for personal hearing.

Instructions

3301. The instructions are set out as follows:

3302–3311	treatment of expenditure generally on master versions of films, tapes or discs
3320–3341	alternative treatment of expenditure on master versions of 'qualifying' films
3342	non-Case I expenditure

Treatment of expenditure generally on films tapes or discs

3302. The expenditure covered by CAA 1990, s 68 is that on the production or acquisition of the master negative of a film, a master tape or a master disc whether the tape or disc is the medium for a film or for an audio product. Expenditure on acquisition includes that on the acquisition of any description of rights in the master version of the film.

Terms used in instructions

References to 'films etc.' in the ensuing paragraphs include references to audio products. References to the production of, or acquisition of rights in, a film, tape or disc are references to the production of, or acquisition of rights in, the master version.

Excluded expenditure

The provisions do not cover expenditure on the purchase of reproductions (such as video cassettes), for examples, by a trader who hires them out to the general public. Thus, if the assets otherwise qualify for capital allowances as plant (by having a life of at least two years, CA 1510) they continue to do so.

Treatment of expenditure generally on films tapes or discs—items deemed to be revenue

3303. Expenditure within IM 3302 which would otherwise have qualified as capital expenditure on the production or acquisition of plant (the master negative etc.) is deemed for all purposes to be revenue expenditure (CAA 1990, s 68(1)). Conversely all income derived from the film etc. (whether, for example, by way of sale, grant of rights or compensation) is to be regarded as a revenue receipt (CAA 1990, s 68(8)).

The rules ensuring that income and expenditure are on revenue account described in the first subparagraph above apply for all tax purposes. Those described below (IM 3304 onwards) allocating production and acquisition expenditure to periods of account, apply only in computing the profits arising from a trade (or business—*see* IM 3342) which includes the exploitation of the master versions of films etc.

Exclusion of trading stock

These allocation rules do not apply where the master version of the film etc. constitutes trading stock. In such cases the ordinary principles for valuing and carrying forward stock and work in progress apply (*see* IM 549 onwards). But generally a film producing company does not hold its films as trading stock. It does not sell the film in its entirety but instead grants exhibition rights, although documents and accounts may well refer to 'sales'. Similarly an audio production company will not usually hold its master tapes or discs as trading stock. The company does not sell these 'masters', but uses them to produce cassette tapes, compact discs etc. and it is these reproductions which are its stock in trade.

Within a group a film production company may make a practice of selling the master negative, with all the rights attached, to an associated distribution company. In that event, the rules in IM 3304 onwards apply to the distribution company.

Allocable expenditure

3304. The expenditure in respect of a film etc. which is allocated under CAA 1990, s 68(3)–(6) is—

    (i) the deemed revenue expenditure described in IM 3303 first sub-paragraph plus

    (ii) actual revenue expenditure on film etc. production (*see* Section 68(3)(*b*))

Particular items included

Items falling under one or other of the two heads include the following—

– the cost of acquiring the master version where another concern makes the film etc.
– the cost of acquiring rights to make a film (whether by way of a lump sum or recurring royalties)
– the cost of adaptation of a story for film purposes
– all normal production expenses such as salaries of production staff, costumes, hire of studios, costs of filming, processing and editing.

Exclusions

On the other hand Inspectors should exclude—

– capital expenditure, such as that on film cameras or sound-recording equipment, which is not used up in the course of a production; this should be dealt with under the capital allowances code in the usual way
– wages of studio technicians charged under general overheads and not attributed to specific productions (as may be the case with the independent television companies) where the accounting treatment should be followed for Case I
– interest on money borrowed to finance the production
– expenditure which is otherwise inadmissible such as entertaining or sums failing the 'wholly and exclusively' test in ICTA 1988, s 74(*a*); this result follows from the wording of CAA 1990, s 68(10).

Abortive expenditure

Where production costs are incurred or rights are acquired, and a decision is taken not to proceed with the project, the expenditure may be charged to revenue for tax purposes at the time when the assets are considered to have no further value.

Timing of expenditure
'Relevant period'

3305.   CAA 1990, s 68(3) provides that expenditure within IM 3304 must be allocated to 'relevant periods. Where the expenditure is incurred in the course of a trade the relevant period will be the period for which accounts are made up. (*See* IM 3342 regarding the expenditure incurred other than in the course of a trade.)

Alternative methods of allocation

There are two methods of allocating expenditure; the **'income matching'** method and the **'cost recovery'** method. Cost recovery only applies if a claim is made (*see* IM 3309) and serves to supplement the expenditure allocated to a period under the income matching method.

Advances received

Under either method the expenditure identified under IM 3304 cannot normally be deducted until the value of the film etc. begins to be realised, typically by earning income on release. Under some distribution agreements non-repayable advances of royalties are received and properly brought into account prior to release. In such cases expenditure may be deducted from the period in which the advances are first brought into account.

Income matching method of allocating production expenditure
Outline

3306.   Under this method expenditure is written off over the period during which the value of the film etc. is expected to be realised in proportion to income earned. CAA 1990, s 68(4) provides that the expenditure to be allocated to a particular period of account is to be such as is reasonable and just having regard to—

(*a*)   the amount of expenditure unallowed at the beginning of the period (calculated by excluding sums deducted in earlier periods not only under Section 68 but also, in the case of 'qualifying films' (IM 3325), under Sections 41–42 F(No 2)A 1992—IM 3328 and 3335);

(*b*)   the proportion which the value of the film etc. realised in the period bears to that value plus the estimated residual value at the end of that period.

Current and residual values

Where a film is produced and exploited by the grant of exhibition rights, the value realised in a period will simply be the receipts referable to that period and the estimated residual value of the film will be the estimated future income (discounted at current rates if appropriate). Estimates of future income will inevitably be revised over the life of a film as its success (or otherwise) become easier to assess.

TV films and leasing transactions

The treatment of certain television films, where the value of the film cannot be measured by income directly derived from them, and that of films exploited by way of a finance lease, where the lessor's return does not depend directly on the success of the film, is discussed in IM 3310 and 3311.

Formula

3307. The income matching method of writing off expenditure as income is earned can be expressed by this formula—

Expenditure to be allowed in period of account $= E \times \dfrac{A}{A + B}$

Where—

E   is the total expenditure on producing a film less any amounts already allowed.

A   is the gross income from the film in that period.

B   is the expected future gross income from the film.

Example 1

A film is in the course of production during year 1 and expenditure of £2.5 m is incurred. The film is completed in year 2 after further expenditure of £1.5 m has been incurred. At the end of year 2 the expected total income from the film is £8 m but at the end of year 3 expected total income has fallen to £6 m.

The amounts of income earned are:		
	Year 2	£3 m
	Year 3	£2 m
	Year 4	£1 m

The expected future income is:		
At the end of year 2	£5 m	(£8 m–£3 m)
At the end of year 3	£1 m	(£6 m–£5 m)
At the end of year 4	negligible	

The treatment of the income and expenditure for tax purposes is as follows—

Year 1	The production costs £2.5 m will be carried forward.	
Year 2	Income brought into account	£3 m
	Expenditure deductible:	
	$£4 \text{ m} \times \dfrac{\text{Income of year £3 m}}{\text{Income of year £ 3m + future income £5 m}}$	(£1.5 m)
Year 3	Income: brought into account	£2 m

Expenditure deductible:

$$(\pounds 4 \text{ m} - \pounds 1.5 \text{ m}) \times \frac{\pounds 2\text{m}}{\pounds 5 \text{ m} + \pounds 1 \text{ m}} \qquad (\pounds 1.7 \text{ m})$$

Year 4   Income brought into account   £1 m

Expenditure deductible

$$(\pounds 4 \text{ m} - (\pounds 1.5 \text{ m} + \pounds 1.7 \text{ m})) \times \frac{\pounds 1 \text{ m}}{\pounds 1\text{m} + \text{nil}} \qquad (\pounds 0.8 \text{ m})$$

Where, at the end of an accounting period, the amount of expenditure not yet written off on the above formula exceeds the estimated future income (because estimates of the total income from the film have been revised downwards), the excess may be written off.

Example 2

Thus, if, in Example 1 above, the income of year 3 were £0.8 m only, and the estimated future income at the end of year 3 were £0.2 m only, the amount to be written off in year 3 would be as follows—

Expenditure written off per formula	£2 m*
Plus excess of expenditure not yet written off over estimated future income	£0.3 m**
Total expenditure written off	£2.3 m

$$\pounds 2.5 \text{ m} \times \frac{\pounds 0.8\text{m}}{\pounds 0.8\text{m} + \pounds 0.2\text{m}} \qquad = \pounds 2 \text{ m*}$$

Expenditure (£m 4) less allowed (£1.5 m × £2 m)	£0.5 m
Estimated future income	(£0.2 m)
Excess of expenditure not yet written off over estimated future income	£0.3 m**

Particular points
'Batching' of films

3308. In the case of individual feature films, it will normally be necessary to estimate the future income separately for each film. In some cases, however, where records show that the income flow follows a fairly regular pattern, and where past experience is likely to apply to current productions, it may be acceptable to write off expenditure on that same basis; but it will be necessary to verify from time to time that the income earning pattern has not changed. (*See* IM 3311 regarding films made by independent TV companies.)

Works by less well-known musicians

In the case of some productions, for example, original master discs for 'singles' in the popular music field where the artist or group is not well known, income from exploitation rights is likely to arise only for a period of a few weeks, or at most months, after release. Where the costs of production are relatively small (say less than about £50,000) and the predicted life is less than 12 months, there will normally be no objection to writing off the cost when the tape or CD is released, and

ignoring the possibility of related income arising in the next accounting period, if
that is the practice followed in preparing the accounts.

'Cost recovery' method
Outline

3309. CAA 1990, s 68(5) and (6) were introduced in 1984 and enable a film etc.
concern to avoid recognising any profit on a production until all the production or
acquisition expenditure described in IM 3304 have been set against the sums
receivable from that production.

Procedure

The provisions enable a claim to be made for a period of account to top up the
amount deductible under the income matching method (CAA 1990, s 68(4), *see* IM
3306–3307) so that the amount set off is equal to the value realised, typically the
receipts recognised, in the period. The claim must be made within two years of the
end of the period of account to which it relates. Informal claims, for example on the
face of the computations, may be accepted.

   In practice it is unnecessary to calculate as a separate step the relief due under the
income matching method to give effect to a 'cost recovery' claim.

Example

A film is in course of production during year 1 and expenditure of £2.5 m is
incurred. The film is completed and released in year 2 after further expenditure of
£1.5 m has been incurred. At the end of year 2 the expected total income from the
film is £8 m.

The amounts of income earned are:

	Year 2	£3 m
	Year 3	£2 m

The expected future income at the end of Year 2 is £5 m (£8 m–£3 m).
Under the income matching method the position is as follows:

Year 1   The production costs of £2.5 m are carried forward.

Year 2   Income brought into account   £3 m

   Expenditure deductible:

   $E \times \dfrac{A}{A = B}$ £4 m $\times \dfrac{£3\ m}{3\ m} = 5\ m$ (£1.5 m)

   Expenditure carried forward

   £4 m – £1.5 m   £2.5 m

Under the cost recovery method a claim can now be made to write off in year 2 a
further £1.5 m; this is the excess of the income brought into account (£3 m) over the
expenditure allocated under the income matching method (£1.5 m).

The figures for year 3 will then be

Year 3   Income brought into account   £2 m

Expenditure deductible:

balance unallowed (£4 m – £3 m) (£1 m)

Where at the end of a period of account after the release of a film etc. the expenditure not yet written off exceeds the estimated future income the claim under the cost recovery rules for that period does not prevent the excess from being written off in the period as it would have been (*see* IM 3307, example 2) if no such claim had been made.

Thus if in the example above the estimated remaining income at the end of year 2 was only £0.5 m, so that a loss of £0.5 m on the total production was expected, the figures would be

Year 2	Income brought into account	£3 m
	Expenditure deductible	(£3.5 m)
	Loss	(£0.5 m)
	Expenditure carried forward	
	£4 m – £3.5 m	£0.5 m
	(that is, limited to the expected future income)	

'Cost recovery' method—finance leases

3310. In principle the rules described above apply to the finance lessor of a film etc. (*See* IM 2670 on finance leasing generally.) Under these arrangements the lessor does not seek a return geared to the success of a film but rather the equivalent of interest on his investment. As a matter of economic substance the risks and rewards of ownership lie with the lessee.

It follows that under the 'income matching' method described in IM 3306–3307 above it would not be 'just and reasonable' (CAA 1990, s 68(3)) to allocate expenditure in accordance with the formula in IM 3307. Instead the amount of expenditure to be deducted should be such as to leave a profit on the transaction (before administrative expenses etc.) equivalent to the rate of interest implicit in the lease.

Approach in practice

In practice it is thought that it will seldom be necessary to calculate this figure. This is because the cost recovery method will be invoked (IM 3309) in order to supplement the deduction available under the income matching method and so to defer recognising a profit until the later years of the lease. If a calculation of implicit interest is required the assistance of Business Profits Division 4 (Schedule D) is available.

'Cost recovery' method—TV films

3311. The application of the rules described in IM 3306–3309 to TV production companies present no special problems where the income from the exploitation of the master negative of a film can be identified. This is understood to be the case where for example an independent television company produces a film for showing on the ITV network.

Where, however a film is primarily exploited by being shown only to the television production company's own audience (for example viewers in the local area of an ITV contractor rather than networked) it will not normally be possible to calculate by reference to the amount of income earned and the estimated future earnings the rate at which the value of the film is realised (*see* IM 3306(*b*)). This is because the film's value takes the form of advertising revenue generally, none of which is directly referable to the film concerned.

In estimating the remaining value of such films for the purpose of CAA 1990, s 68(4)(*b*) Inspectors should consider in particular whether a film is likely to be repeated or otherwise generate income after its first showing. If not, then it can be accepted that the whole of the film's value was realised at its first showing and that therefore the whole of the expenditure can be deducted for the period when shown. But where further income in some form is likely to be generated it should be contended that a proportion of the expenditure on production or acquisition should be carried forward.

Claims under the cost recovery rules should be resisted unless it can be shown that the revenues (including advertising revenues) referable to a film can be specifically identified.

Example

An independent television company makes a six part film at a cost of £800,000. The production is started in year 1 and completed in year 2. The film is primarily of local interest, so it plans to show it in its local area in year 2 with a repeat in year 4. Fees of £100,000 are earned in year 2 from the grant of exhibition rights to the ITC with the franchise for the adjacent area. At the end of year 2, it is estimated that only 20 per cent of the value of the asset will remain and after the second showing the value will be negligible. The company earns most of its income from advertising revenue.

The production costs in year 1 will be carried forward to year 2. In year 2 £600,000, being 80 per cent of the production costs, will be charged against advertising revenue and the income from the grant of the rights to other ITV companies. The balance of the expenditure will be written off on the second showing in year 4.

Approach in practice

In strictness the provisions require each film etc. production to be considered separately. In practice, however, in the case of the independent television companies (and others responsible for a large number of productions) a standard basis of write off should if possible be agreed either for all productions or for particular ranges.

3312–3324. . . .

'Qualifying films'

3325.   Under the Films Act 1985 the Secretary of State is empowered to certify for tax purposes films (but not audio works) meeting the necessary conditions. These conditions ensure a minimum level UK / Commonwealth / European Community participation in the film and are described further in IM 3337 below. Avenues of relief for expenditure on the production or acquisition of a qualifying film are set out below.

Qualifying films—avenues of relief

In summary—

(*a*)   qualifying films (that is, those certified as qualifying by the Secretary of State) completed (*see* IM 3326) **prior to 10 March 1992** are automatically outside the CAA 1990, s 68 regime so that expenditure on them normally qualifies for capital allowances—*see* IM 3327

(*b*)   film concerns may elect for qualifying films completed **on or after 10 March 1992** to receive the treatment set out in (a)—IM 3328; otherwise Section 68 applies with the additional options described in (c) and (d) below

(*c*)   expenditure on a qualifying film **completed on or after 10 March 1992** may be written off in three annual instalments starting in the period in which it is completed—IM 3329

(*d*)   preliminary expenditure incurred **on or after 10 March 1992** on a qualifying film may be written off immediately—IM 3335–3338.

'Qualifying films'—when film completed

3326.   To determine what reliefs are available it is necessary to establish when a qualifying film was completed. For this purpose a film is completed when it is first in a form in which it can reasonably be regarded as ready for presentation to the general public (CAA 1990, s 68(9B) introduced by F(No 2)A 1992, s 69(9)). But if it is acquired after completion the date of acquisition is substituted for the date of completion.

In the case of a cinema film the date of completion will normally be when it has been edited and is ready to be delivered to the distributor even if, exceptionally, it is later sent back to the producer for changes.

Presentation to 'general public'

The condition that a film has to be ready for presentation to the general public should not be regarded as failed simply because it is not put on general release. This situation may arise if it is for example a training film or plans for a general release are abandoned at the last minute.

. . .

*Qualifying films completed or acquired **on or after 10 March 1992***
Election for CA treatment

3328. Where the qualifying film is completed or (if later) acquired on or after 10 March 1992 capital allowances treatment as described in IM 3327 remains available subject to the making of an irrevocable election.

Substantive conditions The substantive conditions for making such an election are:

- the tests described in IM 3327 must be satisfied
- none of the expenditure on the film concerned can have been relieved under CAA 1990, s 68 or F(No 2)A 1992, s 41–F(No 2)A 1992, s 43.

Procedural requirements

For Income Tax the time limit for claims to elect for capital allowances treatment under CAA 1990, s 68(9) depends on whether or not the period is one to which self-assessment applies.

Where the period of account in which film is completed (*see* IM 3326) ends in 1997–98 or later (1996–97 for trades commencing on or after 6 April 1994) the election must be made by 31 January in the next but one year of assessment after the year of assessment in which that period of account ends. If therefore the film is completed in the period of account to 30 April 1997 the election must be made by 31 January 2000.

Where the period of account in which the film is completed (*see* IM 3326) ends in an earlier year of assessment the claim must be made within two years of the end of that period of account.

The time limit for corporation tax remains two years from the end of the period of account to which the claim relates.

The other procedural requirements are that the election must—

- identify the film and state the amount of the expenditure (the election must cover all the expenditure on the film)
- be accompanied by a copy of the Secretary of State's certificate that the film is a qualifying film
- be signed, as the case may be, by the individual claimant, by the company secretary in the case of a company or in the case of a partnership, by the partner signing the partnership tax return.

3329. Where no election is made the rules in CAA 1990, s 68 (IM 3302–IM 3311) apply. In addition, however, a claim may be made to write off production or acquisition expenditure on a qualifying film on the alternative basis described below. *See also* IM 3335–IM 3338 regarding relief for preliminary expenditure.

Alternative method of writing off production and acquisition expenditure

This alternative basis is set out in F(No 2)A 1992, s 42. It was introduced in response to film industry representations that there was often a significant interval between the completion of a film and its release during which no relief for production expenditure was due.

Under F (No 2)A 1992, s 42 production or acquisition expenditure, subject to a claim, first qualifies as a deduction in computing profits for the period of account in which the film was completed or acquired (*see* IM 3326 for meaning of completion etc.). The relief available is one third of the total expenditure on the film in that and, subject to appropriate claims, subsequent periods.

Points to watch

The following points should be noted—

(*a*)   the total expenditure should be reduced by any preliminary expenditure on the film relieved under F(No 2)A 1992, s 41 (*see* IM 3335–IM 3338)

(*b*)   where the period of account is less than twelve months the relief is reduced pro rata; but the relief is not increased if the period of account exceeds twelve months

(*c*)   relief is not due under CAA 1990, s 68 (IM 3302–IM 3311) for the period for which a F(No 2)A 1992, s 42 claim is made but CAA 1990, s 68 relief may still be given for other periods in respect of the same film

(*d*)   the relief cannot exceed the expenditure at the beginning of the period which has not yet been allowed.

Procedural requirements

Where there is any doubt over whether the film is a qualifying film (IM 3325) the Inspector should call for a copy of the Secretary of State's certificate.

For Income Tax the time limit for claims to deduct production expenditure under F(No 2)A 1992, s 42 depends on whether or not the period is one to which self-assessment applies.

Where the period of account to which the claim relates ends in 1995–96 or earlier the claim must be made within two years of the end of that period of account.

Where the period of account to which the claim relates ends in 1996–97 or later the claim must be made by 31 January in the next but one year of assessment after the year of assessment in which that period of account ends. If therefore the expenditure relates to the period of account to 30 April 1997 the claim must be made by 31 January 2000.

The time limit for Corporation Tax remains two years from the end of the period of account to which the claim relates.

3330–3334. . . .

Preliminary expenditure incurred on or after 10 March 1992 on qualifying films
Outline

3335.   F(No 2)A 1992, s 41 introduced a further relaxation in the rules governing the timing of deductions for production expenditure relating to qualifying films. This enables a claim to be made, in computing profits from a trade—or business (*see* IM 3342)—which includes the exploitation of films, to write off particularly high risk expenditure (up to a ceiling) on a qualifying film for the period of account in which it is incurred (that is, becomes payable). The expenditure covered is described in more detail in IM 3336 below but in broad terms the relief covers expenditure incurred before it is clear the film will actually be produced. This is referred to as 'preliminary expenditure' in the Board's Statement of Practice (SP 1/93) (*see* IM 3300) but is also termed 'pre-production' or 'development' expenditure in the film industry.

Conditions

3336. The sums covered represent production expenditure within IM 3304 which meets condition (*a*) or (*b*), and all the other conditions set out below—

(*a*)   (if the film has been completed when the claim is made) the film is a qualifying film

(*b*)   (if the film has not been completed when the claim is made) the film is reasonably likely to be a qualifying film

(*c*)   the expenditure can reasonably be said to have been incurred to enable a decision to be taken whether or not to go ahead with the film

(*d*)   the sums concerned are incurred before the first day of principal photography

(*e*)   the total amounts deducted for the period of account in question and earlier periods must not exceed 20 per cent of the film's budget as at the start of principal photography

(*f*)   the expenditure is not incurred in circumstances where it is repayable if production of the film fails to go ahead

(*g*)   the expenditure is incurred (that is, becomes payable) in the period of account for which the claim is made or in an earlier period

(*h*)   relief for the expenditure has not already been given.

Conditions for qualifying status

3337. In considering whether the requirements set out in IM 3336 are satisfied Inspectors should bear in mind the following points.

Condition (b) in 3336

Where the film has not been completed when the claim is made it is necessary to consider whether it is reasonably likely that the film, if in fact completed, would be a qualifying film. In these circumstances it will not be possible to rely on certification by the Secretary of State that the film is a qualifying film. Instead it will normally be appropriate to accept assurances from the film concern that it is using its best endeavours to ensure the film meets the necessary conditions.

Summary of conditions for qualifying status

If, exceptionally, it is considered necessary to examine the position in more detail Inspectors should refer initially to the brief outline of the conditions on which qualifying status depends set out below. If necessary, Business Profits Division (Schedule D) should be consulted. Those conditions are—

(i)   where the film is made by a company that company must have been both registered and centrally managed and controlled in the UK or another member State of the EC throughout the period the film was being made

(ii)   an unincorporated film maker must have been ordinarily resident in the UK or another EC member State

(iii)   the studio used must have been in the UK, another Commonwealth country or the Republic of Ireland

(iv) 75 per cent of the labour costs must have been represented by payments to Commonwealth citizens (including British subjects), citizens of EC member States or to ordinary residents of those countries.

Condition (c) in 3336—Contributions towards preliminary expenditure

For this purpose the decision to go ahead with a film should not be regarded as taken until (at the earliest) all the necessary elements, and particularly finance, are in place.

It should be noted that the film in question need not be that of the trader laying out the expenditure. A contribution towards the preliminary expenditure of a film-maker may itself qualify for relief as preliminary expenditure (though only in computing the profits from the contributor's trade of exploiting films) so long as all the conditions set out in IM 3336 are satisfied.

Condition (d) in 3336—'Principal photography'

Principal photography is a well-understood term in the film industry and begins when the main filming project gets underway. This date is used as a trigger for a number of contractual arrangements. If exceptionally it is considered necessary to look closely at the date put forward by a film-maker the documentation should make it clear what corroborative evidence can reasonably be sought.

Condition (f) in 3336—Repayable expenditure

This condition is intended to bolster the Exchequer's defences against attempts to dress up as preliminary expenditure qualifying for immediate write off expenditure which would normally have been incurred only after the decision to go ahead with a film has been taken. A 'commitment fee' paid to (say) a lead actress will be excluded from preliminary expenditure if the fee is refundable in the event that the film does not go ahead. A non-refundable fee on the other hand would satisfy the condition.

Condition (h) in 3336—Interaction with other provisions

The legislation provides that expenditure allowed under other provisions cannot be relieved under Section 41 F(No 2)A 1992. Conversely, expenditure relieved under Section 41 cannot also be relieved under other provisions. *See also* IM 3329(*a*) regarding the treatment of Section 41 expenditure in calculating the deduction for other production expenditure under Section 42.

Preliminary expenditure—procedural requirements

3338. Claims to deduct preliminary expenditure under Section 41 F(No 2)A 1992 should be made within two years of the end of the period of account in which the expenditure becomes payable. Thus for example, while a claim may be made to deduct expenditure incurred in period 1 in computing profits for period 2, the claim still has to be made by the end of period 3.

Claims should

– be signed by the person mentioned in IM 3328
– specify the period for which relief is claimed
– identify the film (or prospective film) concerned.

Theatre backers
General

3155. A theatre backer or 'angel' advances an agreed sum of money towards the financing of a theatre production. In return, if the play is successful, he may recover his money plus a share in the profits of the production. If the play is unsuccessful, he may lose the whole or part of his advance.

Any amount received which exceeds the amount advanced in a theatre backing transaction is—

(*a*)   normally in law income within Case III of Schedule D, on the authority of dicta in *Purchase v Stainer's Executors* (1951) 32 TC 367 and in *Mitchell v Rosay* (1954) 35 TC 496 or

(*b*)   possibly, and *in very exceptional cases*, a professional or trading receipt.

Any case of doubt or difficulty on this point should be submitted to BPD Literary and Artistic Profits once all the facts have been established.

If the surplus of return over investment is assessed under Case III, no relief is available for any amount by which sums recovered fall short of sums advanced unless the backer can establish that the shortfall constitutes a capital loss for CGT purposes. In order to afford Income Tax relief for such losses, the Board has sanctioned the practice of assessing surpluses arising from backing transactions under Case VI of Schedule D. The income so assessable is not to be regarded as earned income. Any deficiencies arising may, on this basis, be treated as Income Tax losses available for relief under ICTA 1988, s 392.

The Case VI basis will normally be advantageous to most angels and its application may be accepted without questions where the theatre backer is resident in the UK. Any request by such a backer for the strict Case III basis of assessment should, however, be met.

Where the backer is resident overseas similar treatment may be given so losses arising from theatre backing may be offset against profits. But since, fundamentally, the income arises under Case III, tax should be deducted at source by incorporated and, as appropriate, unincorporated payers.

Deduction of tax—annual payments
(ICTA 1988, s 348–ICTA 1988, s 350)
General position of Revenue

3900. An opinion as to the existence in a particular case of a right of deduction of tax should be given only with the reservation that the question is primarily one between payer and payee with which the Revenue is not immediately concerned.

It may happen very exceptionally that Value Added Tax (VAT) has to be charged on the consideration for goods or services and Income Tax is deductible from the consideration as a charge. Where a dispute arises about the amount from which Income Tax is deductible in such cases, BPD (Value Added Tax) should be consulted. Where, however, payments such as patent royalties are made in such circumstances that—

(*a*) VAT is chargeable in respect thereof and

(*b*) Income Tax is deductible in accordance with ICTA 1988, s 348 or ICTA 1988, s 349

then, although the Board has been advised that the deduction or Income Tax should be computed by reference to the full amount of the payment (inclusive of VAT) no objection should be raised if the payer and recipient agree to make and accept a deduction of Income Tax calculated by reference to the net payment exclusive of the VAT. In such cases, however, Inspectors should reserve the right to review the position at a future date in the light of actual experience in the operation of VAT.

3901. ICTA 1988, s 348 and ICTA 1988, s 349(1) apply to:—

(1) Annuities

(2) Annual payments

(3) Royalties or other sums in respect of the user of a patent

(4) Rents, royalties which by virtue of ICTA 1988, s 119–ICTA 1988, s 120 are subject to deduction of tax under ICTA 1988, s 348–ICTA 1988, s 349.

Payments excluded from ICTA 1988, s 348–ICTA 1988, s 349 ICTA 1988, s 347A

3902. ICTA 1988, s 347A removes most annual payments made by individuals from ICTA 1988, s 348 and ICTA 1988, s 349 so that deduction of tax will not apply. The main exceptions which are still treated as annual payments within ICTA 1988, s 348–ICTA 1988, s 349 are:—

(1) payments made under existing obligations—broadly binding obligations made before 15 March 1988

(2) covenanted donations to a charity

(3) payments made for genuine commercial reasons in connection with the covenantor's trade, profession or vocation.

ICTA 1988, s 347A does not apply to interest payments. These are still subject to deduction of tax by virtue of ICTA 1988, s 349(2).

3903–3909. . . .

Wholly paid out of profits or gains brought into charge, ICTA 1988, s 348

3910. Where the annuity etc. is payable wholly out of profits or gains brought into charge ICTA 1988, s 348 applies and the payer is entitled to deduct tax on making payment. Tax should be deducted at the basic rate for the year in which the amount payable becomes due.

3911–3919. . . .

Not wholly paid out of profits or gains brought into charge, ICTA 1988, s 349

3920. Where the payment is not payable or not wholly payable out of profits or gains brought into charge, ICTA 1988, s 349(1) applies and the payer is under an obligation to deduct tax. Where the payment is only partly paid out of profits or gains brought into charge, the whole amount falls within ICTA 1988, s 349(1) and tax is deductible at the basic rate in force for the year of payment.

Payments made by companies

3921. By virtue of ICTA 1988, s 7(1) no payment made by a UK resident company can be treated as paid out of profits or gains charged to Income Tax. Annuities etc. paid by UK resident companies are, therefore, governed by ICTA 1988, s 349 and the deduction of tax is mandatory.

Patent royalties

3922. The expression 'any royalty or other sum in respect of the user of a patent' in ICTA 1988, s 349(1) applies to income payments as distinct from capital payments (see *British Salmson Aero Engines Ltd v CIR*, at 22 TC 39 and 22 TC 42). Whether a payment is of an income nature of a capital nature depends upon the particular facts of each case, including the contractual relationship between the parties.

A lump sum payment in respect of the past user of a patent, or for the future user to a limited extent (that is, restricted to the amount or quantity), where there is no acquisition of a defined portion of the property in the patent but merely a personal right of user, should be regarded as an income payment.

Lump sum payments which are in respect of the acquisition of

(*a*) a patent outright by assignment

(*b*) the exclusive user of a patent for the whole of its unexpired life

(*c*) the future unlimited user of a patent for a term of years, should be regarded as capital payments.

The expression 'exclusive user' should be taken as applicable to the sole right to use a patent for a particular country or countries. The expression 'unlimited user' should be taken as applicable to the right to use a patent, without quantitative restriction, for a particular country or countries.

As to liability under ICTA 1988, s 349 in respect of capital sums paid for the purchase from a person not resident in the United Kingdom of rights in a United Kingdom patent, *see* IM 3660 onwards. As to liability to tax generally on capital sums received in respect of patent rights, *see* IM 3650 onwards. As to patent royalties paid to residents of double taxation countries and exempt from the United Kingdom tax *see* DT 1820 onwards.

3923–3939. . . .

Copyright and design right royalties etc. paid to persons abroad (ICTA 1988, s 536 and ICTA 1988, s 537B)

'Copyright'

4000. For the purposes of ICTA 1988, s 536, the term 'copyright' includes copyright in—

(*d*)   any literary work (including maps, charts, tables, computer programs and compilations such as encyclopedias, dictionaries etc.)

(*e*)   any dramatic work (excluding cinematograph productions—see third sub-para)

(*f*)   any musical work (including music intended to be used in a 'talking film')

(*g*)   any artistic work (including works of painting, drawing, sculpture, architectural works of art, engravings etc., but excluding photographs intended to be used for cinematograph purposes)

(*h*)   any design registered under the Registered Designs Act 1949 (*see* IM 1033).

ICTA 1988, s 537B applies provisions mirroring those in ICTA 1988, s 536 to design right which is the property right which subsists in original designs. 'Design' is defined by Section 213(2) of the Copyright, Designs and Patents Act 1988 as, 'the design of any aspect of the shape or configuration (whether internal or external) of the whole or part of an article'. This right exists whether or not the design is registered. The instructions in this section should be applied, suitably amended, to payments for design right.

Under ICTA 1988, s 536(2), copyright in a cinematograph film or video recording or the sound-track of such a film or recording is excluded from the provisions of the Section. It is, however, considered that the words refer to the copyright of the owner of the film as such and not, for example, to the literary copyright of the author of the scenario or shooting script upon which the film is based. It follows therefore that such literary copyright falls within the general provisions of the Section.

Public Lending Right (IM 2701) is treated in the same way as copyright by virtue of ICTA 1988, s 537.

Types of payment liable

4001. ICTA 1988, s 536 applies where the payment is—

(*a*)   itself a royalty or other sum, for example, one computed on a profit-sharing basis, payable periodically or

(*b*)   a lump sum advance on account of, or, in general, a composition for, sums falling within (*a*). (*See CIR v Longmans Green & Co Ltd*, 17 TC 272.)

(Throughout the remainder of this section, any instructions relating to a royalty should be regarded as equally applicable to the other payments described in (*a*) and (*b*) above.)

Most double taxation agreements have a clause dealing with copyright royalties. Where payments to which ICTA 1988, s 536 would otherwise apply are made to the resident of a country with which we have a double taxation agreement, FICO (International), on receipt of a competent claim from the overseas party, is usually able to authorise the payer not to deduct tax.

Where it is claimed that tax should not be deducted from a payment within (*a*) or (*b*) above, on the grounds that the recipient is a professional author, composer etc., the fact should be reported to BP3 (Literary and Artistic Profits).

ICTA 1988, s 536 does not apply to a lump sum payment made in outright purchase of a copyright or of serial rights as distinct from a lump sum advance within (*b*) above.

Normally tax is not deductible by proprietors of newspapers or periodicals from payments made by them to contributors abroad for news, articles, essays etc.

Care is needed in considering the application of ICTA 1988, s 536 to computer software. Where software is purchased it is often accompanied by a licence entitling the purchaser to use the software and giving him a limited right to copy it to facilitate its use. In these circumstances we do not usually argue that any part of the payment for the software is a payment to which ICTA 1988, s 536 applies. It is only where, exceptionally, the purchaser has acquired a right of reproduction in order to make several copies as a way of exploiting the software that ICTA 1988, s 536 applies. Careful consideration of the agreement will also be necessary to ensure that it grants rights of reproduction of the software and not merely the right to distribute copies supplied by the owner of the copyright. BP3 (Literary and Artistic Profits) should be consulted in cases of doubt.

Publisher acting as mere selling agent

4002. Payments made by virtue of an agreement under which the sole copyright remains the property of the author or composer, the work being altogether financed by him and the publisher acting as a mere selling agent, should not be regarded as payments in respect of copyright at all.

A non-resident author or composer who has entered into such an agreement may, however, be exercising a trade in the United Kingdom through the publisher as his agent (*see* IM 170 onwards).

Sales, performances etc. in UK

4003. The royalties within the scope of ICTA 1988, s 536 are those relating to sales of books or music, performances of plays etc. within the United Kingdom only.

Advances

4004. Where an advance is made on account of royalties, tax is deductible on the whole of the advance, irrespective of the question where the future sales, performances etc. may take place. Relief by way of repayment can be claimed afterwards to the extent that the royalties covered by the advance are found to relate to sales, performances etc. abroad. Any claim to such a relief should be made through the payer or agent and dealt with in the payer's or agent's District.

A publisher may be in a position to estimate that a part of the advance will (as a minimum) be covered by sales etc. abroad within a reasonably short period after publication. No objection need ordinarily be taken to the part so estimated being provisionally excluded from the amount to be returned for assessment, so long as the person accounting clearly recognises that, in the event of any part of the estimate not being covered, he will be required to make good to the Revenue the corresponding deficiency of tax.

Where it is represented that the whole of an advance relates to sales etc. abroad, and the question is raised whether tax should be deducted from the advance, the matter should be referred to BP3 (Literary and Artistic Profits).

'Usual place of abode'

4005. The term 'usual place of abode' should be interpreted in the light of the intention of ICTA 1988, s 536, which is to enable tax in respect of income from a copyright in this country to be collected both where the copyright owner lives wholly abroad and also where his visits to the United Kingdom are not of sufficient duration to enable the tax to be collected with any ease under the ordinary machinery.

A person may be regarded as having his usual place of abode in this country if he usually or habitually lives here for considerable periods each year, for example, for an unbroken period of three or four months, or for broken periods amounting to five or six months. A person with a house in this country, but habitually here for so short a time that there is or has been difficulty in collecting tax under a direct assessment upon him, should not be considered as having his usual place of abode here. If, however, the conditions are such that tax can clearly be collected without difficulty, no objection need be taken to regarding the person as having his usual place of abode in this country.

It will be observed that it is possible for a person who has a house here to be 'resident'—and also 'ordinarily resident'—and yet not to have his 'usual place of abode' here.

(If a copyright owner's usual place of abode is in the United Kingdom this fact connotes that he is resident and carries on his vocation of author etc. in this country. He is consequently liable to direct assessment on the whole of his profits, including any lump sum payments and payments from abroad.)

Tax deductible whether payments direct or through agent

4006. Where the 'usual place of abode' of the copyright owner is not within the United Kingdom, tax is deductible whether the payment is made directly to him or indirectly, for example, to a literary agent or other representative in this country, or to a banking or other account here.

Deduction of Tax

Arrangement Between Initial Payer and Agent

4007. Where, having regard to the statutory provision for the allowance of an agent's commission, an initial payer and an agent agree in desiring that tax should be deducted (and the necessary account rendered) by the latter, the Board offers no objection to such an arrangement. But they look to the initial payer to provide the agent with such information as may be necessary to enable the latter properly to carry out his obligations, and reserve their legal right to require the initial payer to deduct and account for tax in any particular case.

Where no such arrangement exists, but an initial payer omits for any reason to deduct tax from a particular royalty, the agent as a person 'by or through whom' (ICTA 1988, s 349) the payment is made is required to deduct and account for the tax thereon.

Amount

4008. Where royalties are paid through an agent resident in the United Kingdom, the tax to be deducted, whether by the initial payer or the agent, is the amount applicable to the net royalty, that is, the amount remaining after deduction of the agent's percentage commission (as distinct from incidental fees for particular services etc.). Where, however, an initial payer who deducts tax is either unaware of the existence of the commission or unaware of its amount, the deduction is to be on the gross amount of the royalty, any relief being given by way of repayment to the agent on behalf of the copyright owner. Any claim to such relief should be dealt with in the agent's District.

In no case is an allowance admissible on the ground that the copyright owner has defrayed or contributed towards the cost of publishing, unless and except so far as any part of the royalty payments may, in accordance with the express terms of an agreement, be in reimbursement of such expenses.

The deduction is to be at the basic rate in force at the date of payment irrespective of the date of the sales, performance etc. concerned. The date of payment should be taken to be the date on which payment is made by the initial payer and not, for example, the date when a remittance is sent to the copyright owner by an agent.

Certificates

4009. Where the copyright owner claims repayment of United Kingdom tax, for example, under Part XVIII or ICTA 1988, s 278, he is required to produce evidence of the tax deducted. No pre-printed forms of certificate of deduction of tax are provided, but to guide publishers etc. in drawing up their own forms, two specimen certificates, one appropriate to publishers, producers etc., the other to literary agents etc., are reproduced below. If enquiry is made as to the manner in which the deduction of tax may be explained, use of the specimen certificates should be suggested. In particular, it is thought that the wording of the certificates will prevent enquiries being addressed by a copyright owner to the person who has deducted tax, and thus save trouble to all concerned.

(a)   Specimen certificate for the use of publishers, producers etc.—

'CERTIFICATE OF DEDUCTION OF INCOME TAX FROM ROYALTIES ETC., IN RESPECT OF COPYRIGHT INCOME AND CORPORATION TAXES ACT 1988, SECTIONS 349 AND 536

We certify that on making payment on (date)..

to...

in respect of the gross sum of . . . £ ....
due as royalty,

we deducted therefrom the sum of . . . £ ....

(being Income Tax at the rate of* . . .) in accordance with the requirements of the Income and Corporation Taxes Act 1988, Sections 349 and 536, and we further certify that this tax will be duly accounted for by us to the proper officer for the receipt of taxes.

For ....

Signed..

NOTE: This certificate will be accepted by the Inland Revenue Department as evidence of the deduction of the above-mentioned tax.

(* Insert the basic rate in force at the time of payment by the originator, unless deduction of tax at a reduced rate has been authorised by the Financial Intermediaries and Claims Office (International) for the purpose of double taxation relief.)'

    (b)   Specimen certificate for the use of literary and dramatic agents etc.—

'CERTIFICATE OF DEDUCTION OF INCOME TAX FROM ROYALTIES ETC., IN RESPECT OF COPYRIGHT INCOME AND CORPORATION TAXES ACT 1988, SECTIONS 349 AND 536

We certify that on making payment on (date)...

to..

in respect of the gross sum of . . . £ ....
due as royalty,

we deducted the sum of . . . £ ....

(being Income Tax at the rate of* . . . on £ . . ., i.e., the gross sum less commission) in accordance with the requirements of the Income and Corporation Taxes Act 1988, Sections 349 and 536, and we further certify that this tax will be duly accounted for by us to the proper officer for the receipt of taxes.

For ....

Signed..

NOTE: This certificate will be accepted by the Inland Revenue Department as evidence of the deduction of the above-mentioned tax.

(* Insert the basic rate in force at the time of payment by the originator, unless deduction of tax at a reduced rate has been authorised by the Financial Intermediaries and Claims Office (International) for the purpose of double taxation relief.)'

As regards the verification of certificates, *see* Rp 6/15 and Rp 6/23.

4010. . . .

Deduction in computing profits

4011. The gross amounts of the royalties in respect of which tax is deductible should be treated as admissible deductions in the computation of the profits of the initial payers.

Payment free, or without deduction, of tax

4012.   Where it is stipulated by contract that payment of royalty is to be made free of Income Tax, or without diminution on account of tax, tax is nevertheless required to be deducted and accounted for; the stipulation is void under ICTA 1988, s 536(6).

For example, where a contract provides for payment by a publisher direct to the copyright owner of a royalty on sales of 10 per cent free of Income Tax and the sales amount to £1,000, the gross royalty is £100 and the tax deductible and chargeable (with Income Tax at 25 per cent) is £25. The deduction to be allowed to the publisher in computing his profits is £100: this remains so, even if the tax, although paid by the publisher, is not in fact deducted from the royalty. If, however, the publisher contends that, by reason of possible litigation abroad, he is bound to pay the royalty in full and that consequently £125 (gross royalty *plus* the tax thereon) should be deducted in computing his profits, the case should be referred to BP3 (Literary and Artistic Profits). If tax has not been deducted from the royalty, *and the royalty has not been returned by the publisher for assessment*, the matter should not be adjusted in the Case I assessment: the amount of the royalty, £100, should be allowed as a deduction and an assessment made on that amount.

Payment of such an amount as, after deduction of tax, equals a percentage of gross receipts etc.

4013.   Where it is stipulated in clear terms that the payment is to be of such an amount as after deductions of tax shall be equal to, for example, so much per cent of the gross receipts or profits, the gross amount of the royalty varies according to the rate of Income Tax in force.

Thus, where a contract provides for payment by a publisher direct to the copyright owner of a royalty of such an amount as after deduction of Income Tax shall be equal to 10 per cent of the sales and the latter amount to £1,000, the gross royalty (with Income Tax at 25 per cent) is £133.33 and the tax deductible and chargeable is £33.33; the deduction to be allowed to the publisher in computing his profits is £133.33.

Enterprise Investment Scheme

Waiver of exclusions in certain cases

7000.   The general exclusion of certain activities is mentioned in IM 6997. The specific circumstances in which the exclusion is waived for certain of those activities are shown below.

FILM PRODUCTION

Under ICTA 1988, s 297(4) a trade is not treated as failing to qualify by reason only of consisting to a substantial extent of receiving royalties or licence fees if—

- all those royalties and/or licence fees are in respect of—
    - (i) films produced by the company in the relevant period, or
    - (ii) sound recordings relating to such films, or

      (iii) other products arising from such films,

and

- throughout the relevant (three year) period the company is engaged in the production of films or the distribution of **those** films.

'Other products' includes such things as merchandise which exploits film characters.

A company may be regarded as engaged in film production, even if it does not do the actual physical work of production, if it has overall control of that work.

There are definitions of 'film' and 'sound recording' in ICTA 1988, s 298(5). 'Film' includes a video tape.

RESEARCH AND DEVELOPMENT

Under ICTA 1988, s 297(5) a trade is not treated as failing to qualify by reason only of consisting to a substantial extent of receiving royalties or licence fees if—

- all those royalties and/or licence fees are attributable to research and development carried out by the company,
  and
- the company is engaged in research and development throughout the relevant (three year) period.

Research and development is defined as any activity which is intended to result in *either* a patentable invention or a computer program. To be patentable an invention must be new, involve an inventive step and be capable of industrial application.

A company should be regarded as engaged in research and development if it directs and supervises the project and the results of the research are its own property. It may if it wishes commission others to carry out laboratory and similar work which needs to be done as part of the research.

As regards raising money for a qualifying business activity of research and development, *see* IM 6973.

Sale by an individual of income derived from his personal activities (ICTA 1988, s 775)

General

4680. ICTA 1988, s 775 is aimed at arrangements where an individual gives up the prospect of future income but, either he or some other person, receives instead a 'capital amount'.

Main conditions

4681. The following conditions must all be present before ICTA 1988, s 775 can operate.

ICTA 1988, s 775(1)(a) (i) The individual must be carrying on an activity or occupation of the kind covered by the Section (IM 4682)

ICTA 1988, s 775(1)(a) (ii) Transactions or arrangements must have been effected putting some other person in a position to exploit the earnings capacity of that individual

ICTA 1988, s 775(1)(b) (iii) A 'capital amount' (IM 4683) must have been obtained by the individual or some other person, as part of, or in connection with, or in consideration of the transactions or arrangements

Main object, ICTA 1988, s 775(1)(c) (iv) the main object, or one of the main objects, of the transactions or arrangements must be the avoidance or reduction of liability to Income Tax.

Schedule of charge, ICTA 1988, s 775(2)

The effect of the section is that the 'capital amount' is chargeable on the individual as income under Case VI of Schedule D in the tax year or years in which it becomes receivable (IM 4684). The 'capital amount' (IM 4683) will not be consideration for Capital Gains Tax purposes (CG 815).

Activities covered, ICTA 1988, s 775(3)(a)

4682. ICTA 1988, s 775 refers to any occupation of an individual and the individual's activities in that occupation. 'Occupation' is defined in ICTA 1988, s 775(3)(a) and embraces all activities which are of a kind pursued in any profession or vocation, irrespective of whether the individual is in fact carrying on a profession or vocation. Thus, although the individual may be an employee of, for example, his service company, if the activities which he performs in the course of his employment are of a kind which are performed as part of a profession or vocation, those activities are within the terms of ICTA 1988, s 775.

The use of the word 'vocation' in the sub-section brings in activities which do not fall within the normal meaning of the work 'profession'. For example, a jockey may well be carrying on a vocation without carrying on a profession. The words 'profession or vocation' embrace not only actors, actresses, pop stars and the usual TV and film personalities but also such people as golfers, tennis players, footballers, boxers and so on.

Capital amount, ICTA 1988, s 775(1)(b) & (2)

4683. An assessment under ICTA 1988, s 775(2) can be made only if there is a 'capital amount' which is obtained by the individual for himself or for any other person'.

Capital amount defined, ICTA 1988, s 777(13)

'Capital amount' is defined in ICTA 1988, s 777(13) as 'any amount, in money or money's worth, which, apart from ICTA 1988, s 775, does not fall to be included in any computation of income for the purposes of the Taxes Acts'.

Capital amount receivable by someone other than the individual, ICTA 1988, s 775(1)(b) & (8)

ICTA 1988, s 775 also catches the case in which the 'capital amount' is receivable not by the individual whose activities are being exploited but by some other person. In such a case, the individual who relinquishes the future income remains the person who is chargeable under the Section.

Postponement of charge, ICTA 1988, s 775(5)

Where the 'capital amount' consists of property the value of which derives substantially from the individual's own activities (for example the shares in his service company), no charge under ICTA 1988, s 775 arises at that point, the charge being postponed until that particular piece of property is converted into some property, the value of which does not derive substantially from the activities of the individual.

Capital amount attributable to value as going concern, ICTA 1988, s 775(4)

ICTA 1988, s 775(4) excludes from charge innocent transactions where the 'capital amount' received is attributable to the value of the profession or vocation or of the company's business as a going concern. For example, an individual entering into an existing firm as a new partner is a capital sum to the existing partners. Inasmuch as the new partner might not become immediately useful to the firm, it might be said that for a short period income or profits which were attributable to the activities of the existing partners were being allocated to the incoming partner, and that a part of the 'capital amount' received by the existing partners was so received because the incoming partner was exploiting the activities of the existing partners. ICTA 1988, s 775(4) removes any doubt that such a case could be caught by ICTA 1988, s 775(1).

Year of assessment, ICTA 1988, s 775(2)

4684.   The year for which an assessment under ICTA 1988, s 775 may be made is the year in which a 'capital amount' is receivable.

ICTA 1988, s 777(13)

Notwithstanding the general rule in IM 4683 above, a 'capital amount' is not to be regarded as having become receivable by some person until that person can effectively enjoy or dispose of it.

Recovery of tax, ICTA 1988, s 777(8)

Where an individual is assessed by reason of ICTA 1988, s 775 in respect of a 'capital amount' receivable by another person, he has power to recover the tax charged from that other person. The Revenue has alternative powers to collect tax from either the individual or the other person.

Non-residents, ICTA 1988, s 775(9)

4685.   Non-residents as well as residents may be liable under ICTA 1988, s 775(9) but only if the 'occupation' (IM 4682) is carried on wholly or partly in the UK.

Deduction of tax from overseas payments, ICTA 1988, s 777(9)

Where a 'capital amount' is payable to a non-resident, the Board may direct that Income Tax shall be deducted on payment, the payer accounting to the Revenue by reference to the ordinary procedure under ICTA 1988, s 349(1) (formerly Section 53, ICTA 1970—*see* AP 96).

Information powers, ICTA 1988, s 778

4686.   Power is given to the Board or an Inspector to obtain, in relation to any arrangement or transaction, information which is thought by the Board or the Inspector to be necessary for the purpose of operating ICTA 1988, s 775. This power should not be exercised by an Inspector without the prior agreement of Special Investigations Section.

4687.   Following the unification of rates of tax on income and capital gains in the Finance Act 1988, the incentive to exploit the arrangements countered by ICTA 1988, s 775 diminished. The section still has a purpose however in deterring exploitation of the different rules for Capital Gains and Income Tax or structuring arrangements so that the capital sum would not otherwise attract Income Tax liability.

Reports to Special Investigation Section

4688.   Although ICTA 1988, s 775 is rarely invoked, all cases where it is considered the Section may apply should be submitted to Special Investigations Section at an early stage and before an assessment is made or a notice under ICTA 1988, s 778 is issued and in particular where:

(*a*)   An individual (whether or not domiciled, resident or ordinarily resident in the UK), carries on an activity wholly or partly in the UK of any of the kinds referred to in IM 4682, and

(*b*)   the earning capacity of that individual is enjoyed by some other person and

(*c*)   money or money's worth becomes receivable in the UK or offshore by the individual or some other person (whether before or after the income is earned) which is not taxable in the UK as income; or, after 5 April 1988, if chargeable as a capital gain, produces a disproportionately small tax liability (either because of capital loss relief or otherwise).

Schedule E Manual (SE)

Film and video workers
Film industry unit at LP10

7321. Employees engaged in film and video production, which includes production of TV commercials, are dealt with by the Film Industry Unit at LP10. Refer to the Unit any enquiries you receive about the Schedule of Charge for film and video workers, or about the operation of PAYE by film and video companies. Tell the Unit about any new production companies you find.

Front of camera workers: schedule of charge

7322. Guidance about the status of actors (and others) who perform in front of camera is given at SE 7333. Generally they will be assessable under Schedule D.

Behind camera workers: schedule of charge

7323. The Revenue has examined the type of work done by those engaged behind the camera in film and video production. Examples of 'behind camera' workers are cameramen, producers, writers, carpenters and electricians. Because of what we understand about certain jobs (called 'grades' in the Industry) we automatically accept that certain grades are assessable under Schedule D. These grades are itemised in a 'grading list' which is usually updated from year to year.

Engagements in a grade outside the list are generally dealt with under Schedule E.

There are also special arrangements to enable payments for certain engagements to be made gross, even though the engagement might be for a grade not on the list. These apply to very short engagements in specified circumstances and also to the engagements of particular individuals who are able to show that their engagements are as individuals in business on their own account in accordance with the decision in *Hall v Lorimer* (TL3382).

Use of service company

7324. To avoid PAYE many film and video workers in Schedule E grades have set up limited companies. Normally the worker is the majority shareholder and a director. It is alleged that the service company supplies the services of the individual to a film or video production company.

An examination of many such cases has shown that such arrangements often fail. The worker remains an employee of the production company. Tell the Film Industry Unit about any service companies of this kind that you find.

Which District is GCD

7325. Cases fall into four groups.

- People who work wholly or mainly in Schedule D grades are dealt with by the district in which their business is located.

- People whose status the Film Industry Unit have reviewed in detail, and are accepted as generally assessable under Schedule D are dealt with by the district in which their business is located.
- People who work wholly or mainly in Schedule E grades are all dealt with by the Film Industry Unit. This includes the directors of service companies of the kind described in SE 7324.
- Where someone works regularly in both Schedule D and Schedule E grades ask the Film Industry Unit which district should act as GCD.

Schedule D: returns under TMA 1970, s 16

7326. Returns under TMA 1970, s 16 (AP4025) of payments to actors and others engaged under contracts for services are made to the Entertainers Information Unit (EIU) at TIDO. The EIU distributes the information to Districts.

Television and radio workers

Television and radio unit at LP12

7327. The Television and Radio Unit at LP12 deals with the employees of

- BBC TV
- BBC Radio
- all the independent TV broadcasting, satellite and cable companies
- all the independent radio companies.

Front of camera workers: schedule of charge

7328. People who appear in front of the television cameras or radio microphones are engaged under a great variety of terms.

Whether they are engaged under contracts of employment or contracts for services will depend on all the facts. See for example the guidance about actors and other performers at SE 7333.

If you are not sure whether a front of camera or microphone worker is an employee or is self-employed, ask the Television and Radio Unit for advice.

Behind camera workers: schedule of charge

7329. The Revenue has examined the type of work done by those engaged behind the camera and microphone in television and radio production. Examples of 'behind camera' workers are cameramen, producers, writers, carpenters and electricians. Because of what we understand about certain jobs (called 'grades' in the Industry) we automatically accept that certain grades are assessable under Schedule D. These grades are itemised in a 'grading list' which is updated from time to time as necessary.

Engagements in a grade outside the list are generally dealt with under Schedule E.

There are also special arrangements to enable payments for certain engagements to be made gross, even though the engagement might be for a grade not on the list. These apply to very short engagements in specified circumstances and also to the engagements of particular individuals who are able to show that their engagements are as individuals in business on their own account in accordance with the decision in *Hall v Lorimer* (TL3382).

Use of service companies

7330. To avoid PAYE many television and radio workers in Schedule E grades have set up limited companies. Normally the worker is the majority shareholder and a director. It is alleged that the service company supplies the services of the individual to the television or radio company.

An examination of many such cases has shown that such arrangements often fail. The worker remains an employee of the television or radio company. Tell the Television and Radio Unit about any service companies of this kind that you find.

Which District is GCD

7331. Cases fall into three groups.

- People who work wholly or mainly in Schedule D grades are dealt with by the District in which their business is located.
- People who work wholly or mainly in Schedule E grades are all dealt with by the Television and Radio Unit at LP12.
- Where someone works regularly in both Schedule D and Schedule E grades, ask the Television and Radio Unit at LP12 which District should act as the GCD.

Theatrical performers/artists

Theatrical performers: schedule of charge—history

7332. Two tax cases and a Special Commissioners' decision explain the history of our general treatment of actors and indeed other performers/artists. The current treatment is explained at SE 7333.

Historically these persons have generally been dealt with under Schedule D. The 1931 case of *Davies v Braithwaite*, 18 TC 198, concerned a professional actress, Lilian Braithwaite, whose activities included stage, film, radio, and gramophone recording performances in the UK as well as stage performances in America. It was held that all her income was assessable under Schedule D as income derived from her profession.

But in 1972 in the case of *Fall v Hitchen*, 49 TC 433, a professional dancer, David Hitchen, was held to be assessable under Schedule E in respect of his income from a standard Equity contract that he held with the ballet company, Sadlers Wells. Following the decision in that case, the Revenue took the view that all standard Equity contracts were contracts of employment.

The Schedule E instructions were amended to reflect our view on status, but these also advised districts only to apply Schedule E/PAYE to newcomers to the industry.

Unfortunately there was some inconsistency in the way in which the instructions were interpreted and implemented.

As a result, and to address the inconsistency, meetings were held with bodies representing workers and engagers in the theatrical industry, and they cooperated in the introduction of PAYE in respect of all standard Equity contracts with effect from 6 April 1990. Established performers were entitled to retain their existing Schedule D treatment under the terms of ESC A75. This was facilitated by a microfiche sent to all districts of eligible persons who were then given an NT tax code in respect of any such contract.

Nevertheless, both sides of the industry maintained their stance against the Revenue's view on the status of actors engaged under standard Equity contracts, and mounted a challenge by sponsoring a test case to the Special Commissioners. The Special Commissioners found for the appellants, Sam West and Alec McCowen, and the matter was not pursued into the Courts. The result is that we now accept that most performers/artists are assessable under Schedule D.

Revised guidance on status for performers/artists was made public in late summer 1994, and this is reproduced in SE 7333.

Schedule of charge—guidance

7333.   Actors, ballet dancers, opera singers, musicians and other performers/artists who appear live in the theatre, opera, ballet, or in clubs, or perform in film, video, radio or television productions may be engaged under either contracts for services (Schedule D) or contracts of employment (Schedule E).

There are a number of standard contracts commonly used to engage performers/artists in these industries. These contracts incorporate a comprehensive range of standard terms and are the result of negotiations between bodies representing engagers and performers/artists in the industry. They are often referred to by reference to the union which has negotiated on behalf of the performers, and accordingly there are a range of contracts known for example as standard Musicians Union contracts and standard Equity contracts. The British Actors' Equity Association is the trade union which represents most performing artists other than musicians.

The unions have been able to secure a package of measures designed to protect their members such as

- minimum rates of pay
- overtime, bank holiday and Sunday premiums
- agreed rates of touring and subsistence allowances
- holiday pay
- agreed disciplinary procedures.

Because these features are more commonly found in an employer/employee relationship, it is natural that an examination of the standard contractual terms may lead to the view that performers/artists so engaged are engaged under contracts of employment. And in the case of *Fall v Hitchen*, 49 TC 433, it was held that a ballet dancer engaged under a standard contract was engaged under a contract of employment and that his pay fell within Schedule E.

However in 1993 two actors, Alec McCowen and Sam West appealed to the Special Commissioners, and successfully argued that their income from standard Equity theatre contracts did not fall within Schedule E. The decisions were given in public and accordingly they can be openly referred to, but they are not binding on other bodies of Commissioners. The Revenue did not pursue these cases to the High Court.

It is clear from these contrasting cases that the terms of the contract may not be decisive by themselves, and in the case of artistic workers, such as theatrical performers/artists, the way in which they generally carry on their profession also needs to be considered.

In *Fall v Hitchen*, Mr Hitchen was engaged for a minimum period of something like six months 'to rehearse, understudy, play and dance as and where required by the Manager'. Both Mr West and Mr McCowen, however, were engaged to play a specific role in a specific play for the run of a play, or a shorter fixed period. And both Mr McCowen and Mr West had a variety of engagements in different media (film, television, radio and theatre), consecutively and sometimes concurrently.

The type of engagement undertaken by Mr McCowen and Mr West is now much more typical of the profession than that undertaken by Mr Hitchen in 1969. These days it is comparatively unusual for a performer/artist to be engaged to play parts as and when cast in a series of different plays or other productions.

The typical performer/artist is likely to have a whole series of separate engagements in different media making up his professional working life, commonly interspersed with periods without paid work, between the end of one engagement and the commencement of another.

Other case law supports the view that, for theatrical performers/artists, independence from a particular regular paymaster may indicate that individual contracts are not contracts of employment, even though the prima facie view based on the particular terms of the particular engagement may suggest otherwise.

Accordingly, Schedule D assessment of a performer's/artist's earnings will normally be appropriate. The sort of engagement where Schedule E and PAYE may be appropriate, is more likely to be in circumstances where a performer/artist is engaged for a regular salary to perform in a series of different productions over a period of time, in such roles as may be from time to time stipulated by the engager, with a minimum period of notice before termination of the contract, as was Mr Hitchen in Fall v Hitchen. This would apply for example to permanent members of some orchestras and permanent members of an opera, ballet or theatre company. Schedule E and PAYE would apply in these cases regardless of the receipt by the performer/artist of other income correctly chargeable under Schedule D.

National insurance position

7334. Any enquiry about the National Insurance position of a performer/artist should be referred to the local Contributions Agency Office.

Reserved Schedule D status ESC A75

7335. Concessional arrangements were introduced with effect from 6 April 1990 to enable established performers to retain Schedule D treatment of their earnings. The conditions to be satisfied were published as ESC A75.

However, the McCowen and West decisions changed our views on the nature of many standard industry contracts (see SE 7332–SE 7333). This means that we accept that performers/artists will generally be assessable under Schedule D as a matter of law rather than concession. The concession will therefore only rarely apply. If in doubt, contact Personal Tax Division (Schedule E), Solihull for advice.

7336–7346. . . .

Fees paid to agents

7347. From 1990–91 onwards a deduction may be given for fees paid to agents by theatrical performers out of earnings taxed under Schedule E.

The deduction applies to fees paid either

- under a contract with an agent holding a licence to carry on an agency under the Employment Agencies Act 1973
  or
- to a Co-operative Society which acts as agent for its members.

To be deductible the fees must be

— paid out of the emoluments of the employment falling to be charged to tax for the year concerned and
— calculated as a percentage of those emoluments or part of them. The amount of the fees which can be deducted including any VAT payable on them is limited to 17.5 per cent.

Agents' fees are usually between 10 per cent and 15 per cent of a performer's income so the limit of 17.5 per cent will normally cover an agent's fee together with any VAT paid on it.

Amounts claimed as deductions by performers should normally be accepted. When, exceptionally, you doubt the bona fides of a claim ask the performer to produce documentary evidence.

7348–7350. . . .

Stage management

7351. Stage managers, deputy stage managers and assistant stage managers are normally Equity members. Many of the standard contracts under which they are engaged provide for them to understudy or appear in minor roles in productions, in addition to their stage management duties.

The guidance on the status of theatrical performers/artists at SE 7333 also applies to stage management engagements.

Other theatrical non-performing workers: box office, stage hands, carpenters, dressers etc and visiting producers

7352. Non-performing theatrical staff include box office staff, carpenters and other technicians, stage hands, dressers. They are usually engaged under contracts of employment (but see SE 7354 below) and the theatre management should operate

PAYE in the normal way. If Schedule E treatment is disputed see SE 541 onwards. There are separate instructions for

- film and video workers—see SE 7321 onwards
- television workers—see SE 7327 onwards.

Occasionally the visiting manager or producer of a show takes over all or some of the staff and is responsible for paying them for the run of the show at that theatre. In such cases try to arrange for the staff to be paid by the resident theatre manager on behalf of the visiting manager. This enables the original deductions working sheet to be used so no movement procedure is necessary. Representatives of the staff and management have agreed in principle to do this.

7353. . . .

Designers, directors and choreographers

7354. Designers, directors and choreographers may be engaged under either contracts for services or contracts of employment. You may assess under Schedule D where a designer, director or choreographer is engaged

- for a specific production
  and
- for a limited period, which normally ends soon after the opening of the production
  and
- is paid both a fee and a royalty (often related to box office receipts).

If you are in doubt about any other form of contract under which a director, designer or choreographer or their assistants are engaged, submit to Personal Tax Division (Schedule E), Solihull.

7355–7362.

Musicians

Schedule of charge

7363. General guidance about the status of musicians is at SE 7333.
Reserved Schedule D status (SE 7335) may be available to a musician engaged under a contract of employment where the necessary conditions are met. These are explained in the concession itself. If in doubt submit to Personal Tax Division (Schedule E), Solihull.

Orchestral players

7364. The status of orchestral players can give rise to problems because of the variety of contracts and circumstances under which they are engaged. The main situations are as follows:

(a)   Musicians engaged to play at musicals, pantomimes and other theatrical performances are covered by the guidance at SE 7333.

(b)   Musicians engaged under 'first call' or 'guarantee' contracts are within Schedule D. These are contracts which
   (i)   give the orchestra the right to call on their services but
   (ii) limit this demand so that they may undertake other work and
   (iii) pay them separately for each performance.
(c)   Musicians who are shareholders in the major London Orchestras (London Philharmonic, London Symphony, New Philharmonia and Royal Philharmonic) are self-employed. These orchestras are run by the members themselves.
(d)   Generally, orchestral players who are paid separately for each performance and are not guaranteed a minimum amount of work by an orchestra may be treated as self-employed.
(e)   Musicians who are not within (b)–(d) above and are permanent members of major orchestras are generally chargeable under Schedule E.

PAYE Procedures Manual

Special circumstances
Taxpayers dealt with under schedule D

9662.   Some taxpayers dealt with under Schedule D may receive taxable Benefits. For example, actors and musicians often pay Class 1 National Insurance contributions and may claim Benefit if unemployed. Any person who becomes unemployed may claim income support.

The Benefit can be included in the Schedule D assessment at Part III. If the assessment is final and conclusive, the Benefit is assessed under Schedule E.

A Schedule D section may ask you to make a formal assessment on taxable Benefits.

Make a DC assessment following the instructions in Chapter 10.

Index